Rick Steves'

EUROPE
THROUGH THE
BACK DOOR

2014

CONTENTS

▶ **Preface** x

Part One: Travel Skills 1

▶ **Introduction** 2
Getting Started 3
Making the Most of Your Trip 8
Rick Steves' Back Door
  Travel Philosophy 13

▶ **Budgeting and Planning** 15
Affording Your Trip 15
Researching Your Trip 21
Creating an Itinerary 33
Prioritizing Your Time 49

▶ **Paper Chase** 54
Travel Documents 54
Travel Insurance 59
Before You Go 66

▶ **Pack Light** 69
One Bag—That's It 69
Packing 101 72

▶ **Flying** 87
Flying to Europe 87
Flying Within Europe 99

▶ **Trains and More** 106
Train Tickets and Passes 108
Train Stations 124
On the Train 132
Buses and Ferries 138

▶ **Driving** 144
Renting a Car 144
Behind the European Wheel 158

▶ **Money** 167
Cash 168
Credit Cards 175
Tipping 181
VAT Refunds and Customs 182

▶ **Sleeping** 187
Finding the Right Room 187
Reserving a Room 191
Types of Accommodations 198

▶ **Phones and Technology** 234
Phoning 234
Getting Online 253
Travel Tools for Portable Devices 258
Travel Photography 263
Sharing Your Trip 272

▶ City Transportation 277
  Subways 279
  Buses 283
  Taxis 285
▶ Sightseeing and Activities 289
  Getting Oriented. 289
  Tours 291
  Sightseeing Strategies 295
  Becoming a Temporary European... 307
  Active Travel 312
  Shopping 319
▶ Theft and Scams 325
  Pickpocketing and Theft 325
  Scams and Rip-Offs. 331
  Losing It All...and Bouncing Back.... 335
▶ Language and
  Communication 340
  Hurdling the Language Barrier.... 340
  Numbers and Stumblers. 357
  Mail and Shipping. 359
▶ Eating 361
  Restaurants 362

Cafés and Bars 373
Budget Food Options 375
Local Specialties. 384
▶ Health and Hygiene. 399
  Staying Healthy. 399
  Laundry. 411
  European Bathrooms 415
▶ Travel Styles 422
  Traveling Solo 422
  Family Travel 432
  Savvy Seniors 450
  Travelers with Disabilities. 454
  Bus Tour Self-Defense. 459
  Cruising in Europe 465
▶ Perspectives 474
  Broadening Your Perspective
    Through Travel 474
  Understanding the
    European Union 477
  European Challenges. 481
  Social Issues in Europe 487
  Socially Responsible and
    Educational Travel 491

Part Two: Back Doors 499

▸ Finding a Back Door
   of Your Own 500

▸ Italy 503
   The Cinque Terre: Italy's Riviera.....503
   Hill Towns of Central Italy............510
   North Italy Choices: Milan,
      Lakes, or Mountains.............517
   Naples, the Amalfi Coast,
      and Pompeii...................524
   Sassy, Spicy Sicily.................529

▸ Portugal, Spain & Morocco ...534
   Lisbon Gold 534
   Portugal's Sunny Salema 538
   The White Villages of Andalucía 542
   Morocco: Plunge Deep 547

▸ France 556
   Paris: A Grand Boulevard
      and a Petite Lane 556
   Alsace and Colmar:
      Vintage France 569
   From France to Italy
      over Mont Blanc 573

▸ Belgium and
   the Netherlands 577
   Bruges: Pickled in Gothic 577
   Amsterdam's Counter-Culture 582

▸ Germany, Austria
   & Switzerland 589
   Rothenburg and
      the Romantic Road 589
   Hallstatt: Austria's Commune-with-
      Nature Lake District............594
   Gimmelwald: The Swiss Alps
      in Your Lap...................597

▸ Eastern Europe 604
   Czech Out Prague 604
   Charming Kraków..................613
   Off the Beaten Path in
      Bosnia-Herzegovina 620
   Communist Sites
      in Eastern Europe..............626

▸ Great Britain 634
   London: A Warm Look
      at a Cold City..................634
   Elegant and Frivolous Bath 642
   York: Vikings, Bygone Days,
      and England's Top Church......645

Blackpool: Britain's Coney Island.... 649
Cotswold Villages:
  Inventors of Quaint 651
Mysterious Britain................. 656
▶ Ireland........................... 661
The Dingle Peninsula:
  A Gaelic Bike Ride 661
Northern Ireland and Belfast........ 669
▶ Scandinavia...................... 675
Norway in a Nutshell:
  Oslo and the Fjords 675
Ærø: Denmark's Ship-in-a-Bottle
  Island 681
▶ A European Sampler 685
Offbeat Europe.................... 685
The Flavors of Europe.............. 693
Alpine Escapes 697
Best Medieval Castle Experiences... 702
Sobering Sites of Nazi Europe 712
▶ East Mediterranean............ 722
Greece's Peloponnesian Highlights.. 722
Turkey's Hot....................... 731
Istanbul Déjà Vu 743
Eastern Turkey..................... 747

Part Three: Appendix 753
▶ Sample Routes 754
Europe's Best Whirlwind
  Two-Month Trip 770
▶ Graffiti Wall..................... 781
▶ Resources....................... 799
Rick Steves' Europe
  on Public Television........... 799
Travel Literature 801
Europe in Film and TV............. 803
European National Tourist Offices.... 810
City Name Variations.............. 810
Metric Conversion 811
Clothes Sizing Conversion.......... 812
European Weather.................. 814
▶ Index............................ 819
▶ Map Index....................... 830

Rick Steves'
EUROPE
THROUGH THE
BACK DOOR
2014

AVALON
TRAVEL

PREFACE

This guidebook, based on lessons learned from more than 30 years of exploring Europe, is your handbook for traveling smart. With the tips and advice I've assembled here, you can plan, create, and enjoy a trip that will live up to your dreams.

My first five trips to Europe were purely for kicks. I made my share of blunders—I missed train connections, wasted money on dreary hotels and bad restaurants, and showed up at sights after they had closed. But each new trip became smoother than the last. It was clear: I was learning from my mistakes.

While traveling, I saw others making the same costly and time-consuming errors that I'd once made. It occurred to me that by sharing the lessons I'd learned, I could help people enjoy better, smoother trips. And I'd have a good excuse to go back to Europe every summer to update my material.

Throughout the late 1970s I taught my "European Travel Cheap" class in Seattle during the school year, and traveled to Europe every summer. I developed a good sense of the fears and apprehensions troubling people before their trips, and I was gathering lots of great "Back Door" discoveries and experiences throughout Europe.

So, in 1980, with all that material, writing the first edition of *Europe*

Through the Back Door was easy. I rented an IBM Selectric typewriter, sweet-talked my girlfriend into typing the manuscript, and cajoled my roommate into sketching the illustrations. I gingerly delivered that precious first pile of pages to a printer, and, on my 25th birthday, picked up 2,500 copies.

I sold all those first editions of *Europe Through the Back Door* through my travel classes. With the second edition, in 1981, I got a bit more professional, taking out my personal poems and lists of the most dangerous airlines. I found a distributor who got the book into stores throughout the Pacific Northwest. The third edition, even though typeset, still looked so simple and amateurish that reviewers repeatedly mistook it for a "pre-publication" edition.

All this time I was supporting myself as a piano teacher. But my recital hall was gradually becoming a travel lecture classroom, and I needed to choose what I would teach: Europe or music. I chose Europe, let my piano students go, and began building my travel business. At the same time, an actual publisher agreed to bring out the fourth edition of *Europe Through the Back Door*. Happily, I could now focus on researching and writing rather than publishing.

Since then I've kept to the same teaching mission—though now this mission is amplified by 80 workmates at my company in Edmonds, Washington, and by technology I never could have dreamed of back when I started. Working together, we've developed a wide-ranging program of travel material—dozens of guidebooks, guided bus tours, a public television series, a weekly public-radio program, information-packed smartphone apps, personally designed gear, a generous website, and more. Everything we do is designed to inform and inspire American tourists to turn their travel dreams into smooth and affordable reality—and this book is the foundation of our work.

The favorite part of my job remains my on-the-ground research. I spend four months every year in Europe: April and May in the Mediterranean, July and August north of the Alps. I use some of that time to film my TV series, but for the majority of it, I'm alone, eyes and ears open: exploring new places, revisiting old favorites, tracking down leads, collecting experiences, and updating my guidebooks. When I get home, I can't wait to splice the lessons I've learned from my most recent travels into the book you're about to read.

I still make mistakes with gusto—and take careful notes. Working up a big thirst after a long day of sightseeing in Naples, I come back to the hotel, order a "margarita"...and get a pizza. Sometimes I pretend to screw up, just to see what'll happen. When I get ripped off, I celebrate—the scammer doesn't know who he just ripped off. I'll learn that scam, and pack that lesson—with all the others—into this book.

You can be your own top-notch tour guide—simply equip yourself with the best information. Expect to travel smart...and you will.

PART ONE
TRAVEL SKILLS

In Europe, life's very good—even if you're on a budget.

INTRODUCTION

Why do I find Europe so endlessly fun and entertaining? Because I know where to look.

Europe is my beat. For more than three decades, it's been my second home. Sure, I love the biggies...from the Eiffel Tower to "Mad" King Ludwig's castles to Michelangelo's *David*. But even more than the must-see sights, I value the Back Door experiences that Europe has to offer: meeting pilgrims at Santiago, sampling stinky cheese in a Czech town, pondering an ancient stone circle in Dartmoor, and cheering for a high-school soccer team with new friends in Turkey. Looking back on my European travels, having spent literally a third of my adult life living out of a carry-on bag, I'm thankful that, for me, Europe never gets old. My curiosity will always take me back to that wonderful continent.

But many American travelers miss the real Europe because they enter through its grand front door. This Europe greets you with cash registers cocked, $8 cups of coffee, high-rise hotels, and service with a purchased smile. You can give your trip an extra, more real dimension by coming with me through the back door, where a warm, relaxed, personable Europe welcomes us as friends. Rather than just part of the economy, we become part of the party.

The first half of this book covers the practical skills of Back Door European travel: how to make a livable budget, plan a smart itinerary, pack light, take advantage of public transportation, find good-value accommodations, eat cheaply but well, stay healthy, use technology wisely, avoid theft and scams, save money and time—and best of all, connect with the locals. Even more important than saving you money, my travel tips will steer you toward matchless experiences that become indelible memories—the kind of souvenirs you'll enjoy for a lifetime.

The second half of the book gives you the keys to more than two dozen of my favorite discoveries, or Back Doors. A more intimate Europe survives in these places, where you can immerse yourself in pure Europe—feeling its fjords and caressing its castles.

Getting Started

Kicking off your European adventure can be a matter of simple logistics (you've got 10 days off in April) or the fulfillment of a lifetime dream (you've always wanted to see where your French grandmother was born). Whether your trip is fueled by practicality or inspiration, the planning part can be instrumental in its success and an enjoyable part of the experience itself. You have a world of options and plenty to consider.

Stoke Your Travel Dreams

Find out all you can about the destinations you'd like to visit. Many resources are standing by to help inform and inspire your planning. For in-depth itinerary-planning advice, see "Creating an Itinerary" on page 33.

Talk with travelers. Firsthand, fresh information can be good stuff—whether you're at home or in Europe. Travelers love to share the tips and lessons they've learned. Take advantage of every opportunity to confer with fellow travelers who've been to your target destination. Solicit tips and ideas from your Facebook friends.

Keep in mind, however, that all assessments of a place's touristic merit are a product of that person's personality and experiences there. It could have rained on her parade or he may have been sick in "that lousy, overrated city." Every year, I find travelers hell-bent on following bad advice from friends at home. Treat opinions as opinions (except, of course, those found in this book).

Look through travel books. Spend a few hours in the travel section of a bookstore, thumbing through guidebooks. Page through coffee-table books with eye-candy pictures of the places you're thinking of visiting. Your hometown library has a lifetime of valuable reading on European culture. Navigate toward nonfiction: Dewey gave Europe the numbers 914 and 940.

Flip through travel magazines. Pick up a few glitzy travel magazines loaded with images of enticing destinations. Try the visually stunning

National Geographic Traveler (travel advice, trip ideas, and money-saving tips), *Travel & Leisure,* and *Smithsonian* (combines beautiful photography with scholarly articles, often on travel-related topics).

Watch travel shows. Enjoy the awe-inspiring art, centuries-old churches, colorful markets, romantically cobbled streets, halcyon lakes, and peaceful vineyards. My public television series, *Rick Steves' Europe,* captures the best of Europe in 100 shows (see page 799).

Explore the Internet. Trip inspiration is on overdrive on the Web, from social networking sites to personal trip blogs to street view in Google. Ogle images of places you might want to visit by finding pictures posted by travelers who've been there (see page 274 for more about online resources).

Watch movies and documentaries set in Europe. The Tuscan picnic scene in *Room with a View* will have you packing your bags for Italy. *The Sound of Music* sends fans singing into the streets of Salzburg, and *Midnight in Paris* will inspire you to stay out after dark in the City of Light. Documentaries can be equally compelling: *The Rape of Europa,* telling the fascinating story of the rescue of Europe's great art from Nazi plunderers and how it got back to its rightful home, adds an extra dimension to your museum going. *The Singing Revolution* gives you stirring background on how the people of Estonia literally—and courageously— sang their way to freedom. (For more recommendations, as well as a list of inspiring travel literature, see page 801.)

Take classes. Understanding a subject makes it interesting. To avoid getting "cathedraled" or "museumed" out, take an art history class, especially if you're going to Italy or Greece. A European history class will bring "dull" museums to life, while a conversational language class can be fun and practical. Some of my slideshow talks are available online (search for "Rick Steves Lecture Series" on YouTube).

Go with a Group or on Your Own?

Putting together a dream trip requires time and skills. As with any do-it-yourself project, at the outset it's wise to honestly assess whether you want to handle your endeavor (in this case, Europe) on your own. Some people are not inclined to figure things out on a trip, and that's OK. They make their living figuring things out 50 weeks a year, and that's not their idea of a good vacation. These people should travel with a tour...or a spouse.

Tours and cruises are an easy way to see Europe and can make a lot of sense for people with limited time. You don't have to waste any mental energy on where to sleep or how to get to the next town. With a

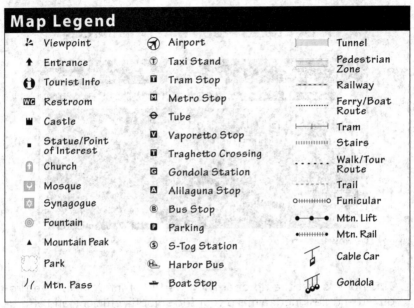

Use this legend to help you navigate the maps in this book.

good tour company, you'll enjoy the insights of local guides who'll bring Roman life alive in Pompeii or help you recall recent history in Berlin. And cruises offer the undeniable efficiency of sleeping while you travel to your next destination, allowing you to tour six dynamically different destinations in a single week—provided you're OK with experiencing Europe as day trips in port rather than as a 24/7 immersion course. (For tips on taking tours and cruises smartly, see the Travel Styles chapter.)

On a bus tour or cruise, you dip into Europe here and there. But these options tend to show you a veneered version of Europe. If you really want to have an intimate challenge, an educational, experiential time, and a break from being surrounded by a bunch of other Americans, you'll get the most satisfaction from traveling independently. Just as someone trying to learn a language will do better by actually experiencing that culture rather than sitting in a classroom for a few hours, I believe that travelers in search of engaging, broadening experiences should eat, sleep, and live Europe.

Can I Afford It?

Europe is expensive. Prices are high for locals—and even steeper for Americans. But the Back Door style of travel is better because of—not in spite of—your budget. Spending money has little to do with enjoying

INTRODUCTION

Rick Steves Free Travel Resources

This book is just the tip of a flying wedge of information I've produced and designed to make your trip smooth, efficient, and affordable. By tapping into the resources listed below, you'll have access to the collective travel experience of my 80-person staff and legions of savvy travelers.

www.ricksteves.com

You'll find my latest guidebook updates (www.ricksteves.com /update), fun articles organized by country, a monthly travel enewsletter (easy and free to sign up), and my travel blog.

Our Travel Forums are an immense (yet well-groomed) collection of message boards, where travelers share their personal experiences on the most important or perplexing travel issues of the day (www.ricksteves .com/forums).

Our Travel Forums let you present a particular travel question or problem you are facing and

Scrawl on our Graffiti Wall.

invite other readers to chime in with advice.

You'll also find information on our small-group European bus tours, railpasses for independent travelers, and a wide array of guidebooks, DVDs, luggage, and accessories for sale.

Rick Steves' Europe on Public Television

My public television series covers my favorite continent in 100 episodes (all available on DVD), and we're working on new shows every year. To watch episodes online, visit www.hulu.com; for scripts, local airtimes, and other details, see www.ricksteves.com/tv.

Travel with Rick Steves on Public Radio

My weekly hour-long radio show is carried by nearly 200 public radio stations across the US. I've interviewed the top experts on world travel. Guests have included European royalty, Irish politicians, and authors such as Salman Rushdie and David Sedaris—and I also take questions from listeners. Years of these interviews have been organized into country-specific playlists, available through my free Audio Europe app (described next).

Rick Steves Audio Europe

This free, online library organizes our vast and varied audio content, including my public-radio interviews and my audio tours of major sights in Europe. Download files to your smartphone or other mobile device, and

Our free audio tours cover the top sights in London, Paris, Rome, Florence, Venice, Vienna, Athens, and others.

with one click, you'll have me as your tour guide anytime. Rick Steves Audio Europe is available at www.ricksteves.com/audio europe, iTunes, or as a smartphone app.

your trip. In fact, as we can learn from Europeans, even those who don't have much money manage plenty of *la dolce vita*.

I've been teaching Americans how to travel smart in Europe on a budget for more than three decades, and the tips in this book are tried and tested on the ground every year. The feedback from my readers makes it clear: Enjoying Europe through the back door can be done—by you. For budget tips, see the next chapter.

When I reread my trip journals, I'm reminded that the less I spend, the richer the experience I have. So often the best travel memories have cost little or nothing. If you see dancers in Barcelona celebrating their Catalan heritage in the *sardana* circle dance, join in. Between Sunday services at Paris' St. Sulpice Church, you can scamper like a 16th note up the spiral staircase into the loft to watch Europe's greatest organist play one of Europe's finest pipe organs...and it doesn't cost a thing. In Rome, go to an English-language Mass, then hang around afterward for coffee and cookies. If you're wandering through Santiago de Compostela and hear music and dancers in a gym, pop in and observe. Even in London— Europe's most expensive city—you can have a world-class experience by soaking up its many free museums: Visiting the Tate Gallery, British Museum, and National Gallery won't cost you a pence.

Participate in sports and games, and everyone wins. Join the Scotsman who runs your B&B in a game of lawn bowling, the Frenchman who runs your *chambre d'hôte* in a game of *pétanque,* or the Greek who runs your *dhomatia* for a game of backgammon. Even if you don't know the rules, you'll end up with a memory that's easy to pack and costs nothing.

Making the Most of Your Trip

On the road, I get out of my comfort zone and meet people I'd never encounter at home. In Europe, I'm immersed in a place where people do things—and see things—differently. That's what distinguishes cultures, and it's what makes travel interesting. By being open to differences and staying flexible, I have a better time in Europe—and so will you. Be mentally braced for some surprises, good and bad. Much of the success of your trip will depend on the attitude you pack.

Don't be a creative worrier. Some travelers actively cultivate pre-trip anxiety, coming up with all kinds of reasons to be stressed. Every year there are air-controller strikes, train wrecks, terrorist attacks, small problems turning into large problems, and old problems becoming new again.

Travel is exciting and rewarding because it requires you to ad-lib, to be imaginative and spontaneous while encountering and conquering surprise challenges. Make an art out of taking the unexpected in stride. Relax—you're on the other side of the world playing games in a continental backyard. Be a good sport, enjoy the uncertainty, and frolic in the pits.

Many of my readers' richest travel experiences were the result of seemingly terrible mishaps: the lost

When I see a bunch of cute guys on a bench, I ask 'em to scoot over...

passport in Slovenia, having to find a doctor in Ireland, the blowout in Portugal, or the moped accident on Corfu.

Expect problems, and tackle them creatively. You'll miss a museum or two and maybe blow your budget for the week. But you may well make some friends and stack up some fond memories. This is the essence of travel that you'll enjoy long after your journal is shelved and your trip is stored neatly in the photo album of your mind.

KISS: "Keep it simple, stupid!" Don't complicate your trip. Simplify! Travelers can get stressed and clutter their minds over the silliest things, which, in their niggling ways, can suffocate a happy holiday: standing in a long line at the post office on a sunny day in the Alps, worrying about the correct answers to meaningless bureaucratic forms, having a picnic in pants that make you worry about grass stains, sending away for Swedish hotel vouchers. Concerns like these are outlawed in my travels.

People can complicate their trips with clunky camera gear, special tickets for free entry to all the sights they won't see in England, inflatable hangers, immersion heaters, instant coffee, and 65 Handi-Wipes. They ask for a toilet in 17 words and carry a calculator to convert currencies to the third digit. Travel more like Gandhi—with simple clothes, open eyes, and an uncluttered mind.

...and 30 years later, I'm still one of the gang.

Head off screwups before they happen. If you make a rental-car reservation six weeks early, have everything in careful order, and show up to pick up your car and it's not there, don't be upset with the car-rental company. You messed up. You didn't confirm the day before. Had you made that smart phone call—even though you shouldn't have to—the problem would have been ironed out in advance and you would have avoided that annoying hiccup in your travel plans. Don't have a trip cluttered by other people's mishaps. As your own tour guide, it's your responsibility to call in advance and double-check things all along the way.

Be militantly humble—Attila had a lousy trip. All summer long I'm pushing for a bargain, often for groups. It's the hottest, toughest time of year. Tourists and locals clash. Many tourists leave soured.

When I catch a Spanish merchant shortchanging me, I correct the bill and smile, *"Adiós."* When a French hotel owner blows up at me for no legitimate reason, I wait, smile, and try again. I usually see the irate ranter come to his senses, forget the problem, and work things out.

"Turn the other cheek" applies perfectly to those riding Europe's magic carousel. If you fight the slaps, the ride is over. The militantly humble and hopelessly optimistic can spin forever.

Ask questions. If you are too proud to ask questions, your trip will be dignified...but dull. Many tourists are too afraid or timid to ask questions. The meek may inherit the earth, but they make lousy travelers. Local sources are a wealth of information. People are happy to help a traveler. Hurdle the language barrier. Use a paper and pencil, charades, or whatever it takes to be understood. Don't be afraid to butcher the language.

Ask questions—or be lost. If you are lost, or just lonely and in need of human contact, take out a map and look lost. You'll get help. Perceive friendliness and you'll find it.

Make yourself an extrovert, even if you're not. Be a catalyst for adventure and excitement. Meet people. Make things happen or often they won't. The American casual-and-friendly social style is charming to Europeans who are raised to respect social formalities. While our slap-on-the-back friendliness can be overplayed and obnoxious, it can also be a great asset for the American interested

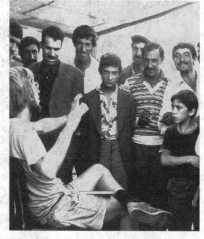

If people stare...sing cowboy songs.

Extroverts Have More Fun

I'm not naturally a wild-and-crazy kind of guy. But when I'm shy and quiet, things don't happen, and that's a bad rut to travel in. So when I'm on the road I make myself an extrovert...and everything changes. Let me describe the same evening twice—first with the mild-and-lazy me, and then with the wild-and-crazy me.

The traffic held me up, so by the time I got to that great museum I'd always wanted to see, it was six minutes before closing. No one was allowed to enter. Disappointed, I walked to a restaurant and couldn't make heads or tails out of the menu. I recognized "steak-frites" and settled for a meat patty and French fries. On the way home I looked into a pub but it seemed dark, so I walked on. A couple waved at me from their balcony, but I didn't know what to say, so I ignored them. I returned to my room and did some laundry.

That's not a night to be proud of. An extrovert's journal entry would read like this:

I got to the museum only six minutes before closing. The guard said no one could enter, but I pleaded with him, saying I'd traveled all the way to see this place. I assured him that I'd be out by closing time, and he gave me a glorious six minutes with a Botticelli painting. At a restaurant that the guard recommended, I couldn't make heads or tails out of the menu. Inviting myself into the kitchen, I met the cooks and got a firsthand look at what was cookin'. What I chose was delizioso! On the way home, I passed a pub, and, while it seemed uninviting, I stepped in anyway, and was greeted by a guy who spoke broken English. He proudly befriended me and told me about his kids (he had pictures), while treating me to his favorite brew. As I headed home, a couple waved at me from their balcony, and I waved back, saying "Buon giorno!" I knew it didn't mean "Good evening," but they understood. They invited me up to their apartment. We joked around—not understanding a lot of what we were saying to each other—and had fun. What a lucky break to be welcomed into a local home! And to think that I could've been back in my room doing laundry!

Pledge every morning to do something entirely different that day. Meet people and create adventure—or bring home a boring journal.

in meeting Europeans. Consider that cultural trait a plus. Enjoy it. Take advantage of it.

Accept that today's Europe is changing. Europe is a complex, mixed bag of the very old and the very new. Among the palaces, quaint folk dancers, and dusty museums, you'll find a living civilization grasping for its future while we romantic tourists grope for its past. This presents us with a sometimes painful dose of truth.

Europe is getting crowded, tense, seedy, polluted, industrialized, hamburgerized, and far from the everything-in-its-place, fairy-tale land so many travelers are seeking. Hans Christian Andersen's statue has four-letter words scrawled across its base. Amsterdam's sex shops and McDonald's share the same streetlamp. In Paris, armies of Sudanese salesmen bait tourists with ivory bracelets and crocodile purses. Drunk punks do their best to repulse you as you climb to St. Patrick's grave in Ireland, and Greek ferryboats dump mountains of trash into their dying Aegean Sea. A 12-year-old boy in Denmark smokes a cigarette like he was born with it in his mouth, and a shoeshine man in Barcelona triple-charges you with a smile. Your must-see cathedral is covered with scaffolding, your must-visit museum is closed for restoration, and your favorite artist's masterpiece is out on loan—probably to the US.

Contemporary Europe is alive and in motion. Keep up! Savor the differences. Even Europeans' eating habits are strange and wondrous. They may have next to nothing for breakfast, mud for coffee, mussels in Brussels, snails in Paris, and dinner at 10 p.m. in Spain. Beer is room-temperature here and flat there, coffee isn't served with dinner, and ice cubes are only a dream.

Germans wait patiently—in the rain—for the traffic light before they cross an empty street, while Roman cars stay in their lanes like rocks in an avalanche. Trains are speedy but rail strikes are as frequent as rain.

On town squares, tattooed violinists play Vivaldi while statue-mime Napoleons jerk into action at the drop of a coin. Locals are more attracted to sidewalk cafés and mobile-phone shops than medieval cathedrals. The latest government tax or austerity measure has everyone talking. Today's problems will fill tomorrow's museums. Feel privileged to walk the vibrant streets of Europe as a student—not as a judge. Be open-minded. Absorb, accept, and learn.

If you can think positively, travel smartly, adapt well, and connect with the culture, you'll have a truly rich European trip. So raise your travel dreams to their upright and locked positions, and let this book fly you away.

Happy travels!

Rick Steves' Back Door Travel Philosophy

Travel is intensified living—maximum thrills per minute and one of the last great sources of legal adventure. Travel is freedom. It's recess, and we need it.

Experiencing the real Europe requires catching it by surprise, going casual..."through the Back Door."

Affording travel is a matter of priorities. (Make do with the old car.) You can eat and sleep—simply, safely, and enjoyably—anywhere in Europe for $120 a day plus transportation costs. In many ways, spending more money only builds a thicker wall between you and what you traveled so far to see. Europe is a cultural carnival, and time after time, you'll find that its best acts are free and the best seats are the cheap ones.

A tight budget forces you to travel close to the ground, meeting and communicating with the people. Never sacrifice sleep, nutrition, safety, or cleanliness to save money. Simply enjoy the local-style alternatives to expensive hotels and restaurants.

Connecting with people carbonates your experience. Extroverts have more fun. If your trip is low on magic moments, kick yourself and make things happen. If you don't enjoy a place, maybe you don't know enough about it. Seek the truth. Recognize tourist traps. Give a culture the benefit of your open mind. See things as different, but not better or worse. Any culture has plenty to share.

Of course, travel, like the world, is a series of hills and valleys. Be fanatically positive and militantly optimistic. If something's not to your liking, change your liking.

Travel can make you a happier American, as well as a citizen of the world. Our Earth is home to seven billion equally precious people. It's humbling to travel and find that other people don't have the "American Dream"—they have their own dreams. Europeans like us, but with all due respect, they wouldn't trade passports.

Thoughtful travel engages us with the world. In tough economic times, it reminds us what is truly important. By broadening perspectives, travel teaches new ways to measure quality of life.

Globetrotting destroys ethnocentricity, helping us understand and appreciate other cultures. Rather than fear the diversity on this planet, celebrate it. Among your most prized souvenirs will be the strands of different cultures you choose to knit into your own character. The world is a cultural yarn shop, and Back Door travelers are weaving the ultimate tapestry. Join in!

BUDGETING AND PLANNING

The best travelers aren't those with the fattest wallets, but those who take the planning process seriously. Jack might jet off to Europe as a free spirit, without much planning and no real itinerary—and return home with a backpack full of complaints about how expensive and stressful it all was. Jill, who enjoys planning and insists on traveling with good information, maps out a detailed day-to-day plan—and returns home with rich stories of spontaneous European adventures. It's the classic paradox of good travel: Structure rewards a traveler with freedom, and "winging it" can become a ball-and-chain of too many decisions, too little information, and precious little time to relax.

In this chapter, I'll help you create a budget for your trip, guide you through the best resources for researching and planning it, give you the scoop on Europe's travel "seasons," and walk you through creating a smart itinerary.

Affording Your Trip

Anticipating costs, knowing your options, and living within your budget are fundamental to a good trip.

I traveled every summer for years on a part-time piano teacher's income (and, boy, was she upset). My idea of "cheap" is simple, not sleazy. I'm not talking about begging and groveling around Europe. I'm talking about enjoying a one-star hotel rather than a three-star hotel ($100 saved), ordering a carafe of house wine at an atmospheric hole-in-the

BUDGETING & PLANNING

wall rather than a bottle of fine wine in a classy restaurant ($40 saved), and taking the shuttle bus in from the airport rather than a taxi ($50 saved). There are plenty of ways to keep your expenses in check without compromising your travel experience. In many ways, the less you spend, the more engaged you are with life around you, and the more you actually experience.

Budget Breakdown

Start penciling out your European budget by getting a handle on your biggest expenses.

Airfare: Prices vary wildly depending on where you're flying from and to, the time of year, and fees (such as airport taxes, fuel surcharges, and baggage fees). For a round-trip flight between the US and Europe, figure about $1,000-1,800 total on average. Understand all of your alternatives (maybe with the help of a good travel agent) in order to make the best choice. Traveling outside of peak season can save you several hundred dollars per ticket.

Transportation Within Europe: This can be reasonable if you use Europe's excellent public transportation system (taking advantage of the best deals) or split a car rental among several people. And cheap flights—about $100 one-way between most major European cities—can save time and money on long journeys. Within cities, figure about $2-3 for each bus or subway ride. Transportation expenses are generally fixed, but your budget should not dictate how freely you travel in Europe. If you want to go somewhere, do it, making the most of whatever money-saving options you can. You came to travel.

Room and Board: The areas that will make or break your budget—over which you have the most control—are your eating and sleeping expenses. In 2014, smart travelers can thrive on $120 a day for room and board: $75 per person in a $150 hotel double with breakfast, $15 apiece for lunch, and $25 for dinner. That leaves you $5 for cappuccino or gelato. Remember that these prices are averages—Scandinavia, Britain, and Italy are more expensive, while Spain, Portugal, Greece, and Eastern Europe are cheaper. Also, as a general rule, you'll pay less in the countryside and more in big cities.

If $120 per day is too steep for your budget, that's no reason to stay home—you can picnic more and stay at simpler accommodations to get by on less. Make your trip match your budget (rather than vice versa). The key is consuming only what you want to consume. If you want real tablecloths and black-tie waiters, your tomato salad will cost 20 times what it costs in the market. If you want a suite with fancy room service

---

Trip Costs

In 2014, you can travel comfortably for a month for $5,600—not including your airfare ($1,000-1,800). If you have extra money, it's more fun to spend it in Europe.

Allow approximately (per person):

$1,000	for a 15-days-in-two-months railpass or shared car rental
800	for sightseeing and entertainment
200	for shopping and miscellany
+3,600	for room and board ($120 a day)
$5,600	

Students or rock-bottom budget travelers can enjoy a month of Europe for about 40 percent less—$3,170 plus airfare.

Allow approximately (per person):

$770	for a one-month youth railpass
500	for sightseeing and entertainment
100	for shopping and miscellany
+1,800	for room and board ($60 a day)*
$3,170	

*$30 for a hostel dorm bed or a bed in a private home with breakfast, $10 for a picnic lunch, $20 for dinner.

---

and chocolate on your pillow, you'll pay in a day for accommodations what many travelers pay in a week.

Sightseeing/Entertainment: Admissions to major attractions are roughly $8-20; smaller sights usually charge $2-5. Concerts, plays, and bus tours cost about $30. Don't skimp here. This category powers most of the experiences that all of the other expenses are designed to make possible. And fortunately, some of the best sights are free.

Shopping/Miscellany: Shopping can vary in cost from nearly nothing to a small fortune. Good budget travelers find that this category has little to do with assembling a trip full of lifelong and wonderful memories.

Budget Tips

We Americans are simply not as rich as we have been conditioned to think we are. For a generation, insiders, politicians, and elites have goosed our economy—and now it just no longer responds to further prodding. We're far from poor. We just need to get real with the fact that rather than hopping into a taxi like a German, we'll stand in line for the bus with the Spaniards. Budget travelers need to seek out money-saving options.

Sleep in cheap hotels. I go to safe, central, friendly, local-style hotels, and I shun swimming pools, people in uniforms, and transplanted American niceties in favor of an opportunity to travel as a temporary European. Hotels are pricey just about everywhere in Europe. But, equipped with good information, you can land some fine deals—which often come with the most memories, to boot.

Try inexpensive, unique alternatives to standard accommodations. On recent visits, I slept well in a former medieval watchtower along Germany's Rhine River (Hotel Kranenturm, $85 double), a room in a private home on the Italian Riviera (Camere Fontana Vecchia in Vernazza, $100 double), and a welcoming guest house in Dubrovnik's Old Town (Villa Ragusa, $100 double). If you're willing to rough it, you'll save even more. Consider a renovated jail in Ljubljana (Hostel Celica, $30 for a bunk in a 12-bed dorm) or a summer-only circus tent in Munich ($10 per mattress).

Patronize family-run restaurants with a local following. The best values are not in the places with glossy menus in six languages out front. I look for family-run restaurants away from the high-rent squares, filled with enthusiastic locals and offering a small, handwritten menu in the local language only. You'll get more for your money at mom-and-pop places; they pay less in labor (family members) and care more about their customers.

You can eat well for under $25 nearly anywhere in Europe by taking advantage of daily specials, lunch deals, and early-bird dinners.

Economize where it's expensive and splurge where it's cheap. The priciest parts of Europe (Scandinavia, Britain, and much of Italy) can be twice as expensive as Europe's cheapest corners (Spain, Portugal, Greece, and Eastern Europe). Exercise budget alternatives where they'll save you the most money. A hostel may save you $10 in Crete but $50 in Finland. In Scandinavia I picnic, walk, and sleep on trains, but I live like a king in Portugal or Poland, where my splurge dollars go the furthest. Those on a tight budget manage better by traveling more quickly through the expensive countries and lingering in the cheap ones.

Lunch for $10, no problema

Comparing *Apfels* to *Pommes*: Relative Prices in Europe's Top Cities

Budget alone should not determine where you go in Europe. People on a shoestring budget can have a blast in Europe's most expensive countries...if they travel smart. But knowing roughly what you'll pay in various destinations can help you craft a more wallet-friendly itinerary. This chart attempts to compare apples to apples by showing rough costs in US dollars for basic tourist expenses in several of Europe's major cities (and, by way of comparison, my hometown in the USA). Note that prices in small towns and the countryside are, as a rule, far lower than in the cities listed here.

	double room at mid-range tour hotel	typical main dish at dinner for a mid-range eatery	one-hour train ride to a nearby town (2nd class)	entrance fee at a top museum
Amsterdam	$165	$22	$15	$18
Athens	$115	$15	$5	$17
Budapest, Kraków, Dubrovnik	$120	$15	$5	$8
Copenhagen, Oslo	$160	$25	$21	$15
London	$200	$20	$39	$25
Madrid, Lisbon	$130	$16	$14	$9
Munich	$125	$21	$28	$10
Paris	$190	$25	$19	$15
Prague	$170	$12	$6	$12
Rome	$210	$15	$13	$17
Vienna	$145	$21	$21	$15
Zürich	$195	$28	$25	$10
Seattle	$150	$15	$14	$15

Eastern European hotels are nearly as pricey as in the West, but other items are a relative steal. A mug of Czech beer—the best in Europe—costs $2 (versus $5 in Britain or Ireland, or $8-10 in Oslo). A ticket for Mozart in a sumptuous Budapest opera house runs $20 (versus $65 in Vienna). And your own private Slovenian guide is $100 for a half-day (versus $200 in London).

Don't take budget tips too far, though. The true "value" of a trip isn't just a function of how cheaply you travel, but how much you enjoy it. If everyone says, "Portugal is cheap," but your travel dreams feature the Swiss Alps, then *your* best value is in Switzerland.

Learn from the locals. When you're in Europe's priciest corners, take the high cost of living gracefully in stride by following the lead of people who live there. Instead of paying dearly for dinner at a restaurant, Norwegians "eat out" in the parks, barbecuing their groceries on disposable "one-time grills" ($4 in supermarkets). The last time I was in a restaurant in Oslo, 16 of 20 diners were drinking only tap water. While you'll see crowds of young people drinking beer along Copenhagen's canals, that doesn't mean consumption is higher in Denmark—it's just that many young adults can't afford to drink in the bars, so they pick up their beer at the grocery store and party

When young Norwegians "eat out," they drop by the grocery store for a disposable "one-time grill" and head for the park.

al fresco. Why not drop by the local equivalent of a 7-Eleven and do the same?

Swallow pride and save money. This is a personal matter, depending largely on how much pride and money you have. Many people cringe every time I use the word "cheap"; others appreciate the directness. Find out the complete price before ordering anything, and say "no thanks" if the price isn't right. Expect equal and fair treatment as a tourist. When appropriate, fight the price, set a limit, and search on. Remember, even if the same thing would cost much more at home, the local rate should prevail. If you act like a rich fool, you're likely to be treated as one.

Spend money to save time. When you travel, time really is money. (Divide the complete cost of your trip by your waking hours in Europe, and you'll see what I mean. My cost: $20 per hour.) Don't waste your valuable time in lines. In Europe's most crowded cities (especially Paris, Rome, and Florence), easy-to-make reservations and museum passes—which pay for themselves in four visits—let you skirt the long ticket-buying lines. If it costs $1 to use your mobile phone to confirm museum times, but it saves you trekking across town to discover the sight is closed, that's a buck very well spent.

Go communal. If you're traveling with a buddy or small group of friends, pool your money for everyday expenses. Separate checks and long lists of petty IOUs are a pain. Plus, combining costs can save you money; for instance, a group of four often travels more cheaply in a shared taxi or rental car than by subway, bus, or train. Note how much each person contributes, and just assume everything equals out in the long run. Keep track of major individual expenses, but don't worry about who got an extra postcard or cappuccino. Enjoy treating each other to taxis and dinners out of your "kitty," and after the trip, divvy up the remains. If one person consumed $50 or $60 more, that's a small price to pay for the convenience and economy of communal money.

Researching Your Trip

Europe is always changing, and it's essential to plan and to travel with the most up-to-date information. Study before you go. Guidebooks, maps, and travel websites are all key resources in getting started.

While information is what keeps you afloat, too much can sink the ship. So winnow down your resources to what best suits your travel needs and interests. For instance, WWII buffs research battle sites, wine lovers brainstorm a wish list of wineries, and MacGregors locate their clan's castles in Scotland.

A word of warning as you hatch your plans: Understand what shapes the information that shapes your travel dreams. Information you seek out yourself is likely to be impartial, whereas information that comes at you is propelled by business (see the sidebar on the next page). Many printed publications and websites are supported by advertisers who have products and services to sell; their information is often useful, but it's not necessarily unbiased. And don't believe everything you read. The power of the printed or pixelated word is scary. Many sources are peppered with information that is flat-out wrong. (Incredibly enough, even this book may have an error.) Some "writers" succumb to the temptation to write travelogues based on hearsay, travel brochures, other books, public-relations junkets, and wishful thinking. A writer met at the airport by an official from the national tourist board learns tips that are handy only for others who are met at the airport by an official from the national tourist board.

Guidebooks and Planning Maps

I am amazed by the many otherwise smart people who base the trip of a lifetime on a borrowed copy of a three-year-old guidebook. The money they save in the bookstore is wasted the first day of their trip, searching for hotels and restaurants long since closed. Guidebooks are $25 tools for

Understanding the Travel Industry

When sorting through all of the options for your trip, you need to understand that we travelers are consumers—and the travel industry is all about selling us things.

Travel media—TV shows, magazines, newspaper articles, and websites—are careful not to offend advertisers. Just like big business lobbies our government, big travel lobbies the travel media. There's a huge appetite these days in travel journalism for lists. "The Best of This" and "Top Fifty That" are what the typical tourist is gobbling up. Plenty of factors that aren't in your interest shape these reports.

The industry in general is geared toward filling resorts, cruise ships, big tour buses, and fancy hotels. There's very little money to be made from independent travel. Consequently, there's little reason to sing its praises in the glossy media that shape many people's travel dreams.

As it's expensive to promote things, attractions and activities that are free or unprofitable are rarely marketed. It's important to be smart about which information you use to determine your itinerary. Don't be too led on by the attractions promoted by leaflets in your hotel lobby, by advertising disguised as tourist information, or by the recommendations of your commission-hungry concierge.

Enjoy the highly publicized attractions—many of them are popular for a reason. But don't let the promotion lead you away from the wonderful world of travel experiences that lie outside the for-profit travel industry—the ones most likely to put you in touch with the people, nature, and culture of Europe. These dimensions, which no big business is pushing with their slick promotional initiatives, are most likely to be the highlights of your trip.

$4,000 experiences. As a writer—and user—of guidebooks, I am a big believer in their worth. When I visit somewhere as a rank beginner, I equip myself with a good, up-to-date guidebook. I travel like an old pro, not because I'm a super traveler, but because I have reliable information and I use it.

With a good guidebook, you can come into Paris for your first time, go anywhere in town for less than $2 on the subway, enjoy a memorable bistro lunch for $20, and pay $150 for a double room in a friendly hotel on a pedestrian-only street a few blocks from the Eiffel Tower—so French that when you step outside in the morning, you feel you must have been a poodle in a previous life.

Never underestimate the value of an up-to-date guidebook.

Before buying any guidebook, check the publication date. If it's last year's edition, find out when the new version is due out. Most guidebooks get an update every two or three years, but a handful of titles (like many of mine) are actually updated in person each year. The rule of thumb: If the year is not printed on the cover, the guidebook is not updated annually. When I'm choosing between guidebooks for a certain destination, the publication date (often on the copyright or title page) is usually the deciding factor.

When you pick up your guidebook, choose a map or two for planning purposes. The *Michelin Map Europe 705* provides an excellent overall view of Europe. Many guidebook publishers (including Rough Guides, Lonely Planet, and Rick Steves) make maps or combination map-guidebooks. For example, my European planning maps are designed to be used with my guidebooks.

If you have a smartphone, ereader, or tablet computer, see "Travel Tools for Portable Devices" (page 258) for advice on using electronic guidebooks, mobile apps, digital maps, and audio tours.

My planning maps highlight what you want to see...not just the biggest cities.

Rick Steves Guidebooks

The book you're holding is the foundation of a series of books—written and refined over the last three decades—that work together to help smooth your travels and broaden your cultural experience. What makes my guidebooks different from the competition? With the help of my research partners, I update my guidebooks lovingly and in person—many of them annually. In order to experience the same Europe that most of my readers do, I insist on doing my research in the peak tourist season—from April through September. And I'm stubbornly selective, writing about fewer destinations than other guidebooks. For example, Italy has dozens of hill towns, but my Italy book zooms in on the handful that are truly worth the trip. I base my depth of coverage on a place's worthiness, rather than its population or fame.

A trio of my books is best read before your trip. *Europe Through the Back Door* teaches you the nuts and bolts of how to travel. **Europe 101: History and Art for the Traveler** (co-authored with Gene Openshaw) helps you achieve a deeper understanding of the story of Europe. *Europe 101* was written for smart people who slept through their art history classes before they knew they were going to Europe...and now they're wishing they knew who the Etruscans were. The book offers a fun and practical sweep through the story of Europe, from the pyramids to Picasso, designed to give meaning to your sightseeing. 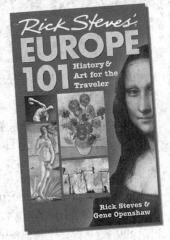 After reading *Europe 101,* you can walk into a Gothic cathedral, excitedly nudge your partner, and marvel, "Isn't this a great improvement over Romanesque?"

The next step, **Travel as a Political Act,** illustrates how Americans who travel with an open mind and a curious spirit can have the time of their lives and come home smarter—with a keener appreciation for the interconnectedness of the world around them. Through a series of field reports from Europe, Central America, Asia, and the Middle East, I explain how you can turn travel into a life-changing experience.

This trilogy forms a pyramid—similar to Abraham Maslow's "hierarchy of needs"—for the thinking traveler. You start off with the basics: Pack light, stay safe, catch the train, and eat and sleep well. When those needs are met, you can enjoy the art, history, and culture. Finally you reach the pinnacle of travel: gaining a deeper understanding of our place on this delightful planet.

But once you're on the road, you need a blueprint for your actual trip. My take-along **guidebooks** weave my favorite sights, accommodations, and restaurants into trip strategies designed to give you the most value out of every mile, minute, and dollar. As a guidebook writer, I focus on helping you explore and enjoy Europe's big cities, small towns, and regions, mixing must-see sights with intimate Back Door nooks and off-

Rick Steves Guidebook Series

Rick Steves City, Regional, and Country Guides

Amsterdam, Bruges & Brussels	*Ireland*
Barcelona	*Istanbul*
Best of Europe	*Italy*
Budapest	*London*
Croatia & Slovenia	*Paris*
Eastern Europe	*Portugal*
England	*Prague & the Czech Republic*
Florence & Tuscany	*Provence & the French Riviera*
France	*Rome*
Germany	*Scandinavia*
Great Britain	*Spain*
Greece: Athens & the Peloponnese	*Switzerland*
	Venice
	Vienna, Salzburg & Tirol

Rick Steves Snapshot Guides

Excerpted from country guidebooks, these slim titles cover many of my favorite destinations, including Lisbon, Scotland, the Cinque Terre, and the Hill Towns of Central Italy.

Rick Steves Pocket Guides

These condensed, colorful guides to Europe's top cities, including Athens, Barcelona, Florence, London, Paris, Rome, and Venice are formatted to slip easily into your pocket.

Rick Steves' Cruise Books

My *Mediterranean Cruise Ports* and *Northern European Cruise Ports* will help you choose and book a cruise, enjoy your time on board, and make the most of your time in port.

Rick Steves Phrase Books

Fun and practical, these guides will help you get along in French, Italian, German, Spanish, Portuguese, and French/Italian/German.

More Rick Steves Books

Europe 101: History and Art for the Traveler
Europe Through the Back Door
European Christmas
Postcards from Europe
Travel as a Political Act

Need help choosing the right Rick Steves guidebook? See www.ricksteves.com/books/update/rightbook.htm

beat crannies. My books cut through the superlatives. Yes, I know you can spend a lifetime in Florence. But you've only got a day and a half, and I've got a great plan. All of my city, regional, and country guides feature engaging, in-depth, self-guided tours of the top sights, highlighting the great art and history with photos and commentary.

If you're planning a wide-ranging trip through the Continent, consider *Rick Steves' Best of Europe.* This "greatest hits" compilation assembles the most popular destinations from my country guidebooks (including many of the Back Doors described in the last half of this book). If its table of contents lists all of your destinations, *Best of Europe* is an all-in-one option that will serve your needs and cost less than several individual country guides.

For some leisure reading laced with inspiration—think of it as a guidebook in disguise—my autobiographical *Rick Steves' Postcards from Europe* takes you on a private tour of my favorite 2,000-mile loop through Europe: from Amsterdam through Germany, Italy, and Switzerland, with a grand finale in Paris. Woven into this fantasy trip are my favorite stories and experiences from over the years, including my first trip to Europe (my parents forced me to go) and my early "Europe Through the Gutter" adventures.

Other Guidebook Series

Every guidebook series has an area of specialization: Some are great for hotels, but fall down on restaurants. Other series can't be beat for history and culture. Some guidebooks (like mine) are more opinionated and selective, choosing only the most worthwhile destinations in each country and covering them in depth. Others seek to cover every possible destination you might find yourself in. When I travel in Europe and beyond—to areas I don't cover in my books—I routinely use guidebooks from these publishers, and find them helpful.

Lonely Planet (www.lonelyplanet.com): The worldwide standard for a solid guidebook, Lonely Planet covers most countries in Europe, Asia, Africa, and the Americas. The Lonely Planet series offers comprehensive, no-nonsense facts, low- and mid-budget listings, and helpful on-the-ground travel tips.

Rough Guides (www.roughguides.com): This British series is written by Europeans who understand the contemporary social scene better than most American writers. While the Rough Guides' hotel listings can be skimpy and uninspired, the historical and sightseeing information tends to offer greater depth than others.

Let's Go (www.letsgo.com): Designed for young train travelers on tight budgets, Let's Go books are written and updated by Harvard students—making them refreshingly youthful and opinionated. Let's Go has retained its super-low-budget approach, is the best resource for shoestring travelers, and offers the best coverage on hosteling and the alternative nightlife scene.

A good guidebook allows you to play "tour guide" and brings Europe's museums to life.

Frommer's Guides (www.frommers.com): Arthur Frommer's books and website are full of listings of hotels, restaurants, and sightseeing tips originally compiled by the father of independent budget travel himself (though new editions are in flux). They're especially well attuned to the needs of older travelers, but some readers may feel like they're being handled with unnecessary kid gloves.

Eyewitness Travel (www.dk.com): These gorgeous visual guides offer appealing color photos and illustrations (like cutaway cross-sections of important castles and churches). They are great for trip planning and visual learners, but the written information is scant—I don't travel with them.

Michelin Green Guides (www.michelintravel.com): From the French publisher Michelin, these famous, tall, green books are packed with full-color maps and photos, as well as small but encyclopedic chapters on history, lifestyles, art, culture, and customs. Recent editions also list hotels and restaurants. The prominence of a listed place on a Green Guide map is determined by its importance to the traveler, rather than its population. This means that a cute, visit-worthy village (such as Rothenburg, Germany) appears bolder than a big, dull city (like Dortmund). The **Michelin Red Guides** are the hotel and restaurant connoisseur's bibles.

Guidebooks: Small, Handy, and Hidden

I often buy several guide-books for each country I visit, rip them up, and staple the pertinent chapters together into my own personalized hybrid guidebook. On the road, I bring only the applicable pages—there's no point in carrying 100 pages of information on Madrid to dinner in Barcelona.

As I travel in Europe, I've met lots of people with clever book treatments. One couple (below left) was proud of the job they did in the name of packing light: cutting out only the pages they'd be using and putting them into a spiral binding. Another couple (below right) put their guidebook in a brown-paper-bag book cover so they wouldn't look so touristy (a smart move, I'll admit).

I love the ritual of customizing the guidebooks I'll be using: I fold the pages back until the spine breaks, then neatly slice out the sections I want with a box-cutter, and pull them out with the gummy edge intact. I use a monster stapler to "rebind" the sections I'm keeping, then finish it off with some clear, heavy-duty packing tape to smooth and reinforce the spine. Another option is to tear out the chapters you don't need and bring the rest in the original binding. To make things even easier, I've created a line of slide-on laminated covers to corral your pages (see www.ricksteves.com).

Blue Guides (www.blueguides.com): Known for a dry and scholarly approach, these guides are ideal if you want a deep dive into history, art, architecture, and culture. With the Blue Guide to Greece, I had all the information I needed about any sight and never needed to hire a guide. Scholarly types actually find a faint but endearing personality hiding between the sheets of their Blue Guides.

Cadogan Guides (www.cadoganguides.com): Readable and thought provoking, Cadogan (rhymes with "toboggan") guides are similar to Blue Guides but more accessible to the typical traveler. They're good pre-trip reading. If you're traveling alone and want to understand tomorrow's sightseeing, Cadogan gives you something productive to do in bed.

Time Out (www.timeout.com): This popular monthly entertainment guide—readily available in Europe—covers many European cities and regions, from Amsterdam to Vienna. Their guidebooks detail sights, entertainment, eating, and sleeping with an insider's savvy. Written with the British market in mind, they have a hard-hitting, youthful edge and assume readers are looking for the trendy scene.

Online Resources

The Internet has taken much of the mystery and uncertainty out of European travel. Wondering where a certain hotel is in Barcelona? Map it online with Google Maps, then check "street view" to get the neighborhood vibe. Thinking about visiting the Eiffel Tower, but worried about getting stuck in a long line? Order up advance tickets online. Want to eat at the latest hot spot in Berlin? Get the inside scoop from a local blog.

Start your Web research with the professionals: Every guidebook publisher has a website (see list of guidebooks, earlier), as do travel magazines and major newspapers with good travel sections. But don't overlook homegrown talent and opinions from other travelers. Here are some sources to consider:

Tourist Information Websites

Just about every European city has a centrally located tourist information office loaded with maps and advice. This is my essential first stop upon arrival in any town, but you don't need to wait until you get to Europe to access

Web Resources

Throughout this book, I've listed helpful websites, including those my staff and I rely on when we're planning our own trips. Here are some that we've found worthwhile. To browse a much more extensive list, visit www.ricksteves.com/links.

General Resources
www.towd.com: Directory of tourism offices worldwide
www.travel.state.gov: US State Department's official travel site, with foreign entry requirements, travel warnings, and more

Air Travel
www.tsa.gov: The latest flight rules and regulations
www.worldtravelguide.net/airport: Arrival information for most of Europe's airports, including how to get into the city center
www.kayak.com: Top site for checking a full range of flight options to and within Europe
www.skyscanner.com: Best search engine for cheap flights within Europe
www.flycheapo.com: Shows which budget airlines fly between any two points

Hotels
www.travelocity.com, **www.expedia.com**, **www.booking.com**, **www.venere.com:** Hotel-booking websites good for initial research (but once you find something that looks interesting, it's best to book direct)
www.mobissimo.com, **www.hotelscombined.com:** Search engines that check multiple hotel sites at once

Trains, Buses, and Boats
www.bahn.com: German Rail timetable, ideal for checking train schedules for anywhere in Europe
www.railfaneurope.net: Links to national rail websites
www.ricksteves.com/rail: Rail guide on railpasses, deals, and point-to-point tickets
www.eurolines.com: Europe's most extensive bus network
www.aferry.co.uk, **www.youra.com/intlferries:** Ferry connections

Driving
www.viamichelin.com, **www.maps.google.com**, **www.theaa.com:** Online maps and a reliable route planner with good estimates of driving times and distances

Travel Tools
www.oanda.com: Currency conversion tool
www.countrycallingcodes.com: International calling made easy

www.howtocallabroad.com: Instructions for dialing internationally from any country

www.translate.google.com: Helpful language translator

www.weather.com: Worldwide weather predictions

www.weatherbase.com: Travel weather and climate averages worldwide

Events

www.timeout.com: Event listings for major European cities

www.ricksteves.com/festivals: Lists of major festivals and national holidays per country

www.sportsevents365.com: Tickets to sporting events and concerts

Social Networking and Traveler Advice

www.gogobot.com: Advice and tips from an extended network of travelers

www.igougo.com: Planning tools, reviews, and photos to spark your wanderlust

www.ricksteves.com/forums: Message boards for swapping tips and tales

www.travellerspoint.com: International meeting point for travelers worldwide

www.tripadvisor.com: Extensive user reviews of hotels and restaurants

www.trippy.com: Tool for creating and sharing travel inspiration boards; also has collaborative trip planner

their information. Each European country has its own official tourism website—often a great place to begin researching your trip. Many of these sites are packed with practical information, suggested itineraries, city guides, interactive maps, colorful photos, and free downloadable brochures describing walking tours and more. In addition, nearly every European country has a national tourist office in the US that you can call or email with specific questions. See page 810 for a list of European tourist offices, and for an even more extensive listing of tourist boards, see www.towd.com.

Local Websites

I'm a big fan of local sites loaded with insider tips. Not only do they fill you in on the latest happenings and hot spots, but they help you feel like a native in no time.

Any major city has a host of online resources dedicated to arts, culture, food, and drink. For instance, AOK is a great city guide to Copenhagen, with helpful information on restaurants, nightlife, and neighborhoods (www.aok.dk). Chew.hu, part of a network of expat sites in Budapest, is a fun read for foodies visiting Hungary. Secrets of Paris, by American-born travel journalist Heather Stimmler-Hall, has a calendar of events, hotel reviews, and a monthly newsletter with dining recommendations and information on exhibits and other Parisian happenings (www.secretsofparis.com).

One of my favorite resources is Matt Barrett's Athens Survival Guide (www.athensguide.com). Matt, who splits his time between North Carolina and Greece, splashes through his adopted hometown like a kid in a wading pool, enthusiastically sharing his discoveries and observations on his generous site. Matt covers emerging neighborhoods that few visitors venture into, and offers offbeat angles on the city and recommendations for vibrant, untouristy restaurants.

Online Traveler Reviews

Review websites, featuring guest opinions from everyday travelers, are changing the travel industry, just as blogs have transformed journalism. These sites are popular tools for finding hotels and restaurants (and in some cases, even sights and activities). They can alert you to some great places to sleep and eat—and warn you about the duds. Using these sites lets you seek a consensus about a business, rather than trusting one travel writer's take.

The biggest of the bunch is TripAdvisor, which maintains a free database of more than 100 million reviews from a wide variety of people.

I find TripAdvisor most useful for hotels, though it also has reviews for restaurants, sights, and tours. Other review websites include Booking.com for hotels and Yelp, which is popular in the US for its restaurant reviews and starting to gain traction in Europe (though the cities covered are limited, and most of the reviews are from tourists rather than locals). For any of these sites, simply look up the place you'll be visiting, and browse for ideas and impressions.

While user reviews allow you to tap into the collective mind of hundreds of people who've traveled before you, they do have their share of drawbacks. European hoteliers and restaurateurs have told me that these reviews (especially on TripAdvisor) can make or break their businesses. But to write a review on TripAdvisor, you need only an email address—making it easy to hide your true identity. Although TripAdvisor works hard to vet reviews, biased ones can make their way through. Also, since reviews come almost exclusively from travelers, "recommendations" tend to skew toward touristy places. I've seen lots of mediocre restaurants with stellar TripAdvisor ratings. How does it happen? Travelers are drawn to glitzy restaurants on the main drag with inoffensive but unexceptional food—creating a self-perpetuating cycle of positive reviews. The so-so place gets more and more popular, while a better, more affordable, and more authentic place may sit ignored, tucked down a side street. (Curious about the reliability of TripAdvisor restaurant ratings, I checked their suggestions for my hometown. The top picks range from truly solid restaurants to touristy places where locals never eat.)

Online travel reviews can be a great place to get information, as long as you use them in conjunction with other resources and don't trust them blindly. But if a hotel or restaurant is well reviewed in a guidebook or two, and also gets good ratings on one of these sites, it's probably a safe bet.

Creating an Itinerary

Each spring through my college years, I'd first determine how much time I could get away for, then I'd buy a cheap plane ticket to Europe—and then I'd figure out where I'd actually go. Filling in the blanks between the flight out and the flight home is one of the more pleasurable parts of trip planning. It's armchair travel that turns into real travel.

I never start a trip without having every day planned out. Your reaction to an itinerary may be, "Hey, won't my spontaneity and freedom suffer?" Not necessarily. Although I always begin a trip with a well-thought-out plan, I maintain my flexibility and make changes as needed. An itinerary forces you to see the consequences of any spontaneous change you make while in Europe. For instance, if you spend two extra days in the sunny Alps, you'll see that you won't make it to the Greek Islands. With the help of an itinerary, you can lay out your goals, maximize their potential, and avoid regrettable changes. (For day-by-day descriptions of my favorite itineraries throughout Europe, see my "Sample Routes," starting on page 754.)

Your itinerary depends on several factors, including weather, crowds, geography, timeline, and travel style (are you antsy to see as much as you can, or do you like settling into a place for a few days?) Take the following considerations into account as you build your European itinerary.

Europe by (Tourist) Season

Some people have flexible enough jobs and lifestyles to cherry-pick when to take their vacations, but many others have less choice. Fortunately, Europe welcomes visitors 365 days a year—and each season offers a different ambience and experience.

In travel-industry jargon, the year is divided into three seasons: peak season (roughly mid-June through August), shoulder season (April through mid-June and September through October), and off-season (November through March). Each has its pros and cons. Regardless of when you go, if your objective is to "meet the people," you'll find Europe filled with them any time of year.

Peak Season

Summer is a great time to travel—except for the crowds and high temperatures. Sunny weather, long days, and exuberant nightlife turn Europe into a powerful magnet. I haven't missed a peak season in 30 years. Families with school-age children are usually locked into peak-season travel. Here are a few tips to help you keep your cool:

In peak season, sunbathers on the beach at Nice are packed like sardines. In shoulder season, it's wide open.

St. Mark's Square in July—no wonder Venice is sinking...

Arrange your trip with crowd control in mind. Go to the busy places as early or late in peak season as you can. Consider, for instance, a six-week European trip beginning June 1, half with a railpass to see famous sights in Italy and Austria, and half visiting relatives in Scotland. It would be wise to do the railpass section first, enjoying fewer crowds, and then spend time with the family during the last half of your vacation, when Florence and Salzburg are teeming with tourists. Salzburg on June 10 and Salzburg on July 10 are two very different experiences.

Seek out places with no promotional budgets. Keep in mind that accessibility and promotional budgets determine a place's fame and popularity just as much as its worthiness as a tourist attraction. The beaches of Greece's Peloponnesian Peninsula enjoy the same weather and water

as the highly promoted isles of Santorini and Ios but are out of the way, underpromoted, and wonderfully deserted. If you're traveling by car, take advantage of your mobility by leaving the well-worn tourist routes. The Europe away from the train tracks is less expensive and feels more peaceful and relaxed. Overlooked by the railpass mobs, it's one step behind the modern parade.

Spend the night. Popular day-trip destinations near

...but any time of the year, walk a few blocks away and it's just you and Venice.

big cities and resorts such as Toledo (near Madrid), San Marino (near huge Italian beach resorts), and San Gimignano (near Florence) take on a more peaceful and enjoyable atmosphere at night, when the legions of day-trippers retreat to the predictable plumbing of their big-city or beach-resort hotels. Small towns normally lack hotels big enough for tour groups and are often inaccessible to large buses. So they will experience, at worst, midday crowds.

Prepare for intense heat. Europeans swear that it gets hotter every year. Even restaurants in cooler climates (like Munich or Amsterdam) now tend to have ample al fresco seating to take advantage of the ever longer outdoor-dining season. Throughout Europe in July and August, expect high temperatures—even sweltering heat—particularly in the south.

Don't discount July and August. Although Europe's tourist crowds can generally be plotted on a bell-shaped curve that peaks in July and August, there are exceptions. For instance, Paris is relatively empty in July and August but packed full in June (conventions) and September (trade shows). Business-class hotels in Scandinavia are cheapest in the summer, when travel—up there, mostly business travel—is down.

In much of Europe (especially Italy and France), cities are partially shut down in July and August, when local urbanites take their beach breaks. You'll hear that these are terrible times to travel, but it's really no big deal. You can't get a dentist, and many launderettes may be closed, but tourists are basically unaffected by Europe's mass holidays. Just don't get caught on the wrong road on the first or fifteenth of the month (when vacations often start or finish, causing huge traffic jams), or try to compete with all of Europe for a piece of French Riviera beach in August.

Some places are best experienced in peak season. Travel in the peak season in Scandinavia, Britain, and Ireland, which rarely have the horrible crowds of other destinations, where sights are too sleepy or even closed in shoulder season, and where you want the best weather and longest days possible. Scandinavia has an extremely brief tourist season—basically from mid-June to late August; I'd avoid it outside this window.

Shoulder Season

"Shoulder season"—generally April through mid-June, September, and October—combines the advantages of both peak-season and off-season travel. In shoulder season, you'll enjoy decent weather, long-enough daylight, fewer crowds, and a local tourist industry still ready to please and entertain.

Shoulder season varies by destination. Because fall and spring bring cooler temperatures in Mediterranean Europe, shoulder season in much of Italy, southern France, Spain, Croatia, and Greece can actually come with near peak-season crowds and prices. For example, except for beach resorts, Italy's peak season is May, June, September, and October, rather than July and August. As mentioned earlier, Paris is surprisingly quiet in July and August.

Spring or fall? If debating the merits of traveling before or after summer, consider your destination. Both weather and crowds are about the same in spring or fall. Mediterranean Europe is generally green in spring, but parched in fall. For hikers, the Alps are better in early fall, because many good hiking trails are still covered with snow through the late spring.

On a budget note, keep in mind that round-trip airfares are determined by your departure date. Therefore, if you fly over during peak season and return late in the fall (shoulder season), you may still pay peak-season round-trip fares.

Off-Season

Every summer, Europe greets a stampede of sightseers. Before jumping into the peak-season pig pile, consider a trip during the off-season—generally November through March.

Expect to pay less—most of the time. Off-season airfares are often hundreds of dollars cheaper. With fewer crowds in Europe, you may find you can sleep for less: Many fine hotels drop their prices, and budget hotels will have plenty of vacancies. And while many B&Bs and other non-hotel budget accommodations may be closed, those still open are usually empty and, therefore, more comfortable.

To save some money, show up late in the day, notice how many open rooms they have (keys on the rack), let them know you're a hosteler (student, senior, artist, or whatever) with a particular price limit, and bargain

Where are the tourists?

from there. The opposite is true of big-city business centers (especially in Berlin, Brussels, and the Scandinavian capitals), which are busiest and most expensive off-season.

Enjoy having Europe to yourself. Off-season adventurers loiter all alone through Leonardo da Vinci's home, ponder in Rome's Forum undisturbed, kick up sand on lonely Adriatic beaches, and chat with laid-back guards by log fires in French châteaux. In wintertime Venice, you can be all alone atop St. Mark's bell tower, watching the clouds of your breath roll over the Byzantine domes of the church to a horizon of cut-glass Alps. Below, on St. Mark's Square, pigeons fidget and wonder, "Where are the tourists?"

Off-season adventurers enjoy step-right-up service at shops and tourist offices, and experience a more European Europe. Although many popular tourist-oriented parks, shows, and tours will be closed, off-season is in-season for high culture: In Vienna, for example, the Boys' Choir, opera, and Lipizzaner stallions are in all their crowd-pleasing glory.

Italy's Cinque Terre villages are empty in the winter...and the good restaurants close for a much-needed extended holiday.

Be prepared for any kind of weather. Because much of Europe is at Canadian latitudes, the winter days are short. It's dark by 5:00 p.m. The weather can be miserable—cold, windy, and drizzly—and then turn worse.

Pack for the cold and wet—layers of clothing, rainproof parka, gloves, wool hat, long johns, waterproof shoes, and an umbrella. Dress warmly. Cold weather is colder when you're outdoors trying to enjoy yourself all day long, and cheap hotels are not always adequately heated in the off-season. But just as summer can be wet and gray, winter can be crisp and blue, and even into mid-November, hillsides blaze with colorful leaves.

Beware of shorter hours. Make the most out of your limited daylight hours. Some sights close down entirely, and most operate on shorter hours, with darkness often determining the closing time. Winter sightseeing is fine in big cities, which bustle year-round, but it's more frustrating in small tourist towns, which can be boringly quiet, with many sights and restaurants closed down. In December, many beach resorts shut up as tight as canned hams. While Europe's wonderful outdoor

In the north, darkness falls early in the winter. This is Oslo at 3:30 p.m.

evening ambience survives all year in the south, wintertime streets are empty in the north after dark. English-language tours, common in the summer, are rare off-season, when most visitors are natives. Tourist information offices normally stay open year-round, but have shorter hours in the winter. Opening times are less predictable, so call ahead to double-check hours and confirm your plans.

Itinerary Considerations

When planning your trip itinerary, deal thoughtfully with issues such as weather, culture shock, health maintenance, fatigue, and festivals—and you'll travel happier.

Establish a logical flight plan. It's been years since I flew into and out of the same city. You can avoid needless travel time and expense by flying into one airport and out from another. You usually pay just half the round-trip fare for each airport. Even if this type of flight plan is more expensive than the cheapest round-trip fare, it may save you lots of time and money when surface connections are figured in. For example, you could fly into London, travel east through whatever interests you in Europe, and fly home from Athens. This would eliminate the costly and time-consuming return to London. Plug various cities into flight websites and check the fares. For more on choosing flights, see page 87.

See countries in order of cultural hairiness. If you plan to see Britain, the Alps, Greece, and Turkey, do it in that order so you'll grow steadily into the more intense and crazy travel. If you've never been out of the US, flying directly into Istanbul can be overwhelming. Even if you did survive Turkey, everything after that would be anticlimactic. Start mild—that means England. England, compared to any place but the United States, is pretty dull. Don't get me wrong—it's a wonderful place to travel. But go there first, when cream teas and roundabouts will be exotic. You're more likely to enjoy Turkey, Naples, or Sarajevo if you gradually work your way south and east.

Match your destination to your interests. If you're passionate about Renaissance art, Florence is a must. England's Cotswolds beckon to those who fantasize about thatched cottages, time-passed villages, and sheep lazing on green hillsides. For World War II buffs, there's no more stirring experience than a visit to Normandy. Beer connoisseurs make pilgrimages to Belgium. If you like big cities, you'll enjoy London, Paris, Rome, and Venice. Want to get off the beaten path? Nothing rearranges your mental furniture like a trip to Bosnia's Mostar or Morocco's Tangier.

If you have European roots, a fun part of travel is to discover a kinship with people from the land of your ancestors. I can't tell you how many American Murphys, Kellys, and O'Somethings I meet in Ireland, in search of their roots and a good beer. When in Scandinavia, I feel like I'm among cousins. Then, when I cross the border into Norway, I feel like I'm among brothers and sisters. Because I'm Norwegian, everyone there looks like family.

Moderate the weather conditions you'll encounter. For 30 years of travels, my routine has been spring in the Mediterranean area and summer north of the Alps. Match the coolest month of your trip with the warmest area, and vice versa. For a spring and early-summer trip, enjoy comfortable temperatures throughout by starting in the southern countries and working your way north. If possible, avoid the midsummer Mediterranean heat and crowds of Italy and southern France. Spend those weeks in Scandinavia, Britain, Ireland, or the Alps (which may also increase your odds of sun in places prone to miserable weather). For average temperatures, see the climate charts in the appendix.

Alternate intense big cities with villages and countryside. For example, break a tour of Venice, Florence, and Rome with an easygoing time in Italy's hill towns or on the Italian Riviera. Judging Italy by Rome alone is like judging America by New York City.

Join the celebration. If you like parties, hit as many festivals, national holidays, and arts seasons as you can (or, if you hate crowds, learn the dates to avoid). This takes some planning. For a calendar of events, try national tourist offices (listed in appendix), www.ricksteves .com/festivals, and official festival websites (the bigger ones have their own). An effort to visit the right places at the right times will drape your trip with festive tinsel. Remember to book your room well in advance.

Take advantage of cheap flights within Europe. The recent proliferation of no-frills, low-budget airlines in Europe is changing the way people design their itineraries. Two decades ago, you'd piece together a trip based on which towns could be connected by handy train trips (or, at most, overnight trains). But these days, it's relatively cheap and easy to combine, say, Portugal, Poland, and Palermo on a single itinerary. For more on cheap flights, see page 102.

Minimize one-night stands. Even the speediest itinerary should be a series of two-night stands. I'd stretch every other day with long hours on the road or train and hurried sightseeing along the way in order to enjoy the sanity of two nights in the same bed. Minimizing hotel changes saves time and money, and gives you the sensation of actually being comfortable in a town on the second night.

Leave some slack in your itinerary. Don't schedule yourself too tightly (a common tendency). Everyday chores, small business matters, transportation problems, constipation, and planning mistakes deserve about one day of slack per week in your itinerary. If your trip is a long one, schedule a "vacation from your vacation" in the middle of it. Most people need several days in a place where they couldn't see a museum or take a tour even if they wanted to. A stop in the mountains or on an island, in a friendly rural town, or at the home of a relative is a great way to revitalize your tourist spirit.

Assume you will return. This "General MacArthur approach" is a key to touristic happiness. You can't see all of Europe in one trip—don't even try. Enjoy what you're seeing. Forget what you won't get to on this trip. If you worry about things that are just out of reach, you won't appreciate what's in your hand. I've taken dozens of European trips, and I still need more time. I'm happy about what I can't get to. It's a blessing that we can never see all of Europe.

Your Best Itinerary in Seven Steps

Trying to narrow your choices among European destinations is a bit like being a kid in a candy shop. The options are endless and everything looks delicious (and consuming too much isn't good for you). Start by listing everything you'd like to visit, then turn that list into a smart itinerary by following these steps.

1. Decide on the places you want to see. Have a reason for every stop. Don't visit Casablanca only because you liked the movie. Just because George Clooney bought a villa on Lake Como doesn't mean you should go there, too.

Minimize redundancy. On a quick trip, focus on only one part of the Alps. England's two best-known university towns, Oxford and Cambridge, are redundant. Choose one (I prefer Cambridge).

Example: Places I want to see— London, Alps, Bavaria, Florence, Amsterdam, Paris, the Rhine, Rome, Venice, Greece.

2. Establish a route and timeline. Circle your destinations on a map, then figure out a logical

Sample Itinerary

To/From USA
London
ENG. Dover
Calais
NETH.
Amsterdam
GERMANY
Koblenz
Bacharach
(Rhine Cruises)
Frankfurt
Bingen
Paris
Rothenburg
Versailles
ROMANTIC ROAD
Munich
Neuschwanstein
Salzburg
FRANCE
SWITZ.
Interlaken
AUSTRIA
Berner Oberland
ITALY
Venice
100 Miles
200 Kilometers
Nice
Florence
Mediterranean Sea
Rome

NT — Night Train
● — Overnight
···· — Rhine Cruise

geographical order and length for your trip. Pin down any places that you have to be on a certain date (and ask yourself if it's really worth stifling your flexibility). Once you've settled on a list, be satisfied with your efficient plan, and focus any more study and preparation only on places that fall along your proposed route.

3. Decide on the cities you'll fly in and out of. Flying into one city and out of another is usually more efficient than booking a round-trip flight. Think carefully about which cities make the most sense as a first stop or a finale.

4. Determine the mode of transportation. Do this not based solely on cost, but by analyzing what's best for the trip you envision. Study the ins and outs of the many ways of getting from point A to point B—whether flying, riding the rails, driving, biking, or hiking.

Example: On this hypothetical trip I'm traveling alone, traversing a huge area, and spending the majority of my time in big cities—so I'd rather not mess with a car. I'll use a railpass and go by train.

5. Make a rough itinerary. Sketch out an itinerary, writing in the number of days you'd like to stay in each place (knowing you'll probably have to trim it later). Carefully consider travel time. Driving, except on expressways, is slower than in the US. Check online to estimate how long various journeys will take by rail (www.bahn.com) or by car (www.maps.google.com). Consider night trains (NT) or overnight boats (NB) to save time and money.

Example: Logical order and desired number of days in each place:

3	*London*
5	*Paris*
3	*Alps*
2	*Florence*
3	*Rome (flight or NB)*
7	*Greece (flight or NB)*
1	*Bologna*
2	*Venice (NT)*
3	*Munich/Bavaria*
3	*Romantic Road/Rhine Cruise*
3	*Berlin*
4	*Amsterdam*

39 TOTAL DAYS

Notes: I have 23 days for my vacation. Greece is time-consuming, even if I fly into one city and out from another. If I eliminate Greece, I'll still need to cut 9

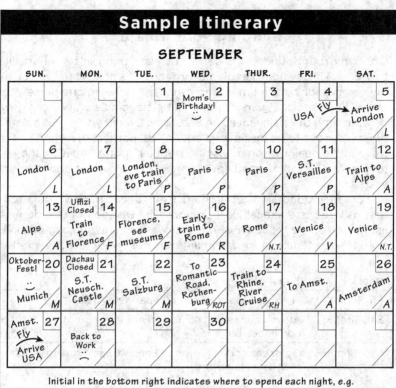

Sample Itinerary

SEPTEMBER

SUN.	MON.	TUE.	WED.	THUR.	FRI.	SAT.
		1	2 Mom's Birthday! :)	3	4 USA Fly → Arrive London	5 Arrive London / L
6 London / L	7 London / L	8 London, eve train to Paris / P	9 Paris / P	10 Paris / P	11 S.T. Versailles / P	12 Train to Alps / A
13 Alps / A	Uffizi Closed 14 Train to Florence / F	15 Florence, see museums / F	16 Early train to Rome / R	17 Rome / N.T.	18 Venice / V	19 Venice / N.T.
Oktober- 20 Fest! :) Munich / M	Dachau 21 Closed S.T. Neusch. Castle / M	22 S.T. Salzburg / M	To 23 Romantic Road, Rothen- burg / ROT	Train to 24 Rhine, River Cruise / RH	25 To Amst. / A	26 Amsterdam / A
Amst. 27 Fly → Arrive USA	28 Back to Work :)	29	30			

Initial in the bottom right indicates where to spend each night, e.g.
L = London   N.T. = Night Train
(S.T. = Side Trip)

days. *Flying into London and out of Amsterdam is economical. Logical order may be affected by night-train possibilities.*

Example: According to the guidebooks, I must keep these points in mind as I plan my trip. London: Theaters closed on Sunday, Speaker's Corner is Sunday only. Paris: Many museums are closed on Tuesday. Versailles and the Orsay Museum are closed on Monday. Florence: Museums are closed on Monday. Concentration-camp memorial in Dachau: Closed on Monday. Note that I'm choosing to pay a little extra on my flight to let my trip stretch over the weekends and minimize lost work time. Yes, I may be a zombie on that first Monday back, but hey, what's more important?

6. Adjust by cutting, streamlining, or adding to fit your timeline or budget. Minimize travel time. When you must cut something, cut to save the most mileage. For instance, if Amsterdam and Berlin are equally important to you and you don't have time for both, cut the destination that saves the most miles (in this case, Berlin).

Minimize clutter. A so-so sight (Bologna) breaking a convenient

Building Your Itinerary

Once my rough itinerary is set, I put everything into a chart like this one. This system keeps me organized, since I can collect all my reservations, train times, and other trip notes in one place. As I travel, I can see at a glance where I'll be sleeping a week from now, or what time the train leaves on Saturday. Even if you're not a detail person, it pays to be disciplined about this, particularly when you're traveling in peak season or visiting popular spots. And it's handy to give to family, friends, and coworkers who are curious about where you'll be.

Create an itinerary like this, then use it to keep track of your progress as you systematically set up your trip. Decide from guidebook listings or online research where you want to stay in each destination. Make a template for an email room-reservation request letter.

Date	Travel
Fri, Sept 4	Fly to London after work (depart 6:00 p.m.)
Sat, Sept 5	Arrive London at 11:45 a.m., check in at hotel, take orientation bus tour
Sun, Sept 6	Sightsee London (Tower of London, Shakespeare's Globe tour, Tate Modern)
Mon, Sept 7	See more London (Westminster Abbey, National Gallery, evening play)
Tue, Sept 8	Wrap up London (St. Paul's/The City, British Museum); take evening train to Paris (6:00-9:20 p.m.)
Wed, Sept 9	Sightsee Paris (historic core, incl. Notre-Dame, Sainte-Chapelle; also Louvre, Eiffel Tower at night)
Thu, Sept 10	Sightsee Paris (Champs-Elysées, Rodin Museum, Orsay)
Fri, Sept 11	Side-trip to Versailles
Sat, Sept 12	Take morning train to Swiss Alps (7:00 a.m.-2:00 p.m. in Interlaken, transfer in Mannheim and Basel); maybe hike in late afternoon
Sun, Sept 13	Sightsee Alps (breakfast at the Schilthorn, Männlichen-Kleine Scheidegg hike)
Mon, Sept 14	Short morning hike and/or visit Trümmelbach Falls, afternoon train to Florence (from Interlaken 1:30-7:00 p.m.)

and so on...

Work your way through your list and request rooms, slogging away until the entire trip is set up. Then...travel, enjoying a well-planned trip.

Notes and Reminders

- Find out if my mobile phone works in Europe.
- Arrange for cat-sitter.
- Reserve Chunnel and overnight trains in advance.
- Make reservations for Eiffel Tower (Sept 9).
- Find out about festivals—check online or call national tourist offices.
- Cancel newspaper, hold mail delivery, prepay bills.
- Double-check the "Before You Go" list (see page 66).

Notes	Sleep
	Plane
Original London Sightseeing Bus Tour is discounted with guidebook	Luna Simone Hotel, London www.lunasimonehotel.com
Many theaters, churches & museums closed today; Speaker's Corner open today only	Luna Simone Hotel, London
Parliament open late; check for discount theater tickets at Leicester Square	Luna Simone Hotel, London
Confirm Paris hotel before leaving London	Grand Hôtel Lévêque, Paris www.hotel-leveque.com
Museums crowded today; Louvre open late	Grand Hôtel Lévêque, Paris
Orsay open late	Grand Hôtel Lévêque, Paris
Reserve train for tomorrow?	Grand Hôtel Lévêque, Paris
Reserve Interlaken-Florence train for Monday?	Olle and Maria's B&B, Gimmelwald oeggimann@bluewin.ch
If rainy, visit Bern	Olle and Maria's B&B, Gimmelwald
If rainy, take morning train to Florence (from Interlaken 8:01 a.m.- 2:00 p.m.); on arrival, do walking tour since most museums closed	Hotel Centrale, Florence, info@hotelcentralefirenze.it

night train (Rome-Venice) into two half-day journeys is clutter.

Trim time from each stop. Five days in Paris would be grand, but you can see the high points in three.

Consider economizing on car rental or a railpass. For instance, try to manage a 23-day trip on a 15-day train pass by seeing London, Paris, and Amsterdam before or after you use the pass.

Example: Itinerary and number of days adjusted to time limitations:

3	London
3	Paris
3	Alps
1	Florence
2	Rome (NT)
2	Venice (NT)
3	Munich/Bavaria
2	Romantic Road/Rhine Cruise
2	Amsterdam

23 *TOTAL DAYS (including 2 travel days)*

7. Fine-tune your itinerary. Study your guidebook. Maximize festival and market days. Be sure crucial sights are open the day you'll be in town. Remember that most cities close many of their major tourist attractions for one day during the week (usually Monday). It would be a shame to be in Paris only on a Tuesday, when the Louvre is *fermé*. Write out a day-by-day itinerary. Note that when flying from the United States, you'll most likely arrive in Europe on the next day. When returning, you arrive home the same day (or so you hope).

The Home-Base Strategy

Staying longer in one spot can be a good way to make your trip itinerary smoother, simpler, and more efficient. Set yourself up in a central location and use that place as a base for day trips to nearby attractions.

The home-base approach minimizes set-up time. Changing hotels frequently can be exhausting, frustrating, and time-consuming. Many hotels give a better price, or at least more smiles, for longer stays. Some B&Bs don't accept those staying only one night.

You are freed from your luggage. Being able to leave your luggage in the hotel lets you travel freely and with the peace of mind that you are set for the night. Bags are less likely to be lost or stolen in your hotel than en route.

You feel "at home" in your home-base town. This comfortable feeling takes more than a day to get, and when you're changing locations every day or two, you may never enjoy this important sense of rootedness. Home-basing allows you to become attuned to the rhythm of daily life.

Day-trip to a village, enjoy the nightlife in a city. The home-base approach lets you spend the evening in a city, where there is more exciting nightlife. Most small countryside towns die after 9:00 p.m. If you're not dead by 9:00 p.m., you'll enjoy the action in a larger city.

Transportation is a snap. Europe's generally frequent and punctual train and bus systems (many of which operate out of a hub anyway) make this home-base strategy practical. With a train pass, trips are "free"; otherwise, the transportation is reasonable, sometimes with reductions offered for round-trip tickets (especially for "same-day return").

Good Home-Base Cities

Here are some of my favorite places to call home, along with the best day trips from each:

Madrid: Toledo, Segovia, El Escorial, and even Sevilla and Córdoba with the AVE bullet trains

Amsterdam: Most of the Netherlands, particularly Alkmaar, Enkhuizen's Zuiderzee Museum, Arnhem's Folk Museum and Kröller-Müller Museum, Scheveningen, Delft/The Hague, and Edam

Copenhagen: Frederiksborg Castle, Roskilde, Helsingør, Odense, and over the bridge to Malmö (Sweden)

Paris: Versailles, Chartres, Vaux-le-Vicomte, Fontainebleau, Chantilly, Giverny, Reims

London: Bath, Stonehenge, Stratford-upon-Avon, Cambridge, York, and many others; even Paris is less than three hours away by train

Arles: Pont du Gard, Nîmes, Avignon, and the rest of Provence

Florence: Siena, Pisa, San Gimignano, and many other hill towns

Venice: Padua, Vicenza, Verona, and Ravenna

Munich: Salzburg, "Mad" King Ludwig's castles (Neuschwanstein and Linderhof), the Wieskirche, Oberammergau, and other small Bavarian towns

Sorrento: Naples, Pompeii, Herculaneum, Mount Vesuvius, Amalfi Coast, Paestum, and Capri

High-Speed Town-Hopping

When I tell people that I saw three or four towns in one day, many think, "Insane! Nobody can really see several towns in a day!" Of course, it's folly to go too fast, but many stop-worthy towns take only an hour or two to cover. Don't let feelings of guilt tell you to slow down and stay longer if you really are finished with a town. There's so much more to see in the rest of Europe. Going too slow is as bad as going too fast.

If you're efficient and use the high-speed town-hopping method, you'll amaze yourself with what you can see in a day. Let me explain with an example:

You wake up early in A-ville. Checking out of your hotel, you have one sight to see before your 10:00 a.m. train. (You checked the train schedule the night before.) After the sightseeing and before getting to the station, you visit the open-air market and buy the ingredients for your brunch, and pick up a B-burg map and tourist brochure at A-ville's tourist office.

From 10:00 to 11:00 a.m. you travel by train to B-burg. During that hour you have a restful brunch, enjoy the passing scenery, and prepare for B-burg by reading your literature and deciding what you want to see. Just before your arrival, put the items you need (camera, jacket, tourist information) into your small daypack. Then, as soon as you get there, check the rest of your luggage in a locker. (Most stations have storage lockers or a baggage-check desk.)

Before leaving B-burg's station, write down the departure times of the next few trains to C-town. Now you can sightsee as much or as little as you want and still know when to comfortably catch your train.

B-burg is great, so you stay a little longer than anticipated. After a snack in the park, you catch the train at 2:30 p.m. By 3:00 p.m. you're in C-town, where you repeat the same procedure you followed in B-burg. C-town just isn't what it was cracked up to be, so after a walk along the waterfront and a look at the church, you catch the next train out at 5:00 p.m.

You arrive in D-dorf, the last town on the day's agenda, by 5:30 p.m. A man in the station directs you to a good budget pension two blocks down the street. You're checked in and unpacked in no time, and, after a few horizontal moments, it's time to find a good restaurant and eat dinner. After a meal and an evening stroll, you're ready to call it a day. As you write in your journal, it occurs to you: This was a great sightseeing day. You spent it high-speed town-hopping.

Prioritizing Your Time

So much to see, so little time. How to choose? It depends on your interest and your tastes. One person's Barcelona is another person's Bucharest.

The Best and Worst of Europe (With No Apologies)

Good travel writers should make hard choices and give the reader solid opinions. Just so nobody will accuse me of gutlessness, I've assembled a pile of spunky opinions. Chances are that you have too many stops on your trip wish list and not enough time. To make your planning a little easier, heed these warnings. These are just my personal feelings after more than 100 months of European travel. And if you disagree with any of them, you obviously haven't been there.

Let's start with the dullest corner of the British Isles, southern Scotland. It's so boring the Romans decided to block it off with Hadrian's Wall. However, like Venice's St. Mark's Square at midnight and Napoleon's tomb in Paris, Hadrian's Wall itself covers history buffs with goose bumps.

London, York, Bath, and Edinburgh are the most interesting cities in Britain. Belfast, Liverpool, and Glasgow are quirky enough to be called interesting. Oxford pales next to Cambridge, and Stratford-upon-Avon is little more than Shakespeare's house—and that's as dead as he is.

Kissing the Blarney Stone: Slathered with spit and lipstick, it's a standard stop for typical big-bus tours in Ireland.

The west coast of Ireland (the Dingle Peninsula), Wales' Snowdonia National Park, and England's Windermere Lake District are the most beautiful natural regions of the British Isles. The North York Moors disappoint most creatures great and small.

Germany's Heidelberg, Ireland's Blarney Stone (slobbered on by countless tourists to get the "gift of gab"), Spain's Costa del Sol, and the French Riviera in July and August are among Europe's most overrated spots. The tackiest souvenirs are found next to Pisa's leaning tower and in Lourdes.

Extra caution is merited in southwest England, a minefield of tourist

Itinerary Priorities, Country by Country

Use this chart to get ideas on how speedy travelers can prioritize limited sightseeing time in various countries. Add places from left to right as you build plans for the best of that country in 3, 5, 7, 10, or 14 days. (These suggestions take geographical proximity into account. In some cases, the plan assumes you'll take a night train.) So, according to this chart, the best week in Britain would be spread between London, Bath, Cambridge, and the Cotswolds.

Country	3 days	5 days	7 days	10 days	14 days
Europe	Forget it	London, Paris	Amsterdam	Rhineland, Swiss Alps	Rome, Venice
Britain	London	Bath	Cambridge, Cotswolds	York	Edinburgh, North Wales
Ireland	Dublin	Dingle Peninsula	Belfast	Galway/the Burren	Antrim Coast, Aran Islands
France	Paris, Versailles	Normandy	Loire	Dordogne, Carcassonne	Provence, the Riviera
Germany	Munich, Bavarian castles	Rhine Valley, Rothenburg	More of Bavaria, Salzburg (Austria)	Berlin	Baden-Baden, Black Forest, Dresden
Austria	Vienna	Salzburg	Hallstatt	Danube Valley, Tirol, Bavaria (Germany)	Innsbruck, Hall, Bratislava (Slovakia)

traps. The British are masters at milking every conceivable tourist attraction for all it's worth. Here are some booby traps: the Devil's Toenail (a rock that looks just like a...toenail), Land's End (pay, pay, pay), and cloying Clovelly (a one-street town lined with knickknack shops selling the same goodies—like "clotted cream that you can mail home"). While Tintagel's castle, famous as the legendary birthplace of King Arthur, offers thrilling wind-

England's Land's End...pay, pay, pay.

Country	3 days	5 days	7 days	10 days	14 days
Switzerland	Berner Oberland	Luzern	Bern, Lausanne	Zermatt, Appenzell, scenic rail trip	Lugano and Zürich
Italy	Florence, Venice	Rome	Cinque Terre	Civita di Bagnoregio, Siena	Sorrento, Naples, Pompeii, Amalfi Coast
Scandinavia	Copen-hagen, side-trips	Stockholm	Oslo	"Norway in a Nutshell" train trip, Bergen	Helsinki, Tallinn
Spain	Madrid, Toledo	Sevilla, Granada	Barcelona	Andalucía	Costa del Sol, Morocco
Portugal	Lisbon, Sintra	The Algarve	Évora, Nazaré	Sights near Nazaré, Coimbra	Porto, Douro Valley
Eastern Europe	Prague	Budapest	Kraków and Auschwitz	Slovenia and Český Krumlov	Dalmatian Coast with Dubrovnik
Croatia & Slovenia	Dubrovnik	Mostar, Split	Korčula/ Hvar or Montenegro	Lake Bled, Plitvice Lakes	Ljubljana, Rovinj
Greece	Athens	Hydra	Delphi	Nafplio, Epidavros, Mycenae	Olympia, Monemvasia, Mani Peninsula

swept and wave-beaten ruins, the town of Tintagel does everything in its little power to exploit the profitable Arthurian legend. There's even a pub in town called the Excali Bar.

Sognefjord is Norway's most spectacular fjord. The Geirangerfjord, while famous as a cruise-ship stop, is a disappointment. The most boring countryside is Sweden's (yes, I'm Norwegian), although Scandinavia's best medieval castle is in the Swedish town of Kalmar.

Norway's Stavanger, famous for nearby fjords and its status as an oil boomtown, is a large port that's about as exciting as...well, put it this way: Emigrants left it in droves to move to the wilds of Minnesota. Time in western Norway is better spent in and around Bergen.

Geneva, one of Switzerland's largest and most sterile cities, gets the "nice place to live but I wouldn't want to visit" award. It's pleasantly situated on a lake—just like Buffalo is. While it's famous, name familiarity is a rotten reason to go somewhere. If you want a Swiss city, see Bern or Luzern. However, it's almost criminal to spend a sunny Swiss day in a city if you haven't yet been high in the Alps.

Geneva's newspaper objects to my "denigrating" its dull city on the Internet.

Bordeaux must mean "boredom" in some ancient language. If I were offered a free trip to that town, I'd stay home and clean the fridge. Connoisseurs visit for the wine, but Bordeaux wine country and Bordeaux city are as different as night and night soil. There's a wine-tourism information bureau in Bordeaux that, for a price, will bus you out of town into the more interesting wine country nearby.

Andorra, a small country in the Pyrenees between France and Spain, is as scenic as any other chunk of those mountains. People from all over Europe flock to Andorra to take advantage of its famous duty-free shopping. As far as Americans are concerned, Andorra is just a big Spanish-speaking outlet mall. There are no bargains here that you can't get at home. Enjoy the Pyrenees elsewhere, with less traffic. Among Europe's other "little countries," San Marino and Liechtenstein are also not worth the trouble.

Germany's famous Black Forest disappoints more people than it excites. If it were all Germany offered, it would be worth seeing. For Europeans, any large forest is understandably a popular attraction. But I'd say the average American visitor who's seen more than three trees in one place would prefer Germany's Romantic Road and Bavaria to the east, the Rhine and Mosel country to the north, the Swiss Alps to the south, and France's Alsace region to the west—all high points that cut the Black Forest down to stumps.

Kraków (Poland) and Budapest (Hungary) are, after Prague, Eastern Europe's best cities. Bucharest, Romania's capital, has little to offer. Its top-selling postcard is of the InterContinental Hotel. If you're heading from Eastern Europe to Greece, skip Thessaloniki, which deserves its place in the Bible but doesn't belong in travel guidebooks.

Europe's most scenic train ride is the Glacier Express, across southern Switzerland from Chur to Zermatt. The most scenic boat ride is from Stockholm to Helsinki—countless islands and blondes. Europe's most underrated sight is Rome's ancient seaport, Ostia Antica, and its most misunderstood wine is Portugal's *vinho verde* (green wine).

The best French château is Vaux-le-Vicomte, near Paris. The best Gothic interior is found in Paris' Sainte-Chapelle church. The top two medieval castle interiors are Germany's Burg Eltz on the Mosel River, and northern Italy's Reifenstein, near the Brenner Pass. Lisbon, Oslo, Stockholm, Brussels, and Budapest are the most underrated big cities.

To honeymoon (or convalesce), try these tiny towns: Beilstein on Germany's Mosel River; Hallstatt on Austria's Lake Hallstatt; Varenna on Italy's Lake Como; Ærøskøbing on an island in south Denmark; and Gimmelwald, high in the Swiss Alps. Have fun (or get well)!

PAPER CHASE

Someday, perhaps, travel will be paperless. But we're not there yet, and you'll want to be prepared with the necessary documents and know your insurance options. Here's how you can stay ahead in the inevitable paper chase.

Travel Documents

Your trip won't get off the ground if you don't prepare these documents well before your departure date. Give yourself plenty of lead time.

Passports

In much of Europe, the only document a US or Canadian citizen needs is a passport. (The US Passport Card works only for those driving or cruising to Canada, Mexico, Bermuda, and the Caribbean.) And for most American travelers, the only time any customs official looks at you seriously is at the airport as you re-enter the United States.

Getting or Renewing Your Passport: US passports, good for 10 years, cost $135 ($110 to renew). The fee for minors under 16 (including infants) is $105 for a passport good for five years—kids under 16 must apply in person with at least one parent and the other parent's notarized permission. (Parents traveling abroad with children should refer to page 435 for other special document needs.)

You can apply at some courthouses and post offices, as well as municipal buildings, such as your City Hall. For details and the location of

Your passport is your most important travel document.

the nearest passport-acceptance facility, see www.travel.state.gov or call 877-487-2778. Processing time varies; the current wait is posted on the State Department website. During busier periods, a six-week wait is common. One or two weeks after you apply, you can check online for the status of your passport application and its estimated arrival date.

If you need your passport in less than six weeks, tack on an additional $60 expediting fee (plus overnight shipping both ways), and you'll get it by mail in two to three weeks (check the State Department's website for current processing times). In a last-minute emergency situation, call the above number and speak to a customer-service representative. If you can prove that you have to leave within two weeks (by showing a purchased airline eticket or a letter from work requiring you to travel overseas on short notice), you may be able to receive a passport in a day or so. Make an appointment to go in person to the nearest US Passport Agency and pay the additional $60 fee; they'll issue your new passport in 24 to 72 hours.

Keep an eye on your passport's expiration date. Many European countries require that your passport be valid for three to six months *after* your ticketed date of return to the United States. This means that even if your passport doesn't expire for a few months, you may still be denied entry to a country. Check your destination country's requirements, and if necessary, get your passport renewed before you go. Other countries can have surprising entry requirements. For example, the Czech Republic and Poland technically require visitors to carry proof of medical insurance (your health insurance card usually suffices). While it's virtually unheard of that a border guard would actually request this, it's worth knowing about. For requirements per country, see www.travel.state.gov.

If you're a frequent international traveler, consider the US Customs' Global Entry Program, which lets you bypass passport control at major US airports ($100 fee, www.globalentry.gov).

Canadian citizens can refer to www.voyage.gc.ca for Canada-specific passport information.

Traveling with your Passport: Take good care of your passport, but relax if a night-train conductor asks you to temporarily give it up. When

European Borders (or Not)

Over the last decade, borders between European countries have faded away. Thanks to a series of treaties known as the Schengen Agreement, today there are no border checks between 25 of Europe's countries: Austria, Belgium, the Czech Republic, Denmark, Estonia, Finland, France, Germany, Greece, Hungary, Iceland, Italy, Latvia, Lithuania, Luxembourg, Malta, the Netherlands, Norway, Poland, Portugal, Slovakia, Slovenia, Spain, Sweden, and Switzerland.

Holdouts include the United Kingdom and the Republic of Ireland, as well as some Eastern European countries (such as Croatia, Bosnia-Herzegovina, Montenegro, and Turkey). Romania and Bulgaria are getting ready to join the Schengen group.

What does Schengen mean for you? When traveling between participating countries, you don't have to stop or show a passport—you'll simply blow past abandoned border posts

Only a few European countries still have border checks.

on the superhighway or high-speed train...souvenirs of an earlier, more complicated era of European travel. Non-Schengen countries still have border checks (for now)—but even in these places, the border crossing is generally just a quick wave-through for US citizens. Schengen or no, you always need to show your passport at your first point of entry into Europe, and to re-enter the US.

you sleep on an international night train to a non-Schengen country (see sidebar), the conductor may take your passport so you won't be disturbed when the train crosses the border at 3:00 a.m. It's also standard for hoteliers to hold onto your passport for a short time so they can register you with the police (for tips and details, see page 203).

If you find yourself in a situation requiring a cash deposit (for bike rentals, audioguides, and so on), a passport can serve as collateral if you don't have cash on hand. You also may need to show your passport if making a purchase for which you'd like to claim a Value-Added Tax refund (see page 182).

Replacing your Passport: If you have to replace a lost or stolen passport in Europe, it's much easier to do if you have a photocopy of it and a couple of passport-type photos, either brought from home or taken in Europe. For details on how to get a replacement, see page 337. For tips on preparing and protecting key documents while traveling, see page 58.

Visas

A visa is a stamp placed in your passport by a foreign government, allowing you to enter their country. Visas are not required for Americans or Canadians traveling in Western Europe and most of the East (includ-

ing the Czech Republic, Slovakia, Poland, Hungary, Slovenia, Croatia, Bosnia-Herzegovina, Montenegro, and the Baltic states).

Both Canadians and Americans need visas to visit **Turkey**, but cruise-line passengers do not need a visa if they are just visiting ports of call and not flying in or out from Turkey. Turkish visas are cheapest and easiest to get upon arrival at the border or airport. You can pay in US currency or euros (US residents pay $20 or €15; Canadians pay $60—US dollars, not Canadian—or €45). For more information, see www.turkishembassy.org (Turkey's embassy in the United States) or www.turkishembassy.com (Turkey's embassy in Canada).

Travelers to **Russia** also need visas. The process can be expensive, and you should begin several weeks in advance. Before applying for a visa, you must first get an official document called a "visa invitation" or a "visa support letter" (generally from a hotel or visa agency). You'll also need to fill out an Electronic Visa Application Form. Since the embassy no longer accepts visa applications in the mail, it's smart to use an agency that specializes in steering your application through the process (Passport Visa Express is one of many, www.passportvisasexpress.com). The costs add up: The visa itself costs $140 (money order or cashier's check only, fee subject to change) and visa agencies charge a service fee of about $50-85. Figure about $250 total per person. For more details, see www.russianembassy.org (which lists Russian consulate locations in Washington, DC; New York; San Francisco; Seattle; and Houston). If you live near one of these consulates, you can save some money (but go through a lot of steps—see website) by applying for your visa in person at the consulate.

For **travel beyond Europe,** get up-to-date information on visa requirements from your travel agent or the US Department of State (www.travel.state.gov).

If you do need a visa, it's usually best to get it at home before you leave (unless you're going to Turkey). If you forget, just about every country has an embassy or consulate (which can issue visas) in the capital of every other European country.

Student Cards and Hostel Memberships

The International Student Identity Card (ISIC), the only internationally recognized student ID card, gets you discounts on transportation, entertainment, and sightseeing throughout Europe, and includes some basic trip insurance. If you are a full-time student (and can prove it), get one. Your ISIC card can also be used as a prepaid phone card. Be aware that if you're older than 26, you might have trouble using the card in some places. Two other varieties of the card, offering similar discounts, are available, though they're often not honored: for teachers of any age (International Teacher Identity Card, or ITIC) and for non-student travelers under age 26 (International Youth Travel Card, or IYTC). Each of these cards costs $25 and is good for one year from the date of issue. Get yours on the ISIC website (www.myisic.com), through STA Travel (www.statravel.com), or from your university foreign-study office.

Travelers who know they'll be staying at least six nights in official HI hostels should get a hostel membership card from a local hostel or Hostelling International (www.hiusa.org, tel. 301/495-1240; for more information on these cards, see page 217).

Railpasses and Car Documents

Most railpasses are not sold in Europe and must be purchased before you leave home (for more on railpasses, see the Trains and More chapter). If you're renting a car, be aware that an International Driving Permit is required in Austria, Bosnia-Herzegovina, Greece, Hungary, Italy, Poland, Slovenia, and Spain (get it at AAA before your departure—for $15 plus tax and the cost of two passport photos, www.aaa.com). For specifics, see the Driving chapter.

Stash Photocopies of Key Documents

Before your trip, make two sets of photocopies of your valuable documents (front and back). Pack a copy and leave a copy with someone at home—to fax or email to you in case of an emergency. (I wouldn't, how-ever, photocopy a debit or credit card—instead, keep just the number in a retrievable place.) It's easier to replace a lost or stolen passport, railpass, or car-rental voucher if you have a photocopy that helps prove you really owned what you lost. Consider bringing a couple of passport-type pic-tures, which can expedite the replacement process for a lost or stolen passport (to replace a passport, see page 337).

While traveling, guard your photocopies as carefully as you would the originals. I hide mine in a second money belt clipped into the bot-tom of my luggage (don't tell anyone). Some people scan their documents and email them to a Web-based account or store them on a site such as Google Docs for easy access from the road (for tips on Internet security, see page 256). If you're concerned about having electronic copies float-ing around in cyberspace, you could put them on a USB flash drive and tuck it into your money belt. If you're traveling with a companion, carry photocopies of each other's passports and other important documents.

It's also smart to have a backup copy of your itinerary in case you lose the information. You can save hotel and car-rental confirmations online, email a copy of your itinerary to yourself, use an itinerary-stor-age website (such as Tripit.com), or at the very least, leave the details at home with a friend. You can also write or print, as small as you can read, any phone numbers or email addresses you might need in an emergency, including a list of your reserved hotels, then store this slip of paper in your money belt.

Travel Insurance

Travel insurance can minimize the considerable financial risks of travel-ing: accidents, illness, missed flights, canceled tours, lost baggage, theft, terrorism, travel-company bankruptcies, emergency evacuation, and getting your body home if you die. Each traveler's potential loss varies, depending on how much of your trip is prepaid, the refundability of the air ticket you purchased, your state of health, the value of your luggage, where you're traveling, the financial health of your tour company and airline, and what coverage you already have (through your medical insur-ance, homeowners' or renters' insurance, and/or credit card).

For some travelers, insurance is a good deal; for others, it's not. What are the chances you'll need it? How willing are you to take risks? How much is peace of mind worth to you? Take these considerations into account, understand your options, and make an informed decision for your trip.

Insurance Basics

The insurance menu includes five main courses: trip cancellation and interruption, medical, evacuation, baggage, and flight insurance. Supplemental policies can be added to cover specific concerns, such as identity theft or political evacuation. The various types are generally sold in some combination—rather than buying only baggage, medical, or cancellation insurance, you'll usually purchase a package that includes most or all of them. If you want just one type of coverage in particular—such as medical—ask for that (though it might come with a little cancellation or baggage insurance, too). "Comprehensive insurance" covers all of the above (plus expenses incurred if your trip is delayed, if you miss your flight, or if your tour company changes your itinerary).

One of the better changes in recent years is that many companies, such as Travelex and Travel Guard, offer comprehensive packages that serve as your primary coverage; they'll take care of your expenses regardless of what other insurance you might have (for instance, if you have health insurance through your job). That means they pay first and don't ask questions about your other insurance. This can be a real plus if you want to avoid out-of-pocket expenses.

Insurance prices can vary dramatically, with most packages costing between 5 and 12 percent of the total trip. Age is one of the biggest factors affecting the price: Rates go up dramatically for every decade over 50, while coverage is generally inexpensive or even free for children 17 and under.

Travel agents recommend that you get travel insurance (because they get a commission when you buy it, and because they can be held liable for your losses if they don't explain insurance options to you). While they can give you information and advice on providers, they are not insurance agents—always direct any specific questions to the insurance provider.

For extensive coverage, go with a big-name company (avoid buying insurance from a no-name company you found online). Consider the package deals sold by Betins (www.betins.com, tel. 866-552-8834 or 253/238-6374), Allianz (www.allianztravelinsurance.com, tel. 800-284-8300), Travelex (www.travelexinsurance.com, tel. 800-228-9792), Travel Guard (www.travelguard.com, tel. 800-826-4919), and Travel Insured International (www.travelinsured.com, tel. 800-243-3174). Insuremytrip.com allows you to compare insurance policies and costs among various providers (they also sell insurance; www.insuremytrip .com, tel. 800-487-4722). The $25 ISIC student identity card (described earlier) includes very minimal travel insurance.

Policies available vary by state. For example, Washington State regulates insurers more strictly than most other states, so Washingtonians may have fewer options than, say, Ohioans. Furthermore, not all insurance companies are licensed in every state. If you have to make a claim and encounter problems with a company that isn't licensed in your state, you don't have a case.

Note that some travel insurance, especially trip-cancellation coverage, is reimbursement-only: You'll pay out-of-pocket for your expenses, then submit the paperwork to your insurer to recoup your money. With medical coverage, you may be able to arrange to have expensive hospital or doctor bills paid directly. Either way, if you have a problem, it's wise to communicate with your insurance company immediately to ask them how to proceed. Many major insurance companies are accessible by phone 24 hours a day—handy if you have problems in Europe.

Types of Coverage

For each type of insurance that follows, I've outlined some of the key legalese. But be warned—these are only guidelines. Policies can differ, even within the same company. Certain companies and policies have different levels of coverage based on whether you purchase the car rental, hotel, or flight directly on your own or through a travel agent. Ask a lot of questions, and always read the fine print to see what's covered (e.g., how they define "travel partner" or "family member"—your great-aunt might not qualify).

Trip-Cancellation or Interruption Insurance

For me, this is the most usable and worthwhile kind of insurance. It's expensive to cancel or interrupt any prepaid kind of travel, and for a fraction of the trip cost, you can alleviate the risk of losing money if something unforeseen gets in the way. This can be a good value or a bad one, depending on the odds that you'll need to use it. If I think there's a greater than 1-in-20 chance I'll need it (for instance, if I have a loved one in frail health at home), trip-cancellation insurance can be a very good value and provide needed peace of mind. But if I'm healthy and hell-bent on making a trip, I'll risk it and not spend the extra. If it turns out that I need to cancel or interrupt, I'll just have to take my financial lumps—I played the odds and lost.

Before purchasing trip-cancellation or interruption coverage, check with your credit-card issuer; yours may offer limited coverage for flights or tours purchased with the card.

A standard trip-cancellation or interruption insurance policy covers the nonrefundable financial penalties or losses you incur when you cancel a prepaid tour or flight for an acceptable reason, such as:

1. You, your travel partner, or a family member cannot travel because of sickness, death, layoff, or a list of other acceptable reasons;
2. Your tour company or airline goes out of business or can't perform as promised;
3. A family member at home gets sick (check the fine print to see how a family member's pre-existing condition might affect coverage);
4. You miss a flight or need an emergency flight for a reason outside your control (such as a car accident, inclement weather, or a strike).

In other words, if you or your travel partner accidentally breaks a leg a few days before your trip, you can both bail out (if you both have this insurance) without losing all the money you paid for the trip. Or, if you're on a tour and have an accident on your first day, you'll be reimbursed for the portion of the tour you weren't able to use.

This type of insurance can be used whether you're on an organized tour or cruise, or traveling independently (in which case, only the pre-paid expenses—such as your flight and any nonrefundable hotel reservations—are covered). Note the difference: Trip *cancellation* is when you don't go on your trip at all. Trip *interruption* is when you begin a journey but have to cut it short; in this case, you'll be reimbursed only for the portion of the trip that you didn't complete. If you're taking a tour, it may already come with some cancellation insurance—ask.

Some insurers won't cover certain airlines or tour operators. Many are obvious—such as companies under bankruptcy protection—but others can be surprising (including major airlines). Make sure your carrier is covered.

It's smart to buy your insurance policy within a week of the date you make the first payment on your trip. Policies purchased later than a designated cutoff date—generally 7 to 21 days, as determined by the insurance company—are less likely to cover tour company or air carrier bankruptcies, pre-existing medical conditions (yours or those of family members at home), or terrorist incidents. Mental-health concerns are generally not covered.

Jittery travelers are fretful about two big unknowns: terrorist attacks and natural disasters. Ask your company for the details. You'll likely be covered only if your departure city or a destination on your itinerary actually becomes the target of a terrorist incident within 30 days of your trip. Even then, if your tour operator offers a substitute itinerary, your coverage may become void. As for natural disasters, you're covered only if your destination is uninhabitable (for example, your hotel is flooded or the airport is gone). A terrorist attack or natural disaster in your hometown may or may not be covered. War or outbreaks of disease generally aren't covered.

You can avoid the question of what is and what isn't covered by buying a costly "any reason" policy. These offer at least partial reimbursement (generally 75 percent) no matter why you cancel the trip. But the premiums are so hefty that these policies appeal mostly to deep-pocketed nervous Nellies prepaying for extremely expensive trips.

The rugged, healthy, unattached, and gung-ho traveler will probably forgo trip-cancellation or interruption coverage. I have skipped it many times, and my number has yet to come up. But if you're paying out a lot of up-front money for an organized tour (which is expensive to cancel), if you have questionable health, or if you have a loved one at home in poor health, it's probably a good idea to get this coverage.

Medical Insurance

Before buying a special medical insurance policy for your trip, check with your medical insurer—you might already be covered by your existing health plan. While many US insurers cover you overseas, Medicare does not.

Even if your health plan does cover you internationally, you may want to consider buying a special medical travel policy. Much of the additional coverage available is supplemental (or "secondary"), so it covers whatever expenses your health plan doesn't, such as deductibles. But you can also purchase primary coverage, which will take care of your costs up to a certain amount. In emergency situations involving costly procedures or overnight stays, the hospital will typically work directly

Some special medical insurance will cover the cost of an emergency-room visit.

with your travel-insurance carrier on billing (but not with your regular health insurance company; you'll likely have to pay up front to the hospital or clinic, then get reimbursed by your stateside insurer later). For non-emergencies, a quick visit to a doctor will likely be an out-of-pocket expense (you'll bring home documentation to be reimbursed). Whatever the circumstances, it's smart to contact your insurer from the road to let them know that you've sought medical help.

Many pre-existing conditions are covered by medical and trip-cancellation coverage, depending on when you buy the coverage and how recently you've been treated for the condition. If you travel frequently to Europe, multitrip annual policies can save you money. Check with your agent or insurer before you commit.

The US State Department periodically issues warnings about traveling to at-risk countries (see www.travel.state.gov). If you're visiting one of these countries, your cancellation and medical insurance will likely not be honored, unless you buy supplemental coverage.

For travelers over 70 years old, buying travel medical insurance can be an expensive proposition. Compare the cost of a travel medical plan with comprehensive insurance (described earlier). The latter plans come with good medical and evacuation coverage that can otherwise be very expensive. A travel-insurance company can help you sort out the options. Check with the AARP for information about foreign medical-care coverage with Medicare supplement plans (www.aarp.com), or call the issuer of your supplemental policy.

Other Insurance

Evacuation insurance covers the cost of getting you to a place where you can receive appropriate medical treatment in the event of an emergency. (In a worst-case scenario, this can mean a medically equipped—and incredibly expensive—private jet.) This is usually not covered by your regular medical-insurance plan back home. Sometimes this coverage can get you home after an accident, but more often, it'll just get you as far as the nearest major hospital. "Medical repatriation"—that is, getting you all the way home—is likely to be covered only if it's considered medically necessary. Ask your insurer exactly what's covered before *and after* you get to the hospital.

Travelers stranded by Cinque Terre floods in 2011 were evacuated by helicopter.

Keep in mind that medical and evacuation insurance may not cover you if you're participating in an activity your insurer considers to be dangerous (such as skydiving, bungee jumping, scuba diving, or even skiing).

Theft Protection

Theft is definitely a concern when you consider the value of the items we now pack along. Laptops, tablets, digital cameras, smartphones, iPods, and ereaders are all much more expensive to replace than the disposable cameras, Walkmans, and paperbacks of yesteryear.

Thieves rifled through this backpack before dumping it—minus any valuables—on the street in Rome.

One way to protect your investment is to purchase travel insurance from a specialized company such as Travel Guard, which offers a variety of comprehensive plans and options that include coverage for theft. Before buying a policy, ask how they determine the value of the stolen objects and about any maximum reimbursement limits for jewelry, electronics, or cameras.

It's also smart to check with your homeowners' or renters' insurance company. Under most policies, your personal property is already protected against theft anywhere in the world—but your insurance deductible still applies. If you have a $1,000 deductible and your $500 iPhone is stolen, you'll have to pay to replace it. Rather than buying separate insurance, it may make more sense to add a rider to your existing policy to cover expensive items while you travel.

Before you leave, it's a good idea to take an inventory of all the items you're bringing. Make a list of serial numbers, makes, and models of your electronics, and take photos that can serve as records. If anything is stolen, this information is helpful to both your insurance company and the police. If you plan to file an insurance claim, you'll need to get a police report in Europe. (If dealing with the police is intimidating, ask your hotelier for help.) For tips on avoiding theft while traveling, see the Theft and Scams chapter.

Some companies sell supplementary adventure-sports coverage.

Baggage insurance—for luggage that is lost, delayed, or damaged—is included in most comprehensive policies, but it's rare to buy it separately. Baggage insurance puts a strict cap on reimbursement for such items as jewelry, eyewear, electronics, and photographic equipment—read the fine print. If you check your baggage for a flight, it's already covered by the airline (ask your airline about its luggage liability limit; if you have particularly valuable luggage, you can buy supplemental "excess valuation" insurance directly from the airline). Check if your homeowners' or renters' insurance covers baggage. Travelers' baggage insurance will cover the deductibles and items excluded from your homeowners' policy. Double-check the particulars with your agent. If your policy doesn't cover railpasses, consider buying the $14-18 insurance deal sold with the pass.

Flight insurance ("crash coverage") is a statistical rip-off that heirs love. It's basically a life insurance policy that covers you when you're on the airplane. Since plane crashes are so rare, there's little sense in spending money on this insurance.

Collision coverage, an important type of insurance for rental cars, is covered on page 153. Collision insurance may be included in some comprehensive travel-insurance plans or available as an upgrade on others.

Before You Go

Quite a few things are worth arranging while you're still at home— lining these up before you leave is a big part of having a smooth trip. I've collected my suggestions here, with references for where to find more detailed information elsewhere in the book.

• Check your **passport expiration**; you may be denied entry into certain European countries if your passport is due to expire within three to six months of your ticketed date of return. Get it renewed if you'll be cutting it close (see page 55).

• Do your homework if you want to buy **travel insurance**. Contact your health-insurance company to see if you are covered in Europe (see page 59).

• If you're bringing the **kids**, make sure you have the right paperwork, including a passport for each one, a letter of consent if only one parent is traveling, and documentation for adopted children (see page 432).

• Make **copies of important travel documents** as a backup in case you lose the originals (see page 58).

• **Students** should get an International Student Identity Card (ISIC) for discounts throughout Europe. **Hostelers** who know they'll be staying at least six nights in official HI hostels should get a membership card (see page 58 for information on both).

• If you need to bridge several long-distance destinations on your trip, look into cheap **flights within Europe.** For the best fares, book these as far in advance as possible (see page 99).

• If you plan on buying a **railpass,** you'll need to get it before you leave the US (see page 115). Railpass or not, it can also be smart to reserve seats on certain trains before you leave (see page 172). If you plan to zip between London and Paris on the **Eurostar,** book tickets in advance (see page 114).

• If you'll be **renting a car,** you'll need a valid driver's license. An International Driving Permit is technically required in Austria, Bosnia-Herzegovina, Greece, Hungary, Italy, Poland, Slovenia, and Spain (see page 150).

• Make **reservations** well in advance, especially during peak season, for accommodations, popular restaurants, major sights (see page 297), and any local guides you plan to hire.

• Call your **debit- and credit-card companies** to let them know the countries you'll be visiting, to ask about fees, and more. Get your bank's emergency phone number in the US (but not its 800 number) to call collect if you have a problem. If you don't know your credit card's PIN code, ask your bank to mail it to you (see page 167).

• If you plan to use your **US mobile phone or smartphone** in Europe, contact your provider to enable international calling or to "unlock" your phone. (Keep in mind that some Verizon or Sprint phones—especially older ones—won't work in Europe.) Consider signing up for an international calling, text, and/or data plan, and be sure to confirm voice- and data-roaming fees (see page 239).

• If you're bringing a **mobile device,** download any apps you might want to use on the road, such as translators, maps, and transit schedules (for a rundown, see page 258). Be sure to check out Rick Steves Audio Europe for free, downloadable audio tours and hours of travel interviews (via the Rick Steves Audio Europe smartphone app, www.ricksteves .com/audioeurope, or iTunes; for details, see page 263).

• Take care of any **medical needs.** Visit your doctor to get a checkup, and see your dentist if you have any work that needs to be done. If you use prescription drugs, stock up before your trip (see page 400). Pack along the prescription, plus one for contact lens or glasses if you wear them.

• Get a proper guidebook. If traveling with one of mine, check the **Rick Steves guidebook updates** page for the latest news about your destination (www.ricksteves.com/update).

• Because **airline carry-on restrictions** are always changing, visit the Transportation Security Administration's website (www.tsa.gov /travelers) for an up-to-date list of what you can bring on the plane with you…and what you must check.

PACK LIGHT

The importance of packing light cannot be overemphasized, but, for your own good, I'll try. You'll never meet a traveler who, after five trips, brags: "Every year I pack heavier." The measure of a good traveler is how light he or she travels. You can't travel heavy, happy, and cheap. Pick two.

One Bag—That's It

My self-imposed limit is 20 pounds in a 9" × 22" × 14" carry-on-size bag (it'll fit in your airplane's overhead bin). At my company, we've taken tens of thousands of people of all ages and styles on tours through Europe. We allow only one carry-on bag. For many, this is a radical concept: 9" × 22" × 14"? That's my cosmetics kit! But they manage, and they're glad they did. After you enjoy that sweet mobility and freedom, you'll never go any other way.

You'll walk with your luggage more than you think you will. Before flying to Europe, give yourself a test. Pack up completely, go into your hometown,

No matter your age, you can travel like college kids: light, mobile, and wearing your convertible suitcase/backpacks.

and practice being a tourist for an hour. Fully loaded, you should enjoy window-shopping. If you can't, stagger home and thin things out.

When you carry your own luggage, it's less likely to get lost, broken, or stolen. Quick, last-minute changes in flight plans become simpler. A small bag sits on your lap or under your seat on the bus, taxi, and airplane. You don't have to worry about it, and, when you arrive, you can hit the ground running. It's a good feeling. When I land in London, I'm on my way downtown while everyone else stares anxiously at the luggage carousel. When I fly home, I'm the first guy the dog sniffs.

These days, you can also save money by carrying your own bag. While it's still free to check one bag on most overseas trips, you'd likely pay a fee to check two. If you're taking a separate flight within Europe, expect to be charged to check even just one bag.

Remember, packing light isn't just about saving time or money—it's about your traveling lifestyle. Too much luggage marks you as a typical tourist. It slams the Back Door shut. Serendipity suffers. Changing locations becomes a major operation. Con artists figure you're helpless. Porters are a problem only to those who need them. With only one bag, you're mobile and in control. Take this advice seriously.

Pack light. You won't have a mule to haul around your bags. (If you do, you're taking advantage of your spouse.)

Baggage Restrictions

Pack light...and pack smart. You can't bring anything potentially dangerous—such as knives, lighters, or large quantities of liquids or gels—in your carry-on bag. (This list can change without notice—for details, see "What Can't I Carry On?" on page 96.) These days I leave my Swiss Army knife at home, bring smaller bottles of toiletries, and carry on my bag as usual.

Be aware that many airlines have additional (and frequently changing) restrictions on the number, size, and weight of carry-on bags. Some European budget airlines, such as Ryanair and Air Berlin, use smaller carry-on dimensions than major airlines. (Restrictions can vary from airport to airport, even on the same airline.) Check your airline's website for details.

When you carry your bag onto the plane, all liquids, gels, and aerosols must be in 3.4-ounce or smaller containers, all of which must fit into one clear quart-size plastic zip-top bag. There are exceptions for certain prescription and over-the-counter medicines, as well as contact-lens solution (see www.tsa.gov/311 for details).

If you check your bag, mark it inside and out with your name, address, and emergency phone number. If you have a lock on your bag, you may be asked to remove it to accommodate increased security checks, or it may be cut off so the bag can be inspected (to avoid this, consider a Transportation Security Administration-approved lock, described in the packing list later in this chapter). I've never locked my bag and never had a problem. Still, just in case, I wouldn't pack anything particularly valuable (such as cash or a camera) in my checked luggage.

Backpack or Rolling Bag?

A fundamental packing question is your choice of luggage. Of all the options, I consider only three: 1) a carry-on-size convertible backpack/suitcase with zip-away shoulder straps; 2) a carry-on-size roll-aboard bag; or 3) an internal-frame backpack.

A convertible backpack/suitcase (see photo on page 73) gives you the best of both worlds—a mobile backpack for traveling and a low-key suitcase when in town. I travel with this bag and keep it exclusively in the backpack mode. While these soft bags basically hang on your shoulders and hips, and are not as comfortable for long hauls as internal-frame backpacks, they work fine for getting from the station to your hotel. And, at 9" × 22" × 14", they fit in the airplane's overhead lockers. I live out of this bag for four months each year—and I absolutely love it.

Carry-on-size roll-aboard bags are well-designed and popular. Many of my staffers prefer this bag; its compact design makes it roomy while keeping it just small enough to fit in the plane's overhead bin (if you don't stuff any expandable compartments). The advantage of a roll-aboard over a convertible is that you can effortlessly wheel your gear around without getting sweaty. The drawbacks: Bags with wheels cost $40-50 extra,

A 9" × 22" × 14" carry-on bag (with or without wheels) is the ideal size.

weigh several pounds more, are awkward to carry up and down stairs, and delude people into thinking they don't need to pack so light. They are cumbersome on rough or uneven surfaces (crowded subways, hiking through a series of train cars, walking to your hotel in villages with stepped lanes, cobbled streets, and dirt paths, and so on)—but they're wonderful in airports, where check-in lines and distances to gates stretch longer than ever. (You can see photos of convertible and roll-aboard bags near the end of this book; they're sold at www.ricksteves.com.) A spin-off option is the hybrid bag, which has both wheels and backpack straps—but the wheels add weight when used as a backpack, and having both wheels and straps eats up interior space. Personally, I'd go with either one or the other.

Some younger travelers backpack through Europe with an internal-frame backpack purchased from an outdoor store. These are the most comfortable bags to wear on your back, as the internal frame keeps the weight off your shoulders and balanced over your hips. However, these bags can be expensive and are often built "taller" than carry-on size.

Base your decision on the strength of your back. The day will come when I'll be rolling my bag through Europe with the rest of the gang. But as long as I'm hardy enough to carry my gear on my back, I will.

Pack your bag only two-thirds full to leave room for souvenirs, or bring along an empty, featherweight nylon bag to use as a carry-on for your return flight, and check your main bag through. Sturdy stitching, front and side pouches, padded shoulder straps (for backpacks), and a low-profile color are virtues. I'm not wild about the zip-off day bags that come with some backpacks—I take my convertible backpack and supplement it with a separate day bag that's exactly to my liking.

Packing 101

How do you fit a whole trip's worth of luggage into a small backpack or suitcase? The answer is simple: Bring very little.

Spread out everything you think you might need on the living-room floor. Pick up each item one at a time and scrutinize it. Ask yourself, "Will I really use this snorkel and these fins enough to justify carrying them around all summer?" Not "Will I use them?" but "Will I use them enough to feel good about hauling them over the Swiss Alps?" Frugal as I may be, I'd buy them in Greece and give them away before I'd carry that extra weight over the Alps.

Don't pack for the worst-case scenario. Pack for the best-case scenario and simply buy yourself out of any jams. Bring layers rather than

One Carry-on Bag

Here's absolutely everything I traveled with for two months (photos taken naked in a Copenhagen hotel room): convertible 9" × 22" × 14" backpack/suitcase; lightweight nylon day bag; ripped-up sections of three guidebooks, notes, maps, journal, tiny pocket notepad; wristwatch; money belt (with debit card, credit card, driver's license, passport, printout of airline eticket, railpass, cash, sheet of phone numbers and addresses); second money belt clipped inside my bag for "semiprecious" documents; toiletries stuff

bag (with squeeze bottle of shampoo, soap in a plastic container, shaver, toothbrush and paste, comb, nail clippers, squeeze bottle of liquid soap for clothes); bag with electronic gear (travel alarm

clock, cable for charging batteries, plug adapter); miscellaneous bag with family photos, tiny odds and ends; light rain jacket; long khaki cotton pants (button pockets), super-light long pants, shorts, five pairs of socks and underwear, two long-sleeved shirts, two short-sleeved shirts, T-shirt; stuff bag with sweater, plastic laundry bag; light pair of shoes; and my smartphone and charger, lightweight laptop, and camera (the only thing not pictured).

take a heavy coat. Think in terms of what you can do without—not what will be handy on your trip. When in doubt, leave it out. I've seen people pack a whole summer's supply of deodorant or razors, thinking they can't get them there. The world is getting really small: You can buy Dial soap, Colgate toothpaste, Nivea cream, and Gillette razors in Sicily and Slovakia. Tourist shops in major international hotels are a sure bet whenever you have difficulty finding a personal item. If you can't find one of your essentials, ask yourself how half a billion Europeans can live without it. Rather than carry a whole trip's supply of toiletries, take enough to get started and look forward to running out of toothpaste in Bulgaria. Then you have the perfect excuse to go into a Bulgarian department store, shop around, and pick up something you think might be toothpaste.

Whether you're traveling for three weeks or three months, pack exactly the same. To keep your clothes tightly packed and well organized, zip them up in packing cubes, airless baggies, or a clothes compressor. The Flat Pack allows you to pack bulky sweaters and jackets without taking up too much space or creating wrinkles (available at www.rick steves.com). Simply put the item in the bag, roll it up to force the air out through the one-way nozzles, and pack it away. I like specially designed folding boards (such as Eagle Creek's Pack-It Folder) to

When getting way off the beaten path—like this traveler, who's staying at a tiny guest house in Italy's Civita di Bagnoregio— you'll be glad you're packing light.

fold and carry clothes with minimal wrinkling. For smaller items, use packing cubes or mesh bags (one for underwear and socks, another for miscellaneous stuff such as a first-aid kit, earplugs, clothesline, sewing kit, and gadgets).

Go casual, simple, and very light. Remember, in your travels you'll meet two kinds of tourists—those who pack light and those who wish they had. Say it out loud: "PACK LIGHT PACK LIGHT PACK LIGHT."

What to Pack

I've broken out the contents of your bag into four major categories: clothing, toiletries, travel documents and important papers (including money), and electronics. My core packing recommendations are all included on my Packing Checklist (see page 82). At the end of this chapter, I've also included a list of optional bring-alongs. Throughout, an asterisk (*) indicates an item you can purchase online at www.ricksteves.com.

Clothing Basics

The bulk of your luggage is filled with clothing. Minimize by bringing less. Experienced travelers try to bring only things that will be worn repeatedly, complement other items, and have multiple uses (for example, since I don't swim much, I let my shorts double as a swimsuit). Pack with color coordination in mind. Neutral colors (black, navy, khaki) dress up easily and can be extremely versatile.

To extend your wardrobe, plan to spend 10 minutes doing a little wash every few nights, or consider a visit to a local launderette, which is in itself a Back Door experience (for details on doing laundry in Europe, see page 411). Choose fabrics that resist wrinkling or look good wrinkled. If you wring with gusto, lightweight clothing should dry overnight in your hotel room.

Many travelers are concerned about appropriate dress. During tourist season, the concert halls go casual. I have never felt out of place at symphonies, operas, or plays wearing a decent pair of slacks and a good-looking sweater or collared shirt. Some cultural events require more formal attire, particularly outside of high season, but the casual tourist rarely encounters these. Women who don't pack a dress or skirt will do just fine with a pair of nice pants.

In Britain, they say there's no bad weather...only inappropriate clothing.

PACK LIGHT

If you're trying to blend in, realize that shorts are not common streetwear in Europe. They're considered beachwear, to be worn in coastal or lakeside resort towns. No one will be offended if you wear shorts, but you might be on the receiving end of some second glances. Shorts are especially uncommon on older women and in big cities, and the cutoff temperature for "hot enough for shorts" is much higher than in the US. Especially in southern Europe, women can blend in with the locals by wearing Capri pants or a skirt instead; men can pack a pair of as-light-as-possible pants.

Shorts, tank tops, and other skimpy summer attire can also put a crimp in your sightseeing plans. Some churches, mostly in southern Europe, have modest-dress requirements for men, women, and children: no shorts or bare shoulders. Except at the strict St. Peter's Basilica (in Rome) and St. Mark's (in Venice), the dress code is often loosely enforced. If necessary, it's usually easy to improvise some modesty (buy a cheap souvenir T-shirt to cover your shoulders, or carry a wide scarf to wear like a kilt to cover your legs). At some heavily touristed churches in southern Europe, people hand out sheets of tissue paper you can wrap around yourself like a shawl or skirt.

It can be worth splurging a little to get just the right clothes for your trip. For durable, lightweight travel clothes, consider ExOfficio (www .exofficio.com), TravelSmith (www.travelsmith.com), Tilley Endurables (www.tilley.com), Eddie Bauer (www.eddiebauer.com), and REI (www .rei.com).

But ultimately—as long as you don't wear something that's outrageous or offensive—it's important to dress in a way that makes you comfortable. And no matter how carefully you dress, your clothes will probably mark you as an American. And so what? Europeans will know anyway. To fit in and be culturally sensitive, I watch my manners, not the cut of my clothes.

Here's a rundown of what should go in your suitcase:

Shirts/blouses. Bring up to five short-sleeved or long-sleeved shirts or blouses (how many of each depends on the season) in a cotton/polyester blend. Shirts with long sleeves that roll up easily can double as short-sleeved. Look for a wrinkle-camouflaging pattern or blended fabrics that show a minimum of wrinkles. Synthetic-blend fabrics (such as Coolmax or microfiber) often dry overnight.

Pants/shorts. Bring two pairs: one lightweight cotton and another super-lightweight pair for hot and muggy big cities. Jeans can be too hot for summer travel (and are slow to dry). Many travelers like lightweight convertible pants/shorts with zip-off legs. While not especially stylish, they're functional in Italy, where you can use them to cover up inside churches while still beating the heat outside. Button-down wallet pockets are safest (though still not nearly as thief-proof as a money belt, described later).

If you bring shorts, one pair is probably enough. Shorts can double as a swimsuit for men when swimming in lakes or the ocean.

Sweater or lightweight fleece. Warm and dark is best—for layering and dressing up.

Jacket. Bring a light and water-resistant windbreaker with a hood. Neutral colors used to look more European than bright ones, but now everything from azure blue to pumpkin orange has made its way into European wardrobes. A hooded jacket of Gore-Tex or other waterproof material is good if you expect rain. (For summer travel, I wing it without rain gear—but always pack for rain in Britain and Ireland.)

Tie or scarf. For instant respectability, bring anything lightweight that can break the monotony and make you look snazzy.

Underwear and socks. Bring five sets (lighter dries quicker). Bamboo or cotton/nylon-blend socks dry faster than 100 percent cotton, which lose their softness when air-dried.

Sleepwear/loungewear. Comfy streetwear—such as shorts, leggings, T-shirts, tank tops, yoga pants, and other lightweight athletic gear—can be used as pajamas, post-dinner loungewear, and a modest cover-up to get you to the bathroom down the hall.

Shoes. Bring one pair of comfortable walking shoes with good traction. Mephisto, Ecco, and Rieker look dressier and more European than sneakers, but are still comfortable. Sturdy, low-profile tennis shoes with a good tread are fine, too. For a second pair, consider sandals in summer. Flip-flops are handy if you'll be using bathrooms down the hall. Whichever shoes you bring, make sure they are well broken in before you leave home. (See page 782 for top reader recommendations on footwear.)

Weather-specific variations. For winter travel, you can pack just about as light. Wear heavier, warmer, waterproof shoes. Add a coat, long johns (quick-drying Capilene polyester or super-light silk), scarf, gloves or mittens, hat, and an extra pair of socks and underwear, since things dry more slowly. Pack with the help of a climate chart (see the appendix). Layer your clothing for warmth, and assume you'll be outside in the cold for hours at a time. On winter trips, I bring comfy slippers with leather soles—great for the flight and for getting cozy in my hotel room.

For warm weather, consider a swimsuit and a light, crushable, wide-brimmed hat for sunny days, especially if you're prone to sunburn. Lightweight, light-colored clothes are more comfortable in very hot weather.

If you expect rain, you can bring a mini-umbrella or plan to buy one in Europe. Umbrella vendors, like worms, appear with the rain. Choose a *collapsible umbrella that's small and compact, but still sturdy enough to withstand strong winds. Hard-core vagabonds use a *poncho—more versatile than a tarp—as protection in a rainstorm, a ground cloth for sleeping, or a beach or picnic blanket.

PACK LIGHT

PACK LIGHT

Packing for Women
Thanks to ETBD tour guides Joan Robinson, Ann Neel, and Margaret Cassady for the following tips. (For a packing list for women, see www.rick steves.com/womenpack.)

Skirts. Some women bring one or two skirts because they're as cool and breathable as shorts, but dressier. A lightweight skirt made with a blended fabric will pack compactly. Make sure it has a comfy waistband. Skirts go with everything and can easily be dressed up with a pair of flats and hose (or warm tights if it's cold).

Underwear and swimsuit. Try silk, microfiber, or stretch lace underwear, which dries faster than cotton, but breathes more than nylon. Bring at least two bras (what if you leave one hanging over your shower rail by accident?). A sports bra can double as a hiking/sunning top. You don't need a bikini to try sunbathing topless on European beaches—local women with one-piece bathing suits just roll down the top.

Toiletries. Before cramming in every facial cleanser, lotion, and cosmetic item you think you might use, ask yourself what toiletries you can live without for a short time. But do estimate how many tampons and pads you might need and bring them with you (unless you're taking a very long trip). Even though many of the same brands are sold throughout Europe, you'll have them when you need them, and it's easier than having to buy a too-small or too-large box in Europe.

Accessorize, accessorize. Scarves give your limited wardrobe just the color it needs. They dress up your outfit, are lightweight and easy to pack, and if purchased in Europe, make a great souvenir. Some women bring a shawl-size scarf or pashmina to function as a sweater substitute, head wrap, skirt at a church, or even a blanket on a train. Functional, cheap, but beautiful imitation pashminas can be found all over Europe. Vests and cardigans can be worn alone or mixed-and-matched with other clothes to give you several different looks as well as layers for cold weather. Leave valuable or flashy jewelry at home.

Documents, Money, and Travel Info
Organizing your travel documents, money, guidebooks, and maps is just as important as assembling your wardrobe.

*Money belt. This flat, hidden, zippered pouch—strapped around your waist and tucked under your clothes—is essential for the peace of mind it brings. You could lose everything except your money belt, and the trip could still go on. Get a lightweight one with a low-profile color (I like beige). For more about money belts, see page 327.

*Small daypack. A lightweight pack is great for carrying your sweater, camera, guidebook, and picnic goodies while you leave your large bag at the hotel or train station. Fanny packs (small bags with thief-friendly zippers on a belt) are an alternative, but they're magnets for pickpockets (never use one as a money belt).

Money. Bring your preferred mix of a credit card, a debit card, and an emergency stash of hard US cash. For detailed recommendations, see page 167.

Documents. Bring your passport, printout of airline eticket, railpass, train reservations, car-rental voucher, driver's license, and any other useful cards (student ID, hostel card, and so on). Photocopies and a couple of passport-type photos can help you get replacements more quickly if the originals are lost or stolen (see page 58 for tips on keeping travel documents safe). In your luggage, pack a record of all reservations (print out your hotels' confirmation emails), along with a trip calendar page to keep things up to date as your trip evolves. For more information on the travel documents you need, see page 54.

Travel information. Pack the guidebooks and maps you'll need on the ground (or download them into your ereader). I like to rip out appropriate chapters from guidebooks and staple them together (see page 28 for a how-to).

Address list. If you'll want to mail postcards, consider printing your mailing list onto a sheet of adhesive address labels before you leave. You'll know exactly who you've written to, and the labels will be perfectly legible.

*Small notepad and pen. A tiny notepad in your back pocket or daypack is a great organizer, reminder, and communication aid.

*Journal. An empty book to be filled with the experiences of your trip will be your most treasured souvenir (for more on journaling, see page 426). Attach a photocopied calendar page of your itinerary. Use a hardbound type designed to last a lifetime, rather than a floppy spiral notebook. My custom-designed Rick Steves Travel Journals are rugged, simple blank books that come in two sizes. Another great brand, with a cult following among travel writers, is Moleskine (www.moleskine.it).

Toiletries and Personal Items

Even if you check your suitcase on the flight, always carry on essential toiletries, including any prescription medications (don't let the time difference trick you into forgetting a dose).

*Toiletries kit. Because sinks in many hotels come with meager countertop space, I prefer a kit that can hang on a hook or a towel bar. For your overseas flight, put all squeeze bottles in sealable plastic baggies, since pressure changes can cause even good bottles to leak. Pack your own bar of soap or small bottle of shampoo if you want to avoid using hotel bathroom "itsy-bitsies" and minimize waste and garbage.

Medicine and vitamins. Keep medicine in original containers, if possible, with legible prescriptions. See the advice on bringing and filling prescriptions in Europe on page 400.

With a hangable toiletries kit, you know the hairs on the toothbrush are yours.

*First-aid kit. See sidebar on next page.

Glasses/contacts/sunglasses. Contact-lens solutions are widely available in Europe. Carry your lens prescription, as well as extra glasses, in a solid protective case. If it's a sunny season, pack along sunglasses, especially if they're prescription.

Sealable plastic baggies. Bring a variety of sizes. In addition to holding your carry-on liquids, they're ideal for packing leftover picnic food, containing wetness, and bagging potential leaks before they happen. The two-gallon jumbo size can be used to pack (and compress) clothing or do laundry. Bring extras for the flight home.

*Laundry soap. A tiny box of detergent or a plastic squeeze bottle of concentrated, multipurpose, biodegradable liquid soap is handy for laundry and more. I find hotel shampoo works fine as laundry soap when I'm doing my wash in the sink (for tips on doing laundry in Europe, see page 411).

*Clothesline. Hang it up in your hotel room to dry your clothes. The twisted-rubber type needs no clothespins.

*Small towel/washcloth. You'll find bath towels at all fancy and moderately priced hotels, and most cheap ones. Although $60-a-day travelers will want to bring their own towel, $120-a-day folks won't. I bring a thin hand towel for the occasional need. Washcloths are rare in Europe, so you might want to pack a *quick-drying microfiber one. Disposable washcloths that pack dry but lather up when wet (such as the ones made by Olay) are another option; cut them in half to make them last longer.

*Sewing kit. Clothes age rapidly while traveling. Take along a few safety pins and extra buttons.

Small packet of tissues. Stick one of these in your daypack, in case you

---

Traveler's First-Aid Kit

You can buy virtually anything you need in Europe. (You might not find Claritin, though you can get the generic equivalent, loratadine.) But if you'd rather stick with a specific name-brand medication, bring it from home. It's also handy to pack:

- Band-Aids
- little container of hand sanitizer
- small tube of antibiotic cream (in Europe, you may need a prescription to buy skin ointments with antibiotics)
- moleskin (to cover blisters)
- tweezers
- over-the-counter pain reliever
- thermometer (if traveling with kids)
- medication for colds and diarrhea (if possible, bring non-liquids)
- prescription medications (preferably in labeled, original containers)

---

wind up at a bathroom with no toilet paper.

Spot remover. Bring a few Shout wipes or a dab of Goop grease remover in a small plastic container.

Hairdryer. These are generally provided in $100-plus hotel rooms. If you can't risk a bad-hair day, buy a cheap, compact hairdryer in Europe (for most people, this makes more sense than toting along a converter to attach to their hairdryer from home).

*Travel alarm/wristwatch. If your phone or watch doesn't have a built-in alarm, pack a small travel alarm clock. At budget hotels, wake-up calls are particularly unreliable.

Earplugs. If night noises bother you, you'll love a good set of expandable foam plugs. They're handy for snoozing on trains and flights, too.

Electronics

Go light with your electronic gear—you want to experience Europe, not interface with it. Of course, some mobile devices are great tools for making your trip easier or better. The lines separating smartphones, tablet computers, portable media players, cameras, GPS devices, and ereaders continue to blur. Think creatively about how you might use your gadgets (especially if Wi-Fi enabled) on the road.

Note that many of these things are high-ticket items; guard them carefully or consider insuring them (see page 65).

Packing Checklist

- ❑ 5 shirts/blouses: long- and short-sleeve
- ❑ 1 sweater or lightweight fleece
- ❑ 2 pairs of pants
- ❑ 1 pair of shorts
- ❑ 5 pairs of underwear and socks
- ❑ 1 pair of shoes
- ❑ 1 rainproof jacket with hood
- ❑ Tie or scarf
- ❑ Sleepwear
- ❑ Swimsuit
- ❑ Money belt
- ❑ Money—your mix of:
  - ❑ Debit card
  - ❑ Credit card(s)
  - ❑ Hard cash ($20 bills)
- ❑ Documents plus photocopies:
  - ❑ Passport
  - ❑ Printout of airline eticket
  - ❑ Driver's license
  - ❑ Student ID, hostel card, etc.

- ❑ Railpass/train reservations/car-rental voucher
- ❑ Hotel-reservation confirmations
- ❑ Insurance details
- ❑ Guidebooks and maps
- ❑ Address list for postcards
- ❑ Notepad and pen
- ❑ Journal
- ❑ Daypack
- ❑ Electronics—your choice of:
  - ❑ Camera (and related gear)
  - ❑ Mobile phone
  - ❑ Portable media player (iPod or other)
  - ❑ Laptop/netbook/tablet
  - ❑ Ebook reader
  - ❑ Ear buds or noise-reduction headphones
  - ❑ Chargers for each of the above
  - ❑ Plug adapter(s)
- ❑ Alarm clock (if not part of phone or watch)
- ❑ Earplugs
- ❑ Toiletries kit
  - ❑ Toiletries
  - ❑ Medicines and vitamins
  - ❑ First-aid kit
  - ❑ Glasses/contacts/ sunglasses (with prescriptions)
- ❑ Sealable plastic baggies
- ❑ Laundry soap
- ❑ Clothesline
- ❑ Small towel/washcloth
- ❑ Sewing kit

Packing light: love it or leave it.

If you plan to carry on your luggage, note that all liquids must be in 3.4-ounce or smaller containers and fit within a single quart-size sealable baggie. For details, see www.tsa.gov/travelers.

Mobile phone/smartphone. Your American mobile phone might work perfectly in Europe, or you can buy one to use while you're there. Smartphones are a nice compromise for travelers who need to stay plugged in, but don't want to lug along a laptop. For more on using mobile phones in Europe, see page 238.

Other mobile devices. Take your pick: tablet, portable media player, ereader. Download apps before you leave home (for a list of useful mobile apps, see page 258).

Digital camera. Take along an extra memory card and battery, and don't forget the charger and a cable for downloading images.

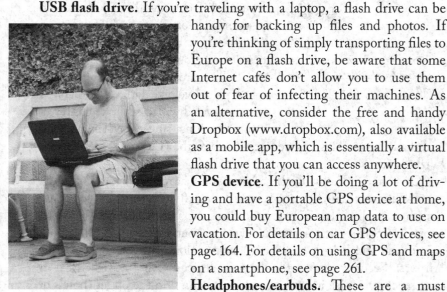

When traveling with a smartphone, it's best to disable data roaming and use Wi-Fi to surf the Web.

PACK LIGHT

Laptop. More and more tourists enjoy bringing their laptop along. For tips on getting online in Europe, see page 253.

USB flash drive. If you're traveling with a laptop, a flash drive can be handy for backing up files and photos. If you're thinking of simply transporting files to Europe on a flash drive, be aware that some Internet cafés don't allow you to use them out of fear of infecting their machines. As an alternative, consider the free and handy Dropbox (www.dropbox.com), also available as a mobile app, which is essentially a virtual flash drive that you can access anywhere.

GPS device. If you'll be doing a lot of driving and have a portable GPS device at home, you could buy European map data to use on vacation. For details on car GPS devices, see page 164. For details on using GPS and maps on a smartphone, see page 261.

Headphones/earbuds. These are a must for listening to music, tuning in to audio tours, or simply drowning out whiny kids on the plane. (I never travel without my

Wireless hotspots allow you to get online from a park bench.

noise-canceling Bose headphones.) Pick up a Y-jack so you and a partner can plug in headphones at the same time.

Chargers and batteries. Bring each device's charger. Look into getting a universal charger, with multiple plugs to fit each device (the octopus-shaped Chargepod is convenient but pricey; www.callpod.com), or a dual charger capable of juicing your iPad and iPod at the same time.

Adapters and Converters

Europe's electrical system is different from ours in two ways: the voltage of the current and the shape of the plug.

American appliances run on 110 volts, while European appliances are **220 volts**. Newer travel accessories and electronic gadgets are "dual voltage," which means they work on both American and European current. If you see a range of voltages printed on the item or its plug (such as "110-220"), you're OK in Europe. Some older appliances have a voltage switch marked 110 (US) and 220 (Europe)— switch it to 220 as you pack.

A few old, cheap American appliances aren't equipped to deal with the voltage difference at all, and they could be damaged or destroyed if plugged directly into a European wall outlet. In these cases, you'll need to buy a separate, bulky converter (about $30). With so many dual-voltage gadgets available, I haven't traveled with a separate converter in years. Still not sure? Travel stores offer

In Europe, two kinds of adapters fit virtually all outlets: two little round prongs for the Continent, three big rectangular ones for Britain and Ireland.

useful advice on plugs and adapters (such as the "Electrical Connection Wizard" at www.magellans.com).

Once you've dealt with the voltage, you'll have to consider the *****plug**. A small adapter allows American-style plugs (two flat prongs) to fit into British or Irish outlets (which take three rectangular prongs) or continental European outlets (which take two round prongs). I bring both continental and British adapters (handy for long layovers at Heathrow Airport). Secure your adapter to your device's plug with electrical or duct tape; otherwise it can easily get left behind in the outlet (hotels or bed and breakfasts sometimes have a box of abandoned adapters—ask). Many sockets in Europe are recessed into the wall; your adapter should be small enough so that the prongs seat properly in the socket. If, for some reason, your adapter doesn't work in your hotel, just ask at the desk for assistance; hotels with unusual sockets will invariably have the right adapter to loan you.

Some budget hotel rooms have only one electrical outlet, occupied by the lamp. Hardware stores in Europe sell cheap three-way plug adapters that let you keep the lamp on and your camera battery and smartphone charged.

Optional Bring-Alongs

I don't advocate bringing everything listed here. Choose the items that fit with your travel style and needs.

Picnic supplies. Bring a plastic plate (handy for dinner in your hotel room), cup, spoon, fork, and maybe salt and pepper. Buy a Swiss Army-type knife with a corkscrew and can opener in Europe (or bring one from home if you're checking your luggage on the plane).

*Water bottle. The plastic half-liter mineral water bottles sold throughout Europe are reusable and work great. If you bring one from home, make sure it's empty before you go through airport security (fill it at a fountain once you're through).

*Inflatable pillow (or neck rest). These are great for snoozing in planes, trains, and automobiles. Many travelers also swear by an ***eye mask** for blocking out early-rising or late-setting sun.

Insect repellent. Bring some along if you're prone to bites and are going somewhere especially bug-ridden.

Office supplies. Bring paper, a few pens, an envelope of envelopes (for letter writers), and some sticky notes (such as Post-Its) to keep your place in your guidebook.

Duct tape. A small roll of duct tape can work miracles—mending a punctured bag, solving an emergency shoe problem, or otherwise saving the day as a temporary fix. Conserve space by spooling only as much as you might need (less than a foot) around a short pencil or dowel.

*Small flashlight. Handy for reading under the sheets after "lights out" in the hostel, late-night trips down the hall, exploring castle dungeons, and hypnotizing street thieves. Tiny-but-powerful LED flashlights—about the size of your little finger—are extremely bright, compact, and lightweight. Camping-type headlamps also do the trick.

*Tiny lock. Use it to lock your backpack zippers shut. Note that if you check your bag on a flight, the lock may be broken to allow the bag to be inspected. Improve the odds of your lock's survival by buying one approved by the Transportation Security Administration—security agents can open the lock with a special master key.

PACK LIGHT

Universal drain-stopper. Some hotel sinks and tubs have no stoppers. This flat, flexible plastic disc—which works with any size drain—allows you to wash your clothes or take a bath.

***Hostel sheet.** These days, sheets are usually included in the price of a hostel, and if they aren't, you can rent one for about $5 per stay. Still, you might want to bring along a sheet (silk is lighter and smaller, cotton is cheaper), which can double as a beach/picnic blanket and cover you up on overnight train rides. See page 218 for hosteling tips.

A good book. There's plenty of empty time on a trip to either be bored or enjoy some good reading. Popular English-language paperbacks are often available in European airports and major train stations (usually for far more than their North American price). An ebook reader carries lots of books without the additional weight (and you can easily buy more as you go).

Gifts. If you'll be the guest of local hosts, show your appreciation with small, unique souvenirs from your hometown.

Postcards/photos from home. A collection of show-and-tell pictures (either digital or paper) is always a great conversation piece with Europeans you meet.

FLYING

Before you can enjoy Europe, you have to get there. And unless you're a romantic who's signing up to crew on a tramp steamer, you'll be riding on a jet plane. This chapter will help you figure out the best way to fly to Europe, when to buy your airline ticket, and how to get the lowest fare, both for transatlantic and intra-European flights.

Flying to Europe

Your plane ticket to Europe will likely be your biggest trip expense. Depending on the time of year, the typical round-trip fare for a basic ticket is $1,000-1,800 (including taxes and fuel surcharges), but fares can run as low as $700 and as high as $2,200. Because airlines offer fewer flights and sales these days, you'll have to be on your toes to get the best deal.

Your first decision when booking flights to Europe is whether to do it yourself or to enlist the help of a travel agent. Each option has pros and cons, but both work well.

Finding Plane Tickets Online
While each airline has its own website, I prefer to begin my search with a site that compares all my options.

Researching Flights
Flight search engines compare fares available at multiple airlines, online travel agencies, or both, and then sort them by price. I've tested a number

FLYING

Flight-Search Guidelines

When searching online for a flight, keep these tips in mind.

- No single flight-search site includes every possible airline—it's always smart to **check more than one website**.
- If you are flying into a city with several airports, select either **"all airports"** or simply the **city name** ("LON" for London) rather than a specific airport name ("LHR" for London Heathrow). Doing so will return more flight options.
- Some websites have a **"nearby airport"** option that broadens your search to include airports easily connected to your main destination by public transportation (for example, Pisa for Florence or Bratislava for Vienna).
- Choosing **"flexible dates"** lets you see what you might save by flying a few days before or after your ideal timeframe.
- If you want to fly into and out of different cities, select the **"multi-city"** option.
- When booking, decline **extras** that you don't want (for example, premium seating—with an extra fee). On each page of the transaction, be sure that no boxes are checked unless you wanted them to be.

---

of them on a variety of journeys, both transatlantic and within Europe. Surprisingly, I've seen that the industry's big sites—like Travelocity.com and Expedia.com—can miss several good-value results that other sites turned up. Overall, **Kayak.com** seems to have the best results for both intercontinental and intra-European flights on a combination of mainstream and budget carriers. (However, for cheap flights within Europe, **Skyscanner.com** has a slight edge—see page 102.)

A couple of sites are better for flights *to* Europe than flights *within* Europe, and some nice features make their results easier to navigate. **Hipmunk.com** has a lively interface (with a cheery cartoon chipmunk and "agony" rating) and a helpful timeline display of available flights, including layovers, to give you an at-a-glance rundown at your options. **Insidetrip.com** assigns each journey a numerical "Overall Trip Quality" score, based on such factors as the total trip time, comfort, and the number, duration, and ease of layovers. You can sort your options either by price or by overall quality.

Booking Your Flight Online

While it's possible to book your flights on search sites (they certainly hope you will, to garner their commission), I use them only as a first step. Once I've zeroed in on which airline has the best deal for my trip, I check the airline's own site to compare fares. You can sometimes avoid third-party service fees by booking direct, and airlines may offer bonuses (such as extra frequent-flier miles) to those who book direct.

On the other hand, the search sites occasionally beat the fares on the airline's official site, sometimes by using "mix and match" journeys to connect the legs of a single trip on multiple airlines. (However, these trips can be difficult to rebook in case of a delay or missed leg—review the schedule carefully, watching out for very tight connections or extremely long layovers.)

For maximum peace of mind, it can be best to book directly through the airline, which can more easily address unexpected problems or deal with rescheduled flights. If you do wind up buying tickets through a third-party site, make sure you have a phone number in hand—you'll need to speak to a person if you have a problem.

More Money-Saving Tips

Here are some additional ideas for finding lower fares online:

Comparison-shop "air plus hotel" promotional deals. Some major Internet travel agencies and airlines offer "getaway" deals on their websites. For one low price, you get a round-trip flight to a European city, as well as a few nights' lodging (generally a soulless business hotel). Given Europe's high accommodations costs—especially in big cities—this can be a good value.

Sign up for email alerts. Many airfare search sites—as well as the official airline sites—will email automated updates about low fares for specific routes.

Consider budget airlines. A few of Europe's low-cost budget carriers have flights between the US and Europe; these include Aer Lingus, airberlin, Brussels Airlines, Condor, Icelandair, TUIfly, and XL Airways (for websites, see the sidebar on page 100). But passenger reviews are mixed regarding their legroom, onboard services, and overall comfort—all of which are more important on a long overseas flight than a quick intra-European hop. Do your homework before committing to a lengthy flight on one of these carriers.

Those with flexibility can score some deals. If your travel dates aren't set, check out the take-what-you-can-get airfares from websites such as Lastminute.com or Lastminutetravel.com; Travelzoo.com also keeps track of the latest deals (though it lacks a flight-search engine). Bing's Flexible Search feature helps you figure out the cheapest travel days (www.bing.com/travel/flight). Enter your departure city and destination,

FLYING

a 30-day range for travel, and the length of your trip. The search results display which dates of travel will yield the lowest fares.

"Bidding-for-travel" sites like Priceline.com and Hotwire.com are also worth checking. But you're just as likely to stumble upon deals on the airlines' own websites—particularly if you sign up for their email alerts. Be aware that deeply discounted fares generally have serious restrictions; for example, you can't always choose the time of day to fly. But the savings could make it worthwhile if your travel dates are flexible.

Using a Travel Agent

While they may seem like an antiquated notion, travel agents are alive and well in the 21st century. I have long thought that I might be the last person still enjoying the services of a living, breathing agent. But, after polling my readers recently, I found quite a few who also appreciate a personal touch. My travel agent is my vital ally—I've never gone to Europe without her help.

When most people imagine a travel agency, they envision a brick-and-mortar shop on Main Street, staffed by professional, experienced travelers who enjoy lavishing personal attention on their clients. But increasingly, travel agencies are large operations that sell most of their products online. These Internet agents can't offer personal service, but they can give you access to some great deals. In many cases, the larger they are, the more leverage they have to negotiate discounted fares with airlines and cruise lines.

If you're seeking a good travel agent, recommendations from other travelers provide excellent leads. But the right agency doesn't guarantee the right agent. You need a particular person—someone whose definition of "good travel" matches yours. Ask for the agency's "independent Europe specialist."

Who should use an agent? You're likely to benefit from the services of an experienced travel agent if you're doing any of the following: coordinating a trip for a small group; booking a complicated, multi-leg journey; taking a cruise (most cruise lines prefer that you book through an agent); or traveling for work (especially if your company contracts with a particular agent).

Travel agents sometimes have access to cheaper fares. A good travel agent—especially one specialized in the region you're traveling to—offers both regular airline fares and discounted consolidator fares that aren't available elsewhere. Consolidators are wholesalers who negotiate with airlines to get deeply discounted fares, which they then sell cheaply (but with a markup) to travelers. Be aware that consolidator

The Fear of Flying

I can understand why many people are afraid to fly. I always think of the little rubber wheels splashing down on a rain-soaked runway and then hydroplaning out of control. Or the spindly landing gear crumbling. Or, if not that, then the plane tilting just a tad, catching a wing tip, and flipping over and bursting into flames.

I overcome these concerns with simple logic. The chances of being in an airplane crash are minuscule. I remind myself that every day, 30,000 commercial planes take off and land safely in the United States alone. While airplanes do crash, entire years go by in which there are no passenger fatalities on any commercial American airline. The pilot and crew fly daily, and they don't seem to be terrified. For more than 30 years, my company has had countless tour-group members fly over to meet us—12,000 tourists a year these days—and, as far as I know, never has one of our travelers even picked up a bruise while flying.

Also consider these statistics: A typical American has a 1 in 375 chance of dying of a heart attack; a 1 in 21,000 chance of being killed in a car accident (or a 1 in 48,000 chance of being hit by a car while walking); a 1 in 6.3 million chance of being killed by lightning...and a 1 in 8 million chance of dying in an airplane accident. Worldwide, more than a million people die each year in road accidents—about the same as if a fully loaded 747 crashed every four hours. If you worry about safety, the real time to panic is during the drive to the airport.

I comfort my nervousness with the knowledge that flying is a matter of physics and aerodynamics. Air has mass, and the plane maneuvers itself through that mass. I can understand a boat coming into a dock—maneuvering through the water. That doesn't scare me. So I tell myself that a plane's a boat with an extra dimension to navigate, and its "water" (air) is a lot thinner. Also, the pilot, who's still "flying" the plane after it lands, is as much in control on the ground as in the air. Only when he's good and ready does he allow gravity to take over.

Turbulence scares me, too. But a United pilot once told me that he'd have bruises from his seat belt before turbulence really bothered him. Still, every time the plane comes in for a landing, I say a prayer, close my eyes, and take my pen out of my shirt pocket so it won't impale me if something goes wrong. And every time I stick my pen back in my shirt pocket, I feel thankful.

FLYING

tickets are "nonendorsable" (meaning that no other airline is required to honor that ticket if your airline is unable to get you home—though this is rarely a problem). And if the airline drops its prices (which often happens), you are stuck with what was, but no longer is, a cheap fare. If buying a consolidator ticket, check cancellation policies and other restrictions carefully.

Use your agent only for arranging transportation. Although many agents can give you tips on Irish B&Bs and sporadic advice on biking in Holland, assume you'll do better if you use your travel agent only to get you to your destination. I use an agent for my plane ticket, railpass or car rental, advice on visas, and possibly travel insurance, but I turn to a good guidebook for everything else (such as hotel advice). For intra-Europe flights, do your own search, as a travel agent's reservations networks don't include most of the cheap, no-frills European airlines (see "Flying Within Europe," later).

Check student travel agencies. Any city with a university probably has a student travel agency. STA Travel offers budget fares to students, anyone age 26 and under, and to teachers (16 offices in the US, www .statravel.com, tel. 800-781-4040).

Travel agent fees are a good investment. Now that airline commissions are a thing of the past, many agents charge a $35-100 fee per ticket. Travel agencies have also had to specialize, offering their customers something beyond just plane tickets—a friendly, knowledgeable human being you can call on in a travel-related emergency or with any last-minute itinerary changes. In the long run, paying a modest fee could be a worthwhile expense to ensure that you have the right—and cheapest— ticket for your trip. Think of it as a consulting cost for your travel agent's expertise.

As a loyal customer, I enjoy the luxury of calling or emailing my agent, explaining my travel plans, getting a briefing on my options, and choosing the best flight. Once you find the right agent, nurture your alliance. Be loyal. Send her a postcard.

Flight-Booking Tips

These days, there's no such thing as a free lunch in the airline industry. (In fact, these days, there's usually no lunch at all.) If you save money, you usually incur some kind of loss. The formula I keep in mind when shopping for a flight is "Dollars saved = discomfort + restrictions + inflexibility." Expensive full-fare tickets offer the ultimate in flexibility, but I've never met anyone spending his or her own money who flies that way. Before grabbing the cheapest ticket you can find, make sure it meets your travel needs with the best combination of reliability, economy, and flexibility.

Airfares flex like crazy—so buy your tickets at the right time. There can be up to 10 different pricing levels for each flight, fares fluctuate throughout the day, and cheap tickets are limited to a few seats. To get the best fare, it's wise to start looking for tickets four to six months before you fly—as soon as you're able to commit to a firm date.

The specific window for optimal booking depends on the season. For spring and summer travel, prime time is January, February, and March. In general, the sooner the better (though that doesn't always mean the best prices are available in January). Fall travel should probably be booked by May or June, because the trend for airfare prices and availability is known by then. If you're traveling in September (particularly the first half of the month)—a very popular time to fly to Europe—start looking even earlier. Travel during winter, November through March, can be purchased a month or so in advance (with the exception of winter breaks and holidays, which require earlier booking).

Find out when "peak season" begins and ends for your travel destination. At certain crucial times, moving your flight by one day (out of peak and into shoulder season) could save you hundreds of dollars. Fares are generally a bit cheaper for travel Monday through Thursday than for weekends (and it's also generally cheaper to book midweek).

Be ready to buy. Given how erratic airline pricing can be, you want to be ready to pounce on a good fare when you see it. Waiting to talk with your travel partner could cost you a good fare. As you delay, dates sell out and prices generally go up. Figure out in advance what constitutes a good fare, then grab it when you find it. Long gone are the days when you or your travel agent could put several different reservations on hold while you made a decision.

Consider flying into one city and out of another. It's probably been

Multiple-City Flights

FROM NORTH AMERICA

OSLO

TO NORTH AMERICA

EXPLORE...

LISBON

10 years since I flew in and out of the same European city. Think cleverly about making what used to be called an "open jaw" itinerary—now dubbed a "multiple-city" trip. Since it rarely makes sense to spend the time and money returning to your starting point, this can be very efficient. In general, the fare is figured simply by taking half of the round-trip cost for each of those ports. I used to fly into Amsterdam, travel to Istanbul,

FLYING

and then ride two days by train back to Amsterdam to fly home (because I thought it was "too expensive" to pay $200 extra to fly out of Istanbul). Now I understand the real economy—in time and money—in breaking out of the round-trip mold. Note that multiple-city flights are cheapest when you use the same airline for each segment.

Pay attention to additional fees. Most airlines levy a hefty "fuel surcharge," which varies depending on the airline and the price of fuel. Charges for checked bags are another headache, although most transatlantic flights do not charge for the first checked bag (ask the airline). Combined with airport taxes (which vary by city), these fees can add hundreds of dollars to your total ticket price. In early 2012, the US government made pricing more transparent by enacting a law that requires the advertised price of a ticket to include all taxes and fees for any flight that includes a stop in the US. Advertised rates don't, of course, include optional add-ins (such as insurance or seat upgrades)—you must opt in for these extras.

Changing or canceling your ticket can be very expensive. Be sure of your dates before you book; airlines can be very aggressive about change fees. Understand your ticket's change policies before you buy. (While cheaper, nonrefundable tickets are the most restrictive, even certain types of business and first-class tickets have penalties for changes.) Most airlines charge a penalty of about $250 per ticket per change. (Sometimes you must rebook new dates immediately or lose the value of your ticket.) Even then, you typically need to make changes at least 24 hours before your departure to avoid losing the entire value of the ticket. If you need to alter your return date in Europe, call (or, if possible, visit) your airline's European office. If you absolutely must get home early, go to the airport. If you're standing at the airport two days before your ticket says you can go home, and seats are available, they may just let you fly.

Reserve a seat for maximum comfort. To avoid being squeezed in the middle of a row, pick a seat as early as possible. Most airlines let you choose your seat when you book (although there may be a charge for roomier seats). If seat assignments aren't available at booking, ask about the earliest possible date that you can call to request your seat (for example, 90 or 30 days before your flight)—and put it on your calendar. For pointers on which seats are best on specific airplanes, see www.seatguru .com. Several airlines have an intermediate class between Economy and Business; it goes by various names, but look for something like Economy Extra. Seats are a bit more expensive, but they're also more comfortable (wider and with more legroom). These are worth considering for larger or taller travelers, or for those who get squirmy on long, intercontinental flights and can afford the extra fee.

Review your ticket information carefully when you book. Double-check your dates, destinations, and exact spelling of your name. Confirm that the name on your reservation exactly matches the one on your passport, which can be an expensive hassle to correct later. A simple second look can give you a chance to fix any mistakes and save you enormous headaches down the road.

Check In and Take Off
To ensure your flight goes as smoothly as possible, heed these tips:

Check in online before heading to the airport. Most carriers' websites allow you to check in and print your boarding pass from home (or from your European hotel) 24 hours before departure time. This is a good way to confirm your flight schedule and seat assignment, and it can save you from a long check-in line at the airport. It can sometimes be a hassle to check in for a connection on two different carriers, even if they're partnered (for example, the first leg on Lufthansa and the second leg on United). First try checking in on the website of the company from which you bought the ticket; if that doesn't work, try the other carrier's site. In a pinch, you can check in for the entire journey at the airport, but in rare cases, you may have to wait until your layover to check in for your connecting flight. Don't dawdle—check in as soon as you possibly can.

Increasingly, airlines are allowing you to download a scannable boarding pass onto your smartphone. I've seen many TSA agents scratching their heads over these at the front of long security lines, so clearly the kinks haven't been worked out yet. But it's certainly going to become a more popular option down the line.

Bring a printout of your eticket and your passport. Even though most airlines no longer issue paper tickets, it's always smart to bring the printed receipt with you in case there are complications at the airport. Be sure the receipt has both your eticket number and the airline's reservation code. When flying to Europe, you're required to show your passport to the airline before boarding the flight.

Fly in comfort, even in economy class. I've never in my life paid for anything more than coach. And many times I've ended up on a full flight, spending nine hours in a middle seat. Here are my tricks for a comfortable flight in cattle-car "luxury": Dress warm and loose. I take off my shoes and belt and then cuddle up with a sweater and scarf. I wear noise-reduction headphones. These mute both the rumble of the engines and the mind-numbing chatter of people around me. And with

FLYING

What Can't I Carry On?

Items prohibited in carry-on luggage on US flights generally include the following:

- **liquids** in containers larger than 3.4 ounces
- **knives** and other sharp items including box cutters and scissors with blades longer than four inches
- **blunt instruments** (ski poles, golf clubs, baseball bats, or martial arts weapons)
- **guns,** ammunition, and explosives
- **tools**—no hammers or saws of any size; no screwdrivers or wrenches longer than seven inches
- **flammable materials** (though one book of safety matches and common lighters are allowed)
- **aerosol containers** greater than 3.4 ounces; self-defense sprays such as mace and pepper spray
- **"disabling chemicals"** such as bleach or chlorine

You can take an entire set of knives or a giant bottle of shampoo to Europe if you like—but you'll have to check your bag. (Certain items—such as fueled lighters or explosives—are not allowed in your checked luggage, either.)

Be warned that this list can change without notice—especially just after a terrorist threat. And be aware that restrictions can differ between the US and Europe, as well as between any two European countries. Don't assume you know what's allowed. Shortly before

headphones on, I get into conversations only if I want to. This makes the flight much more restful. I have a full charge on my laptop and lots of reading or writing to do. This provides me with a mental escape and an opportunity to prepare for my upcoming travels, and it makes the time race by. And I take a nap with the help of Ambien (the generic name for this prescription drug for insomnia is Zolpidem). For me, just a quarter-tablet is good for a couple of blissful hours. When I wake up, I have to work the kink out of my sore neck, but I'm thankful for the shut-eye. It enables me to function much better on my first day in Europe.

Frequent-Flier Miles

Personally, I don't collect frequent-flier miles. (It's my own quirky hang-up, but I view frequent-flier programs as a cynical way for airlines to produce nothing while prodding their customers to jump through needless hoops and compromise flexibility.) However, for a traveler who's willing to play the game, it can be a useful budget tool. While far from a sure

your flight, check the websites for your airline and any airports you're flying through. (This is an especially good idea if you're flying through London, which often enforces tighter restrictions than other European hubs.) Most of Europe follows security rules similar to the US and Canada. For the latest regulations, check www .tsa.gov/travelers. For the United Kingdom, see www.gov.uk /hand-luggage-restrictions.

You might be tempted to pick up some **duty-free booze** or **perfume** on your way back home—but before you do, think about your flight plan. You might see signs reassuring you that duty-free liquids—if purchased at the airport and sealed in a special bag—can be carried on board your flight. But your purchases may not be allowed on a connecting flight. If you have a layover, you'll often have to pass through a new round of security checks, and duty-free liquids that were fine on your first leg may be seized when you change planes. If you have a US connection, duty-free liquids (even in the special sealed bags) will not be allowed as a carry-on item through the security checkpoint. You can get around this by checking your bag when you leave Europe: Because you'll retrieve your suitcase at the first US airport you land in (to go through customs), you'll have an opportunity to place the duty-free liquor or perfume in your bag before re-checking it to your final destination.

FLYING

thing—and the rules are constantly changing—using your frequent-flier miles to get to Europe can save you a bundle.

What began as a way to reward customer loyalty has evolved into a profitable side-business for the airlines, who sell "award miles" to credit-card and other companies (who pass along those miles as incentives to their own customers). But as more people earn piles of miles, airlines are bumping up the restrictions and additional fees required to claim a seat. Here are some strategies for getting the most travel out of your miles. For more tips, check out www.flyertalk.com.

Book as far ahead as possible. Airlines reserve only a handful of "award seats" on each flight—and they go fast. The further ahead you book (ideally months in advance), the more likely you'll get your choice of flights for the fewest miles.

Maximize the miles you earn. For example, booking direct with the airline, rather than on a third-party booking site, might earn you bonus miles. Many credit cards allow you to accrue miles with each purchase you make, flight-related of not. But watch out if you buy your tickets on discount sites—depending on the seat code, some airlines may not credit the full amount of miles to your account.

Know about alliances. Most major airlines belong to one of three gigantic frequent-flier collectives (but these partnerships are as slippery as political alliances). The Star Alliance includes North American airlines (United, US Airways, Air Canada) as well as European carriers both big (Germany's Lufthansa, SAS Scandinavian, LOT Polish Airlines) and small (TAP Air Portugal, Greece's Aegean Airlines, Croatia Airlines, Slovenia's Adria Airways). Other alliances include SkyTeam (Delta, KLM, Air France, Alitalia, Czech Airlines) and OneWorld (American Airlines, British Airways, Air Iberia, Finnair). If you have miles on one airline in the alliance, you can redeem them on any of the others. So, for example, if you're headed to Prague, try using your Delta miles first (allied with Czech Airlines).

Use airline alliances to collect miles smartly. The same alliances work for collecting miles. You might not care about earning miles for an SAS or Air Portugal flight, but if you give them your United frequent-flier number, the miles go into your United pot.

To redeem miles, check online first, then call. Check if the flight you want is available on the airline's website. If not, don't give up. Call to speak with an airline agent. While this can come with a small additional fee, it's worth it to talk with a live person who has all your options at his or her fingertips—especially if you...

Do some research and know your options. There are a variety of ways to connect any two points. When you try to redeem miles, the agent might simply try the most straightforward route. If that route is sold out, ask him to check other ways. Better yet, do some homework before you call, and make a list (in order of preference) of the connections that would work for your trip. For example, if I'm flying from Seattle to London, it's easiest to take a direct, nonstop flight. But if that's full, I'd be willing to settle for any one of the dozens of other possible connections through other cities.

If you're short on miles, you still have options. Look into buying miles from the airline or paying a fee to transfer them from someone else (such as a spouse or relative). While it wouldn't be cost-effective to do this for the entire value of a ticket, it can be worthwhile if you're, say, 2,000 miles short on a 50,000-mile fare. Many airlines also allow you to "pay" for one leg of the ticket with miles and the other in cash.

Watch the expiration date. For many airlines, miles expire at a certain point after you accrue them (usually one to two years) or if your frequent-flier account remains inactive for too long. Typically the miles must be redeemed for a ticket before the expiration date, but the flight can occur anytime—even months later.

You're still responsible for taxes and fees. What were once "free" award seats can now cost as much as $300, depending on the airline and destination. But you're still flying for a fraction of the full fare.

Flying Within Europe

For most of my traveling life, I never would have considered flying point-to-point within Europe. It simply wasn't affordable. But today that kind of thinking seems *so* 20th century.

With the deregulation of airlines and the proliferation of extremely competitive discount carriers, suddenly Europe's vagabonds are jetsetters. New no-frills airlines take off every year. Before buying a long-distance train ticket, first do a search on Skyscanner.com. You might be surprised. Even some major European airlines (including British Airways, Lufthansa, Air France, Alitalia, SAS, KLM, LOT, and Croatia Airlines), faced with competition from budget carriers, have joined the discount-airfare game.

Using Budget Airlines

Since Europe deregulated its airways in the 1990s, a flock of budget-conscious, no-frills airlines have taken flight. Some of the most established (such as easyJet and Ryanair) have route maps that rival their mainstream competitors. Meanwhile, dozens of smaller, niche airlines stick to a more focused flight plan. For a list of many of these carriers—including websites and which hubs they primarily use—see the sidebar on page 100.

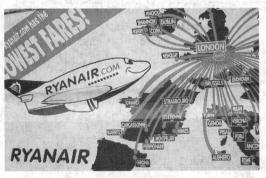

Europe's no-frills, smaller airlines offer cut-rate fares and scaled-down services.

Many budget airlines offer flights between major European cities for about $100, but you can find some remarkable, it-must-be-a-typo deals if your timing is right (for example, Ryanair routinely flies from London to any one of dozens of European cities for less than $20). Even after adding taxes and airport fees, these flights are a

Budget Airlines in Europe

These are just a few of the budget airlines taking to the European skies. To discover more, check out Skyscanner.com, or simply do an online search for "cheap flights" plus the cities you're interested in

Airline	Hub(s)
Aer Lingus www.aerlingus.com	Dublin, Shannon, Cork, Belfast
airBaltic www.airbaltic.com	Riga (Latvia)
airberlin www.airberlin.com	Multiple German cities
Air One www.flyairone.com	Milan, Venice, Pisa
Blue Air www.blueairweb.com	Bucharest, Bacău (Romania)
Brussels Airlines www.brusselsairlines.com	Brussels
CityJet www.cityjet.com	London City Airport
Condor www.condor.com	Multiple German cities
Danube Wings www.danubewings.eu	Bratislava (Slovakia)
Darwin Airline www.darwinairline.com	Geneva, Lugano
easyJet www.easyjet.com	London, Milan, Berlin, Paris, Liverpool, Geneva, Basel, Nice, Toulouse, Edinburgh, Madrid, and more
Estonian Air www.estonian-air.com	Tallinn
Flybe www.flybe.com	Newquay, Exeter, Southampton, London (southern England); Jersey, Gurnsey (Channel Islands)
Germanwings www.germanwings.com	Multiple German cities
Helvetic Airways www.helvetic.com	Zürich, Bern
Icelandair www.icelandair.com	Reykjavik

FLYING

flying to/from. Note that new airlines appear—and old ones go out of business—all the time.

Airline	Hub(s)
Jet2 www.jet2.com	Multiple British cities
Jetairfly www.jetairfly.com	Brussels, Liège, Ostend (Belgium)
Meridiana www.meridiana.it	Olbia, Cagliari (Sardinia); Rome and other Italian cities
Monarch Airlines www.monarch.co.uk	Multiple British cities
Niki www.flyniki.com	Vienna, Salzburg
Norwegian www.norwegian.no	Oslo, Bergen, Copenhagen, and Stockholm
Pegasus Airlines www.flypgs.com	Istanbul, Antalya (Turkey)
Ryanair www.ryanair.com	Point-to-point system focusing on London, Dublin, and several other cities
SmartWings www.smartwings.net	Prague, Ostrava (Czech Republic), Budapest
Thomsonfly http://flights.thomson.co.uk	Connects various British cities to Mediterranean resorts
Transavia www.transavia.com	Amsterdam, Rotterdam, Eindhoven
TUIfly www.tuifly.com	Multiple German cities
Vueling www.vueling.com	Multiple Spanish cities, Amsterdam, Toulouse (France)
Widerøe www.wideroe.no	Oslo
Wind Jet www.volawindjet.it	Catania, Palermo (Sicily); Rimini (Italy)
Wizz Air www.wizzair.com	Budapest and many other Eastern European cities
XL Airways www.xlairways.com	Paris

FLYING

great value. To get the lowest fares, book long in advance. The cheapest seats sell out fast (aside from occasional surprise sales), leaving the pricier fares for latecomers. Of course, there are caveats with flying budget airlines (described later, under "What's the Catch?").

One-way flights on low-cost airlines are just as economical as round-trips. Consider linking cheap flights, either with the same or different airlines. But be very careful to leave plenty of time for connections—you're on your own if a delay causes you to miss your next flight on a different airline. If you're using a budget carrier to connect to your US-bound flight, allow enough of a layover to absorb delays—maybe even an overnight.

Most low-cost airlines are primarily Web-based; it's easy to check schedules and book etickets online (described later). Interactive route maps offer an at-a-glance summary of your options.

Smart vagabonds use low-cost airlines to creatively connect the dots on their itinerary. If there's no direct cheap flight to Florence, maybe there's an alternative that goes to Pisa (1.5 hours away by train); remember that many flight-search websites have a "nearby airports" option that broadens your search. Even adding the cost of the train ticket from Pisa to Florence, the total could be well below the price of a long overland journey, not to mention several hours faster.

Searching for Cheap Flights Within Europe

Most budget airlines focus on particular hubs (for instance, Norwegian Air has hubs in Oslo, Bergen, Copenhagen, and Stockholm). When looking for cheap flights, first check airlines that use either your starting point or your ending point as a hub. For example, for a trip from Berlin to Oslo, I'd look at Air Berlin (with a hub in Berlin) and at Norwegian (which has a hub in Oslo). But some airlines forego this "hub-and-spoke" model for a less predictable "point-to-point" schedule.

To find out all your options, it's smart to use an online search engine that covers everything. My first stop when seeking budget flights is **Skyscanner.com**; this no-frills website specializes in European budget airlines, and it's a fast way to determine if any of them serve the route you're eyeing. Skyscanner also includes major non-budget carriers.

Another good option is the all-purpose **Kayak.com** (which also works well for flights *to* Europe). The visually engaging **Momondo.com** automatically searches for flights at nearby airports; read the results carefully to be clear on which airport it's using. **Dohop.com** has a clean interface and generally good results. You can also check **Flycheapo.com**, which doesn't include full flight schedules but can tell you which budget airlines fly between any two points. To find the right connection, it helps to search several sites.

Once I've determined which airline covers the trip, I book on that airline's website. For general pointers on using flight-search sites, see the sidebar on page 88.

What's the Catch?

With cheaper airfares come potential pitfalls. These budget tickets are usually nonrefundable and nonchangeable. Many airlines take only online bookings, so you won't have a travel agent to go to bat for you, and it can be hard to track down a staff member to talk to if problems arise. (Read all the fine print carefully, so you know what you're getting into.) Flights are often tightly scheduled to squeeze more flying time out of

Even if the name of your budget airline (such as Wizz Air) doesn't exactly inspire confidence, these carriers can get you to many destinations cheaper and a whole lot faster than the train.

each plane, which can exaggerate the effects of delays. Deadlines are strictly enforced: If they tell you to arrive at the check-in desk an hour before the flight, and you show up 10 minutes late, you've just missed your flight. And, as these are relatively young companies, it's not uncommon for budget carriers to go out of business or cancel a slow-selling route unexpectedly—leaving you scrambling to find an alternative.

Since budget airlines are not making much money on your ticket, they look for other ways to pad their profits—bombarding you with ads, selling you overpriced food and drinks on board (nothing's included), and gouging you with fees for everything—you'll get dinged for paying with a credit card (even though there's no option for paying cash), checking in and printing your boarding pass at the airport (instead of online), "priority boarding" ahead of the pack, reserving a specific seat, carrying an infant on board, or—of course—checking bags. The initial fare you see on the website can be misleadingly low, and once you begin the purchasing process, each step seems to come with another unexpected charge.

As in the US, baggage restrictions can be expensive. Not only will you pay a fee to check each bag, but you may have to pay extra if it's over a certain (relatively low) weight limit. Don't assume your bag qualifies as carry-on in Europe; many budget airlines use smaller dimensions than other carriers. To avoid unpleasant surprises, read the baggage policy carefully before you book.

Ryanair, one of the biggest budget carriers, is as famous for its low fares as it is for the creative ways it's devised to nickel-and-dime passengers. For instance, their complicated checked-luggage price schedule varies depending on how many bags you have, how heavy they are, and whether you prebook online—ranging from about $20 for a small bag prebooked off-season to $180 for a bigger bag booked at the airport in peak season, plus about $30 per extra kilogram over 20 kilos (44 pounds).

Another potential headache: Budget airlines sometimes use obscure airports. For example, one of Ryanair's English hubs is Stansted Airport, one of the farthest airports from London's city center. Ryanair's flights to "Frankfurt" actually take you to Hahn, 75 miles away. Sometimes you may even wind up in a different (though nearby) country: For example, a flight advertised as going to Copenhagen, Denmark, might go to Malmö, Sweden, or a flight bound for Vienna, Austria, might land in Bratislava, Slovakia. These are still safe and legal airstrips, but it can take money and time to reach your final destination by public transportation. On the other hand, the money you save on your ticket (compared to using a mainstream carrier into a major airport) often more than pays for the difference.

Flight vs. Train?

The availability of inexpensive flights is changing the way travelers plan their itineraries. A decade ago, it would have been folly to squeeze Italy and Norway into a single two-week trip. Today that plan is easy and cheap. So to connect two far-flung cities, what's better? Hopping a flight or riding the rails?

Flying can save both time and money, especially on long journeys. A cheap flight can help a light sleeper avoid spending the night on a rattling train. But if you're focusing on a single country or region and connecting destinations that are closer together, the train is still more practical.

Europe's high-speed train network is getting faster and faster, covering even long distances in a snap. From London to Paris, the Eurostar train can be faster than flying when you consider the train zips you directly from downtown to downtown. Train and car travel, unlike flights, keep you close to the scenery, to Europe, and to Europeans. Ground transportation is also less likely to be disrupted by bad weather, mechanical problems, or scheduling delays.

If you're environmentally minded, you already know that the greenest way to move your body around Europe is by train. Taking the train leaves a carbon footprint that's 70 to 90 percent smaller than if you fly. For that reason alone, some travelers choose to spend more time and money to ride the rails.

TRAINS AND MORE

In Europe, public transportation *works*. Europeans have invested hugely in their public transit, and it's generally fast and effective. Of course, digging the English Channel Tunnel, building a bridge between Denmark and Sweden, and adding bullet trains all cost money, and train travel is no longer as cheap as it once was. But savvy travelers can still get around on a tight budget.

Europe's commitment to public transportation is not just limited to populated areas; it's widespread. For example, in Scotland's Highlands—way up north—if the population is too sparse to justify a public bus service, citizens needing to get to a remote farmstead are welcome to ride with the postman for the cost of a bus ticket. In Europe, I use this rule of thumb: If there are people here and people there, there's a way to get between them by public transit. I can't think of a favorite European sight that you can't reach by bus, boat, or train.

This chapter pays special attention to the pros and cons of buying railpasses and point-to-point tickets, figuring out train schedules, and navigating Europe's train stations. Travel by bus and ferry is covered at the end of the chapter; for information on subways, city buses, and taxis, see the City Transportation chapter.

The Benefits of Train Travel

The European train system shrinks what is already a small continent, making the budget whirlwind or far-reaching tour a reasonable and exciting possibility for anyone. The system works great for locals and travelers alike, with well-signed stations, easily accessed schedules, and efficient connections between popular destinations. First-time train travelers get the hang of it faster than they expect. Generally, European trains go where you need them to go and are fast, frequent, and affordable. Lace

this network together to create the trip of your dreams.

For many travelers, the pleasure of journeying along Europe's rails really is as good as the destination. Train travel, though not as flexible as driving, can be less stressful. On a train, you can forget about parking hassles, confusing road signs, speed limits, bathroom stops, or Italian drivers. Watch the scenery instead of fixing your eyes on the road, and

Trains connect big cities, but also small towns—such as Manarola, in Italy's Cinque Terre.

maybe even enjoy a glass of the local wine. Compared to flying, rail travel allows more spontaneity. If a town looks too cute to miss, hop out and catch the next train.

It's also quite time-efficient, especially with Europe's ever-growing network of super-fast trains. With night trains, you can easily have dinner in Paris, sleep on the train, and have breakfast in Venice, Munich, or Madrid. And (with the exception of the Eurostar Chunnel

TRAINS AND MORE

train) you don't need to show up early. As long as you're on board when the train leaves, you're on time.

As Americans, we're accustomed to being shoehorned into a cramped car or an economy-class airline seat. On the train, you can walk around, spread out in comparatively wide seats, and easily retrieve an extra sweater from your luggage. The popularity of clean-air laws has made trains even more comfortable, as most of Western Europe's trains are now smoke-free.

Trains remain the quintessentially European way to go, and the best option for romantics. Driving to the Austrian lakeside hamlet of Hallstatt

Free Guide to European Railpasses

If you're planning to do Europe by rail on limited money, it's worth spending some time on www.ricksteves.com/rail. It's the only information source that compares rail deals available in the US with rail deals available in Europe. My staff and I research and produce this guide annually. Our goal is to create smart consumers (as well as sell a few passes). My rail guide covers everything you need to know to select and order the best railpass for your trip. While this chapter provides a good start in planning your train travel, my online railpass guide has even more details: current pass prices, region-specific ticket-price maps, a list of trains that require reservations (and how much they cost), and a handy link to the best European train schedule site.

is easy, but arriving by train is magical: Hop off at the hut-sized station across the lake, catch the waiting boat, and watch the town's shingled roofs and church spires grow bigger as the mist lifts off the water.

Train Tickets and Passes

A train traveler's biggest pre-trip decision is whether to get a railpass or stick with point-to-point tickets. Many travelers make a costly mistake by skipping over the details of this decision, as railpasses are no longer the sure bet they once were. It pays to know your options and choo-choose what's best for your trip.

Tickets or Pass?

Point-to-point tickets are just that: Tickets bought individually to get you from Point A to Point B. It's simplest to buy these in train stations as you travel, but they're becoming easier to purchase online, which can be handy if you need to secure an advance reservation for a certain train.

By contrast, a railpass covers train travel in one or more countries for a certain number of days (either a continuous span of days or a number of days spread out within a wider window of time). Most railpasses available to non-Europeans can only be bought outside Europe, so before your trip, you'll need to sketch out your itinerary, then answer the following questions:

On how many calendar days do you expect to ride the train? If you'll be on the train for just one or two days, you almost certainly won't benefit from a pass. The more time you expect to spend on the train, the more likely it is that you'll want a pass.

In how many countries will you be riding the train? If it's three or more, you are a likely candidate for a pass. If you'll be in fewer countries but on the train for at least three days, it's worth doing the math to see whether a pass makes sense. You get the most value out of a railpass when you use it for long travel days and in countries where train travel is expensive.

Roughly how much would your point-to-point tickets cost? You don't have to laboriously look up exact train fares online—to get a rough idea of what you'd pay for bigger journeys, check the map on page 111. If you're traveling in just one or two countries, you can check the more detailed regional maps at www.ricksteves.com/rail. Connect the dots and add up the fares to get an approximate cost for your tickets. Don't worry if one of your destinations isn't shown on this map: Ticket prices are mostly based on distance, so you can estimate fares. For example, if you're going to Germany's Rothenburg ob der Tauber, about halfway between Frankfurt and Munich, it's safe to assume the train fare to Rothenburg from Frankfurt or Munich is about half the total shown for the whole Frankfurt-Munich stretch.

How does your point-to-point ticket cost compare to the price of a pass? Look up the cost of a pass that covers the region you'll be in and the number of days you'll be on the train (see "Choosing Between Passes" on page 117). You may notice that several countries, mostly in southern and eastern Europe, have train fares so low that railpasses rarely beat out point-to-point tickets (you'd need to do a whole lot of train travel in a short time to make a pass worthwhile). If you're sticking to moderate distances in Italy, for example, it's unlikely a pass will save you money. If you're traveling in Germany, however, a pass is quite likely a smart move.

If your price comparison doesn't produce an obvious winner, take a closer look at factors that could tilt your decision one way or another, such as:

• *Sparse rail coverage:* In some areas, such as southern Spain, coastal Croatia, much of Scotland, most of Greece, and all of Ireland, railpasses make little sense because trains don't reach a lot of places you're planning to go. (To check whether your destinations are served by train, check online train schedules, described later, or the rail route maps at www .ricksteves.com/rail.)

• *Pricey fast-train supplements:* Passes lose their luster when fees are tacked on. In some countries, passholders are required to pay extra for each trip on a high-speed train. In Italy, for instance, it costs about an additional $15 per ride for mandatory fast-train reservations on most convenient connections between major cities. On the Thalys train that monopolizes direct service from Paris to Brussels or Amsterdam, passholders are forced to pay substantial extra fees of up to $55 in second class and $95 in first class.

• *First-class-only passes:* Many railpasses don't offer a second-class option for adult travelers. If a first-class pass costs about the same as traveling with second-class tickets, go with the pass for comfort. (For more on the differences between classes, see the sidebar on page 112.)

• *Advance-purchase discounts:* If you don't mind forgoing some spontaneity, you might be able to save money with advance-purchase discounts on point-to-point tickets. But unless you're taking just a few train trips, these discounts aren't worth the bother. While passes are flexible, these point-to-point discounts are usually valid only for nonrefundable, nonchangeable reserved tickets.

• *Convenience:* In countries or regions where reservations are not required, a pass allows you to hop on and off trains without fussing with multiple tickets; if all other things are even, a pass can make sense for ease of travel.

Point-to-Point Tickets

If a railpass doesn't pencil out for your trip, you can buy individual tickets for each leg of your journey. Tickets are sold in Europe's train stations, at some European travel agencies, on the websites of Europe's national railways, and through US-based retailers.

Unreserved, one-way tickets within a single country require your travel to be completed within a day, but allow stops and connections along the way. Unreserved international tickets (such as those commonly available in Germany, Austria, and Eastern Europe) allow two months to complete a journey with unlimited stopovers along the most direct route; if you want to reserve a seat or sleeper, you'll pay for it separately.

You're commonly required to reserve point-to-point tickets for the faster trains, such as the TGV, Eurostar Italia, Thalys, and AVE (see "Seat Reservations," later).

Point-to-Point Rail Tickets: Cost & Time

This chart shows the cost of second-class train tickets. Connect the dots of your itinerary, add up the cost, compare it with a railpass, and see what is better for your trip.

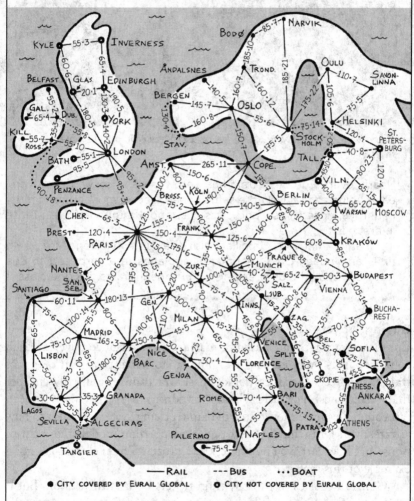

——— RAIL ‑‑‑ BUS •••BOAT
● CITY COVERED BY EURAIL GLOBAL   ○ CITY NOT COVERED BY EURAIL GLOBAL

The **first number** between cities = **Approximate cost** in $US for a one-way, second class ticket.

The **second number** = Number of **hours** the trip takes.

Important: These fares and times are for express trains where applicable and are based on European sources. Actual prices may vary due to currency fluctuations, advance purchase, and local promotions. For approximate first-class rail prices, add 50 percent. For shorter routes, see more cost comparison maps at www.ricksteves.com/rail.

First or Second Class?

First class—plusher, roomier, and less crowded—costs 50 percent more than second.

Nearly every European train has both first- and second-class cars, each going at precisely the same speed. Yet on most trains in most countries, tickets in second class cost about a third less than those in first class.

Many Americans, familiar with the huge difference between first- and coach-class seating on airplanes, are surprised to see just how small the difference is on European trains. Second class is

Buying Tickets

European train fares are based primarily on the distance traveled. Each country has its own "euros per kilometer" formula, though the type of train also affects the price (logically, slower trains are usually cheaper than faster ones). For faster classes of trains, however, many European rail companies have moved to a dynamic pricing system (similar to how airfares work), in which a fare can vary depending on demand, restrictions, and how early you purchase; the Eurostar Chunnel train is a good example of this system.

Generally, it's easiest to buy train tickets right at the station. But if your dates are set and you don't want to risk a specific train journey selling out—or if you're hoping to land an advance-purchase discount—it can be smart to buy in advance. Your three options are described next.

National Railway Websites: Many European national rail companies allow customers to buy tickets online at the going European price (usually for faster classes of trains for which reservations are required or at least recommended). Your "ticket" may be a barcode on your smart phone, an emailed confirmation code redeemable at the station, or a print-at-home document. Online tickets are valid for a specific date and

plenty comfortable, with way more legroom than you'd get on any economy-class airplane seat; it's generally a no-brainer for anyone on a budget. It can also be more fun. Many first-class travelers are business people looking to get work done; you'll have an easier time striking up a conversation in second class. Most Europeans don't travel in first class unless someone else is paying for it.

The biggest advantage to riding first class is that it's less crowded, which can be a significant plus at peak times on popular routes, when it can be harder to find a seat in second class. First class also has wider seats and wider aisles, and is more likely to have amenities such as air-conditioning and power outlets (though outlets are still rare on Europe's trains, no matter which class). While first class is less conducive to conversation, it's more conducive to napping.

With some railpasses, anyone age 26 or older must buy a first-class pass (youth passes, however, always have a second-class option). Those with first-class passes may travel in second-class compartments (although the conductor may give you a puzzled look). Those with second-class passes can pay the difference in ticket price to upgrade to first (except in Britain).

time and have strict refund restrictions, so read the fine print carefully. Not all national-railway sites are created equal: While some are fairly easy to navigate (such as the French, German, Italian, Swiss, British, Austrian, Swedish, and Irish railway sites), some are difficult (or impossible) for foreigners to use (such as the unreliable Spanish railway site).

Agents in the US: It's possible to purchase train tickets through your hometown travel agent or at RailEurope.com (most US-based agents or websites are essentially middlemen for Rail Europe). But tickets purchased this way are often expensive than those bought in Europe or from the European websites. Also, most US-based sellers exaggerate the importance of advance-purchase tickets and the need for seat reservations. I generally don't get my tickets through a US retailer unless I need a reserved seat on a particular train that I just can't miss (and I can't book it directly through a European website).

In Europe: Once in Europe, you can simply get tickets at the station, usually without much fuss (for tips, see page 125). You can even get tickets for trains in another country: For example, if your trip starts in Paris, you can buy your Berlin-to-Prague ticket at any Parisian train station (as any Parisian would). You can sometimes avoid trekking to the

Eurostar: Speeding from Great Britain to France or Belgium

If you factor in the time wasted in airports, the fastest and most convenient way to get from Big Ben to the Eiffel Tower is by rail. Eurostar, a joint service of the Belgian, British, and French railways, is the speedy passenger train that zips you (and up to 800 others in 18 sleek cars) from downtown London to downtown Paris. The train goes 190 mph both before and after the English Channel crossing. The actual tunnel (a.k.a. the Chunnel) is a 20-minute, black, silent, 100-mile-per-hour nonevent. Your ears won't even pop.

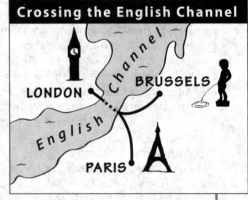

Crossing the English Channel

Unlike most trains in Western Europe, Eurostar always requires a separate, reserved ticket. Though it is not covered by a railpass, passholders may be able to get discounts. Eurostar fares (essentially the same between London and Paris or Brussels) vary depending on how far ahead you reserve, whether you can live with restrictions, and whether you're eligible for any discounts (such as those for early purchase or round-trip travel).

A one-way, full-fare ticket (with no restrictions on refundability) runs about $425 for first class and $310 for second class, but discounts can lower those fares substantially. Within each discount category, multiple fares exist (figure $90-200 for second-class, one-way), and the early bird gets the best price. If you're ready to commit, you can book some tickets up to nine months in advance at www.eurostar.com, but more commonly starting six months out.

Eurostar's monopoly on using the Chunnel track expired at the beginning of 2010. Deutsche Bahn—Germany's state-run railway company—is negotiating to run competing high-speed trains between London and Frankfurt and Amsterdam.

train station by visiting a neighborhood travel agency or branch office of the national railroad. Sometimes this convenience comes with an extra fee, but it can save lots of time and hassle (and travel agents may have more time and English-language skills than station counter agents).

Ticket Discounts

If you're buying point-to-point tickets, be aware of the ways you can qualify for a discount.

Advance purchase (a week to three months in advance) can save you money in certain countries (most notably Britain, France, Germany, and Spain), especially for faster or longer rides. In other parts of Europe (such as Switzerland, Austria, Italy, and most eastern countries), advance-purchase deals either don't exist or aren't worth the hassle. For regional or medium-speed trains in most places, tickets cost the same whether they're bought two months or two minutes before the train leaves.

Round-trip tickets can be cheaper than two one-way tickets in some countries (Britain, France, Germany, the Netherlands, and Spain; sometimes in combination with advance purchase). For many trips within Britain, for example, a "day return" (round-trip in a single day) can be just a bit more expensive than a single one-way ticket.

Children get ticket discounts in most of Europe (typically about 50 percent off for ages 4-11, sometimes free with an adult). Whether you're traveling with tickets or a railpass, kids under 4 always travel free on your lap (though if there's an empty seat, feel free to use it).

Youths ages 12-25 can buy discount cards in Austria, Belgium, Britain, France, Germany, and Italy.

Seniors can find a few ticket deals, most of which require a discount card purchased in Europe (discounts start between ages 60 and 67; for details, see page 453).

Off-peak travel (such as midday or midweek) can be cheaper than peak-time journeys (mainly in Britain and France).

Railpasses

Armed with a railpass, the independent traveler has Europe as a playground. You can travel virtually anywhere, anytime, often without any seat reservations. Just step on the right train, sit in an unreserved seat, and when the uniformed conductor comes, flash your pass. High-speed, international, or overnight trains are more likely to require reservations, but despite that chore, a railpass is still a joy.

Although the array of railpasses seems daunting, every pass has these features: It covers a specific geographical area (one or more countries); it

Do You Speak Railpass?

When choosing a railpass, you're likely to come across some unfamiliar terms. Here's what they mean in plain English:

Global Pass: The classic "Eurail" pass, letting you travel freely throughout most of continental Europe, from Portugal to Finland to Greece.

Select Pass: Unlike the Global Pass, covers just three, four, or five neighboring countries in continental Europe.

Eurail: Brand name under which many European railpasses are sold—but more commonly used as a generic term for any European railpass.

Continuous Pass: Gives you unlimited train travel for the duration of the pass.

Flexipass: Lets you pay for just a certain number of train travel days within a specified window of time (for example, any 10 days within a two-month period).

Saverpass: A single ticket printed with at least two people's names on it (code for "group discount"—even if your group is just two people).

Youth Pass: Discounted pass for travelers ages 12-25.

Rail-and-Drive: Flexipass letting you prepay for a mix of train days and car-rental days.

Railpass Bonuses: Certain boat, bus, and non-rail trips that are either covered or discounted with a railpass.

Benelux: Belgium, the Netherlands, and Luxembourg—collectively treated as one country by railpasses.

Couchette (koo-SHET): A night-train bunk bed in a lockable compartment (with a blanket, pillow, clean linen, and up to five compartment mates).

Sleeper: Berth with more privacy than a *couchette,* with one, two, or three beds.

Point-to-Point Ticket: Covers travel from Point A to Point B (may be an open-date ticket, or for a certain train at a certain time).

Reservation: Not only a good idea on a can't-miss train, but also required on many of Europe's faster trains.

Validation: Step required before using your pass—have it stamped by someone behind a station counter.

has a fixed number of travel days; and it's either good for a continuous block of time (continuous pass) or selected days in a window of time (a flexipass). Most passes offer "saverpass" deals to people traveling together.

Choosing Between Passes

It's wise to carefully compare passes to find the best fit for your itinerary and style of travel. The range of options may seem intimidating, but mostly it's a matter of simply knowing which countries you intend to travel in and for how many days.

Where To? First find the pass that best matches the area you'll be traveling in. If you're planning on covering a lot of ground by train, you probably want one of the multi-country passes described below; it generally makes little sense to cobble together several single-country passes.

A **Global Pass,** covering the widest area, gives you most of Europe by the tail, buying you unlimited travel on all public railways in most of Europe (Britain is the big exception). If you've got a whirlwind trip planned, the Global Pass is probably the best way to go. (You need to essentially travel from Amsterdam to Rome to Madrid and back to Amsterdam to justify the purchase of a one-month Global Pass.)

For a less ambitious multi-country trip, consider a **Select Pass,** which lets you preselect three, four, or five adjoining countries (though not including France). If you're traveling just a tad beyond five main countries and for fewer than 10 travel days, consider whether buying one or two extra point-to-point tickets might be cheaper than bumping up to a Global Pass (see "Getting the Most out of a Railpass," later). If a certain **regional pass,** such as for Scandinavia, happens to fit your plans, it can be even cheaper than a Select Pass.

Virtually every European country has its own **single-country pass.** These are especially important in Britain, which does not participate in the Global Pass or Select Pass. Several **two-country passes** are available

Eurail Countries

Note: France & Slovakia are not Select Pass options
Serbia & Montenegro are not part of Global Pass

*A **Global Pass** covers most of Europe except Great Britain, Poland, and some nations in Eastern Europe. A **Select Pass** lets you narrow the scope to three, four, or five adjacent countries.*

A Sample Select Pass

EURAIL   CIV No. 73030621*A |IEL| R   181925   R
                                            E   E
                                            I   06 Jan 2013   I
                                            Issuing Stamp

EURAIL SELECT PASS 5 COUNTRIES   FLEXI
Valid in: **AUSTRIA - BENELUX - GREECE - GERMANY - ITALY**

Category: Adult   Validity: 5 days within 2 Months   Class 1   MUST BE VALIDATED
                                                                          BEFORE 05 JUL 2013
First   Name: **STEVES, R MR**
Day   Day Month Year   Country of Residence: USA
Last   Passport #: _____   VOID
Day   Day Month Year   Travel Calendar below must be filled in: STAMP
           1   2   3   4   5
Day: |__|__|__|__|__|
Mth: |__|__|__|__|__|
This coupon is only valid with EURAIL cover and passport. Please see conditions of use.   EUR 415.00

70285451

Don't write anything on your railpass before it's validated. When you're ready to use it, the ticket agent will fill in validity dates and your passport number, and stamp the validation box on the far right. Each day when you take your seat on the train, write down the date in ink (day first, then month) before the conductor comes around.

for specific country pairs (for example, France and Italy).

Flexipass or Continuous? If you plan to linger for a few days at most of your destinations, a **flexipass** is the better choice, letting you pay only for the days on which you actually travel. Most railpasses are this type. You don't have to decide beforehand which days you'll travel on, but you do have a certain window in which you must use up your train days (usually two months after you start using the pass). You can take as many trips as you like within each travel day, which runs from midnight to midnight (most direct overnight rides count as one travel day on a flexipass).

A **continuous pass** makes sense if you plan to travel nearly daily and cover a lot of ground. Global, BritRail, and Swiss passes offer this option. If you have a 15-day continuous pass, you can ride the trains as many times as you like for 15 days. The length of a one-month pass depends on the month you start traveling. If you set off on any day in February, the pass is only good for the next 28 days. If you start in July, it's good for 31 days.

For those with open-ended plans, continuous passes can be worth the extra cost. Let's say you're planning a three-week trip and choosing between two versions of a Global Pass: a 21-day continuous pass and a cheaper 10-days-in-two-months flexipass. For not much more, the continuous pass gives you the freedom to take any train without wondering if a particular trip justifies the use of a travel day.

Rail-and-drive passes combine train and car travel, providing you with a railpass and vouchers for a few Hertz or Avis car-rental days. This can be convenient if you plan to drive in areas poorly served by trains—but for most, it's no easier than simply arranging for a separate, short-term car rental.

Using Your Railpass

Railpasses are pretty straightforward but come with a lot of fine print (worth reading). It's important to understand at least the basics before your first day of train travel.

Validate your pass before your first use. You must activate your railpass, in person at a European train station, for it to be valid for train travel. Your pass comes printed with an issue date (usually the day you bought it) and must be validated within six months. For example, if May 24 is stamped on your railpass as the issue date, you must start the pass by November 23. Never write anything on your railpass before it's been validated.

Validation is easy: At any European train station, present your railpass and passport to a railway official at a ticket or information window. The ticket agent (not you) writes in your passport number, and the first and last dates of your travel period, and stamps the validation box on the far right. For example, a two-month validity period starting May 15 will end at midnight on July 14. Agents will assume that you intend to use the pass on the same day you are presenting it, so if you're validating it a few days beforehand, write your desired dates (European style, e.g., 15/05/14 - 14/07/14) on a slip of paper to show the agent. All train trips and non-train "bonuses" (trips on covered or discounted boats and buses) must be started and finished within the valid life of your railpass. If you have a group pass (i.e., a saverpass), all group members must be present when the railpass is validated.

You may validate your country railpass before arriving in that country. Let's say you're in Copenhagen with a German railpass, you're heading to Berlin, and you want the German portion of your route to be covered by your railpass. At the Copenhagen train station, buy a ticket to the German border and have the agent validate your railpass at the same time. Don't get caught with an unvalidated pass: If you forget to do it before boarding, approach the conductor right away to have it validated on board (don't be surprised if you're charged a fee of $5-30).

Fill in travel days (for flexipasses) and trip details. With a continuous railpass, nobody counts how many days you travel during the validated period. But if you're using a flexipass, you'll have to fill in your travel days as you go. On your flexipass, you'll see a string of blank boxes, one for each travel day available to you. Either just before or after boarding, fill in that day's date in ink in one of the blank boxes on your pass before the conductor reaches you. (Don't fill out the dates any further in advance, in case your plans change.)

Note that a travel day is a calendar day, running from midnight to midnight. You can take as many trips as you like within each travel day that you've marked on your pass. A nice bonus is that a direct overnight train uses up only one flexipass travel day (not two), as long as you board after 7 p.m. and do not change trains before 4 a.m. (you just write the arrival date on your flexipass).

Some passes (continuous or flexi) also require you to fill in your trip destinations on the foldout sheets of your pass cover.

Show your pass if asked. After the train starts, the conductor heads down the aisle, asking for tickets and passes, and checking that they are dated correctly. You may be asked to present your passport, too.

Keep your pass in your money belt. Your railpass is a valuable slip of paper—if you lose it, it's gone. (Even if you bought "railpass insurance" when you got your pass, a lost or stolen pass presents a logistical headache.) While some national railways are slowly moving toward paperless ticketing, all railpasses are still only available in old-fashioned hard-copy form. Guard yours carefully.

Getting the Most out of a Railpass

Many people spend more on their railpass than they have to. Consider the following tips before you make your purchase:

Stretch a flexipass by paying out of pocket for shorter trips. If you plan to ride the train on, say, eight different days, but two of those days are very short trips, you may save money by getting a six-day pass and buying point-to-point tickets at the station on your short-haul days. Use your flexipass only for those travel days that involve long hauls or several trips. To determine whether a trip is a good use of a travel day, divide the cost of your pass by the number of travel days (or look at what it costs to add a day onto the pass's base price). If the pass you're considering costs about $60 per travel day, it makes no sense to use one of your days for a trip that would otherwise cost $10.

With careful juggling, a shorter pass can cover a longer trip. For example, if you're on a one-month trip, you don't necessarily need a one-month pass. You may be able to get by with a 21-day continuous pass by starting and/or ending your trip in a city where you'd like to stay for several days or in a country not covered by your pass. On, say, a one-month London-Vienna trip, you could spend a few days in London, pay to take the Eurostar train to Paris (see page 114), sightsee in Paris for several days, then validate your pass when you leave Paris. Plan for your pass to expire in Vienna, where you can easily spend a few days without the use of a railpass.

It can make sense to buy a longer pass for a shorter trip. One long, expensive train ride at the end of a 25-day trip can justify jumping from a 21-consecutive-day railpass to a one-month pass.

More travel days on a pass = cheaper cost per day. Compared to shorter passes, longer railpasses are cheaper per travel day. For example, a 15-consecutive-day Global Pass costs $775, the equivalent of about $50 a day. With a three-month Global Pass for $2,100, you're paying about $25 a day. (Most one-hour train rides cost more than that.) Similarly, many single-country passes start at a base price of about $70 each for three travel days, but allow you to buy extra days for as low as $20 each.

One railpass is usually better than two. To cover a multiple-country trip, it's almost always cheaper to buy one Select Pass or Global Pass with lots of travel days than to buy several country passes with a few high-cost travel days per pass. If you travel over a border (such as Germany to Switzerland) using separate country railpasses, you'll use up a day of each pass.

Understand your bonuses. Some boat, bus, and other non-train rides—called "bonuses"—are either covered or discounted with any rail-pass that covers the appropriate country. A bonus trip is no different from a train trip: To use your flexipass to cover the cost of a bonus boat or bus, you must fill in a travel day on your pass (and you can take as many trips, whether train or non-train, in one travel day as you can squeeze in). These include German Rhine boats, Swiss lake boats, and Italy-Greece ferry crossings. Trips offered only at a discount (rather than those that are completely covered by the pass) usually don't cost you a travel day, but you must use the discount while your pass is valid.

Looking up Train Schedules

Riding the rails has become even easier with the advent of user-friendly online timetables. While maps can be helpful, they can't do what a good online schedule can: instantly show you the fastest connections, frequency, and length of a train trip (and whether reservations are required).

Each country's national rail company has its own website, but the one operated by German Rail (Deutsche Bahn, www.bahn.com) has

---

Using the Deutsche Bahn Website

No matter where you're traveling in Europe, the German railway's website at www.bahn.com should be your first stop for timetable information. Here's how to use it:

Start with a station-to-station search. Enter just the city name, unless you know the name of the specific station you want. Remember to use local spellings. For example, Prague is "Praha," Rome is "Roma," and Florence is "Firenze" (see "City Name Variations" on page 810). Replace umlauts with an e: Cologne is "Köln" in German, but you can spell it as "Koeln" to avoid having to figure out how to type ö. Enter the time you think you might be traveling (using the 24-hour clock) and the date, if you know it. Though schedules for most trains aren't available more than three months out, they generally don't vary much (Sundays are the major exception). If you're looking up a connection several months ahead, try a closer date on the same day of the week you'll be traveling.

Skip the extra search fields. If you're just looking up schedules, there's no need to fill out any fields beyond the top ones: Once you've entered the stations, date, and time, just skip right to "Search."

If prompted, choose a station. Many cities have several stations, and you may be asked to specify which station you want from

---

train schedules for virtually all of Europe. I use this site to plan my connections for almost every trip in Europe; see the sidebar above for tips on using it. Their DB Navigator app is a boon for train travelers with smartphones and tablets.

The Deutsche Bahn's site doesn't show fares for most trains outside Germany and Austria. I wouldn't bother checking exact ticket prices on each country's own national railway site; for estimates, use the map on page 111.

Printed schedules can also be helpful. Many railpasses come with a schedule booklet listing major (but by no means all) routes. For a more comprehensive printed resource, consider the frequently updated *Thomas Cook European Rail Timetable* (www.thomascookpublishing.com). For tips on gathering schedule information while you're on the go in Europe, see page 126.

Seat Reservations

Depending on the route and type of train, reservations (which guarantee you a specific seat) can either be required, a good idea, a pointless

a drop-down menu. If one of the options is the city's name spelled in capital letters, go with that one (it'll look up the best connections for that city, regardless of the station). In cities with several major stations (such as London, Paris, Barcelona, and Madrid), your choice of station may depend on the specific direction of travel or the location of your hotel—refer to your guidebook.

Review your options. You'll be given a range of possibilities for your journey. Each one shows the start and end points (with stations specified), the departure and arrival times, the duration of the trip, the number of changes, the types of trains, and whether the train requires a reservation (indicated by a circled "R").

Know where to find more details. Clicking the arrow symbol next to any of the trip connections will give you more detail, including all transfer points. If you click "Show intermediate stops," you can see every stop on that route. Clicking the train number shows all the stops for the entire route, including those before and/or after your stations.

Check for reservation info. "Compulsory reservation" means what it says, while "Please reserve" means that reservations are recommended but optional (see "Seat Reservations" below). "International supplement" doesn't apply to travelers with railpasses.

hassle, or not even an option. Many American travelers waste money and surrender their flexibility after being swayed by US-based agents who profit from exaggerating the need for reservations. The Deutsche Bahn's online schedule, described above, is objective and complete—it's your best resource for identifying trains that truly require a reservation.

Reservations typically cost anywhere from $5 to $35 (with a few more expensive exceptions; in Britain they're free). When a reservation is required, the cost is included in the price of a point-to-point ticket, but railpass holders pay extra for it. When it's optional, it costs extra with either a point-to-point ticket or a railpass. Slower regional trains do not accept reservations.

When Reservations Are Required: Certain types of trains always require reservations and can sell out (much like an airplane). These include privately run high-speed trains such as the Brussels-based Thalys and the London-Paris/Brussels Eurostar, certain country-specific high-speed trains (especially in France, Italy, Spain, and Sweden), some of Switzerland's just-for-tourists scenic trains, and beds on overnight trains.

When Reservations Are Optional but a Good Idea: Most of the time, there's plenty of seating for everyone. But it's wise to reserve at least several days ahead if you are traveling during a peak time (summer, weekends, holidays); on a route with infrequent service; if you need several seats together (a family with children); or for a train you simply cannot afford to miss.

How Soon to Reserve: Dates, times, and seat assignments are built into some tickets at the time of purchase. If you have an unreserved ticket or a railpass, you can purchase seat or sleeper reservations anywhere from a few hours to several months in advance. Most trains that require reservations limit the number of seats available to passholders (most notoriously France's TGV trains), saving the remaining places for full-fare ticket buyers. Your decision of how soon to reserve depends on how firm your itinerary is (do you have hotel reservations or a flight to catch?), how many departures in a day could get you there on time (2 or 20?), and other factors mentioned above. One of the most popular train routes for my readers is between Paris and Italy, where direct trains run only a few times per day, can sell out weeks ahead, and generally don't accept railpasses.

Where to Reserve: You can get reservations either in European stations or ahead of time through US-based agents (Rail Europe is the largest). Reservations made in the US cost a little more and are less likely to be changeable or refundable.

Train Stations

Great European train stations stir my wanderlust. Stepping off a train in Munich, I stand under the station's towering steel and glass rooftop and study the big, black schedule board crowned by the station clock.

Whether old or new, bustling European train stations are temples of travel. Just pick a platform...and explore Europe.

It lists two dozen departures. Every few minutes, the letters and numbers on each line spin and tumble as one by one cities and departure times work their way to the top and flutter away.

Surrounded by Germany on the move, I notice businessmen in tight neckties, giddy teenage girls, and a Karl-Marx-like bum leaning on a *Bierstube* counter. The fast and the slow, the young and the old, we're all in this together—working our way up life's departure board.

There's plenty of romance here, but the hustle and bustle at train stations can also be confusing. Here are some tips on navigating Europe's temples of travel.

Europe is becoming automated. Anyone insisting on talking to a real person at a ticket window will stand in long lines and pay a premium. Savvy travelers figure out the machines: Choose English, follow the step-by-step instructions, and get comfortable swiping your credit card and keying in your PIN.

Buying Tickets at the Station

Nearly every station has old-fashioned ticket windows staffed by human beings, usually marked by long lines; avoid them by using ticket machines, which almost always offer instructions in English.

The downside to ticket machines: Some won't take American credit cards (even if they claim to), or accept them only if you type in your card's PIN (for more on dealing with credit-card hassles in Europe, see page 178). If the machines aren't cooperating with your card, try cash (most machines are labeled according to the kind of payment they accept), or head for the ticket window.

In person, bridge any communication gap by writing out your plan: departure and destination, date, time (if you want a reservation and/or a printout of your departure options), how many people, first or second class.

A Typical Train Ticket

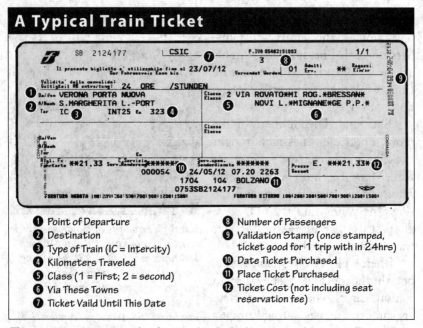

1. Point of Departure
2. Destination
3. Type of Train (IC = Intercity)
4. Kilometers Traveled
5. Class (1 = First; 2 = second)
6. Via These Towns
7. Ticket Vaild Until This Date

8. Number of Passengers
9. Validation Stamp (once stamped, ticket good for 1 trip with in 24hrs)
10. Date Ticket Purchased
11. Place Ticket Purchased
12. Ticket Cost (not including seat reservation fee)

This is a point-to-point ticket for travel in Italy, but train tickets across Europe have the same kind of information.

If you do opt for using a ticket window, be sure you select the appropriate line—larger stations may have different windows for domestic, international, sleeper cars, or immediate departures. When buying tickets, you can most clearly communicate your intentions by writing them out and showing them to the ticket agent (see photo on previous page). If there's a problem, she'll solve it.

It's often possible to buy tickets aboard the train, but expect to pay an additional fee for the convenience. Be sure to have enough cash in case the conductor can't use your American credit card. If you're buying on board, find the conductor before he finds you; otherwise, your "fee" could turn into a much heftier "fine" for traveling without a valid ticket. Be aware that on most local trains (especially commuter lines), all trains in Switzerland, and many others around Europe, you can be fined for traveling *sans* ticket, no matter what. Look for warning signs on train doors.

Schedule Information

Even if you've already looked up your train schedules online, always confirm your plans at the station. Every station has some kind of schedule information available, whether it's in printed or electronic form, or at

Key Train Vocabulary

	French	Italian	German
train	train	treno	Zug
ticket	billet	biglietto	Fahrkarte
station	gare	stazione	Bahnhof
main station	gare centrale	stazione centrale	Hauptbahnhof
platform/track	quai/voie	binario	Bahnsteig/ Gleis
timetable	horaire	orario	Fahrplan
supplement	supplément	supplemento	Zuschlag
delay	retard	ritardare	Verspätung
strike	grève	sciopero	Streik
reservation	réservation	prenotazione	Reservierung
berth/couchette	couchette	cuccetta	Liegeplatz

information counters staffed by people eager (or at least able) to help you. All European timetables use the 24-hour clock (see page 357).

Learning to decipher printed schedules makes life on Europe's rails easier. Posters list all trains that arrive at and depart from a particular station each day. This information is clearly shown in two separate listings: Departures are usually in yellow, and arrivals are normally in white. In some stations, you'll find free schedule booklets listing all their daily departures.

In Munich's train station, departures and arrivals are clearly listed on easy-to-read electronic boards. Railroad staff is standing by to answer your questions.

Familiarize yourself with the symbols in schedules that indicate exceptions: Crossed hammers, for instance, mean the train goes only on workdays (daily except Sundays and holidays); a cross signifies that it runs only on Sundays and holidays. Most other symbols are easy enough to guess at: A little bed means the train has sleeping

TRAINS AND MORE

compartments, and crossed silverware indicates a dining car.

Many stations also have either video screens or big flippy boards that list the next several departures. These often befuddle travelers who don't realize that all over the world, the same five easy-to-identify columns are listed: destination, major stops along the way, type of train, track number, and departure time. I don't care what language they're in; without much effort you can accurately guess which column is which.

17.26 ⊖3 'X außer Sa 2.Kl	Schwabach 17.44 – **Roth 17.54**	2
17.28 ⊖2 2.Kl	N.-Frankenstadion 17.35 – Feucht 17.43 – Altdorf 18.00	3
17.29 ICE 1519/ ICE 1719 🍴	Augsburg 18.29 – M.-Pasing 18.57 – **München 19.09** ⊙	9
17.34 IC 2366 Sa, So* 🍴	Ingolstadt 18.39 – **München 19.37** ⊙ *auch 1.Nov	13
17.34 EC 24 🍴🛪	*FRANZ LISZT* Würzburg 18.26 – Aschaffenburg 19.08 – Frankfurt (M) 19.41 – Frankfurt (Airport) 19.57 – Mainz 20.18 – Koblenz 21.10 – Bonn 21.43 – Köln 22.06 – Solingen-Ohligs 22.27 – Wuppertal 22.41 – Hagen 22.59 – **Dortmund 23.21** ⊙	7

Posted train schedules clearly mark the departure times, destinations, arrival times, and track numbers.

Stations may also have self-service computer terminals—many of which are ticket machines—where you can look up schedule information. These computers are almost always multilingual and can be real time-savers. Use them to understand all your options. Many even print out a schedule tailored to your trip.

Of course, your best authority is the person at the train station information window. Uniformed employees on the platforms or on board the trains can also help.

Other Services

Besides offering travel-related services, most stations are great places to take care of your basic to-do list, with ATMs, grocery stores (usually with longer hours than you'll find in the town center), restaurants, bike-rental kiosks, and shops selling calling cards and/or mobile-phone SIM cards.

Baggage Check: Most major stations have storage lockers and/or a luggage-checking service where, for about $3 to $8 a day, you can leave your bags. People traveling light can fit two bags into one storage locker, cutting their storage costs in half. In some security-conscious train stations, lockers are no longer in use, and travelers must check their bags at a luggage-deposit desk—often after going through an airport-type security check. This service is expensive; you'll pay $5 to $15 per bag. Lock your bag and don't leave valuables inside—both for your own security and because some luggage desks won't accept unlocked bags. In extreme cases, they don't take laptop computers. (I once spent a day in Marseille carrying around my laptop.) Allow plenty of time to retrieve

Train stations often have good, long-hours grocery stores. This one in Vienna is open every day, 5:30 a.m.-11:00 p.m.

your bag before boarding your train. Bag-check desks come with lines, can close for lunch in smaller stations, and usually aren't open all night—confirm opening and closing times before storing your bag. If the station doesn't offer a place to leave your bags, head to a nearby tourist-information office, hotel, or gift shop: Ask nicely, offer your most charming smile (or a small fee), and you'll likely find someone willing to keep an eye on your things for a few hours.

Internet Access: You can usually get online at major train stations throughout Western Europe, often for a fee. Internet cafés offer Wi-Fi for those with mobile devices and computer terminals to those without. Wi-Fi is sometimes free in the first-class lounge; some bars and cafés may offer it free to paying customers. Finding Wi-Fi on trains is still more serendipitous than reliable, with the exception of high-speed trains on some of the most common business routes.

Tourist Information: Many stations have a tourist information office either in the station or very nearby. Pick up a map, find out about local transit, and double-check the hours of your must-see sights (for more on these offices, see page 290).

Waiting Rooms: Most stations have comfortable waiting rooms, and travelers with fancy tickets often enjoy fancy business or VIP lounges. Before you spend hours idling in one of these rooms, take advantage of the station's services (look up schedules for the next leg of your trip, get groceries) or explore the area around the station. You may well find yourself within a short walk of something really cool. For example, if you're changing trains in Köln, even on a tight schedule you can easily pop outside for a jaw-dropping look at its cathedral, just across the square. Waiting rooms can be decent last-ditch sleeping options (but guard your valuables).

Bus Connections: Train stations are also major bus stops, so connections from train to bus are generally no more difficult than crossing the street. Buses go from the stations to nearby towns that lack train service. If you have a bus to catch, be quick, since many are intended for commuters and are scheduled to connect with the train and leave

TRAINS AND MORE

promptly. If an airport is nearby, you'll find bus or rail airport shuttle services (usually well marked) at the train station.

Getting on the (Right) Train

For many Americans, Europe presents their first experience with a bustling train station, and the task of navigating the system and finding the right train can sound daunting—but it's not. Anyone who's managed to find their way in a sprawling American airport will find Europe's train stations a snap. Managing in the stations and on the trains is largely a matter of following signs, asking questions, letting people help you, and assuming things are logical. As you head for your train, ticket or pass in hand, keep these pointers in mind.

Get yourself to the right station. Many cities have more than one train station: Paris has six, Brussels has three, and even Switzerland's little Interlaken has two. Be sure you know whether your train is leaving from Interlaken East or Interlaken West, even if that means asking what might seem like a stupid question.

Train cars are usually labeled with pertinent information. This is a non-smoking second-class car with video surveillance and room for wheelchairs but not bikes. The eye (top left) means you'll be fined if a ticket patroller catches you without a valid ticket or pass.

Ask for help. I always ask someone on the platform if the train is going where I think it is. Uniformed train personnel can answer any question you can communicate. Speak slowly, clearly, and with caveman simplicity. Resist the urge to ask, "Pardon me, would you be able to tell me if this train is going to Rome?" Just point to the train or track and say, "Roma?"

Be observant. If the loudspeaker comes on while you're waiting for your train at track 7, gauge by the reaction of those around you whether the announcement affects you. If, after the babble, everyone dashes over to track 15, assume your train is no longer leaving from track 7.

Allow yourself sufficient time to navigate the station. Stations are generally laid out logically, with numbered tracks lined up in a row. But the biggest stations are so extensive they can take time to cross. Some large stations have entirely separate sections for local trains and long-distance trains. For example, Madrid's Atocha station is divided

The train on track 4 will stop at three Berlin stations. It was due to leave 10 minutes ago, but the sign notes it'll be 20 minutes später.

according to which kind of train it serves: *cercanías* (local trains) and *AVE* (high-speed, long-distance trains). A Paris train station might have some tracks devoted to *Grandes Lignes* ("grand lines" to other cities), and others for *Transilien* (local milk-run trains). At the Frankfurt airport, regional trains depart from the *Regionalbahnhof,* while long-distance trains use the *Fernbahnhof.* Many large stations also have vast sections devoted to subway trains or regional buses.

Where required, validate your ticket or reservation before boarding. In France and Italy, point-to-point tickets and seat reservations must be validated by inserting them into a machine near the platform. If you have multiple parts to your ticket (for example, a ticket and a reservation), each one must be validated. Watch (or ask) others, and imitate— but don't assume that you can skip this step just because others have, as locals traveling with commuter passes won't be date-stamping them.

Expect no-hassle boarding. For the vast majority of Europe's trains, you stroll (or dash) right to your boarding platform, ticket or pass in hand, without any check-in formalities. The main exception is the Eurostar Chunnel train, which has an advance check-in deadline (30 minutes before departure) and an airline-style security procedure. You may find simple preboarding security or ticket checks in a few other places. In Spain, for instance, your tickets will be checked and luggage scanned before you access the platform to board fast AVE trains. Many stations in Britain now require you to slide your paper ticket or tap your barcode on a turnstile reader both to enter and exit the boarding areas. (Railpass travelers show their passes to the attendants at these gates.) Some night trains have conductors checking tickets at the doors to each car.

TRAINS AND MORE

A handy diagram showing the configuration of your train (and at which platform section each car will arrive) posted at the platform can help you decide where to stand while waiting for your train. Understanding this could make the difference between snagging a great seat...or hoofing it to the other end of the train and scrambling for what's left.

Scope out the train ahead of time. The configuration of many major trains is charted in display cases on the platform. As you wait, study the display to note where the first-class, second-class, restaurant, and sleeping cars are, and which cars are going where. First-class cars are always marked with a "1" on the outside, second-class cars with a "2." Some train schedules will say, in the fine print, "Munich-bound cars in the front, Vienna-bound cars in the rear." Knowing which cars you're eligible for can be especially handy if you'll be competing with a mob for a seat. When expecting a real scramble, I stand on a bench at the far end of the track and study each car as the train rolls by, looking in the windows to note where the empty places are. If there are several departures within an hour and the first train looks hopeless, I'll wait for the next.

Never assume the entire train is going where you are. For long hauls, each car is labeled separately, because cars are usually added and dropped here and there along the journey. I'll never forget one hot afternoon in the center of Spain. My train stopped in the middle of nowhere. There was some mechanical rattling. Then the train pulled away leaving me alone in my car—in La Mancha. Ten minutes later, another train came along, picked up my car, and I was on my way. To survive all this juggling without any panic, be sure that the city on your car's nameplate is your destination. The nameplate lists the final stop and some (but not all) of the stops in-between.

On the Train

Once you're on board, it's time to sit back and enjoy the journey.

Find a seat. If you have a seat assignment, locate it and plop yourself down. If you're traveling without a seat reservation, you can claim any unreserved seat. If these are in short supply, take a closer look at the reservation tags posted above the seats or on compartment doors. Each tag shows which stretch of the journey that seat is reserved for. You may well

Strikes

Some travelers worry about getting stranded somewhere because of a strike. But in general, they're nothing to stress about.

Strikes can affect rail service anywhere in Europe (especially in Italy). They're usually announced long in advance in stations and online. Most last just a day, or even just several hours. Anticipate strikes—ask your hotelier, talk to locals, look for signs, check online—but don't feel bullied by them. In theory, train service shuts down, but in reality, sporadic trains lumber down main-line tracks during most strikes (preserving "essential service").

If a strike occurs on your travel day, head to the station anyway, where the few remaining station personnel can tell you the expected schedule. You'll likely find a workable train to your destination, though it may involve a wait (stay near the station). While it's usually possible to get a refund for reservations affected by a strike, there are no refunds for partially used railpasses.

Know the local word for "strike": sciopero (Italian), grève (French), apergia (Greek), and so on. They're a nuisance but, in many countries, a normal part of life.

be getting off the train before the seat owner even boards. For example, if you're headed from Luzern to Lugano, and you see a seat that's reserved from Lugano to Milan, it's all yours.

Stow your luggage. In more than 30 years of train travel, I've never checked a bag. Simply carry it on and heave it up onto the rack above the seat or wedge it into the triangular space between back-to-back seats. I've seen Turkish families moving all their worldly goods from Germany back to Turkey without checking a thing. People complain about the porters in the European train stations. I think they're great—I've never used one.

Be savvy with your bags. I assume every train has a thief planning to grab a bag. Store your luggage within sight, rather than at the end of a train car. Before leaving my luggage in a compartment, I establish a relationship with everyone there. I'm safe leaving it among mutual guards. I don't lock my bag, but to be safe, I often clip my rucksack straps to the luggage rack. When a thief makes his move in the darkness of a train tunnel, and the bag doesn't give, he's not going to ask, "*Scusi,* how is your luggage attached?"

Europe's trains are fast—pulling into the station with squashed birds on their windshields. You'd wait all your life to see a bird squashed onto the windshield of a train back home. I guess with Europe's impressive transportation infrastructure, "DB" stands for "dead bird."

Use train time wisely. The time you spend on long train rides can be an opportunity to get organized or make plans for your next destination. Read ahead in your guidebook, write journal entries, delete yesterday's bad photos, double-check your connection information with the conductor, organize your daypack, or write an email home (you don't have to be online to write one). If the train has power outlets (rare but becoming more common), charge your gadgets. Don't, however, get so immersed in chores that you forget to keep an eye out the window for beautiful scenery around the next bend.

Use WCs—they're free: To save time and money, use the toilets on the train rather than those in the station (which can cost money). Toilets on first-class cars are a cut above second-class toilets. I "go" first class even with a second-class ticket. Train toilets are located on the ends of cars, where it's most jiggly. A trip to the train's john always reminds me of the rodeo. Some toilets empty directly on the tracks. Never use a train's WC while stopped in a station (unless you didn't like that particular town). A train's WC cleanliness deteriorates as the journey progresses.

Follow local train etiquette. Pay attention to the noise level in your car. If everyone else is speaking in hushed tones, follow suit. Watch for signs indicating that you're sitting in a designated quiet car, where business people come to work and others to nap. No matter where I'm sitting, I make an effort not to be the loudest person in earshot (easily done on the average Italian train, but takes extra awareness in, say, Germany). Resting your feet on the seat across from you without taking your shoes off is perhaps an even graver faux pas.

Talk to locals or other travelers. There is so much to be learned.

Europeans are often less open and forward than Americans. You could sit across from a silent but fascinating and friendly European for an entire train ride, or you could break the ice by asking a question, quietly offering some candy, or showing your Hometown, USA, postcards. This can start the conversation flowing and the friendship growing.

Pack a picnic. For the best dining value and variety, stock up at a local deli, bakery, supermarket, or wine cellar before you board; most train stations offer at least one of these. Food sold on the train costs more, with options ranging from a basic coffee and sandwich cart to a more extensive bar car or sit-down dining car (noted on most schedules when available). A few trains offer a "complimentary" meal, in first class only, usually covered by a higher seat-reservation fee.

Strategize your arrival. Use your guidebook to study up on your destination city while you're still on board—it's far more time-efficient and less overwhelming to arrive in a station already knowing how you plan to reach the city center (or your hotel). If you're trying to make a tight connection, it's good to know which platform your next train leaves from. If you don't already have that information, flag down a conductor, who either knows the answer or should be able to look it up for you.

As you approach your destination, have a game plan ready for when you get off the train. Know what you need to accomplish in the station before heading out—e.g., looking up the schedule (and perhaps making seat reservations) for the next leg of your train trip, picking up a map from a trackside information office, hitting an ATM, buying a transit pass, or grabbing provisions from a grocery store (especially if you're arriving late, after most city-center shops and restaurants have closed). If you'll depart from the same station later, pay attention to the layout.

Know where to get off. In Dresden, I twice got off my train too early—at two different suburban stations—before arriving at the central station. Know which station you need before you arrive, and be patient. When arriving in a city (especially on a commuter train), you may stop at several suburban stations with signs indicating your destination's name and the name of the neighborhood (e.g., Madrid Vallecas, Roma Ostiense, or Dresden Neustadt). Don't jump out until you've reached the central station (Madrid Chamartín, Roma Termini, or Dresden Hauptbahnhof)—ask fellow passengers or check your guidebook to find out which name to look for. Learn the local word for "main station."

Be aware that some trains (especially express trains) stop only at a major city's suburban station—if you stay on board, expecting to get off in the center a few minutes later, you'll bypass your destination city altogether. For instance, several trains to "Venice" leave you at Venice's suburban station (Venezia Mestre), where you'll be stranded without a glimpse of a gondola. (You'll have to catch another train to reach the main Venezia Santa Lucia station, on the Grand Canal.) On the other hand, it can be handy to hop out at a suburban station if it's closer to your hotel than the main station. Many trains headed for Barcelona's big Sants station also stop at the Plaça de Catalunya subway station, which is near many recommended accommodations. If you do find yourself at the wrong station, don't despair: It's a safe bet that a city's stations are connected by frequent trains, and probably subway or buses as well.

Check your seat before leaving. Before you depart any train, turn around and check your seat for anything you might have left behind: sunglasses, guidebook, or the sweater you shed when the sun came out.

Sleeping on Trains

The economy of night travel is tremendous. Sleeping while rolling down the tracks saves time and money, both of which are limited resources. For every night you spend on the train, you gain a day for sightseeing and avoid the cost of a hotel.

The first concern about night travel is usually, "Aren't you missing a lot of beautiful scenery? You just slept through half of Sweden!" The real question should be, "Did the missed scenery matter, since you gained an extra day for hiking the Alps, biking through tulips, or island-hopping in the Greek seas?" The answer: No. Maximize night trips.

When you're checking schedules for night trains, pay attention to the details. A connection doesn't have to be direct to be a workable overnight option—it all depends on the timing. If you need to change trains a half hour after boarding, it's no problem. But if the connection involves getting off at 2:00 a.m....and waiting till 5:30 a.m. for the next leg, that's not a night train, it's a nightmare.

Book your night-train reservation at least a few days in advance. On some popular routes, particularly between Paris and Italy, reservations can sell out weeks in advance, making it worthwhile to commit before you even leave for Europe. Spanish international hotel trains also tend to be booked up well ahead. For advice on making reservations, see page 122.

Some train travelers are ripped off while they sleep—they're usually the ones who haven't safely stashed their money and valuables in a money belt. You'll hear stories of entire train cars being gassed and robbed in Italy, Spain, and Eastern Europe. It's extremely rare and I wouldn't lose sleep over it.

Types of Compartments

Most overnight trains offer one or two different ways to sleep; the more comfortably you sleep, the more you pay. For much more on night trains in Europe, go to www.seat61.com and search on "sleeper."

Couchettes: To ensure a safer and uninterrupted night's sleep, you can reserve a sleeping berth known as a *couchette* (koo-SHET). For a sur-

charge of about $35, you'll get sheets, a pillow, and blankets on a bunk bed in a compartment with three to five other people—and, hopefully, a good night's sleep.

Some trains have more spacious four-berth *couchettes* (two sets of doubles rather than triple bunks for about $50 apiece). This exception aside, most *couchettes* are the same in first and second class.

You can rent a couchette *(bunk bed) on your overnight train. Top bunks give you a bit more room and safety—but B.Y.O.B.& B.*

When booking your *couchette,* you can request the top, middle, or bottom berth. While the top bunk gives you more privacy and luggage space, it can be hotter and stuffier than lower bunks and a couple of inches shorter (a concern if you're six feet or taller). Compartments may be coed or single gender, depending on the route. On the rare train that still permits smoking, you can request smoking or non-smoking.

As you board, you'll give the attendant your *couchette* voucher and railpass or ticket. This is the person who deals with the conductors and keeps out the thieves so you can sleep uninterrupted. In case of a border check (rare in most of Europe these days), you'll either be woken up to show your passport, or your attendant will ask for your passport in advance and handle this task for you.

Private Sleepers: These sleeper compartments are more comfortable but pricier than *couchettes*. Compartments with two or three beds range from about $40 to $150 per person. Single-sleeper surcharges range from $70 to $190.

If you're on a budget, avoid the fancy Spanish hotel trains. Running between Spain and France, these overnight hotels-on-wheels are comfortable but expensive (even if discounted with a railpass).

Sleeping Free

Shoestring travelers just sack out for free, draping their tired bodies over as many unoccupied seats as possible. But trust me: Trying to sleep over-night without a bed can be more lumpy than dreamy. And even free seat "sleeping" isn't always an option, since not all night trains offer standard seats—and many that do require a paid seat reservation. One night of end-less head-bobbing, very swollen toes, glaring overhead lighting, a screaming tailbone, sitting up straight in an eternity of steel wheels crashing along rails, try-

They didn't rent a couchette.

ing doggedly—yet hopelessly—to get comfortable, will teach you the importance of finding a spot to stretch out for the night. (If you decide you want a *couchette* after all, seek out a conductor—provided there's a *couchette* available, you can book one onboard.)

Some older trains have seats that you can pull out to make a bed—assuming your compartment isn't too full. Skilled shoestring travelers know to look for traditional train cars: the kind that have about 10 com-partments, each with six or eight seats (three or four facing three or four). Some have seats that pull out and armrests that lift, turning your compartment into a bed on wheels. These cars make sleeping free quite manageable, but they're increasingly rare.

If you're determined to avoid paying for a *couchette*, head to the sta-tion a day or two ahead of your departure, a few minutes before that night train is scheduled to pull out, and see for yourself if fold-out com-partment seats will be an option on your train. If they won't be, book a *couchette*—what you'll spend is less than what you'd waste by arriving at your next destination too fatigued to enjoy it.

Buses and Ferries

Trains go a lot of places, but they don't go everywhere. Europe's buses and ferries help fill in the gaps.

Buses

In most countries, trains are faster, more comfortable, and have more extensive schedules than buses. But in some countries—especially

Greece, Turkey, and parts of Ireland, Croatia, the Czech Republic, Portugal, Spain, and Morocco—buses are often the better (or only) option. Bus trips are usually less expensive than trains—especially in the British Isles—and are occasionally included on your railpass (where buses are operated by train companies, as many are in Germany, Switzerland, and Belgium). Note that in Great Britain and Ireland, a long-distance bus is called a "coach," while a "bus" provides only in-city transit.

Use buses mainly to pick up where Europe's great train system leaves

Buses can help you reach places trains don't go.

off. Buses fan out from the smallest train stations to places trains can't get to. For towns with train stations far from the center (such as hill towns), buses are often scheduled to meet each arrival and shuttle passengers to the main square (often at no extra cost—show your train ticket to the bus driver and see what happens). Many bus connections to nearby towns not served by train are timed to depart just after the train arrives. Miss that connection in a remote place and you'll wait with the ghosts in an empty station until the next train arrives. Bus service can be less frequent on holidays, Saturdays, and especially Sundays.

Schedules
In most countries, bus routes are operated by multiple companies, each with its own timetables and fares. Finding a unified source for schedule and price information can be next to impossible. If you're lucky, the city you're traveling from will have one main bus station that can offer consolidated timetables online. But it's more likely that you'll have to check several websites, run by the various companies that serve the cities you're connecting. If you're going from a small town (with no online timetable) to a big city, try checking the "arrivals" schedules on the big city's website instead. Always confirm the schedule in person.

Learn the code words for deciphering local schedules. For example, in Spain, *pista* or *autopista* means the bus takes the freeway—the fastest option. Buses that are *directa* (direct) are faster than those labeled *semi-directa* or *ruta* (roundabout journeys with several stops en route). Posted schedules list many, but not all, stops on each route. If your intended destination isn't listed, ask at the ticket/information window.

If your trip involves a connection at an intermediate station, don't be surprised if it's difficult to get schedule details for your onward journey. Try calling the tourist information office or bus station in the transfer town (or at your final destination) for details.

Stations and Tickets

It's common for a big city to have a number of smaller bus stations serving different regions, rather than one terminal for all bus traffic. Sometimes a bus "station" can just be an open parking lot with lots of stalls and a tiny ticket kiosk. Your hotel or the local tourist information office can usually point you in the right direction. Larger bus stations have an information desk (and, often, a telephone number) with timetables. In smaller stations, check the destinations and schedules posted on the window of each company's office. Bus-station staffers are less likely to speak English than their train-station counterparts. Bus stations have WCs (often without toilet paper) and cafés that offer quick, forgettable, slightly overpriced food.

For popular routes during peak season, ensure you'll get a seat by dropping by the station to buy your ticket a few hours in advance. If you're downtown, need a ticket, and the bus station isn't central, save time by asking at the tourist information office about travel agencies that sell bus tickets. If you arrive in a city by bus, and plan to leave by bus, it can be convenient to buy your outbound ticket when you arrive.

Riding the Bus

Before you get on a bus, ask the ticket seller and the conductor if you'll need to transfer. If so, pay attention (and maybe even follow the route on a map) to be sure you don't miss your change. When you transfer, look for a bus with the same name/logo as the company you bought the ticket from.

For long trips, your ticket might include an assigned seat. If your bag doesn't fit in the overhead storage space, you may be required to check it under the bus (sometimes for a small fee). Your ride likely will come with a soundtrack: recorded pop music, radio, sports games, or movies or TV shows. Earplugs and/or headphones can go a long way toward preserving your sanity. In most of Europe, smoking is no longer allowed on buses.

Drivers may not speak English. Buses generally lack toilets, but they stop every two hours or so for a short break. Drivers announce how long the stop will be, but if in doubt, ask the driver so you know if you have time to get out. Listen for the bus horn as a final call before departure.

Package bus excursions from big cities into the countryside are designed for sightseeing, but can also serve as useful transportation. For example, if you're about to spend $75 for a train ticket—let's say, from London to Bath—why not spend $115 for a one-day bus tour from London that visits Salisbury, Stonehenge, and Bath? Bring your luggage and leave the tour in Bath before it returns to London, having enjoyed a day of transportation and information for not much more than the cost of a train ticket.

Cheap, long-haul buses, such as Eurolines (www.eurolines.com), and hippie-type "magic buses," such as Busabout (www.busabout.com), are a good option for the very budget-conscious. For example, Eurolines' priciest one-way bus fare from Amsterdam to Paris is $60 (compared to $175 second class by train); from Barcelona to Madrid, it's $42 ($165 by train).

Crossing the Channel by bus and ferry takes more than twice as long as the Eurostar train, but costs a fraction of the price (London to Paris by Eurolines bus: about $30-65 one-way for economy fares booked at least three days in advance).

Ferries

Boats can be a romantic mode of European travel. They're particularly useful for Greek or Croatian island-hopping, for Norwegian fjord gawking, or for connecting Scandinavian destinations overnight—saving both time and the expense of a pricey hotel room.

Terminology helps differentiate your options: Most boats labeled as ferries carry cars as well as passengers. Ferries move slowly but can run in almost any weather. While the number of cars is limited, there's virtually unlimited deck space for walk-on passengers. Much faster catamarans carry only passengers. They're faster but smaller, so they may indeed sell out their limited seating. While catamarans are time-efficient, they have to slow down (or sometimes can't run at all) in bad weather. Because of the high speeds, you'll likely have to stay inside the boat while en route. On many islands, the big car ferries arrive at a different point (usually farther from the main town) than the smaller catamarans (which may drop you right in the town center).

Some countries have a national ferry company (such as Croatia's Jadrolinija), but in most places, routes are operated by a variety of smaller companies. You can usually find schedules online; however, particularly in Mediterranean countries, they may not be posted more than a few days before the season starts, making it challenging to plan your midsummer trip in the springtime. Service to the smaller Mediterranean islands is particularly seasonal: Routes which run once daily in summer may drop to four days per week in shoulder season and two days per week in winter. To search for schedules, check www.aferry.co.uk for most of Europe, www.greekferries.gr for Greek island services, and www.visitnorway.com/us for Norwegian fjord boats; you can also try searching for the name of the company (if you know it) that operates a particular route.

In some cases, you can buy tickets online or at a travel agency; for others, you simply show up at the ticket window an hour before departure. During peak times in popular destinations (August, Croatia's Dalmatian Coast), get advice from your hotel or the local tourist information office about how far ahead you should book your ticket. Otherwise, the ferry could sell out and you'll be stranded on a castaway isle for longer than you intended. This is particularly important if you're driving a car onto a ferry—in which case you may need to line up hours in advance. (If it's possible to book a space in advance, do so.) Some international ferry routes are covered or discounted with a railpass (such as Ancona or Bari, Italy, to Patra, Greece; and Sweden to Germany or Denmark).

If you're taking an overnight ferry, consider your sleeping options. A basic passenger ticket is "deck class," meaning you'll simply have to camp out wherever you can find room. You can pay a little more for a seat. A "berth" (bed) costs more, similar to a night train. The more private your lodgings, the more you'll pay, especially if a toilet and shower are included in the compartment. You usually can (and should) reserve overnight accommodations in advance. Some Greek island ferries only allow you to reserve beds upon boarding.

On the ferry, you may be able to stow your luggage on a public rack on the boarding level; otherwise you'll haul it up several flights of stairs to the passenger decks. You can buy food and drinks on board most boats. It's not too expensive, but it's usually not top quality, either. Bring your own snacks or a picnic instead. Dining is a featured attraction on just a few ferries, such as the *smörgåsbord* service on Scandinavian overnight cruises.

For information about taking a cruise in Europe, see page 465.

DRIVING

While most European travel dreams come with a clickety-clack rhythm of the rails soundtrack—and most first trips are best by train—you should at least consider the convenience of driving. Behind the wheel you're totally free, going where you want, when you want.

Driving is ideal on countryside-focused trips. The super mobility of a car saves you time in locating budget accommodations in small towns and away from the train lines. This savings helps to rationalize the "splurge" of a car rental. You can also play it riskier in peak season, arriving in a town late with no reservation. If the hotels are full, simply drive to the next town. And driving is a godsend for those who don't believe in packing light—you can even rent a trailer.

Every year, as train prices go up, car rental becomes a better option for budget travelers in Europe. While solo car travel is expensive, three or four people sharing a rented car will usually travel cheaper than the same group using railpasses.

Renting a Car

Renting a car in Europe tends to be more expensive and more complicated than in the US, thanks to byzantine insurance options and other additional fees. But once you're free and easy behind the wheel of a European car, it's worth the hassle.

Car or Train?

Consider these variables when deciding if your European experience might be better by car or train:

Concern	By Car	By Train
Packing heavy:	• no problem	• must go light
Scouring one area:	• best	• frustrating
All over Europe:	• too much driving	• great
Big cities:	• pointless	• ideal
Camping:	• perfect	• more like boot camp
One or two people:	• expensive	• probably cheaper
Three or more:	• probably cheaper	• more expensive
With young kids:	• survivable	• miserable
Environmental:	• less green	• more green

Car-Rental Costs

European cars are rented for a 24-hour period, usually with a 30- to 59-minute grace period. Cars are most economical when rented by the week with unlimited mileage (sometimes five or six days cost the same as a week). Daily rates are generally quite high; typically, the longer you rent for, the less it'll cost per day. You'll get the best deal on long-term rentals by booking a car in advance (either online or through a travel agent). Another option is a rail-and-drive pass, which combines a certain number of days of train travel with a few days of car rental within a certain region (see page 119).

There's no way to chart the best car-rental deals. Rates vary from company to company, month to month, and country to country. The cheapest company for rental in one country might be the most expensive in the next. You'll need to do some comparison-shopping to figure out which one is best for your trip (see "Booking a Car," later).

Be aware that the true cost of the rental far exceeds the weekly unlimited-mileage rate. Some extras are predictable, like gas and parking, but others,

Small car, big scenery...but shut the sunroof!

Cost of Car Rental

This very rough estimate for a one-week car rental includes unlimited mileage.

Ford Fiesta (including tax): $375/week
CDW insurance: $175/week ($15-35/day)
Fuel: $160/week ($7/gallon, 30 mpg, 100 miles/day)
Parking in big cities: $25-40/day
Freeway tolls: $4-9/hour (Mediterranean countries only)
Total: About $800 a week

---

like airport fees, can be a rude shock. Most problems I hear about from readers relate to add-on charges concealed in the fine print. Car-rental companies—including the biggies—have various quasi-legitimate ways to pad their profits, so it pays to be informed, ask a lot of questions when arranging your rental, and read everything carefully before finalizing your reservation.

Tax: The tax, clear and consistent within each country, generally runs 18-25 percent (while tax is only 8 percent in Switzerland, Swiss rental rates are that much higher).

Insurance: Your biggest potential extra cost when renting a car is insurance, even if the rental price supposedly "includes" insurance. Figure on paying roughly 30 percent extra, or about $15-35 a day, for a collision damage waiver supplement (described later).

Fuel: Paying about $160 a week will get you roughly 700 miles; most rental agencies offer "green" cars with better fuel efficiency—ask.

Tolls: You'll pay tolls figured on the distance you drive (about $4-9 per hour) for expressways in certain countries. Countries that have toll-free highways often require drivers to buy a sticker ("vignette") for their window (for more on tolls, see page 160).

Parking: Estimate $25-40 a day in big cities; otherwise it's usually free, or at least very cheap.

Theft Protection: This charge, about $20/day, is required in Italy (most companies include this in their advertised rates for Italy).

Airport Fees: In some countries, you'll pay more to pick up a car at the airport or train station than in the town center (10-20 percent extra, or a flat fee of $30-50). When you're calling about prices, rental agents usually quote you this pricier airport pickup rate. Ask if they have a cheaper, downtown-pickup price. Some companies deliver the car to your hotel for free.

Refueling Fees: In Britain, National requires renters to prepay for a full tank of fuel at the start of the rental, which means you can return the vehicle on empty. In other countries (as in the US), this charge is usually optional. If you decide to pass on the prepaid option and then forget to fill your tank before returning the car, you will be charged for a full tank no matter how much gas is actually left. If you wait until you're almost at the rental office to look for a gas station, it can be stressful; since fuel gauges are very forgiving, I start watching for a convenient fill-up point miles before I reach my final stop.

From sleek German autobahns to windy, cliffside Irish lanes, driving is a fun part of European travel.

International Drop-Off Fees: It will generally cost an extra $100-300 to drop the car in a different country. You'll find exceptions, some happy (free) and some outrageous ($1,000+). The farther the distance between your start and end points, the higher the fee. While there's usually no fee to drop the car at a different location in the same country, it's always smart to double-check.

Booking a Car

For the best deal on long-term rentals, book in advance from home. If you decide to rent a car while in Europe, try calling around to local car-rental agencies, or book through a local travel agency (though it will probably cost more than it would if you'd done it in advance). When renting a car, you'll need to make a few decisions, including whom to rent from, what kind of car to get, and where to pick it up.

Which Rental Company?

Most of the major US rental agencies (including National, Avis, Budget, Hertz, and Thrifty) have offices throughout Europe (see sidebar on next page). If you have a favorite agency at home, consider using the same company in Europe, or the two major Europe-based agencies, Europcar and Sixt. To comparison-shop, you can request a quote from each company or search on a travel-booking site such as Expedia, Travelocity, Kayak, or AAA. After you determine which companies offer the best combination of rates, service, and pickup/drop-off locations (with long office hours) for

DRIVING

Leading Car-Rental Companies

Contact your favorite rental company directly, or try a consolidator, which compares rates at major companies to find you the best deal.

Major Car-Rental Companies

Avis	800-331-1212	www.avis.com
Budget	800-472-3325	www.budget.com
Europcar	877-940-6900	www.europcar.com
Hertz	800-654-3001	www.hertz.com
National	877-222-9075	www.nationalcar.com
Sixt	888-749-8227	www.sixt.com
Thrifty	800-847-4389	www.thrifty.com

Consolidators

Auto Europe	888-223-5555	www.autoeurope.com
Europe by Car	800-223-1516	www.ebctravel.com
Kemwel	877-820-0668	www.kemwel.com
Renault Eurodrive	888-532-1221	www.renaultusa.com (leasing only)

your trip, visit their individual websites or call for more details.

Consolidators, such as Auto Europe (www.autoeurope.com) or Europe by Car (www.ebctravel.com), compare rates among various companies (including many of the big-name firms), find the best deal, and—because they're wholesalers—pass the savings on to you. You pay the consolidator, and they issue you a voucher to pick up your car in Europe. While this can be cheaper than booking direct, my readers have reported problems with consolidators, ranging from misinformation to unexpected fees. Because you're working with a middleman, ask ahead of time about add-on fees and restrictions or you might not learn this critical information until you pick up the car. If any dispute arises when you show up at the rental desk, call the consolidator's toll-free line to try to resolve the issue. Once you sign off on something with the vendor, it's difficult for the consolidator (or anyone else) to reverse what you agreed to. If you have a problem with the rental agency, the consolidator may not be able to intervene to your satisfaction.

Car-Sharing Programs: Like Zipcar in the US, Hertz On Demand (www.hertzondemand.com) places cars throughout a city and lets users rent them for just a few hours or days (currently available in London,

Before you commit, ask about:
- weekly unlimited mileage rate
- age restrictions
- insurance costs
- CDW options ("super CDW" or "zero-deductible" coverage)
- theft insurance (required in Italy)
- cost of adding another driver
- drop-off fees within a country or in another country
- office locations in the countries you're visiting (consider the most efficient pickup and drop-off points, and their hours)
- whether it's cheaper to pick up the car at the airport or downtown
- if there is a covered trunk
- availability of extras, such as automatic transmission, child safety seats, or GPS
- restrictions on driving the car in any countries (particularly in far-eastern Europe)
- additional charges or taxes, such as VAT (value-added tax), mandatory winter tire or equipment fee, or refueling fee

Paris, Madrid, and Berlin). You book your car online, pick it up at one of their set locations, drive it, then return it to the nearest location. The fee includes insurance, fuel, and GPS, so you can avoid extra insurance charges or having to fill the tank before you return the car. There are no enrollment or annual fees, and prices are relatively reasonable—in London a Fiat 500 costs about $9 per hour or $70 per day. These rentals could possibly be fun for day trips, but are not practical for use within the big cities, where public transportation is a breeze.

Choosing a Car

Most rental cars in Europe have manual transmissions. Automatics are more expensive and may only be available if you upgrade to a bigger, pricier car. However, some people find automatics worthwhile in Great Britain and Ireland, where it can be enough of a challenge just to learn to drive on the left. Since supplies are limited, if you must have an automatic, you'll need to arrange it further in advance. Ideally, skip the automatic and brush up on your shifting skills. It's worth doing some lurching through your hometown parking lot to save the expense or to be prepared in case your reserved automatic doesn't materialize.

DRIVING

I normally rent the smallest, least-expensive model with a stick shift—not just to save money, but because larger cars are not as maneuverable on narrow, winding roads found throughout Europe.

Where to Pick Up (and Drop Off)

It's best and less stressful to begin your driving experience away from big cities, so try picking up your car away from major destinations. A pleasant scenario for a trip to England would be to start your trip in the small town of Bath, rent a car when leaving Bath, explore Britain at your leisure by car, then drop off the car in York and take the train into London, where you can rely on the excellent public transportation system. (That way you'd enjoy the three major city stops on your England itinerary—where the last thing you'd want is a car—without paying for one.)

Picking up a car at an airport usually costs more than picking it up downtown. But also consider traffic—it may be easier to drive away from an airport than a parking garage in the heart of the city. Also, when choosing where to pick up your rental car, remember that a downtown branch can be on the outskirts of the city limits—a long, costly taxi ride from the center. Before choosing a rental location, find it on a map. You may find that the train-station office is handier than the downtown one.

Many central car-rental locations have shorter hours (and may close at midday) or are buried in a maze of narrow streets. Don't plan to pick up or drop off your car in a small town on a Saturday afternoon or Sunday—or anywhere on a holiday, when offices are likely to be closed.

Just as it can make sense to fly into one city and out of another, you can start and end your car rental in different cities. For maximum options, use a bigger company with offices in many cities. While dropping off in another country can incur an extra fee, there's typically no extra charge to do this within the same country—but always ask when you reserve, just in case. Also, know your options in case you change your plans en route and want to drop off your car at an office in another city or on a different date.

Red Tape and Restrictions

Every country has its own take on who can drive—and who can rent—a car. Follow these tips to make sure you'll be able to take the wheel at your destination.

Passports, Driver's Licenses, and International Driving Permits: Whether you're American or Canadian, your passport and driver's license are all you need in most European countries. However, some countries

Car vs. Train: Comparing Rough Costs

When comparing the costs of renting a car, leasing a car, using a railpass, or buying point-to-point train tickets, consider these factors:

- the **duration** of your trip (dramatically affects the cost of car rental; less important for train tickets or railpasses)
- the **miles** you'll cover (important for point-to-point train tickets; irrelevant to railpasses and car rental/leasing, except for fuel costs)
- the **countries** you'll be visiting (very important for a railpass; less critical for car rental/leasing, unless you pick up in one country and drop off in another).

Here are sample **per-person** prices for a three-week trip from Amsterdam to Rome to Paris, covering about 2,000 miles:

Means of Transport	Cost per Person
Railpass (first class)	$750
Point-to-point train tickets (second class)	$950
Subcompact car rental (2 people)	$1,050
Subcompact car lease (2 people)	$900
Midsize car rental (4 people)	$600
Midsize car lease (4 people)	$575

Fine Print

Railpass: This is the approximate cost of a pass covering 10 days of train travel (not necessarily in a row), valid across continental Europe, and priced assuming that two or more people are traveling together. Seat or overnight-berth reservation fees are not included.

Car Rental/Lease: These prices are for cars with manual transmission and include tax, the fee for drop-off in a different country ($100-300), and gas costs of about $7/gallon at 35 mpg for smaller cars (30 mpg for midsize). Rental rates also include CDW supplements (but not "super CDW") and fees for an airport pickup (about 10 percent); leased cars do not come with these expenses.

DRIVING

also require you to have an International Driving Permit (IDP), which provides an official translation of your license—making it easier for the cop to write out the ticket. You can get an IDP at your local American Automobile Association or Canadian Automobile Association office ($15 plus the cost of two passport-type photos, www.aaa.com or www.caa.ca). AAA is authorized by the US State Department to issue permits; avoid scam artists peddling overpriced, fake international licenses.

You may hear contradictory information on exactly where you need an IDP. People who sell them say you should have them almost everywhere. People who rent cars say you need them almost nowhere. People who drive rental cars say the IDP is overrated, but can come in handy as a complement to your passport and driver's license. Those driving in Austria, Bosnia-Herzegovina, Greece, Hungary, Italy, Poland, Slovenia, and Spain are technically required to carry a permit and could be fined if found without one. If all goes well, you'll likely never be asked to show this permit—but it's a must if you end up dealing with the police. Even if you have an IDP, remember that you must carry your American or Canadian driver's license as well.

Age Limits: Minimum and maximum age limits for renting a car vary by country, type of car, and rental company. Younger renters can get stuck with extra costs, such as being required to buy extra insurance or pay a surcharge of $15-40/day (fortunately, there are usually maximum surcharge limits). Most companies will not rent a car to someone under 21 (there are exceptions, depending on the country and type of car), but those who are at least 25 years old should have no problem. The student-oriented STA Travel is a good option for young renters (www.statravel .com, tel. 800-781-4040).

Drivers over 70 may have trouble renting in the Czech Republic, Great Britain, Greece, Northern Ireland, Poland, Slovakia, Slovenia, and Turkey. If you're over 69, you may pay extra to rent a car in the Republic of Ireland, where the official age limit is 75 (but people 75-79 can rent if they provide extensive proof of good health and safe driving). If you're considered too young or too old, look into leasing (explained later), which has less stringent age restrictions. (If you're traveling to Ireland, the closest leasing option is in London.)

In the mountainous northwest corner of Slovenia, you're just a few miles' drive from both Austria and Italy—and these days, you can cross those borders without stopping.

Crossing Borders: As Europe's internal borders fade, your car comes with the paperwork you need to drive wherever you like in Western and much of Eastern Europe (always check when booking). But if you're heading to a country in far eastern or southeastern Europe that still has closed borders (such as Croatia, Bosnia-Herzegovina, or Montenegro), state your travel plans up front to the rental company when making your reservation. Some companies may have limits on eastward excursions because of the higher incidence of car thefts (for example, you can only take cheaper cars, and you may have to pay extra insurance fees). When you cross these borders, you may be asked to show proof of insurance (called a "green card"). Ask your car-rental company if you need any other documentation for crossing the borders on your itinerary.

Some rental companies allow you to take a rental car from Britain to the Continent or to Ireland, but be prepared to pay high surcharges and extra drop-off fees. If you want to drive in Britain, Ireland, and on the Continent, it's usually cheaper to rent three separate cars than one, thanks to the high cost of taking cars on ferries (between Ireland and Britain) and crossing under the English Channel via the pricey Eurostar car train.

Insurance and the Collision Damage Waiver (CDW)

When you rent a car, you are liable for a very high deductible, sometimes equal to the entire value of the car. There are various ways you can limit your financial risk in case of an accident. Those needing a car for at least three weeks should look into leasing (described later), which is tax-free and includes zero-deductible collision and theft insurance.

Car-Rental Company CDW: The simplest solution is to buy a collision damage waiver (CDW) supplement from the car-rental company.

This technically isn't insurance; rather, it's a waiver: The car-rental company waives its right to collect a high deductible from you in the event the car is damaged. CDW covers everything except the undercarriage, roof, tires, and windshield. While each company has its own variation of CDW, it generally costs $15-35 a day (figure roughly 30 percent extra) and reduces the

Luckily, Bud paid extra for full insurance.

deductible, but does not eliminate it. Many rental companies have inclusive plans that come with both theft/loss insurance and a more reasonable CDW—ask. In general, it's cheaper to pay for this kind of coverage when you book than when you pick up the car.

DRIVING

Note that it can be even cheaper to buy all your travel insurance—including collision coverage—from a travel insurance company (rather than buying some insurance from a car-rental company and other portions from a travel insurance company). If you do, be sure to add the travel insurance company's name to your rental agreement when you pick up the car. For more on travel insurance, see page 59.

When purchasing CDW, the reduced deductibles can be substantial, with most hovering at about $1,000-1,500 (or more, depending on the car type). So, when you pick up the car, the counter agent might try to sell you a second tier of coverage (called "super CDW" or "zero-deductible") to buy down the deductible to or near zero. This is pricey—figure about an additional $10-30 per day—but, for some travelers, it's worth the peace of mind.

Since most of the major car-rental companies come with these astronomical deductibles, the alternatives to CDW are worth considering carefully.

Credit-Card Coverage: Many credit-card companies offer their own type of zero-deductible collision coverage (comparable to CDW). By paying for your car rental with a credit card that offers this coverage, you can choose to decline the car-rental company's CDW coverage. Dealing with credit-card coverage can be a hassle if you do wind up needing it, but since rental companies' CDW costs can stack up, it can be a worthwhile trade-off.

Basically, if your car is damaged or stolen, your credit card will cover whatever cost you're liable for. Of course, restrictions apply and coverage varies between issuers (for example, lately American Express has been offering its cardholders "premium" car rental insurance for about $25 per rental—not per day—that covers more than just CDW). If you opt for this coverage, get a complete description of it from your credit-card company, and ask in which countries it is applicable, the maximum number of rental days they'll cover, and the types of vehicles that are eligible. Have them explain the worst-case scenario to you.

To use the coverage provided by your credit card, you'll have to decline the CDW offered by your car-rental company. Therefore, as far as some rental companies are concerned, you're technically liable for the full deductible (which can equal the cost of the car). Because of this, the car-rental company may put a hold on your credit card for the full value of the car. This is bad news if your credit limit is low—particularly if you plan on using that card for other purchases during your trip. (Consider bringing two credit cards—one for the rental car, the other for everything else.) If you don't have enough credit on your card to

The Accidental Tourist

Some travelers obsess about the possibility of a car accident while driving in Europe. Most come back bragging about their road skills and missing the freedom of the autobahn. Those who do have a mishap usually tell me it was the result of a tight squeeze in a parking garage (ask for a small car). If there's major damage to your vehicle or a flat tire, your rental company includes 24-hour emergency roadside assistance. In the unlikely event your accident involves another car, you'll need to show your driver's license and insurance "green card" to the other driver and/or the police. Fill out the European Accident Report form that the agency includes with your rental documents. If you're going to submit an insurance claim, make sure you file a police report (and get copies of that report), even if no other cars are involved. If the police refuse to write up a report ("it's only a scrape"), ask your hotelier to help you type up a report, take it to the police station, and ask them to stamp it. It's a good idea to take photos of the damage to your car and the license plate of any other vehicles involved.

cover the car's value, the rental company may require you to purchase CDW insurance.

If you have an accident, the rental company will charge your credit card for the value of the damage (up to the deductible amount) or, if the vehicle is stolen, the value of the deductible associated with theft. It's up to you to seek reimbursement for these charges from your credit-card company when you get home (you'll need to submit the police report and the car-rental company's accident report). American-based rental companies can be easier to work with if you have a claim to resolve.

Be warned that if you accept any coverage offered by the car-rental company, you automatically forego any coverage provided by your credit card. (In other words, if you buy CDW that comes with a $1,000 deductible, don't expect your credit card to cover it.) This may also be the case if you book and prepay for a rental that already includes CDW and/or theft coverage.

Travel Guard Collision Insurance: Travel Guard sells renter's collision insurance at very affordable rates ($9/day plus a one-time $3 service fee for coverage up to $35,000, $250 deductible, www.travelguard.com, tel. 800-826-4919). It's valid everywhere in Europe except the Republic of Ireland, and some Italian car-rental companies refuse to honor it. If your car-rental company doesn't accept this coverage, and you have to

DRIVING

buy other coverage to replace it, Travel Guard will refund your money. Note that various US states differ on which providers and policies are available to their residents.

Remember that some comprehensive travel insurance policies include collision coverage if you rent your car through a travel agent.

Exceptions for Italy and Ireland: If you rent a car in Italy, you're required to have theft insurance, and most car-rental company rates automatically include CDW coverage (which you sometimes can't decline). Even if you decline CDW when you reserve your Italian car (because you've arranged other coverage), you may discover—when you show up at the counter—that you must buy it after all.

Car-rental companies in the Republic of Ireland are less amenable to letting renters waive CDW insurance in favor of credit-card coverage; some companies will only allow specific credit-card brands to be used for that purpose. Check with your issuing bank to see if you are covered in Ireland, and bring written confirmation with you. Also unique to Ireland is that you sometimes have the option of buying down the deductible on your CDW at the time of booking (for an additional $15-30/day), rather than when you pick up the car.

Liability Insurance: It's unusual to purchase additional liability insurance when renting a car in Europe. With most European car-rental companies, any liability coverage you might need is already included in the price, as the coverage is required under local law. But if you're concerned about this, ask for details when you rent.

The Final Say: Buying CDW—and the supplemental insurance to buy down the deductible, if you choose—is the easiest but priciest option. Using the coverage that comes with your credit card is cheaper, but can involve more hassle (call your credit-card company and check the fine print before you depart). If you're taking a short trip (but not in Italy or Ireland), the simplest solution is to buy Travel Guard's very affordable CDW. For longer trips, leasing is the best way to go.

Picking Up and Returning Your Car

When picking up your car, always check the entire vehicle for scratches, dings, and the gas level. If anything is not noted on the rental agreement, return to the counter to make adjustments.

Before you drive off, get to know your car. This is tough when you're aching to get out on the road—but take a few minutes, while you're still in the rental agency's parking lot, to try out all the features and gadgets: Turn on the radio, run the front and rear windshield wipers and sprayers, figure out whether the headlights come on automatically with the engine, switch the headlights to high-beam, get comfortable with the gearshift, and so on.

This is also a good time to quiz the rental agent on a few things, including:

- local laws you might not be aware of (for example, whether headlights must be on at all times, where and how kids ride, etc.)
- length of the grace period for drop-off (can be 30-59 minutes)
- how to use anything you can't figure out, such as the wipers, alarm system, lights, radio, GPS (including how to set the language to English), etc.
- what type of fuel the car takes (diesel vs. unleaded), the local term for that fuel type, and how to release the gas cap
- location of insurance "green card" and other paperwork
- info on making repairs and any included emergency roadside services
- how to change the tire

Before leaving, get instructions for driving to your next stop (or at least to the expressway). Then drive around the parking lot for a few minutes to test rearview mirrors, the gearshift and clutch, and the lights and signals.

When you drop off the car, walk around the car again with the attendant to be sure there are no new problems. Some drivers take pictures of the returned vehicle as proof of its condition. Otherwise, unexpected charges might show up on your credit-card statement. These are easier to dispute when the information is documented. Ask for a copy of the final condition report and keep it until you've seen your credit-card statement. On that same note, try to avoid dropping off your car after hours (at a drop box); it's best to finalize the rental and receive the paperwork in person. If you are bringing the car back with a full tank, keep your fuel receipt from the final fill-up.

Leasing and Buying

Leasing (technically, buying the car and selling it back) gets around many tax and insurance costs and is a great deal for people needing a car for three weeks or more. For trips of eight weeks and longer, leasing can be more economical than buying a railpass. Leases are available for periods of up to six months. Prices include all taxes, as well as zero-deductible theft and collision insurance (comparable to CDW), and you get to use a new car. Leased cars can most easily be picked up and returned in France, but for an additional fee you can also lease cars in the Netherlands, Belgium, Germany, Spain, Portugal, Italy, and Great

DRIVING

Britain.

Europe by Car, which invented leasing more than 50 years ago, still offers good deals. For example, you can lease a Citroen C3 in France for as few as 21 days for about $1,030—about $49 a day. Renault Eurodrive offers similar deals. In general, the longer you lease the car, the lower the price (a 60-day lease can be as inexpensive as $31 per day).

Although Americans rarely consider this budget option, it's possible to buy a used car for your trip and sell it when you're done. The most common places to buy cars are Amsterdam, Frankfurt, London, and US military bases. In London, check Craigslist (london.craigslist.co.uk), the used-car market on Market Road (Tube: Caledonian Road), and look in London periodicals such as *Loot* (www.loot.com), which lists used cars as well as jobs, flats, cheap flights, and travel partners.

Campers: Consider the advantage of a van or motor home, which gives you the flexibility to drive late and just pull over and camp for free. Fairly cheap to run, these vehicles use diesel—which costs a little less than gasoline—and have much better mileage. For tips on camping and camper-van rentals, see page 228.

Behind the European Wheel

Horror stories about European traffic abound. They're fun to tell, but driving is really only a problem for those who make it one. The most

dangerous creature on the road is the panicked foreign visitor. Drive defensively, observe, fit in, avoid big-city driving when you can, and wear your seat belt.

Some places are easier to handle than others. The British Isles are good for driving— reasonable rentals, no language barrier, exciting rural areas, and fine roads...and after one near head-on collision scares the bloody heck out of you, you'll have no trouble remembering which side of the road to drive on.

Other good driving areas are Scandinavia (hug the lip of a majestic fjord as you meander from village to village); Belgium and the Netherlands (yield to bikes—you're outnumbered); Spain and Portugal (explore out-of-the-way villages and hill towns); Germany (enjoy wonderfully engineered freeways much loved by wannabe race-car drivers); Switzerland and Austria (drive down sunny alpine valleys with yodeling on the stereo for auto ecstasy); and Slovenia (a picturesque country with many diverse sights hard to reach by public transit).

Once you're behind the wheel, you may curse the traffic jams, narrow roads, and macho habits, but driving in Europe carbonates your experience. Driving at home is mundane; driving in Europe is memorable.

Driving Tips and Road Rules

Drive European. After a few minutes on the autobahn, you'll learn that you don't cruise in the passing lane. Cruise in the right-hand lane on the Continent and the left-hand lane in Britain and Ireland. For an A-to-Z index of European-country driving tips, see the website of the British Automobile Association (www.theaa.com, "Driving" tab).

Drive defensively. Be warned that some Europeans, particularly Italians, make up their own rules of the road. In Rome, red lights are considered "discretionary." On one trip, my cabbie went through three red lights. White-knuckled, I asked, "*Scusi*, do you see red lights?" He said, "When I come to light, I look. If no cars come, red light *stupido*, I go through. If policeman sees no cars—*no problema*. He agree—red light *stupido*."

Know the laws. Many European countries require you to have your headlights on anytime the car is running, even in broad daylight. Nearly all countries forbid talking on a cell phone without a hands-free headset. In Europe, it's illegal to turn right on a red light, unless there is a sign or signal specifically authorizing it (most common in Germany). Most countries require safety seats for children under age three, but a few—including Ireland and Germany—require booster seats for kids under age 12 or under 4'11" (or under 4'5" in Sweden). In nearly all countries, children under 12 aren't allowed to ride in the front seat without a booster seat; a few ban kids from the front seat no matter what, and some have these front-seat rules for teens up to age 18. Other laws are more obscure: Austria, Belgium, France, Italy, Norway, and Portugal require each driver to carry a reflective safety vest or kit with a reflecting triangle (typically supplied by the rental company). In many German cities, cars must meet a certain emission standard in order to enter. Your car-rental company should be aware of these rules—just ask. Or you can research them on the US State Department website: go to www.travel.state.gov, click on "International Travel," then specify your country of choice and click "Traffic Safety and Road Conditions."

DRIVING

Learn the signs. All of Europe uses the same simple set of road symbols. Just take a few minutes to learn them. Many major rest stops have free local driving almanacs (or cheap maps) that explain such signs, roadside facilities, and exits.

Find the center. You can drive in and out of strange towns fairly smoothly by following a few basic signs. Most European towns have signs directing you to the "old town" or the center (such as *centrum, centro, centar, centre-ville, Zentrum, Stadtmitte*). The tourist office, normally right downtown, will usually be clearly signposted (*i, turismo, VVV,* or various abbreviations that you'll learn in each country). The

AND LEARN THESE ROAD SIGNS

Speed Limit (km/hr) · Yield · No Passing · End of No Passing Zone

One Way · Intersection · Main Road · Freeway

Danger · No Entry · No Entry for cars · All Vehicles Prohibited

Parking · No Parking · Customs · Peace

tallest spire often marks the center of the old town. Park in its shadow and look for the tourist information office.

Avoid heavy traffic times. Big cities are great fun and nearly traffic-free for Sunday drives. Mediterranean resort areas are extremely congested on summer weekends.

To save time, use the expressway. The shortest distance between any two European points is found on the *autobahn/strada/route/cesta.* Most international European expressways are designated with an "E" (similar to the "I" designation on American freeways), but they can also be named using national letters (for example, the main route between Paris and Lyon is known as both A-6 and E-15). Some prefer the more scenic national highway systems (*route nationale* in France). These small roads can be a breeze, or they can be dreadfully jammed up.

Better roads often come with tolls. It's free to drive on expressways in some countries, such as most roads in Great Britain or Germany's famous autobahn. In other countries, you'll pay for the privilege. Sometimes you'll have to buy a toll sticker (usually called a "vignette") to display in your window. You'll pay about $44 for the highway permit decal as you enter Switzerland; about $11 apiece for Austria and the Czech Republic; $14 each for Hungary and Slovakia; and $21 for Slovenia. You can usually buy the toll sticker at border crossings, gas stations, and post offices (check to see if your rental car already has one that hasn't yet expired). If you don't have one, you'll soon meet your first local...in uniform. In most Mediterranean countries—including Italy, France, Spain, Portugal, Greece, and Croatia—you'll periodically encounter tollbooths on major expressways (charges are based on the distance you drive; figure about $4-9 per hour). Although tolls can add up (for example, it's about $90 to get from Paris to the French Riviera), the fuel and time saved on European expressways justifies the expense. Note that in any country, if you're skipping the expressways and sticking to secondary roads, you don't need to buy a toll sticker or otherwise pay for road use.

You'll pay to drive in some big cities. To drive in downtown London or Stockholm, you'll pay a "congestion charge." You'll pay a toll to drive into Oslo and Bergen—but because of their automated systems, you may not know it until you get a bill two months later.

Big Brother is watching. In many countries, traffic is monitored by automatic cameras that check car speed, click photos, and send speeders tickets by mail. It's smart to know—and follow—the area speed limit.

Car traffic is banned in many Italian city centers, including Rome, Naples, Florence, Pisa, Lucca, Siena, San Gimignano, Orvieto, and Verona. Don't drive or park anywhere you see signs

reading *Zona Traffico Limitato* (ZTL, often shown above a red circle). If you do, even briefly by accident, your license plate will be photographed (usually without your knowledge) and a hefty $150 ticket will be waiting for you at home. It can be an unpleasant ending to your trip. If your hotel is within a restricted area, ask your hotelier to register your car or direct you to legal parking.

Passing is essential. Don't be timid about passing other drivers—be bold, but careful. On winding, narrow roads, the slower car ahead of you may use turn-signal sign language to indicate when it's OK to pass. This is used inconsistently. Don't rely on it blindly. Be sure you understand the lane markings—in France a single, solid, white line in the middle of the road means no passing in either direction; in Germany it's a double white line.

Explore the roundabouts. In roundabouts, traffic continually flows in a circle around a center island. While you'll see them sporadically throughout continental Europe (where vehicles move counterclockwise), roundabouts are everywhere in the British Isles (where traffic flows clockwise). These work wonderfully if you follow the golden rule: Traffic in roundabouts always has the right-of-way, while entering vehicles yield.

For many, roundabouts are high-pressure circles that require a snap decision about something you don't completely understand: your exit. To replace the stress with giggles, make it standard operating procedure to take a 360-degree case-out-your-options exploratory circuit. Discuss the exits with your navigator, go around again if necessary, and then confidently wing off to the exit of your choice. (Don't worry. No other cars will know you've

A roundabout: Take a spin...or two.

been in there enough times to get dizzy.) When approaching an especially complex roundabout, you'll first pass a diagram showing the layout and the various exits. And in many cases, the pavement is painted with the name of the particular road or town to which the lane leads.

In a big city, park carefully. Don't use a car for city sightseeing. Park it and use public transportation or taxis. City parking is a pain. Find a spot as close to the center as possible, grab it, and keep it. For overnight stops, it's crucial to choose a safe, well-traveled, and well-lit spot. A tourist's car parked overnight in a bad urban neighborhood will almost certainly be vandalized (for safe-parking tips, see page 330). In cities with the worst traffic (Rome, Paris, Milan), look for huge government-sponsored (cheap) park-and-rides on the outskirts, where a bus or

Much of Europe uses cardboard or plastic "parking clocks" instead of parking meters. They often come with rental cars or can be bought cheaply at gas stations, newsstands, or tobacco shops. Park, set the clock for the current time, and leave it on your dashboard. A street sign indicates how much time you have (according to this sign, parking is limited to 60 minutes, Mon-Fri, 8:00 a.m.-6:00 p.m.). The clock establishes when you arrived. In Germanic countries, where they're widely used, ask for a Parkscheibe.

subway will zip you easily into the center. It's often worth paying to park in a garage ($25-40 a day). Ask your hotelier for advice.

Filling the Tank

The cost of fuel in Europe ($7-8 a gallon) sounds worse than it is. Distances are short, the petite cars get great mileage, and, when compared to costly train tickets (for the price of a two-hour train ride, you can fill your tank), expensive gas is less of a factor. You'll be impressed by how few miles you need to travel to enjoy Europe's diversity. To minimize fuel costs, consider renting a car that takes diesel, which costs slightly less per liter and gets much better mileage.

Pumping gas in Europe is as easy as finding a gas station (the word "self-service" is universal), sticking the nozzle in, and pulling the big trigger. Paying can be more complicated, because some pay-at-the-pump machines won't accept most American credit cards (most common in the UK, France, and Scandinavia, see page 178). Be prepared to pay cash. If you're traveling on rural highways, automated gas stations may be the only ones open on Sundays, holidays, and late at night—fill up ahead of time.

Fuel prices are listed by the liter (about a quart, four to a gallon). As in the US, most cars take unleaded, but diesel is widely in use. In many countries, the pumps are color-coded to help you find the right kind of gas. In Europe, regular gas is marked "95" while super or premium gasoline is usually designated "97" or "98." Unleaded gas is called *essence*, *petrol*, or *benzine*, while diesel is known as *gasoil, gasol, gaz-oil, gasolio, gasóleo, dieselolie, mazot, motorina, nafta*, or just plain *diesel* (ask about the proper local term when you rent your car). Pay extra attention in Spain, where gasoline is *gasolina* and diesel is sometimes called *gasóleo*.

Freeway gas stations are more expensive than those in towns, but sometimes (e.g., during lunchtime siesta) only freeway stations are open. Giant suburban supermarkets often offer the cheapest gas.

Navigating

After more than 30 years of driving in Europe—pre- and post-GPS—I've collected a carload of knowledge and tricks for navigating the roads.

Paper Maps

Drivers need detail, especially when focusing on a specific region. The free maps you get from your car-rental company usually don't cut it. Better maps and atlases are sold at European gas stations, bookshops, newsstands, and tourist shops.

I like Michelin maps, but the cost for individual maps can add up. Consider the popular and relatively inexpensive Michelin road atlases for each country (with good city maps and detailed indexes). Though they can be heavy, atlases are compact, a good value, and easier for drivers to use than big foldout maps.

Sometimes the best regional maps are available locally. For example, if you're exploring your roots in the Norwegian fjord country, Cappelens 1:200,000 maps are detailed enough to help you find Grandpa Ole's farm. Other quality European brands include Hallwag, Freytag Berndt, Marco Polo, Berndtson & Berndtson, AA (Britain's AAA-type automobile club), Road Editions (for Greece), and Kod & Kam (for Croatia and Slovenia).

Each map has a legend that indicates navigational as well as sightseeing information, such as types of roads, scenic routes and towns, ruined castles, hostels, mountain huts, viewpoints, and so on. Good maps even include such specific details as tolls and opening schedules of remote mountain roads.

21st-Century Maps

If you can get online before your road trip, it's a good idea to look up your route. Mapping websites suggest the fastest way between Point A and Point B, and offer fairly accurate estimates of how long the drive will take, barring traffic delays. Check www.viamichelin .com, Google Maps (www.maps .google.com), www.theaa.com, or www.mappy.com.

Some drivers like to have a GPS unit for navigating unfamiliar European roads. A GPS helps determine the best route for your journey using preloaded maps. Then, using satellite technology to track your precise location, it leads you turn-by-turn to

Like most goats, I appreciate a good, old-fashioned map.

your destination with a small LCD map and voice instructions.

You have three options for using GPS in Europe: You can sometimes get a GPS unit with your rented or leased vehicle for an additional fee (around $15/day; be sure it's set to English and has all the maps you need before you drive off). If you have a portable GPS device at home, you can take it to Europe. Or you can rent a GPS unit in the US to bring with you.

Many American GPS devices come loaded with US maps only. If

you want to bring your unit along, buy and upload European maps before your trip. (Check with your device's manufacturer to find maps compatible with your unit and for details on how to load them.) Note that some GPS mapping packages are designed for regional driving and might not have detailed street-by-street maps for a specific city; before you buy, be sure the maps will fit your travel needs.

Once on the road, stay on your toes, and remember that your GPS is fallible. Check the settings to see whether it's defaulting to the "most direct" or the "most scenic" route—a distinction that can translate to hours of extra driving. Some GPS units receive wireless traffic reports, then modify your route to help you avoid upcoming traffic jams; however, these automated detours onto back roads can wind up costing you even more time.

That's why, even if I'm using a GPS, I make it a point to also have a road map handy and at least a vague sense of my route. One time, driving from St. Moritz to Lugano via Italy's Lake Como, I realized my GPS had just directed me right past the Lugano turnoff. Hitting the brakes and checking my map, I figured out it was aiming to send me on the freeway, then on a ferry across the lake. I stuck with the "slower" roads on the correct side of the lake—and got in an hour earlier. The lesson: GPS is most useful in conjunction with a good map and some common sense.

Though many smartphones have GPS built in, they're not as helpful as a dedicated GPS device, since it takes an Internet connection to update their maps, which could lead to some exorbitant data-roaming charges. However, you can still download driving directions or a map of your region in the morning using your hotel's Wi-Fi connection and then refer to it—without having to be online—throughout your drive (explained on page 260).

Trip Tips

Here are some general tips for finding your way:

Navigate intelligently. Study the roads and major interchanges you'll be using before you set out. If you're headed for a small or midsize town, know which big city is nearby (and most likely to be signposted) to keep you headed in the right direction. In some countries, road numbers can help you find your way: For example, take road A-1 to London, then B-23 to Bristol, then C-456 to Bath. In other countries, locals (and local signs) ignore the road numbers, so you'll navigate by town name. Signs are often color-coded: yellow for most roads, green or blue for expressways, and brown for sightseeing attractions. When leaving a city, look for "all directions" signs (*toutes directions, Alle Richtungen,* etc.) pointing you out of town.

Know the local road-naming conventions. Normally, the more digits the road number has, the smaller it is. In Britain, M-1 is a freeway, A-34 is a major road, and B-4081 is a secondary road. Roads are labeled on many maps with both national and European designations—for example, the same expressway from Madrid to Sevilla may be labeled A-4, E-5, or both. Since road numbers can change, you should also navigate by town names.

Get directions. When you call ahead to confirm your room, ask your hotelier for detailed directions on how to reach the place. Many hotels give precise driving directions and/or GPS coordinates on their websites. If possible, figure out your arrival route on a map before you enter the city limits. While some cities helpfully post signs directing you to individual hotels, in many cases you're on your own.

Consider hiring cabbies. Even if you have a rental car, cabbies can be handy when you're driving lost in a big city. Many times I've hired a cab, showed him an elusive address, and followed him in my car to my hotel.

Think metric. Outside of the UK, you'll be dealing with kilometers. To convert kilometers to miles, cut the kilometers in half and add 10 percent of the original number (90 km/hour = 45 + 9 miles = 54 miles—not very fast in Europe). Do the math yourself: 140 km/hour = 84 mph. Or 360 km = 216 miles. Some people prefer to drop the last digit and multiply by 6 (if 80 km, multiply 8 × 6 = 48 miles), though this can be challenging with large numbers (340 km × 6 = ?). Choose whichever formula works for you.

Figure out the length of your trip. When estimating how long a drive will take, figure you'll average 100 kilometers per hour on expressways (about the same as going 60 mph back home). Determining how much ground you can cover off the freeway is a crapshoot. I use a trick an Irish bus driver taught me: Figure a minute for every kilometer (covering 90 km will take you about an hour and a half). Double that for slow, curvy roads, such as in Italy's Dolomites or Amalfi Coast.

MONEY

Life in 21st-century America has become a plastic experience. For many of us, days can go by at home when we don't use any cash. We swipe our credit card at the drug store or push our debit card's PIN code at the gas pump, and we're on our way.

In Europe, however, day-to-day spending is much more cash-based. There I rely mostly on cash, though I appreciate the convenience that credit cards offer.

Pay with Plastic or Cash?

For me, it all comes down to maximizing ease and minimizing fees. I pay for as much as possible with cash, using a bank that charges low rates for international ATM transactions and withdrawing large amounts at each transaction. I never exchange dollars for foreign cash at a currency exchange booth, and I don't bother getting euros, pounds, or whatever prior to my trip. When I arrive in Europe, I head for an ATM at the airport, load up on cash, and keep it safe in my money belt.

I use my credit card to book reservations by phone (for hotel rooms and a rental car), to cover major expenses (such as plane tickets and long hotel stays), and to pay for things near the end of my trip (to avoid another visit to the ATM). If you'll be shopping a lot or settling bills at pricey business-class hotels, you might use your credit card more than I do—but you'll still be better off using cash for smaller purchases.

Because merchants pay sky-high commissions to credit-card companies, small European businesses (hotels, restaurants, gift shops, and more) often prefer that you pay in cash. Vendors might offer you a discount for paying with cash, or they might not accept credit cards at all. And having enough cash on hand can help you avoid a stressful predicament, especially in countries where chip-and-PIN cards (explained later) are common, as you may find yourself in a place that won't accept your credit card.

A dependence on plastic reshapes the Europe you experience. Pedro's Pension, the friendly guide at the cathedral, and most merchants in the market don't take credit cards. Going through the Back Door requires hard local cash. Minimizing debit- and credit-card use also guards against card fraud or theft: The less you use your cards, the less likely your information will be stolen.

Remember, you're on vacation. Don't get stressed about money in Europe; just spend it wisely.

Use euros in €uroland: Austria, Belgium, Cyprus, Estonia, Finland, France, Germany, Greece, Ireland, Italy, Luxembourg, Malta, the Netherlands, Portugal, Slovakia, Slovenia, and Spain. Even though Montenegro and Kosovo are not in the EU, they use the euro as their official currency.

Cash

When I first started traveling in Europe, I'd convert my traveler's checks into cash at American Express—the convivial, welcoming home to American travelers abroad. When changing dollars into francs in Paris, it felt so good to lose money to that smiling, English-speaking person at the desk. Now with ATMs, the euro, and the general shrinking of the economic world, AmExCo is a dinosaur.

Cash Machines (ATMs)

Throughout Europe, cash machines (ATMs) are the standard way for travelers to get local currency. European ATMs work like your home-town machine and always have English-language instructions. Using your debit card at an ATM takes dollars directly from your bank account

MONEY

Welcome to €uroland

Seventeen EU member countries—and more than 330 million people—use the same currency, the euro. With euros, tourists and locals can easily compare prices of goods between countries. And we no longer lose money or time changing money at borders.

Not all European countries have switched to euros. As of now, major holdouts include the United Kingdom, Denmark, Norway, Sweden, Switzerland, and Croatia. Despite the currency's recent trouble, several Eastern European countries that have joined the European Union—including the Czech Republic, Poland, Hungary, Latvia, and Lithuania—are committed to adopting the euro sometime in the future. For now, these countries still use their traditional currencies.

Even in some non-Euroland countries, the euro is commonly used. For example, in Switzerland, some ATMs give euros, most prices are listed in both Swiss francs and euros, and travelers can get by with euro cash. But if you pay in euros, you'll get a rotten exchange rate. Ideally, if you're in the country for more than a few hours, stow your euros and get some local currency instead.

at home and gives you foreign cash. You'll pay fees, but you'll still get a better rate than you would exchanging cash dollars at a bank.

Ideally, use your debit card with a Visa or MasterCard logo to take money out of ATMs. Before you go, confirm with your bank that your debit card will work in Europe and alert them that you'll be making withdrawals while traveling—otherwise, they might freeze your card if they detect unusual spending patterns.

ATM transactions made with bank-issued debit cards come with various fees. Your bank may levy a flat $2-5 transaction fee each time you use an ATM, and/or may charge a percentage for the currency conversion (1-3 percent), on top of Visa and MasterCard's 1 percent fee for international transactions. Most bank ATMs in Europe don't charge a usage fee, but watch out for "independent" ATMs, which have high fees. Run by companies such as Travelex, Euronet, or Forex, these machines are often found next to bank ATMs in the hope that travelers will be too confused to notice the difference.

If your US bank charges a flat fee per transaction, make fewer visits to the ATM and withdraw larger amounts. (Some major US banks partner with European bank chains, meaning that you can use those

MONEY

ATMs with no fees at all—ask your bank.) Quiz your bank to figure out exactly what you'll pay for each withdrawal (for a list of questions, see page 177).

Since European keypads have only numbers, you'll need to know your personal identification number (PIN) by number rather than by letter; to determine this, just take a close look at your hometown bank's keypad. Plan on being able to withdraw money only from your checking account. You are unlikely to be able to dip into your savings account or transfer funds between accounts from a European ATM.

Bringing an extra ATM card provides a backup if one is demagnetized or eaten by a machine. Make sure your card won't expire before your trip ends. You do not need a chip-and-PIN card (described later) to use a European ATM—your standard magnetic strip card will work fine.

Ask your bank how much you can withdraw per 24 hours, and consider adjusting the amount. Some travelers prefer a high limit that allows them to take out more cash at each ATM stop, while others prefer to set a lower limit as a security measure, in case their card is stolen. To

How to use a European cash machine: Insert card, pull out cash.

avoid excess per-transaction fees, I usually go with a higher maximum.

Be aware that many foreign ATMs have their own limits. If the ATM won't let you withdraw your daily maximum, you'll have to make several smaller withdrawals to get the amount you want. Note that few ATM receipts list the exchange rate, and some machines don't dispense receipts at all.

In some countries (especially in Eastern Europe), an ATM may give you high-denomination bills, which can be difficult to break. My strategy: Request an odd amount of money from the ATM (such as 2,800 Czech *koruna* instead of 3,000). If the machine insists on giving you big bills, go to a bank or a major store to break them.

If you're looking for an ATM, ask for a *distributeur* in France, a cashpoint in the UK, and a *Bankomat* just about everywhere else. Many European banks have their ATMs in a small entry lobby, which protects users from snoopers and bad weather. When the bank is closed, the door to this lobby may be locked. In this case, look for a credit-card-size slot

ATM Basics

Before you go:
- Call your bank to let them know your travel dates in Europe and to find out more about using your debit card abroad (see sidebar on page 177 for a list of questions).
- Since European ATMs will only take funds from checking accounts—not savings—make sure you have enough in your checking account before you go.
- Bring at least one credit card and one debit card, ideally with a Visa or MasterCard logo. Some travelers carry an extra card, in case one gets demagnetized or eaten by a temperamental machine.
- Make sure you have a four-digit PIN number (no letters) for all of your cards. Allow time for your bank to mail you a PIN if you don't know it.

When making a withdrawal:
- Try to use ATMs at banks during banking hours. If there's a problem, someone in the bank can probably help.
- Avoid ATMs that are not provided by a bank. Independent ATMs—such as the Travelex Money Machine, Fast Cash Bank Machine, or Euronet Bankomat—charge outrageous fees.
- Grab your cash and card quickly; some ATMs suck back the cash after 30 seconds.
- Try to take out large amounts of money at one time to avoid frequent ATM trips and repeated withdrawal fees.
- Don't use your credit card to withdraw cash unless it's an emergency. You'll be charged a high cash-advance interest rate from the minute you pull out the money.

If your card doesn't work:
- Try a different ATM. (Do not re-enter your PIN if the ATM eats your card.)
- Try a lower amount; the ATM may have a withdrawal limit.
- Try later. Your card's 24-hour withdrawal maximum is based on US time, or your bank's network may be temporarily down.

If all else fails:
- Use your emergency dollars stashed in your money belt.
- Use your credit card to get a cash advance (you'll need your credit-card PIN for the ATM).
- Have a friend or relative wire you money via Western Union (explained later).
- Contact the nearest American embassy/consulate; they can help arrange a wire transfer.

MONEY

next to the door. Simply insert or swipe your debit or credit card in this slot, and the door should automatically open.

Cash and Currency Tips

Avoid (or at least minimize) cash exchange. The financial industry does a masterful job of hiding the fact that you lose money each time you change it. On average, at a bank you lose 8 percent when you change dollars to euros or other foreign currency. When you use currency exchange booths such as Forex or Travelex at the airport, you lose around 15 percent. If you must change cash in Europe, the postal banks inside post offices usually have the best rate.

Don't buy foreign currency in advance. Some tourists just have to have euros or pounds in their pockets when they step off the airplane, but smart travelers don't bother and know better than to get lousy stateside exchange rates. Wait until you arrive at your destination; I've never been to an airport in Europe that didn't have plenty of ATMs.

Leave the traveler's checks at home. I cashed my last traveler's check long ago. They're a waste of time (long lines at slow banks) and money (fees to get them, fees to cash them). ATMs are the way to go.

For information about using traveler's checks... see the 1995 edition of this book.

Use local cash. Many Americans exclaim gleefully, "Gee, they accept dollars! There's no need to change money." But the happy sales clerk doesn't tell you that your purchase is costing about 20 percent more because of the store's private exchange rate. Without knowing it, you're changing money—at a lousy rate—every time you buy something with dollars.

Figure out currency conversions. To "ugly Americans," foreign money is "funny money." They never figure it out, get no respect from the locals, and are constantly ripped off. Local currencies are all logical. Each system is decimalized just like ours. There are a hundred "little ones" (cents, pence, groszy, stotinki) in every "big one" (euro, pound, złoty, lev). Only the names have been changed—to confuse the tourist. Examine the coins in your pocket soon after you arrive, and in two min-

utes you'll be comfortable with the nickels, dimes, and quarters of each new currency.

You don't need to constantly consult a currency converter. While you can get the exact exchange rate at www.oanda.com, I've never bothered. You'll know the rough exchange rates when you're in a country, and I see no need to have it figured to the third decimal.

Very roughly determine what the unit of currency (euros, kroner, Swiss francs, or whatever) is worth in American dollars. For example, let's say the exchange rate is €1 = $1.40. If a strudel costs €5, then it costs five times $1.40, or about $7. Ten euros is about $14, and €250 = $350 (figure about 250 plus a little less than one-half). Quiz yourself. Soon it'll be second nature. Survival on a budget is easier when you're comfortable with the local currency.

Assume you'll be shortchanged. In banks, restaurants, at ticket booths, everywhere—expect to be shortchanged if you don't do your own figuring. Some people who spend their lives sitting in booths for eight hours a day taking money from strangers have no problem stealing from clueless tourists who don't know the local currency. For 10 minutes I observed a man in the Rome subway shortchanging half of the tourists who went through his turnstile. Half of his victims caught him and got their correct change with apologies. Overall, about 25 percent didn't notice and probably went home saying, "*Mamma mia*, Italy is really expensive."

Coins can become worthless when you leave a country. Since big-value coins are common in Europe, exporting a pocketful of change can be an expensive mistake. Spend them (on postcards, a

Avid coin collectors have the joy of filling in coin books, as the eight denominations of euro coins from 19 different countries make for a fun frontier in coin collecting. Europhiles can buy these books in Europe and chart their travels by gradually completing the collection.

newspaper, or food or drink for the train ride), change them into bills, or give them away. Otherwise, you've just bought a bunch of souvenirs. Note, however, that while euro coins each have a national side (indicating where they were minted), they are perfectly good in any country that uses the euro currency.

Bring along some US dollars. While you won't use it for day-to-day purchases, American cash in your money belt comes in handy for emergencies, such as when banks go on strike or your ATM card stops working. I carry several hundred US dollars as a backup (in denominations of easy-to-exchange 20s or less bulky 50s, though don't bring 100s—popular with counterfeiters and not always accepted for exchange). I've been in Greece and Ireland when every bank went on strike, shutting down without warning. But hard cash is hard cash. People always know roughly what a dollar is worth, and you can always sell it.

Get back to dollars at the end of your trip. If you have any foreign cash left before you fly home, change it into dollars at the European airport or simply spend it at the airport. You might get a few more dollars from your hometown bank for that last smattering of foreign bills, but it's clean and convenient to simply fly home with nothing but dollars in your pocket.

Wiring Money

What if your credit and debit cards don't work, you're out of emergency cash, and you don't have a travel partner who can loan you money? Don't panic. It's easy for someone in the US to wire you some cash. Western Union has thousands of agents at banks, travel agencies, post offices, train stations, airports, currency exchange offices, and supermarkets in Europe. As long as you still have your passport, a friend or relative can go online at www.westernunion.com, transfer money with a credit card, and call you back with your Money Transfer Control Number (MTCN). Then you present your passport and the control number to a Western Union agent, who gives you the cash. If your friend or relative prefers, he or she can make the transfer in person at a Western Union office in the US or by calling toll-free 800-225-5227. There's a hefty fee and a lousy exchange rate, but the cash can be ready for pickup in a matter of hours.

It's trickier if you've lost your passport. Western Union lets your financial angel set up a "secret question" that only you can answer to confirm your identity. Or you can use a slower US State Department service that wires money to an embassy or consulate for pickup during business hours (see www.travel.state.gov/travel). For more on what to do if you've lost your passport, see page 337.

Credit Cards

American credit cards work throughout Europe (at hotels, larger shops and restaurants, travel agencies, car-rental agencies, and so on); Visa and MasterCard are the most widely accepted. American Express is less common (because it costs merchants more) but is popular with some travelers for its extra services. The Discover card is unknown in Europe. It's a good idea to bring an extra card as a backup (especially if you're renting a car and using your card to cover CDW insurance—see page 154 for more). Although most of Europe is switching to new technology that may cause your US card to be rejected in a few automated machines, it shouldn't cause you too much hassle (see "Chip-and-PIN Cards," later).

Plastic fans should realize that when you use your credit card, you're buying from businesses that have enough slack in their prices to absorb the fees the credit-card company charges the merchant (2-5 percent). In other words, those who travel on their plastic may be enjoying the convenience, but at a worse price. While more consumers believe they are getting "free use of the bank's money," we all absorb the percentage the credit-card companies are making in higher purchase prices.

Fees (and How to Avoid Them)

Travelers returning from Europe often open their mail to discover they paid more for their trip than they thought they had. Over the last decade, banks have dramatically increased the fees they charge for overseas transactions. While these fees are legal, they're basically a slimy way for credit-card companies to wring a few more dollars out of their customers. About a decade ago, a class-action settlement forced many banks to refund some of these fees, and most have (slightly) reduced what they charge for international transactions.

Visa and MasterCard levy a 1 percent fee on international transactions, and some banks that issue those cards also tack on a currency conversion fee (additional 1-3 percent). These are similar to the fees associated with using your debit card for ATM withdrawals (described earlier).

So, how can a smart traveler avoid—or at least reduce—these fees? Here are a few suggestions.

Ask about fees. Banks are now required to break out international transaction fees as line items on your statement, helping you to see exactly

---

Transaction Fees Add Up

It pays to shop around for the best rates, both for debit-card ATM withdrawals and credit-card transactions. Consider these examples and you'll see how these fees can really add up over the length of your trip.

$300 ATM withdrawal (with debit card)

	Bank A	Bank B
Flat fee	$3	$5
Currency conversion fee	$6 (2%)	$0 (0%)
ATM noncustomer fee	$2	$2
Total fees	$11	$7

$600 credit-card purchase

	Bank A	Bank B
International transaction fee	$6 (1%)	$6 (1%)
Bank currency conversion fee	$12 (2%)	$0 (0%)
Total fees	$18	$6

---

what you're paying. But by the time you get your statement, it's too late—so it's smart to make a call before your trip to get the whole story. Quiz your bank or credit-card company about the specific fees that come with using their card overseas (see sidebar on page 177).

If you're getting a bad deal, get a new card. Some companies offer far lower international fees than others—and a handful don't charge any at all. If you're going on a long trip, do some research and consider taking out a card just for international purchases. Capital One has a particularly good reputation for no-fee international transactions on both its credit cards and its debit cards linked to a checking account (www.capitalone.com). Most credit unions have low-to-no international transaction fees. Bankrate has a good comparison chart of major credit cards and their currency-conversion fees (search "conversion fees" at www.bankrate.com).

Avoid dynamic currency conversion (DCC). Some European merchants—capitalizing on the fact that many Americans are intimidated by unusual currencies—cheerfully charge you for converting their prices to dollars before running your credit card. This may seem like a nice service, but you'll actually end up paying more. Usually the dollar price is based on a lousy exchange rate set by the merchant, and to make matters worse, even though you're paying in "dollars," your credit-card issuer may still levy its standard foreign-transaction fee. The result: the

MONEY

Questions to Ask Your
Credit-Card Company and Bank

Before your trip, call your credit-card company and your bank (for debit cards) to let them know you'll be using the cards in Europe. This will ensure that they don't decline foreign transactions. While you have them on the phone, ask these questions. If the person doesn't know the answers, ask to speak to someone who does.

The Basics:
- Will my card work in Europe? (Specify which countries you're traveling to.)
- What do you charge for withdrawals or purchases in Europe? Is it a percentage, flat fee, or both?
- Are other currency conversion or foreign transaction fees tacked on?
- What will the total charge be on my card—including all fees— if I take out €100 at an ATM with my debit card? Or if I pay for a €100 purchase with my credit card?
- If my credit/debit card is lost or stolen, what is my liability?
- What phone number should I call is there's an emergency?

Specific to Debit Cards:
- What is my daily limit for ATM withdrawals in Europe? (If you want to change the limit, ask if you can.)
- Do you have any partner banks in Europe where I can use my debit card at an ATM without paying an extra fee?

Specific to Credit Cards:
- Can you mail my credit card's PIN to me? (If you don't know it; you might need it for some purchases in Europe.)

"convenience" of seeing your charge in dollars comes at a premium.

Some merchants may disagree, but according to DCC provider Planet Payment, you have the right to decline this service at the store and have your transaction go through in the local currency. If you're handed a receipt with two totals—one in the local currency and the other in US dollars—circle or check the amount in the local currency before you sign. If your receipt shows the total in dollars only, ask that it be rung up again in the local currency.

Don't bother with prepaid cards. It's possible to buy prepaid "cash cards"—which you load with funds before you leave, then use like any other credit or debit card—but they come with high fees and aren't worth considering for most trips.

The Bottom Line: Here's the best formula for saving money as you travel. Pay for as much as possible with cash (use a bank that charges low rates for international ATM transactions, and withdraw large amounts at each transaction—keeping the cash safe in your money belt). When using a credit card, use a card with the lowest possible international fees, and make sure your transactions are charged in the local currency—not dollars. Then smile and enjoy your trip, feeling very clever for avoiding so much unnecessary expense.

Chip-and-PIN Cards

Europe—and the rest of the world—is adopting a new system for credit and debit cards. While handy for locals, these chip-and-PIN cards are causing a few headaches for American visitors: Some machines that are designed to accept chip-and-PIN cards simply don't accept US credit cards. This news is causing some anxiety among American travelers, but really: Don't worry. While I've been inconvenienced a few times with automated machines that wouldn't accept my card, it's never caused me any serious trouble. Here's the scoop:

When Europeans buy something with their chip-and-PIN card, they insert the card in a machine like this one, then type in their PIN.

Today, outside the US, nearly half of all cards are chip cards. These "smart-cards" come with an embedded micro-chip that enhances their security. When making a purchase, the cardholder must enter a PIN (similar to using a debit card in the US) while the card stays in its slot in the sales terminal. The chip inside the card then authorizes the transaction.

Readers tell me they've had cards rejected by a few machines in Great Britain, Ireland, Scandinavia, France, Switzerland, Belgium, Austria, Germany, and the Netherlands. This is especially common with auto-mated machines, such as those at train and subway stations, toll roads, parking garages, luggage lockers, bike-rental kiosks, and self-serve gas pumps. For example, after a long flight into Charles de Gaulle Airport, you find you can't use your credit card in the ticket machine for the train into Paris. Or, while driving in rural Switzerland on a Sunday afternoon, you discover that the automated gas stations only accept chip-and-PIN cards.

In most of these situations, a cashier is nearby who can process your magnetic-strip card manually by swiping it and having you sign the receipt the old-fashioned way. Many automated machines take cash as well as credit cards; other machines might take your US credit card if you also know the card's PIN. Every card has one—ask your bank for the number before you leave (since they will not tell you over the phone, allow time for the bank to mail you the PIN).

Most hotels, restaurants, and shops that serve Americans will gladly accept your US credit card. During the transaction, they may ask you to type in your PIN rather than sign a receipt. Some clerks off the beaten track may not be familiar with swiping a credit card—be prepared to give them a quick lesson—or pay with cash.

In a few cases, you might need to get creative; drivers in particular need to be aware of potential problems when filling up at an automated gas station, entering an unattended parking garage, or exiting a toll road...you might just have to move on to the next gas station or use the "cash only" lane at the toll plaza.

Those who are really concerned can apply for a chip card in the US, but I think this is overkill. Major US banks, such as Chase, Citi, Bank of America, US Bank, and Wells Fargo, are beginning to offer credit cards with chips—but most of these come with a hefty annual fee or are exclusive to corporate accounts.

Also, while these cards have chips, they are not presently configured for offline transactions (in which the card is securely validated for use without a real-time connection to the bank). So although these American chip cards will work for most European transactions, such as in the Paris Metro or the London Tube stations, they might not work at an out-of-the-way gas station in Provence, where the gas pump is probably offline. If you really want a chip card, ask your financial institution if it plans to offer one soon, and if their cards are offline-capable.

Some credit unions are beginning to roll out true chip-and-PIN cards that work for all transactions, online or offline. One attractive no-fee card is the GlobeTrek Visa, offered by Andrews Federal Credit Union in Maryland (open to all US residents, see www.andrewsfcu.org).

In the future, chip cards could well become standard issue in the US. Visa and MasterCard have asked US merchants to start making chip-based transactions by late 2015 or assume the liability for fraud. Over the next three years, when your bank renews your credit card, it's likely there will be a chip in it.

MONEY

Bank Card Scams

As with preventing other kinds of theft, the key to averting fraud is to protect your personal information. For information on Internet security (such as checking bank statements online from the road), see page 256.

Protect your credit and debit cards. Take to Europe only the credit and debit cards that you expect to use, plus a backup, and keep them safely in your money belt. Upon returning home, verify the balance and charges on your debit and credit cards. For a longer trip, monitor balances as you travel. (If you lose a card, see page 336; for more tips on money belts and foiling pickpockets, see page 327.)

Safeguard your PIN code. Memorize your personal identification number; you'd be surprised how many people write it on their card (which is extremely risky). "Shoulder surfing"—a thief watching you as you type your PIN into a keypad—is a common problem. When entering your PIN, carefully block other people's view of the keypad, covering it with your free hand.

Ask your bank about an international travel account. Some banks, such as Wells Fargo, can set up a special travel account that links to your debit card. If a thief steals your card or number while you're traveling, he'll have access only to the funds in this account, and the bank can easily close it; none of your other accounts will be compromised. You'll have to make sure to keep enough funds in the account; if you need to transfer funds, you can do it online from a secure computer. Close the account when you return.

Use your credit card sparingly. Restaurant servers and shop clerks might try to steal your credit-card information, sometimes by swiping it in a special machine that reads the card or by surreptitiously snapping a photo of it with their mobile phone. Most European restaurants have portable card readers that waiters bring to the table; it's more secure since your card never leaves your sight. In most cases, it's safest to pay with cash.

Use your debit card even more sparingly. Use your debit card to withdraw sizable amounts of local cash from ATMs (and then stow it in your money belt to protect against pickpockets) so you can pay with cash whenever possible. Use your debit card only for cash-machine withdrawals. To make purchases, pay with cash or your credit card. Because a debit card pulls funds directly out of your bank account, potential charges incurred by a thief are scary—it's *your* money that's gone, not the credit-card company's. If you establish that your card is lost or stolen, report it immediately, as your liability is linked to timely reporting (you'll likely be on the hook for only $50, but it's still worrisome). If you're concerned about this, talk to your bank about setting a daily withdrawal limit for your ATM or debit card; you'll have to weigh the convenience of withdrawing large amounts of euros from your accounts...against the risk of a crook doing the same. Note that this limit applies to cash-machine withdrawals, not purchases.

Watch out for ATM skimming. Thieves can place an illegal card reader over the slot of an ATM and make it look like it's part of the equipment. Some aim tiny cameras at the keypad to record your fingers typing the PIN. Inspect the card slot carefully for signs of tampering. Look for a color difference in the material or a gap where something appears to be glued onto the slot. If the entry to the card slot bulges out dramatically from the surface of the machine, it might be a skimming device. If a bank machine eats your ATM card, see if there's a thin plastic insert with a tongue hanging out that crooks use to extract it. (A similar scam is to put something sticky in the slot.) Try to use ATMs at banks—since a thief has to attach a skimming device, he's less likely to target an ATM near surveillance cameras.

What to do if your card is stolen: If your credit or debit card is stolen, call these 24-hour US numbers collect—Visa: tel. 303/967-1096, MasterCard: tel. 636/722-7111, American Express: tel. 336/393-1111 (see sidebar on page 336).

Tipping

Tipping in Europe isn't as automatic and generous as it is in the United States, but in many countries, tips are appreciated, if not expected. As in the US, the proper amount depends on your resources, tipping philosophy, and the circumstances. That said, there are big tippers and there are misers the world over. Tipping varies widely by country, but some general guidelines apply.

At restaurants, check the menu to see if service is included; if it isn't, a tip of 5-10 percent is normal (for more on tipping at restaurants, see page 372). For taxis, round up the fare (see page 285). At hotels with porters, pay the porter a euro for each bag he carries; it's nice (but not required) to leave a small tip in your room for the housekeeping staff when you depart.

Tipping for special service is optional. Guides who give talks at public sights or on bus or boat tours often hold out their hands for tips after they give their spiel. If I've already paid for the tour or admission to the sight, I don't tip extra (but if you feel you must tip, a euro or two is enough for a job well done). In general, if someone in the service industry does a super job for you, a tip of a couple of euros is appropriate...but

MONEY

not required.

When in doubt, ask. The French and British generally tip hairdressers, the Dutch and Swedish usually don't. If you're not sure whether (or how much) to tip for a service, ask your hotelier or the tourist information office; they'll fill you in on how it's done on their turf.

VAT Refunds and Customs

For serious shoppers it's worth knowing the ins and outs of tax refunds on your major purchases, and how to bring these items home. For general shopping tips, see page 319.

Claiming Back Value-Added Tax (VAT)

Every year, tourists visiting Europe leave behind millions of dollars of refundable sales taxes. For some, the headache of collecting the refund is not worth the few dollars at stake. But if you do any extensive shopping, consider that the refund is hard cash—free and fairly easy to claim. You just have to bring your passport along on your shopping trip, get the necessary documents from the retailer, and track down the right folks at the airport, port, or border when you leave. (This gives you something to do while you're hanging around waiting for your flight.)

The standard European Union Value-Added Tax ranges from 15 to 25 percent per country. Exact rates change; you can double-check with merchants when you're there.

Unlike business travelers, tourists aren't entitled to refunds on the tax they spend on hotels and meals. Still, you can get back most of the tax you paid on merchandise such as clothes, cuckoos, and crystal. You're not supposed to use your purchased goods before you leave Europe—if you show up at customs wearing your new Italian shoes, officials might look the other way, or they might deny you a refund.

To get any refund, your purchase has to be above a certain amount—ranging from about $30 to several hundred dollars, depending on the country (except in Ireland, which has no minimum). Typically, you must ring up the minimum at a single retailer—you can't add up your purchases from various shops to reach the required amount—so if you're doing a lot of shopping, you'll benefit from finding one spot where you can buy big. If you'll be in Europe for a long time, shop near the end of your trip. You need to collect your refund within three months of your purchase.

The details on how to get a refund vary per country, but generally you'll need to follow the same basic steps:

VAT Rates and Minimum Purchases Required to Qualify for Refunds

Country of Purchase	VAT Standard Rate*	Minimum in Local Currency	Approx. Min. in US Dollars
Austria	20%	€75.01	$105
Belgium	21%	€125.01	$175
Croatia	25%	740 HRK	$148
Czech Republic	21%	2,001 CZK	$112
Denmark	25%	300 DKK	$51
Estonia	20%	€38.36	$55
Finland	24%	€40	$56
France	19.6%	€175.01	$245
Germany	19%	€25	$35
Great Britain	20%	£30	$48
Greece	23%	€120	$168
Hungary	27%	50,000 HUF	$240
Ireland	23%	No minimum	No minimum
Italy	23%	€155	$217
Latvia	21%	30.50 LVL	$60
Lithuania	21%	200 LTL	$82
Luxembourg	15%	€74	$104
Netherlands	21%	€50	$70
Norway	25%	315 NOK	$63
Poland	23%	200 PLN	$67
Portugal	23%	€61.35	$84
Romania	24%	250 RON	$83
Slovakia	20%	€175	$245
Slovenia	20%	€50.01	$70
Spain	21%	€90.15	$126
Sweden	25%	200 SEK	$33
Switzerland	8%	300 CHF	$273
Turkey	18%	118 TRY	$71

* The VAT Standard Rates listed above—while listed as exact amounts—are intended to give you an idea of the rates and minimums involved. But VAT rates fluctuate based on many factors, including what kind of item(s) you are buying. Your refund will likely be less than the above rate, especially if it's subject to processing fees.

MONEY

Bring your passport along. You'll likely be asked to present your passport when you make the purchase, in order to start the refund process.

Shop at stores that know the ropes. Retailers choose whether to participate in the VAT-refund scheme. Most tourist-oriented stores do; often you'll see a sign in the window or by the cash register (if not, ask). It'd be a shame to spend big bucks at a place and not have a chance of getting a refund.

Get the documents. When you make your purchase, have the merchant fill out the necessary refund document, often called a "cheque." Make sure the paperwork is done before you leave the store so there's nothing important missing. If they leave any blanks for you to fill out, be sure you understand what goes where. Attach your receipt to the form and stash it in a safe place.

Some stores may offer to handle the rest of the hassle for you (if they provide this service, they likely have some sort of "Tax Free" sticker in the window). If you're charming and at the right store, try talking the merchant into mailing your documents for you and reimbursing your credit card on the spot. (To ensure their records are legally above-board, the merchant may ask you to get the documents stamped at the border, then mail them back to the store.)

If the store ships your purchase to your home, you can still collect a refund (or you may even be able to avoid paying the VAT in the first place). However, shipping fees can be pricey enough to wipe out most of what you'd save in VAT. I wouldn't mail a purchase home just to avoid paying the VAT, but if you're having things shipped anyway, ask for the refund at the shop. (Depending on the country, you may still have to handle some VAT-related red tape—ask the merchant.)

Bring your paperwork and purchases to the airport or border crossing, and arrive early. Assuming you left the store with your purchase, receipt, and VAT paperwork (but no refund), you'll need to get the refund processed before going home. If you've bought merchandise in a European Union country, process your documents at your last stop in the EU, regardless of where you made your purchases. So if you buy sweaters in Denmark, pants in France, and shoes in Italy, and you're flying home from Greece, get your documents stamped at the airport in Athens. (If the currencies are different in the country where you made your purchase and where you process your refund—say, pounds and euros—you may have to pay an extra conversion fee.) And don't forget—Switzerland, Norway, and Turkey are not in the EU, so if you buy in one of those countries, get your documents stamped before you cross the border.

Get your documents stamped at customs. Before checking in, find the local customs office, and be prepared to stand in line. In smaller airports, ports, and less-trafficked border crossings, finding the right customs agent can be tough. If you run out of time and have to leave without the stamp, you're out of luck. At customs, an export officer will stamp your documents and may ask you to present your unused goods to verify that you are, indeed, exporting your purchase. (Some retailers, particularly those in Scandinavia, will staple and seal the shopping bag to keep you from cheating.) It's best to keep your purchases in your carry-on for viewing, but if they're too large or dangerous to carry on (such as knives), have your purchases easily accessible in the bag you're about to check, ready to show the customs agent.

Collect the cash—sooner or later. Once you get your form stamped by customs, it takes one more step to get your money back. If your purchases were bought from a merchant who works with a refund service such as Global Blue or Premier Tax Free, find their offices inside the airport (either before or after security). These services take a cut of your refund (about 4 percent), but save you further fuss and delay. Present your stamped document, and they'll likely give you your refund in cash, right then and there. If they'll only issue your refund in the local currency, you can either exchange that cash at home, save it for your next trip, or try spending it at the airport. (Look—there's a duty-free shop next door!) Otherwise, they'll credit the refund to your credit card (within two billing cycles, see www.global-blue.com or www.premiertaxfree.com).

If the retailer handles VAT refunds directly, you don't have the option of using a refund service—it's up to you return your stamped documents to the merchant for your refund. You can mail the documents from home, or more quickly, from the airport or border (using a stamped, addressed envelope you've prepared, or one that's been provided by the merchant). Then you wait. It could take months. Look for a refund on your credit-card statement, or for a check in the mail. If the refund check comes in a foreign currency, you may have to pay $30 or so to get your bank to cash it.

Don't count on it. My readers have reported that, even when following all of the instructions carefully, sometimes the VAT refund just doesn't pan out. (For example, they have all the paperwork ready when they get to the airport—but can't find the customs official to process it.) These problems seem most prevalent in Italy. Your best odds are to buy from a merchant who knows how to deal with the red tape for you—but even that is not infallible.

Only you can decide whether VAT refunds are worth the trouble. As for me, my favorite trip souvenirs are my photos, journal, and memories. These are priceless—and exempt from taxes and red tape.

Customs for American Shoppers

You are allowed to take home $800 worth of items per person duty-free, once every 30 days (family members can combine their individual $800 exemptions on a joint declaration). The next $1,000 is taxed at a flat 3 percent. After that, you pay the individual item's duty rate. You can also bring in duty-free a liter of alcohol (slightly more than a standard-size bottle of wine; you must be at least 21), 200 cigarettes, and up to 100 non-Cuban cigars.

Because food items can carry devastating diseases or pests, they are strictly regulated. You may take home vacuum-packed cheeses; dried herbs, spices, or mushrooms; and canned fruits or vegetables, including jams and vegetable spreads. Baked goods, candy, chocolate, oil, vinegar, mustard, and honey are OK. Fresh fruits and vegetables (even that banana from your airplane breakfast) are not permitted. Meats are generally not allowed, though canned pâtés from some countries are usually permitted if made from geese, duck, or pork—but not beef. Just because a duty-free shop in an airport sells a food product, it doesn't mean it will automatically pass US customs. Be prepared to lose your investment.

Of course, you'll need to carefully pack any bottles of wine, jam, honey, oil, and other liquid-containing items in your checked luggage, thanks to limits on liquids in carry-ons. For tips on bringing duty-free liquids onto the plane, see "What Can't I Carry On?" on page 96.

To check US customs rules and duty rates, visit www.cbp.gov, click on "Travel," and then "Know Before You Go." For details about mailing items from Europe to yourself or somebody else, see page 359.

SLEEPING

Europe offers a wide range of accommodations: hotels (from small to large, and simple to swanky), cozy B&Bs, characteristic guest houses, cheap hostels, and rental apartments, plus creative accommodations such as monasteries, campgrounds, free couches, and house-swaps. There's certain to be a perfect home-away-from-home for you. First we'll cover the basics of choosing and reserving a room. Then we'll take a spin through the various types of lodging.

Finding the Right Room

Whether you're booking accommodations for your entire trip months in advance, or rolling into town after dark and finding a room on the fly, these tips will help you choose what's best for you and your budget.

Independent Traveler Seeks Good-Value Accommodations

People often ask me how I choose which hotels to list in my guidebooks. There's no secret trick to it: I walk through the most inviting neighborhood in town, snoop around each hotel and grab their price lists, and jot down some

SLEEPING

notes. By the end of the day, the best-value hotels stand out. What's striking to me is how little correlation there is between what you pay and what you get. I recently spent a day in Amsterdam, scaling the stairs and checking out the rooms of 20 different hotels, all offering double rooms for $100-230 a night. What I found is that you are just as likely to spend $150 for a big, impersonal place on a noisy highway as you are to spend $100 for a charming, family-run guest house on a bikes-only stretch of canal.

I look for places that are clean, central, relatively quiet at night, reasonably priced, friendly, small enough to have a hands-on owner and stable staff, run with a respect for local traditions, and not listed in other guidebooks. Obviously, meeting every criterion is rare, and many hotels fall short of perfection—sometimes miserably. But if I can find a place with, say, six of these eight criteria...it's a keeper. I'm more impressed by a handy location and a fun-loving philosophy than flat-screen TVs and shoeshine machines.

My favorite type of European hotel: well-located, small, friendly, charming, and moderately priced

It pays to choose your accommodations thoughtfully. Expensive hotels can rip through a tight budget like a grenade through a dollhouse. I hear people complaining about that "$300 double in Frankfurt" or the "$400-a-night room in London." They come back from their vacations with bruised and battered pocketbooks, telling stories that scare their friends out of international travel and back to Florida or Hawaii one more time. True, you can spend $400 for a double, but I never have. That's three days' accommodations for me.

As far as I'm concerned, spending more for your hotel just builds a bigger wall between you and what you traveled so far to see. If you spend enough, you won't know where you are. Think about it. "In-ter-con-ti-nen-tal." That means the same everywhere—designed for people who deep-down inside wish they weren't traveling, people spending someone else's money, people who need a strip of paper over the toilet promising them no one's sat there yet. It's uniform sterility, a lobby full of Stay-Press Americans, English menus, and lamps bolted to tables.

Europe's small, mid-range hotels may not have room service, but their staffs are more interested in seeing pictures of your children and helping you have a great time than in thinning out your wallet.

Budget Tips

The majority of Americans traveling in Europe want to sleep in moderately priced hotels. Most of the accommodations I recommend in my guidebooks fall into this category. Here are a few factors to weigh when searching for a good-value hotel that suits your budget:

Comparison shop. These days, many hotels change prices from day to day according to demand. Given the economic downturn, hoteliers are often willing and eager to make a deal. I'd suggest emailing several hotels to ask for their best price. Compare their offers and make your choice.

Book direct. Skip the middleman, such as a hotel-booking website or the tourist information office's room-finding service. If you book direct, the hotel doesn't have to pay a cut to that intermediary. This might make the hotelier more open to giving you a deal. For tips on getting the best deals online, see page 202.

Try to wrangle a discount for a longer stay or payment in cash. If you plan to stay three or more nights at a place, or if you pay in cash rather than by credit card (saving the hotelier the credit-card company's fee), it's worth asking if a discount is available.

If it's off-season, bargain. Prices usually rise with demand during festivals and in July and August. Off-season, try haggling. If the place is too expensive, tell them your limit; they might meet it. Or consider arriving without a reservation and dropping in at the last minute to try and score a deal.

Think small. Larger hotels are usually pricier than small hotels or

Europe's cheap, no-character hotels cater to local business travelers interested in going home with some of their per diem still in their pockets.

B&Bs, partly because of taxes (for example, in Britain, once a B&B exceeds a certain revenue level, it's required to pay an extra 15 percent tax to the government). Hoteliers who pay high taxes pass their costs on to you.

Know the exceptions. Hotels in northern Europe are pricier than those in the south, but you can find exceptions. In Scandinavia, Brussels, and Berlin, fancy "business hotels" are desperate for customers in the summer and year-round on weekends, when their business customers stay away. Some offer some amazing deals through the local tourist information offices. The later your arrival, the better the discount.

Don't consume above your needs. Know the government ratings. A three-star hotel is not necessarily a bad value, but if I stay in a three-star hotel, I've spent $60 extra for things I don't need. Amenities such as air-conditioning, elevators, private showers, room service, a 24-hour reception desk, and people in uniforms each add $10 apiece to your room cost. Before you know it, the simple $90 room is up to $150. Then, additional charges can pile on top of this already inflated room rate. For example, most moderately priced hotels offer Wi-Fi free to their guests, while the expensive places are more likely to charge for it.

Check the prices on the room list, and figure out how to get the best-value rooms. Room prices can vary tremendously within a hotel according to facilities provided. On their websites (and near their reception desks), most places post a room summary that lists each room, its bed configuration, facilities, and maximum price (for one and for two people), sometimes broken down by season (low, middle, high). Also read the breakfast, tax, and extra-bed policies. By studying this information, you'll see that, in many places, a shower costs less than a bath, and a double bed is cheaper than twins. In other words, an inattentive couple who would have been just as happy with a shower and a double bed can end up paying more for an unneeded tub and twins. If you want a cheap room, say so. Many hoteliers have a few unrenovated rooms without a private bathroom; they usually don't even mention these, figuring they'd be unacceptable to Americans.

Put more people in a room. Family rooms are common, and putting four in a quad is much cheaper than two doubles. Many doubles come with a small double bed and a sliver of a single, so a third person pays very little. A family with two small children can ask for a triple and bring a sleeping bag for the stowaway.

Avoid doing outside business through your hotel. Go to the flamenco show and get the ticket yourself. You'll learn more, save money, and be more likely to sit with locals than with a bunch of tourists. So often, tourists are herded together—by a conspiracy of hotel managers and tour organizers—at gimmicky folk evenings featuring a medley of cheesy cultural clichés kept alive only for the tourists. You can't relive your precious nights in Sevilla. Do them right—on your own.

Avoid hotels that require you to buy meals. Many national governments regulate hotel prices according to class or rating. In order to overcome this price ceiling (especially at resorts in peak season, when demand exceeds supply), hotels might require you to buy dinner—or your choice of lunch or dinner—in their dining room. It's generally called "half board," "half pension," or *demi-pension*. While this might not be expensive, I prefer the freedom to explore and sample the atmosphere of restaurants in other neighborhoods. Breakfast is often included in the room rate, but in some countries it's an expensive, semi-optional tack-on. If you want to opt out of a pricey hotel breakfast, ask if it's possible when you book the room.

Reserving a Room

I used to travel with absolutely no reservations. A daily chore was checking out several hotels or pensions and choosing one. Europe was ramshackle, things were cheap, and hotel listings were unreliable and unnecessary. Now, like hobos in a Jetsons world, budget travelers need to think one step ahead.

To Reserve or Not to Reserve?

Every Europe-bound traveler has to make a decision: Am I willing to sacrifice spontaneity for the comfort of knowing exactly where I'll sleep each night? Decide which of the following scenarios best suits your style.

Want maximum choice and peace of mind? Book far in advance. Most travelers find that it's worth booking ahead to get into the most popular, best-value hotels. In fact, lately I've been getting aced out by my own readers at my favorite accommodations. So when I want to be certain to get my first choice, I reserve several weeks (or even months) in advance. For peak-season travel, on national holidays, during big festivals, and when visiting big, popular cities (such as London, Paris, Madrid, Venice, and so on), I make my reservations as soon as I can pin down a date. (To check holiday and festival dates, go to www.ricksteves.com/festivals.)

Family-run hotels offer the warmest welcome and the best value.

SLEEPING

Happy with a mix of predictability and flexibility? Call ahead as you travel. If you don't want to book everything far in advance, but also don't want to simply show up without a room, calling a day or two ahead while on the road can be a good compromise. This works best when there's relatively little demand for rooms (in shoulder or off-season, or in less-crowded places). In these situations, my standard room-finding tactic is to telephone in the morning to reserve my room for that night. I travel relaxed, knowing a good place is holding a room for me.

Prefer maximum spontaneity? Find rooms as you travel. There's nothing more liberating than choosing which town to visit only when you step onto the rail platform, or veering off course from your itinerary just to get away from the clouds or crowds. But doing this makes it less likely you'll find a room that matches your budget and priorities. Even those who generally skip reservations should at least reserve their arrival night in Europe (as jet-lagged room-finding can be stressful). Several tips for this strategy are explained later, under "Reserving Rooms as You Travel."

Making Reservations

If you decide to reserve rooms in advance, here are the basics. Remember to book direct with the hotel or B&B.

Requesting a Reservation: These days, virtually every European hotel and B&B has a website, many with reservation-request forms built right in. Just type in your preferred dates, and the website will automatically display a list of available rooms and prices (simpler websites will send an email to the hotelier with your request).

When making reservations, communicate your needs clearly to your hotelier.

If there's no reservation form, or for complicated requests, send an email in simple English. The hotelier wants to know these key pieces of information (also included in the sample request form on page 194):

- number and type of rooms (e.g., "1 double room")
- number of nights
- date and estimated time of arrival
- date of departure
- any special needs (e.g., bathroom in the room or down the hall, twin

beds vs. one big bed, air-conditioning, quiet, view, ground floor/no stairs, etc.)

To avoid confusion, use the European style for writing dates: day/month/year. For example, a couple reserving a two-night stay would write the following: "Please reserve 1 double room for 2 nights, arriving 16 July 2014, departing 18 July 2014." Consider in advance how long you'll stay; don't just assume you can tack on extra days once you arrive, especially if you're traveling in peak season. Mention any discounts offered—for Rick Steves readers or otherwise—when you make the reservation.

If you don't get a response to your email, it usually means the hotel is already fully booked—but try sending the message again or call to follow up. Use the phone if you want an immediate response.

Confirming a Reservation: Most places will request your credit-card number for a one-night deposit to hold the room. To confirm a room using a hotel website reservation form, enter your contact information and credit-card number; the hotel will send you a confirmation via email. Before entering your credit-card number, make sure the site is secure (check for *https:* in your browser's address bar). And be sure you use the hotel's official site and not a booking agency's site—otherwise you may pay higher rates than you should.

If you sent an email to request a reservation, the hotel will reply with its room availability and rates for your dates. This is not a confirmation. You must email back to say that you want the room at the given rate. While you can email your credit-card information (I do), it's safer to share that personal info via phone call, fax, two successive emails, or the hotel's secure online reservation form.

Small B&Bs, which often don't accept credit cards, may not require a deposit; however, in places where no-shows are epidemic, some B&B owners request that you put money down to hold a room (it's becoming easier to do this, thanks to PayPal). Especially during slow times, some establishments will hold a room without a deposit if you promise to arrive early in the day. The earlier you arrive, the better your chances of a room being held for you. If you end up running a little late, call again to assure the owners that you're coming.

Canceling a Reservation: If you must cancel a reservation, it's courteous to do so with as much notice as possible. Simply make a quick phone call or send an email. Family-run places and small B&Bs lose money if they turn away customers while holding a room for someone who doesn't show up. Your prompt cancellation gives them time to fill that room. (Don't let these people down—I tell my recommended places that you'll call if you can't make it.)

Hotel Reservation

To: _____   _____
              hotel   *email or fax*

From: _____   _____
              name   *email or fax*

Today's date: _____ / _____ / _____
                      day   *month*   *year*

Dear Hotel _____ ,

Please make this reservation for me:

Name: _____

Total # of people: _____   # of rooms: _____   # of nights: _____

Arriving: _____ / _____ / _____   My time of arrival (24-hr clock): _____
                day   *month*   *year*   (I will telephone if I will be late)

Departing: _____ / _____ / _____
                 day   *month*   *year*

Room(s): Single ____   Double ____   Twin ____   Triple ____   Quad ____

With: Toilet ____   Shower ____   Bath ____   Sink only ____

Special needs: View ____   Quiet ____   Cheapest ____   Ground Floor ____

Please email or fax confirmation of my reservation, along with the type of room reserved and the price. Please also inform me of your cancellation policy. After I hear from you, I will quickly send my credit-card information as a deposit to hold the room. Thank you.

_____
Name

_____
Address

_____
City   **State**   **Zip Code**   **Country**

Before hoteliers can make your reservation, they want to know the information listed above. You can use this form as the basis for your email, or you can photocopy this page, fill in the information, and send it as a fax (also available online at www.ricksteves.com/reservation).

Understandably, many hotels bill no-shows for one night. Cancellation policies can be strict: For example, you might lose a deposit if you cancel within two weeks of your reserved stay, or you might be billed for the entire visit if you leave early. Internet deals may require prepayment, with no refunds for cancellations. Especially if your plans are in flux, carefully confirm the hotel's cancellation policy when you book.

A hotel might lose track of your cancellation, then charge you when you don't show up. Make sure to get a written record (via email) of your cancellation. (You might have to request this more than once, but it's worth it.)

Reconfirming a Reservation: Hotels make mistakes. Always call to reconfirm your room reservation a day or two in advance. (This gives you time to improvise in the unlikely event that something goes wrong.) I even call again on the day of arrival to tell my host what time I expect to get there (especially for a small hotel or B&B that may not have a 24-hour reception desk). If you'll be arriving late (after 17:00), let them know. It's smart to carry a printed copy of your confirmation—both to keep track of where you're staying and as recourse on the small chance that the hotel loses your reservation.

Reserving Rooms as You Travel

While most travelers prefer to nail down room reservations long in advance, you can blow like the wind freely through Europe if you want, finding beds on the fly.

Your approach to room-finding will be determined by whether it's a "buyer's market" or a "seller's market"—based on the current demand. These trends can be obvious (a beach resort will be crowded in summer, empty in winter); in other cases, a guidebook or local tourist information office can tip you off. Sometimes you can arrive late, be selective, and even talk down the price. Other times you'll happily accept anything with a pillow and a blanket.

These tricks work for me:

Travel with a good list of hotels. Even the most footloose and fancy-free traveler shouldn't totally wing it. Bring along a good guidebook so you at least have a sense of your options (and the general price range in town) when you begin your search.

The early bird gets the room. If you anticipate crowds (weekends are worst), go to great lengths to arrive in the morning when the most—and best—rooms are available. For instance, I would leave Florence at 7 a.m. to arrive in popular, crowded Venice early enough to get a decent choice of rooms. If the rooms aren't ready until noon, take one anyway. Leave your luggage behind the desk; you can relax and enjoy the city, then move in later. Consider the advantage of overnight train rides—you'll arrive, if not bright, at least early.

Shop around. When going door-to-door, the first place you check is rarely the best. It's worth 20 minutes of shopping around to find the going rate before you accept a room. You'll be surprised how prices vary as you walk farther from the station or down a street strewn with B&Bs. Never judge a hotel by its exterior or lobby. Lavish interiors with shabby exteriors are a cultural trait of Europe (blame the landlord who's stuck with rent control and therefore doesn't invest in fixing it up, not the hotel). If you're traveling with a companion, one of you can watch the bags over a cup of coffee while the other runs around.

Ask to see the room before accepting. Then the receptionist knows the room must pass your inspection. He'll have to earn your business. Notice the bellhop is given two keys. You asked for only one room. He's instructed to show the room that's harder to rent first. It's only natural for the hotel receptionist to try to unload the most difficult-to-sell room on the easiest-to-please traveler. Somebody has to sleep in it. If you ask to see both rooms, you'll get the better one. When you check out a room, point out anything that deserves displeasure. The price may come down, or they may show you a better room. Think about heat and noise. Some towns never quiet down. I'll climb a few stairs to reach cheaper rooms higher off the noisy road. A room in back may lack a view, but at least you'll sleep in peace.

Consider hotel runners. As you step off the bus or train, you'll sometimes be met by hotel and B&B runners wielding pictures of their rooms for rent. My gut reaction is to steer clear, but these people are usually just hardworking entrepreneurs who lack the location or write-up in

a popular guidebook that can make life easy for a small hotel or B&B owner. If you like the guy and what he promises, and his rooms aren't too far away, follow him to take a look. You are obliged only to inspect the room. If it's good, take it. If it's not, leave. You're probably near other budget accommodations anyway. Before setting out, establish the location very clearly, as some of these people have good places located miserably far out of town. Especially in Eastern Europe, room hawkers might

not be affiliated with a hotel at all; they're simply renting out vacant rooms in their own homes. If nothing else, taking the room for a night is an easy way to buy more time to seek out an even better option for the remainder of your stay.

Use room-finding services only if necessary. Popular tourist cities usually have a room-finding service at the train station or tourist information office. They have a listing of that town's "acceptable" available accommodations. For a fee of a few dollars, they'll get you a room in the price range and neighborhood of your choice. Especially in a big city, the service can be worth the price to avoid the search on foot.

But I generally avoid room-finding services unless I have no listings or information of my own. Their hotel lists normally make no judgments about quality, so what you get is potluck. The stakes are too high for this to be acceptable. Remember the exception: In certain northern European cities—such as Brussels and some Scandinavian capitals—room-booking services can sometimes land you a deeply discounted room in an upscale business-class hotel.

Since most room-finding services profit from taking a "deposit" that they pocket, hotel managers may tell the room-finding service they're full when they aren't. These places know they'll fill up with travelers coming direct, allowing the hotelier to keep 100 percent of the room cost.

In recent years, many tourist information offices have lost their government funding and are now privately owned. This creates the absurdity of a profit-seeking tourist information "service." Their previously reliable advice is now colored with a need to make a kickback. Some room-finding services work for a group of supporting hotels. Only if you insist will you get information on cheap sleeping options such as dormitories or hostels. And beware: Many offices labeled "tourist information" are just travel agencies and room-booking services in disguise.

Follow taxi tips. A great way to find a place in a tough situation is to let a cabbie take you to his favorite hotel. They are experts.

Let hotel managers help. Have your current hotelier call ahead to make a reservation at your next destination. If you're in a town and having trouble finding a room, remember that nobody knows the hotel scene better than hotel managers do. If one place doesn't have a vacant room, the manager often has a list of neighborhood accommodations or will even telephone a friend's place around the corner. If the hotel is too expensive, there's nothing wrong with asking where you can find a budget place. The priciest hotels have the best city maps (free, often with other hotels listed) and an English-speaking staff who can give advice to the polite traveler in search of a cheap room. I find hotel receptionists to be understanding and helpful.

Leave the trouble zone. If the room situation is impossible, don't struggle—just leave. An hour by car, train, or bus from the most miserable hotel situation anywhere in Europe is a town—Dullsdorf or Nothingston—with the

Ask your friend who runs today's hotel to call tomorrow's hotel to make you a reservation in the native language.

Dullsdorf Gasthaus or the Nothingston Inn just across the street from the station or right on the main square. It's not full—never has been, never will be. There's a guy sleeping behind the reception desk. Drop in at 11:00 p.m., ask for 14 beds, and he'll say, "Take the second and third floors—the keys are in the doors." It always works. Oktoberfest, Cannes Film Festival, St-Tropez Running of the Girls, Easter at Lourdes—your bed awaits in nearby Dullsdorf. If you anticipate trouble finding a room, consider staying at the last train stop before the crowded city.

Types of Accommodations

Hotels

I normally stay in a hotel. But rather than the predictable cookie-cutter comfort of a modern chain hotel, I prefer a small, independently owned hotel in the center of town. Perhaps the single most important factor for me in selecting a hotel—assuming it's in my price range—is location. I also count on character. Part of the fun of travel is enjoying a friendly and characteristic hotel in an exciting destination.

Room Types and Costs: Most European hotels have lots of doubles and a few singles, triples, and quads. Traveling alone can be expensive, especially when staying in older hotels, where singles (except for the rare closet-type room that fits only one twin bed) are simply doubles used by one person—so they cost about the same as a double. Most hotels offer family deals, which means that parents with young children can easily get a room with an extra child's bed or a discount for larger rooms. Teenagers are generally charged as adults, while kids under age five sleep almost free. Hotels cannot legally allow more people in the room than are shown on their price list. Hotels often charge a daily room tax of about €1-2 per person per day. Some hotels include it in the price list, but most add it to your bill.

Room prices vary within each hotel depending on size and whether the room has a tub or a shower, and twin beds or a double bed. A room with a bathtub costs €10-15 more than a room with a shower and is generally larger. Hotels are inclined to give you a room with a tub because they often have more rooms with tubs than with showers; be sure to specify if you have a preference.

A room with a European double bed (which is smaller than an American queen) is usually cheaper than one with twins, though twin rooms tend to be larger. If you want any room for two but you say "double," they'll think you'll only take a double bed. To keep all my options open (twin and double), I ask for "a room for two people." On the other hand, it can also help to specify "one big bed for two people" if you want the cost benefit of a double bed. (Most hoteliers understand "double bed" in English, but here's some local lingo: *französische Liege* in German, *un lit de cent-soixante* in French, *matrimoniale* in Italian, and *matrimonial* in Spanish). At many hotels—especially in the north and in Eastern Europe—a "double bed" is two twin beds pushed together, sometimes sheeted as one big bed.

A triple comes with a double or queen-size bed plus a sliver-sized single (or sometimes with three singles). Quad rooms usually have two double beds.

Breakfast: Hotels generally offer some kind of breakfast, usually served from about 7:30 to 10:00 a.m. in the breakfast room near the front desk. Continental breakfast is usually coffee, tea, or hot chocolate and a roll that's firmer than your mattress. Breakfasts in Eastern Europe and northern countries can be a bit heartier, with fruit, yogurt, cereal, and more. (For details, see page 374.) Breakfast may or may not be included in room rates: Pay attention when comparing prices between hotels. This per-person charge can add up, particularly for families. While hotels hope you'll buy their breakfast, it's optional unless otherwise noted; to save money, head to a nearby bakery or café instead.

Budget Hotels: What's a Cheap Room?

Europe has many traditional old hotels—dingy, a bit run-down, central, friendly, safe, and government-regulated, offering good-enough-for-the-European, good-enough-for-me beds. In a typical budget European hotel, a double room costs an average of $100 a night. You'll pay about

$80 at a pension in Madrid, $90 at a simple guest house in rural Germany or a B&B on the Croatian coast, and $130 for a two-star hotel in Paris or a private room in a Bergen pension. This is hard-core Europe: fun, cheap, and easy to find, particularly in Italy, France, Spain, Portugal, and Greece.

A typical budget hotel room: tidy, small, affordable

A typical room in an old-fashioned, low-end hotel has a simple bed (occasionally a springy cot, so always test it out before accepting the room); a rickety, old, wooden (or new, plastic) chair and table; a freestanding closet; a small window; old wallpaper; a good sink under a fluorescent light; a mysterious bidet; a view of another similar room across a tall, thin interior courtyard; peeling plaster; and a tiled or wood floor. The light fixtures are very simple, often with a weak ceiling light. Naked fluorescent is common in the south.

1977: It slowly dawns on Rick that cheap beds aren't always good beds.

While non-smoking places are increasingly common (and, in many countries, legally mandated), a lot of cheap rooms still come with ashtrays. You might have a TV, but likely not a telephone. While more and more European hotels are squeezing boat-type prefab showers and toilets into their rooms, the cheapest rooms still offer only a toilet and shower or tub down the hall, which you share with a handful of other rooms.

You'll climb lots of stairs, as a hotel's lack of an elevator is often the only reason it can't raise its prices. You'll be given a front-door key because the desk is not staffed all night. At some hotels, you'll need to press a button to be buzzed into the lobby.

Cheap hotels usually have clean-enough but depressing shower rooms, with hot water normally free and constant (but, in very rare cases, available only through a coin-op meter or at certain hours). The WC has toilet paper, but might have a missing, cracked, or broken lid. At a few hotels, you might be charged $3-5 for a towel and a key to the shower room. The cheapest hotels are run by and filled with people from the Two-Thirds World.

I want to stress that there are places I find unacceptable. I don't mind dingy wallpaper, stairs, and a bathroom down the hall, but I won't compromise when it comes to safety and being able to get a decent night's sleep.

The hotel I'm describing may be appalling to many Americans; to others, it's charming, colorful, or funky. To me, "funky" means spirited and full of character(s): a caged bird in the TV room, grandchildren in the backyard, a dog sleeping in the hall, no uniforms, singing maids, a night-shift man tearing breakfast napkins in two so they'll go further, a handwritten neighborhood history lesson on the wall, different furniture in each room, and a willingness to buck the system when the tourist board starts requiring shoeshine machines in the hallways. An extra $40-50 per night will buy you into cheerier wallpaper and less funkiness.

Unfortunately, cheap hotels are becoming an endangered species. As Europe becomes more affluent, land in big cities is becoming so expensive that cheap hotels can't survive and are bought out, gutted, and turned into modern hotels. More and more Europeans are expecting what were once considered "American" standards of plumbing and comfort. A great value is often a hardworking family-run place that structurally can't fit showers in every room or an elevator up its spiral staircase. Prices are regulated, and regardless of how comfy and charming it is, with no elevator and a lousy shower-to-room ratio, it is—and will remain—a cheap hotel.

Big, Good-Value, Modern Chains

More and more hotel chains—offering cheap or moderately priced rooms—are springing up throughout Europe. Hotels that allow up to four people in a room are great for families. You won't find character at chain hotels, but you'll get predictable, Motel 6-type comfort. The huge Accor chain offers a range of options, from the cheap Formule 1 Hotels (mostly in France, www.hotelformule1.com) to the mid-range Ibis Hotels (sterile, throughout Europe, www.ibishotel.com) to the pricier, cushier Mercure and Novotel Hotels (for all Accor Hotels, see www.accorhotels.com). Britain has Travelodge (www.travelodge.co.uk), Premier Inn (www.premierinn.com), Holiday Inn Express (www.hi express.co.uk, a Holiday Inn lite with cheaper prices and no restaurant),

SLEEPING

and Jurys Inn (www.jurysinn.com, also found throughout Ireland). The easyHotel chain—based on the pay-as-you-go business model of their sister airline, easyJet—rents cheap and extremely basic rooms in major European cities, including London, Berlin, Zürich, and Budapest (www .easyhotel.com).

Finding a Hotel

Your hotel, and the neighborhood it inhabits, can color your travel experience. Landing in the right place merits a little research.

Guidebooks: A trusted guidebook remains the best place to start your search for a great hotel. Professional guidebook writers take their jobs seriously, offering detailed hotel reviews and their best advice on the sleeping scene. Find and use a guidebook whose travel philosophy matches yours. (For a rundown of various guidebooks, see page 21.) Get the most current edition possible—but even with the newest editions, don't be surprised if rates have increased slightly since the book was published.

Hotel Websites: If a guidebook's write-up of a particular hotel appeals to you, visit the hotel website to glean additional information, check prices, and view photos of the rooms. Some hotels (especially chain or business hotels) offer discounts only if you book on their website. Here are some tips for getting the best deal online: Midweek prices are generally higher than weekend rates, and Sunday nights can be shockingly cheap. The rates for a particular room for a specific date can change from day to day or week to week (like airline tickets), making it difficult to know when to book. On the hotel's online reservation form, punch in the dates you're considering to see what the going rate is. Look for special offers. For the best deals, book at least three weeks in advance, prepay in full, and hope you don't have to change your plans (since promotional rates are often nonrefundable).

Hotel-Booking Websites: The big hotel-booking websites, such as Travelocity.com, Expedia.com, Booking.com, and Venere.com, can provide a wealth of information about the types of hotels available and the range of prices. But what you won't easily find on these sites are links to individual hotels—that's because the big guys want you to book through them (or their partners) for a fee. Using a booking service costs the hotel about 20 percent and logically closes the door on special deals. Instead, once you've identified a promising option, do a Google search to find the hotel's own website. You'll get more complete information, and you may save money by booking direct.

Traveler Reviews: To read reviews from other travelers, check sites such as Tripadvisor.com. Generally the more individual reviews a place has, the more reliable the information. But don't trust everything you read (for more on TripAdvisor and other review websites—and their pitfalls—see page 32). The Travel Forum at www.ricksteves.com/forums is another option.

Other Online Sources: Sites such as Mobissimo.com and Hotelscombined.com compile prices from travel agencies, consolidators, and hotel websites. (If you find a deal you like, still go to the hotel's website to book direct.) If your travel dates are flexible, consider the deep discounts available on sites such as www.priceline.com, www.euro cheapo.com, and www.ratestogo.com. Also consider the "air plus hotel" packages described on page 89.

Hotel Tips

This section covers what you can expect—and what may be unexpected—when it comes to European hotels. Many of these tips also apply to the other types of accommodations described later in this chapter.

Check-in: When you check in at a hotel, with or without an advance reservation, establish the complete and final price of your room. Know what's included and what taxes and other charges (breakfast, extra fee for air-conditioning) will be added. More than once, when checking out, I've been given a bill that was double what I expected. Dinners were required, and I was billed whether I ate them or not, or so I was told—in very clear Italian.

At check-in, hotels may take your passport for the night so they can register you with the police. This is normal. Hotels throughout Europe must do this paperwork for foreign guests, and busy receptionists like to gather passports and register them all at the same time when things are quiet. Although it's unreasonable to expect a receptionist to drop whatever he or she is doing to register me immediately, I politely ask if I can pick up my passport in two hours. I just don't like having my passport in the hotel lobby's top drawer all night long.

Reconfirm how long you intend to stay when you check in. If you think you may want to stay a night or two longer than your reservation allows, discuss it with the receptionist up front. Don't assume your room is yours indefinitely once you're in.

Your Room: In a typical room, you'll find a TV and phone, and you'll usually have either wired Internet access or Wi-Fi. To turn on your TV, press the channel-up or channel-down button on the remote. If it still doesn't work, see if there's a power button on the TV itself, then press the up or down button again.

The  to Keys

Tourists spend hours fumbling with old skeleton keys in rickety hotel doors. The haphazard, nothing-square construction of old hotels means the keys need babying. Don't push them in all the way. Lift the door in or up. Try a little in, quarter turn, and farther in for full turn. Always turn the top of the key away from the door frame to open it. Some locks take two key revolutions to open. Leave the key at the desk before leaving for the day. I've never had my room broken into in Europe. Confirm closing time. Some hotels lock up after their restaurant closes, after midnight, or during their weekly "quiet day" and expect you to keep the key to the outside door with you to get in after hours.

Plastic key cards (the size of a credit card) are becoming standard at many European hotels. If there's no slot to insert the card into, try simply touching the card to your door's keypad. Once inside the room, you may have to insert your card into a slot near the door to turn on the lights. This green measure is intended to prevent potentially energy-wasting guests from leaving the lights on when they're not in the room.

As Europe gets hotter, more hotels are offering rooms with air-conditioning. (But be aware that regulations may prohibit turning on the air-conditioning between October and May.) Most A/C units come

An A/C remote lets you cool off the room without even getting out of bed.

with a remote control, similar to one for a TV. The various remotes have basically the same features, including: a fan icon (click to toggle through wind power), louver icon (click for steady air flow or waves), sunshine and snowflake icons (generally just cold or hot is possible: cool in summer, heat in winter), two clock settings (to determine how many hours the air-conditioning will stay on

French hotels sometimes come with Lincoln Log pillows.

before turning off, or stay off before turning on), and temperature control (20 degrees Celsius is comfortable).

Be prepared for regional differences in bedding. In France, some hotel beds have irregular pillows (shaped like a wedge or a log). To get an American-style pillow or extra blankets, look in the closet or ask at the desk. In alpine countries and in northern Europe, many hotels use covered duvets instead of a top sheet; don't be confused if your top sheet is "missing."

For details on hotel-room bathrooms, see page 415.

Hotel Help: In the lobby, there's nearly always a lounge with a TV, a phone, and a clerk at the desk who can be a great help and source of advice. Hotels are in the business of accommodating people. If you need another blanket or an electrical adapter, just ask. Hoteliers can point you to the nearest Internet café, launderette, grocery store, restaurant, or show. They'll call a taxi for you, make restaurant reservations, telephone your next hotel, or give you driving instructions for your departure.

Pick up the hotel's business card. In the most confusing cities, the cards come with a little map. Even the best pathfinders can get lost in a big city, and not knowing where your hotel is can be scary. With the card, you can hop into a cab and be home in minutes. Most hotels give out free city maps.

Many hoteliers can book bus tours for you (though they usually get a commission, so they might be biased in their recommendation). In Florence, hoteliers can make museum reservations for the Uffizi Gallery and for Michelangelo's *David*; ask when you book your room. If you arrive in town early or need to leave late, any good hotel will store your bag for you (without charge) while you sightsee.

Hotel Hassles: Even at the best hotel, things can go awry. You may be on your dream trip, but you're still in the real world. Take a deep breath, and remember that things go wrong at home, too. If you state your concern to your hotelier politely, you'll more likely be dealt with kindly.

When you enter a hotel room for the first time, survey it for problems. Is the bathroom dirty and moldy? Is the window latch broken and unsafe? Are you next to a noisy elevator? Is the room too small? If the room you're shown doesn't meet your standards, ask to see a different one. It's easier to change rooms before you've settled in.

It can be disappointing to arrive at a hotel and find that your room is in a less desirable annex or in a partner hotel. If you feel the hotel has misrepresented its offer, it can help (though it's not essential) to show them a copy of their confirmation email. You don't need to stay.

Just as it happens at your house, hotels experience mechanical breakdowns from time to time. Sinks get clogged, hot water turns cold, toilets gurgle and smell. The air-conditioning dies when you need it most. The Wi-Fi doesn't work. The elevator refuses to budge. Report your concerns calmly at the front desk. For more complicated problems, don't expect instant results. In the rare case that something is stolen from your room, talk to the hotelier (see page 328 for tips on safeguarding your hotel-room belongings).

Occasionally travelers encounter bedbugs—tiny blood-sucking insects that live in bedding and come out at night. Bedbugs may be visible in the seams of the mattress, but often the first signs of trouble are mysterious, itchy welts (similar to mosquito bites) on your legs and arms. These critters are a nuisance, but they don't spread disease. Bedbugs can show up even at fine hotels, brought in by the last guest. Don't automatically assume that the hotel is overrun with them. Report the problem, and see how it's dealt with. Changing rooms should be enough.

Mosquitoes can also be pests. In warm climates, make sure there's a window screen; if there isn't, think twice about leaving your window open all day for ventilation. Insect repellant can help. Warning: If you leave your window open and forget to close it when darkness falls, the light of your room can attract a vast swarm of bugs.

Europe seems to excel in thin-walled rooms, narrow streets that amplify traffic noise, and people who party until the wee hours in formerly romantic piazzas. I always consider these problems before settling into a room. If you suspect night noise will be a problem, ask for a room in the back or on an upper floor. Some travelers customarily ask for a quiet room when they book or reconfirm their reservation; if you wait to ask until you arrive, the quietest rooms might already be occupied. On the other hand, if you'd happily put up with some street noise to look out onto a square, be sure to ask for a view (which might cost extra). If you're a light sleeper, skip the view (and bring earplugs, too).

"Too many stairs!" is a common complaint. In general, European hotels have more stairs and fewer elevators than we're used to. Think of it as exercise, and pack light. On the bright side, higher floors generally have better views and less street noise than lower ones. If you must have an elevator or ground-floor room, confirm that one is available when you book. And be aware that European hotel elevators can be miniscule.

If you're trying to dial out from your room but the phone won't work, try calling (or visiting) the reception desk. They might have to open up an outside line for you on the switchboard, or they can tell you if you have to dial an access number first. If the hotel has Wi-Fi, ask whether you need to pay to use it, and request the network name and password. (For a rundown on telephones and Internet access, see the Phones and Technology chapter.)

If you're in southern Europe and having trouble getting a problem solved at your hotel, ask to see the complaint book, which the hotelier is legally required to show you on request. Sometimes even just asking to see the complaint book will inspire the hotelier to see that your problem is fixed. If you've had a good experience, jot a friendly note in the hotel's guest book; conscientious hoteliers love to show these off to arriving guests.

Unfriendly staff can taint your stay, but don't let them ruin your trip. If you have difficulties to bring up, keep checking to see if a sympathetic or more capable staff member comes on shift, or just be persistent (kind but firm) with whomever you have to deal with. Generally the hotel staff doesn't like to have complainers overheard by other customers, so it can be effective to state your problems clearly and reasonably with witnesses around. The staff may accommodate you just to shut you up.

Above all, keep a positive attitude. After all, you're on vacation. If your hotel is a disappointment, spend more time out enjoying the city you came to see.

Checkout: When you pay for your room is up to the hotel and you (normally I pay upon departure). If surprise charges pop up on your bill, ask the hotelier to explain each item you're not sure about. Some charges are legitimate; for example, in some touristy areas, hotels charge a per-day tax that everyone has to pay. To avoid preventable charges, don't use the hotel-room phone to make international calls unless you have an international calling card (described on page 250) and even then, ask first to be sure the hotel won't charge you to dial that "toll-free" access number.

Some hoteliers have credit-card readers that mysteriously break when you want to check out, requiring you to pay in cash. Or you might be charged extra if you want to pay with your credit card. If you settle up your bill the night before you leave—or even better, the day before, when there's a manager present—you'll have time to discuss and address any points of contention.

SLEEPING

Bed & Breakfasts

Between hotels and hostels in price and style is a special class of accommodations: bed-and-breakfasts (B&Bs). These are small, warm, and family-run, and offer a personal touch at a reasonable price. They are the next best thing to staying with a family, and even if hotels weren't more expensive, this budget alternative can be your best bet.

Don't confuse European bed-and-breakfasts with their rich cousins in America. B&Bs in the US are usually frilly, fancy places, very cozy and colorful, but as expensive as hotels. In a

Bed-and-breakfasts offer double the cultural experience for half the price of a hotel.

European B&B, rather than seven pillows and a basket of jams, you get a warm welcome and a good price.

Each country in Europe has these friendly accommodations in varying degrees of abundance, facilities, and service. While we commonly refer to them as bed-and-breakfasts, some include breakfast and some don't. They have different names from country to country, but all have one thing in common: They satisfy the need for a place to stay that gives you the privacy of a hotel and the comforts of home at a price you can afford.

While information on more established places is available in many budget-travel guidebooks, the best leads are often found locally, through

tourist information offices, or even from the man waiting for his bus or selling apples. Especially in the British Isles, each B&B host has a network of favorites and can happily set you up in a good B&B at your next stop.

Many times, the information is brought to you. I'll never forget struggling off the plane on my arrival in Santorini. Fifteen women were begging me to spend the

A special bonus when enjoying Britain's great B&Bs: You get your own temporary mother.

night. Thrilled, I made a snap decision and followed the most attractive offer to a very nice budget accommodation.

The "part of the family" element of a B&B stay is determined entirely by you. Chatty friendliness is not forced on guests. Depending on my mood and workload, I am often very businesslike and private during my stay. On other occasions, I join the children in the barn for the sheep-shearing festivities.

B&Bs by Region

The British Isles: Britain's B&Bs are the best of all. As the name indicates, a breakfast comes with the bed, and (except in London) this is no ordinary breakfast. Most B&B owners take pride in their breakfasts. Their guests sit down to an

In most British towns, B&Bs line up along the same street—find one, and you've found a dozen.

elegant and very British table setting and feast on cereal, juice, bacon, sausage, eggs, broiled tomatoes, mushrooms, toast, marmalade, and coffee or tea. While you are finishing your coffee, the landlady (who by

Never judge a B&B by its name. Like most in Britain, this one is non-smoking and comes with numerous pleasant extras.

this time is probably on very friendly terms with you) may present you with her guest book, inviting you to make an entry and pointing out others from your state who have stayed in her house. Your hostess will sometimes cook you a simple dinner for a good price, and if you have time to chat, you may get in on an evening social hour. When you bid her farewell and thank her for the good sleep and full stomach, it's often difficult to get away. Determined to fill you with as much information as food, she wants you to have the best day of sightseeing possible.

If you're going to the normal tourist stops, your guidebook will list some good B&Bs. If you're venturing off the

SLEEPING

beaten British path, you don't need (or want) a listing. The small towns and countryside are littered with places whose quality varies only in degrees of wonderful. I try not to choose a B&B until I have checked out three. Styles and atmosphere vary from house to house, and besides, I enjoy looking through European homes.

Britain rates its B&Bs using a diamond system (1-5) that considers cleanliness, furnishings, and decor. But diamond definitions are pretty squishy. Few B&Bs make a big deal of the ratings, and fewer tourists even know the system exists.

Ireland has essentially the same system of B&Bs. They are less expensive than England's and if anything, even more "homely" (cozy). You can expect a big breakfast and comfortable room, often within an easy walk of the town center.

Germany, Switzerland, and Austria: Look for *Zimmer Frei* or *Privatzimmer.* These are very common in areas popular with travelers (such as Austria's Salzkammergut Lake District and Germany's Rhine, the Romantic Road region, and southern Bavaria). Signs will clearly indicate whether rooms are available (green) or not (orange). Especially in Austria, one-night stays are discouraged. Most *Privatzimmer* cost about $40 per person and include a hearty continental breakfast. *Pensions, Gasthauses,* and *Gasthöfe* are similarly priced small, family-run hotels. Don't confuse *Privatzimmer* with *Ferienwohnung,* which is a self-catering apartment rented out by the week or fortnight.

France: The French have a growing network of *chambres d'hôte* (CH) where residents, mainly in the countryside and in small towns, rent double rooms for about the price of a cheap hotel ($75-120), but with breakfast included. Some CHs post *chambre* signs in their windows, but most are listed only through tourist information offices. While your hosts likely won't speak English, they will almost always be enthusiastic and happy to share their home.

Italy: Check out Italy's good alternatives to its expensive hotels— *albergo, locanda,* and *pensione.* (While these are technically all bunched together now in a hotel system with star ratings, you'll still find these traditional names to be synonymous with simple, budget beds.) Private rooms, signposted as *camere libere* or *affitta camere,* are fairly common in Italy's small towns. Small-town bars are plugged into the B&B grapevine. Breakfasts are usually included, and you'll sometimes get a kitchenette in the room. Drivers can try *agriturismi,* rooms in farmhouses in the countryside. Weeklong stays are preferred in July and August, but shorter stays are possible off-season. For a sampling, visit www .agriturismoitaly.it or do an Internet search for *agriturismo.*

Private Rooms to Rent

Private rooms throughout Europe can cost as little as $40-60 per person, which sometimes includes breakfast and sometimes does not—confirm when you reserve. (For more on staying in European homes, see page 224.)

In...	Look for...
Great Britain & Ireland	bed-and-breakfast
Norway/Sweden	*rom* or *rum*
Denmark	*værelser*
Germany/Switzerland/Austria	*Zimmer*
France	*chambre (d'hôte)*
Italy	*(affitta) camere*
Spain	*casa particular*
Portugal	*quarto*
Greece	*dhomatia*
Croatia/Slovenia	*sobe*
Poland	*pokoje*
Eastern Europe	*Zimmer* or "rooms"

Scandinavia: These usually luxurious B&Bs—called *rom, hus rum,* or, in Denmark, *værelser*—cost about $40-60 per person. By Scandinavian standards, these are incredibly cheap (well, not so incredibly, when you figure it's a common way for the most heavily taxed people in Europe to make a little money under the table). Unfortunately, many Scandinavian B&Bs are advertised only through the tourist information offices, which very often keep them a secret until all the hotels are full. If your

Bed-and-breakfast travelers scramble at the breakfast table.

Scandiavian B&B is serving breakfast, eat it. Even at $15, it's a deal by local standards and can serve as your best big meal of the day. Some hosts provide a roll of foil so you can pack up a lunch from the breakfast spread. If that sounds like a good idea, just ask.

Spain and Portugal: Travelers get an intimate peek into their small-town, whitewashed worlds by renting *camas* and *casas particulares* in Spain and *quartos* in Portugal. In rural Iberia, wherever there's tourism, you'll find these budget accommodations. Breakfast is rarely included. *Hostales* and *pensiones* are easy to find, inexpensive, and, when chosen properly, a fun part of the Spanish cultural experience. These places are often family-owned, and may or may not have amenities like private bathrooms and air-conditioning. Don't confuse a *hostal* with a hostel. A *hostal* is an inexpensive hotel, not a hostel with bunks in dorms.

Greece: You'll find many $60-per-room *dhomatia*. Especially in touristy coastal and island towns, hardworking entrepreneurs will meet planes, ferries, and buses as they come into town at any hour. In Greek villages with no hotels, ask for *dhomatia* at the town *taverna*. Forget breakfast.

Croatia and Slovenia: In these countries—where mass tourism and overpriced resort hotels reign—private rooms are often the best deal in town (no breakfast). You'll notice

Guidebook listings will lead you to friendly Croatian sobe hosts eager to invite you into their homes.

signs advertising *sobe* (rooms) everywhere you look, or you can book one through a travel agency (10-30 percent extra). You'll generally pay extra if you stay less than three nights. Along the Dalmatian Coast, *sobe* skimmers meet every arriving ferry, targeting backpackers and eager to whisk you away to see their room. In the Slovenian countryside, look for tourist farms *(turistične kmetije)*, where you can sleep in a family's farmhouse for remarkably low prices. Croatia's Istria region has similar *agroturizam*s.

Apartment Rentals

Whether you're in a city or the countryside, renting an apartment, house, or villa can be a fun and cost-effective way to delve into Europe. A short-term rental is a great alternative to a hotel, especially if you plan to settle in one location for several nights. Options run the gamut, from French *gîtes* to Tuscan villas to big-city apartments in the heart of town. Prices vary depending on the season, size, location, and quality of the accommodation. For stays longer than a few days, you can usually find a rental that's comparable to—or even cheaper—than a hotel room with similar amenities.

Apartments and houses for rent are generally roomier than hotel rooms and come with kitchens and common areas to gather in; some have laundry facilities. Rentals can be especially cost-effective for groups. Two couples traveling together can share a two-bedroom apartment, which often ends up being less expensive than a pair of hotel rooms. Groups of backpackers find that splitting the price of a cheap apartment can cost less than paying for several bunks at a youth hostel. You can further your savings by cooking your own meals instead of going out. If you enjoy eating in restaurants, consider stocking your kitchen with breakfast food or picnic-lunch supplies and saving your money for nice dinners out.

For families, an apartment is a huge benefit. Kitchens make it easier and cheaper to dine in and feed picky eaters. Laundry machines let you do the family wash. With more than one room, parents of younger children can hang out and chat while their kids slumber (as opposed to being trapped in a hotel room with the lights out at 8 p.m.). If you have teenagers, you can leave them to eat dinner in the apartment while you go out to a restaurant—they'll feel independent (perhaps enjoying a little screen time without parents), and you'll get a night on the town with your partner.

In general, I find that if you're staying somewhere for four nights or longer, it's worth considering an apartment or rental house. Three nights is borderline. To me, anything less than that isn't worth the extra effort involved in settling into an apartment (arranging key pickup, buying groceries, figuring out the neighborhood without the help of a hotelier, etc.). Plus, many apartments require minimum stays—typically three to seven nights (note that you'll likely pay more per night if staying less than a week, and you can sometimes negotiate better deals if renting for longer). If you can work it into your itinerary, consider settling in a rental for a full week. This gives you an opportunity to really get to know the town and take advantage of day-trip possibilities. (Good home-base cities are also ideal apartment-rental cities—see the list on page 47.)

The rental route isn't for everyone. First off, you're generally on your own. While the apartment owner or manager might offer some basic assistance, don't expect them to provide all the services of a hotel reception desk. If you like fresh towels and daily sheet changes, stay in a hotel. Your apartment likely won't be serviced or cleaned during a one-week stay unless you pay extra (though places generally have cleaning supplies—ask about this when you check in). Remember that the lack of these services is what keeps rentals affordable.

Finding an Apartment

Sometimes you'll deal directly with the apartment owner; in other cases, you might work with an agency that maintains a network of rentals. (Agencies may actually own the apartments, or they can act as a go-between.)

Direct-Booking Websites: Websites such as HomeAway.com and its sister site VRBO.com let you correspond directly with European property owners or managers. Owners pay a fee to list their places and include photos and loads of other information (number of bedrooms and bathrooms, amenities, etc.) to help you make your decision. VRBO lists many properties, but their results appear in a long list that can be overwhelming to sort through. HomeAway is more user-friendly, letting you narrow down a search to number of bedrooms or price range. GreatRentals.com, also part of the HomeAway network, is worth a peek as well.

Sites such as Roomorama.com and Airbnb.com list houses and apartments, as well as rooms in someone's pad (for more on using Airbnb to stay in someone's home, see page 225). Both websites charge a booking fee (from 6-12 percent) but alleviate worries about fraud by collecting payment when you book, then waiting until you check in to release the funds to owners. Airbnb leans more toward budget listings while Roomorama tends to have nicer places, many of which are handled by management companies.

Once you've found some options that look appealing, contact the owner for more information. Most sites provide a form for entering your contact info, travel dates, and number of people. Your details are sent to the owner, who should respond directly to you within a few days to let you know whether the place is available and how much it will cost.

These sites have their pros and cons. Booking direct takes a little more effort, but cutting out the middleman also decreases cost and bureaucracy. Because you're working directly with the owner, you'll probably get a slightly better deal than if you go through an agency, which takes a commission. On the flip side, these sites require a little more legwork. You have to filter through a lot of properties, and you'll probably have a lot of back-and-forth with several owners about availability, amenities, policies, and other info.

Rental Agencies: If combing through listings and contacting homeowners sounds like too much effort, consider going through a rental agency. Using an agency is convenient, the places they list have been pre-screened, and their staff will work with you to find an appropriate accommodation. For instance, if you have a larger family or you're not sure what neighborhood you want to be in, it might be easier to talk to a rental agency, convey your needs, and see what they come up with. The downside is that you'll pay more for the rental to cover the agency's costs.

Rental agencies such as Interhome.us and the more upscale Rentavilla.com list places all over Europe. Other agencies concentrate on a certain region or city. For example, Prague-stay.com focuses on apartments in Prague while France: Homestyle (www.francehomestyle .com) lists Parisian apartments and country houses in the Loire. To find a rental in a specific region, simply search for "vacation rental" or "holiday rental" and the town you're interested in, then browse your options.

Renting an Apartment

Before you commit to a rental, be clear on the details. Check out the location on a map so you know how convenient—or inconvenient—it is. Ask about the neighborhood and what's nearby. If you plan on driving, find out about parking. If you have kids, ask if there are playgrounds or parks nearby. Many European apartments involve some climbing; confirm what floor the apartment is on and whether the building has an elevator. If the owner or agency is anything but helpful, skip to the next place on your list.

When you make a reservation, you'll probably have to pay a deposit, which can range from 10 to 50 percent of the rental cost. Many places require you to pay the entire balance before your trip (such as 30 days prior to your stay), or upon arrival. Ideally the owner will accept credit cards (which offer some fraud protection), but some places will add a credit-card fee. And some rentals don't accept credit cards and will instead ask you to make your deposit securely online via PayPal, or to send a personal check.

Be warned: You're renting a place sight unseen, so check for scams before sending money. You can do this by searching online for the lister's name, address, or email to see if anything suspicious pops up. For a fee, VRBO, HomeAway, and GreatRentals offer a rental guarantee that protects you for up to $10,000 if you're the victim of fraud, or if the owner misrepresented the property (for example, if your 200-square-foot studio facing a dumpster looks nothing like the photos of the spacious two-bedroom apartment with "lovely garden views" you thought you were renting). The fee for the guarantee starts at $39 and depends on the price of the rental.

Most places will provide you with a rental agreement (either via email or a website), which usually includes the house rules and the cancellation policy. Read the document carefully and clear up any questions you have with the owner or agency. Rentals tend to have much more rigid cancellation policies than hotels (30 days is common, but it can be longer), even in circumstances beyond your control. For example, when the volcano erupted in Iceland in 2010, one of my staffers had to delay her trip to Spain by a few weeks. While the apartment she had booked in Madrid was able to accommodate her new itinerary, she was still charged for the original dates (even though she ended up staying two fewer nights). Some homeowners might be more lenient and let you out of your contract in an emergency. It's always worth asking.

If you think your plans might change, consider staying in a hotel, where you can usually cancel just a few days beforehand without paying a penalty. You can also protect your investment by purchasing trip-cancellation insurance (see page 61).

Upon Arrival

Apartments, especially those in big cities, can be tricky to find. Unlike hotels, you can't expect taxi drivers and people on the street to be able to point you in the right direction. Make sure you nail down directions to the rental prior to your arrival.

You'll also need to arrange a time and place to meet the property owner or manager and pick up the keys. That person will show you around the rental and may be able to give you tips about the neighborhood (grocery stores, pharmacies, and good places to eat). But once they leave, you probably won't see them again.

On departure, it's generally expected that you leave the place clean and in good condition. If you don't, you may lose some or all of your security deposit. Some places may ask you to do minimal cleaning before you leave (for instance, stripping off bed linens or emptying the fridge).

Hostels

Europe's cheapest beds are in hostels. Several thousand hostels provide beds throughout Europe for $20-40 per night. Most hostels are set in good, easily accessible locations.

As Europe has grown more affluent, hostels have been remodeled to provide more plumbing and smaller rooms. Still, hostels are not hotels— not by a long shot. Many people hate hostels. Others love them and will be hostelers all their lives, regardless of their budgets. Hosteling is a philosophy. A hosteler trades service and privacy for a chance to live simply and communally with people from around the world.

For students, travelers on a budget, solo travelers, groups or families who can take a whole room, and those hoping to meet other travelers, hostels can be a great option.

Official Hostels vs. Independent Hostels

There are two different types of hostels: official and independent.

Official hostels belong to the same parent organization, Hostelling International, and share an online booking site (www.hihostels.com). They used to adhere to various rules (such as a 17:00 check-in, lockout during the day, and a curfew at night), but nowadays are more flexible. If you plan to spend at least six nights at official HI hostels, you'll save money if you buy a membership card before you go ($28/year for full benefits, free if you're under 18 and $18 if you're 55 or over, stripped-down $18 emembership does not include frills such as insurance and currency exchange; available at your local student-travel office, any HI hostel office, or Hostelling International; www.hiusa.org, tel. 301/495-1240). If you think you may not spend six nights at HI hostels, don't buy the card in advance. Nonmembers who want to stay at HI hostels can usually get an "international guest card" at their first hostel. You'll pay about $5 extra per night for a "welcome stamp" to stick to this card, and once you buy six welcome stamps, you become a member. As independent hostels become a more popular option, this "pay-as-you-go" system for official hostels makes sense for many travelers (rather than buying your membership up front).

Independent hostels tend to be more easygoing and colorful, run

Hosteling Terms

Dormitory: Group room with multiple beds, usually bunk beds, and lockers for storage. You'll pay to rent one bed and will sleep in a room shared with strangers.

Private/Family Room: Private rooms with one, two, three, or more beds. You'll pay to rent every bed in the room, which will be used only by you and your traveler partners.

Mixed Dorm: Dormitory open to both genders.

Shared Bathroom: You'll share a bathroom down the hall (like the locker room at the gym).

En Suite: The room has a private bathroom, not one down the hall. This can apply to either a dorm room or a private/family room.

by people who prefer to avoid the occasionally heavy-handed bureaucracy of HI. These non-HI hostels are looser and more casual, but not as predictably clean or organized as official hostels. Independent hostels don't require a membership card or charge extra for nonmembers, and generally have fewer rules. Many popular European destinations have wild and cheap student-run hostels that are popular with wild and cheap student travelers, but some independent hostels are tame and mature. Various sites promote independent hostels, including www.hostelz.com, www.hostels.com, and www.hostelbookers.com. There's also www.hostelworld.com, a hostel website geared for "flashpackers." These younger, tech-savvy travelers are basically 21st-century vagabonds with credit cards and iPhones.

If you're staying at a mix of both official and independent hostels—as most hostelers do—Let's Go guidebooks offer the best all-around listings (www.letsgo.com).

Hosteling Tips

Unless noted, these tips apply to both official and independent hostels.

A youth hostel is not limited to young people. You may assume hostels aren't for you because, by every standard, you're older than young. Well, many countries have dropped the word "youth" from their hostels, and for years Hostelling International has given "youths" over the age of 54 a discount on the membership card. Even the last holdout, the German state of Bavaria, has finally dropped its youths-only restriction. If you're alive, you're young enough to hostel anywhere in Europe (with the rare exception of some independent hostels that have age cutoffs of around 40). The average hosteler is 18-26 years old, but every year there are more seniors and families hosteling. As a reader wrote on my website: "My partner and I stayed in a 'youth' hostel for the first time by Lake Como and thought we'd be the oldest people there. Not so! At our table was a 60-ish couple from Sydney and a 79-year-old British woman who was backpacking alone through Europe. All three were a delight, but especially the backpacker, who said she stays in hostels for the evening company."

Cooking in the hostel members' kitchen, this traveler lives in Europe on $25 a day for his bed, plus the price of groceries.

Hostels provide "no frills" accommodations in clean dormitories. Hostels were originally for hikers and bikers, but that isn't the case these days—some newer hostels are downright plush. Still, expect humble conditions. At official hostels, the sexes are segregated, with 4 to 20 people packed in a room full of bunk beds. Many independent hostels have both segregated and mixed dorms. Hostels often have a few doubles for group leaders and couples, and rooms for families are increasingly common (and affordable). Strong, hot showers (a few with coin-op meters) are the norm, but some very rustic, off-the-beaten-path hostels (or mountain huts) might have no showers at all.

Bedding is usually included. Pillows and blankets are provided. Sheets are typically included in the cost, but occasionally you'll be asked to pay about $5 extra to rent them. Hostelers who are used to bringing their own sleep sack should check ahead before packing it. Concerned about bedbugs, many hostels now require you to use their linens even if you have your own.

Many hostels offer meals, meeting places, and information. A simple breakfast is often included in the price of your bed. Hearty, super-cheap meals are served at an extra cost, often in family-style settings. A typical dinner is fish sticks and mashed potatoes seasoned by conversation with new friends from Norway to New Zealand. The self-service kitchen, complete with utensils, pots, and pans, is a great budget aid that comes with most hostels. Larger hostels even have small grocery

SLEEPING

stores. International friendships rise with the bread in hostel kitchens.

The hostel's recreation and living rooms are my favorite. People gather, play games, tell stories, share information, read, write, and team up for future travels. Solo travelers find a family in every hostel and can always find a new travel partner; those with part-

Hostels: Meet, drink, and be merry.

ners do well to occasionally stay in a hostel to meet some new companions.

Most hostel lobbies are littered with brochures and posters about local tours, events, and public transportation. There's generally Wi-Fi or an Internet terminal.

Get to know your host. The people who live in and run hostels (sometimes called "wardens" in Britain) do their best to strictly enforce rules, quiet hours, and other regulations. Some are loose and laid-back, others are like Marine drill sergeants, but they all work toward the noble goal of enabling travelers to better appreciate and enjoy that town or region. While they are often overworked and harried, most hostel employees are fine people who enjoy a quiet cup of coffee with an American and are happy to give you some travel tips or recommend a special nearby hostel. Be sensitive to the many demands on their time, and never treat them like hotel servants.

One of Europe's hostels—$25 a night, your own kitchen, a million-dollar view of the Swiss Alps, and lots of friends. Note the worldwide triangular hostel symbol.

Hostels have drawbacks. Some hostels—especially official ones—have strict rules. Some lock up during the day (usually from 10:00 a.m. to 5:00 p.m.), and a few may have a curfew at night, when the doors are locked. Keep in mind that a curfew can be a big advantage—hostels that don't have curfews, especially in big cities, are more likely to have hostelers (often drunk and rowdy) returning at ungodly hours. The sounds you'll hear just after everyone's turned in remind me of summer camp—giggles, burps, jokes, and strange noises in many languages. Snoring is permitted and practiced openly.

Hostel rooms can be large and packed. School groups (especially German) can turn hostels upside down (typically weekends during the school year and weekdays in the summer). Try to be understanding (many groups are disadvantaged kids); we were all noisy kids at one time. Get to know the teacher and make it a "cultural experience."

Stockholm's floating youth hostel, the af Chapman

Theft can be a problem in hostels, but try this simple safeguard: Wear your money belt (even while sleeping), and don't leave valuables lying around (but no one's going to steal your tennis shoes or journal). Use the storage lockers that are available in most hostels.

Be skeptical about hostel ratings. The ratings on hostel-booking websites can help you get a feel for a hostel, but shouldn't be the end-all in your decision making. What matters most to me are a hostel's ratings in the areas of safety, location, and character. Seek a hostel where you and your belongings will be secure, in a central location (or easily linked to the center by public transit), and with a good vibe (if other people enjoy their time there, you likely will too). I don't pay much attention to ratings for cleanliness or helpfulness of the staff (which can be negatively influenced by former 5-star hotel guests who weren't ready for a hostel experience).

Hostel selectively. I've hosteled mostly in northern Europe, where hostels are more comfortable and the savings over hotels more exciting. (This is particularly true in Scandinavia, where you find lots of Volvos in hostel

INFORMATION			
YOUNG	£3.50	SHEET	80p
JUNIOR	£4.40	SHOWERS	FREE
SENIOR	£5.50		
DINNER	£3.00		
BREAKFAST	£2 30		
LUNCH PACK	£1.60		
DOORS OPENED		7.30 AM	
RISING BELL & OFFICE OPEN		8.00	
BREAKFAST		8.30	
HOSTEL CLOSES		10.00	
HOSTEL REOPENS		5.00 PM	
DINNER		7.00	
HOSTEL CLOSES		11.00	
LIGHTS OUT		11.30	
WARDENS			
KEITH & JOAN BENNETT			
ASSISTANT WARDEN JAN VAN KAAM			
WE HOPE YOU ENJOY YOUR STAY AT			
STOW — ON — THE — OLD			

SLEEPING

parking lots; locals know that hostels provide the best—and usually only—$30 beds in town.) I rarely hostel in the south, where hostels are less common and two or three people can sleep just as cheaply in a budget hotel.

Big-city hostels are the most overrun by young backpackers. Rural hostels, far from train lines and famous sights, are usually quiet and frequented by a more mature crowd. If you have a car, use that mobility to visit places without train service and enjoy some of Europe's overlooked hostels.

Getting a hostel bed in peak tourist season can be tricky. The most popular hostels fill up every day. Most hostels will take telephone or email reservations. I always call or email ahead to try to reserve and at least check on the availability of beds. But don't rely solely on advance reservations, because many hostels hold some beds for drop-ins. Try to arrive early. If the hostel has a lockout period during the day, show up before the office closes in the morning; otherwise, line up with the scruffy gang for the 5:00 p.m. reopening, when any remaining beds are doled out.

Some hostels have a reservation system where, for a small fee, you can reserve and pay for your next hostel bed before you leave the last one.

In most hostels, there are dorm rooms for boys... and dorm rooms for girls.

You can also book Hostelling International locations online (www.hihostels.com, $3 nonrefundable booking fee plus 5 percent nonrefundable deposit per location booked, balance due at hostel on arrival, $3 refund for HI members at hostel); they accept Visa and MasterCard and also sell hostel membership cards. Book at least a day ahead.

Hostel bed availability is unpredictable. Some obscure hostels are booked out on certain days six months in advance. But I stumbled into Oberammergau one night during the jam-packed Passion Play festival and found beds for a group of eight.

Look for unique hostel experiences. Hostels come in all shapes and sizes, and some are sightseeing ends in themselves. There are castles (Bacharach, Germany), moored ships and a converted jumbo jet (Stockholm), alpine chalets (Gimmelwald, Switzerland), huge modern buildings (Frankfurt), lakefront villas (Lugano, Italy), former prisons (Stockholm and Ljubljana, Slovenia), medieval manor houses (Wilderhope Manor, England), former choirboys' dorms (St. Paul's, London), country estates (Loch Lomond, Scotland), and former royal residences (Holland Park, London). Survey other hostelers and hostel employees for suggestions.

Hostel-Style Alternatives

Hostels aren't the only places to find low-cost rooms in Europe. Depending on where you're traveling, you might wrangle a bed in a convent, school, or youth camp.

In Italy, some cities have convents that rent out rooms. The beds are twins and English is often in short supply, but the price is right. If you're going to Rome, see the Church of Santa Susanna's website for a list (www.santasusanna.org, select "Coming to Rome").

If you can't bunk with pilgrims, try snoozing with students. In London, which seems to have the highest hotel prices in Europe, the University of Westminster opens its dorm rooms to travelers from mid-June through late September. Located in several high-rise buildings scattered around central London, the rooms—some with private baths—come with access to well-equipped kitchens and big lounges (www.westminster.ac.uk/business). University College London (www.ucl.ac.uk/residences) and the London School of Economics (www.lsevacations.co.uk) also rent out dorm space in the summer.

In the cheap-sleeps circus, nothing beats Munich's venerable International Youth Camp Kapuzinerhölzl (a.k.a. "The Tent"). From June to early October, they offer 400 spots on the wooden floor of a huge circus tent—and they never fill up. You can rent a mattress or bed, or you can pitch your own tent. Blankets, hot showers, lockers, a kitchen, and Wi-Fi are all included; breakfast is a few euros extra. It can be a fun but noisy experience—kind of a cross between a slumber party and Woodstock (www.the-tent.com).

Staying in European Homes

There is no better way to get to know a new country than to stay in a home. Whether paying a host for a spare room or crashing on your neighbor's cousin's couch, bunking with locals can provide some of the richest, most memorable travel experiences (and it's cheap, to boot). For those aware of the trade-offs, it can be a great option.

Being a guest in a European home isn't all that different from being a guest in an American one. That said, clear communication and a focus on being considerate are even more critical when trying to bridge a linguistic or cultural divide. People who are OK with welcoming strangers in their home are usually friendly, interested in others, and eager to show off their town. You'll likely be greeted with genuine enthusiasm, whether you're paying a fee or staying for free. Many hosts happily provide maps, sightseeing and transit information, and advice on how to make the most of your time.

But some awkwardness is inevitable—expect to make a faux pas or two. Limit your embarrassing blunders by doing your cultural homework—ask around and look online for pointers on guest etiquette in the country you're visiting. Follow your host's lead—if they're not wearing shoes in their house, leave yours at the door. Be aware of what makes for touchy conversation, and do your best to get squared away on geopolitical basics—e.g., Scotland isn't in England, and Bratislava is no longer in "Czechoslovakia." To bridge a wide language gap, try to learn the elements of that country's nonverbal communication: What means "OK" in the US can mean something quite the opposite in some parts of Europe. Communicate your plans clearly: how long you expect to stay, whether you'll be there for dinner in the evening, and where to leave the key in the morning.

Before you arrange to stay with someone in their house, be aware of the potential downsides. Consider what you may have to give up for your free or cheap bed. At a hotel, B&B, or hostel, you have no social obligations to your host. But if someone's offering to put you up, it could be perceived as rude to return late at night and leave first thing in the morning. If your host invites you to dinner, do your best to accept—but remember to budget your sightseeing time accordingly. If you accept a bed from someone (especially if it's free), it's polite to give your hosts plenty of advance warning of your arrival and not flippantly change plans at the last minute.

If you're sleeping where others live, there's a decent chance you'll find yourself in a workaday suburb, or at least far from old-town charm or sights you came to see. Thanks to Europe's excellent public-transit network, you'll probably be able to reach the city center on your own, but that commute will cost you time and money.

Room-Finding Services

If you're looking for a cheap or free home to call home, consider one of the services that mediate between travelers and hosts.

Cheap Beds in Private Homes: Airbnb (www.airbnb.com) makes it reasonably easy to find a place to sleep in someone's home. Beds range from air-mattress-in-living-room basic to plush-B&B-suite posh. Most listings offer at least a spare room to yourself, and many are for entire apartments. The listings have plenty of pictures, easy ways to sort your options according to your preferences, and feedback from previous travelers. All arrangements, including payment, are handled via their website, and safety is taken seriously. The site provides a round-the-clock emergency hotline and waits until after you've checked in to pay the host, giving you a chance to back out. Hosts tend to be convivial and accommodating, but are usually more interested in earning some money with their spare square footage than making new friends. A similar site worth checking out is 9flats.com.

CouchSurfing: This free-to-join network of travelers is a vagabond's alternative to Airbnb (www.couchsurfing.org). It lists millions of outgoing members—more than two million in Europe alone—who host fellow "surfers" in their homes for free. Most do this out of a sincere interest in meeting interesting people, and many of them are in it for the good karma, having couch-surfed themselves. This service is a boon for laid-back, budget-minded extroverts who aren't too picky about where they rest their head. Most surfers are young (the average age is 28) and traveling solo, but plenty are a decade or two older, or traveling in small groups.

Travelers and hosts alike post profiles on the website, listing basic information (usually a photo, age, languages spoken, and interests). Potential hosts post invitations, offering their "couch" (often precisely that, but can be anywhere from floor space to a spare room), or just the chance to meet up for a cross-cultural conversation. Travelers search on the city they're headed to, then browse the listings, which focus primarily on the host, not on the quality or location of the accommodation. Surfers contact a potential host based on a sense of compatibility, whether several months or several days in advance, and ask them about the bed specifics (if not included in the profile). Once you're in town, the host usually makes time to introduce you to the city, whether taking you on a walk past the big sights or out on the town to introduce you to friends (everyone pays their own way, though many surfers buy their host a thank-you drink or gelato). Most surfers will tell you that they enjoy the conviviality even more than the free accommodation.

Safety is, of course, a concern of any smart couch surfer. While the CouchSurfing site makes an effort toward this end (offering plenty of safety tips, providing a forum for travelers and hosts to rate each other, and allowing hosts to pay for name and address verification), travelers must still be on alert for creeps and scammers—they're certainly out there. My best tip for crashing with strangers: Always arrive with a backup hostel, hotel, or CouchSurfing host in mind; if you don't feel comfortable with your host, just leave (after all, it's free). Don't worry about hurting their feelings. Never let budget concerns take you outside your comfort zone.

Other Options: If you've got more time and stamina than money, consider Workaway.info, which connects you with families or small organizations offering room and board in exchange for volunteer work, usually manual labor (gardening, carpentry, painting) for about five hours a day, five days a week. For more on volunteer opportunities, see page 492.

If you believe that travel is about bringing people together, consider joining a cultural-exchange organization, which lets you stay with hosts in their home (described on page 492). Note that while travelers do get a free bed with their hosts, the focus is much less about providing accommodation than an opportunity to connect. Guests are there to spend the bulk of their visit with their hosts, not off sightseeing.

Crashing with Friends and Family

Staying with a friend, relative, or friendly stranger not only stretches your budget (usually along with your belly), but your cultural horizons. And now that it's so easy to connect and stay in touch online, travelers are finding more and more chances to crash with old or new friends.

Try and dig up some European relatives, friends, friends of relatives, or relatives of friends. No matter how far out on the family tree they are, unless you're a real jerk, they're tickled to have an American visitor in their nest. I email my potential host, telling them when I'll arrive and asking if they'd be free to meet for dinner while I'm there. They answer with "Please come visit us" or "Have a good trip." It's obvious from their response (or lack of one) if I'm invited to stop by and stay awhile.

Especially if you're traveling solo and reasonably extroverted, you're likely to make new friends on the

The Europeans you visit don't need to be next-of-kin. This Tirolean is the father of my sister's ski teacher. That's close enough.

road. When people meet, they invite each other to visit. Exchanging email addresses or Facebook names is almost as common as a handshake in Europe. If you have a business or personal card, bring a pile. Some travelers even print up a batch of personal cards for their trip. Once invited to visit, I warn my new friends that I may very well show up some day at their house, whether it's in Osaka, Auckland, Santa Fe, or Dublin. When I have, it's been a good experience.

Don't be afraid to follow up with indirect contacts. I have dear "parents away from home" in Austria and London. My Austrian "parents" are really the parents of my sister's ski instructor. In London, they are friends of my uncle. Neither relationship was terribly close—until I visited. Now we are friends for life.

If you're afraid of being perceived as a freeloader, remember that both parties benefit from such a visit. A Greek family is just as curious and interested in me as I am in them. Equipped with hometown postcards, pictures of my family, and a bag of goodies for the children, I make a point of giving as much from my culture as I am taking from the culture of my host. I insist on no special treatment rather than to be treated simply as part of the family. If I ask for a favor, I make it as easy as possible for my host to say no. I try to help with the chores, I don't wear out my welcome, and I follow up each visit with postcards or emails to share the rest of my trip. I reimburse my hosts for their hospitality with a bottle of wine, a bunch of flowers, or a thank-you letter from home, possibly with photos of all of us together.

House Swapping

Many families enjoy this great budget option year after year. They trade houses (sometimes cars, too—but most draw the line at pets) with someone at the destination of their choice. People who've tried house swapping rave about the range of places they've enjoyed for free, and about the graciousness and generosity of their swap-mates.

Swapping works best for people with an appealing place to offer, and who can live with the idea of having strangers in their home, touching their stuff. Unsurprisingly, those living in swanky Manhattan apartments and beachside villas have the best pick of options in Europe, but you don't need to live in an obvious vacation spot or a mansion to find a workable exchange. Your guests may appreciate the pace of a smaller town (especially if you offer your car) and may be less interested in luxury or location than in finding a suitable place that's available when they are.

Good places to start are HomeLink (www.homelink.org/usa), HomeExchange (www.homeexchange.com), or Intervac Home Exchange (www.intervacus.com). Once you've found a potential host, expect to be in fairly close contact with them as you finalize the swap. Be very clear about your expectations, agree on how you'll handle worst-case scenarios, and get the details pinned down before you leave. Be triple-sure about where to find the key and how to open the door, find out beforehand how to get to the nearest grocery store, make sure your host family leaves instructions for operating the appliances, make arrangements in advance for phone and Internet charges, and ask about any peculiarities with the car you'll be driving. Veteran house swappers report that by the time these logistics are all worked out, it usually feels less like you'll be swapping with strangers, and more like you've made a new, conveniently located friend.

Camping European Style

Camping, like hosteling, is a great way to meet Europeans. But although camping is the middle-class European family way to travel—and can be the cheapest way to see Europe—relatively few Americans take advantage of Europe's 10,000-plus campgrounds. Those who do camp in Europe give it rave reviews.

"Camping" is the international word for campground. In the US, we think of campgrounds as being picturesque outposts near a lake or forest. By contrast, European campings are often located on the outskirts of an urban center and can range from functional

Many campgrounds offer bungalows with kitchenettes and four to six beds. Comfortable and cheaper than hotels, these are particularly popular in Scandinavia.

(like park-and-rides) to vacation extravaganzas, with restaurants and mini water-parks. In general, European campgrounds are less private than the American version and forbid open fires. But they rarely fill up, and if they do, the "Full" sign usually refers to motorhomes and trailers. A small tent can almost always be squeezed in somewhere.

Campgrounds generally mirror their surroundings: If the region is overcrowded, dusty, dirty, unkempt, and chaotic, you're unlikely to

Camping Resources

The **Let's Go** guides give good instructions on getting to and from European campgrounds. **Eurocampings** has details and user reviews on more than 8,000 campgrounds (www.euro campings.co.uk). Once in Europe, campings are well-signed, and local tourist information offices have guides and maps listing spots at nearby campgrounds.

Helpful Books

Europe by Van and Motorhome (David Shore and Patty Campbell, 2012). Renting, buying, or shipping an RV; plus what to take and where to camp. The purchase price includes a free, personal consultation (free shipping for Rick Steves' readers, also available for download, www.roadtripeurope.com, tel. 800-659-5222, shorecam@aol.com).

Caravan & Camping Europe (2011). Excellent resource from Britain's AAA-type automobile club with detailed Western Europe campground listings and color maps. Separate editions available for France and Britain/Ireland.

Camping Europe (Carol Mickelsen, 2008). Tips for car camping, bringing your bike from home, and driving directions to major destinations. Includes Scandinavia, Central, and Eastern Europe.

RV and Car Camping Vacations in Europe (Mike and Terri Church, 2004). Two-week itineraries, campground listings, and advice for both RV and tent campers.

find an oasis behind the campground's gates. A sleepy Austrian valley will probably offer a sleepy Austrian campground. "Weekend campings" are rented out on a yearly basis to local urbanites. Too often, weekend sites are full or don't allow what they call "stop-and-go" campers (you). Camping guidebooks indicate which places are the "weekend" types.

Prices: Prices vary according to facilities and style—sometimes it's by the tent, the person, or the vehicle. Expect to spend $10-12 per night per person.

Registration and Regulations: Camp registration is easy. As with most hotels, you show your passport, fill out a short form, and learn the rules. Quiet is enforced beginning at 10:00 or 11:00 p.m., and checkout time is usually noon. English is the second language of campings throughout Europe, and most managers will understand the monoglot American.

Out of Options (or Money)?

This book is not a vagabonding guide, but things happen: You run out of money, you get into town too late to find a room, or volcanic ash strands you somewhere without a place to stay. I once went 29 out of 30 nights without paying for a bed. It's not difficult...but it's not always comfortable, convenient, clean, safe—or legal.

I no longer lug a sleeping bag around, but if you'll be vagabonding a lot, bring a light bag—you'll find plenty of places to roll it out. Just keep your passport with you, attach your belongings to you so they don't get stolen, and use good judgment in your choice of a free bed. Faking it until the sun returns can become, at least in the long run, a good memory.

A bench with a view

The Great Outdoors: Some large cities, such as Amsterdam and Athens, are flooded with tourists during peak season—and some of those tourists spend their nights dangerously in city parks. Most cities enforce their "no sleeping in parks" laws only selectively. Away from the cities, in forests or on beaches, you can pretty much sleep where you like. In my vagabonding days, I found summer nights in the Mediterranean part of Europe mild enough that I was comfortable with just my jeans, sweater, and hostel sheet.

Train Stations: Assuming the station stays open all night, it can be a free, warm, safe, and uncomfortable place to hang your hat. Most popular tourist cities in Europe have stations whose concrete

Services: There's usually space to pitch a tent or park a camper van, motorhome, or trailer (caravan). Most campgrounds have laundry facilities and great showers with metered hot water—carry coins and scrub quickly. Larger campgrounds may have a grocery store and café (a likely camp hangout with an easygoing European social scene).

Equipment: You can bring your gear with you—or buy it when you get there. Tents, sleeping bags, and cooking supplies are cheaper at large European superstores (found in Britain, France, Germany, and Spain) than at specialty backpacking stores. European campers prefer a very lightweight "three-season" sleeping bag and a closed-cell sleeping pad.

floors are painted nightly with a long rainbow of sleepy vagabonds. Some stations close for a few hours in the middle of the night, and everyone is always cleared out at dawn before the normal rush of travelers converges on the station. Any ticket or train pass entitles you to a free night in a station's waiting room: You're simply waiting for your early train. For safety, lock your pack in a station locker or check it at the baggage counter.

Trains: Success hinges on getting enough room to stretch out, and that can be quite a trick (see page 138). It's tempting but risky to sleep in a train car that seems to be parked for the night in a station. No awakening is ruder than having your bedroom jolt into motion and roll toward God-knows-where. If you do find a parked train car to sleep in, check to see when it's scheduled to leave. Some railpass holders get a free if disjointed night's sleep by riding a train out for four hours and catching a different train back for another four hours.

Airports: After a late landing, crash on an airport sofa rather than waste sleeping time looking for a place that will sell you a bed for the remainder of the night. Frankfurt's airport is served conveniently by the train and is great for sleeping free—even if you aren't flying anywhere. A few large airports have sterile, womblike "rest cabins" that can be rented for as few as four hours or overnight at the price of a cheap hotel room (for example, see www.yotel.com for London's Heathrow and Gatwick airports and Amsterdam's Schiphol airport).

Tents and Dorms: Big, crowded cities such as London, Paris, Munich, Venice, and Copenhagen run safe, legal, and nearly free sleep-ins (in tents or huge dorms) during peak season.

I'd start without a stove, keeping meals simple by picnicking and enjoying food and fun in the campground café. You can always buy a stove later.

Safety: Campgrounds, unlike hostels, are remarkably theft-free. Campings are full of basically honest, middle-class European families, and someone's at the gate all day. Most people just leave their gear in their vans or zipped inside their tents.

Kids: A family can sleep in a tent, van, or motorhome a lot cheaper than in a hotel. Camping offers plenty to occupy children's attention, namely playgrounds that come fully equipped with European kids. As your kids make friends, your campground social circle widens. Campgrounds are filled with Europeans in the mood to toss a Frisbee with a new American friend (bring a nylon "Woosh" Frisbee).

Tent Camping: Tent-and-train can be a money-saving combination, though it can be challenging to connect the train station and the camp-

For a "room" with a view on a tight budget, pitch your tent in a secluded mountain valley.

ground with bulky equipment. In some cases, buses shuttle campers from train station to campground. Tents and bikes are an even cheaper way to go, if you don't mind the weight. Bikers enjoy the same we-can-squeeze-one-more-in status as hikers and are very rarely turned away. Camping by car is my favorite combination. A car carries all your gear and gets you to any campground quickly and easily. In big cities, the money you save on parking alone will pay for your campsite (leave your car at the campground and take the bus downtown).

RV Camping: David Shore, author of *Europe by Van and Motorhome* (see sidebar on page 229), gives consults on finding and renting the right camper vehicle (shorecam@aol.com). Each country has companies specializing in camper van and motorhome rentals. Look for one with a pick-up and drop-off location that makes sense for your itinerary. For example, Origin Campervans is centrally located in Lille, France (www.origin-campervans.com). McRent (www.mcrent.eu) has 43 rental depots across Germany. London-based Wild Horizon (www.wildhorizon.co.uk) can meet you at any airport in the UK.

Turn-Key Camping: Some services offer virtually turn-key camping, renting sites already set up for you with a tent, trailer, or mobile home outfitted with linens and kitchen gear. Two British companies are a good place to start: Eurocamp (www.eurocamp.co.uk) and Canvas Holidays (www.canvasholidays.co.uk) contract with campgrounds across continental Europe.

Free Camping: Low-profile, pitch-the-tent-after-dark-and-move-on-first-thing-in-the-morning free camping is usually allowed even in countries where it is technically illegal. Use common sense, and don't pitch your tent in carefully controlled areas such as cities and resorts. It's a good idea to ask permission when possible. Never leave your gear and tent unattended without the gates of a formal campground to discourage thieves. With a camper van or motorhome, no stealthiness is required—you can sleep overnight in any legal parking space.

SLEEPING

PHONES AND TECHNOLOGY

With my mantra being "Pack Light," I used to be against packing electronics of any kind. But now, I bring my laptop, iPhone, digital camera, and a slew of cables, chargers, and adapters—and I wouldn't consider leaving any of these behind. In this chapter, I cover telephoning in Europe (with a mobile phone, over the Internet, or on a landline); how to get online during your trip; mobile apps and other tools for techie travelers; tips for shutterbugs; and the best ways to share pictures and memories of your trip.

Phoning

When traveling, it pays to use the telephone. Call tourist offices to smooth out sightseeing plans, train stations to confirm timetables, museums to see if an English tour is scheduled, restaurants to check if they're open, hotels to confirm reservations, and so on. The more I travel, the more I use the telephone (for tips on communicating over the phone with someone who speaks another language, see page 354).

How to Dial

Many Americans are intimidated by dialing European phone numbers. You needn't be. It's simple, once you break the code.

Note that whether you're calling from the US or from within Europe, calls to a European mobile phone are substantially more expensive than calls to a fixed line. Off-hour calls are generally cheaper. Also, remember that from most of Europe, it's usually six hours earlier in New York and nine hours earlier in California.

Dialing Domestically

About half of all European countries use area codes (like we do); the other half uses a direct-dial system without area codes.

To make calls within a country that uses a direct-dial system (Belgium, the Czech Republic, Denmark, France, Greece, Italy, Norway, Poland, Portugal, Spain, and Switzerland), dial the same number whether you're calling across the country or across the street.

In countries that use area codes (such as Austria, Croatia, Britain, Finland, Germany, Hungary, Ireland, the Netherlands, Slovakia, Slovenia, Sweden, and Turkey), dial the local number when calling within a city, and add the area code if calling long-distance within the country. Example: To call a Munich hotel (tel. 089/264-349) within Munich, dial 264-349; to call it from Frankfurt, dial 089/264-349. In some countries, particularly those with area codes, phone numbers can have varying lengths. For instance, a hotel might have a seven-digit phone number and an eight-digit fax number.

Relatively few phone booths remain in Europe...and those that do, generally take phone cards rather than coins.

These instructions apply to dialing from a landline (such as a pay phone or your hotel-room phone) or a European mobile phone. If you're dialing domestically in a European country using your US mobile phone, you may need to dial as if it's a domestic call, or you may need to dial as if you're calling from the US (see "Dialing Internationally," next). Try it one way, and if it doesn't work, try it the other way.

Dialing Internationally

Calling Europe from Another Country: Always start with the international access code: 011 if you're calling from the US or Canada, 00 from anywhere in Europe. Then dial the country code of the country you're calling (see chart on page 236). If you're dialing from a mobile phone, you can replace the international access code with +, which works

European Calling Chart

Just smile and dial, using this key:
AC = Area Code, LN = Local Number.

European Country	Calling long distance within ...	Calling from the US or Canada to ...	Calling from a European country to ...
Austria	AC + LN	011 + 43 + AC (without initial zero) + LN	00 + 43 + AC (without initial zero) + LN
Belgium	LN	011 + 32 + LN (without initial zero)	00 + 32 + LN (without initial zero)
Bosnia-Herzegovina	AC + LN	011 + 387 + AC (without initial zero) + LN	00 + 387 + AC (without initial zero) + LN
Britain	AC + LN	011 + 44 + AC (without initial zero) + LN	00 + 44 + AC (without initial zero) + LN
Croatia	AC + LN	011 + 385 + AC (without initial zero) + LN	00 + 385 + AC (without initial zero) + LN
Czech Republic	LN	011 + 420 + LN	00 + 420 + LN
Denmark	LN	011 + 45 + LN	00 + 45 + LN
Estonia	LN	011 + 372 + LN	00 + 372 + LN
Finland	AC + LN	011 + 358 + AC (without initial zero) + LN	999 + 358 + AC (without initial zero) + LN
France	LN	011 + 33 + LN (without initial zero)	00 + 33 + LN (without initial zero)
Germany	AC + LN	011 + 49 + AC (without initial zero) + LN	00 + 49 + AC (without initial zero) + LN
Gibraltar	LN	011 + 350 + LN	00 + 350 + LN
Greece	LN	011 + 30 + LN	00 + 30 + LN
Hungary	06 + AC + LN	011 + 36 + AC + LN	00 + 36 + AC + LN
Ireland	AC + LN	011 + 353 + AC (without initial zero) + LN	00 + 353 + AC (without initial zero) + LN
Italy	LN	011 + 39 + LN	00 + 39 + LN

European Country	Calling long distance within ...	Calling from the US or Canada to ...	Calling from a European country to ...
Latvia	LN	011 + 371 + LN	00 + 371 + LN
Montenegro	AC + LN	011 + 382 + AC (without initial zero) + LN	00 + 382 + AC (without initial zero) + LN
Morocco	LN	011 + 212 + LN (without initial zero)	00 + 212 + LN (without initial zero)
Netherlands	AC + LN	011 + 31 + AC (without initial zero) + LN	00 + 31 + AC (without initial zero) + LN
Norway	LN	011 + 47 + LN	00 + 47 + LN
Poland	LN	011 + 48 + LN	00 + 48 + LN
Portugal	LN	011 + 351 + LN	00 + 351 + LN
Russia	8 + AC + LN	011 + 7 + AC + LN	00 + 7 + AC + LN
Slovakia	AC + LN	011 + 421 + AC (without initial zero) + LN	00 + 421 + AC (without initial zero) + LN
Slovenia	AC + LN	011 + 386 + AC (without initial zero) + LN	00 + 386 + AC (without initial zero) + LN
Spain	LN	011 + 34 + LN	00 + 34 + LN
Sweden	AC + LN	011 + 46 + AC (without initial zero) + LN	00 + 46 + AC (without initial zero) + LN
Switzerland	LN	011 + 41 + LN (without initial zero)	00 + 41 + LN (without initial zero)
Turkey	AC (if no initial zero is included, add one) + LN	011 + 90 + AC (without initial zero) + LN	00 + 90 + AC (without initial zero) + LN

- The instructions above apply whether you're calling to or from a European landline or mobile phone.
- If calling from any mobile phone, you can replace the international access code with "+" (press and hold 0 to insert it).
- The international access code is 011 if you're calling from the US or Canada.
- To call the US or Canada from Europe, dial 00, then 1 (country code for US and Canada), then the area code and number. In short, 00 + 1 + AC + LN = Hi, Mom!

regardless of where you're calling from. (On many phones, to insert a +, press and hold the 0 key.)

Exactly what you dial after the international access code and country code depends on the phone system of the country you're calling. If the country uses area codes, you'll generally drop the initial zero of the area code, then dial the rest of the number. Example: To call the Munich hotel (tel. 089/264-349) from Italy, dial 00 (or +), then 49 (Germany's country code), then 89/264-349.

Countries that use direct-dial systems vary in how they're accessed internationally by phone. If you're making an international call to Denmark, the Czech Republic, Italy, Norway, Poland, Portugal, or Spain, simply dial the international access code, country code, and phone number. Example: To call a Madrid hotel (tel. 915-212-900) from Germany, dial 00 (or +), 34 (Spain's country code), then 915-212-900. But if you're calling Belgium, France, or Switzerland, drop the initial zero of the phone number. Example: To call a Paris hotel (tel. 01 47 05 49 15) from London, dial 00 (or +), then 33 (France's country code), then 1 47 05 49 15 (phone number without initial zero).

For online instructions on calling between any two countries, see www.countrycallingcodes.com or www.howtocallabroad.com.

Calling the US from Europe: To dial the US direct, first enter the international access code (00 from Europe, or + from anywhere), then the country code of the US (1), then the area code and the seven-digit number. To call my office in Edmonds, Washington, from France, dial 00-1-425-771-8303.

Mobile Phones

Traveling with a mobile phone provides the best combination of practicality and flexibility. Most travelers find it's worth the slight additional effort and expense to equip themselves with a mobile phone that works in Europe. With a mobile phone, you can call to get driving instructions as you approach your hotel, reserve restaurants on the fly, locate a lost travel partner, or chat with family and friends at home as you roam the streets of Rome.

Mobile phones aren't for everyone. Some travelers simply don't want to hassle with figuring out how to use their phone in Europe. Others like having an excuse to be out of touch. It's OK—you still have other options for contacting people, from using hotel-room phones to pay phones to Internet calling apps on a mobile device (all explained later).

If you do want to go mobile, you have several options: Bring your American phone (if it works in Europe), buy a phone to use in Europe,

Mobile phones give B&B owners the freedom to run errands and their business at the same time.

or rent a phone. If you bring your own phone, it's easiest to roam with your US phone number—but it's more expensive. An "unlocked" phone allows you to switch out SIM cards as you travel from one country to another, giving you cheap pay-as-you-go calls (to learn the lingo, see the sidebar, next page). This takes a bit more effort but can be a huge money saver—especially if you'll be making lots of calls. You can buy an unlocked phone, or you may be able to unlock your own, depending on your model and carrier. I explain all of these options later.

No matter what kind of phone you use, as you cross each border, you'll usually receive a text message welcoming you to the new country's network and explaining how to use their services. If you're traveling within the European Union, the message will indicate how much it costs to make and receive calls in the country you're in. Remember, having people call you on your European mobile phone number typically costs them much more than calling a fixed line (the rates can be as much as double). It might be cheaper for them to phone you at your hotel, rather than calling your mobile.

Roaming with Your Own Mobile Phone

Many AT&T and T-Mobile phones work fine abroad, while only specialized phones from Verizon or Sprint do—check your operating manual (look for "tri-band" or "quad-band"). If your Verizon phone doesn't work in Europe, they'll loan you one that does for a one-time shipping fee (described later, under "Renting a Mobile Phone"). Note that some older iPhones from Verizon don't work in Europe.

The simplest way to travel with your own phone is to set up an international plan with your carrier. This is a good choice if you don't plan on making many calls, you'll only be away for a short time, or you want people to be able to reach you on your US phone number. It's also the best solution for those who value ease over expense. Most US providers offer an international plan that charges $1.29 to $1.99 per minute to make or receive calls in Western Europe, and 20 to 50 cents to send or receive text messages. (Rates for roaming in Eastern Europe

Mobile Phones 101

The standard mobile-phone network in Europe, and much of the world, is called **GSM**. Some American mobile-phone companies—most notably AT&T and T-Mobile—use the same GSM technology as in Europe. Others (including Verizon and Sprint) use a different system, called CDMA, which is not compatible with European networks (if you want to use Verizon or Sprint abroad, you'll need a global phone with GSM capabilities).

Within the GSM network, different regions operate on different **bands.** The United States uses two bands, and most of Europe uses two other bands. A GSM phone that's **tri-band** or **quad-band** oper-ates on both US bands, plus one or both European bands—so it works at home and abroad.

The "identity" of a GSM mobile phone—your phone number and account informa-tion—is stored on a removable fingernail-sized chip, called a **SIM card,** which slides into the phone. (Some phones, such as the iPhone, come with a newer, miniature version called a **micro-SIM card.**) Mobile phones won't work without a SIM card (except for emergency calls).

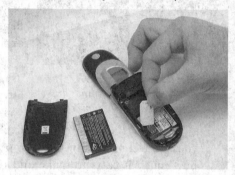

Your phone's SIM card is sometimes hiding behind the battery.

Some phones are electronically **"locked"** so that you can't switch SIM cards—therefore, you must stay loyal to your original

are generally higher.)

Before you leave, call your mobile-phone provider to find out whether your phone will work in Europe and to ask about dialing instructions. In addition, ask if you need to activate international calling. Get rates for each country you'll be visiting and ask about other fees (such as for text messaging and data roaming—explained later). While it's typically free to enable international calling, many companies also offer the option of paying an additional monthly fee to lower the per-minute charges. Similar deals exist for text messaging (for example, $10 for 100 texts abroad). These services can often be worth it, but remember to deac-tivate the service when you return. (On the other hand, you can call your mobile-phone company and ask them to disable both international

service provider. But it's possible to get your phone **"unlocked"**—allowing you to replace the original SIM card with a local European one. This is especially useful if you want to use the phone in multiple countries, as you can buy a different SIM card in each one.

If you venture outside your mobile phone's home area, you're **roaming.** Making calls when you're roaming in a foreign country can be expensive. To avoid high roaming fees, some Europeans switch SIM cards as they cross borders. (The European Union caps roaming fees within their territory—but if you're roaming with a non-EU SIM card, or if you're traveling in a country not in the EU, it can get very pricey.) You can use a SIM card outside its original country until you run out of credit; to extend its life, just text or make quick calls.

Texting (which Europeans often call SMS, or short message service) is much cheaper than calling—usually 5 to 10 cents to send and nothing to receive (potentially more if you're roaming outside your SIM card's home country—but still cheap).

Smartphones (such as the iPhone, Android, Windows Phone, or BlackBerry) have similar calling and texting features to conventional phones, but can access the Internet via a mobile-phone network or over Wi-Fi. If you're outside your home coverage area and go online using a mobile network (such as 3G or 4G), you are **data roaming**—which can be very expensive without a plan. Save your downloading for when you are on Wi-Fi.

Europeans might not understand the American term "cell phone." Try **"mobile"** (pronounce it the way Brits do—rhymes with "smile") or **"handy"** (most common in German-speaking areas).

calling and data roaming; when you get to Europe, you're still free to use your smartphone's Wi-Fi capabilities.)

Mobile-phone companies have received furious complaints from customers who've rung up huge bills because they didn't realize they were incurring roaming charges, so they can be a little over-the-top in making sure you understand all the potential costs. But it's better to be informed.

Note that you'll be charged for incoming calls, even if you don't answer them (and, in some cases, even if your phone is turned off)—so tell your friends and co-workers not to call except in emergencies. If you want to have your US phone with you for making calls or texting, but do not want to receive expensive calls, ask your provider about setting up automatic call forwarding so that calls to your mobile phone are automatically rerouted to your home phone.

Data Roaming with a Smartphone

My iPhone—whose phone capabilities I disable in Europe, essentially turning it into an iPod Touch—has quickly become my favorite travel companion, whether it's keeping me on top of my work, keeping me in touch with my kids, or simply keeping me entertained. For instance, if I'm in a café in Paris that has free Wi-Fi, I can pop onto the Internet and check sports scores back home. If an impromptu soccer game breaks out on a piazza in Naples, I can record a video of it, then use the Dropbox application to send it to my assistant, who can post it to my Facebook page. Using Skype on my phone, I can connect to Wi-Fi and call my daughter in the US for free (for more on Internet calling, see page 247).

While a smartphone is a great tool for overseas travel, it can also run up your cell phone bill sky-high if you're not careful. That's because carriers charge outrageous data roaming fees, which accrue whenever you use the mobile network (rather than Wi-Fi) to access the Internet or download emails.

For example, if you roam with a smartphone from most US providers, you'll pay about $20 per megabyte used in Europe. This means it costs about $40 to watch a three-minute video clip from YouTube, stream a four-minute song, or email a large digital image (each of these eats up around 2 megabytes). Even an average-size Web page costs around $3 to view. While downloading a few emails (figure around 40 cents to send or receive a basic message) doesn't involve such large kilobyte loads, these charges can add up fast. For tips on making data roaming more affordable, see later. (The European Union is attempting to more strictly regulate data-roaming fees, but this applies primarily to EU residents—not to visitors.)

Also note that many smartphone apps—such as news readers, flight trackers, and so on—automatically access the Internet to download content or updates. This means you can accidentally rack up data charges, even if you're not actively checking emails or using a browser. (For more on smartphone apps, see page 258.)

Avoiding Data-Roaming Charges: To avert the risk of accidentally running up a huge tab, call your mobile-service provider to make sure data roaming is turned off, or disable data roaming on the phone itself (look under the "Network" or "Roaming" menu). It's also possible to block data by switching your phone to airplane mode, but this option turns off Wi-Fi and the ability to make voice calls.

Since smartphones are Wi-Fi enabled, and hotspots are easy to find in most of Europe, you can simply wait until you reach a free hotspot to download emails or get online (for more on Wi-Fi in Europe, see page 253).

Affordable Data Roaming: Data roaming becomes far more affordable if you buy a plan from your provider before your trip. Many US carriers offer an international data-roaming plan for $25-30 per month, which includes up to 100 megabytes of usage (enough for about 100 website views or 1,000 text emails). Larger plans are also available (carrier websites have data usage calculators to help you figure out how much you'll need). You pay the monthly fee whether or not you use all the available data, and going over the plan limit can be costly (the per-megabyte rate increases). Therefore, it's important to keep track of usage: Reset your phone's data counter to zero (look for this under the "Usage" menu), and check it periodically. Some companies automatically send you a text message warning if you exceed your limit. Remember to deactivate the plan when you get home.

To keep data usage on a leash, make adjustments to your smartphone. When you're not actively using the Internet, it's smart to manually turn off the data-roaming feature (under the "Network" or "Roaming" menu). You can also change the way your smartphone receives emails. Smartphones either "fetch" emails from the server or have the server "push" emails to the phone. If your phone is set to "push," it will download emails as they come in, potentially gobbling up precious bytes of your data plan. But if you set it to "fetch," you can manually retrieve your emails when you want, such as when you're on Wi-Fi, then save your kilobytes for times that you're truly out of reach. Adjust the push/fetch settings in your phone's "Mail" menu.

Using an Unlocked Phone

With an unlocked mobile phone, you've got Europe at your beck and call. No contracts are necessary; all you have to do is buy a SIM card, pop it in your phone, and you'll instantly have access to European calling and texting rates, as well as your very own European phone number. You can unlock your US phone or buy an unlocked phone (either before your trip or once you've reached your destination).

Getting Your US Phone Unlocked: Most mobile phones sold in the US are electronically locked to work exclusively with the carrier that sells them. However, any GSM phone—which all use SIM cards—can be unlocked for use with other providers (remember, some phones from Verizon or Sprint don't have SIM card slots). Just call your provider, ask if your phone will work in Europe, and see if they will send you an unlock code. If they agree, you'll receive a long code that you can punch into your phone. Some providers are willing to give you a code after you've been under contract for 90 days, while others wait until your phone's contract has expired. (Sometimes they won't do it at all, though companies seem to be gradually loosening up on this.) You can also go through back channels to get an unlock code (either on the Internet or at a back-alley mobile phone shop), but this is less reliable and in some situations may even be illegal.

Buying an Unlocked Phone in the US: As the world shrinks, unlocked phones are becoming more and more affordable. Go to Amazon.com or your favorite online shopping site and search for "unlocked quad-band GSM phone." As long as the phone has each of those attributes, it should work with European SIM cards. Phones range in features and price, but they don't have to cost much at all. I recently bought a basic unlocked phone for less than $40 and was able to start using it immediately throughout Europe. Some companies specialize in selling unlocked phones to travelers (sometimes bundled with SIM cards), but I'd avoid them since they often come at a higher price.

Buying a Phone in Europe: At your destination, shop around at the ubiquitous corner phone marts or at mobile-phone counters in big department stores. Many airports and train stations have hole-in-the-wall mobile phone shops. You'll get the most versatility from an unlocked phone (generally $60 and up), but many shops sell even cheaper locked phones (starting around $20) that you'll have to use with a single provider. To save even more, look for special promotions or shops that sell used phones.

Buying and Using SIM Cards

Once you have an unlocked phone, you'll need to buy a SIM card to make it work anywhere in Europe. A SIM card is a small, fingernail-size chip that stores your phone number and other information. With an unlocked phone, you can buy a SIM card at your destination and have your very own European phone number at local calling rates. I've bought SIM cards for my unlocked phone in two dozen different countries, and it's become a convenience I can't live without.

While some online companies in the US sell European SIM cards, these tend to be outrageously marked up (to prey on nervous travelers who don't realize how easy it is to buy SIM cards in Europe). For the best deal, just buy one when you arrive in Europe. Each country has various service providers, all of whom sell their own SIM cards. Since these companies are very competitive, they're pretty much the same—just look for the best rates. SIM cards, which generally cost around $5-15, come with a European phone number and starter credit. These days, mobile-phone companies are working hard to attract customers, and you'll often get the SIM card free when you buy calling credit. I've even bought a few SIM cards that came with more credit than the cost of the card (for example, a €5 card that includes €7 of credit).

Rates: If you're calling from the SIM card's home country, you'll generally pay around 10 to 20 cents per minute for domestic calls to fixed lines, and nothing to receive calls. (Calls to mobile phones tend to be more expensive.) Calling the US can cost $1 per minute or more, though some providers offer extremely cheap rates. For example, Lebara—which sells SIM cards in several European countries—typically lets you call the US for around 10 cents per minute. You can also use an international phone card (described later) with your mobile phone to call internationally for pennies.

A SIM card works most affordably in the country where you buy it. If you roam with the SIM card in another country, call prices go up, and you pay to receive incoming calls. If your SIM card is from a European Union country, fees are regulated when roaming anywhere within the EU: You'll pay no more than about 30 cents per minute to make calls, 10 cents per minute to receive calls, or 10 cents to send a text message (plus tax); receiving text messages is free. If your SIM card is from a non-EU country—or if you're traveling in one—roaming fees can be dramatically higher. If you'll be making a lot of calls, it can be cheaper to buy a new SIM card for that country.

Shopping for a SIM Card: In some places, getting a SIM card is as simple as buying a pack of gum. In Greece, I walked up to a newsstand and bought a SIM card for about $5; in the Brussels train station, I got one from a vending machine. But other countries (including Italy and Germany) regulate SIM cards more carefully, so you might have to fill out some paperwork and show your passport before activating the card.

Though you can buy SIM cards at newsstands in many countries, don't expect much help from the newsstand vendor. For first-timers, it's probably worth the extra time to go to a mobile-phone shop, where an English-speaking clerk can help you explore your options, get your SIM card inserted and set up, and show you how to use it. (The mobile-phone desk in a big department store can be another good place to check.) Note that some mobile-phone shops sell SIM cards for only one provider, while others offer a wide range. Unless you're certain you want a particular company, look for a place that gives you several options, then ask the clerk which one is best for the types of calls you're going to make.

(Mostly domestic or international calls? Are you using it only in that country, or planning to "roam" with it across a border?) Also ask for a list of calling rates: for making phone calls and sending text messages—both domestic and international—and for roaming (if you'll be leaving the country).

Setting Up Your Phone: Installing a SIM card is quite simple. First, locate its slot—usually on the side of the phone or behind the battery. If you already have a card installed, pop it out, then put in the new one. When you first insert a new SIM card, you might be prompted to enter the "SIM PIN" (a code number that came with your card). In some cases, you'll be asked for this every time you turn on the phone, though this feature can usually be disabled (look through your phone's menu for security features, or ask the shop clerk for help).

If buying a card from a mobile-phone shop, ask the salesperson to walk you through the entire process, from turning on the phone to making a call. If texts, recorded messages, and other instructions are in another language, ask the clerk to help you switch it to English.

Buying More Credit: Learn how to check your remaining credit balance to avoid running out at an inopportune time. This is different for each phone company, but typically you'll enter a three-digit number, then #, then hit "send." The remaining amount should pop up on your screen. Ask how to do this when you buy your SIM card.

If you start running low, you can top up your credit at any newsstand, tobacco shop, mobile-phone shop, or many other businesses (look for the SIM card's logo in the window). Typically you'll tell the clerk how much credit you want; the clerk will print out a paper voucher with instructions for how to add the amount to your total—usually by punching in a long string of numbers. (I punch in the numbers before I leave the shop, in case it doesn't work or if I need the clerk to help me interpret the instructions.) Once you've entered the code, the credit is instantly added to your account. You'll often receive a text message confirming the new amount.

If you can't find a shop, you have other options: Many ATMs let you buy credit, and some providers let you top up on their website.

Tips: Be aware that most European SIM cards expire after a certain period of inactivity (typically 3 to 12 months)—including any credit you have left on the card. So saving your Italian SIM card for next year's trip isn't a sure thing. Use it up or hand it off to another traveler.

Remember to store your phone numbers in the phone itself, rather than on the SIM card; otherwise, you'll lose access to them when you switch SIMs. When storing phone numbers, include the plus (+) sign and the country code so your calls will go through, regardless of where you're calling from.

Renting a Mobile Phone

Many car-rental companies, mobile-phone companies, and even some hotels offer the option to rent a mobile phone with a European number. While this seems convenient, hidden fees (such as high per-minute charges or expensive shipping costs) can add up—which usually makes it a terrible value. You can probably buy a similar unlocked phone on Amazon.com for the price you'd pay to rent one.

However, one option worth considering is Verizon's Global Travel Program (available only to Verizon customers). While this doesn't save you money or let you use cheap European SIM cards, it does give you the convenience of traveling with your own phone number (including all your contacts). If your Verizon phone won't work in Europe, you can pay a one-time $20 shipping fee to borrow a Europe-compatible phone that can make calls at the regular international rates (generally $1.29 to $1.99 per minute). As long as you send it back within 30 days, there are no additional rental fees or charges.

The Bottom Line on Mobile Phones

When deciding whether to roam with your US provider or use a cheap unlocked phone with European-purchased SIM cards, consider the following questions: 1) How much will you use a phone? 2) How many countries will you be visiting, and for how long?

If you're the type of person who dials ahead to confirm each hotel, makes nightly restaurant reservations, or regularly calls for info about tours and sightseeing, using an unlocked phone with local SIM cards will be much more affordable. If you won't be making a lot of calls, or you just want something for emergencies, you should be able to roam with your US phone without racking up a huge bill.

Internet Calling

Some things that seem too good to be true...actually are true. If you're traveling with a laptop, tablet, or smartphone, you can make calls over the Internet to another wireless device, anywhere in the world, for free. (Or you can pay a few cents to call from your device to a telephone.) Officially dubbed Voice over Internet Protocol (VoIP), Internet calling can save you a ton of money. Simply put, this is *the* cheapest way to stay in touch with folks back home while you're on the road.

The major providers are Skype (www.skype.com, also available as a smartphone app), Google Talk (www.google.com/talk), and FaceTime (preloaded on most Apple devices). Other variations include Rebtel (www.rebtel.com), which can also be used in combination with mobile minutes (not just Wi-Fi or 3G) and Viber (www.viber.com).

To get started, visit the service's website to download the free application and register. Once you're signed up, you can talk online via your computer to a buddy with a computer running the same program—just look for them on your list of contacts, and click "Voice Call" or "Video Call." Call recipients need to be online with the app launched, so it's best to set up a time to talk in advance.

Internet calling makes it easy to keep in touch via your computer or wireless device for free.

The program uses your computer's built-in speakers and microphone, if it has them. If your computer lacks a microphone, or if you want to improve the voice and sound quality, you can buy an operator-type headset for around $20. If both of you have webcams, you can see each other while you chat. (If your laptop doesn't already have one, a basic webcam costs about $20.) You can even show off the perfect piazza view out your hotel-room window. If you have a good Internet signal, the sound quality is generally at least as good as a standard phone connection (although video can be choppy).

Many Internet calling programs also work for making calls from your computer to telephones worldwide. This service is not free, but the rates are very reasonable (generally a few cents per minute). To make phone calls, you have to buy credit. Then just click on "Call" and punch the number in the keypad. I use Skype both in the US and in Europe to make cheap phone calls. When I'm at home, I can sit at my computer and use Skype to call phone numbers all over Europe to reserve hotels for my whole trip, quickly and affordably. And when I'm in Europe, I can get online and make calls to phone numbers in the US—or call ahead to confirm tomorrow's hotel in Europe—for pennies a minute. With Skype, you can also buy an "Online Number" in your home country that links to your computer wherever you are traveling. Your grandma makes a "local phone call" in Phoenix, and you "pick up" on your laptop in Barcelona. Google Talk has a similar feature, called Google Voice. This and other features are explained on each company's website; while they have to be set up online, they are fairly user-friendly.

Most providers also have apps that let you use the service on a mobile device (such as a smartphone, a tablet computer, or most portable media players with Wi-Fi access). For example, if you have the Skype app on your smartphone, you can get online at a café or any Wi-Fi hotspot to make calls. Fring (www.fring.com) allows you to use other VoIP providers—including Google Talk—on your smartphone. You can make Internet calls even if you're traveling without your own mobile device: Many European Internet cafés already have Skype, as well as microphones and webcams, built into their machines—just log on and chat away.

Internet calling does have its negatives. You're tethered to one spot while you talk. And in order for it to work, you need a very strong Internet connection. If your hotel's Wi-Fi signal is weak or spotty, these programs can be frustrating to use: The video freezes, the sound cuts out intermittently, or the person on the other end can't hear you.

Even if you're not using Internet calling, it's worth knowing about because of its increasing popularity in Europe. It's only a matter of time before a new European friend who wants to keep in touch asks you, "Are you on Skype?"

Landline Telephones

Each country's phone system is different, but each one works—logically. The key to figuring out a foreign phone is to approach it without comparing it to yours back home. It works for the residents, and it can work for you.

As in the US, these days many Europeans do most of their phoning on mobile telephones. But for those sticking with landlines, here are the different places from which to make landline calls.

Hotel-Room Phones: Phones in your hotel room can be great for local calls and for calls using cheap international phone cards (described later). Otherwise, they can be an almost criminal rip-off. I use hotel phones only when I'm feeling flush and lazy, for a quick "Call me in Stockholm at this number" message. Many hotels charge a fee for local and "toll-free" as well as long-distance or international calls—always ask for the rates before you dial.

Types of Telephone Cards

You can save plenty of money on your calls, especially international calls, by using a telephone card purchased in Europe. (Don't use expensive calling-card services offered by US companies such as Sprint and AT&T; these are a rotten value.)

Insertable Phone Cards: These cards, which can only be used at pay phones, are common throughout Europe (except Britain). They are easy to use and sold conveniently at post offices, newsstands, street kiosks, tobacco shops, and train stations. Simply take the phone off the hook, insert the card, wait for a dial tone, and dial away. The phone displays your credit ticking down as you talk. While you can use these cards to call anywhere, they're only a good  deal for making quick local calls. Each European country has its own phone card—so your German card won't work in an Austrian phone. The cheapest cards can cost $5—more phone time than you may need in that country. You can always blow through the remaining telephone time by calling home, or pass your card to another traveler.

International Phone Cards: These cards can be used to make inexpensive calls from nearly any phone, including the one in your hotel room or a mobile phone that has a European SIM card. (Without a European SIM card, you'd pay high international rates just to connect to the phone card's access number, negating any cost savings.)

With these cards, phone calls from Europe to the US can cost less than a nickel a minute. You can also use the card to make calls within the same country and to other countries in Europe. Cards are generally marked as national or international. All cards work for both domestic or international calls, but you get better rates if you use the card for the purpose it was intended.

International cards all work the same way and are simple to use.

These prepaid cards come with a toll-free number and a PIN code (similar to cheap calling cards widely available in the US). The back of the card often contains basic instructions in English on how to make calls. Scratch off the back to reveal your PIN, then dial the toll-free number to reach an automated operator (if calling from your hotel-room phone, check first with the desk to see if there's a fee to call toll-free numbers). Punch in your PIN code at the prompt, then dial the number you want to call. Before you're connected, a voice tells you how much is left in your account. The prompts are nearly always in English, but if they aren't, experiment: Dial your code, followed by the pound sign (#), then the phone number, then pound again, and so on, until it works. If you're making lots of calls, you can avoid redialing the access number and PIN code by pressing whichever key (usually #) allows you to launch directly into your next call—just follow the instructions on the card.

International phone cards are sold at many kiosks, newsstands, long-distance phone shops, youth hostels, and Internet cafés, but the best selection is usually at hole-in-the wall calling shops that cater to immigrants—the leading experts on phoning home cheaply. Tell the vendor you want the cheapest card for making calls to the US. Most cards work only in the country where you buy them, but some cards can be used in multiple countries; if traveling to Norway, Denmark, and Sweden, look for a card that will function in all three places. Buy a lower-denomination card in case the card is a dud. Many shops also sell cardless codes, printed right on the receipt.

There's one catch: International phone cards are such a good deal that the national telecom companies in some countries (including Germany and Great Britain) have cracked down. In these places, using one of these cards at a pay phone comes with a hefty surcharge that effectively eliminates any savings. However, even in these countries, international phone cards are still a good deal for making calls from your hotel room (or any landline other than a pay phone). In Eastern Europe, these cards are harder to find—and rarely as cheap.

Because you don't need the actual card to use your account, it's shareable. You can write down the access number and PIN code and share it with friends.

You'll never be charged for receiving calls, so having someone from the US call you in your room can be a cheap way to stay in touch (provided they have a long-distance plan with good international rates). Give your family a list of your hotels' phone numbers before you leave. While you're on the road, you can set up calling times by email, text messages, or quick pay-phone calls. Then relax in your room and wait for the ring.

Public Pay Phones: While pay phones are on the endangered species list, you'll still see phone booths (in most European languages, these are called *cabina,* kah-bee-nah) and banks of phones in post offices and train stations. Pay phones generally come with multilingual instructions. If you follow these step-by-step, the phone will work—usually. Operators generally speak some English and are helpful. International codes, instructions, and international assistance numbers are usually on the wall (printed in several languages) or in the front of the phone book. If I have problems, I ask a local person for help.

Most public phones in Europe work with insertable phone cards that you buy locally (described earlier). While some card phones also accept coins, most don't. Great Britain, an exception to the norm, doesn't sell insertable phone cards. Their pay phones accept coins or major credit cards. A few other European countries also have a smattering of coin-operated phones. If you use one, have enough small change to complete your call. Only entirely unused coins will be returned—so don't plug in large coins until it's clear that you'll be having a long conversation. The digital countdown meter warns you when you're about to be cut off. Many phones allow follow-on calls, so you won't lose your big-coin credit—look for this button and push it (rather than hanging up), then dial the next number.

Call Shops: Cheap call shops that advertise low rates to faraway lands have popped up all over Europe, often in immigrant neighborhoods. While these target immigrants from the developing world who want to call home cheaply, tourists can use them, too. (A few European post offices have old-fashioned metered phones that work similarly.) The clerk assigns you a booth and can help you with your long-distance prefixes. You sit in your private sweatbox, make the call, and pay the bill when you're done. Sometimes (especially at post offices), calls cost the same as from a public phone, but most of the calling shops specialize in long-distance calls and can have cheaper rates. Before using any metered phone service, be completely clear on the rates. For example, the listed price may be per *unit,* rather than per minute—if there are 10 "units" in a minute, your call costs 10 times what you expected.

Getting Online

To get online in Europe, you have two choices: Bring your own wireless portable device to access Wi-Fi hotspots, or use public Internet terminals (such as the ones at an Internet café, library, or your hotel).

Wi-Fi Access in Europe

More and more travelers are bringing along smartphones, tablet computers, laptops, and other wireless devices to enhance their trips. While Wi-Fi (sometimes called "WLAN" in Europe) is readily available in many areas, in my experience, the quality of the signal is potluck. For instance, it can slow down or speed up suddenly, or just decide to conk out every few minutes. Have some patience and keep your Internet chores to a minimum.

These days, the majority of accommodations in Europe offer Wi-Fi, as do many cafés. Access is often free, but occasionally you will have to pay a fee. Strangely, while many budget and mid-range hotels offer free Wi-Fi to their guests, the pricier places are more likely to charge.

If hotel Wi-Fi is important to you, ask about it when booking your accommodations—and be specific with your questions. For instance, many accommodations are located in historic old buildings with thick walls. This means that well-intended Wi-Fi signals often can't penetrate past the lobby area. Even if your hotel advertises Wi-Fi, don't assume you can get online in your room. Make sure you ask when you book. Once I get to a hotel, I ask at the desk for the network name (in case several are in range) and password so I can log on right away. If your hotel lacks Wi-Fi, the staff can tell you where to get online nearby.

When you're out and about, your best bet for finding Wi-Fi is often at a café. If you sit down, you can usually just buy a drink in exchange for use of their network (you may need to request a password from the cashier). More sneaky—but also effective—is to stroll down a café-lined street, smartphone in hand, checking for available networks every few steps until you find one that works. (I've also found that free Wi-Fi at executive lounges in airports often leaks into the main hall. Just sitting against the wall, I can get online for free.)

Some towns have public Wi-Fi hotspots scattered around highly trafficked areas. Sometimes this is free, or you may have to pay at the tourist office or an Internet café to get the password. Just find whichever idyllic spot you like best—a bench overlooking a sandy beach, on a floodlit piazza, or along a bustling people-watching boulevard—then log on and surf away.

Translating Foreign Websites

Monolinguists will appreciate the fact that many European websites offer the option to view their pages in English. For those that don't, a website translator can help.

Google's Chrome browser (free, available for Windows and Mac) automatically detects when a Web page is in a foreign language and asks if you want it translated to English. While the translation is automated (and can be less than perfect), this opens up a whole new world of local information for travelers. For example, while preparing for my last trip to Copenhagen, I used this feature to read piles of restaurant reviews written by Danish users.

Google lends a hand even if you use a different browser (such as Windows Internet Explorer). Whenever you Google a page that's in a foreign language, you'll see a "Translate this Page" button next to the URL. Click on it for a rough version in English. You can also cut and paste any text into Google Translate (www .translate.google.com) for an instant translation; click the speaker icon to hear the foreign words spoken aloud.

Other Ways to Get Online

While Wi-Fi is the most convenient method for getting online with your laptop, you do have a few other options.

High-Speed Cable Internet: Many hotel rooms and some Internet cafés have high-speed Internet jacks that you can plug into with an Ethernet cable (with an RJ45 plug; looks like an oversized phone cord)—no special software or password required. You could travel with a small length of Ethernet cable just in case, but most hotels will loan you one if you ask. Again, while this is usually free, some hotels charge a fee for access.

Cellular Modems: For those who need more consistent Internet access than scattered Wi-Fi hotspots will provide, cellular modems (also known as wireless modems or mobile broadband) may be worth considering. A mobile phone company routes your Internet connection over its high-speed data network—it's essentially like turning your computer into a cell phone. Usually you buy a "dongle"—it looks like a USB flash drive—that you insert into your laptop's USB slot. In the UK, Vodafone offers a variety of pay-as-you-go mobile broadband packages, some as low as $40 for up to 500 megabytes of data (www.vodafone.co.uk). T-Mobile has similar plans in the UK and Germany (www.t-mobile.co.uk).

Typing @ on Keyboards

Language and Name	Pronounced	How It's Typed
French		
signe arobase	seen ah-roh-bahs	Alt Gr + 0
German		
At-zeichen; also *Klammeraffe* ("monkey hug") or *A-Affenschwanz* ("A with a monkey tail")	"at"-tsei-khehn	Alt Gr + Q
Italian		
chiocciola ("snail")	kee-OH-choh-lah	Alt Gr + @
Spanish and Portuguese		
arroba	ah-ROH-bah	Alt Gr + 2

Public Internet Terminals

If you don't bring your own wireless gadgets, no worries—finding public Internet terminals in Europe is a breeze. These days, many hotels and hostels have a computer in the lobby for guests to use (sometimes free, sometimes for a fee). Otherwise, head for an Internet café (also called a cybercafé). While these places don't always serve food or drinks—sometimes they're just one big, functional, sweaty room filled with computers—they are an easy and affordable way to get online. Large European chains offer inexpensive access in big cities.

Even if a small town lacks an Internet café, there's almost always some way to get online—at libraries, bookstores, post offices, copy shops, and so on. Ask the tourist office, your hotelier, fellow travelers, or any young person for the nearest place to access the Internet.

European computers typically use non-American keyboards. Most letters are the same as back home, but a few are switched around, and many of the command keys are labeled in a foreign language. It takes time to find the right keys. Many European keyboards have an "Alt Gr" key (for "Alternate Graphics") to the right of the space bar; press this to insert the extra symbol that appears on some keys. Europeans have different names for, and different ways to type, the @ symbol; above are a few. If you can't locate a special character (such as the @ symbol), simply copy it from a Web page and paste into your email message.

Many computers have a box in the lower right-hand corner of the

PHONES & TECHNOLOGY

screen where you can click and select which type of keyboard you prefer. If not, ask the clerk for help. Often a simple keystroke or click of the mouse can make the foreign keyboard work like an American one.

Internet Security

Whether you're accessing the Internet with your own wireless device or at a public terminal, using a shared network or computer comes with the potential for increased security risks. In general, accessing Wi-Fi is safer than logging on to a public computer—but anything you do online can open you up to cyber attacks. Protect your computer and your personal information by heeding the following tips.

Wi-Fi Safety: Start by configuring your computer for maximum security. Before your trip, make sure that your antivirus and firewall software are up-to-date and activated (this helps prevent hackers from gaining access to your machine). Many computers have a file sharing option. Though it's often off by default, it's a good idea to check that this option is not activated so that people on the same network can't access your files (to find out how to do this on your machine, do a search for your operating system and "turn off file sharing"). Newer versions of Windows have a "Public network" setting (choose this when you first join the network) that automatically configures your computer so that it's less susceptible to invasion.

Once on the road, use only legitimate hotspots. Ask the hotel or café for the specific name of their network, and make sure you log onto that exact one. In an effort to gain access to your computer, hackers sometimes create a bogus hotspot with a similar or vague name (such as "Hotel Europa Free Wi-Fi") that shows up alongside a bunch of authentic networks. It's better if a network uses a password (especially a hard-to-guess one) rather than being open to the world. If you're not actively using a hotspot, turn off Wi-Fi so that your computer is not visible to others.

Security for Public Internet Terminals: You have no idea who used that hotel-lobby computer last—or who will hop on next. Assume that anyone who touches that computer will have access to anything that you have or will enter on it. Public computers may be loaded with damaging malware, such as key logger programs that keep track of what you're typing—including passwords.

Many Web-based email servers, ecommerce, and other sites store your user name by default to make it easier to log in again later. Whenever you sign in, click the box for "public or shared computer" (if given the option) to ensure that the browser forgets your user name and password

Europe's Internet cafés, often open long hours, allow travelers to get online.

after you log out. It also makes me feel better to clear out my Internet browser's cache, history, and cookies after I'm done using a public computer so that fewer artifacts of my surfing session remain (under your browser's "Options" settings, look for a "Privacy" or "Security" category).

Sending Personal Information Online: While you're away, you may be tempted to check your online banking or credit-card statements, or to take care of other personal-finance chores. Internet security experts advise against accessing these sites entirely while traveling. Even if you're using your own computer at a password-protected hotspot, any hacker who's logged on to the same network can see what you're up to. If you need to log on to a banking website, try to do so on a hard-wired connection (i.e., using an Ethernet cable in your hotel room). Ultimately, the chances are remote that your hotspot will happen to be under scrutiny by a hacker—but it's possible.

Still, there are times when you may need to use a site that exposes sensitive personal information (for instance, if booking tickets to a museum or the theater). In those cases, make sure that the site is secure. Most browsers display a little padlock icon, and the URL begins with *https* instead of *http*. Never send a credit-card number over a website that doesn't begin with *https*. While this provides some confidence, it isn't foolproof. Remember, the safest option is to avoid accessing any sites that could be sensitive to fraud.

Experts also recommend using complicated passwords for email accounts and other online services, and changing them frequently so they're harder to crack. Passwords should include a combination of upper- and lowercase letters, and numbers or special characters.

It's also important to be careful if emailing personal information. Don't send your credit-card number in one email message. It's better to call or fax. Some people send their credit-card number in two halves, via two separate email messages. For extra security, a few banks, such as Citi and Bank of America, allow their customers to create virtual account numbers, which are one-time or short-term numbers linked to your regular credit card.

Travel Tools for Portable Devices

From apps to maps, a whole world of tools awaits the savvy traveler. This section explains how to use smartphones, portable media players (such as the iPod Touch), tablet computers, and ereaders to enhance your trip (for a list of gear to consider bringing along, as well as advice on using adapters to charge your devices in European outlets, see page 83).

Mobile Apps

Apps for smartphones and tablets can be useful both before you leave and while you're traveling. Most devices are preloaded with apps that can come in handy on a trip (such as an alarm clock, compass, calculator, weather, and so on). But you can greatly extend your device's usefulness by downloading additional tools, such as restaurant reviews, translators, and transportation apps.

While it's convenient to be able to access this type of information, there is a catch: For many mobile apps, you need to be online to download the latest information. With the prevalence of Wi-Fi in most corners of Europe, this is generally not a problem—just find a hotspot and browse away. But if you have a smartphone or tablet with mobile data capabilities, you can incur outrageously high data roaming fees if you try to access these apps while not logged in to a hotspot. To be sure you understand your options, see page 242.

I've recommended some of my favorite mobile apps below. All of these are available on Apple's iOS devices through their app store, and many of them are also available for Android, Windows Phone, and BlackBerry platforms. I've noted whether they're free or must be paid for, and whether they're self-contained (Internet connection not necessary after the initial download) or require ongoing Internet access. While it's possible to download these apps over any Wi-Fi network, plan ahead and try to grab the ones you want while you're still at home. This is by no means a comprehensive list. New apps are hitting the market every day. To find the latest, browse the iTunes App Store or the Android Market (look under "Travel"), or search for tips on travel blogs and websites.

Trip Planning and Management

From booking flights and hotels to managing your itinerary, these apps can help you plan your trip.

Travel Booking: Orbitz, Priceline, Booking.com, Expedia's TripAssist, and Travelocity (free, Internet) allow you to search for flights, hotels, rental cars, and more. Skyscanner (free, Internet) helps you survey a wide variety of European budget airlines to find the cheapest connection between any two points.

Airlines: Each airline has its own app; these usually allow you to search for and book flights, check in, and track the status of a flight. While you can do many of these same activities through the airline's website on your phone's browser, the apps are generally faster and more user-friendly.

Flight Trackers: Plug your flight details into FlightTrack (pay, Internet) or Kayak (free, Internet), and these apps will keep track of whether your plane is on time. Folks back home can even track your plane's progress on a map.

Itinerary Organizers: Apps like TripIt (free, Internet) save all your trip details in one convenient place. Forward reservation emails to your TripIt account, and it automatically adds them to your itinerary.

Audio Tours, Transit, Restaurants, Money, Weather, and More

The following tools run the gamut, from Europe-specific advice to apps that help document your travels.

General Europe: Rick Steves Audio Europe (free, self-contained) has hundreds of radio interviews and dozens of audio walking tours of Europe's top sights, organized by destination for easy browsing (for more info, see "Audio Tours," later). Download the playlists that interest you and fit your itinerary before your trip, then listen to them offline as you travel.

Smart Traveler (free, Internet), from the US State Department, includes basic information on each country, plus travel advisories.

Public Transportation: Various subway map apps for the London Tube, Paris Métro, and others (pay, self-contained) have detailed, digital plans of public transit networks that save you from having to unfold an unwieldy map on a busy platform. The free, self-contained MetrO is a handy route-planner for public transit in dozens of European cities, but does not have maps.

DB Navigator (free, Internet), German Rail's comprehensive train timetables, includes connections for all of continental Europe. For the UK, try thetrainline (free) or UK Train Times (pay).

Restaurants and Reviews: TripAdvisor's app (free, Internet) gives you access to millions of user reviews of restaurants, hotels, and sights (though TripAdvisor ratings should never be taken as gospel—see page 32). Some users prefer Yelp (free, Internet), which is just catching on in Europe; unlike back home, where most Yelp reviewers are locals, European Yelp reviews tend to come from travelers.

Currency and Conversions: Oanda Currency Converter, Currency, or XE Currency (free, Internet) instantly tells you today's exchange rate. Measures (pay, self-contained) converts various European units (metric measurements, clothing sizes, even currency) to American ones.

Weather: Take a walking tour or hit a museum? You can better plan your day with The Weather Channel, AccuWeather, and other forecast apps (free, Internet).

Medical Help: mPassport (pay, self-contained) are city-specific apps that direct you to English-speaking doctors and hospitals, as well as local names for prescription medications.

Journaling: Note-taking apps such as All-in Notes and Microsoft OneNote (pay, self-contained) let you combine photos, recorded sounds, and written notes to keep a multimedia journal of your trip.

Translation

These amazing apps are helpful for navigating in a country where you don't speak the language.

With Google Translate (free, Internet), you can type something in a foreign language (or have someone speak clearly into your microphone) for an immediate translation. You can also say or type a sentence in English, and a computer voice actually says the translation (or hold up the screen to show someone the written translated message).

Digital phrase books, such as Lonely Planet Audio Phrasebooks (pay, self-contained), allow you to simply press a button to hear the phrase you're struggling to pronounce.

With Word Lens (pay, Internet), you can aim your smartphone's camera at a sign in a foreign language, and it'll instantly translate it for you (available for Spanish, French, German, and Italian).

Maps and Navigation

With the help of mapping apps, you can navigate Europe more easily than ever. Smart smartphone users have become accustomed to having local maps at their fingertips and to downloading route information, including maps, turn-by-turn directions, and estimated trip duration. But there's a catch to using mapping apps overseas: Since base maps must be downloaded and continually updated on the Internet, you'll either have to wait until you reach a hotspot or pay international data roaming fees in order to call up a new map.

To avoid these fees, download a map or driving route when you're on Wi-Fi (for instance, from your hotel), then use it to navigate all day long. This can be useful whether driving through Burgundy or walking around Barcelona. And since the GPS signal does not utilize the Internet (instead, it uses a combination of satellites and cell phone towers to triangulate your precise location), it will continue to track your location on the map, even when you're offline.

To download a map on your iPhone, simply punch in the start and end points of your route or the city or town's name. The map remains available on your phone, and you can zoom in and out, even if you go offline. Note, though, that maps are downloaded at a fairly low resolution (you can only zoom in so far before it becomes unreadable); route time estimates are based on the initial request and don't adjust as you travel; and it can only remember one route at a time—so you can't switch to another route without a Wi-Fi hotspot or paying for data roaming. GPS also gobbles battery life, so you may want to bring a car charger.

The iPhone app OffMaps (pay) will store multiple maps for later use. You need an Internet connection to download maps, but once that's done, the maps are accessible anywhere. Google Maps for Android phones have a similar capability that lets you download and cache (save) several maps for use offline (free). For much more fully featured GPS apps for your mobile phone, check out those from TomTom, Garmin, and other GPS device makers, though European maps for these tend to be very expensive (for more on bringing dedicated GPS devices to Europe, see page 164).

Keeping in Touch
Stay connected to home with these apps.

Social Media: Using Facebook, Twitter, Instagram, and other social networking apps (free, Internet), you can post descriptions and photos of your trip while keeping track of what your friends are up to back home. For details, see "Sharing Your Trip" on page 272.

Internet Calls and Texting: Skype or Fring (free, Internet) lets you make free voice or video calls over Wi-Fi to fellow users' computers and smartphones, and cheap calls to other phones (see "Internet Calling," earlier). Text Plus and Textfree (free, Internet) work similarly for text messaging (note that both parties need to have the app installed).

News: New York Times, ESPN ScoreCenter, NPR News, and other news/information readers (free, Internet) help you keep track of news and scores back home.

PHONES & TECHNOLOGY

File Sharing: Dropbox (free, Internet) saves files from your computer in an online account, which you can access from anywhere on your smartphone or a computer.

Postcards: Using apps like SnapShot Postcard (pay, Internet), you can snap a photo with your phone and turn it into a custom postcard, which will be printed and sent via snail mail to anywhere you want. Various digital postcard apps (including fCards) will let you email your postcard instead.

Electronic Guidebooks

With ebook readers such as the Kindle and Nook becoming more affordable, electronic books are getting more popular. Plus, many ereaders are available as mobile apps, allowing you to turn your tablet or smartphone into a digital book. Though the majority of ebooks being read are fiction, ereaders can also be useful as a travel tool. Many guidebook series, including most of my titles, are available as ebooks (check out Amazon, Barnes & Noble, and Apple's electronic bookstores).

While I still consider myself a paper guy, I can see the advantages to ebooks. An ereader or smartphone is smaller and lighter than a guidebook. You can effortlessly carry a number of ebooks without adding weight to your bag, which is great for long, multi-destination trips. And with built-in Wi-Fi, you can buy books from anywhere, convenient for spur-of-the-moment detours. Eventually ebooks will offer other advantages impossible for traditional paper books—including customizing content to cover precisely the destinations you want and linking maps to GPS technology so you'll never get lost.

But for now, ebooks have their limitations. Though they work well for novels, they're not quite in sync yet with the needs of guidebook users. It can be difficult to find the information you're looking for; flipping from page to page can be awkward; and maps—often designed to run across two pages—don't always appear correctly.

Ebook apps, offered by various travel publishers—including Lonely Planet and Frommer's—are guidebooks in app format. These are similar to an ebook but don't require an ereader, allowing them to be more customized and, in many cases, easier to navigate (for example, interactive maps).

While currently only 10 percent of guidebook sales are electronic, ebooks are here to stay, and they'll only gain in popularity. But until the perfect digital solution arrives, the most practical guidebook format remains the one you're holding in your hands.

Audio Tours

With an audio tour, you can immerse yourself in a wonderful sight, enjoying its visual wonder while listening to information that gives it all meaning. Before you leave for Europe, it's worth checking online to see what kinds of digital content you can find to enhance your trip. Using Google or the iTunes store, search for sights and cities you'll be visiting. For instance, Versailles offers informative podcasts for touring the extensive palace grounds (www.chateauversailles.fr). Remember to bring earbuds.

I've produced free, self-guided audio versions of my tours of the major sights in Athens, Florence, London, Paris, Rome, Venice, Vienna, and several other places (download them via www.ricksteves.com/audio europe, iTunes, or the Rick Steves Audio Europe free smartphone app). These user-friendly, easy-to-follow, fun, and informative audio tours are available for museums (for instance, Paris' Louvre and Orsay, Florence's Uffizi), churches (St. Paul's in London, St. Peter's in Rome, the Basilica of St. Francis in Assisi), ancient sights (Athens' Acropolis, Rome's Colosseum), my favorite neighborhood walks and tours (historic Paris, London's Westminster, Venice's Grand Canal), and much more. Compared to live tours, these audio tours are hard to beat: No guide will stand you up, the quality is reliable, you can take the tour exactly when you like, and they're free.

Some European museums offer room-by-room audioguide tours that you can download on the spot to your mobile device (rather than borrowing a physical audioguide). To access the tour, simply log onto the museum's Wi-Fi network with your device. While this sounds complicated, it generally works great.

Travel Photography

If my hotel was burning down and I could grab just one thing, it would be my digital camera with its memory card filled with photos. Every year I ask myself whether it's worth the worry and expense of mixing photography with my travels. After I return home and relive my trip through those pictures, the answer is always "Yes!"

Since I spend four months a year in Europe, I usually prefer to bring a compact point-and-shoot camera to keep things as lightweight as possible. There are trade-offs—smaller cameras have smaller lenses, and the image quality can suffer slightly. But many people find that since they can slip the camera into a pocket, they're more likely to take it everywhere...and use it more. Serious photographers can consider more elaborate digital SLR cameras (with interchangeable lenses and a satisfying, old-fashioned shutter click). These cameras are bulky, but produce beautiful, professional-looking images. If you prefer the portability of a point-and-shoot but the advanced features of a DSLR, consider a compact interchangeable lens digital camera. These cameras offer better image quality than point-and-shoots, but aren't as large as DSLRs and allow you to swap out lenses. If shopping for a camera, check out reviews on www.cnet.com, www.steves-digicams.com, and www.dpreview.com.

Some people prefer to capture Europe in motion. A video camera used to be a big, heavy lug-along that weighed down day bags and compromised footloose and fancy-free travel. But thanks to pocket-sized video cameras (such as ones from Sony, Panasonic, and Kodak), along with the proliferation of high-definition video cameras built into smartphones and still cameras, shooting and sharing vacation videos is easier than ever.

Accessories and Gadgets

Like many hobbies, photography allows you to spend endless amounts of money on accessories. The following are particularly useful to the traveling photographer. But be careful not to take so much gear on your trip that you become a slave to your gadgets.

Memory: Travel with enough digital memory to cover your entire trip. Memory cards come in different types (Secure Digital is most common, but there's also CompactFlash and Sony's Memory Stick) and different sizes (from 2 to 16 gigabytes). Memory is so cheap now, I'd spring for one of the bigger cards, but buy the cards at home; although they're readily available in Europe, they're more expensive. Higher-capacity cards are necessary if you plan to record lots of video. For more tips on saving and backing up images—especially on a long trip—see "Managing Images on the Road," later.

Batteries: Some digital cameras come with a battery that can be recharged; others take AA batteries (which the camera will burn through amazingly quickly). Rechargeable or lithium AA batteries last much longer than disposable alkalines and are significantly cheaper in the long run—you can buy a good set of rechargeable nickel-metal hydride (NiMH) batteries and a charger for about $20. Before you buy, make sure the charger will work in Europe (look for the voltage numbers "110V" and "220V"), and take an adapter to plug it in (for details, see "Electronics," page 81). Be aware that you cannot pack loose lithium batteries in your checked luggage—but you can carry spare rechargeable

A mini-tripod is light and easy to carry, and allows you to take remarkably clear low-light shots—like this serene twilight image of Moscow's Red Square.

batteries in your carry-on as long as they're sealed inside a plastic zip-lock bag or in their original packaging.

Mini-tripod: Because the flash on my camera gives a harsh image, I prefer to use existing light—which often requires a tripod. A conventional tripod is too large to lug around Europe. A mini-tripod screws into most cameras, sprouts three legs, and holds everything perfectly still for slow shutter speeds, timed exposures, and automatic shutter-release shots. (About five inches high, it looks like a small lunar-landing module; some are flexible enough to wrap around posts.) Those without a mini-tripod use a tiny beanbag or a sock filled with rice, or get good at balancing their camera on anything solid and adjusting the tilt with the lens cap or strap. If you're planning to use a mini-tripod, master your delayed shutter release button or consider bringing a shutter release cable (if your camera accepts one).

Telescoping Extender: An extendable, hand-held camera arm allows you to securely take photos of yourself (and your travel partners) without handing the camera to a stranger or leaving it propped on a bench. Also called a "monopod," a telescoping rod screws into the tripod mount on the bottom of most cameras and can extend out as far as three feet. Some even come with a mirror so you can see yourself (this is unnecessary on cameras with dual or rotating screens). When not in use, the telescoping rod collapses down to a compact eight inches in length. Some are as thin as a pencil; others can clip to your smartphone.

SLR Lenses and Filters: No-frills photographers will stick with the mid-range lens that comes with the camera; serious shutterbugs can look into zoom, wide-angle, or image stabilization lenses. If you invest in a zoom lens, get one that covers both ends of the visual range—close-ups to long shots. A 24-105 mm lens gives you a great medium-wide angle that zooms to a medium-telephoto. Make sure all your lenses have a haze or UV filter. It's better to bang and smudge up your filter than your actual lens. The only other filter you might use is a polarizer, which eliminates reflections and enhances color separation, but you can lose up to two stops of light with it. Don't use

SLR cameras give you the maximum in adaptability, including interchangeable lenses.

more than one filter at a time, and don't go cheap. You're placing another layer of glass in front of your shooting lens. If the filter is poor, your images will not be as sharp as they should be. Some photographers suggest using a lens shade in daylight; it keeps stray light off the front of the camera to prevent "lens flare" and enhances the color saturation of your images.

Tissue, Cleaner, and Lens Cap: A lens-cleaning tissue and a small bottle of cleaning solution are wise additions (use cleaning solution sparingly and only for greasy spots—too much cleaner can damage your lens). If you have an SLR, protect your lens with a cap that dangles on its string when you're shooting.

TV Adapter Cable: Many cameras come with a cable that allows you to plug directly into a TV set. If you're staying at a hotel in Europe with a modern TV, you can enjoy a big-screen digital slideshow while you're still on the road.

There are several different types of memory cards. Figure out which one your camera uses, get the highest-capacity one you can afford, and consider buying an extra one for additional storage.

Camera Case: When you're not using your camera or camcorder, keep it in a small, padded case inside your day bag. If you have a DSLR or extra accessories, you may need a dedicated bag. A functional and economical way to tote your gear is in a small nylon stuff bag (the type made for hikers). I steer clear of formal camera bags, which are bulky and attract thieves.

Managing Images on the Road

Even if you have plenty of space on your camera's memory card, it's always wise to back up your images. One year, I took some of the best photos I can remember at Chartres Cathedral in France, when the setting sun brought life to the expressions on the delicately carved faces of the Gothic statues. Afterwards, I celebrated with a *salade de gésiers* of bouncy lettuce and chicken innards, washed down with a life-is-good carafe of red house wine. Back at my hotel, as I sorted through my intimate moments with those statues through the viewing screen of my camera, I accidentally erased everything on my memory card. That night, I learned several important lessons: 1) Never cull photos with a wine buzz, and 2) Be vigilant about backing up. You never know what might happen, from leaving your camera on a train to dropping your memory card in a puddle. Here are some tips for dealing with images while you travel.

Be selective. Travelers who are taking an extended trip, recording a lot of video, or just plain shutter happy may run out of card space. If that happens, the easiest solution is to edit your images ruthlessly and often, keeping only the very best shots. (The people who wind up watching your slideshow will thank you for it.) Get in the habit of doing this periodically, even if space isn't an issue, to avoid bringing home an overwhelming number of photos. If you cull photos and are still short on space, you may need to transfer your photos onto another medium (see tips below), then empty your memory card so you can reuse it.

Dump images onto a laptop. Since I usually travel with a laptop, I can simply upload my photos to my computer every so often (if your computer lacks a card reader, remember to bring a cable so you can connect your camera to your laptop). For added safety, you can back up photos from your laptop to a high-capacity USB flash drive, burn them to a CD or DVD, or upload them to a photo-sharing service such as Flickr or Snapfish (see 274, later).

Use other media. If you want to save or back up photos, but you're traveling *sans* laptop, you have several options. Many European photo stores and Internet cafés can burn your images to a DVD or CD for about $10. (Be mindful of how much memory you need; there's no point burning three CDs when one DVD would do the job.) If you have an iPad, you can purchase Apple's camera connection kit, which lets you transfer photos from an SD card or camera directly to your device. You can also consider a photo backup device like the HyperDrive Colorspace UDMA (www.hypershop.com), a palm-sized (but pricey) gadget that has a memory-card reader, hard drive, and color screen.

Consider lower resolution. If you plan to use your photos only for emailing or posting to a website, and if you're certain you won't want to print any of your photos, you can squeeze more images on your memory card by taking photos at a lower resolution. In order to get double the shots on my memory card, I sometimes shoot at the grainier "basic" level rather than the memory-gobbling fine-resolution level. But I've sometimes regretted taking lower-resolution images—such as when I've captured a really great shot, but the resolution is too low to make a large framed print.

Remember the cloud. Companies like Apple and Amazon are trying to entice consumers to store their music, books, images, and videos in their "clouds" (their networks). With Apple's iCloud, owners of a newer iPhone have an automatic image backup system built in. All you have to do is enable Apple's Photo Stream app on your iPhone (under iCloud settings). Then, whenever you're at a Wi-Fi hotspot, your phone will automatically send your latest pictures to the cloud, which in turn pushes those images to other iCloud-enabled devices (iPad, home computer, etc.) the next time they're connected to the Internet. The iCloud will hold your last 1,000 images and saves new photos for 30 days (so eventually you must edit and permanently save the images you want). With both Apple and Amazon, the first 5 GB of storage is free (about 2,000 photos), and additional storage is available at a price.

Tricks for a Good Shot

Most people are limited by their photographic skills, not by their camera. Understand your camera. Devour the manual. Take experimental shots, make notes, and see what happens. If you don't understand f-stops or depth of field, find a photography class or book and learn (for tips on taking better pictures, visit www.photosecrets.com and www.bbc.com /travel/photography). Camera stores sell good books on photography in general and travel photography in particular. I shutter to think how many people are underexposed and lacking depth in this field.

A sharp eye connected to a wild imagination will be your most valuable piece of equipment. Develop a knack for what will look good and be interesting after the trip. The skilled photographer's

Find a creative angle.

The Vatican Museum staircase: Have fun with composition and find creative new angles.

eye sees striking light, shade, form, lines, patterns, texture, and colors.

Look for a new slant to an old sight. Postcard-type shots are boring. Everyone knows what the Eiffel Tower looks like. Find a unique or different approach to sights that everyone has seen. Shoot the bell tower through the horse's legs or lay your camera on the floor to shoot the Gothic ceiling.

Capture the personal and intimate details of your trip. Show how you lived, whom you met, and what made each day an adventure (a close-up of a picnic, your favorite taxi driver, or the character you befriended at the launderette).

Vary your perspective—add extra depth with a foreground.

Vary your perspective. You can shoot close, far, low, high, during the day, and at night. Don't fall into the rut of always centering a shot. Use foregrounds to add color, depth, and interest to landscapes.

Maximize good lighting. Real photographers get single-minded at the "magic hours"—early morning and late afternoon—when the sun is very low, light is rich and diffused, and colors glow. Plan for these times. Grab bright colors. Develop an eye for great lighting; any time of day, you may luck into a perfectly lit scene. Some of my best photos are the result of great lighting, not great subjects.

Get close. Notice details. Eliminate distractions by zeroing in on your subject. Get so close that you show only one thing. Don't try to show it all in one shot. For any potentially great shot, I try several variations—then delete the ones that don't pan out.

Fill the lens with your subject.

People are the most interesting subjects. It takes nerve to walk up to people and take their picture. It can be difficult, but be nervy. Ask for

The best people shots are up close and well lit, with a soft background.

permission. (In any language, point at your camera and ask, "Photo?") Your subject will probably be delighted. Try to show action. A candid is better than a posed shot. Even a "posed candid" shot is better than a posed one. Give your subject something to do. Challenge the kid in the market to juggle oranges. Many photographers take a second shot immediately after the first portrait to capture a looser, warmer subject. The famous war photographer Robert Capa once said, "If your pictures aren't good enough, you're not close enough." My best portraits are so close that the entire head can't fit into the frame.

Buildings, in general, are not interesting. It does not matter if Karl Marx or Beethoven was born there—a house is as dead as its former resident. As travel photographers gain experience, they take more people shots and fewer buildings or general landscapes.

Expose for your subject. Even if your camera is automatic, your subject can turn out to be a silhouette. Get those faces in the sun or (even better) lit from the side.

When shooting a portrait, the sun should be behind you. Have the sunlight hit the subject's face at an angle by making sure it's coming over your right or left shoulder. This creates dramatic highlights and shadows on the subject's face. Avoid shooting outdoor portraits during the lighting "dead zone," between 11:00 a.m. and 2:00 p.m. If you have to shoot then, use your camera's flash to fill the shadows that form in the eye sockets, under the nose, and under the chin. High-end cameras have an adjustable power setting on the flash. Use it to get the right ratio of sunlight to fill light.

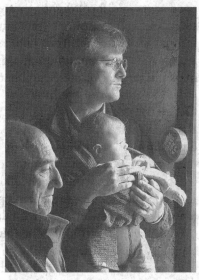

Capture the magic with just the right light.

Don't be afraid to handhold a slow shot. Tripods enable you to take professional shots that could compete with those at the museum gift shop. But most major museums prohibit you from using a tripod or a flash (which ages paintings). Despite these restrictions, you can take good shots by holding your camera as still as possible. If you can lean against a wall, for instance, you become a tripod instead of a bipod. Placing your elbows on a flat surface also helps. Wait until you breathe out to take the picture (when you hold your breath, your body shakes more). Use a self-timer or a shutter release cable, which clicks the shutter more smoothly than your finger can. With these tricks, I get good pictures inside a museum at 1/30 of a second. Many digital cameras nowadays use "image stabilization" to help in these situations. (And if you still can't get that perfect shot, go to the gift store. Nearly every important museum has a good selection of top-quality cards and prints at reasonable prices.)

Back lighting "puts an edge" on ice-cream lickers.

Bracket shots when the lighting is tricky. The best way to get good shots in difficult lighting situations is to "bracket" your shots (take several different pictures of the same scene, slightly varying the exposure settings for each one). You can simply delete the unsuccessful attempts. Automatic cameras usually meter properly up to 8 or 10 seconds, which makes night shots easy, though bracketing may still be necessary.

Once Back Home...

Relive your trip by organizing, editing, improving, and sharing your digital images.

First, come up with a system to keep your photos organized on your computer. You can simply create folders and subfolders, or you can use a more advanced photo-organizing program, such as Google's free Picasa (described later), which also includes editing and sharing features.

It's always smart to look at your pictures and see if you can improve them. While a basic photo-editing program probably came with your camera, serious shutterbugs use Adobe Photoshop Elements (an easy-to-use program for novices) or Adobe Photoshop (for more advanced work). You can't imagine how much better your photos will look until you use this software.

When it comes time to share your images, you have many options, from making prints of your favorite shots to putting them online (see the next section).

Sharing Your Trip

Back in the '70s and '80s, I eagerly shared my travel experiences through slideshows. Even that method was high-tech compared to my earliest travels—on my first trip at age 14, I collected and logged my experiences in a file of several hundred numbered postcards, each packed with notes. Those days of slow, static 20th-century methods are now long gone, replaced by a slew of fast, interactive advancements in social media, online programs, and websites.

Social Media

While on the road and back at home, I interact with more than 80,000 readers via my Facebook page. Each night, my favorite bedtime reading has been the Facebook comments from my followers. It's become a fun way for us to experience Europe together. With social-networking sites like Facebook and Google+, you can share real-time travel stories by posting quick updates—a simple task thanks to worldwide Internet access and social-media mobile apps.

You can post photos and videos, add brief captions, and receive instant feedback in the form of comments and likes. Easy uploading and drag-and-drop photo placement in Facebook makes it ideal for the non-tech-savvy. If frustrated by the one-at-a-time photo uploading on the Facebook mobile app, an application such as iLoader2 will let you upload multiple pictures or videos to your page at once.

As you update, try to avoid mundane or chronological statements of your journey ("Explored Rome today"). Aim to be witty and insightful ("Climbed all 138 Spanish Steps!"). You want to fascinate, not bore or annoy your friends and family.

Twitter.com lets you share (or tweet) interesting tidbits, humorous instances, and awe-inspiring pictures. With the 140-character limit of each tweet, focus on the little, entertaining things and quick updates. If you bring your mobile phone or buy one in Europe, you can text in your tweets as you travel (but beware of texting costs, explained earlier).

With any of these sites, it's important to not share your whereabouts with strangers (or advertise that your home is unguarded), especially when you're traveling. Under Facebook's Privacy settings, you can make yourself unsearchable on public search engines. You can also make your profile, including your wall, information, profile pictures, tagged photos, and individual albums, viewable by friends only (or certain individuals, networks, or lists). The Activity Log on your Facebook profile page allows you to change the visibility of each and every post. Similarly, on Google+ consider selecting specific circles to control the visibility of individual posts (note that your name and any other public fields you share will appear in Google's search results). On Twitter, you can protect your tweets so that only those you approve can receive them.

Blogs

While social media is optimal for quick updates, blogging is the best option for lengthy storytelling. Maintaining a blog of your travels is the perfect way to document your journey, as well as entertain family and friends with your adventures.

First, decide on a blog host. Popular choices include WordPress.com and Blogger.com. Both are free, relatively easy to use, and suitable for on-the-go writing. WordPress allows for complete customization—you can choose from more than 100 themes or design your own, as well as create supplementary pages to detail your experiences.

Tumblr.com lets you easily post media, including text, photos, audio, video, slideshows, links, and more. The site can be synced with Facebook or Twitter to publish directly to them, and multiple people can contribute to one blog. If you're going to be away from your computer, you can use Tumblr's queue option to automatically publish your blog posts at staggered times, or consider texting and emailing posts directly from your mobile phone. You can even dictate your posts over the phone if you're feeling ambitious (or lazy).

Several travel-oriented sites are geared specifically toward trip sharing, with features such as maps, statistics, and itineraries to document your travels. TravelPod.com and MapQuest Travel Blogs (http://travel blogs.mapquest.com) offer free hosting for travel blogs and journals, with quick and easy sharing to outlets like Facebook and Twitter. You can build your itinerary, chart your route on an interactive map, and add photos, videos, and stories to create a shareable overview of your journey. Mobile applications allow you to update either site on the go, and each also offers the option to print your trip as a book. Other hosts include TripNTale.com and MyTripJournal.com, both of which let you create a personal travel profile.

Whichever host you choose, creating a memorable blog requires sticking to a few guidelines:

• It's best to write your blog entries in a non-Web-based program first so that you can edit and reword your thoughts to perfection.

• When posting stories online, think about interactive elements that combine entertaining, insightful text with engaging videos and photos.

• Consider embedding slideshows (a presentation-sharing site like SlideShare.net can help) or links to related websites and resources.

• Include fascinating factoids, amusing tidbits, or interesting quotes to spice up your stories. Be intimate. Share your feelings.

• If struggling for inspiration, consider implementing a certain theme or ongoing elements like a "picture of the day."

Online Photo and Video Sharing

Photos and videos take you there in a way that words cannot. Multimedia-sharing sites let you unleash your images to friends and family—without holding them captive in a dark room. With any of these trip-sharing possibilities, editing your photos before posting online will improve their impact (see page 272).

Picasa.com: This popular photo site has organizing and editing features that allow you to create stunning images, which you can then share through Web albums or import into your social networking sites. You can also create videos from your photos and upload them straight to YouTube.

Flickr.com: You can upload pictures to Flickr from your browser, email, or phone, then share them through email or directly to your social media and blog accounts. Flickr's Organizr lets you label, tag, and arrange your photos into sets, then group those sets into collections so others may view and comment.

LiveShare.com: This site is geared toward creating social albums—ideal if traveling with a group. Upload photos from your computer or through a mobile application, then drop them into photo albums. The whole group can contribute and comment.

Instagram: This app for iPhone and Android phones lets you put fun filters on images and share them with friends.

YouTube.com: The de facto video-sharing site, YouTube offers high-quality, free video hosting with detailed privacy control. You can also try Vimeo.com, which has no bandwidth or time limits, so you can customize your videos and embed them into any website or blog.

Scrapbooks and Photo Books

Creating a tangible scrapbook of travel photos and anecdotes allows you to personally share your journey with loved ones at home. It's simple—a few clicks and personal touches, and you've got your own coffee-table masterpiece.

Your friends will enjoy seeing photos of the different characters you meet.

After selecting the best photos from your trip, you can either visit an online publishing service to create a custom book, or you can make a scrapbook the old-fashioned way (print your favorites and paste them into an album or book). Snapfish.com and Shutterfly.com are two easy-to-use printing sites where you can upload, view, and edit photos, then order prints, photo books, cards, gifts, calendars, mugs, posters, home décor, and beyond. It takes about a week to receive your custom product.

One of my favorite tools is MyPublisher (www.mypublisher.com), which lets you create high-quality, custom-bound, professional-looking scrapbooks. Download the site's free photo book application and customize to your heart's desire.

Slideshows

If you'd like to do a slideshow (to be viewed with a digital projector or on a TV), Google's Picasa (described earlier) and other photo-organizing programs can help you. Microsoft PowerPoint works as well for vacation photos as it does for dry financial reports (though you might need to shrink the slideshow's resolution to help it load and advance more quickly).

Like PowerPoint on steroids, Prezi.com is an online tool for creating multimedia presentations. You can use its templates and shapes to guide you, or build your own to create a display of your trip that is as simple or detailed as you want. After embedding photos, videos, and text, you can show off your Prezi directly at their website or download finished Prezis to present them offline.

When putting your slideshow together, be mindful that no one wants to suffer through an endless parade of lackluster and look-alike shots. Set a limit and prune your show until it bleeds. Keep it tight. Keep it moving. Leave the audience crying for more...not for mercy.

CITY TRANSPORTATION

Shrink and tame big cities by mastering their subway and bus systems—you'll save time, money, and energy. Europe's public-transit systems are so good that many urban Europeans go through life never learning to drive. Their wheels are trains, subways, trams, buses, and the occasional taxi. If you embrace these forms of transportation when visiting cities, you'll travel smarter.

Buses can give you a tour of the town on the way to your destination. Subways are speedy and never get stuck in traffic jams. With the proper attitude, taking public transit can be a cultural experience, plunging you into the people- and advertisement-filled river of workaday life.

This chapter offers tips on using subways, buses, and taxis. If you'd rather get around by bicycle (especially fun in bike-friendly cities like Amsterdam and Copenhagen), see page 317. For information on taking trains, long-distance buses, and ferries, read the Trains and More chapter.

Public Transit Tips

Even if you've never used public transit in your hometown, these tricks can help you quickly master your transportation options in Europe's cities. You'll have the city by the tail, without having to shell out for taxis.

Get a transit map. With a map, anyone can decipher the code to easy, affordable urban transportation. Paris and London have the most extensive—and the most needed—subway systems. Pick up a schematic map at the tourist office or subway ticket window, ask for one at your

Public transit—the European treat

hotel, or print one off a website. Many city maps, even free ones, include a basic transit map. To help you plot your travel, some transit systems (such as London's) offer online journey planners, and many sights list the nearest bus or subway stop on their websites and brochures.

Learn what's covered by a ticket. In many cities, the same tickets are good on the subway, trams, and buses, and include transfers between the systems; in other places, you'll need to buy a new ticket each time you transfer. If a ticket seems expensive, ask what it covers—$4 may seem like a lot until you learn it's good for a round-trip, two hours, or several transfers.

Consider your ticket options. Your choices, which vary per city, are individual tickets, multi-ticket deals, passes, and reloadable cards. You'll pay the most per ride by buying individual tickets, but this can be the way to go if you'll be taking only a few rides or prefer to get around mainly on foot.

If you're committed to using public transit, the following options will cut your per-ride costs and save you time (because you won't have to stand in a ticket line every time you travel):

Multi-ticket deals offer you a set number of tickets—most notably Paris' 10-ticket *carnet*—that you can use anytime and share with companions, even on the same ride (unlike passes and cards, which can be used by only one person at a time).

Passes allow unlimited travel on all public transport for a set number of hours or days; a 24-hour pass usually costs less than four single fares. Some passes cover sights as well (for more on these, see page 298).

If you take advantage of public transportation, you can zip quickly, effortlessly, and inexpensively around Europe's most congested cities.

Before you buy, plan how you'll get the most use out of your pass during its period of validity.

Reloadable cards, such as London's prepaid Oyster card, require a deposit to buy, subtract the cost of your rides when you use it, and can be topped off when the balance runs low.

You can buy tickets, passes, and cards at subway ticket-machines or windows, and, depending on the city, on the bus (usually for exact change and at a slightly higher cost than the ticket-machine price), at newsstands, or in tourist offices. Ask about discounts if you're young, old, or traveling with children.

Don't try to travel for free. Many European subways, buses, and trams use the honor system, patrolled sporadically by ticket checkers—some are in uniform, others rove incognito, but all mean business. If you're caught without a valid ticket, you'll most likely have to pay a hefty fine.

If confused, ask for help. Europe's buses and subways are filled with people who are more than happy to help lost tourists locate themselves. Confirm with a local that you're at the right platform or bus

stop before you board. If you tell them where you're going, the driver or passengers sitting around you will gladly tell you where to get off.

Expect pickpockets. While public transportation feels safe, savvy riders are constantly on guard. Per capita, there are more pickpockets on Europe's subway trains and buses than just about anywhere else. They congregate wherever there are crowds or bottlenecks: on escalators, at turnstiles, or at the doors of packed buses or subway cars as people get on and off. If there's a hubbub, assume it's a distraction for pickpockets—put a hand on your valuables. Be on the lookout, wear your money belt, and you'll do fine. (For tips on avoiding theft, see the Theft and Scams chapter.)

Subways

Most of Europe's big cities are blessed with an excellent subway system, and wise travelers know that learning this network is key to efficient sightseeing. European subways go by many names: "Metro" is the most

CITY TRANSPORTATION

common term on the Continent, but Germany and Austria use "U-Bahn." For Scandinavia, it's the "T-bane" in Oslo, "T-bana" in Stockholm, and "S-tog" in Copenhagen. In London, it's the "Tube" (to the British, a "subway" is a pedestrian underpass). In big subway systems, shops are clustered at larger stops.

Subways generally operate from about 6 a.m. until midnight. They rarely follow a specific schedule, but just pass by at frequent but irregular intervals. Newer systems have electronic signs noting when the next train will arrive.

Here are tips for smooth sailing on Europe's subways:

Study your map. Subway maps are usually included within city maps and are posted prominently at the station and usu-

As you'll constantly be reminded on London's Tube...mind the gap.

ally on board. A typical subway map is a spaghetti-like tangle of intersecting, colorful lines. The individual lines are color-coded, numbered, and/or lettered (and even named, in the case of London); their stations, including those at either end of the line, are also indicated. These end stations—while probably places you'll never go—are important, since they tell you which direction the train is headed and appear (usually) as the name listed on the front of the train.

A few cities (like Rome) have just two or three subway lines, while London has over a dozen. Some cities' subways share the tracks with express commuter trains (such as Paris' RER and Germany's S-Bahn), which make fewer stops and can usually get you across town faster.

Plan your route. Determine which line you need, the name of the end station in the direction you want to go, and (if necessary) where to transfer to another line. In the station, you'll use this information to follow signs to reach your platform. (See the sidebar for a step-by-step sample trip.) When in doubt, just ask someone.

Validate your ticket. Once you buy a ticket, you may need to validate it in a turnstile slot (don't forget to retrieve it)—watch to see what others do. If you have an all-day or multi-day ticket, you may need to validate it only the first time you use it, or not at all (ask when you buy it). If there's no turnstile at the station, it doesn't mean the subway is free; if you're caught traveling without a valid ticket, you'll be fined,

A Sample Subway Trip

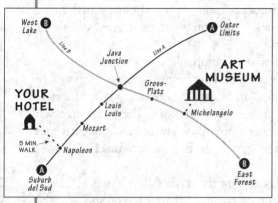

Let's say you want to go from your hotel to the art museum on the other side of town. Your hotel is a five-minute walk from the Napoleon station on the A line. Note that the A line has two end stations: Outer Limits to the north and Suburb del Sud to the south. The art museum is on the B line, so you'll need to transfer at the station where these two lines intersect: Java Junction.

Here's how you'll do it:

1. Entering the subway at the Napoleon station, follow signs to trains going in the direction of *Outer Limits* (the northern end station).
2. Ride three stops to Java Junction, where you get off to transfer to line B.
3. Follow signs to line B, in the direction of *East Forest* (the end station).
4. Ride the train two stops to the Michelangelo station.
5. Use the neighborhood map in the station to choose the exit closest to the museum.

Congratulations—you've survived your first European subway trip!

usually on the spot. Don't throw away your ticket too soon—you might need to insert it in a turnstile to exit the system (the machine might keep your ticket if it's used up). Once you're out, toss or tear used tickets to avoid confusing them with unused ones.

As you enter the subway station, insert your ticket into the slot to open the turnstile. After validating your ticket, remember to reclaim it.

Keep alert. Follow signage carefully as you navigate through the station. Confirm that you're at the right platform—heading in the right direction—before boarding. Subways can get packed during rush hour. Try to steer clear of crowds and commotion; there are usually fewer people in the first and last cars.

Stick together. If you're with a companion or group, make sure everyone knows the name of your final stop before boarding, stays close together, and agrees on a game plan in case you get separated. If a subway is about to depart as you arrive on the platform, don't rush to catch it and risk leaving behind your companions; subways run frequently and it's far easier to wait for the next departure than to reconnect with your split-up group.

Get off at the right place. Once on the train, follow along with each stop on your map. Newer cars may have an electronic screen showing the next stop. Sometimes the driver or an automated voice announces the upcoming stop—but don't count on this cue, as a foreign name spoken by a native speaker over a crackly loudspeaker can be difficult to understand. Keep an eye out the window as you pull into each station; the station's name will be posted prominently on the platform or along the wall. If the train is crowded, move close to the doors one stop before you want to exit. When the train stops, the doors may open automatically, or you may need to open them yourself by pushing a button or pulling a lever. Don't panic—watch others and imitate.

Before exiting a major subway system like the Paris Métro, take a moment to familiarize yourself with the neighborhood map (plan du quartier), posted by the exits. Choose your exit smartly to surface closer to your destination.

If you need to transfer, follow the signs. Changing from one subway line to another can be as easy as walking a few steps to an adjacent platform—or a bewildering wander via a labyrinth of stairs and long passageways. Subway systems are clearly signed—just follow along (or ask a local for help).

Exit the station. When you arrive at your destination station, follow exit signs up toward street level, keeping an eye out for posted maps of the surrounding neighborhood to help you get your bearings. Bigger stations have multiple exits, signposted

> ## Subway Etiquette
>
> - On escalators to and from platforms, stand on the right, pass on the left.
> - When waiting at the platform, stand to either side of the opening doors, out of the way of people exiting the train. Board only after everyone who wants to leave is off.
> - Talk softly on board. Listen to how quietly Europeans communicate and follow their lead.
> - On a crowded train, try not to block the exit (unless your stop is next). If you're at the door of a packed train when it reaches a stop, step out of the car and off to the side, let others off, then get back on.

by street name or nearby landmarks. Choosing the right exit will help you avoid extra walking and unnecessary forays through busy intersections. Some travelers carry a pocket compass to help them get oriented when they surface from the subway.

Buses

Getting around town on city buses is a little more complicated than using the subway, but has its advantages. Since you're not underground,

it's easier to stay oriented, see the landmarks, and enjoy the vibrant street life out the window. In fact, some public bus routes are downright scenic—Paris' bus #69 gives you a great sightseeing introduction for just the cost of a transit ticket. Bus stops are more closely spaced than subway stops—meaning the bus is useful even for short hops and usually gets you closer to where you need to go. Some buses go where the subway can't, such as the top of Castle Hill in Budapest. Like subways, city buses run frequently, especially during peak hours (if a bus is packed, wait for the next one). Although night buses run less frequently and follow limited routes, they're useful for night owls who don't want to spring for a taxi. The main disadvantage of buses is that they're slowed down by traffic, so try to avoid taking them during rush hour.

In many cities, you'll see hop-on, hop-off tourist buses connecting the major sights; these are generally privately operated (for details, see page 292). The focus of this section is on public city buses.

To travel smartly by bus, follow these tips:

Plan your route. You can usually get a bus map and schedule from local tourist or transit offices, or print them off the bus system's website. Many bus stops have their routes and timetables posted, and some have electronic signs noting how many minutes until the next bus arrives.

Confirm the essentials before you board. Find out if you need to have a ticket in advance or if you can buy it on the bus. Make sure you're getting on the right bus going in the right direction.

Posted bus schedules tell you when the next bus should be coming...and where it's going.

If your destination is obvious— such as Florence's Duomo— choosing the right stop is easy; otherwise, ask fellow passengers for help.

Before you get on, mention your destination to a local or the driver. Smile and ask, for example, "Vaticano?"

Validate your ticket. Usually you enter at the front of the bus and show your ticket to the driver, or validate it by inserting it into an automated time-stamp box. Observe and imitate what the locals do.

Get off at the right stop. Bus stops, like subway stops, are named (usually for a cross street or nearby landmark), but their names are often difficult to see from a moving bus. It can be tricky to get off where you intend, so it pays to stay alert: Have a sense of how long a ride is going to take, and know the names of the stops coming up right before yours (and the one right after yours, so you'll know if you've gone too far). If possible, sit near the door, so you can hop out easily. On a cross-town trip, you'll have time to enjoy the sights. As you ride, follow along the route on your map, looking for landmarks along the way: monuments, bridges, major cross streets, and so on. If you're uncertain about your stop, get the attention of the driver or another passenger and ask, "Prado?" (For extra credit, preface your request with the local word for please.) Then wait for them to signal to you when the bus reaches the Prado.

In bike-friendly cities such as Amsterdam and Copenhagen, buses often let you off directly into busy bicycle lanes. Look carefully, in both directions, as you exit.

You may have to signal for your stop. Some buses pull over at every stop, while others only stop by request; this means you can't necessarily navigate by counting stops. If in doubt, look for a pull cord or a button with the local word for "stop," and use it to signal that you want to get off at the next stop.

Taxis

Taxis are underrated, scenic time savers that zip you effortlessly from one sight to the next (except during rush-hour traffic, when they're stuck like everyone else). I enjoy cab rides.

These Sorrento cabbies hire by the hour and would love to show you around.

Many of my favorite insider tips and most interesting conversations have come from chatting up taxi drivers. But don't trust their advice blindly; cabbies can get kickbacks for recommending (and delivering you to) a particular restaurant or attraction.

While cabs are expensive for the lone budget traveler, a group of three or four people can often travel cheaper by taxi than by buying bus or subway tickets. Taxis are especially cheap in Mediterranean countries and Eastern Europe. You can go anywhere by cab in downtown Lisbon or Athens for about $15.

Tipping: For a typical ride, round up to the next euro on the fare (to pay a €13 fare, give €14); for a long ride, to the nearest 10 (for a €76 fare, give €80). If the cabbie hauls your bags and zips you to the airport to help you catch your flight, you might want to toss in a little more. But if you feel like you're being driven in circles or otherwise ripped off, skip the tip.

Avoiding Taxi Scams

Though many Americans are wired to assume that taxi drivers in other countries are up to no good, I've also found that most drivers are honest. Sure, scams happen. But with the right tips and a watchful eye, you'll get where you want to go without being taken for a ride.

Be extra careful at airports and train stations. Dishonest cabbies often lurk at major transit points, ready to take advantage of travelers who are jet-lagged and travel-weary—just when they're most susceptible to getting ripped off. If you don't want to worry about getting conned the minute you arrive at a new destination, plan ahead. In many cities, you can arrange for an airport shuttle bus to pick you up at the airport and zip you straight to your hotel (you can ask your hotelier for a recommended service). Another option, much cheaper than a taxi ride, is taking public transportation into town. Recently, I took a speedy train from Rome's airport to the train station downtown, then caught a bus from there to my hotel. It took me less than an hour, and while a taxi would have cost me about $65, I paid about $38—for the train fare and a handy transit pass that lasted me all week. If you want to take a taxi from the airport, it's better to head for the official taxi stand and join the queue rather than flag one down.

Always choose a well-marked cab. It should have a big, prominent taxi-company logo and telephone number. Avoid using unmarked beaters with makeshift taxi lights on top.

In some cities, it's easy to flag down a cab; in any city, you can find cabs at a taxi stand. These stands are often listed as prominently as subway stations on city maps; look for the little *T*s (or ask a local to direct you to the nearest one).

When you need a ride from a hotel or restaurant, you can have the staff call a taxi for you (or you can phone a taxi yourself). This can dramatically decrease your odds of getting ripped off, but be aware that in many places, the meter starts ticking from the time the call is received. Note that if you have an early-morning flight to catch, it'll save you some stress (and cost nothing beyond the usual supplements) to have your hotelier book a cab for you the day before.

Establish a price or rough estimate up front. It's usually best to make sure the cabbie uses the taxi meter. But for certain standard trips (such as to or from the airport), it can be common for the cabbie to use a set price. Know the going rate—ask your hotelier or the tourist office in advance how much a taxi ride should cost to your destination. You can check your guidebook or www.worldtaximeter.com for estimated taxi fares in larger cities.

Sometimes tourists wrongly accuse their cabbies of taking the long way around or adding unfair extras. But what can seem like a circuitous route may still be the shortest, given pedestrianized zones and one-way streets. And many supplements are legit, based on the time of day (nights, early mornings, and weekends), amount of baggage, extra people, airport taxes, port fees, and so on.

In cities such as London, Paris, and Barcelona, meters are tamper-proof. That said, even cabbies with honest meters have ways of overcharging tourists. One common trick is for cabbies to select the pricier "night and weekend" rate on their meter during a weekday. An explanation of the different meter rates should be posted somewhere in the cab, often in English; if you're confused about the tariff, ask your cabbie to explain. If you suspect foul play, following the route on your map or conspicuously writing down the cabbie's license information can shame a cad into being honest.

Pay with small bills. Using small bills minimizes your chance of getting ripped off. If you only have a large bill, state the denomination out loud as you hand it to the cabbie. They can be experts at dropping your €50 note and then showing you a €20. Count your change. If, for whatever reason, I'm charged a ridiculous price for a ride, I put a reasonable sum on the seat and say good-bye. Don't be intimidated by a furious cabbie.

Taking a Taxi Between Cities

While a budget traveler would generally never dream of hiring a taxi for a trip between cities, it can actually be a fairly good value. For example, if you're headed somewhere that's a long train trip but a short drive away, a taxi can be an affordable splurge, especially if the cost is split between two or more people.

Consider the time you'll save over public transportation—for example, one hour of sweat-free, hotel-door-to-hotel-door service versus two sticky hours on stop-and-go public transit, including transfers to and from the train or bus station. Simply ask any cabbie what they'd charge (it could be an hourly rate or even an off-meter flat rate—they know you have a cheap public-transit alternative and might be willing to strike a deal if they want the work). Or ask at your hotel if they have a line on any car or taxi services that do the trip economically. See if you can find a driver who's accustomed to taking tourists on these trips. While not technically guides, these drivers are often willing to provide some basic commentary on what you're seeing and might even suggest some interesting stops along the way.

SIGHTSEEING AND ACTIVITIES

After months of planning, you're finally on the ground in Europe, and the real work begins: sightseeing. This is when it pays to have a thoughtful plan. The pointers in this chapter will help you get oriented to your surroundings, use your sightseeing hours wisely, and find your way off the beaten path. I also include tips for energetic travelers, from hikers to bikers and even shoppers.

Getting Oriented

Whether tackling big cities or quaint villages, you don't want to feel like a stranger in a strange land (even though that's exactly what you are). Getting oriented is especially important in big cities—which, for many travelers, are the most intimidating part of a European trip. Visitors who decide to wing it in Europe's large cities invariably waste time—and miss out. Here are your best resources for getting acclimated to a new place.

Guidebook and Map

Have a good guidebook for wherever you're traveling. If you haven't shown up with one, get one; they're sold at newsstands, major sights, English bookstores, and the English sections in large bookstores (see page 21 for a rundown of guidebooks).

While guidebooks come with basic maps of big cities, these are generally small and intended only to give you an overview. A detailed, foldout map can save you endless time and frustration; I make a point of picking one up immediately upon arrival. (You can almost always get a decent map free or cheaply at the local tourist office—described next.) If choosing a city sightseeing map, make sure the city center is detailed enough, because that's where you'll be spending most of your time. If you'll be relying heavily on public transit, get a map that shows not just subway stations, but bus and tram lines and stops. For an extended stay in a sprawling city, it can be worth paying extra for a sturdier, more detailed map.

Study your map to understand the city's layout. Relate the location of landmarks—your hotel, major sights, the river, main streets, the train station—to each other. Use any viewpoint, such as a church spire, tower, or hilltop, to understand the lay of the land and see where you're going next.

Tourist Information Offices

No matter how well I know a town, my first stop is always the tourist information office. Nearly any place with a tourist industry has an information service for visitors on the main square, in the City Hall or public library, at the train station, or sometimes at airports or freeway entrances. You don't need the address—just follow the signs. A normally busy but friendly and multilingual staff gives out sightseeing information, reserves hotel rooms, sells concert or theater tickets, and answers questions.

Your first stop in a new town: the tourist information office

Prepare a list of questions ahead of time. Write up a proposed sightseeing schedule. Find out if it's workable or if you've left out any important sights. Confirm closed days and free-admission days. If necessary, get ideas on where to eat and sleep, though keep in mind that their advice can be biased. Many tourist offices aren't nonprofit services—they're businesses that sell things and work on fees and commissions.

Entertainment Guides

Big European cities bubble with entertainment, festivities, and nightlife. But these events won't come to you. New in town and unable to speak the native language, travelers can be oblivious to a once-in-a-lifetime event erupting just across the bridge. A periodical entertainment guide is the key. Every big city has one, either in English (such as *What's On in Oslo* or *Time Out*, which has editions in many cities) or in the local language, but easy to decipher (such as the *Pariscope* weekly in Paris). Most are also on the Internet, with many going online-only.

You can find printed guides at the tourist office (where they're often free), at newsstands, English-language bookstores, or at the front desk of big, fancy hotels (look like a guest and help yourself). Events are posted on city walls everywhere. They are in a foreign language, but that really doesn't matter when it reads: *Weinfest, Música Folklórica, 9 Juni, 21:00, Piazza Maggiore, Entre Libre,* and so on. Figure out the signs—or miss the party.

Other Resources

If you find yourself in a town with no guidebook coverage or tourist office, glance through a postcard rack to get a quick overview of the town's most famous sights. Even the most mundane town will feature whatever's worth seeing on its postcards.

Firsthand advice is available from hotel information desks, B&B hosts, hostel employees, and other travelers. Glean advice from the couple seated next to you at breakfast, chat with the waiter who serves you lunch, or ask a shop owner for tips.

You can also find help online: Search Twitter for the scuttlebutt on local events, poll your social-network friends for advice, or choose restaurants with the help of user-review sites like Yelp and TripAdvisor (see page 32).

Tours

Organized tours are a great way to acclimate to a new city and learn about its history and highlights. Not only do tours provide a city overview, but they also give you an idea of what to revisit later in your stay. Especially in big cities, you'll find tours of all kinds, from organized walks to bus rides that let you hop on and off at will.

Walking Tours

These are my favorite introduction to a city. Since they focus on just a small part of a larger whole (generally the old town center), they are thorough. The tours are usually conducted in English by well-trained guides who are sharing their town for the noble purpose of giving you an appreciation of its history, people, and culture—not to make a lot of money. Walking tours are personal, inexpensive, and a valuable education. They're nearly always time and money well spent.

On your travels, you might run across start-up companies advertising "free" walking tours in major European cities. While the tours are indeed free, tipping is expected; in fact, the guides don't earn money unless you tip. Personally, I avoid these tours. They're usually light on history, and the guides spend your valuable time heavily promoting their company's other tours (which are not free). I'd rather support tours offered by established companies, and pay up front for hardworking guides whose goal is to make the city's history come alive.

Try a guided walk to learn about a town that's probably a thousand years older than your hometown.

Many tourist offices rent audioguides you can take for a walk or provide do-it-yourself walking-tour leaflets. The avid walker should

Audioguides...for all the hair-raising details on Europe's historic sights

consider purchasing one of the many "turn right at the fountain"-type guidebooks that are carefully written collections of self-guided walks through major cities. Many of my guidebooks include these types of walking tours. If you have a mobile device, you can download my free audio tours of major sights and walks in Europe (for details, see page 263).

Bus Orientation Tours

Many cities have fast-orientation bus tours that take you around the city on a double-decker bus. Riding in the open air atop a two-story bus, you get a feel for the city's layout as the major sights roll on by; most buses include live or tape-recorded narration. Many are structured as hop-on/hop-off tours with a circular route that connects the top sights; with an all-day pass, you can hop off to visit a sight, then catch a later bus to

A minibus tour of Bruges—name your language

continue the route.

Bus tours usually cost about $30-40. Some can be a disappointing rip-off; others are a great sightseeing tool. If you're short on time, have limited mobility, or would appreciate an overview before diving into a city, they can be worth the money. If I had only one day in a big city, I might spend half of it on one of these tours.

But before you shell out for a ticket, consider a few key factors: route, quality of narration, and for hop-on/hop-off buses, frequency. The best-value hop-on/hop-off tours leave several times an hour, visit sights I actually want to see, and feature an engaging live guide (if the guide is good, I'll stay on for the entire route). Be wary of overcrowded buses—if space is full on top, you may have no choice but to be crammed into the (potentially hot and stuffy) lower level. It's worth waiting for the next bus if that will get you space on an upper level, where views come from a higher vantage point and aren't marred by smeared windows. The best scenario is enjoying the view from a topless bus on a sunny day.

Many cities also offer a public bus (e.g., Berlin's bus #100 or Paris' bus #69) or boat route (Amsterdam has several) that connects many of the city's major sightseeing attractions; you can ride these as if they were low-cost (unguided) tour buses/boats. Tourists buy the one-day pass and make the circuit at their leisure (for more on city buses, see page 283.)

Local Guides

For the price of four seats on a forgettable tape-recorded city bus tour, you can often hire your own private guide for a personalized city tour (most cost-effective if you're traveling with a group). Every city has a long list of English-speaking professional guides who earn their living giving tours. They

Guides bring museums and castles to life.

hire out by the day or half-day and generally follow a national guide service fee schedule (about $200 per half-day, which can mean two to four hours—ask when you book). In my research, I've grown accustomed to relying heavily upon these experts and generally find them well worth the investment. You can find and book guides by calling the local tourist information office (or visiting its website) in advance, or even by dropping by and arranging a guide upon arrival in a town. Although you can get the contact information from the tourist office, you typically book the guide by emailing or calling the person directly. When I meet particularly good independent guides, I include their contact information in my guidebooks.

Hiring a private guide is an especially good value in Eastern Europe, where guides tend to be young, intelligent, and enthusiastic—and charge half as much. The best guides are often those whose tours you can pick up at a specific sight. They usually really know their museums, castles, cathedrals, or town.

Minivan Excursions

Some of Europe's top sights are awkward to reach by public transportation, such as the *châteaux* in the Loire, the *Sound of Music* sights outside Salzburg, the D-Day beaches of Normandy, the rural meadows of Cornwall, or the Lascaux cave paintings in France's Dordogne. For roughly $50 per half-day, an organized tour not only whisks you effortlessly from one hard-to-reach-without-a-car sight to the next, but gives you lots of information as you go. (Or, if you have a car, consider picking up the brochure for a well-thought-out tour itinerary and doing it on your own.)

Minivan tours—such as this one, to the Irish countryside—can be an ideal way for non-drivers to reach far-flung sights.

If you have a choice between a big, 50-seat bus (a "coach") and a minivan, I'd generally recommend the minivan. While typically a bit more professional and comfortable, big-bus tours are often also boring and impersonal. With a smaller group, you're likely to have a more engaging, entertaining guide and more camaraderie as you roll.

Sightseeing Strategies

Westminster Abbey, the Eiffel Tower, the Sistine Chapel—these are the reasons you came to Europe. They're also the reason millions of other tourists are here as well. Nothing kills a sightseeing buzz like waiting in line for hours to get into a popular sight or being crammed into a room, squinting up at Michelangelo's masterpiece. If you plan ahead, the sights you dreamed of seeing won't disappoint.

Be Strategic and Selective

Set up an itinerary that allows you to fit in your must-see sights, but be realistic about what you can accomplish in a day. As you make your plan, note the specifics of the sights on your list, especially their closed days and any evening hours (which can help extend your sightseeing day). Check the weather report a few days out and plan your indoor/outdoor time accordingly. Arrange your sightseeing to cover a larger city systematically and efficiently, one neighborhood at a time.

Save yourself for the biggies. Don't overestimate your powers of absorption. Rare is the tourist who doesn't become somewhat jaded after several weeks of travel. At the start of my trip, I'll seek out every great painting and cathedral I can. After two months, I find myself "seeing" cathedrals with a sweep of my head from the doorway, and I probably wouldn't cross the street for another Rembrandt. Don't burn out on mediocre castles, palaces, and museums. Sightsee selectively.

When possible, visit major sights in the morning (when your energy is best), and save other activities for the afternoon. Don't put off visiting a must-see sight; even if you've double-checked hours, places can close unexpectedly for a strike or restoration. On holidays, expect reduced hours or closures. In summer, some sights may stay open late. Off-season, many attractions have shorter hours.

Avoiding Lines and Crowds

Plenty of people queue up in long lines at Europe's most popular sights. As far as I'm concerned, there are two IQs for travelers: those who queue...and those who don't. If you plan ahead, you can avoid virtually every line that tourists suffer through. The following tricks aren't secrets. They're in any good, up-to-date guidebook. Just read ahead.

Timing is Everything

In many cities, a number of sights tend to be closed on the same day of the week (usually Sunday, Monday, or Tuesday). In high season, any major sight that's open when everything else is closed is guaranteed to be crowded. For example, Versailles is very crowded on Tuesdays, when many of the biggest museums in Paris are closed.

Many museums are free one day a month—a great deal for locals who can nip in and see small parts of a museum without paying the full fare. But for visitors, it's generally worth paying the entrance fee to avoid the hordes on a museum's free day. The Sistine Chapel feels more like the Sardine Chapel when it's open and free on the last Sunday of the month.

At popular sights, it can help to arrive early or go late. This is especially true at places popular with cruise excursions and big-bus tour groups. At 8:00 in the morning, Germany's fairy-tale Neuschwanstein Castle is cool and easy, with relaxed guides and no crowds; come an hour later and you'll either wait a long time, find that tickets are sold out, or both.

It's Tuesday at Versailles, and these people now have time to read their guidebooks, which warn: "On Tuesday, many Paris museums are closed, so Versailles has very long lines."

Many sights are open late one or two nights a week—another pleasant time to visit. For instance, London's Tate Modern stays open Friday and Saturday evenings, when you'll enjoy Matisse and Dalí in near solitude. Very late in the day—when most tourists are long gone, searching for dinner or lying exhausted in their rooms—I linger alone, taking artistic liberties with some of Europe's greatest works in empty galleries.

Shortcuts

Even at the most packed sights, there's often a strategy or shortcut that can break you out of the herd, whether it's a side entrance with a shorter wait, a guided tour that includes last-minute reservations, a better place in town to pick up your ticket, or a pass with line-skipping privileges (explained later).

Grand as the Louvre's main entrance is, that glass pyramid stops looking impressive as you wait—and wait—to get through security. Lines are shorter if you go in through the less crowded underground entrance.

In Milan, you can take a bus tour that includes an easy stop at

Leonardo's *Last Supper*, normally booked up more than a month in advance.

At St. Mark's Basilica in Venice, you can either snake slowly through an endless line, or go instead to a nearby church to check a bag—then walk right to the front of the basilica's line, show your bag-claim tag, and head on in (go figure). Check your guidebook for sight-specific insider tips.

Making Advance Reservations

Certain sights are almost always jammed, all day long, throughout

most of the year (many in older edifices that weren't built to accommodate the demands of mass tourism). Fortunately, many popular sights sell advance tickets that guarantee admission at a certain time (often with a small booking fee that's well worth it). While hundreds of tourists are sweating in long lines, those who've booked ahead can just show up at their reserved entry time and breeze right in. It's worth giving up some spontaneity in order to save time. In some cases, buying in advance can

The Eiffel Tower comes with long lines for those who didn't book online in advance. With my reservation and appointment in hand, I zigzagged through a long row of empty stanchions and was escorted directly to the elevator, while this long queue of tourists waited. (None of them had my guidebook.)

simply mean getting your ticket earlier on the same day. In London, buying a Fast Track ticket at a souvenir stand allows you to skip the long line at the Tower of London.

Some sights are notorious for grueling waits. These include the Eiffel Tower, Rome's Vatican Museum, Barcelona's Picasso Museum, and Florence's famous galleries—the Accademia (Michelangelo's *David*) and the Uffizi (the showcase for Italian Renaissance art). At these places, lines are completely avoidable by making advance reservations. After learning how simple this is and seeing hundreds of annoyed tourists waiting in lines without a reservation, it's hard not to be amazed at their cluelessness. As soon as you're ready to commit to a certain date, book it.

Note that some sights require reservations, such as the Reichstag in Berlin, Leonardo's *Last Supper* in Milan, Giotto's Scrovegni Chapel in

Padua, and the Borghese Gallery in Rome. For some of these, the reservations system is aimed not so much at coping with vast crowds, but toward moving people in and out efficiently.

At many great galleries, such as the Uffizi in Florence, you can wait in line for two hours...or book ahead for an appointment and walk right in. Remember: Lines like this are not for the entry turnstile, but for the ticket booth.

Sightseeing Passes and Combo-Tickets

Most tourist destinations offer a citywide sightseeing pass (or "tourist card"), which includes free or discounted entrance to many or most sights for a certain amount of time (usually intervals of 24 hours). Many of these deals also include free use of public transit, a brief explanatory booklet, and a map.

In some places, passes can save you serious time and money; in others, you'd have to sightsee nonstop to barely break even. Do the math: Compare the price of the pass to the total of what you'd pay for individual admissions. But remember: Time is money. These passes are almost always worthwhile if they allow you to bypass long admission lines. For instance, Paris' Museum Pass covers many top sights (the Louvre, Orsay, Notre-Dame, and Versailles) and allows you to skip ticket-buying lines at the same time. The Madrid Card may not save you a lot of money, but it can help you avoid the lines at the Royal Palace and the Prado in high season.

For Rome's Colosseum, buy a combo-ticket 150 yards away at the Palatine Hill—which never has a line—and skip directly past the not-so-smart travelers pictured here.

Combo-tickets combine admission to a larger sight with entry to a lesser sight or two that few people would pay to see. The bad news: You have to pay for multiple sights to visit one. The good news: You can bypass the line at the congested sight by buying your ticket at a less-popular sister sight. You can wait up to an hour to get into

Popular Sights with Advance Reservations

At some of Europe's most popular sights, reservations are required; at others, reservations are very smart. This list includes many major sights you can book ahead, but it isn't comprehensive; check your guidebook for details on the sights you plan to visit.

Austria
Schönbrunn Palace, Vienna

Great Britain
Lennon and McCartney Homes, Liverpool
Madame Tussauds Waxworks, London
Tower of London
London Eye
Stonehenge, near Salisbury (required to enter the stone circle)
Jorvik Viking Center, York

France
Château de Chenonceau, Chenonceaux
Cro-Magnon Caves, Dordogne region
Château de Versailles, near Paris
Eiffel Tower, Paris
Musée d'Orsay, Paris

Germany
Reichstag, Berlin (required)
Neuschwanstein Castle, Bavaria region

Italy
Accademia Gallery, Florence
Brancacci Chapel, Florence (required)
Uffizi Gallery, Florence
Last Supper, Milan (required)
Scrovegni Chapel, Padua (required)
Borghese Gallery, Rome (required)
Vatican Museum (including Sistine Chapel), Rome

The Netherlands
Anne Frank House, Amsterdam
Rijksmuseum, Amsterdam
Van Gogh Museum, Amsterdam

Spain
Casa Mila, Barcelona
Picasso Museum, Barcelona
Sagrada Família, Barcelona
Salvador Dalí House, Cadaqués
Alhambra, Granada
Altamira Caves, near Santillana del Mar

Rome's Colosseum or Venice's Doge's Palace—or buy a combo-ticket (at another participating yet less-crowded site) and scoot inside.

Whether you have a combo-ticket or pass, never wait at the back of the line if there's any chance you can skip it. Don't be shy: March straight to the front and wave your pass or ticket. If you really do have to wait with everyone else, they'll let you know.

Visiting Sights Smartly

Some people walk into Europe's major museums, churches, and ancient sights, gawk for a few minutes, then walk out. But with a little preparation and know-how, your sightseeing will go much smoother—and take on more significance.

General Tips

Here's what you can expect at Europe's major sights.

Security Check: Some important sights have metal detectors or conduct bag searches that will slow your entry, and a rare few will confiscate the same sharp items that you're not allowed to carry on board a plane.

Tickets: As you approach the ticket window, study the list of prices. You could have a choice of individual tickets, combo-tickets, or passes. You may be eligible for discounts if you're young, old, or with children (have proof of ID, student card, etc.). Be prepared to pay cash, particularly for inexpensive sights.

Museums may have special exhibits in addition to their permanent collections. Some exhibits are included in the entry price, while others come at an extra cost (which you may have to pay even if you don't want to see the exhibit).

Your ticket may allow in-and-out privileges (e.g., if you want a lunch break outside the museum); if this is important to you, ask.

Entry Procedure: Entering a major sight is similar to arriving at a new town—you need to get oriented. Hit the information desk for a brochure or map, find out about any special events and tours, and ask about any temporary room or wing closures.

Checkroom: Most sights offer a checkroom or lockers (usually free or with a small deposit), and many require you to check daypacks and coats. They'll be kept safely. If you have something you can't bear to part with, stash it in a pocket or purse. To avoid checking a small backpack, carry it under your arm like a purse as you enter. (From a guard's point of view, a backpack is generally a problem while a purse is not.)

Touring the Sight: Many sights have audioguide tours with recorded descriptions in English. If the audioguide isn't included with admission, you can ask to listen to it for a couple of minutes to gauge the quality before paying for it. If you bring along a Y-jack and an extra pair of earbuds, you may be able to share the same audioguide with a companion.

Guided tours in English are most likely to be available during peak season (they may be included with your admission). If you're interested, check online or call ahead to be sure your visit will coincide with a tour.

Some sights run short films that are generally well worth your time. I make it standard operating procedure to ask when I arrive at a sight if there is a film in English.

Once inside, hit the highlights first, then go back to other things if you have the time and stamina. Expect changes—items can be on tour, on loan, out sick, or shifted at the whim of a curator. If the painting you crossed the Atlantic to see isn't on the wall, ask a museum staffer if it's been shifted to another location.

Most sights stop selling tickets and start shutting down rooms or sections 30 to 60 minutes before closing. Guards usher people out,

Stroll with a chatty curator through Europe's greatest art galleries, thanks to digital audioguides.

so don't save the best for last. Get to the far end early, see the rooms that are first to shut down, and work your way back toward the entry.

My favorite time at a major sight is the lazy last hour, when the tourists clear out. On a recent visit to the Acropolis, I showed up late and had the place to myself in the cool of early evening. Other blockbuster sights like St. Peter's Basilica and the Palace of Versailles can be magical just before closing.

Photography: Flashes are often banned in museums, but taking photos without a flash is usually allowed. Look for signs or ask. Flashes damage oil paintings and delicate artifacts, and distract others in the room. Even without a flash, a handheld camera will take a decent picture (or buy postcards or posters at the museum bookstore).

Services: Bigger sights will have an on-site café or cafeteria (usually a good place to rejuvenate during a long visit). The WCs at sights are free and usually clean; make a point of using them whether you think you need to or not.

Museums

Europe is a treasure chest of great art and history. For some, visiting the world's greatest museums is the highlight of a European trip. For others, "museum" spells "dull." But don't forget that you don't need to know how a 747 works to enjoy the ride. Paintings really aren't any different.

You can just stroll through a gallery and bask in the color scheme. That said, it doesn't hurt to keep in mind the following.

Learn about art and history. In my student days, I had to go to the great art galleries of Europe because my mom said it would be a crime not to. Touring places like the National Archaeological Museum in Athens, I was surrounded by people looking like they were having a good time—and I was convinced they were faking it. I thought, "How could

At the Louvre, it's worth fighting through crowds of amateur paparazzi to see the Venus de Milo...*who's ready for her close-up.*

anybody enjoy that stuff?" Two years later, after a class in classical art history, that same museum was a fascinating trip into the world of Pericles and Socrates, all because of some background knowledge. Pre-trip studying makes art and artifacts more fun. When you understand the context in which things were made, who paid for it and why, what the challenges of the day were, and so on, paintings and statues become the closest thing to a time machine Europe has to offer.

Don't miss the masterpieces. A common misconception is that a great museum has only great art. But only a fraction of a museum's

With a good guidebook, you stand a chance of finding Michelangelo's Slaves *in the Louvre.*

pieces are masterpieces worthy of your time. You can't possibly cover everything—so don't try. With the help of a tour guide or guidebook, focus on just the museum's top attractions. Most of Europe's great museums provide brief pamphlets recommending the best basic visit. With this selective strategy, you'll appreciate the highlights while you're fresh. If you have any energy left afterward, you can explore other areas of specific interest to you. For me, museum going is the hardest work I do in Europe, and I'm rarely good for more than two or three hours at a time. If you're determined to cover a large museum thoroughly, try tackling it in separate visits over several days.

Don't miss your favorites. On arrival, look through the museum's collection handbook or the gift shop's postcards to make sure you won't miss anything of importance to you. For instance, I love Salvador Dalí's work. One time I thought I was finished with a museum, but as I browsed through the postcards...Hello, Dalí. A museum guide was happy to show

me where this Dalí painting was hiding. I saved myself the disappointment of discovering too late that I'd missed it.

More and more museums offer a greatest-hits plan or brochure. Some (such as London's National Gallery) even have a computer study room where you can input your interests and print out a tailored museum tour.

A victim of the Louvre

Eavesdrop. If you're especially interested in a particular piece of art, spend a half hour studying it and listening to each passing tour guide tell his or her story about *David* or the *Mona Lisa*. They each do their own research and come up with a different angle to share. Much of it is true. There's nothing wrong with this sort of tour freeloading. Just don't stand in the front and ask a lot of questions.

Take advantage of my free audio tours of Europe's finest museums. My Rick Steves Audio Europe smartphone app now includes self-guided tours of museums in many of Europe's greatest cities. These can make your museum going easier and more meaningful (see page 263).

Churches, Synagogues, and Mosques

European houses of worship offer some amazing art and architecture—not to mention a welcome seat and a cool respite from the heat. You may be there just to see the Caravaggio over the side altar, but others are there as worshippers. Be a respectful visitor.

A modest dress code (no bare shoulders or shorts) is encouraged at most churches, but is enforced at some larger churches and most mosques. If you are caught by surprise, you can improvise, such as using maps to cover your shoulders and tying a jacket around your hips to cover your knees. (Throughout the Mediterranean world, I wear a super-lightweight

SIGHTSEEING & ACTIVITIES

pair of long pants rather than shorts for my hot and muggy big-city sight-seeing.) At Turkish mosques, women must cover their heads and wear clothing that shields their legs and arms; everyone needs to remove their shoes.

At active places of worship, visitors may not be allowed inside for one or more time periods throughout the day. If you are already inside, you may be asked to leave so as not to disturb the congregation. Check your guidebook's listing to avoid showing up at a church or mosque when it's closed for worship. Some services are open to the public. One of my favorite experiences in Great Britain is to attend evensong—a daily choral service—at a grand cathedral.

Some churches have coin-operated audio boxes that describe the art and history; just set the dial on English, insert your coins, and listen. Coin boxes near a piece of art illuminate the work (and present a better photo opportunity). I pop in a coin whenever I can. It improves my experience, is a favor to other visitors trying to appreciate a great piece of art in the dark, and is a little contribution to that church. Whenever possible, let there be light.

Ancient Sights and Ruins

Climbing the Acropolis, communing with the druids at Stonehenge, strolling the Croatian shore in the shadow of Emperor Diocletian's palace in Split, tracing the intricate carvings on a Viking ship—the remnants of Europe's distant past bring a special thrill to those of us from the New World.

But the oldest sights are also the most likely to be initially underwhelming, especially if it's been a while since your last history class. On its own, the Roman Forum is just a cluster of crumbling columns and half-buried foundations. You've heard about it all your life, you've spent good money to get here, and your first thought upon entering is..."This is it?"

Ancient sights come to life with your imagination, aided by information. Bring a guidebook that's heavy on historical background, and consider hiring a local guide. For some well-known places you can get books that cleverly use overlays to visually mesh the present with the past. To fire up your imagination before your trip, watch a movie or read a book set in the time and place of any sight you're excited to see. Once you're there, mentally reconstruct arches and repaint facades. Clad your fellow tourists in togas. Fill a ruined cathedral with the chants of cowled monks while inhaling imaginary incense.

Many major ancient sights (such as the Acropolis and Delphi in

Greece) have both an archaeological site and a nearby museum full of artifacts unearthed there. You can choose between visiting the museum first (to mentally reconstruct the ruins before seeing them) or the site first (to get the lay of the ancient land before seeing the items found there). In most cases, I prefer to see the site first, then the museum. However, crowds and weather can also help determine your plan. If it's a blistering hot afternoon, tour the air-conditioned museum first, then hit the ruins in the cool of the early evening. Or, if rain clouds are on the horizon, do the archaeological site first, then duck into the museum when the rain hits.

Open-Air Folk Museums

Many people travel in search of the old life and traditional culture in action. While we book a round-trip ticket into the romantic past, those we photograph with the Old World balanced on their heads are struggling to dump that load and climb into the modern world. In Europe, most are succeeding.

Traditional culture is kept alive in Europe's open-air folk museums.

The easiest way to see the "real local culture" is by exploring open-air folk museums. True, it's culture on a lazy Susan, with an often sanitized, romanticized version of an area's preindustrial lifestyle. But these museums can be simultaneously fun and enlightening—a magic carpet ride through a culture's past. In more and more places they provide your only chance for a close-up look at the "Old World."

An open-air folk museum collects traditional buildings from every corner of a country or region, then carefully reassembles them in a park, usually near the capital or a major city. Log cabins, thatched cottages, mills, old schoolhouses, shops, and farms come complete with original furnishings and usually a local person dressed in the traditional costume who's happy to answer any of your questions about life then and there. In the summer, these museums buzz with colorful folk dances, live music performances, and craft demonstrations by artisans doing what they can to keep the cuckoo clock from going the way of the dodo bird. Some of my favorite souvenirs are those I watched being dyed, woven, or carved

SIGHTSEEING & ACTIVITIES

Europe's Best Open-Air Folk Museums

Popularized in Scandinavia, these folk museums are now found all over the world, though the best ones are still in the Nordic capitals.

Scandinavia

Skansen (Stockholm, Sweden): One of the best in Europe, with more than 100 buildings from all over Sweden, craftspeople at work, feisty folk entertainment, and an Arctic camp complete with reindeer and Lapp dancing.

Funen Village (Den Fynske Landsby, near Odense, Denmark): Life in the 18th century.

The Old Town (Den Gamle By, Århus, Denmark): Danish town life between 1580 and 1850.

Norwegian Folk Museum (Bygdøy, near Oslo, Norway): Norway's first, with 150 old buildings from all over Norway and a 12th-century stave church.

Maihaugen Folk Museum (Lillehammer, Norway): Norway's best, with folk culture of the Gudbrandsdal Valley.

Seurasaari Island (near Helsinki, Finland): Reconstructed buildings from all over Finland.

The Netherlands, Germany, and Switzerland

Dutch Open-Air Folk Museum (Arnhem, Netherlands): Holland's first and biggest.

Zuiderzee Open-Air Museum (Enkhuizen, Netherlands): Lively reconstruction of Dutch traditions lost forever to land reclamation.

Vogtsbauernhof Black Forest Open-Air Museum (Gutach, Germany): Farms filled with exhibits on traditional dress and lifestyles.

by folk-museum artists. To get the most out of your visit, start by picking up a list of that day's special exhibits, events, and activities at the information center, and take advantage of any walking tours.

Folk museums teach traditional lifestyles better than any other kind of museum. As our world hurtles past 250 billion McDonald's hamburgers served, these museums will

At Stockholm's open-air folk museum, you may be entertained by this rare band of left-handed fiddlers.

Ballenberg Swiss Open-Air Museum (near Interlaken, Switzerland): Fine collection of old Swiss buildings, arranged roughly as if in a huge map of Switzerland.

Hungary

Skanzen (Szentendre, near Budapest, Hungary): Traditional architecture from around Hungary.

Hollókő (near Budapest, Hungary): Old-fashioned village where people still live.

Great Britain and Ireland

Blists Hill Victorian Town (Ironbridge Gorge, England): Unrivaled look at life in the early days of the Industrial Revolution, with the world's first iron bridge and a glimpse at the factories that lit the fuse of our modern age.

Beamish Open-Air Museum (northwest of Durham, England): Life in northeast England in 1900.

St. Fagans National History Museum (near Cardiff, Wales): Traditional Welsh ways of life.

Ulster Folk and Transport Museum (near Belfast, Northern Ireland): Traditional Irish lifestyles and buildings from all over Ireland.

Bunratty Folk Park (near Limerick, Ireland): Buildings from the Shannon area and artisans at work.

Muckross Traditional Farms (near Killarney, Ireland): Six vintage farmhouses from the early 20th century.

SIGHTSEEING & ACTIVITIES

become even more important. Of course, they're as realistic as Santa's Village, but how else will you see the elves?

Becoming a Temporary European

Many travelers tramp through Europe like they're visiting the cultural zoo. "Ooh, that guy in lederhosen yodeled! Excuse me, could you do that again in the sunshine so I can get a good picture?" It's important to stow your camera, roll up your sleeves, and enjoy the real thing.

By developing a knack for connecting with locals and their culture, we become temporary Europeans, members of the family—approaching Europe on its level, accepting and enjoying its unique ways of life. When I'm in Europe, I become the best German or Spaniard or Italian I can be. I consume wine in France, beer in Germany, and small breakfasts in Italy. While I never drink tea at home, after a long day of sightseeing in England, "a spot of tea" really does feel right. Find ways to really be there. Here are some ideas to consider:

Hit the back streets. Many people energetically jockey themselves into the most crowded square of the most crowded city in the most crowded month (St. Mark's Square, Venice, July)—and then complain about the crowds. If you're in Venice in July, walk six blocks behind St. Mark's Basilica, step into a café, and be greeted by Venetians who act as though they've never seen a tourist.

Play where the locals play. A city's popular fairgrounds and parks are filled with families, lovers, and old-timers enjoying a cheap afternoon or evening out. European commu-nities provide their heavily taxed citizens with wonderful athletic facilities. Check out a public swimming pool, called a "leisure center" in Britain. While tourists outnumber locals five to one at the world-famous Tivoli Gardens, Copenhagen's other amusement park, Bakken, is enjoyed purely by Danes. Disneyland Paris is great, but Paris' Parc Astérix is more French.

Connect with people. Greeks and Turks love a game of backgammon.

Take a stroll. Across south-ern Europe, communities have a *paseo*, or stroll, in the early evening. Stroll along. Join a *Volksmarch* in Bavaria to spend a day on the trails with people singing "I love to go a-wandering" in its original language. Mountain huts across Europe are filled mostly with local hikers. Most hiking centers have alpine clubs that welcome foreigners and offer orga-nized hikes.

Go to church. Many regular churchgoers never even consider a European worship service. But any church would welcome a traveling American. And an hour in a small-town church provides an unbeat-able peek into the community, especially if you join them for coffee and cookies afterwards. I'll never forget going to a small church on the south coast of Portugal one Easter. A tourist stood at the door videotaping the "colorful natives" (including me) shaking hands with the priest after the service.

Be an early bird. Throughout Europe—on medieval ramparts, in

Mass with the sun's rays, daily in St. Peter's

churches, produce markets, alpine farmsteads, and Riviera villages—the local culture thrives while the tourists sleep. In Germany, walk around Rothenburg's fortified wall at breakfast time, before the tour buses pull in and turn the town into a medieval theme park. Crack-of-dawn joggers and walkers enjoy a special look at wonderfully medieval cities as they yawn and stretch and prepare for the daily onslaught of the 21st century. By waking up with the locals on the Italian Riviera in the off-season, you can catch the morning sun as it greets a sleepy village, breathe in the damp, cool air...and experience a rare Italian silence. Among travelers, the early bird gets the memories.

Root for your team. For many Europeans, the top religion is soccer. Getting caught up in a sporting event is going local. Whether enjoying soccer in small-town Italy or hurling in Ireland, you'll be surrounded by a stadium crammed with devout fans. Buy something to wear or wave with the hometown colors to help you remember whose side you're on. In Dublin, I joined 60,000 locals to watch a hurling match at Croke Park. Taking my seat, I was among new Irish friends. They gave me a flag to wave and taught me who to root for, the rules of the game... and lots of creative ways to swear.

Challenge a local to the national pastime. In Greece or Turkey, drop into a teahouse or *taverna* and challenge anyone to a game of backgammon. You're instantly a part (even a star) of the café or bar scene. Normally the gang will gather around,

Make your trip worth more by cranking up the experiences. Attending a sporting event anywhere in Europe—like this soccer match in Germany—puts you in touch with the local spirit for little money. If you're wearing a lei with colors, be sure you root for the right team. Auf geht's Deutschland!

Connecting with the Culture

Generally speaking, Europeans enjoy getting to know Americans—all it takes to connect is a friendly smile and genuine curiosity. Take advantage of one of the many programs and organizations set up to help bridge the cultural divide.

Meet-the-Locals Programs: Several European cities have English-speaking volunteer greeters who belong to the Global Greeter Network (www.globalgreeternetwork.com). Greeters are screened extensively, but aren't trained as historical experts. Instead, they introduce visitors to their city by spending a few hours sharing their insider knowledge—their favorite hidden spots, how to navigate public transit, where to find the best bargains, etc.

A few bigger cities have more formal programs that put travelers in direct touch with locals. Dublin, the City of a Thousand Welcomes, brings volunteers and first-time visitors together for a cup of tea or a pint (free, www.cityofathousandwelcomes.com). In Paris, the group Meeting the French organizes dinners in private homes and workplace tours to match your interests or career (fee, www.meetingthefrench.com). Visitors to Copenhagen can enjoy a home-cooked meal with a family through Dine with the Danes (fee, www.dinewiththedanes.dk).

Conversation Clubs: Across Europe, most large cities, and even many small towns, have informal English-language conversation

and what starts out as a simple game becomes a fun duel of international significance.

Contact an equivalent version of your club. If you're a member of a service club, bridge club, professional association, or international organization, make a point to connect with your foreign mates.

See how the locals live. Residential neighborhoods rarely see a tourist; ride a city bus or subway into the suburbs. Browse through a department store. Buy a copy of the local *Better Homes and Thatches* and use it to explore that particular culture. Get off the map. In Florence, most tourists stick to the small section of the city covered by the ubiquitous tourist maps. Wander beyond

Blend into Europe: Shop at the town market.

clubs, usually meeting weekly or monthly in a public space (search online or ask at the tourist information office). You may well be the only native speaker there—if so, expect an especially warm welcome. For instance, in Rothenburg, Germany, the English Conversation Club meets on Wednesdays at Mario's Altfränkische Weinstube am Klosterhof. After 9 p.m., when the beer starts to sink in, the crowd grows, and everyone seems to speak that second language a bit more easily.

Casual Meetups: While primarily designed to connect travelers with overnight hosts, CouchSurfing also lists "day hosts" who are happy to just meet up with like-minded visitors and swap travel stories (see page 225). Meetup.com is another free means of finding people with shared interests in a given city. Sponsored events include picnics, museum tours, cocktail evenings, and more (www .meetup.com).

Cooking Schools: These give you not just a taste of the culinary traditions of the area you're visiting, but also a hands-on feel for what happens in European kitchens—along with a skill you can take home. Many include a trip to local markets. You can find one-day European cooking classes at the International Kitchen (www.the internationalkitchen.com) or get recommendations from my readers at www.ricksteves.com (search for "cooking").

that, and you'll dance with the locals or play street soccer with the neighborhood gang. In Helsinki, rather than sweat with a bunch of tourists in your hotel's sterile steam room, ride the public bus into a working-class neighborhood to a rustic-and-woody $14 sauna. Surrounded by milky steam, knotty wood, stringy blond hair, and naked locals, you'll have no idea which century you're in. But one thing is clear: You're in Finland.

Drop by a university. Mill around a university and check out the announcement boards. Eat at the college cafeteria. Ask at the English-language department if there's a student learning English whom you could hire to be your private guide. Be alert and even a little bit snoopy. If you stumble onto a grade-school talent show—sit down and watch it.

Join in. When you visit the town market in the morning, you're just another hungry shopper, picking up your daily produce. Traveling through the wine country of France during harvest time, you can be a tourist taking photos—or you can pitch in and become a grape-picker. Get more than a photo op. Get dirty. That night at the festival, it's just grape-pickers dancing—and their circle could include you.

If you're hunting cultural peacocks, remember they fan out their tails best for people...not cameras. When you take Europe out of your view-finder, you're more likely to find it in your lap.

Active Travel

Sightseeing can actually be quite sedentary. If you're an energetic person, make a point to be active in Europe. There are plenty of ways to get your heart pumping and, at the same time, inhale some of Europe's natural wonders.

Hiking and Walking

From casual city strolls to pleasant day hikes to multi-day alpine treks, Europe is a walker's paradise.

City Walking (and Dodging)

It's easy to get in a lot of walking time in Europe's cities and towns. Skip public transport (or save it for the end of the day, when your feet are crying for mercy), and get a literal feel for a place.

When putting together a walking itinerary, look for ways to splice in some top sights. In Rome, for example, winding up to the top of Gianicolo Hill rewards you with a lovely park and superb city views—and along the way you can knock off Bramante's Tempietto church, one of the jewels of the Italian Renaissance. For help weaving sightseeing into your walking plans, you can also join a walking tour (described earlier, under "Tours").

But be on your toes: Walking in cities can be dangerous, and jaywalking can have serious consequences (scores of pedestrians are run down on the streets of Paris each year). Drivers are aggressive, and politeness has no place on the roads of Europe. Cross streets carefully, but if you wait for a break in the traffic, you may never make it to the other side. Look for a pedestrian underpass, or when all else fails, just shadow a local—one busy lane at a time—across that seemingly impassable street. In some cities, such as Amsterdam, bikes can mow you down as easily as cars—and without the warning noise of an engine.

Be prepared—bring good, well-broken-in walking shoes, and realize that pounding the pavement all day can result in blisters (see page 408 for remedies). Pace yourself—concrete takes its toll on feet much sooner than dirt trails do.

Day-Hiking

You don't need to go far into the wild to find a slice of natural Europe to explore on foot. A two-hour trek connecting two thatched-roof towns

in England's Cotswolds affords backyard glimpses of farms in action, ancient wind-sculpted trees, and slate church spires. Southern France's Cap Ferrat has well-maintained foot trails, perfect for short, view-struck walks above the Mediterranean. In Italy, a delightful trail at the base of the cliffs of Orvieto gives you a peaceful and memorable hour-long circuit of that dramatic hill town.

Thanks to well-maintained trails, walking in Italy's Dolomites can be a walk in the park—with more spectacular scenery.

Perhaps my favorite place to hike is in Italy's Cinque Terre. The five towns that make up the Cinque Terre are strung together by a series of trails that form a national park. Hiking these trails—a seven-mile, five-hour journey—is one of the most exhilarating experiences in Italy. Take it slow...smell the cactus flowers and herbs, listen to birds, and enjoy spectacular vistas on all sides. (For more on the Cinque Terre, see page 503.)

If you plan on taking some day hikes, look for walking and hiking books on that region. Tourist offices often have booklets of local self-guided hikes. You can also look into local groups that offer walks to see if one of their scheduled hikes fits with your itinerary. In Great Britain, for example, the Ramblers extend guest privileges to nonmembers who want to try one of the group walks they lead every week, ranging from short strolls to bracing treks (www .ramblers.org.uk).

Hard-Core Hiking

Imagine hiking along a ridge high in the Swiss Alps. On one side of you, lakes stretch all the way to Germany. On the other stands the greatest mountain panorama in Europe—the peaks of the

Eiger, Mönch, and Jungfrau. And up ahead you hear the long, legato tones of an alphorn, announcing that a helicopter-stocked mountain hut is open, it's just around the corner...and the coffee schnapps is on. That's the kind of magic that awaits anyone who makes the effort to get high in the Alps.

Outstanding national parklands are scattered throughout Europe, offering wonderful ways for visitors to commune with nature. Hikers enjoy nature's very own striptease as the landscape reveals itself in an endless string of powerful poses. Most alpine trails are free of snow by July, and lifts take less rugged visitors to the top in a sweat-free flash. Trails are generally well kept and carefully marked, and precise maps are readily available. Throughout the Alps, trail markers are both handy and humiliating. Handy, because they show hours to hike rather than kilometers to walk to various destinations. Humiliating, because these times are clocked by local senior citizens. You'll know what I mean after your first hike.

Alpine trail signs show where you are, the altitude in meters, and how long in hours and minutes it takes to hike to nearby points.

If you're serious about hiking, do some research before you leave. Buy an appropriate hiking guidebook. Ask for advice from the national tourist offices of the countries you will visit (find a list on page 810). Invest in detailed maps (1:100,000 or 1:50,000)—look for OS Ordnance Survey (Britain), Michelin (throughout Europe), IGN's Blue series (good for France), Touring Club Italiano (Italy), and Die Generalkarte (Germany). Make sure the map shows general elevation gain with contour lines and/or indicates the steepness of roads.

Travelers who want to make walking a focus of their European trip will find several series of books aimed at them. Look into guidebooks published by Lonely Planet (www.lonelyplanet.com), Sunflower Books (www.sunflowerbooks.co.uk), Interlink Books (www.interlinkbooks.com), and Cicerone Press (www.cicerone.co.uk). Another good resource for long-distance walkers is the European Ramblers' Association, whose website (www.era-ewv-ferp.com) has country-specific advice and maps of Europe's walking paths. In the United Kingdom, try the Long Distance Walkers Association (www.ldwa.org.uk). A search online before your

Lift Lingo

Europeans, and especially the Swiss, have come up with a variety of ways to conquer alpine peaks and reach the best viewpoints and trailheads with minimum sweat. Known generically as "lifts," each of these contraptions has its own name and definition.

Cogwheel Train: A train that climbs a steep incline using a gear system, which engages "teeth" in the middle of the tracks to provide traction. Also known as "rack-and-pinion train" or "rack railway." In German, it's a *Zahnradbahn* (*train à cremaillère* in French and *ferrovia a cremagliera* in Italian).

Funicular: A car that is pulled by a cable along tracks up a particularly steep incline, usually counterbalanced by a similar car going in the opposite direction (meaning you'll pass the other car exactly halfway through the ride). Funiculars, like cogwheel trains, are in contact with the ground at all times. In German, it's a *Standseilbahn* (*funiculaire* in French and *funicolare* in Italian).

Cable Car: A large passenger car, suspended in the air by a cable, which travels between stations without touching the ground. A cable car is generally designed for skiers and holds a large number of people (sometimes dozens at a time), who generally ride standing up. When a cable car reaches a station, it comes to a full stop to allow passengers to get on and off. In German, it's a *Seilbahn* (*téléphérique* in French and *funivia* in Italian).

Gondola: Also suspended in the air by a cable, but smaller than a cable car—generally holding fewer than 10 people, who are usually seated. Gondolas move continuously, meaning that passengers have to hop into and out of the moving cars at stations. Also, while cable-car lines usually have two big cars—one going in each direction—gondolas generally have many smaller cars strung along the same cable. In German, it's a *Gondel* (*télécabine* in French and *telecabine* in Italian).

trip should turn up other local organizations as well as tour companies (such as Country Walkers—www.countrywalkers.com) offering guided or self-directed hiking itineraries.

Hut Hopping

The hikers' shelters spaced along the European trail system make walking trips a simpler proposition: There's no need to carry a tent, stove, or cooking utensils. Hundreds of huts exist to provide food and shelter for hikers. Using a smart network of trails and mountain huts spaced one convenient day's hike apart, you could walk from France to Slovenia without ever coming out of the Alps. At mountain villages, you can replenish your food supply or enjoy a hotel bed and a restaurant meal.

Alpine huts are generally spaced four to six hours apart. Most serve hot meals and provide bunk-style lodging. Many huts require no linen and wash their blankets annually. I'll never forget getting cozy in my top bunk while a German in the bottom bunk said, "You're climbing into zee germs of centuries." Serious hut-hoppers hike with their own sheets or hostel-style sheet sack.

In the Alps, look for the word *Lager*, which means they have a coed loft full of $25-a-night mattresses. The Swiss Alpine Club runs more than 150 hiker huts (www.sac-cas.ch); the Austrian Alpine Club has a helpful English website with links to other national alpine clubs and hut directories by country (www.aacuk.org.uk). Among many good books on hut hopping, consider *100 Hut Walks in the Alps* (Kev Reynolds, 2010).

Biking

Some travelers are surprised when I tell them to consider biking in Europe. I explain that it gets you close to the ground and close to the people. Europeans love bicycles, and they are often genuinely impressed when they encounter Americans who reject the view from the tour-bus window in favor of huffing and puffing on two wheels. Your bike provides an instant conversation piece, the perfect bridge over a maze of cultural and language barriers.

City Biking

While my schedule usually won't allow a week-long pedal in the Loire Valley, I'll often do day trips in or around cities. I feel local, efficient, and

even smug with my trusty and well-fitted bike. Especially during rush hour, I can get across town faster on my bike than by taxi or tram.

Europe's cities are striving to become more bike-friendly. Dozens of them have joined a European Union initiative to make bicycles on par with cars as a form of urban transport. The progress is gradual. Some cities (such as Rome and Athens) are not yet set up well for bikers, but quite a few (including Stockholm, Amsterdam, Copenhagen, Lucca, Florence, Salzburg, Munich, and Bruges) are a delight on two wheels, offering an extensive network of well-marked bike lanes. In these cities, rather than relying on walking or public transportation, consider making a bike your mode of transport. Bikes cut transit times in half compared to walking, giving you more time to spend at the sights.

Rental bikes are bargains at $12-15 per day (the best deals are for multiple days). Bike rental shops generally provide strong locks. Always lock the frame (not the wheel) to the permanent rack. Bike thieves can be bold and brazen.

Many places (including Barcelona, Copenhagen, Dublin, London, Paris, Stockholm, and Vienna) have citywide programs in which hundreds of free or very cheap loaner bikes are locked to racks around town. While tourists can easily take advantage of these programs in

Use your bike lock correctly. I learned this lesson the hard way...and suffered the embarrassment of returning just one wheel to my bike-rental place.

cities like London and Vienna, in other places (Dublin), the systems are designed mostly for residents (some require a membership or only take European-style chip-and-PIN credit cards). Also, the bikes are very basic, sometimes in disrepair, and often plastered with ads. If you're serious about biking, pay to rent a good one from a shop instead.

For a quick but meaningful spin around town, consider a bicycle tour. Guided bike tours are popular in cities throughout Europe (including Amsterdam, Barcelona, Bruges, Paris, Munich, Berlin, and Budapest), as well as many bike-friendly countryside areas. You'll get a young, entertaining, often foul-mouthed, sometimes informative guide who will give you a breezy introduction to the city and a close-up look at back streets few tourists ever see. The various companies (generally started by disgruntled employees of other bike-tour companies) are highly competitive, and come and go all the time. Tours are typically fun, reasonable (about $25-30), good exercise, and an easy way to meet other travelers as well as get a fresh angle on an old city.

Bike tours are a fun, informative, and healthy way to see great cities with an entertaining guide.

Countryside Biking

Biking in the boonies (using a small town as a springboard) is extremely popular in Europe. Thanks to the law of supply and demand, you can generally count on finding bike-rental shops wherever there are good bike-tripping options: along the Danube, the Rhine, and other idyllic river valleys; around Ireland's Dingle Peninsula; on Greek islands; and in the Alps for mountain biking on service roads.

In many countries (especially France, Germany, Austria, Belgium, and the Netherlands), train stations rent bikes and sometimes have easy "pick up here and drop off there" plans. For instance, if you ride the train into Amsterdam, rent a bike at the station for a few days to get around the city...and out into the tulip fields and windmills.

Wherever biking is fun, you'll find shops renting bikes and helmets.

Longer Bike Trips

If you're interested in long-distance biking, figure out how much of Europe you want to see. With an entire summer free, you can cover a lot of ground on a bike. But with a month or less, it's better to focus on a single country or region.

Consider bringing your bike from home. Bikes are less expensive in the US, and you'll know the bike works well for you. Carry along the tools you'll need to get your bike back into riding form, so you can ride straight out of your European airport.

Anyone can enjoy a gentle pedal through some of Europe's flat and inviting countryside.

Unless you love camping, it makes sense to stay in hostels, hotels, or B&Bs, since it frees you from lugging around a tent and sleeping bag. If you'd rather let someone else carry your gear, try a bike tour (offered by REI and many other companies).

Don't be a purist. Taking your bike on a train can greatly extend the reach of your trip, and there's nothing so sweet as taking a train away from the rain and into a sunny place.

You can find many good books on cycling in Europe, along with online info (such as www.europebicycletouring.com).

Shopping

Shopping in Europe can be fun, but don't let it overwhelm your trip. All too often, slick marketing and clever displays can succeed in shifting the entire focus of your vacation toward things rather than experiences. I've seen half the members of a guided tour of the British Halls of Parliament skip out to survey an enticing array of plastic "bobby" hats, Big Ben briefs, and Union Jack panties. Stay in control, and don't let your trip become just one more glorified shopping spree.

The thrill of where you bought something can fade long before the item's usefulness does. Even thoughtful shoppers go overboard. I have several large boxes in my attic labeled "great souvenirs." On the other hand, a few well-chosen items—a hand-painted tile from Siena, Provençal fabric from Nice, a fine old print from Rome—can help you capture the essence of a place for years to come.

Where to Shop

Avoid the souvenir carts outside of big monuments, where the goods tend to be overpriced and cheesy. Do your shopping in places that offer a fun cultural experience as well.

Outdoor Markets: The most colorful shopping in Europe—and a fun way to feel the local vibe—is at its lively open-air markets. A stroll along Portobello Road, arguably London's best street market, has you rubbing elbows with antique buffs and people who brake for garage sales. In Florence, the elegant iron-and-glass-covered Mercato Centrale is a wonderland of picturesque produce. Even a place as overrun with international visitors as Istanbul's Grand Bazaar still has tourist-free nooks and crannies that offer a glimpse into the real Turkey. Jump into the human rivers that flow in these venues.

Other good markets are Amsterdam's Waterlooplein, Madrid's El Rastro, and Paris' Puces St. Ouen. Remember that flea markets anywhere have soft prices. Bargain like mad (see my haggling strategies, later). Pickpockets love flea markets—wear your money belt and watch your day bag.

Department Stores: While these large stores may seem daunting at first, they're generally laid out much like ours. Most are accustomed to wide-eyed foreign shoppers and have some English-speaking staff. The store directory (usually near the elevators or escalators) often includes English. Many department stores have a souvenir section, with standard local knickknacks and postcards at prices way below the cute little tourist shops.

In Paris, visit Galeries Lafayette or Printemps. Harrods is London's most famous and touristy department store, but locals prefer Liberty on Regent Street. In Italy, an upscale department chain is La Rinascente, and in Spain, El Corte Inglés is everywhere. Berlin's mammoth Kaufhaus des Westens (KaDeWe) has a staff of 2,100 to help you sort through its vast selection of 380,000 items.

Neighborhood Shops and Boutiques: The best shopping districts not only offer interesting stores, but also let you feel the pulse of the city. In Rome, an early evening stroll down Via del Corso takes you past affordable shops—and the city's beautiful people. For top fashion—and top people watching—stroll the streets around the Spanish Steps.

The narrow streets near Vienna's cathedral are sprinkled with old-fashioned shops that seem to belong to another era—just the place to pick out an old print or an elegant dirndl. London's best and most convenient shopping streets are in the West End and West London (roughly between Soho and Hyde Park).

In Paris, a stroll from the Bon Marché department store to St. Sulpice allows you to sample smart clothing boutiques and clever window displays while enjoying one of the city's more attractive neighborhoods. For more eclectic, avant-garde boutiques, peruse the artsy shops of the Marais. Or head to the Champs-Elysées and peek into Louis Vuitton, Guerlain, and Mercedes-Benz; you don't have to buy the glitz to feel *très* French.

Souvenir Strategies

Shop smart, and remember that your most prized souvenirs are your memories.

Comparison shop at home. Do some research if you're looking for a particular high-end item overseas (and be aware that you can often find a similar item of better quality for a cheaper price at home). Before heading off to buy a Turkish carpet in Istanbul, learn the going rate, types of materials, and signs of quality, if only to avoid advertising your inexperience.

Concentrate your shopping in countries where your dollar will stretch. You'll find the best bargains in Turkey, Morocco, Portugal, Spain, Greece, and Eastern Europe. For the price of a skimpy doily in Britain, you can get a lace tablecloth in Spain.

Boxloads of Davids *await busloads of tourists.*

Restrict your shopping to a stipulated time. Form an idea of what you want to buy in each country. Set aside one day to shop in each country, and stick to it. This way you avoid drifting through your trip thinking only of souvenirs.

Lighten your load. Larger stores can arrange shipping for you, or you can ship packages home yourself through the post office (see page 359 for details on mailing packages). Or simply wait to go hog-wild until the last country you visit and fly home heavy. One summer I had a 16-pound backpack and nothing more until the last week of my trip, when I hit Spain and Morocco and managed to accumulate two sets of bongos, swords, a mace, and a camelhair coat...most of which are now in boxes in my attic.

Don't forget about the paperwork. If you intend to claim a Value-Added Tax (VAT) refund, you'll need to get the right documents from the merchant. For details on VAT as well as US customs regulations, see page 182.

Choose good souvenirs. My favorites are books; these are a great value all over Europe, with many editions that are impossible to find in the US. I look for local crafts, such as hand-knit sweaters in Portugal or Ireland, glass in Sweden, painted beehive panels in Slovenia, or lace in Belgium. I also like strange stuffed animals (at flea markets), CDs of music I heard live, posters (one sturdy tube stores 8-10 posters safely), clothing, photographs I've taken, and memories whittled lovingly into my journal.

Clothes Shopping

Many travelers enjoy shopping for wearable souvenirs in Europe, where the fashions can be quite different from back home. Options range from hole-in-the-wall boutiques to grand department stores to colorful street markets.

Europe-wide chains such as H&M and C&A have stylish, affordable selections. They can offer good value, especially for designer-inspired

clothing. In addition, each country has its own popular chains (such as Topshop in Britain). Fashions vary by store and by country, so if you see an item you like, grab it rather than wait to pick it up at a later stop—you might never see that same style or color again. Some women like buying high-quality underwear and camisoles in Italy or France; browse for them at any large department store.

European department stores (such as Paris' regal Galeries Lafayette) can be as interesting as what's on sale.

Street markets also offer clothing. Remember that prices are often soft—especially if it's near the end of the day, you're paying cash, and you're buying multiple items (such as three scarves). Don't be afraid to bargain.

No matter where you buy, be aware that the US, the UK, and continental Europe all use slightly different sizing conventions. For specifics, see the clothing-size conversion chart on page 812. Also note that European clothes are generally cut to fit more tightly than American clothes. Be prepared to swallow your pride and go up a size or two. If you wear a size medium leather jacket back home, you might need a large or extra-large in Italy.

Successful Haggling

In much of the Mediterranean world, the price tag is only an excuse to argue. Bargaining is the accepted and expected method of finding a compromise between the wishful thinking of the merchant and the tourist. In Europe, bargaining is common only in the south, but you can fight prices at flea markets and with street vendors anywhere.

Here are a few guidelines to help you get the best bargain.

Determine if bargaining is appropriate. It's bad shopping etiquette to "make an offer" for a tweed hat in a London department store. It's foolish not to at a Greek outdoor market. To learn if a price is fixed, show some interest in an item but say, "It's just too much money." You've put the merchant in a position to make the first offer. If he comes down even 2 percent, there's nothing sacred about the price tag. Haggle away.

You can troll for quirky souvenirs at flea markets.

Shop around to find out what locals pay. Prices can vary drastically among vendors at the same flea market, and even at the same stall. If prices aren't posted, assume there's a double price standard: one for locals and one for you. If only tourists buy the item you're pricing, see what an Arab, Spanish, or Italian tourist would be charged. I remember thinking I did well in Istanbul's Grand Bazaar, until I learned my Spanish friend bought the same shirt for 30 percent less. Merchants assume American tourists are rich, and they know what we pay for things at home.

Determine what the item is worth to you. Price tags can be meaningless and serve to distort your idea of an item's true worth. The merchant is playing a psychological game. Many tourists think that if they can cut the price by 50 percent they are doing great. So the merchant quadruples his prices and the tourist happily pays double the fair value. The best way to deal with crazy price tags is to ignore them. Before you even see the price tag, determine the item's value to you, considering the hassles involved in packing it or shipping it home.

Determine the merchant's lowest price. Merchants hate to lose a sale. Work the cost down, but if it doesn't match with the price you have in mind, walk away. That last amount the merchant hollers out as you turn the corner is often the best price you'll get. If *that* price is right, go back and buy. Prices often drop at the end of the day, when merchants are considering packing up.

Curb your enthusiasm. As soon as the merchant perceives the "I gotta have that!" in you, you'll never get the best price. He assumes Americans have the money to buy what they really want.

Employ a third person. Use your friend who is worried about the ever-dwindling budget or who doesn't like the price or who is bored and wants to return to the hotel. This trick can work to bring the price down faster.

Impress the merchant with your knowledge. He'll respect you, and you'll be more likely to get good quality. Istanbul has very good leather coats for a fraction of the US cost. Before my trip I talked to some leather-coat sellers and was much better prepared to confidently pick out a good coat in Istanbul.

Obey the rules. Don't hurry. Bargaining is rarely rushed. Make sure you are dealing with someone who has the authority to bend a price downward. Bid carefully. If a merchant accepts your price (or vice versa), you must buy the item.

Show the merchant your money. Physically hold out your money and offer him "all you have" to pay for whatever you are bickering over. He'll be tempted to just grab your money and say, "Oh, OK."

If the price is too much, leave. Never worry about having taken too much of the merchant's time. Merchants are experienced businesspeople who know they won't close every deal.

THEFT AND SCAMS

The odds are in your favor for enjoying a perfectly safe and incident-free trip to Europe. But anybody, whether at home or abroad, can experience unexpected problems, from inadvertently leaving your backpack on the train to getting pickpocketed. By taking a few common-sense precautions, you'll greatly improve your chances of having a smooth trip.

Pickpocketing and Theft

Europe is safe when it comes to violent crime. But it's very "dangerous" in terms of petty theft: Purse-snatching and pickpocketing are rampant in places where tourists gather. Thieves target Americans—not because they're mean, but because they're smart. Americans have all the good stuff in their bags and wallets. Loaded down with valuables, jetlagged, and bumbling around in a strange new environment, we stick out like jeweled thumbs. If I were a European street thief, I'd specialize in Americans—my card would say "Yanks R Us."

If you're not constantly on guard, you'll have something stolen. One summer, four out of five of my traveling companions lost cameras in one way or another. (Don't look at me.) In more than 30 summers of travel, I've been mugged once (in a part of London where only fools and thieves tread); my various rental cars were broken into a total of six times (broken locks, shattered windows, lots of nonessential stuff taken); and one car was hot-wired (and abandoned a few blocks away after the thief

Tourists are often targets at major sights in Italy, especially around Rome's Forum and Florence's train station. Many thieves pose as beggars, using newspapers or even babies to distract you while they pilfer your pocket or bag.

found nothing to take). But not one of my hotel rooms was ever rifled through, nor any of my money-belt-worthy valuables ever stolen.

Many tourists get indignant when ripped off. It's best to get over it. You're rich and thieves aren't. You let your guard down and they grab your camera. It ruins your day and you have to buy a new one, while they sell it for a week's wages on their scale. And the score's one to nothing. It's wise to keep a material loss in perspective.

Remember, nearly all crimes suffered by tourists are nonviolent and avoidable. Be aware of the pitfalls of traveling, but relax and have fun. Limit your vulnerability rather than your travels.

Be Prepared

Before you go, you can take some steps to minimize your loss in case of theft.

Make photocopies of key documents—your passport, railpass, car-rental voucher, itinerary, and more (see page 58 for details).

If you have expensive electronics (camera, netbook, smartphone, etc.), consider getting theft insurance (see page 65) and back up your files and photos frequently as you travel.

Leave your fancy bling at home. Luxurious luggage lures thieves. The thief chooses the most impressive suitcase in the pile—never mine.

Avoiding Theft

If you exercise adequate discretion, stay aware of your belongings, and avoid putting yourself into risky situations (such as unlit, deserted areas at night), your travels should be about as dangerous as hometown grocery shopping. Don't travel fearfully—travel carefully.

Here's some advice given to me by a thief who won the lotto.

Wear a money belt. A money belt is a small, zippered fabric pouch on an elastic strap that fastens around your waist, under your pants or skirt. I never travel without one—it's where I put anything I really, really don't want to lose. Wear it completely hidden from sight, tucked in like a shirttail—over your undies and shirt, under your pants. Most people wear the pouch over their stomach, but if you find it more comfortable, slide it around to the small of your back. (And some people prefer to use a neck pouch instead, worn like a necklace but under their shirt.) Each traveler should carry his or her own credit and debit cards and a stash of emergency cash in their own money belt.

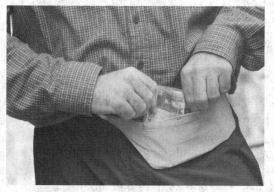

If you need to access your money belt, just reach casually into your pants (ignoring the curious glances of onlookers) and pull it out.

THEFT AND SCAMS

With a money belt, all your essential documents are on you as securely and thoughtlessly as your underwear. Have you ever thought about that? Every morning you put on your underpants. You don't even think about them all day long. And every night, when you undress, sure enough, there they are, exactly where you put them. When I travel, my valuables are just as securely out of sight and out of mind, around my waist in a money belt. It's luxurious peace of mind. I'm uncomfortable only when I'm not wearing it.

Those who travel with nothing worth stealing except for what's in their money belt are virtually invulnerable. But money belts don't work if they're anywhere but under your clothes. I once met an American woman whose purse was stolen, and in her purse was her money belt (that juicy little anecdote was featured in every street-thief newsletter). If you pull out your money belt to retrieve something, always remember to tuck it back in. And don't use a fanny pack as a money belt—thieves assume this is where you keep your goodies.

Tour of a Money Belt

Packing light applies to your money belt as well as your luggage. Here's what to keep in it:

Passport: This is probably the item you least want to lose en route.

Railpass: It's as valuable as cash.

Driver's License: It's helpful to use as non-passport collateral in rental situations (bikes, audioguides, and so on), and necessary if you want to rent a car.

Credit Card

Debit Card

Cash: Keep big bills in your money belt (with change and a few small bills in your pocket).

Plastic Sheath: Keep money-belt contents dry by placing them in something protective—even a plain old plastic baggie.

Just-in-Case Information: List of important phone numbers, email addresses, hotels, and any other itinerary details.

Never leave a money belt "hidden" on the beach while you swim (ideally, leave it locked up in your room). In hostels or on overnight trains, wear your money belt when you sleep. You can shower with it (hang it—maybe in a plastic bag—from the nozzle or curtain rod). Keep your money-belt contents dry and sweat-free by slipping them into a plastic sheath or baggie before zipping them into the belt.

You don't need to get at your money belt for every euro. Your money belt is your deep storage—for select deposits and withdrawals. For convenience, carry a day's spending money in your pocket (a button-down flap or Velcro strip sewn into your front or back pocket slows down fast fingers). Make sure it's an amount you're prepared to lose. Lately, I haven't even carried a wallet. A few bills in my shirt pocket—no keys, no wallet—I'm on vacation!

Leave your valuables in your hotel room. Your expensive gear, like a laptop, is much safer in your room than with you in a day bag on the streets. While hotels often have safes in the room (or at the front desk), I've never bothered to use one, though many find them a source of great comfort. Theft happens, of course, but it's relatively rare—hoteliers are quick to squelch a pattern of theft. That said, don't tempt sticky-fingered staff by leaving your camera or laptop in plain view; tuck your enticing things well out of sight.

Establish a "don't lose it" discipline. Travelers are more likely to inadvertently lose their bags than to have them stolen. I've heard of people leaving passports under pillows, bags on the overhead rack on the bus, and cameras in the taxi. Always take a look behind you before leaving any place or form of transport. At hotels, stick to an unpacking routine, and don't put things in odd places in the room. Have a mental checklist to use every time you pack up again: money belt, passport, cell phone, electronic gear, charging cords, toiletries, laundry, and so on. Before leaving a hotel room for good, conduct a quick overall search—under the bed, under the pillows and bedspread, behind the bathroom door, in a wall socket....

When you're out and about, never idly set down any small valuable item, such as a camera, ereader, wallet, or railpass. Either hold it in your hand or keep it tucked away. At cafés, don't place your phone on the tabletop where it will be easy to snatch—leave it in your front pocket (then return it to a safer place before you leave). Make it a habit to be careful with your things; it'll become second nature.

Secure your bag. Thieves want to quickly and unobtrusively separate you from your valuables, so even a minor obstacle can be an effective deterrent. If you're sitting down to eat or rest, loop a strap of your daypack around your arm, leg, or chair leg. If you plan to sleep on a train (or at an airport, or anywhere in public), clip or fasten your pack or suitcase to the seat, luggage rack, or yourself. Even the slight inconvenience of undoing a clip deters most thieves. While I don't lock the zippers on my bag, most zippers are lockable, and even a twist-tie, paper clip, or key ring is helpful to keep your bag zipped up tight—the point isn't to make your bag impenetrable, but harder to get into than the next guy's.

Stay vigilant in crowds and steer clear of commotions. Go on instant alert anytime there's a commotion; it's likely a smokescreen for theft. Imaginative artful-dodger thief teams create a disturbance—a fight, a messy spill, or a jostle or stumble—to distract their victims. For more on this, see "Scams and Rip-Offs," later.

Crowds anywhere, but especially on public transit and at flea markets, provide bad guys with plenty of targets, opportunities, and easy escape routes.

Be on guard in train stations, especially upon arrival, when you may be overburdened by luggage and overwhelmed by a new location. Take turns watching the bags with your travel partner. Don't absentmindedly set down a bag while you wait in line at the train station; always be in physical contact with your stuff. If you check your luggage, keep the claim ticket or locker key in your money belt; thieves know just where to go if they snare one of these. On the train, be hyper-alert at stops, when thieves can dash on and off—with your bag.

City buses that cover tourist sights (such as Rome's notorious #64) are happy hunting grounds. Be careful on packed buses or subways; to keep from being easy pickings, some travelers wear their day bag against their chest (looping a strap around one shoulder). Some thieves lurk near subway turnstiles; as you go through, a thief might come right behind you, pick your pocket and then run off, leaving you stuck behind the turnstile and unable to follow. By mentioning these scenarios, I don't want you to be paranoid...just prepared. If you keep alert, you'll keep your valuables, too.

Theft-Proofing Your Rental Car

Thieves target tourists' cars—especially at night. Don't leave anything even hinting of value in view in your parked car. Put anything worth stealing in the trunk (or, better yet, in your hotel room). Leave your glove compartment open so the thief can look in without breaking in. Choose your parking place carefully. Your hotel receptionist knows what's safe and what precautions are necessary.

Make your car look as local as possible. Leave no tourist information lying around. Put a local newspaper under the rear window. More than half of the work that European automobile glass shops do is repairing windows broken by thieves. Before I choose where to park my car, I check to see if the parking lot's asphalt glitters. In Rome, my favorite hotel is next to a large police station—a safe place to park.

You can judge the safety of a European parking lot by how it glitters.

If you have a hatchback, leave the trunk covered during the day. At night, roll back the cover so thieves can see there's nothing stored in the car. Many police advise leaving your car unlocked at night. "Worthless" but irreplaceable things (journal, memory cards full of photos, etc.) are stolen only if left in a bag. It's better to keep these things with you, or if need be, lay them loose in the trunk.

Be alert to "moving violations." In some urban areas, crude thieves reach into windows or even smash the windows of occupied cars at stoplights to grab a purse or camera.

Scams and Rip-Offs

Europe is a surprisingly creative place when it comes to travel scams. Many of the most successful gambits require a naive and trusting tourist. But don't think it can't happen to more sophisticated travelers too. There are many subtle ways to be scammed—a cabbie pads your fare, a shop clerk suddenly inflates prices, or a waiter offers a special with a "special" increased price. Be smart: Know what you are paying for before handing over money, and always count your change. (For tips on avoiding taxi scams, see page 286.)

Thieving moms with their babies are hard at work. Be careful. The wrap—not her left arm—is holding the baby...freeing that hand to pick your pocket.

Scam artists come in all shapes and sizes. But if you're cautious and not overly trusting, you should have no problem. Here are some clever ways European crooks bolster their cash flow. (For more examples, look in the "Graffiti Wall" section of the appendix for excerpts from my online Travel Forums.)

Such a Deal!
If a bargain is too good to be true...it's too good to be true.

The "Found" Ring: An innocent-looking person picks up a ring on the ground in front of you and asks if you dropped it. When you say no, the person examines the ring more closely, then shows you a mark "proving" that it's pure gold. He offers to sell it to you for a good price—which is several times more than he paid for it before dropping it on the sidewalk.

The "Friendship" Bracelet: A vendor approaches you and aggressively asks if you'll help him with a "demonstration." He proceeds to make a friendship bracelet right on your arm. When finished, he asks you to pay a premium for the bracelet he created just for you. And, since

THEFT AND SCAMS

you can't easily take it off on the spot, you feel obliged to pay up. (These sorts of distractions by "salesmen" can also function as a smokescreen for theft—an accomplice is picking your pocket as you try to wriggle away from the pushy vendor.)

Leather Jacket Salesman in Distress: A well-spoken, well-dressed gentleman approaches you and explains that he's a leather jacket sales-man, and he needs directions to drive to a nearby landmark. He chats you up ("Oh, really? My wife is from Chicago!") and gives you the feel-ing that you're now friends. When finished, he reaches in his car and pulls out a "designer leather jacket" he claims is worth hundreds of dol-lars, which he gives to you as a gift for your helpfulness. Oh, and by the way, his credit card isn't working, and could you please give him some cash to buy gas? He takes off with the cash, and you later realize that you've paid way too much for your new vinyl jacket.

Money Matters

Any time money changes hands, be alert. For advice on avoiding credit-card scams, see page 180.

Slow Count: Cashiers who deal with lots of tourists thrive on the "slow count." Even in banks, they'll count your change back with odd pauses in hopes the rushed tourist will gather up the money early and say *"Grazie."* Also be careful when you pay with too large a bill. Waiters seem to be arithmeti-cally challenged. If giving a large bill for a small payment, clearly state the value of the bill as you hand it over. Some cabbies or waiters will pretend

Don't confuse the €2 coin (left, value $2.80) with the old 500-lira coin (right, value $0).

to drop a large bill and pick up a hidden small one in order to short-change a tourist. Get familiar with the currency and check the change you're given: The valuable €2 coin resembles several coins that are either worthless or worth much less: the 500-lira coin (from Italy's former cur-rency), Turkey's 1-lira coin, and Thailand's 10-baht coin.

Talkative Cashiers: The shop's cashier seems to be speaking on her phone when you hand her your credit card. But listen closely and you may hear the sound of the phone's camera shutter, as she takes a picture of your card. It can make you want to pay cash for most purchases, like I do.

Meeting the Locals

I want my readers to meet and get to know Europeans—but watch out for chance encounters on the street.

The Attractive Flirt: A single male traveler is approached by a gorgeous woman on the street. After chatting for a while, she seductively invites him for a drink at a nearby nightclub. But when the bill arrives,

In Berlin, the police teach the public the latest shell-game scam. On the streets of Europe, anything that seems too good to be true...is.

it's several hundred dollars more than he expected. Only then does he notice the burly bouncers guarding the exits. There are several variations on this scam. Sometimes, the scam artist is disguised as a lost tourist; in other cases, it's simply a gregarious local person who (seemingly) just wants to show you his city. Either way, be suspicious when invited for a drink by someone you just met; if you want to go out together, suggest a bar (or café) of your choosing instead.

Oops! You're jostled in a crowd as someone spills ketchup or fake pigeon poop on your shirt. The thief offers profuse apologies while dabbing it up—and pawing your pockets. There are variations: Someone drops something, you kindly pick it up, and you lose your wallet. Or,

In your wallet, you've got a little cash, a phone card...and this funny note to the thief. Cut it out and take it along.

DEAR THIEF...

ENGLISH: Sorry this contains so little money.
Consider changing your profession.

ITALIANO: Mi dispiace per te che ci siano così pochi soldi.
Sara' meglio che cambi lavoro.

FRANCAIS: Je suis désolé d'avoir si peu d'argent.
Considérez un changement de carrière.

DEUTSCH: Tut mir leid dass meine Geldbörse so wenig Geld
enthält. Vielleicht sollten Sie sich einen neuen Beruf auswählen.

ESPAÑOL: Lamento que encuentre tan poco dinero.
Vaya pensando en cambiar de trabajo.

THEFT AND SCAMS

even worse, someone throws a baby into your arms as your pockets are picked. Assume beggars are pickpockets. Treat any commotion (a scuffle breaking out, a beggar in your face) as fake—designed to distract unknowing victims. If an elderly woman falls down an escalator, stand back and guard your valuables, then...carefully...move in to help.

The "Helpful" Local: Thieves posing as concerned locals will warn you to store your wallet safely—and then steal it after they see where you stash it. If someone wants to help you use an ATM, politely refuse (they're just after your PIN code). Some thieves put out tacks and ambush drivers with their "assistance" in changing the tire. Others hang out at subway ticket machines eager to "help" you, the bewildered tourist, buy tickets with a pile of your quickly disappearing foreign cash. If using a station locker, beware of the "Hood Samaritan" who may have his own key to a locker he'd like you to use. And skip the helping hand from official-looking railroad attendants at the Rome train station. They'll help you find your seat...then demand a "tip."

Young Thief Gangs: These are common all over urban southern Europe, especially in the touristy areas of Milan, Florence, and Rome. Groups of boys or girls with big eyes, troubled expressions, and colorful raggedy clothes play a game where they politely mob the unsuspecting tourist, beggar-style. As their pleading eyes grab yours and they hold up their pathetic message scrawled on cardboard, you're fooled into thinking that they're beggars. All the while, your purse or backpack is being expertly rifled. If you're wearing a money belt and you understand what's going on here, there's nothing to fear. In fact, having a street thief's hand slip slowly into your pocket becomes just one more interesting cultural experience.

Travel smart — keep what matters in your moneybelt.
www.ricksteves.com

Appearances Can Be Deceiving

The sneakiest pickpockets look like well-dressed businesspeople, generally with something official-looking in their hand. Some pose as tourists, with daypacks, cameras, and even guidebooks. Don't be fooled by looks, impressive uniforms, femme fatales, or hard-luck stories.

Fake Police: Two thieves in uniform—posing as "Tourist Police"—stop you on the street, flash their bogus badges, and ask to check your wallet for counterfeit bills or "drug money." You won't even notice some bills are missing until after they leave. Never give your wallet to anyone.

Groups of teenagers, using newspapers to distract their prey, pickpocket tourists strolling the beach promenade in Nice. Not nice.

Room "Inspectors": There's a knock at your door and two men claim to be the hotel's room inspectors. One waits outside while the other comes in to take a look around. While you're distracted, the first thief slips in and takes valuables left on a dresser. Don't let people into your room if you weren't expecting them. Call down to the hotel desk if "inspectors" suddenly turn up.

The Broken Camera: Everyone is taking pictures of a famous sight, and someone comes up with a camera or cell phone and asks that you take his picture. But the camera or cell phone doesn't seem to work. When you hand it back, the "tourist" fumbles and drops it on the ground, where it breaks into pieces. He will either ask you to pay for repairs (don't do it) or lift your wallet while you are bending over to pick up the broken object.

The Stripper: You see a good-looking woman arguing with a street vendor. The vendor accuses her of shoplifting, which she vehemently denies. To prove her innocence, she starts taking off her clothes—very slowly. Once she's down to her underwear, the vendor apologizes and she leaves. Suddenly all the men in the crowd find out that their wallets have "left," too, thanks to a team of pickpockets working during the show.

Losing It All...and Bouncing Back

You're winging your way across Europe, having the time of your life, when you make a simple mistake. You set your bag down next to your café chair, and before you know it...your bag is gone. Unfortunately, today's

THEFT AND SCANS

> ## Lost It All? Follow These Steps
>
> 1. File a police report, either on the spot or later. You'll need it to file an insurance claim for a lost railpass or travel gear.
> 2. Replace your passport at the nearest embassy or consulate (find locations online: www.travel.state.gov for Americans, www.passportcanada.gc.ca for Canadians).
> 3. Cancel and replace your credit and debit cards. Toll-free numbers (listed by European country) are available at the websites for Visa and MasterCard. You can also call these 24-hour US numbers collect:
>   Visa: 303/967-1096
>   MasterCard: 636/722-7111
>   American Express: 336/393-1111

the day you tucked your passport, credit cards, and extra cash in your bag instead of in your money belt. That sinking feeling is the realization that you've lost everything, except for the euro or two in your pocket.

Odds are, this won't ever happen to you. But a little bit of advance preparation can make even this worst-case scenario a minor bump in your European adventure.

Don't panic. First of all, take a breath. Panic clouds your judgment. And don't beat yourself up: No matter how careful, any traveler can get ripped off or lose a bag. I once met a family in Amsterdam who managed to lose all their bags between the airport and their first hotel, and they went on to have a very successful trip. A positive attitude can be a great asset.

Ask for help. If you're in a country where little English is spoken, enlist the help of a local English speaker to assist you in making phone calls or explaining the situation to officials. Try your hotelier or someone at the tourist office: Even in the smallest towns, someone is likely to know at least a little English. Fellow travelers you've met and even family or friends back home can also be sources of help.

For emergency help (for any reason—police, medical, and fire), dial 112 from any phone. This toll-free number is the European Union's version of 911. In many cases, operators are able to answer in English.

File a police report. Find a police officer and report the theft or loss. Having a police report may help with replacing your passport and credit cards, and is a must if you file an insurance claim for a lost railpass or expensive travel gear. The police may be able to direct you to a local travelers' aid office or Red Cross-like organization. And if you're lucky, someone may actually turn in your bag. That happened to me one time. My stolen bag showed up at the police station—turned in by a Good Samaritan who found it discarded after the thief rifled through its contents. Thieves don't want your clothes or your bag. They want only what they can resell and they discard the rest.

Gather critical information. In the best situation, you've got photocopies of your important documents on you. If you don't have your bank or embassy's contact information, look it up online (if Internet access is a problem, explain the situation to your hotelier or a staffer at the tourist office, and ask if you can use their office computer). Your hotelier or a tourist-office staffer should also be able to help you place necessary collect or toll-free calls. Retrieve information you've stored online, or solicit help from folks back home. Be careful about emailing passport and credit-card numbers. If you need important documents, have them sent by fax to a trusted location.

Replace your passport. This is top priority. Without a passport, you can't leave the country, and you'll find it difficult to check into a new hotel or receive wired funds. You'll need to go in person to the closest embassy (usually in the capital) or consulate (in major cities).

You may be able to make an appointment at the embassy or consulate, or you may need to show up during open hours and wait your turn. If you can, save time by printing the required forms off their website and filling them out before you go. Having a photocopy of your passport can help; if you don't, embassy staff can look up your previous passport records, interview you and your travel partners, and even call contacts at home to verify your identity.

Americans can find embassy and consulate information at www .travel.state.gov. Every US consulate operates an American Citizen Services (ACS) office, which aids Americans traveling abroad in coping with natural disasters, receiving money, and replacing passports (if calling from overseas, dial 202/501-4444; in the US, call 888/407-4747). A replacement passport costs $140 and can generally be issued within a few days, or faster if you make a good case that you need it right away. If you don't have the funds, the embassy will help you contact someone at home who can wire money directly to the embassy. If no one can wire the money, the embassy staff may waive the fee or give you a "repatriation loan"—just enough funds to cover the new passport and get you back home.

If you're Canadian, you'll need to report the loss or theft to the local police, as well as your nearest embassy or consulate. Canadian authorities will conduct an investigation into the circumstances, which may delay the processing of your request. You must complete an application form and a statutory declaration concerning the lost/stolen passport, supply two passport photos and documentary proof of Canadian citizenship, and pay a C$100 fee (for more information, see www.passportcanada .gc.ca).

Cancel debit and credit cards. Within two days, cancel your lost or stolen debit and credit cards (meeting this deadline limits your liability to $50) and order replacements. Visa, MasterCard, and American Express all have global customer-assistance centers, reachable by collect call from anywhere (see sidebar on page 336). You'll need to know the name of the bank that issued the card; the card type (classic, platinum, or whatever); the card number; the primary and secondary cardholders' names; the cardholder's name exactly as printed on the card; billing address; home phone number; circumstances of the loss or theft; and identification verification (your birth date, your mother's maiden name, or your Social Security number—memorize this, don't carry a copy). If you are the secondary cardholder, you'll also need to provide the primary cardholder's identification-verification details.

Your bank can generally deliver a new card to you in Europe within two to three business days. Some may even be able to wire cash to keep you going or pay for your hotel room directly. Ask about these extra services. It's also possible to transfer money from a bank in the US to a bank in Europe, but this may take several days to accomplish—you'll probably have the new cards faster. (For information on wiring money, see page 174.)

Replace travel documents. Point-to-point rail etickets can often be reprinted from any computer or at the station, but tickets purchased at the station and printed on special ticket paper probably can't be replaced. Unfortunately, you can't replace a railpass—you'll need to either purchase a new pass (most likely sent from home) or new tickets to complete your trip. (If you bought railpass insurance, you may be able to get a partial refund when you get home.) There's no need to replace printed copies of airline reservations—once you have your new passport, the airline can easily look up your reservation when you arrive at the airport.

Try to regenerate any other documents you might have stuffed in your pack, such as hotel and car-rental confirmations. If you don't have these stored somewhere, such as in your email or with a friend at home, call the hotel or car-rental agency and explain your predicament.

Rearrange travel plans. Depending on how long it takes to get your passport replaced—and how far you have to travel to get to an embassy or consulate—you'll probably need to rearrange your travel plans. Call or email to cancel and reschedule hotels and flights as soon as possible to avoid losing deposits or paying change fees (explaining the situation may help). If you're stuck without cash or credit cards for a few days, see if your bank or a family member back home can pay for your hotel stay.

Replace travel gear. Once you've started the process of replacing your passport and credit and debit cards, you can think about restoring gear such as your camera, phone, laptop, or iPod. Depending on your insurance policy, you may be able to get reimbursed for part of the replacement cost when you get home (see page 65). Decide which items are critical enough to your trip to replace immediately (flea markets and cheap department stores are great for bargains).

Refill prescriptions. Bring in a copy of your prescription to a pharmacy—if you don't have it, try contacting your doctor's office by phone or email. They can usually fax or email a copy to you in Europe (see page 410 for more on filling prescriptions). Your optometrist can do the same for your prescription eyewear.

Replace a rental-car key. If you lose the key to your rental car, call the car-hire company with your rental agreement number and your exact location. Be prepared for considerable expense and a delay: You will be charged $200 or more for a replacement key, and you may need to wait 24 to 48 hours for delivery of new keys or even a different vehicle.

Make the best of the situation. Getting everything straightened out can take a while. Be flexible and patient. It may not help at the time, but try to remember that your loss will make for a good story when you get home. Like a friend of mine says, "When it comes to travel, Tragedy + Time = Comedy."

THEFT AND SCAMS

LANGUAGE AND COMMUNICATION

You're probably wondering: How can you connect with the locals if you can't communicate in their language? You'll be surprised at how easy it is. Over the years, I've collected tips and tricks on how travelers who speak only English can step right over that pesky language barrier. Still, it always helps to be able to communicate—even just a few phrases—in the local tongue. In this chapter, you'll learn how to simplify your English and communicate creatively to get your points across and your needs met.

Communication also goes beyond words: It helps to know the meaning of various common gestures (and what to avoid doing) and, on a very practical level, the different ways that Europeans use numbers for dates, times, and more.

Your trip isn't all about communicating in Europe. You'll also want to connect with your friends back home. Phoning and email are covered in another chapter, but here, I'll cover snail mail. Nothing quite beats the Grand Tour romance of colorful postcards sent home the old-fashioned way.

Hurdling the Language Barrier

A fear of the language barrier keeps many people (read: English speakers) out of Europe, but the "barrier" is getting smaller every day. Over the last 30 years, an entire generation of Europeans has grown up speaking more English than ever. English really has arrived as Europe's

New signs in Amsterdam's airport don't even bother with Dutch.

second language. According to studies, half of all Europeans now speak English. Historically, many European signs and menus were printed in four languages: German, French, English, and—depending on where you were—Italian, Spanish, or Russian. But there's been a shift. In the interest of free trade and efficiency, the European Union has established English as Europe's standard language of commerce. Now most signs are printed in just two languages: the native language for locals and English for everyone else. In some airports, signs are now in English only.

Confessions of a Monoglot

While it's nothing to brag about, I basically speak only English. Of course, if I spoke more languages, I could enjoy a much deeper understanding of the people and cultures I visit. Still, speaking only English, I've enjoyed researching my guidebooks, leading tours, and making my TV shows, as well as navigating through wonderful vacations—getting transportation, finding rooms,

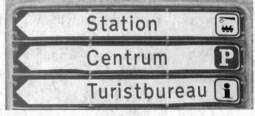

You don't have to speak Danish to understand this sign.

eating well, and seeing the sights. However, while you can manage decently with the blunt weapon of English, you'll get along in Europe better if you learn and use a few basic phrases and polite words.

Having an interest in the native language wins the respect of those you'll meet. Pocket-size two-language dictionaries are cheap and sold throughout Europe. Get a good phrase book, and start your practical vocabulary growing right off the bat. My **phrase books** (for French, Italian, German, Spanish, Portuguese, and French/Italian/German) are the only ones on the market designed by a guy who speaks just English (that's why they're so helpful). They are both fun and practical, with a meet-the-people and stretch-the-budget focus. Mr. Berlitz knew the languages, but he never stayed in a hotel where he had to ask, "Where can I hang my laundry?" These phrasebooks—written by travelers for travelers—have what you need to communicate during your vacation.

If your taxi driver is going too fast, my phrase books will help you say, "If you don't slow down, I'll throw up."

Spend bus and train rides learning. Start studying the language when you arrive—or sooner. I try to learn five new words a day. You'd be surprised how handy it is to have a working vocabulary of even 50 words. Take advantage of everyday conversations to learn the language. You're surrounded by expert, native-speaking tutors in every country. Let them teach you.

While Americans are notorious monoglots, many Europeans are very good with languages. Make communication easier by choosing a multilingual person to speak with. Businesspeople, urbanites, well-dressed young people, students, and anyone in the tourist trade are most likely to speak English. Many Swiss grow up trilingual, and many young Scandinavians and Eastern Europeans speak several languages. People speaking minor languages (Dutch, Norwegians, Czechs, Hungarians, Slovenes) have more reason to learn English, German, or French since their linguistic world is so small. All Croatians begin learning English in elementary school, and—since their TV programming is subtitled—they listen to Americans talk for hours each day. Scandinavian students of our language actually decide between English and "American." My Norwegian cousin speaks with a touch of Texas and knows more slang than I do.

Dutch is close enough to English that most any tourist can decipher this sign: It tells the opening hours (10:00 a.m. to 12:00 p.m., then 2:00 p.m. to 5:00 p.m.) on Maandag (Monday), Woensdag (Wednesday), Vrydag (Friday), and Zaterdag (Saturday).

We English speakers are the one group that can afford to be lazy, because English is the world's linguistic common denominator. When a Greek meets a Norwegian, they speak English. (What Greek speaks Norwegian?)

Imagine if each of our states spoke its own language. That's close to the European situation, but they've done a great job of minimizing the communication problems you'd expect to find on a small continent with such a Babel of Tongues. Most information a traveler must understand (such as road signs, menus, telephone instructions, and safety warnings) is printed either in English or in universal symbols. Europe's uniform road-sign system (see page 160) enables drivers to roll right over the language barrier. And rest assured that any place trying to separate tourists from their money will explain how to spend it in whatever languages are necessary. English always makes it.

Dominant as English may be, it's just good manners to start every conversation by politely asking, "Do you speak English?," *"Parlez-vous anglais?," "Sprechen Sie Englisch?,"* or whatever. If they say "No," then I do the best I can in their language. Usually, after a few sentences they'll say, "Actually, I do speak some English." (One thing Americans do well is put others at ease with their linguistic shortcomings.) Your European friend is doing you a favor by speaking your language. The least we can do is make our English simple and clear.

Using Simple English

English may be Europe's lingua franca, but communicating does require some skill. If you have a trip coming up and don't speak French yet, be realistic, and don't expect to become fluent by the time you leave. Rather than frantically learning a few more French words, the best thing you can do at this point is to learn how to communicate in what the Voice of America calls "Special English."

Speak slowly, clearly, and with carefully chosen words. Assume you're dealing with someone who learned English out of a book—reading British words, not hearing American ones. They are reading your lips, wishing it were written down, hoping to see every letter as it tumbles out of your mouth. If you want to be understood, talk like a Dick-and-Jane primer. Choose easy words and clearly pronounce each syllable (po-ta-to chips.) Try not to use contractions. Be patient—when many Americans aren't easily understood, they speak louder and toss in a few extra words. (Listen to other tourists talk, and you'll hear your own shortcomings.) For several months out of every year, I speak with simple words, pronouncing...very...clearly. When I return home, my friends say (very deliberately), "Rick, you can relax now, we speak English fluently."

Can the slang. Our American dialect has become a super-deluxe

Europeans: Babel of Tongues

Most of Europe's many languages can be arranged into one family tree. Many of them have the same grandparents and resemble each other more or less like you resemble your siblings and cousins. But occasionally, an oddball uncle sneaks in whom no one can explain.

Romance Countries: Italy, France, Spain, and Portugal

The Romance family evolved out of Latin, the language of the Roman Empire ("Romance" comes from "Roman"). Few of us know Latin, but being familiar with any of the modern Romance languages helps with the others. For example, your high school Spanish will help you learn some Italian.

Germanic Countries: British Isles, Germany, Netherlands, and Scandinavia

The Germanic languages, though influenced by Latin, are a product of the tribes of northern Europe (including the Angles and Saxons)—people the ancient Romans called "barbarians" because they didn't speak Latin. German is spoken by all Germans and Austrians, and by most Swiss. The people of Holland and northern Belgium speak Dutch, which is very closely related to German. While Dutch is not *Deutsch*, a Hamburger or Frankfurter can almost understand an Amsterdam newspaper. The Norwegians, Danes, and Swedes can read each other's magazines and enjoy their neighbors' TV shows.

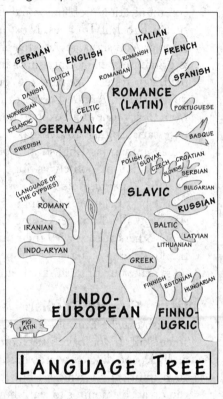

GERMAN ENGLISH ITALIAN FRENCH ROMANSH ROMANIAN SPANISH
DUTCH DANISH ROMANCE (LATIN) PORTUGUESE
NORWEGIAN CELTIC
ICELANDIC GERMANIC BASQUE
SWEDISH
POLISH SLOVAK CZECH CROATIAN SLOVENE SERBIAN
(LANGUAGE OF THE GYPSIES) SLAVIC BULGARIAN
ROMANY RUSSIAN
IRANIAN BALTIC LATVIAN
INDO-ARYAN LITHUANIAN
GREEK
FINNISH ESTONIAN HUNGARIAN
INDO-EUROPEAN FINNO-UGRIC
PIG LATIN

LANGUAGE TREE

Slavic Countries: Czech Republic, Poland, Slovakia, Slovenia, Croatia, and More

Most Eastern European countries (except Hungary, Romania, and the Baltics) speak Slavic languages. While these languages are more or less mutually intelligible, spellings change as you cross borders; for example, Czech *hrad,* or castle, becomes Croatian *grad.* Farther east—in Serbia, Russia, Ukraine, Bulgaria, and elsewhere—the language sounds similar, but is written with the Cyrillic alphabet. The Baltic languages, Latvian and Lithuanian, are distantly related to Slavic tongues.

Finno-Ugric Countries: Hungary, Finland, and Estonia

Hungarian, Finnish, and Estonian are more closely related to Asian languages than to European ones—likely hinting that the Hungarians, Finns, and Estonians all share ancestors from Central Asia.

Multilingual Countries and Regions

Switzerland has four official languages: German, French, Italian, and Romansh (an obscure Romance tongue); most Swiss are at least bilingual. Because the region of Alsace, on the French-German border, has been dragged through the mud during several tugs-of-war, most residents speak both languages. Belgium waffles (linguistically), with the southern half (the Walloons) speaking French and the rest speaking Dutch.

Europe's Underdog Languages

Every year on this planet, a dozen or so languages go extinct. But thanks to Europe's recent determination to celebrate diversity, its underdog languages—once endangered—are thriving once more.

The Basques, who live where Spain, France, and the Atlantic all touch, speak Euskara—mysteriously unrelated to any other European language.

England is surrounded by a "Celtic Crescent." In Scotland, Ireland, Wales, and Brittany (northwestern France), the old Celtic language survives. Seek out these die-hard remnants in proud gift shops and bookstores, Gaelic pubs, and the Gaeltachts (districts, mostly in Western Ireland, where the old culture is preserved by the government).

COMMUNICATION

slang pizza not found on any European menu. The sentence "Can the slang," for example, would baffle the average European. If you learned English in a classroom for two years, how would you respond to the American who uses expressions such as "sort of like," "pretty bad," or "Howzit goin'?"

Keep your messages grunt-simple. Make single nouns work as entire sentences. When asking for something, a one-word question ("Photo?") is more effective than an attempt at something more grammatically correct ("May I take your picture, sir?"). Be a Neanderthal. Strip your message naked and drag it by the hair into the other person's mind. But even Neandertourists will find things go easier if they begin each request with the local "please" (e.g., "*Bitte,* toilet?").

Use internationally understood words. Some Americans spend an entire trip telling people they're on *vacation*, draw only blank stares, and slowly find them-

Öffnungszeiten vom 4. Juli an

Montag: 9⁰⁰ - 11⁰⁰ und 16⁰⁰ - 18⁰⁰
Dienstag: 9⁰⁰ - 11⁰⁰ und 16⁰⁰ - 18⁰⁰
Mittwoch: 9⁰⁰ - 11⁰⁰ nachmittag geschlossen
Donnerstag: 9⁰⁰ - 11⁰⁰ und 16⁰⁰ - 18⁰⁰
Freitag: 9⁰⁰ - 11⁰⁰ und 16⁰⁰ - 18⁰⁰
Samstag: 8⁰⁰ - 12⁰⁰ und 14⁰⁰ - 16⁰⁰

*Hurdle the language barrier by thinking of things as multiple-choice questions and making educated guesses. This is a sign on a shop in Germany. It lists times. The top word can only mean "open times" or "closed times." I'd guess it lists hours open from (*vom = from, if it rhymes, I go for it*) the Fourth of July. Those six words on the left, most of which end in* tag, *must be days of the week (think guten tag or soup of the tag). Things are open from 9:00–11:00* und *from 16:00–18:00 (24-hour clock). On* Mittwoch *(midweek), in the afternoon...something different happens. Since it can only be open or closed, and everything else is open, you can guess that on Wednesdays,* nach Mittag, *this shop is* geschlossen!

selves in a soundproof, culture-resistant cell. The sensitive communicator notices that Europeans are more likely to understand the word *holiday*—probably because that's what the English say. Then she plugs that word into her simple English vocabulary, makes herself understood, and enjoys a much closer contact with Europe. If you say *restroom* or *bathroom*, you'll get no relief. *Toilet* is direct, simple, and understood. If my car is broken in Portugal, I don't say, "Excuse me, my car is broken." I point to the vehicle and say, "Auto kaput."

Tips on Creative Communication

Even if you have no real language in common, you can have some fun communicating. Consider this profound conversation I had with a

International Words

As our world shrinks, more and more words leap their linguistic boundaries and become international. Sensitive travelers develop a knack for choosing words most likely to be universally understood ("auto" instead of "car"; "kaput" rather than "broken"; "photo," not "picture"). They also internationalize their pronunciation. "University," if you play around with its sound (oo-nee-vehr-see-tay), can be understood anywhere. The average American really flunks out in this area. Be creative.

Communication by analogy is effective. Anywhere in Europe (except in Hungary), "Attila" means "crude bully." When a bulky Italian crowds in front of you, say, "*Scusi,* Ah-tee-la" and retake your place. If you like your haircut and want to compliment your Venetian barber, put your hand sensually on your hair and say "Casanova." Nickname the hairstylist "Michelangelo."

Here are a few internationally understood words. Remember, cut out the Yankee accent and give each word a pan-European sound ("autoboooos," "Engleesh").

Hello	Autobus	Europa
No	Taxi	Disneyland
Stop	Tourist	(wonderland)
Kaput	Beer	Nuclear
Ciao	Coke, Coca-Cola	Toilet
Bye-bye	Tea	Police
OK	Coffee	English
Mañana	Vino	Telephone
Pardon	Chocolate	Photo
Rock 'n' roll	Picnic	Photocopy
Mamma mia	Self-service	Disco
No problem	Yankee, Americano	Computer
Super	Hercules (strong)	Sport
Sex/Sexy	Casanova	Internet
Oo la la	(romantic)	Central
Moment	Attila (mean, crude)	Information
Bon voyage	Fascist	University
Restaurant	Elephant (a big	Passport
McDonald's	clod)	Bill Gates
Bank	Michelangelo	Obama
Hotel	(artistic)	Holiday (vacation)
Post (office)	Rambo	Gratis (free)
Camping	Communist	America's favorite
Auto	Amigo	four-letter words

cobbler in Sicily:

"Spaghetti," I said, with a very saucy Italian accent.

"Marilyn Monroe," was the old man's reply.

"Mamma mia!" I said, tossing my hands and head into the air.

"Yes, no, one, two, tree," he returned, slowly and proudly.

By now we'd grown fond of each other, and I whispered, secretively, *"Molto buono,* ravioli."

He spat, "Be sexy, drink Pepsi!"

Waving good-bye, I hollered, *"No problema."*

"Ciao," he said, smiling.

Risk looking goofy. Even with no common language, rudimentary communication is easy. Butcher the language if you must, but communicate. I'll never forget the clerk in the French post office who flapped her arms and asked, "Tweet, tweet, tweet?" I understood immediately, answered with a nod, and she gave me the airmail stamps I needed. At the risk of getting birdseed, I communicated successfully. If you're hungry, clutch your stomach and growl. If you want milk, "moo" and pull two imaginary udders. If the liquor was too strong, simulate an atomic explosion starting from your stomach and mushrooming to your head. If you're attracted to someone, pant.

Be melodramatic. Exaggerate the native accent. In France, you'll communicate more effectively (and have more fun) by sounding like Maurice Chevalier or Inspector Clouseau. The locals won't be insulted; they'll be impressed. Use whatever French you know. But even English spoken with a sexy French accent makes more sense to the French ear. In Italy, be melodic and exuberant, and wave those hands. Go ahead, try it: *Mamma mia!* No. Do it again. *MAMMA MIA!* You've got to be uninhibited. Self-consciousness kills communication.

Make logical leaps. Most major European languages are related, coming from (or at least being influenced by) Latin. Knowing that, words become meaningful. The French word for Monday (our "day of the moon") is *lundi* (lunar day).

Make an educated guess and go for it. Can you read the Norwegian: "Central Sick House"? Too many Americans would bleed to death on the street corner looking for the word "hospital."

Tongue-Twisters (or "Tongue-Breakers")

These are a great way to practice a language—and break the ice with the Europeans you meet. Here are some that are sure to challenge you and amuse your new friends.

German	Fischer's Fritze fischt frische Fische, frische Fische fischt Fischer's Fritze.	Fritz Fischer catches fresh fish, fresh fish Fritz Fischer catches.
	Ich komme über Oberammergau, oder komme ich über Unterammergau?	I am coming via Oberammergau, or am I coming via Unterammergau?
Italian	Sopra la panca la capra canta, sotto la panca la capra crepa.	On the bench the goat sings, under the bench the goat dies.
	Chi fù quel barbaro barbiere che barberò così barbaramente a Piazza Barberini quel povero barbaro di Barbarossa?	Who was that barbarian barber in Barberini Square who shaved that poor barbarian Barbarossa?
French	Si ces saucissons-ci sont six sous, ces six saucissons-ci sont trop chers.	If these sausages are six cents, these six sausages are too expensive.
	Ce sont seize cents jacinthes sèches dans seize cent sachets secs.	There are 1,600 dry hyacinths in 1,600 dry sachets.
Spanish	Un tigre, dos tigres, tres tigres comían trigo en un trigal. Un tigre, dos tigres, tres tigres.	One tiger, two tigers, three tigers ate wheat in a wheatfield. One tiger, two tigers, three tigers.
	Pablito clavó un clavito. ¿Qué clavito clavó Pablito?	Paul stuck in a stick. What stick did Paul stick in?
Portuguese	O rato roeu a roupa do rei de Roma.	The mouse nibbled the clothes of the king of Rome.
	Se cá nevasse fazia-se cá ski, mas como cá não neva não se faz cá ski.	If the snow would fall, we'd ski, but since it doesn't, we don't.

Excerpted from Rick Steves' Phrase Books—*full of practical phrases, spiked with humor, and designed for budget travelers who like to connect with locals.*

COMMUNICATION

Happy Talk

English	French	Italian	German	Spanish
Good day.	Bonjour.	Buon giorno.	Guten tag.	Buenos dias.
How are you?	Comment allez-vous?	Come sta?	Wie geht's?	¿Cómo está?
Very good.	Très bien.	Molto bene.	Sehr gut.	Muy bien.
Thank you.	Merci.	Grazie.	Danke.	Gracias.
Please.	S'il vous plaît.	Per favore.	Bitte.	Por favor.
Do you speak English?	Parlez vous anglais?	Parla inglese?	Sprechen Sie Englisch?	¿Habla usted inglés?
Yes./No.	Oui./Non.	Si./No.	Ja./Nein.	Sí./No.
My name is...	Je m'appelle...	Mi chiamo...	Ich heisse...	Me llamo...
What's your name?	Quel est votre nom?	Come si chiama?	Wie heissen Sie?	¿Cómo se llama?
See you later.	Á bientôt.	A più tardi.	Bis später.	Hasta luego.
Good-bye.	Au revoir.	Arrivederci.	Auf Wiedersehen.	Adiós.
Good luck!	Bonne chance!	Buona fortuna!	Viel Glück!	¡Buena suerte!
Have a good trip!	Bon voyage!	Buon viaggio!	Gute Reise!	¡Buen viaje!
OK.	D'accord.	Va bene.	OK.	De acuerdo.
No problem.	Pas de problème.	Non c'è problema.	Kein Problem.	No hay problema.
Everything was great.	C'était super.	Tutto magnifico.	Alles war gut.	Todo estuvo muy bien.
Enjoy your meal!	Bon appétit!	Buon appetito!	Guten Appetit!	¡Qué aproveche!
Delicious!	Délicieux!	Delizioso!	Lecker!	¡Delicioso!
Magnificent!	Magnifique!	Magnifico!	Wunderbar!	¡Magnifico!
Bless you! (after sneeze)	À vos souhaits!	Salute!	Gesundheit!	¡Salud!
You are very kind.	Vous êtes très gentil.	Lei è molto gentile.	Sie sind sehr freundlich.	Usted es muy amable.
Cheers!	Santé!	Salute!	Prost!	¡Salud!
I love you.	Je t'aime.	Ti amo.	Ich liebe dich.	Te quiero.

COMMUNICATION

The Germans say the same thing—*Montag*. *Sonne* is sun, so *Sonntag* is Sunday. If *buon giorno* means good day, *zuppa del giorno* is soup of the day. If *Tiergarten* is zoo (literally "animal garden") in German, then *Stinktier* is skunk and *Kindergarten* is children's garden. Think of *Vater, Mutter, trink, gross, gut, rapide, grand, económico, delicioso*, and you can *comprender mucho*.

Many letters travel predictable courses (determined by the physical way a sound is made) as related languages drift apart over the centuries. For instance, *p* often becomes *v* or *b* in the neighboring country's language. Italian menus always have a charge for *coperto*—a "cover" charge.

Read and listen. Read time schedules, posters, multilingual signs (and graffiti) in bathrooms and newspaper headlines. Develop your ear for foreign languages by tuning in to the other languages on a multilingual tour. It's a puzzle. The more you play, the better you get.

This is Danish for "tour bus." These days most come with air-conditioning.

A notepad can work wonders. Words and numbers are much easier to understand when they're written rather than spoken (especially if you mispronounce them). My back-pocket notepad is my constant travel buddy. To repeatedly communicate something difficult and important (such as medical instructions, "I'm a strict vegetarian," "boiled water," "well-done meat," "your finest ice cream," or "I am rich and single"), have it written in the local language on your notepad.

Assume you understand and go with your educated guess. My master key to communication is to treat most problems as multiple-choice questions, make an educated guess at the meaning of a message (verbal or written), and proceed confidently as if I understood it correctly. At the breakfast table the waitress asks me a question. I don't understand a word she says, but I tell her my room number. Faking it like this applies to rudimentary things like instructions on customs forms, museum hours, and menus. With this approach I find that 80 percent of the time I'm correct. Half the time I'm wrong, but I never know it, so it doesn't really matter. So 10 percent of the time I really blow it. My trip becomes easier—and occasionally much more interesting.

A Yankee-English Phrase Book

Oscar Wilde said, "The English have really everything in common with the Americans—except, of course, language." On your first trip to Britain, you'll find plenty of linguistic surprises. I'll never forget checking into a small-town bed-and-breakfast as a teenager on my first solo European adventure. The landlady cheerily asked me, "And what time would you like to be knocked up in the morning?" I looked over at her husband, who winked, "Would a fry at half-eight be suit-

Hmm... Where's the "exit"?

able?" The next morning I got a rap on the door at 8:00 and a huge British breakfast a half hour later.

Traveling through Britain is an adventure in accents and idioms. Every day you'll see babies in prams and pushchairs, sucking dummies as mothers change wet nappies. Soon the kids can trade in their nappies for smalls and spend a penny on their own. "Spend a penny" is British for a visit to the loo (bathroom). Older British kids enjoy candy floss

(cotton candy), naughts and crosses (tic-tac-toe), big dippers (roller coasters), and iced lollies (popsicles), and are constantly in need of an Elastoplast or sticking plaster (Band-Aid).

It's fun to browse through an ironmonger's (hardware store) or chemist's shop (pharmacy), noticing the many familiar items with unfamiliar names. The school-supplies section includes sticky tape or Sellotape (adhesive tape), rubbers (erasers), and scribbling blocks (scratch pads). Those with green fingers (a green thumb) might pick up some courgette (zucchini), swede (rutabaga), or aubergine (eggplant) seeds.

In Britain, fries are chips and potato chips are crisps. A beefburger, made with mince (hamburger meat), comes on a toasted bap (bun). For pudding (dessert), have some gateau or sponge (cake).

The British have a great way with names. You'll find towns with names like Upper and Lower Piddle, Once Brewed, and Itching Field. This cute coziness comes through in their language as well. Your car is built with a bonnet and a boot rather than a hood and trunk. You drive on motorways, and when the freeway divides, it becomes a dual carriageway. And never go anticlockwise (counterclockwise) in a roundabout. Gas is petrol, a truck is a lorry, and when you hit a tailback (traffic jam), don't get your knickers in a twist (make a fuss), just queue up (line up).

A two-week vacation in Britain is unheard of, but many locals holiday for a fortnight in a homely (homey) rural cottage, possibly on the Continent (continental Europe). They might pack a face flannel (washcloth), torch (flashlight), and hair grips (bobby pins) in their bum bag (never a fanny pack!) before leaving their flat (apartment). On a cold evening it's best to wear the warmest mackintosh (raincoat) you can

Don't take British road signs personally.

find or an anorak (parka) with press studs (snaps). You can post letters in the pillar box and give your girlfriend a trunk (long distance) call. If you reverse the charges (call collect), she'll say you're tight as a fish's bum. If she witters on (gabs and gabs), tell her you're knackered (exhausted) and it's been donkey's years (ages) since you've slept. After washing up (doing the dishes) and hoovering (vacuuming), you can go up to the first floor (second floor) with a neat (straight) whisky and a plate of biscuits (cookies) and get

Somehow, "Broken TV" just doesn't have the same ring to it.

goose pimples (goose bumps) just enjoying the view. Too much of that whisky will get you sloshed, paralytic, bevvied, wellied, popped up, ratted, or even pissed as a newt.

All across the British Isles, you'll find new words, crazy humor, and colorful accents. Pubs are colloquial treasure chests. Church services, sporting events, the Houses of Parliament, live plays featuring local comedy, the streets of Liverpool, the docks of London, and children in parks are playgrounds for the American ear. One of the beauties of touring Great Britain is the illusion of hearing a foreign language and actually understanding it—most of the time.

COMMUNICATION

Desperate Telephone Communication

Getting a message across in a language you don't speak requires some artistry. It takes something closer to wizardry on a telephone, where you won't have any visual aids (your dynamic hand and facial expressions, for example). In attempting a phone conversation, speak slowly and clearly, pronouncing every syllable. Keep it very simple—don't clutter your message with anything more than what's essential. Don't overcommunicate—many things are already understood and don't need to be said. (See? Those last six words didn't need to be written.) Use international or carefully chosen English words. When all else fails, let a local person on your end (such as a hotel receptionist) do the talking after you explain to him (with visual help, if needed) the message.

Let me illustrate with a hypothetical telephone conversation. I'm calling a hotel in Barcelona from a phone booth in the train station. I just arrived, read my guidebook's list of budget accommodations, and I like Pedro's Hotel. Here's what happens:

Pedro answers, "Hotel Pedro, grabdaboodogalaysk."

I ask, "Hotel Pedro?" (Question marks are created melodically.)

He affirms, already a bit impatient, "*Sí*, Hotel Pedro."

I ask, "*Habla* Eng-leesh?"

He says, "No, dees ees Ehspain." (Actually, he probably would speak a little English or would say "*momento*" and get someone who did. But we'll make this particularly challenging. Not only does he not speak English, he doesn't want to...for patriotic reasons.)

Remember not to overcommunicate. You don't need to tell him you're a tourist looking for a bed. Who else calls a hotel speaking in a foreign language? Also, you can assume he's got a room available. If he's full, he's very busy and he'd say "complete" or "no hotel" and hang up. If he's still talking to you, he wants your business. Now you must communicate just a few things, like how many beds you need and who you are.

I say, "OK." (OK is international for, "Roger, prepare for the next transmission.") "Two people"—he doesn't understand. I get fancy, "*Dos* people"—he still doesn't get it. Internationalize, "*Dos* pehr-son"—*no comprende*. "*Dos hombre*"—nope. Digging deep into my bag of international linguistic tricks, I say, "*Dos* Yankees."

"OK!" He understands that you want beds for two Americans. He says, "*Sí*," and I say, "Very good" or "*Muy bien*."

Now I need to tell him who I am. If I say, "My name is Mr. Steves, and I'll be over promptly," I'll lose him. I say, "My name Ricardo (ree-KAR-do)." In Italy I say, "My name Luigi." Your name really doesn't matter; you're communicating just a password so you can identify yourself when you walk through the door. Say anything to be understood.

He says, "OK."

You repeat slowly, "Hotel, *dos* Yankees, Ricardo, coming *pronto*, OK?"

He says, "OK."

You say, "*Gracias, adiós!*"

Twenty minutes later you walk up to the reception desk, and Pedro greets you with a robust, "Eh, Ricardo!"

European Gestures

In Europe, while some gestures can help you communicate, others can contribute to the language barrier. For example, if you count with your  fingers, start with your thumb, not your index finger (if you hold up your index finger, you'll probably get two of something). If you make a "peace" sign to indicate the number two, you may get three— or a punch in the nose in parts of Britain, where it's an obscene gesture.

The "thumbs up" sign popular in the United States is used widely in France and Germany to say

The "V for victory" sign is international. "OK" (it also represents the number one when counting throughout Europe). The "V for victory" sign is used in most of Europe as in the United States. (But beware—making the V with your palm toward you is the rudest of gestures in Britain.)

Some cultures also indicate "yes" and "no" differently: In Turkey, they shake their heads as Americans do, but someone may also signal "no" by tilting their head back. In Bulgaria and Albania, "OK" is indicated by happily shaking your head left and right—as if you were signaling "no" in the US.

Here are a few more common European gestures, their meanings, and where you're likely to see them.

Fingertips Kiss: Gently bring the fingers and thumb of your right hand together, raise to your lips, kiss lightly, and joyfully toss your fingers and thumb into the air. This gesture is used commonly in France, Spain, Greece, and Germany as a form of praise. It can mean sexy, delicious, divine, or wonderful. Be careful—tourists look silly when they

COMMUNICATION

overemphasize this subtle action.

Hand Purse: Straighten the fingers and thumb of one hand, bringing them all together and making an upward point about a foot in front of your face. Your hand can be held still or moved a little up and down at the wrist. This is a common and very Italian gesture for a query. It is used to say "What do you want?" or "What are you doing?" or "What is it?" or "What's new?" It can also be used as an insult to say "You fool." The hand purse can also mean "fear" (France), "a lot" (Spain), and "good" (Greece and Turkey).

Hand Shake: "Expensive" is often indicated by shaking your hand and sucking in like you just burned yourself.

Cheek Screw: Make a fist, stick out your index finger, and (without piercing the skin) screw it into your cheek. The cheek screw is used widely and almost exclusively in Italy to mean good, lovely, beautiful. Many Italians also use it to mean clever. But be careful: In southern Spain, the cheek screw is used to call a man effeminate.

Eyelid Pull: Place your extended forefinger below the center of your eye and pull the skin downward. In France and Greece this means "I am alert. I'm looking. You can't fool me." In Italy and Spain, it's a friendlier warning, meaning "Be alert, that guy is clever."

Very delicious!

Forearm Jerk: Clench your right fist and jerk your forearm up as you slap your right bicep with your left palm. This is a rude phallic gesture that men throughout southern Europe often use the way many Americans "give someone the finger." This jumbo version of "flipping the bird" says "I'm superior" (it's an action some monkeys actually do with their penises to insult their peers). This "get lost" or "up yours" gesture is occasionally used by rude men in Britain and Germany as more of an "I want you" gesture about (but never to) a sexy woman.

Chin Flick: Tilt your head back slightly and flick the back of your fingers forward in an arc from under your chin. In Italy and France, this means "I'm not interested, you bore me," or "You bother me." In southern Italy it can mean "No."

Numbers and Stumblers

Europeans convey numerical information differently than we do, from measurements to schedules and even dates. As simple as these things are, they can be frustrating barriers and cause needless, occasionally serious problems.

Time and Date

The 24-hour clock (military time) is used in any official timetable. This includes bus, train, and tour schedules. Learn to use it quickly and easily. Everything is the same until 12:00 noon. Then, instead of starting over again at 1:00 p.m., the Europeans keep on going—13:00, 14:00, and so on. For any time after noon, subtract 12 and add p.m. (18:00 is 6:00 p.m.).

To figure out the time back home, remember that European time is generally six/nine hours ahead of the East/West Coasts of the US. (These are the major exceptions: British, Irish, and Portuguese time is five/eight hours ahead; Greece and Turkey are seven/ten hours ahead.) Europe observes Daylight Saving Time (called "Summer Time" in the UK), but on a slightly different schedule than the US: Europe "springs forward" on the last Sunday in March (three weeks after most of North America) and "falls back" the last Sunday in October (one week before North America). For a handy online time converter, try www.timeand date.com/worldclock.

When it comes to dates, it's critical to remember—especially when making reservations—that European date order is written day/month/ year. Christmas, for example, is 25/12/14 instead of 12/25/14, as we would write it.

Written Numbers

A European's handwritten numbers look different from ours. The number 1 has an upswing ($\mathit{1}$). The number 4 often looks like a short lightning bolt ($\mathit{4}$). If you don't cross your 7 ($\mathit{7}$), it may be mistaken as a sloppy 1, and you could miss your train. Don't use "#" for "number"—it's not common in Europe.

On the continent, commas are decimal points and decimals commas, so a euro and a half is €1,50 and there are 5.280 feet in a mile. (Britain and Ireland use commas and decimal points like North America.)

The Metric System

European countries (except the UK) use kilometers instead of miles.

A kilometer is six-tenths of a mile. To quickly translate kilometers to miles, cut the kilometer figure in half and add 10 percent of the original figure (e.g., 420 km = 210 + 42 = 252 miles). Some people prefer to drop the last digit and multiply by six: Quick, what's 150 km? (15 × 6 = 90 miles.) "36-26-36" means nothing to a European (or metric) girl-watcher. But a "90-60-90" is a real pistachio.

Here are some easy ways to guesstimate metric measurements: Since a meter is 39 inches, just consider meters

This birth-announcement sign doubles as a lesson in European measurements: Little Martin weighed 4,370 grams (1,000 grams = 1 kilo = 2.2 pounds, so he weighed about 4.3 times 2.2, or around 9.5 pounds) and was 53 centimeters long (100 cm = 1 meter = 39 inches, so 53 cm is just over 20 inches). He was born on 14.7.95 (July 14, 1995) at 21:09 (9:09 p.m.).

roughly equivalent to yards. A hectare equals about 2.5 acres. A liter is about a quart (1.056 quarts, to be exact)—four to a gallon. A centimeter (cm) is about half the distance across a penny, while a millimeter (mm) is about the thickness of a penny.

Converting Temperatures

Europeans measure temperatures in degrees Celsius (zero degrees C = 32 degrees Fahrenheit). You can use a formula to convert temperatures in Celsius to Fahrenheit: Divide C by 5, multiply by 9, and add 32 to get F. If that's too scary, it's easier and nearly as accurate to double the Celsius temperature and add 30. So if it's 27° C, double to 54 and add 30 to get 84° F (it's actually 81° F, but that's close enough for me). Chilly 10° C comes out to 50° F either way, and comfy 20° C is about 70° F (actually 68° F). To convert Fahrenheit to Celsius, subtract 32, divide by 9, then multiply by 5; or take the easy route—just subtract 30 and divide by 2. A memory aid: 28° C = 82° F—balmy summer weather. And a rhyme: 30 is hot, 20 is nice, 10 is cold, 0 is ice.

Addresses and Floors of Buildings

House numbers often have no correlation to what's across the street. While in America, an odd-numbered house is usually on one side of the street and an even-numbered is on the other, in Italy #28 may be directly across from #2.

Floors of buildings are numbered differently in Europe. The bottom floor is called the ground floor, and what we call the second floor is a European's first floor. So if your room is on the second floor (European), bad news—you're on the third floor (American). On the elevator, push whatever's below "1" to get to the ground floor.

Mail and Shipping

It's been years since I've communicated via snail mail in Europe, but it can be done. Here are some tips for dealing with the European postal service:

Post Offices and Stamps: European post offices can be handy and efficient or jam-packed and discouraging, depending on the country. In general, small-town post offices can be less crowded and more user-friendly. If possible, avoid the Italian male...I mean, mail. Service is best north of the Alps.

Don't assume you have to wait in a long line for a few postcard stamps—they're often sold in machines at post offices. Sometimes you can buy them at neighborhood newsstands, gift shops that sell cards, or your hotel's front desk. (Write your postcards before getting stamps— you may be in the next country by the time you're ready to mail them.)

Receiving Letters and Packages: If you need to have something sent from home, have it addressed to you at a hotel you'll arrive at when it does; your hotelier will be happy to hold it for you. Allow 10 days for a letter; to speed things up, try second-day US-Europe services (such as DHL, www.dhl.com), though figure on four days for delivery to a small town. If you're not staying at a hotel (for instance, if you're camping or caravanning), you can have mail sent to any city's post office, addressed to you in care of "Poste Restante"; if possible, pick a small town with only one post office and no crowds.

Sending Packages: Shoppers needing to ship packages home can usually buy boxes and tape at the post office. Postage is expensive—a box the size of a small fruit crate costs about $40 by slow boat. Post offices in some countries have limits on how big or heavy your packages can be. In Germany and Great Britain, any surface-mail package for overseas delivery is limited to 2 kilograms, or about 4.5 pounds (but for books only, Great Britain allows up to 5 kilograms, or 11 pounds). For heavier packages, you must use their postal services' affiliated package services. From France, you can ship surface packages up to 30 kilograms (about 66 pounds). The fastest way to get a package home from Italy is to use the Vatican post office—or take it home in your suitcase. Every box I've ever mailed has arrived—bruised and battered but all there—within six weeks. To send precious things home fast, I use DHL; they have offices in any big city.

Shipping Guidelines: Customs regulations amount to 10 or 15 frustrating minutes of filling out forms with the normally unhelpful postal clerk's semi-assistance. Be realistic in your service expectations. European postal clerks are every bit as friendly, speedy, and multilingual as American postal clerks.

You can mail one package per day to yourself worth up to $200 duty-free from Europe to the US (mark it "personal purchases"). If you mail an item home valued at $250, you pay duty on the full $250, not $50. When you fill out the customs form, keep it simple and include

If you accumulate a shoebox's worth of dead weight, mail it home and keep on packing light.

the item's value (contents: clothing, books, souvenirs, poster, value $50). For alcohol, perfume containing alcohol, and tobacco valued at more than $5, you will pay a duty. You can also mail home all the "American Goods Returned" you like (e.g., clothes you packed but no longer need) with no customs concerns—but note that these goods really must be American (not Bohemian crystal or a German cuckoo clock), or you'll be charged a duty. If it's a gift for someone else, they are liable to pay customs if it's worth more than $100 (mark it "unsolicited gift"). For details, visit www.cbp.gov and search for "Know Before You Go."

COMMUNICATION

EATING

Eating in Europe is sightseeing for your taste buds. Every country has local specialties that are good, memorable, or both. Whether it's Wiener schnitzel in Vienna, *salade niçoise* in Nice, or wurst in Würzburg, a country's cuisine is as culturally important as its museums. But just as there are

A fun neighborhood restaurant: no English menus, no credit cards, but good food, good prices, and a friendly staff

tricks for sightseeing, there are also ways to maximize your culinary journey.

Much of my experience lies in eating well cheaply. Galloping gluttons thrive on $25 a day—by picnicking. Those with a more refined palate and a little more money can mix picnics with atmospheric and enjoyable restaurant meals and eat well for $45 a day.

This $45-a-day budget includes a $15 lunch (cheaper if you picnic or eat fast food), a $25 good and filling restaurant dinner (more with wine or dessert), and $5 for your chocolate, cappuccino, and gelato needs. (This assumes that breakfast is included with your hotel room; if you have to buy breakfast, have a picnic lunch...or eat less gelato.) If your budget requires, you can find a satisfying dinner for $20 or less anywhere in Europe. If you have more money, of course, it's delightful to spend it dining well.

Restaurants

Restaurants are the most expensive way to eat. They can pillage and plunder a tight budget, but it would be criminal to pass through Europe without sampling the specialties served in good restaurants.

The truth is that European restaurants are no more expensive than American ones. The cost of eating is determined not by the local standard, but by your personal standard. Many Americans can't find an edible meal for less than $30 in their hometown, but their next-door neighbors enjoy eating out for half that. If you can enjoy a $15 meal in Boston, Detroit, or Seattle, you'll eat well in London, Rome, or Helsinki for the same price. Every year I eat about 100 dinners in Europe. My budget target is $15 for a simple, fill-the-tank meal; $25 for a good restaurant dinner; and $50 for a splurge feast. Forget the scare stories. People who spend $60 on dinner in Dublin and then complain either enjoy complaining or are fools. Let me fill you in on filling up in Europe.

Finding a Restaurant

Average tourists are attracted—like moths to a lightbulb—to the biggest neon sign that boasts, *We speak English and accept credit cards*. Wrong! I look for a handwritten menu in the native language only, with a small selection. This means the kitchen is cooking what was fresh in the market that morning for loyal return customers (and not targeting tourists).

Restaurants listed in your guidebook are usually fine, but too often when a place becomes famous this way, it goes downhill. You don't need those listings to find

A small, handwritten menu in the local language is a good sign.

your own good restaurant. Ask your hotel receptionist or even someone on the street for a good place—not a good place for tourists, but a place they'd take a friend. Or leave the tourist center and stroll around until you find a restaurant with a happy crowd of locals. Be snoopy; look at

EATING

Brussels' "restaurant row," Rue des Bouchers, is fun for a walk. And, if you understand the prices thoroughly, it's not a bad place to dine.

what people are eating. After a few days in Europe, you'll have no trouble telling a genuine hangout from a tourist trap.

Many European cities have a bustling, colorful "restaurant row," a street or square lined with characteristic eateries—such as Rue des Bouchers in Brussels, Rue Mouffetard in Paris, Rua das Portas de Santo Antão in Lisbon, Leidsedwarsstraat in Amsterdam, Campo de' Fiori in Rome, Adrianou street in Athens, and Prijeko street in Dubrovnik. The restaurants usually have straightforward menus of tourist-pleasing dishes, superficial elegance, and gregarious hawkers out front trying desperate sales pitches to lure in diners. Some of the restaurants are tourist traps with overpriced food and rotten service; others are frequented by natives and can offer great ambience and decent value. A good guidebook, a tip from a trusted native, or simply an eye for choosing the local favorite can help you figure out which is which.

Techie travelers report they're generally pleased with the restaurant advice they've found on Yelp and TripAdvisor (for more on review-type sites, see page 32). And many cities have websites where residents post their own restaurant reviews; you can ask locals for their recommended sites, but be aware that these sites often are not designed for English speakers.

Keep in mind that restaurants and pubs in Europe don't usually serve meals continuously throughout the day. They typically close in the late afternoon (about 2 p.m.) and then reopen at dinner. In between meals, you'll find plenty of snack bars or cafés happy to feed you.

Restaurant Etiquette

When entering a restaurant, feel free to seat yourself at any table that isn't marked "reserved." I try to catch a server's eye and signal to be sure it's OK for me to sit there. It also lets him know I'm ready to look at a menu. If the place is full, you're likely to simply be turned away: There's no "hostess" standing by to add your name to a carefully managed waiting list. Since European diners take their time with a meal, it's impossible

EATING

Vegetarians

Vegetarians find life a little frustrating in Europe. Very often, Europeans think "vegetarian" means "no red meat" or "not much meat." If you are a strict vegetarian, you'll have to make things very clear. Write the appropriate phrase (see opposite page), keep it handy, and show it to each waiter before ordering your meal.

Vegetarians have no problem with continental breakfasts, which are normally meatless anyway. Meat-free picnic lunches are delicious, since bread, cheese, and yogurt are wonderful throughout Europe. Have some healthy snacks (such as nuts or fresh produce) on hand, in case you can't find a suitable meal.

Salad bars are abundant and great for vegetarians.

It's in restaurants that your patience may be minced. Big-city tourist office brochures list restaurants by category. In any language, look under "V." For a good meal, vegetarians basically have two options: Seek out a vegetarian restaurant (most big cities have them), or browse the menus at some fine-dining restaurants, many of which pride themselves on offering at least one good vegetarian option. (In my guidebooks, whenever possible, I make it a point to list a good vegetarian restaurant in each city.)

Cafeterias (such as the bright, cheery, fresh, affordable ones you'll find on the top floor of major department stores) are a good spot for vegetarians, since you can see exactly what you're getting

to predict how quickly the tables will turn over. You might see people milling around outside a popular place hoping for a table to free up, but it's basically a chaotic, self-managing system—not monitored by any restaurant staff.

While portions may be expensive, they're often huge and splittable. A key challenge of budget eating is ordering just enough to fill you, while leaving nothing on your plate. If a single main dish is enough for 1.5 people (as many are), split it between yourself and your travel partner, and supplement it with a bowl of soup or something small. Waiters are generally understanding and accommodating; the prices are high for Europeans, too. But be careful in France, where splitting meals at

and select an assortment of foods that suit your diet.

Each country has its own quirks: Italy seems to sprinkle a little meat in just about everything. German cooking normally keeps the meat separate from the vegetables. Hearty German salads, with beets, cheese, and eggs, are a vegetarian's delight. Vegetarians enjoy *antipasti* buffets, salad bars, and ethnic restaurants throughout Europe.

A big plate of veggies makes for an energizing lunch...even if you're not a vegetarian.

Key Vegetarian Phrases

We are (I am) vegetarian. We (I) do not eat meat, fish, or chicken. Eggs and cheese are OK.

German: *Wir sind (Ich bin) Vegetarier. Wir essen (Ich esse) kein Fleisch, Fisch, oder Geflügel. Eier und Käse OK.*

French: *Nous sommes (Je suis) végétarien. Nous ne mangeons (Je ne mange) pas de viande, poisson, ou poulet. Oeufs et fromage OK.*

Italian: *Siamo vegetariani (Sono vegetariano/a). Non mangiamo (mangio) nè carne, nè pesce, nè polli. Uova e formaggio OK.*

Spanish: *Somos vegetarianos (Soy vegetariano/a). No comemos (No como) ni carne, ni pescado, ni pollo. Los huevos y el queso OK.*

restaurants can be frowned upon; instead, head for a café, where it's perfectly acceptable to share meals or order just a salad or sandwich, even for dinner. At any place, it's fine to split a dessert, saving money and calories.

In Europe, the meal is routinely the event of the evening.

These days, the Germans are splitting their bratwurst and kraut, too.

EATING

Share fine things. Restaurateurs are happy to bring one dessert and as many spoons as needed.

At good restaurants, service will seem slow. Meals won't always come simultaneously—it's fine to start eating when served. Europeans will spend at least two hours enjoying a good dinner, and, for the full experience, so should you. Fast service is rude service. If you need to eat and run, make your time limits very clear as you order.

Of course, each country has its own quirks when it comes to dining. Spaniards eat dinner very late (after 9 p.m.). In Italy, it's common to be charged a *pane e coperto* ("bread and cover" charge) just to sit down. In Portugal, appetizers (olives, bread, etc.) that are automatically brought to your table are not free—you touch them, you pay for them. If you see a *Stammtisch* sign hanging over a table at a German restaurant, it means that it's reserved for regulars.

The no-smoking rules seem to be working in restaurants all over Europe these days, but watch out if you're seated outdoors, where smokers congregate to light up.

Ordering Your Meal

Finding the right restaurant is only half the battle. You also need to order a good meal. European restaurants post their menus outside.

Check the price and selection before entering. If the menu's not posted, ask to see one. Just be aware that in France, the word *menu* means a fixed-price meal; instead you want *la carte* (to order à la carte). Several other countries also use variations on the word "card" to mean "menu": *Speisekarte* in Germany, *la carta* in Spain, and so on.

Ordering in a foreign

Young taste buds having their horizons gently stretched

language can be fun, or it can be an ordeal. Ask for an English menu—if nothing else, you might get the waiter who speaks the most English. Many waiters can give at least a very basic translation—"cheekin, bunny, zuppa, green salat," and so on. A phrase book or menu reader is helpful for those who want to avoid ordering sheep stomach instead of lamb chops. If you have allergies, carry a handwritten card in the local language that states "I am allergic to" followed by the problem foods; a native speaker (such as your hotelier) can help you with this.

If you don't know what to order, go with the waiter's recommendation or look for your dream meal on another table and order by pointing. People are usually helpful and understanding of the poor and hungry monoglot tourist. If they aren't, you probably picked a place that sees too many of them. Europeans with the most patience with tourists are the ones who rarely deal with them.

People who agonize over each word on the menu season the whole experience with stress. If you're

Picking green peppers off their pizzas, my kids discover that in Italy, peperoni *doesn't mean spicy sausage.*

in a good place, the food's good. Get a basic idea of what's cooking, have some fun with your server, be loose and adventurous, and just order something.

To max out culturally, my partner and I order two different meals: one high risk and one low risk. We share, sampling twice as many dishes. At worst, we learn what we don't like and split the chicken and fries. My tour groups cut every meal into bits, and our table becomes a lazy Susan. If anything, the waiters are impressed by our interest in their food and very often they'll run over with a special treat for all of us to sample— like squid eggs. With a gang of 10 travelers, I once ordered all 10 pizzas on the menu to come one after the other, each cut into 10 slices. We took our time, the waiters had fun, we savored a great variety, and everything was hot...it was the cheapest 10-course meal in Rome.

The "tourist *menu*" (*menu* in France, *menù turistico* in Italy) is popular in restaurants throughout Europe's tourist zones, offering confused visitors a no-stress, three-course meal for a painless price that usually includes service, bread, and a drink. You normally get a choice of several

EATING

MENU TURISTICO €19,00

ANTIPASTO di MARE

PRIMI PIATTI

RISOTTO alla PESCATORA
SPAGHETTI alla MARINARA
SPAGHETTI allo SCOGLIO
TRENETTE al PESTO

SECONDI PIATTI

PESCE ai FERRI
FRITTO MISTO
GRIGLIATA di CARNE

CONTORNI

PATATE FRITTE o INSALATA

This Italian menu turistico *includes a seafood starter plate* (antipasto di mare), *then you get to choose a first course* (primi piatti), *a second course* (secondi piatti), *and a side dish* (contorni, *either French fries or salad)...all for €19.*

options for each course. Locals rarely order this, but if the options intrigue you, the tourist *menu* can be a convenient way to sample some regional flavors for a reasonable, predictable price.

The daily special is a great value. Small eateries in most countries offer this fresh, economical "*menu* of the day." Recognize the native term (*menu del día* in Spain, *plat du jour* in France, *menù del giorno* in Italy, *dagens rett* in Sweden). These are often limited to early seatings (with the time—usually before 7:30 p.m.—posted on the door and in the menu).

If you're a foodie, do some research and learn what's in season (or ask your server). In the summer, French onion soup and cheese fondue are only for tourists. White asparagus and porcini mushrooms are a treat for your palate in season... but come out of the freezer the rest of the year.

The best values in entrées are usually chicken, fish, and veal. Sometimes, rather than getting entrées, my travel partner and I share a memorable little buffet of appetizers—they're plenty filling, less expensive, and more typically local than entrées. Drinks (except for wine in southern Europe) and desserts can be the worst value. Skipping those, you can enjoy some surprisingly good $15 meals.

Drinks

If your budget is tight and you want to save $5-10 a day, never buy a restaurant drink. Beverages can sink a tight budget.

Europeans generally drink bottled water—for taste, not health. But as their

For a good dining value, I look for a chalkboard daily special (menu del día).

Tap Water in Five Languages

Italian: *acqua del rubinetto*
French: *une carafe d'eau*
German: *Leitungswasser*
Spanish: *agua del grifo*
Portuguese: *água da torneira*

In other languages, just do the international charade: Hold an imaginary glass in one hand, turn on the tap with the other, and make the sound of a faucet. Stop it with a click of your tongue and drink it with a smile.

cost of living increases, so do their requests for tap water. Once in an Oslo restaurant, I counted 16 of 20 diners drinking tap water. They were charged $1 a glass, but it was still a substantial savings over a $6 Coke.

To get tap water at a restaurant, you may need to be polite, patient, inventive, and know the correct phrase. Availability of (and willingness to serve) tap water varies from country to country; in Belgium they'll make you pay for it. It's sometimes considered a special favor, and while your glass or carafe of tap water is normally served politely, occasionally it just isn't worth the trouble, and it's best to put up with the bottle of Perrier or order a drink from the menu.

Bottled water is served crisp and cold, either with or without carbonation, usually by happier waiters. Some Americans don't like the bubbly stuff, but I do. Learn the local phrase for *con/avec/mit/con/*with gas or *senza/sans/ohne/sin/*without gas (in Italian, French, German, and Spanish, respectively), and you'll get the message across. Acquire a taste for *acqua con gas*. It's a lot more fun (and read on the label what it'll do for your rheumatism).

Drink like a European. Cold milk, ice cubes, and coffee with (rather than after) your meal are American habits. Insisting on any of these in Europe will get you strange looks and a reputation as a crazy American. Order local drinks, not just to save money but to experience the culture and to get the best quality and service. The timid can always order the "American waters" (Coke, Fanta, and 7-Up), sold everywhere.

EATING

Trying regionally produced alcohol can be a great cultural experience—and brings out fun and fascinating facets of my favorite continent. In Scotland, locals are passionate about finding and describing the whisky that fits their personality. Each guy in the pub has "his" whisky. And the flavors (fruity, peppery, peaty, smoky) are much easier to actually taste than their wine-snob equivalents.

In France, geography plays a big part in their liquid pride. *Terroir* (pronounced "tehr-wah") is a uniquely French concept. *Terroir* is "somewhere-ness," a combination of the macro- and microclimate, soil, geology, and culture (the accumulated experience of the people and their craft). The French don't call a wine by the grape's name. Two wines can be made of the same grape, but be of very different character because of their *terroir*. A real Chablis made from the Chardonnay grape is better than Chardonnays made elsewhere because of its *terroir*.

German pubs don't serve minors beer—but many locals do.

Drinking locally produced alcohol has another advantage: It's cheaper than your favorite import. A shot of the local hard drink in Portugal will cost a dollar, while an American drink would cost more than the American price. Drink the local stuff with local people in local bars; it's a better experience than having a Manhattan in your hotel with a guy from Los Angeles. Drink wine in wine countries and beer in beer countries. Sample the regional specialties. Let a local person order you her favorite. You may hate it, but you'll never forget it.

Paying the Bill

To get the bill, you'll have to ask for it (catch the waiter's eye and, with raised hands, scribble with an imaginary pencil on your palm). Before it comes, make a mental tally of roughly how much your meal should cost. The bill should vaguely resemble the figure you expected. (It should at least have the same number of digits.) If the total is a surprise, ask to have it itemized and explained. Some waiters make the same "innocent" mistakes repeatedly, knowing most tourists are so befuddled by the money and menu that they'll pay whatever number is scrawled across the

Interpreting the Bill

Examine this sample Italian restaurant bill to get used to the charges you'll see in Europe.

Check each line item. Be sure you understand what each charge was for. You don't have to speak fluent Italian to recognize *minestrone* or *spaghetti carbonara*. Even *insalata mista* isn't a stretch if you remember that you ate a mixed salad. But if it says *"4 birre"* and you don't remember drinking four beers, ask for an explanation (or an apology).

Pane e coperto ("bread and cover" charge) is a mandatory amount charged per customer just to sit down. Common in Italy, this is relatively rare in other countries—though (sadly) it's beginning to catch on at touristy restaurants in popular destinations (such as Prague).

A legitimate **servizio** (service) charge of 10 percent has been added. You don't need to leave a big tip (but if you were pleased with the service, you'd add a euro or two for each person in your party). In many cases, rather than adding the 10 percent at the end of the bill, the menu prices already include the service charge (in which case, the menu might say *"servizio incluso."*)

```
VIA GARIBALDI 37, ROMA

Ristorante  Colosseo

DI RICARDO STEFANO
                           IMPORTO
pan e coperto (x2)... 4,00

insalata caprese..... 6,00
ins. mista.......... 4,00

spaghetti carbonara... 6,00
minestrone ........ 8,00

frutta .......... 4,00
tiramisú ......... 5,00

vino rosso (bottiglia) ... 12,00
acqua min. (litro)..... 4,00

totale ........... 53,00

servizio 10% ....... 5,30

totale ........ €58,30
documento

        RICEVUTA FISCALE
        COPIA PER IL CLIENTE
```

Also notice that Europeans use a comma as a decimal point—so €58,30 is the same as €58.30.

Now hand over your cash and wait for the change...and don't leave until you get the correct amount back. When you collect your change, you can leave the tip on the table, or better, give the tip directly to your server.

Or you can pay with exact change, including the tip, and indicate you don't need any back. For this meal, I'd hand the server €60, smile, say *grazie*, and wave my hand to suggest she should keep the change.

EATING

bottom of the bill.

I pay cash for my meals. But if you use a credit card, don't be surprised if your waiter brings a mobile card reader to the table. These machines cut down on fraud since your card never leaves your sight. Be aware that you may have to enter the card's PIN rather than sign a receipt (see page 178). Many restaurants in Germany won't take a credit card, and in Denmark they may tack on an extra fee if you use one—ask.

Tipping

Restaurant tips are more modest in Europe than in America. In most places, 10 percent is a big tip. If your bucks talk at home, muzzle them on your travels. As a matter of principle, if not economy, the local price should prevail. Please believe me—tipping 15 or 20 percent in Europe is unnecessary, if not culturally insensitive.

Tipping is an issue only at restaurants that have waiters and waitresses. If you order your food at a counter (in a pub, for example), don't tip.

At table-service restaurants, the tipping etiquette and procedure vary slightly from country to country. But in general, European servers are well paid, and tips are considered a small "bonus"—to reward great service or for simplicity in rounding the total bill to a convenient number. In many countries, 5 percent is adequate and 10 verges on excessive.

In Mediterranean countries, the "service charge" (*servizio* in Italian, *service* in French, *servicio* in Spanish)—usually figured at 10 or 15 percent of your total bill—can be handled in different ways. Sometimes the menu will note that the service is included ("*servizio incluso*"), meaning that the prices listed on the menu already have this charge built in. When the service is not included ("*servizio non incluso*"), the service charge might show up as a separate line item at the end of your bill. Fixed-price tourist deals (a.k.a. *menu*) include service.

In northern and eastern Europe, the menu or bill is less likely to address the "service charge," but you can usually assume that it's included in the prices.

Virtually anywhere in Europe, you can do as the Europeans do and (if you're pleased with the service) add a euro or two for each person in your party. In very touristy areas, some servers have noticed the American obsession with overtipping—and might hope for a Yankee-size tip. But the good news is that European servers and diners are far more laid-back about all this than we are. Any tip is appreciated, the stakes are low, and it's no big deal if you choose the "wrong" amount.

Typically, it's better to hand the tip to the waiter when you're paying your bill than to leave it on the table, particularly in busy places where the wrong party might pocket the change. Servers prefer to be tipped in cash even if you pay with your credit card (otherwise the tip may never reach your server); in many cases, there isn't even a line on the credit-card receipt for a tip.

In Germanic countries, it's considered discreet and classy to say the total number of euros you'd like the waiter to keep (including his tip) when paying. So, if the bill is €42, hand him €50 while saying, "45." You'll get €5 back and feel pretty European.

Cafés and Bars

On my last trip to Italy, I savored a peaceful moment in Siena's great square, Il Campo, sipping a glass of *vin santo* as the early evening light bathed the red-brick stone. My five-euro drink gave me a front-row seat at the best table on the square, and for a leisurely hour I soaked up the promenading action that nightly turns Il Campo into "Il Italian Fashion Show."

In European cafés, menus are two-tiered: cheaper at the bar, more expensive at a table.

Public squares like Il Campo are the physical and cultural heart of Europe's cities and towns. For Europeans, these bustling squares proclaim "community." Defined by stately architecture and ringed by shops and cafés, squares are the perfect venue for café-sitting, coffee-sipping, and people-watching. Promenaders take center stage, strolling and being seen, while onlookers perch on the periphery. To play your part, tether yourself to one of the café tables parked around any square, order a drink, and feel the pulse of the passing scene. Don't be in a hurry—spending endless hours sitting in an outdoor café is the norm.

In many countries, you'll pay less to stand and more to sit. In general, if you simply want to slam down a cup of coffee, it's cheapest to order and drink it at the bar. If you want to sit a while and absorb that last museum while checking out the two-legged art, grab a table with a view, and a waiter will take your order. This will cost you about double what it would at the bar. (Sometimes an outdoor table is more expensive than an indoor

Breakfast Basics

The farther north you go in Europe, the heartier the breakfasts. Heaviest are the traditional British fry (described on page 385) and Scandinavian buffet breakfasts. Throughout the Netherlands, Belgium, Germany, Austria, Switzerland, and Eastern Europe, expect a more modest buffet—but still plenty of options (rolls, bread, jam, cold cuts, cheeses, fruit, yogurt, and cereal). In these countries, there's a good chance of finding hard-boiled eggs, but scrambled or fried eggs are relatively rare. As you move south and west (France, Italy, Spain, and Portugal), skimpier "continental" breakfasts are the norm. You'll get a roll with marmalade or jam, occasionally a slice of ham or cheese, and coffee or tea.

The continental breakfast: bread, jam, cheese, and coffee

If your breakfast is sparse, supplement it with a piece of fruit and a wrapped chunk of cheese from your rucksack stash. Orange juice fans pick up liter boxes in the grocery store and start the day with a glass in their hotel room. If you're a coffee drinker, remember that breakfast is the only cheap time to caffeinate yourself. Some hotels will serve you a bottomless cup of a rich brew only with breakfast. After that, the cups acquire bottoms. Juice is generally available at breakfast, but in Mediterranean countries, you have to ask...and you'll probably be charged.

In many countries, breakfast is included in your hotel bill, though if you make prior arrangements with the hotelier, you may be able to skip breakfast and pay a lower price for the room. If breakfast costs extra, it's often optional, and you can usually save money and gain atmosphere by buying coffee and a roll or croissant at the café down the street or by brunching picnic-style in the park.

I'm a big-breakfast person at home. But when I feel the urge for a typical American breakfast in Europe, I beat it to death with a hard roll. You can find bacon, fried eggs, and orange juice, but it's nearly always overpriced and disappointing.

Few hotel breakfasts are worth waiting around for. If you need to get an early start, skip the breakfast.

EATING

one.) If you're on a budget, always confirm the price for a sit-down drink. While it's never high profile, there's always a price list posted somewhere inside with the two- or three-tiered price system clearly labeled (cheap at the bar, more at a table, still more at an outside table). If you pay for a seat in a café with an expensive drink, that seat's yours for the afternoon if you like. Lingering with your bar-priced drink on a nearby public bench or across the street on the beach is usually OK—just ask first.

If you're a coffee lover, it pays to know the grounds rules. In some coffee bars (especially in Italy), you pay for your drink at the cash register, then take your receipt to the bar, where you'll be served. In Italy, if you ask for *un caffè*, you'll get espresso. Cappuccino is served to locals before noon and to tourists any time of day. (To an Italian, cappuccino is a breakfast drink, and drinking anything with milk or cream after eating anything with tomatoes is a travesty.) A *caffè latte* is an espresso mixed with hot milk with no foam and served in a tall glass (ordering just a *latte* gets you only hot milk). While the French call espresso with lots of steamed milk *un café au lait*, you can get specific by asking for *un grand crème* if you want a big cup or *un petit crème* for a smaller one.

If you're hankering for the closest thing to brewed coffee in Italy, try a *caffè americano*, which is espresso diluted with hot water. A similar drink in France is called *un café allongé*. Cafés in Britain, Germany, and Scandinavia are more likely to serve brewed coffee, though there are plenty of espresso places these days. Turkish coffee is unfiltered coffee, with the grounds mixed right in. It's popular in the eastern Mediterranean—typically drunk as a digestive after dinner and sometimes after lunch.

As a traveler, you naturally want to take in as many sights as you can every day. But make time in your itinerary to simply drop yourself into a café chair for a few hours. Enjoying life like the Europeans do— watching the world go by—is one of the best and most relaxing ways to go local.

Budget Food Options

There are plenty of strategies for stretching your food budget on the road. While cafeterias, street stands, and "to go" meals are not high cuisine, they're undeniably cheap. And in my book, there's no better travel experience than a picnic sourced from local markets and grocers.

Cheap Eats

Europe offers a bounty of options for eating inexpensively:

Cafeterias: "Self-service" is an international word. You'll find self-service restaurants in big cities everywhere, offering low-price, low-risk, low-stress, what-you-see-is-what-you-get meals. A sure value for your euro is a department-store cafeteria. These places are designed for the shopper who has a sharp eye for a good value. At a salad bar, grab the small (cheap) plate and stack it like the locals do—high. Hungry sightseers also appreciate the handy, moderately priced cafeterias they'll find in larger museums.

Cafeteria leftovers: even cheaper than picnics...

Institution-Affiliated Eateries: If your wallet is as empty as your stomach, find a cheap, humble cafeteria that's associated with (and subsidized by) a local institution—such as a university, city hall, church, hospital, charity, senior center, fire station, union of gondoliers, retired fishermen's club, and so on. (These are sometimes called "mensas.") Profits take a back seat to providing good food at a good price—and many of these eateries welcome the public to pull up a chair. Options range from a semi-swanky City Hall cafeteria in Oslo, to student canteens in university towns (such as Salzburg, Austria), to Poland's dreary-looking but cheap-and-tasty "milk

For restaurant food at halfway-to-picnic prices, visit the neighborhood rosticcería *or take-out deli.*

bars." Don't be afraid to take advantage of these opportunities to fill yourself with a plate of dull but nourishing food for an unbeatable price in the company of locals. University cafeterias (generally closed during summer holidays) also offer a surefire way to meet educated, English-speaking young people with open and stimulating minds. They're often eager to share their views on politics and economics, as well as their English, with a foreign friend.

Bakeries and Sandwich Shops: Bakeries are a good place to pick up basic sandwiches, tiny pizzas, or something equally cheap and fast but with more of a regional flavor (such as savory pasties in England or a *croque-monsieur* sandwich in France). Britain's Pret à Manger, Norway's Deli de Luca, and Spain's Pans & Company are chains that sell good, healthful sandwiches, salads, and pastries. Local deli-like shops are popular in many parts of Europe; try a *traiteur* in France or a *rosticceria* in Italy. The busi-

For a good-value lunch in England (or most anywhere), follow the local business crowd to find the best sandwiches.

ness lunch crowd invariably knows the best place for an affordable fill-the-tank bite.

Street Food: Every country has its own equivalent of the hot-dog stand, where you can grab a filling bite on the go—French *crêperies,* Greek souvlaki stands, Danish *pølse* (sausage) vendors, Italian *pizza rustica* take-out shops, Dutch herring carts, and Turkish-style kebab and falafel kiosks in Germany (and just about everywhere else). A falafel (fried chickpea croquettes wrapped in pita bread) is a good vegetarian option that's also popular with meat eaters. Of all of these options, the ubiquitous kebab stand is my favorite. The best ones have a busy energy, and a single large kebab wrapped in wonderful pita bread can feed two hungry travelers for €4. Don't miss the *ayran*—a healthy yogurt drink popular with Turks—which goes well with your kebab. In general, if there's a long line at a particular stand, you can bet that customers appreciate the value that vendor provides.

Ethnic Eateries: Through-out wealthy northern Europe, immigrant communities labor at subsistence wages. Rather than eat bland and pricey local food, they (along with savvy residents and travelers) go cheap and spicy at simple diners, delis, and take-away stands serving Middle Eastern, Pakistani, and Asian food. These places usually offer the cheapest hot meals in town.

Eat where the immigrants do, and you'll save plenty.

EATING

McEurope: Fast-food restaurants are everywhere. Yes, the hamburgerization of the world is a shame, but face it—the busiest and biggest McDonald's in the world are in Tokyo, Rome, and Moscow. The burger has become a global thing. You'll find Big Macs in every language—it isn't exciting (and costs more than at home), but at least at McDonald's you know exactly what you're getting, and it's fast. A hamburger, fries, and shake can be fun halfway through your trip.

American fast-food joints are kid-friendly and satisfy the need for a cheap salad bar and a tall orange juice. They've grabbed prime bits of real estate in every big European city. Since there's no cover charge, this is an opportunity to savor a low-class paper cup of coffee while enjoying some high-class people-watching. Many offer free Wi-Fi as well.

Each country has its equivalent of the hamburger stand (I saw a "McCheaper" in Switzerland). Whatever their origin, they're a hit with youths and a handy place for a quick, cheap bite to eat.

Picnics, Markets, and Supermarkets

There is only one way left to feast for $10-15 anywhere in Europe: picnic. You'll eat better, while spending half as much as those who eat exclusively in restaurants.

I am a picnic connoisseur. While I'm the first to admit that restaurant meals are an important aspect of any culture, I picnic almost daily.

This is not solely for budgetary reasons. It's fun to dive into a marketplace and actually get a chance to do business. Europe's colorful markets overflow with varied cheeses, meats, fresh fruits, vegetables, and still-warm-out-of-the-bakery-oven bread. Many of my favorite foods made their debut in a European picnic.

To busy sightseers, restaurants can be time-consuming and frustrating. After waiting to be served, tangling with a menu, and consuming a budget-threatening meal, you walk away feeling unsatisfied, knowing your money could have done much more for your stomach if you had invested it in a picnic.

You can save on your food budget by visiting the corner bakery and picnicking on the steps of the church.

Nutritionally, a picnic is unbeatable. Consider this example: cheese, thinly sliced ham, fresh bread, peaches, carrots, a cucumber, a half-liter of milk, and fruit yogurt or a freshly baked pastry for dessert.

To bolster your budget, I recommend picnic dinners every few nights. At home, we save time and money by raiding the refrigerator to assemble a pickup dinner. In Europe, the equivalent is the corner deli, bakery, or grocery store. When staying several nights, I cozy up a hotel room by borrowing plates, glasses, and silverware from the breakfast room and stocking the closet with my favorite groceries (juice, fruits and vegetables, cheese, and other munchies). If your hotelier posts signs prohibiting picnicking in rooms (most likely to occur in France), you'll easily be able to find plenty of other atmospheric places to eat. But if you picnic in your room anyway,

A quick dashboard picnic halfway through a busy day of sightseeing

be discreet and toss your garbage in a public waste-can.

There is nothing second-class about a picnic. A few special touches will even make your budget meal a first-class affair. Proper site selection can make the difference between just another meal and *le pique-nique extraordinaire*. Since you've decided to skip the restaurant, it's up to you to create the atmosphere.

Try to incorporate a picnic brunch, lunch, or dinner into the day's sightseeing plans. For example, I start the day by scouring the thriving market with my senses and my camera. Then I fill

Throughout France, signs direct you to the most scenic places to "pique-nique."

up my shopping bag and have breakfast on a riverbank. After sightseeing, I combine lunch and a siesta in a cool park to fill my stomach, rest my body, and escape the early afternoon heat. It's fun to eat dinner on a castle wall enjoying a commanding view and the setting sun. Some of my all-time best picnics have been lazy dinners accompanied by medieval fantasies in the quiet of after-hours Europe.

Mountain hikes are punctuated nicely by picnics. Food tastes even better on top of a mountain. Europeans are great picnickers. Many picnics become potlucks, resulting in new friends as well as full stomachs.

Only a glutton can spend more than $15 for a picnic feast. In a park in Paris, on a Norwegian ferry, high in the Alps, at an autobahn rest stop, on your convent rooftop, or in your hotel room, picnicking is the budget traveler's key to cheap and good eating.

Picnic Tips

Here are some tricks for picnicking like a pro:

Picnic Supplies: Pack resealable plastic baggies (large and small). Buy a good knife with a can opener and corkscrew in Europe (or bring it from home, if you plan to check your luggage on the plane). In addition to being a handy plate, fan, and lousy Frisbee, a plastic lid makes an easy-to-clean cutting board. A dishtowel doubles as a small tablecloth, and a washcloth helps with cleanup. A disposable shower cap contains messy food nicely on your picnic cloth. Bring a plastic, airline-type drink cup and spoon for cereal and a fork for take-out salad. Some travelers get immersion heaters (buy in Europe for a compatible plug) to make hot drinks to go with munchies in their hotel room.

Kick back and munch a picnic dinner in your hotel room.

Drinks: There are plenty of cheap ways to wash down a picnic. While Europeans don't generally drink milk by the glass like Americans do, it's always cheap and available in quarter, half, or whole liters. Be sure it's normal drinking milk. Strange white liquid dairy products in look-alike milk cartons abound, ruining the milk-and-cookie dreams of careless tourists. Look for local words for "whole" or "light," such as *voll* or *lett*. Nutritionally, a half-liter provides about 25 percent of your daily protein needs. Get refrigerated, fresh milk. Or look on

This happy gang is living simply and well on the cheap: enjoying a picnic in Assisi, the hometown of St. Francis.

the (unrefrigerated) shelves for the common-in-Europe but rarer-in-America "long life" milk. This milk—which requires no refrigeration until it's opened—will never go bad...or taste good.

European yogurt is delicious and can usually be drunk right out of its container. Fruit juice comes in handy liter boxes (look for "100% juice" or "no sugar" to avoid Kool-Aid clones). Buy cheap by the liter, and use a reusable half-liter plastic mineral-water bottle (usually found next to the soft drinks) to store what you can't comfortably drink in one sitting. Liter bottles of Coke are cheap, as is wine in most countries. Local wine gives your picnic a nice touch. Any place that serves coffee has free boiling water. Those who have more nerve than pride get their plastic water bottle (a sturdy plastic bottle will not melt) filled with free boiling water at a café, then add their own instant coffee or tea bag later. Many hotels or cafés will fill a thermos with coffee for about the price of two cups.

Farmer's markets are a fun source for healthy picnic snacks.

Stretching Your Money: Bread has always been cheap in Europe. (Leaders have learned from history that when stomachs rumble, so do the mobs in the streets.) Cheese is a specialty nearly

EATING

everywhere and is, along with milk, one of the Continent's cheapest sources of protein. The standard low-risk option anywhere in Europe is Emmentaler cheese (the kind with holes, what we call "Swiss"). Buy fruit and veggies that are in season; see what's cheap and plentiful in the produce section or market. Anything American is usually expensive and rarely satisfying. Cultural chameleons eat and drink better and cheaper.

Markets

Nearly every town, large or small, has at least one colorful outdoor or indoor marketplace. Assemble your picnic here. Make an effort to communicate with the merchants. Know what you are buying and what you are spending. Whether you understand the prices or not, act like you do (observe the weighing process closely), and you're more likely to be treated fairly.

Learn the measurements. The unit of measure throughout the Continent is a kilo, or 2.2 pounds. A kilo (kg) has 1,000 grams (g or gr). One hundred grams (a common unit of sale) of cheese or meat tucked into a chunk of French bread gives you about a quarter-pounder.

Food can be priced in different ways. Watch the scale when your food is being weighed. It'll likely show grams and kilos. If dried apples are priced at €2 per kilo, that's $2.80 for 2.2 pounds, or about $1.25 per pound. If the scale says 400 grams, that means 40 percent of €2 (or 80 euro cents), which is a little over $1.

Not everything is strictly priced by the kilogram. Read the little chalkboard price carefully: Particularly in the case of specialty items, you might see things priced by the 1/4 kg, 1/2 kg, 100 g, 500 g, and so on. Or an item could be priced by the piece (*Stück* in German, *la piéce* in French, *pezzo* in Italian), the bunch, the container, and so on. If the pâté seems too cheap to be true, look at the sign closely. The posted price is probably followed by "100 gr."

If no prices are posted, be wary. Travelers are routinely ripped off by market merchants in tourist centers. Find places that print the prices. Assume any market with no printed prices has a double price standard: one for locals and a more expensive one for tourists.

I'll never forget a friend of mine who bought two bananas for our

Europe's grocery stores have some surprisingly addictive snacks.

London picnic. He grabbed the fruit, held out a handful of change, and said, "How much?" The merchant took the equivalent of $4. My friend turned to me and said, "Wow, London really is expensive." Anytime you hold out a handful of money to a banana salesman, you're just asking for trouble.

Point, but don't touch. Most produce stands and outdoor markets are not self-service: Tell the vendor (or point to) what you want, and let the merchant bag it and weigh it for you. It's considered rude for a customer to touch the goods.

Want only a small amount? You'll likely need only one or two pieces of fruit, and many merchants refuse to deal in such small quantities. The way to get what you want and no more is to estimate what it would cost if the merchant were to weigh it and then just hold out a coin worth about that much in one hand and point to the apple, or whatever, with the other. Have a Forrest Gump look on your face that says, "If you take this coin, I'll go away." Rarely will he refuse the deal.

Appreciate the cultural experience. Shopping for groceries is an integral part of everyday European life for good reasons: People have small refrigerators (kitchens are tiny), value fresh produce, and enjoy the social interaction.

Supermarkets

I prefer local markets, but American-style supermarkets, many of which hide out in the basements of big-city department stores, are a good alternative. Some of them are getting very yuppie—offering salads, quiche, fried chicken, and fish, all "to go." Common European chains include Aldi, Carrefour, Coop, Despar, Konzum, Lidl, Migros, Monoprix, Morrisons, Sainsbury's, Spar, and Tesco.

If it's late in the day, you may be able to score some deals. One night in Oslo I walked into an ICA supermarket just before closing to discover that they'd marked down all the deli food by 50 percent. Back in my hotel room, I ate my cheapest meal in Norway—roast chicken and fries at almost US prices.

Don't be intimidated by the produce section; it's a cinch to buy a

EATING

tiny amount of fruit or vegetables. Many have an easy push-button pricing system: Put the banana on the scale, push the picture of a banana (or enter the banana bin number), and a sticky price tag prints out. You could weigh and sticker a single grape.

Bring your own shopping bag or expect to pay extra for the store's plastic bags. It's easiest to pay cash at checkout, but if you want to use your credit card, be sure you know the PIN—the clerk may ask you to enter it.

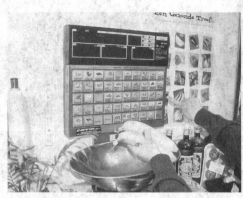

At the supermarket, put your banana in the bin, push the banana button, rip off the price sticker, and stick it on your banana.

Local Specialties

Here are some tips to help you eat, drink, and be merry in Europe. At least once, seek out and eat or drink the notorious "gross" specialties: ouzo (Greece), horse meat (France), snails (Spain and France), raw herring (Scandinavia), blood sausage (Britain), haggis (Scotland), fried fish sperm (Czech Republic), tripe stew (best in eateries near meat markets), and so on. All your life you'll hear references to them, and you'll have actually experienced what everyone's talking about. For more on the delicious and diverse tastes of Europe—especially France and Italy—see "The Flavors of Europe" on page 693.

Belgium

Belgians boast that they eat as heartily as the Germans and as well as the French.

Nobody does chocolate like the Belgians. There's something elegant about dropping in on the most expensive chocolate maker in town— there's one in every Belgian burg. Find a place that's family-run, where locals buy their chocolate fresh and people expect the shop to close on hot days because quality chocolate can't survive the heat.

Seafood—fish, eel, oysters, and shrimp—is especially well prepared in Belgium. Mussels are served everywhere. You get a big-enough-for-two bucket and a pile of fries. Go local by using one empty shell to tweeze out the rest of the *moules*.

Belgian fries (*Vlaamse frites*, or "Flemish fries") taste so good because they're deep-fried twice—once to cook, and once to brown. The natives dunk them in mayonnaise...especially delicious if the mayo is flavored with garlic.

Belgium has more varieties and brands of beer than any other country—and the locals take their beers as seriously as the French do their wines. For my favorite budget meal, I head to an atmospheric old pub to enjoy their finest beer (I love Chimay) and some simple pub grub with a gaggle of "beer pilgrims" who've flocked to Belgium

According to Belgians, the best part of the crab is the guts.

from around the world to appreciate some of Europe's best brew.

Britain and Ireland

The British Isles' reputation for miserable food is now dated, and today's cuisine scene is lively, trendy, and surprisingly good. (Unfortunately, it can also be expensive.)

The traditional "fry," or "full English breakfast"—generally included in the cost of your room—is famous as a hearty way to start the day. Also known as a "heart attack on a plate," the standard fry includes cereal or porridge, a fried egg, Canadian-style bacon or sausage, a grilled tomato, sautéed mushrooms, baked beans, and fried bread or toast. This protein-stuffed meal is great for stamina and tides many travelers over until dinner. There's nothing wrong with skipping some or all of the fry—just let your hosts know in advance so they don't have to throw out uneaten food. Better B&Bs often serve local specialties such as porridge, haggis, or mackerel. Come to breakfast with an adventurous spirit.

While you can seek out fine cuisine in Britain and Ireland, it's cheaper and easier to enjoy decent cuisine in a great atmosphere. That means pub grub. For $15-20, you'll get a basic, budget, hot lunch or dinner in friendly surroundings.

British pubs generally serve traditional dishes, like fish-and-chips, roast beef, and meat pies. "Crisps" are potato chips. Irish pubs often serve Irish stew (mutton), chowders, pork dishes, and lots of potatoes. For something more refined, try a gastropub, which serves higher-quality meals for a bit more.

Pub meals are usually served from noon to 2:00 p.m. and from 6:00

EATING

p.m. to 8:00 p.m. Because pubs make far more money selling beer, they're quick to shut down their kitchen and fill the place with drinkers, rather than eaters, later in the evening. There's usually no table service. Order at the bar, then take a seat and they'll bring the food when it's ready (or sometimes you pick it up at the bar). Pay at the bar. Don't tip unless it's a place with full table service. Pubs that advertise their food and are crowded with regulars are less likely to serve only lousy microwaved snacks.

Of course, in any town you'll find alternatives to pub grub. At classier restaurants, look for early-bird specials, allowing you to eat well and affordably, but early (at about 5:30-7:00 p.m., last order by 7:00 p.m.). A top-end restaurant often serves a two-course lunch deal for a third the price you'd pay at dinner.

Picnickers and serious sightseers can grab gourmet sandwiches and sides from chains such as Pret à Manger, Tesco, Sainsbury's, and Marks & Spencer (or follow businesspeople on their lunch break to the best hole-in-the-wall sandwich shops). For a distinctive local flavor, try a Marmite sandwich; the brown yeasty-salty spread is every young Brit's peanut butter. But beware...a little Marmite goes a long way.

Ethnic restaurants from all over the world add spice to England's cuisine scene. Eating Indian or Chinese is cheap (even cheaper if you take it out). Middle Eastern stands sell gyro sandwiches and *shwarmas* (lamb in pita bread).

The British take great pride in their beer. Many Brits think that drinking beer cold and carbonated, as Americans do, ruins the taste.

At pubs, long-handled pulls are used to pull the traditional, rich-flavored "real ales" up from the cellar. Shorthand pulls at the bar mean colder, fizzier, mass-produced, and less interesting keg beers. Try the draft cider (sweet or dry)...carefully.

When you say "a beer, please" in an Irish pub, you'll get a pint of Guinness (the black beauty with a blonde head). If you want a small beer, ask for a glass or a half-pint. Never rush your bartender when he's pouring a Guinness. As pints cost exactly double what a half-pint does, you can enjoy a broader experience for no extra cost by drinking smaller glasses of each type of beer. (But, if you're a guy, you'll have to endure a little subtle ridicule.)

If you're in Scotland and want a nonalcoholic drink, try Irn-Bru (pronounced "Iron Brew"). This bright-orange beverage tastes not like orange soda, but like bubblegum with a slightly bitter aftertaste. Be cautious sipping it—as the label understates, "If spilt, this product may stain."

Scotland's also the place to try the famous haggis, a rich assortment of oats and sheep organs stuffed into a chunk of sheep intestine, liberally seasoned and boiled. Usually served with "neeps and tatties" (turnips and potatoes), it's tastier than it sounds and worth trying...once.

Eastern Europe
Eastern Europe offers good food for relatively little money—especially if you venture off the main tourist trail. The cuisine here is generally heavy, hearty, and tasty. Expect lots of meat, potatoes, and cabbage. Still, there's more variety in the East than you might expect.

Czech food is heavy on pork and kraut, but more modern eateries are serving up pasta and salads. Czechs are among the world's most enthusiastic beer *(pivo)* drinkers. The pub is a place to have fun, complain, discuss art and politics, talk hockey, and chat with locals and visitors alike.

In Poland, try the hearty soups (such as the red-beet borscht, or *barszcz*), tasty sauerkraut stew, and pierogi (ravioli-like dumplings with various fillings). Take advantage of Poland's amazingly cheap, government-subsidized milk bars *(bar mleczny)*, which usually offer tasty traditional specialties. And be sure to sample the national drink, *wódka*. Locals cut it with apple juice to make a cocktail they call *szarlotka* ("apple cake").

The quintessential ingredient in Hungarian cuisine is spicy paprika, which appears in red shakers alongside salt and pepper on tables. Meat of all kinds (especially goose liver) is popular. Seek out the sweet, creamy cold fruit soup *(hideg gyümölcs leves)*.

Slovenia and Croatia offer more variety. Choosing between strudel and baklava on the same menu, you're constantly reminded that this is a land where the Germanic world meets the Eastern Mediterranean.

EATING

Slovenia has hearty, German-style food, with lots of sausage and buckwheat. In Croatia, the seafood is succulent and plentiful. Both countries have been influenced by Italian cuisine, with lots of pasta, pizza, and gelato.

France

France is famous for its cuisine—and rightly so. Dining in France can be surprisingly easy on a budget, especially in the countryside. Small restaurants throughout the country love their regional cuisine and take great pride in serving it. France is known for particularly slow (as in polite) service. If you need to eat and run, make it clear from the start.

The *plat du jour* (daily special), salad plate, and *menu* (fixed-price, three- to six-course meal) are often good deals. To get a complete list of what's cooking, remember to ask for *la carte* (not the *menu*). Order the house wine *(vin du pays)*. Wine is the cheapest drink, and every region has its own wine and cheese. The cheese boards that come with multicourse

Cheers!

meals offer the average American a new adventure in eating. When it comes, ask for "a little of each, please" *(un peu de chaque, s'il vous plaît).*

Classy restaurants are easiest to afford at lunchtime, when meal prices are usually reduced. If a restaurant serves lunch, it generally begins at 11:30 a.m. and goes until 2:00 p.m., with last orders taken at about 1:30. If you want to eat a late lunch or early dinner, you'll have better luck at cafés or brasseries, which serve food throughout the day. Compared to restaurants, they may have a more limited menu (such as omelets, salads, and sandwiches, including the *croque-monsieur*—grilled ham and cheese) but are less formal; you're welcome to order just a bowl of soup, even for dinner.

French food, while delicious, at times stretches your culinary horizons. A few words to look out for: *cervelle* (brains), *ris de veau* (calf pancreas or thymus), *viande de cheval* (horse meat), *andouillette* (intestines), *langue* (tongue)...and, of course, *escargot* (snails) and *cuisses de grenouilles* (frog's legs).

Degustation gratuite is not a laxative, but an invitation to a free wine-tasting. You'll find *D/G* signs throughout France's wine-growing regions.

Croissants are served warm with breakfast, and baguettes (long, skinny loaves of French bread) are great for sandwiches. When buying cheese, be sure to ask for samples of the specialties.

For a royal tour of French delicacies—regardless of your budget—assemble a gourmet picnic. Make a point of visiting the small specialty shops and picking up the finest (most expensive) pâtés, hors d'oeuvres, and sweets. As you spread out your tablecloth, passersby will wish you a cheery *"Bon appétit!"*

Germany

Germany is ideal for the "meat-and-potatoes" person. With straightforward, no-nonsense food at budget prices, Deutschland feeds me very well. Small-town restaurants serve up wonderful plates of hearty specialties for $12-20.

Ein *Beer*, ein *Pretzel*, und *Thou*

The classic dish is sausage. Hundreds of varieties of *Bratwurst*, *Weisswurst*, and other types of wurst are served with sauerkraut as an excuse for a vegetable. The generic term *Bratwurst* means "grilled sausage," but there are many regional variations. For example, *Nürnberger* bratwurst are short and spicy, and usually browned and served over sauerkraut or with horseradish for lunch or dinner (generally, the darker the weenie, the spicier it is). The boiled *Weisswurst* (white sausage) is traditionally consumed before noon, with sweet mustard and a fresh soft pretzel; make sure you peel off the casing before eating it. Only a tourist puts the sausage in a bun like a hot dog. Munch alternately between the meat and the bread ("that's why you have two hands"), and you'll look like a local.

Potatoes are the standard vegetable, but *Spargel* (giant white asparagus) is a must in-season (early summer). The bread and pretzels in the basket on your table often cost extra.

When I need a break from pork, I order the *Salatteller* (big, varied dinner-size salad). For budget (and palate) relief in big-city Germany, find a Greek, Turkish, or Italian restaurant. Fast-food stands are called *Schnell Imbiss*.

EATING

German wine (85 percent white) is particularly good from the Mosel and Rhine River Valleys. The Germans enjoy a tremendous variety and quantity of great beer. The average German drinks 30 gallons of beer a year.

Traditional restaurants go by many names. For basic, stick-to-the-ribs meals—and plenty of beer—look for a beer hall *(Bräuhaus)* or beer garden *(Biergarten)*. *Gasthaus, Gasthof, Gaststätte,* and *Gaststube* all loosely describe an informal, inn-type eatery. A *Kneipe* is a bar, and a *Keller* (or *Ratskeller*) is a restaurant or tavern located in a cellar. A *Weinstube* serves wine and, usually, traditional food as well.

Browse through supermarkets and see what Germany eats when there's no more beer and pretzels. Gummi bears, the bear-shaped jelly bean with a cult following, go by the name brand Goldbären here in their native land. Another sweet staple is Nutella, a sensuous chocolate-hazelnut spread (originally from Italy) that turns anything into a first-class dessert.

A few unusual German flavors are worth sampling. *Handkäse* is an especially pungent cheese, sometimes pickled in vinegar. Tourists flock to Rothenburg to buy, sample, and immediately throw away the notorious *Schneeballs*—made of balled-up strips of dough. *Schmalz,* a popular spread, is pure lard...literally. And at Bavarian beer halls, you're likely to see people munching on *Steckerlfisch*—an entire mackerel fish on a stick, roasted over a fire.

Greece

Greek food is simple...and simply delicious. The four Greek food groups are olives (and olive oil), salty feta cheese, tasty tomatoes, and crispy phyllo dough. Virtually every dish is built on a foundation of these four building blocks.

Menus are usually written in both Greek and English, but you're welcome to go into the kitchen and point to the dish you'd like. This is a good way to make some friends, sample from each kettle, get what you want (or at least know what you're getting), and have a truly memorable meal. (The same is true in Turkey.) Be brave.

The best snack deal in Europe—a Greek souvlaki

Every meal seems to start with a classic Greek village salad: ripe tomatoes chopped up just so, rich feta cheese (sometimes in a long, thick slab that you break apart with your fork), olives, and onions, all drenched with olive oil. The best strategy at most tavernas is to split a salad and a few *meze* dishes (appetizers) to taste several different flavors. If you're still hungry, split a main dish or two. Dunk your bread into *tzatziki,* the ubiquitous and refreshing cucumber-and-yogurt dip. (Tourists often call it *tzitziki,* which sounds like the Greek word for crickets—a mispronunciation that endlessly amuses local waiters.)

My favorite on-the-go Greek snack is souvlaki pita, a tasty shish kebab wrapped in flat bread. Souvlaki stands are all over Greece. Savory, flaky phyllo-dough pastries called "pies" (*pita,* not to be confused with pita bread) are another budget staple of Greek cuisine; the most common are *spanakopita* (spinach), *tiropita* (cheese), *kreatopita* (lamb), and *meletzanitopita* (eggplant).

For dessert, don't miss the creamy yogurt with honey. The Greeks throw together honey, nuts, and phyllo dough to create delectable desserts—from baklava to *kataifi* (similar to shredded wheat, doused in honey).

Retsina is a pine-resin-flavored wine that is a dangerous taste to acquire. Ouzo is a powerful, love-it-or-hate-it, licorice-flavored apéritif. While there's espresso and American-style coffee, try the potent, grainy Greek coffee for a real kick. Eat when the locals do—late.

Italy

Italians eat huge meals consisting of a first course of pasta and a second plate of meat, plus a salad, fruit, and wine. The pasta course alone is usually enough to fill the average tourist. You'll save money by ordering pasta as your main course. Some fancier restaurants won't serve just pasta; find one that will, and you'll enjoy a reasonably priced meal of lasagna or minestrone and a salad.

Veggie lovers enjoy the restaurants that have self-serve *antipasti* buffets. These offer a variety of cooked appetizers spread out like a salad bar (pay per plate, not weight). A single plate of *antipasti* combined with a pasta dish makes a healthy, affordable, interesting meal for two.

Note that anytime you eat or drink at a table, you'll be charged a cover *(pane e coperto)* of a couple of dollars. That, plus service *(servizio),* makes even a cheap, one-course restaurant meal cost at least $15.

For inexpensive Italian eateries, look for the term *osteria, tavola calda, rosticceria, trattoria, pizzeria,* or "self-service." A meal-size pizza (sold everywhere for less than $12) and a cold beer is my idea of a good, fast, cheap Italian dinner. For a stand-up super-bargain meal, look for a *pizza rustica* shop, which sells pizza by weight. Just point to the best-looking pizza and tell them how much you want (200 grams is a filling meal). They weigh, you pay. They heat it, you eat it. *Panini* (sandwiches)—*calda* (toasted) if you ask—are cheap and widely available at bars.

For the best budget gourmet meal in Italy, I find an *enoteca* (wine bar). Buy the best glass of fine wine you can afford (I like it *corposo*—full-bodied), and nibble the snacks that come with it and are designed to complement the wine. This ingredient-driven light meal is similar in price to a full meal at a mid-range restaurant, but can be a gourmet experience.

For dessert any time of the day, Italy's gelato is probably the best ice cream you'll ever taste. A big cone or cup containing a variety of flavors costs $3-5.

Cappuccino, rich coffee with a frothy head of steamed milk, is very popular, and it should be. Tiny coffee shops are tucked away on just about every street.

Two fine reasons to savor Italy: gelato and the Riviera

All have a price list, and most require you to pay the cashier first and then take the receipt to the man who makes the drinks. Experiment. Try coffee or tea *freddo* (cold) or *frappé* (blended with ice). Discover a new specialty each day. Bars sell large bottles of cold mineral water, with or without gas, for about $2.

Bar-hopping is fun. A carafe of house wine serves four or five people for about $10. Many bars have delicious *cicchetti*, local toothpick munchies. While *cicchetti* are traditionally from Venice, it's trendy lately throughout Italy for bars to offer an enticing spread of free *cicchetti*-style dishes to anyone buying a drink during happy hour. Just follow the locals and eat dinner for the cost of a cocktail.

The Netherlands

Traditional Dutch food is basic and hearty, with lots of bread, cheese, soup, and fish. Dutch treats include pancakes, "syrup waffles," and cheese. An experience you owe your tongue in Holland: slurping down raw herring at an outdoor herring stand.

My favorite Dutch food is Indonesian. Indonesia, a former colony of the Netherlands, gained its independence but left behind plenty of great restaurants. The cheapest meals, as well as some of the best splurges, are found in these "Indisch" or "Chinese-Indisch" restaurants. The famous rijsttafel ("rice table") is the ultimate Indonesian meal, with as many as 36 delightfully exotic courses, all eaten with rice. One meal is plenty for two, so order carefully. In a small-town restaurant, a rijsttafel can be a great bargain—two can split 12 exotic courses with rice for $30-40. *Bami* or *nasi goreng* are smaller and cheaper but still filling versions of a rijsttafel.

Order a beer, and you'll get a *pils*, a light lager. (While Belgian beer is gourmet, Dutch beer is pretty basic.) *Jenever* is Dutch gin flavored with juniper berries (and often other botanicals). While cheese gets harder and sharper with age, *jenever* grows smooth and soft. Old *jenever* is best.

Portugal

Portugal has some of the most enjoyable and cheapest eating I've found in Europe. Find a sailors' hangout and fill up on fresh seafood, especially

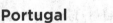

clams, cockles, and fish soup. The young *vinho verde* ("green wine") is an addictive specialty and a favorite of visiting wine buffs. In fishing towns, you'll find boiled *percebes* (barnacles) sold on the street; these are the Portuguese answer to beer nuts. Let a local show you how to strip and eat one. A fun excuse to visit the fine bakeries is to go on a quest for the best *pastéis de nata*.

These delightful mini cream-pies are sold everywhere, but they originated near Lisbon in Belém, where you can visit the famous Pastéis de Belém bakery and try the original.

Be warned that in restaurants, pricey little appetizers—or even just bread and olives—might be placed at your table as if they're free. These are fun and tasty, but if you nibble even one you'll be charged for the entire lot. To clear out the temptation, ask to have them taken away.

Scandinavia

Most Scandinavians avoid their highly taxed and very expensive restaurants. The cost of alcohol alone is sobering. The key to hearty and reasonable eating in Nordic Europe is to take advantage of the *smörgås-bord*. For about $20 (cheap in Scandinavia), breakfast *smörgåsbords* will fill you with plenty of hearty food. I opt for the budget breakfast meal over the fancier, more expensive ($30) *middag*, or midday, *smörgåsbord*, since both meals are, by definition, all-you-can-eat. Many train stations and ferries serve *smörgåsbords*.

Smörgåsbord: *enough food to sink a Viking ship*

For a budget lunch in Denmark, find a *smörrebrød* (open-face sandwich) shop. These places make artistic and delicious sandwich picnics to go. Or munch on a *pølse*, the Danish version of a hot dog.

All over Scandinavia, keep your eyes peeled for daily lunch specials called *dagens rett*. You can normally have all the vegetables (usually potatoes) you want when you order a restaurant's entrée. Just ask for seconds. Many Scandinavian pizzerias offer all-you-can-eat deals and hearty salad bars. (Your bill will double if you order a beer.) The cheapest cafeterias often close at about 5:00 or 6:00 p.m.

Fresh produce, colorful markets, and efficient supermarkets abound in Europe's most expensive corner. Liver paste is curiously cheap but tastes powerfully nutritious. The rock-bottom, bilge-of-a-Viking-ship-cheap meal is a package of cracker bread and a tube of sandwich spread. Handy tubes of cheese, shrimp, and even caviar spread are popular. To save money and enjoy the great Nordic outdoors, have a picnic of Scandinavian goodies or take-out food from one of the many ethnic eateries.

Licorice is a popular Scandinavian snack. Finland's distinctive *salmiakki* is a salty licorice, popularized after World War II when sugar was carefully rationed.

Spain

Spaniards eat to live, not vice versa. The Spanish diet—heavy on ham, deep-fried foods, more ham, weird seafood, and ham again—can be brutal on Americans more accustomed to salads, fruit, and grains. But it's relatively cheap—you can eat well in restaurants for $20.

The Spanish eating schedule—lunch from 1:00 p.m. to 4:00 p.m., dinner after 9:00 p.m.—frustrates many visitors. Most Spaniards eat one major meal of the day: lunch *(comida)* around 2:00 p.m., when stores close, schools let out, and people gather with their friends and family for the so-called siesta. Because most Spaniards work until 7:30 p.m., a light supper *(cena)* is usually served at about 9:00 p.m. or 10:00 p.m.

At a traditional Spanish small-town bar, $3 buys you a glass of wine—and might even include a tapa.

To get by in Spain, either adapt to the Spanish schedule and diet, or do the tapa tango. Bars and coffee spots serve tapas (hors d'oeuvres), sandwiches, and *tortillas* (omelets, great for a hearty breakfast). On my last trip, I ate at least one easy, quick, and cheap tapas meal a day.

Two famous Spanish dishes are gazpacho (chilled tomato soup) and paella (saffron-flavored rice with seafood, chicken, and sausage). While paella can be expensive as a restaurant dish, bars love to cook up a big batch and serve it in smaller, cheaper tapa portions. *Platos combinados* (combination plates of three or more items) are a reasonable way to sample Spanish cuisine. For a more unusual Spanish taste, seek out *pulpo* (octopus)—especially popular in the northwest region of Galicia.

Spain is one of the world's leading producers of grapes, and that means lots of excellent wine. For a basic glass of red wine, you can order *un tinto*. But by asking for *un crianza*, you'll get a quality aged wine for little or no extra money. Rioja is a full-bodied wine from the north of Spain. Sangria (red wine mixed with fruit juice) is popular and refreshing. Sherry is the fortified wine from the Jerez region, and *cava* (from Catalunya) is Spain's answer to champagne.

Switzerland

Here at a crossroads of Europe, the food has a wonderful diversity: heavy *Wurst-und-Kraut* Germanic fare; delicate, subtle French cuisine; and pasta dishes *all'Italiana*. But Swiss restaurant prices can ruin your appetite and send you running to a grocery store. Even locals find their restaurants expensive. The Migros and Co-op stores sell groceries for about

EATING

Tapas Tips

You can eat well any time of day in Spain's tapas bars. Tapas are small appetizer portions of seafood, salads, meat-filled pastries, deep-fried tasties, and on and on—normally displayed under glass at the bar.

Tapas typically cost about $2-3, up to $14 for seafood. Most bars push larger portions called *raciones* (dinner-plate size) rather than smaller tapas (saucer size). Ask for the smaller tapas portions or a *media-ración* (listed as ½ *ración* on a menu), though many bars simply don't serve anything smaller than a *ración*.

Eating and drinking at a bar is usually cheapest if you sit or stand at the counter *(barra)*. You may pay a little more to eat sitting at a table *(mesa)* and still more for an outdoor table. Locate the price list (often posted in fine type on a wall somewhere) to know the menu options and price tiers. In the right place, a quiet snack and drink on a terrace on the town square is well worth the extra charge. But the cheapest seats sometimes get the best show. Sit at the bar and study your bartender—he's an artist.

Be assertive or you'll never be served. *Por favor* (please) grabs the guy's attention. Don't worry about paying until you're ready to leave (he's keeping track of your tab). To get the bill ask: *"¿La cuenta?"*

the same prices you find in America—reasonable by Swiss standards.

Aside from clocks, banks, and knives, Switzerland is known for its cheeses: strong-flavored Gruyère, mild Emmentaler, and pungent Appenzeller, with a smell that verges on nauseating...until you taste it.

Two of Switzerland's best-known specialties are cheese-based: fondue and raclette. You eat fondue with a long fork, dipping cubes of bread into a pot of melted cheese and wine. Raclette is melted cheese over potatoes, pickled onions, and gherkins.

(I have fun with my pet alternative, *"¿La dolorosa?"* Literally meaning "the pained one"—roughly, "What's the damage?"—it's a colloquial way to ask for the bill.)

Chasing down a particular bar for tapas nearly defeats the purpose and spirit of tapas—they are impromptu. Just drop in at any lively place. I look for the noisy spots with piles of napkins and food debris on the floor (go local and toss your trash, too), lots of customers, and the TV blaring. Popular television-viewing includes bullfights and soccer games, American sitcoms, and Spanish interpretations of soaps and silly game shows (you'll see Vanna Blanco). While tapas are served all day, the real action begins late—9:00 p.m. at the earliest. But for beginners, an earlier start is easier and comes with less commotion.

Get a fun, inexpensive sampler plate. Ask for *una tabla de canapés variados* to get a plate of various little open-face sandwiches. Or ask for a *surtido de* (an assortment of...) *charcutería* (a mixed plate of meat) or *queso* (cheese). *Un surtido de jamón y queso* means a plate of different hams and cheeses. Order bread and two glasses of red wine on the right square—and you've got a romantic (and $25) dinner for two.

Another must-try dish, most typical in the mountains of the German-speaking areas, is *Rösti:* traditional hash browns with alpine cheese, sometimes served with an egg cracked over the top...yum.

And, of course, there's chocolate. The Swiss changed the world in 1875 with their invention of milk chocolate. Today, the vast variety of chocolate flavors available in any Swiss supermarket—let alone a specialty chocolate shop—is staggering. The big-name brands such as Lindt, Toblerone, and Cailler are everywhere; keep your eyes peeled for lesser-known brands like Läderach, a favorite among many Swiss. If you prefer milk chocolate, look for bars marked *Vollmilch* or *Alpenmilch*; dark chocolate fans want the *edelbitter* or *dunkeler* stuff, and *weisse Schokolade* is white chocolate. Bars with percentages printed on them are boasting their high cocoa content (the higher the number, the more bitter the chocolate). Other popular varieties include *Haselnuss* (hazelnuts), *Mandeln* (almonds), *Trauben* (grapes/raisins), and *Joghurt* (guess).

Turkey

Bring an appetite and order high on the menu in nice restaurants. Eating's cheap in Turkey. The typical eatery is a user-friendly cafeteria with giant bins of lots of delicacies you always thought were Greek. Kebabs are a standard meaty snack. *Pide,* fresh out of the oven, is Turkish pizza. *Sütlaç* (rice pudding) and baklava will satisfy your sweet tooth. Munch pistachios by the pocketful. Tea in tiny hourglass-shaped glasses is served constantly everywhere. A refreshing, milky yogurt drink

called *ayran,* cheap boxes of cherry juice, and fresh-squeezed orange juice make it fun to quench your Turkish thirst. Or try the *rakı* (Turkish ouzo). Let a local show you how to carefully create a two-layered *rakı* drink by slowly dribbling the anise-flavored spirit into a glass of water. For breakfast, get ready for cucumbers, olives, tomatoes, and lots of goat cheese and bread.

HEALTH AND HYGIENE

Understandably, two big concerns of American travelers are staying healthy and adjusting to European plumbing. Take comfort: Doctors, hospitals, launderettes, and bathrooms aren't *that* different in Europe. And dealing with them is actually part of the fun of travel. This chapter provides information on staying healthy while traveling, dealing with jet lag, and finding medical treatment, along with tips on hygiene—from doing your laundry to mastering European bathrooms.

Staying Healthy

Before You Go

When you're scrambling around before a trip, the last thing you want to do is to get your medical business in order, but your health is critical to your enjoyment of your trip.

Get a checkup. Just as you'd give your car a good checkup before a long journey, it's smart to meet with your doctor before your trip, particularly if you have any medical concerns. Ask for advice on maintaining your health on the road. Obtain recommended immunizations and discuss proper care for any pre-existing medical conditions while traveling. Get any prescriptions you might need (described next). If you have heart concerns, pack a copy of a recent EKG. Avoid having major procedures right before you leave, in case any complications arise during your travels.

It's also a good idea to figure out if your health insurance covers you internationally or whether you might need to buy special medical insurance (for details, see page 63).

Pack prescriptions If you have any health problems or issues that could flare up on your trip, bring a letter from your doctor describing the condition and any prescription medications you may need—including the generic names of the drugs. It's best to bring a big enough supply to cover your entire trip, along with a copy of your prescription just in case you need more while you're abroad (if you'll be gone for an extended period of time, talk to your pharmacist and/or doctor ahead of time). Bring pharmaceuticals in their original containers (clearly labeled), and pack them in your carry-on bag (don't stow them in checked luggage in case it gets lost).

Visit the dentist. Get a dental checkup well before your trip. Emergency dental care during your trip can be expensive, time consuming...and painful. I once had a tooth crowned by a German dentist who knew only one word in English, which he used in question form—"Pain?"

Take extra precautions for exotic locations. No vaccinations are required for travel in Europe. But if you're heading to more exotic destinations, such as Morocco, Russia, or Turkey, ask your doctor about any shots or medicine you might need, or consult a travel-medicine physician. Only these specialists keep entirely up-to-date on health conditions for travelers around the world. Tell the doctor about every possible destination on your vacation itinerary, confirmed or not. Then you can have the flexibility to take that impulsive swing through Turkey or Morocco knowing that you're prepared medically and have the required shots. Ask the doctor about vaccines against hepatitis A (food- or water-borne virus) and hepatitis B (virus transmitted by bodily fluids), antidiarrheal medicines, and any additional precautions. Countries "require" shots in order to protect their citizens from you and "recommend" shots to protect you from them. If any shots are recommended, take that advice seriously. The Centers for Disease Control offers updated information on every country (www.cdc.gov/travel).

Conquering Jet Lag

Anyone who flies through multiple time zones has to grapple with the biorhythmic confusion known as jet lag. Flying from the US to Europe, you switch your wristwatch six to nine hours forward. Your body says, "Hey, what's going on?" Body clocks don't reset so easily. All your life you've done things on a 24-hour cycle. Now, after crossing the Atlantic, your body wants to eat when you tell it to sleep and sleep when you tell

Health Resources

Centers for Disease Control and Prevention (CDC, www.cdc.gov /travel): Gives health-related information and advice by country, plus trip preparation and health tips for travel worldwide.

International Association for Medical Assistance to Travelers (IAMAT, www.iamat.org): Directory of English-speaking doctors around the world.

Shoreland's Travel Health Online (www.tripprep.com): Offers health advice for travelers, a planning guide, and information for more than 200 countries.

U.S. Department of State (www.state.gov/travel): Provides an overview of the quality of medical care available in each country and points out areas of concern.

it to enjoy a museum.

Too many people assume their first day will be made worthless by jet lag. Don't prematurely condemn yourself to zombiedom. Most people I've traveled with, of all ages, have enjoyed productive—even hyper— first days. You can't avoid jet lag, but with a few tips you can minimize the symptoms.

Leave home well rested. Flying halfway around the world is stressful. If you leave frazzled after a hectic last night and a wild bon-voyage party, there's a good chance you won't be healthy for the first part of your trip. An early-trip cold used to be a regular part of my vacation until I learned this very important trick: Plan from the start as if you're leaving two days before you really are. Keep that last 48-hour period sacred (apart from your normal work schedule), even if it means being hectic before your false departure date. Then you have two orderly, peaceful days after you've packed so that you

Jet lag hits even the very young.

are physically ready to fly. Mentally, you'll be comfortable about leaving home and starting this adventure. You'll fly away well rested and 100 percent capable of enjoying the bombardment of your senses that will follow.

HEALTH AND HYGIENE

Use the flight to rest and reset. The in-flight movies are good for one thing—nap time. With a few hours of sleep during the transatlantic flight, you'll be functional the day you land. When the pilot announces the European time, reset your mind along with your wristwatch. Don't prolong jet lag by reminding yourself what time it is back home. Be in Europe.

On arrival, stay awake until an early local bedtime. If you doze off at 4:00 p.m. and wake up at midnight, you've accomplished nothing. Plan a good walk until early evening. Jet lag hates fresh air, daylight, and exercise. Your body may beg for sleep, but stand firm: Refuse. Force your body's transition to the local time. You'll probably awaken very early on your first morning. Trying to sleep later is normally futile. Get out and enjoy a "pinch me, I'm in Europe" walk, as merchants set up in the marketplace and the town slowly comes to life. This will probably be the only sunrise you'll see in Europe.

Consider jet-lag cures. The last thing I want to do is promote a pharmaceutical, but I must admit that the sleep aid Ambien (generic name Zolpidem) has become my friend in fighting jet lag. Like all prescription medications, Ambien can have side effects—read and follow the directions, and carefully discuss using it with your doctor. The stuff is powerful (almost comically so). I use it very sparingly. Generally I fall asleep without a problem on my first night in Europe, but wake up wired after only four hours. So I keep a half-tablet of Ambien on my bedside table and pop it when I awaken to enjoy about three more solid hours of sleep. Managing a good seven hours of sleep a night in Europe (or after flying home) hastens my transition to local time. That way, I'm not disabled by sleepiness that first afternoon and can stay awake until a decent bedtime. (I also use a quarter-tablet of Ambien to get some sleep during the long flight over, in a noisy hotel, or if I'm coming down with a cold and want to sleep it off.) Other travelers rave about melatonin, a hormone that is supposed to help recalibrate your internal clock (available over-the-counter in the US, but illegal in some European countries).

Bottom Line: The best prescription is to leave home unfrazzled, minimize jet lag's symptoms, force yourself into European time, and give yourself a chance to enjoy your trip from the moment you step off the plane.

Staying Healthy While Traveling

Using discretion and common sense, I eat and drink whatever I like when I'm on the road. I've stayed healthy throughout a six-week trip traveling from Europe to India. By following these basic guidelines, I

European Water

I drink European tap water and any water served in restaurants. Read signs carefully, however: Some taps, including those on trains and airplanes, are not for drinking. If there's any hint of nonpotability—a decal showing a glass with a red "X" over it, or a skull and crossbones—don't drink it. Many fountains in German-speaking countries are for drinking, but others are just for show. Look for *Trinkwasser* ("drinking water") or *Kein Trinkwasser* ("not drinking water").

The water at many European public fountains is safe to drink...unless your travel partner has dirty hands.

The water (or, just as likely, the general stress of travel on your immune system) may, sooner or later, make you sick. It's not necessarily dirty. The bacteria in European water are different from those in American water. Our bodily systems—raised proudly on bread that rips in a straight line—are the most pampered on earth. We are capable of handling American bacteria with no problem at all, but some people can go to London and get sick. Some French people visit Boston and get sick. Some Americans travel around the world eating and drinking everything in sight and don't get sick, while others spend weeks on the toilet. It all depends on the person.

East of Bulgaria and south of the Mediterranean, do not drink untreated water. Water can be sanitized by boiling it for 10 minutes or by using purifying tablets or a filter. Bottled water, beer, wine, boiled coffee and tea, and bottled soft drinks are safe as long as you skip the ice cubes. Coca-Cola products are as safe in Egypt as they are at home.

never once suffered from Tehran Tummy or Delhi Belly.

Take precautions on the flight. Long flights are dehydrating. I ask for "two orange juices with no ice" every chance I get. Eat lightly, stay hydrated, and have no coffee or alcohol and only minimal sugar until the flight's almost over. Avoid the slight chance of getting a blood clot in your leg during long flights by taking short walks hourly. While seated, flex your ankles and don't cross your legs. Some people are more prone to clots (factors include obesity, age, genetics, smoking, and use of oral contraceptives or hormone replacement therapy).

Eat nutritiously. The longer your trip, the more you'll be affected by an inadequate diet. Budget travelers often eat more carbohydrates and less protein to stretch their travel dollars. This is the root of many health problems. Protein helps you resist infection and rebuilds muscles. Get the most nutritional mileage from your protein by eating it with the day's largest meal (in the presence of all those essential amino acids). Supplemental super-vitamins, taken regularly, help me to at least feel healthy.

Use good judgment when eating out (and outside Europe). Avoid unhealthy-looking restaurants. Meat should be well cooked (unless, of course, you're eating sushi, carpaccio, etc.) and, in some places, avoided altogether. Have "well done" written on a piece of paper in the pertinent language and use it when ordering. Pre-prepared foods gather germs (a common cause of diarrhea). Outside of Europe, be especially cautious. When in serious doubt, eat only thick-skinned fruit...peeled.

Keep clean. Wash your hands often, keep your nails clean, and avoid touching your eyes, nose, and mouth. Hand sanitizers, such as Purell, can be helpful. However, since they target bacteria, not viruses, they really should be used as an adjunct to, rather than a replacement for, hand washing with soap and warm water.

Practice safe sex. Sexually transmitted diseases are widespread. Obviously, the best way to prevent acquiring an STD is to avoid exposure. Condoms (readily available at pharmacies and from restroom vending machines) are fairly effective in preventing transmission. HIV is also a risk, especially among prostitutes.

Exercise. Physically, travel is great living—healthy food, lots of activity, fresh air, and all those stairs! If you're a couch potato, try to get in shape before your trip by taking long walks. People who regularly work out have plenty of options for keeping in shape while traveling. Biking is a great way to burn some calories—and get intimate with a destination. Though running is not as widespread in Europe as it is in the US, it's not considered weird either. Traveling runners can enjoy Europe from a special perspective—at dawn. Swimmers will find that Europe has plenty of good, inexpensive public swimming pools. Whatever your racket, if you want to badly enough, you'll find ways to keep in practice as you travel. Most big-city private tennis and swim clubs welcome foreign guests for a small fee, which is a good way to make friends as well as stay fit.

Get enough sleep. Know how much sleep you need to stay healthy (generally 7-8 hours per night). If I go more than two nights with fewer than six hours' sleep, I make it a priority to catch up—no matter how busy I am. Otherwise, I'm virtually guaranteed to get the sniffles.

Give yourself psychological pep talks. Europe can do to certain travelers what southern France did to Vincent van Gogh. Romantics can get the sensory bends, patriots can get their flags burned, and anyone can suffer from culture shock.

Europe is not particularly impressed by America or Americans. It will challenge givens that you always assumed were above the test of reason, and most of Europe on the street doesn't really care that much about what you, the historical and cultural pilgrim, have waited so long to see.

Take a break from Europe, whether it's a long, dark, air-conditioned trip back to California in a movie theater; a pleasant sit in an American embassy reading room surrounded by eagles, photos of presidents, *Time* magazines, and other Yankees; or a visit to the lobby of a world-class hotel, where any hint of the traditional culture has been lost under a big-business bucket of intercontinental whitewash. It can do wonders to refresh the struggling traveler's spirit.

Women's Health Issues

For specific advice on women's health, I turned to Europe Through the Back Door *researcher Risa Laib, who wrote the following section based on her experiences traveling solo (and pregnant) through Europe.*

You can find whatever medications you need in Europe, but you already know what works for you in the US. It's easiest to B.Y.O. pills, whether for cramps, yeast infections, or birth control. Some health-insurance companies issue only a month's supply of birth control pills at a time; ask for a larger supply for a longer trip. Tampons and pads, widely available in Europe, are sold—for more than the US price—at supermarkets, pharmacies, and convenience stores. You may not see the range of brands and sizes typical in American supermarkets, so if you're used to a particular type, it's simpler and cheaper to bring what you'll need from home.

Yeast and Urinary Tract Infections: Women prone to yeast infections should bring their own over-the-counter medicine (or know the name and its key ingredient to show a pharmacist in Europe). Some women get a prescription for fluconazole (Diflucan), a powerful pill that cures yeast infections more quickly and tidily than creams and suppositories. If you get a yeast infection in Europe and need medication, go

HEALTH AND HYGIENE

to a pharmacy. If you encounter the rare pharmacist who doesn't speak English, find an English-speaking local woman to write out "yeast infection" for you in the country's language to avoid the embarrassing charade.

You can treat minor urinary tract infections with unsweetened cranberry juice (available in northern Europe) or with cranberry pills (made from cranberry juice concentrate) sold at health food stores. If you often get urinary tract infections, bring antibiotics and a prescription from your doctor. If you forget, a pharmacist in Europe should be able to help.

Traveling When Pregnant: Some couples want to time conception to occur in Europe so they can name their child Paris, Siena, or wherever. (Be thoughtful about this, or little Zagreb may harbor a lifelong grudge against you.) Consider bringing a pregnancy test from home to help you find out when you can celebrate.

If you'll be traveling during your first pregnancy, rip out a few chapters from a book on pregnancy to bring along; it can be hard in Europe to find books in English on pregnancy. If you want certain tests done (such as an amniocentesis), ask your doctor when you need to be home.

Traveling in the first trimester can be rough for some women: Morning sickness can make bus or boat rides especially unpleasant, and climbing all those stone stairs can be exhausting. Packing light is more essential than ever. You might find it easier to travel in the second trimester, when your body's used to being pregnant and you're not yet too big to be uncomfortable.

Wear comfortable shoes that have arch supports. If you'll be traveling a long time, bring loose clothing (with elastic waistbands) and shoes a half size larger to accommodate your changing body. Keep your valuables (cash, passport, etc.) in a neck pouch rather than a constricting money belt.

Pace yourself and allow plenty of time for rest. If problems pop up, go to a clinic or hospital (for more, see "Medical Care in Europe," later).

Seek out nutritious food (though some of it may make you nauseated, just as in America). Picnics, with drinkable yogurt, are often healthier than restaurant meals. Pack baggies for carrying snacks. Bring prenatal vitamins from home, plus a calcium supplement if you're not a milk drinker.

It's actually pleasant to be pregnant in Europe. People are particularly kind. And when your child is old enough to understand, she'll enjoy knowing she's already been to Europe—especially if you promise to take her again.

Basic First Aid

Be proactive to stay well. If you do get sick, take action to regain your health. For a list of first-aid items to pack from home, see page 81.

Headaches and Other Aches: Tylenol (or any other over-the-counter pain reliever) soothes headaches, sore feet, sprains, bruises, Italian traffic, hangovers, and many other minor problems. If you're buying it overseas, Europeans may be more familiar with the term "paracetamol" (pare-ah-SEET-ah-mall).

Swelling: Often accompanying a physical injury, swelling is painful and delays healing. Ice and elevate any sprain periodically for 48 hours. A package of frozen veggies works as a cheap ice pack. If your foot or leg is swollen, buy or borrow a bucket and soak the affected area in cold water, or sit on the edge of a cool swimming pool. Take an anti-inflammatory drug like ibuprofen (Advil, Motrin). Use an Ace bandage to immobilize, reduce swelling, and provide support. It is not helpful to "work out" a sprain—instead, cut back on activities that could aggravate the injury.

Fever: A high fever merits medical attention. A normal temperature of 98.6° Fahrenheit equals 37° Celsius. If your thermometer reads 40°C, you're boiling at 104°F.

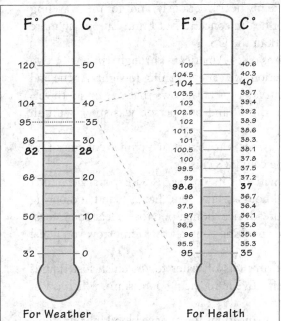

For Weather   For Health

Europe takes its temperature using the Celsius scale, while we opt for Fahrenheit. For weather, remember that 28°C is 82°F—perfect. For health, 37°C is just right.

Colds: It's tempting to go, go, go while you're in Europe—but if you push yourself to the point of getting sick, you've accomplished nothing. Keep yourself healthy and hygienic. If you're feeling run-down, check into a good hotel, sleep well, and force fluids. (My trick during the hectic scramble of TV production is to suck on vitamin C with zinc tablets.) Stock each place you stay with boxes of juice upon arrival. Sudafed (pseudoephedrine) and other cold capsules are usually available, but may not come in as many varieties.

HEALTH AND HYGIENE

Abrasions: Clean abrasions thoroughly with soap to prevent or control infection. Bandages help keep wounds clean but are not a substitute for cleaning. A piece of clean cloth can be sterilized by boiling for 10 minutes or by scorching with a match.

Blisters: Moleskin, bandages, tape, or two pairs of socks can prevent or retard problems with your feet. Cover any irritated area before it blisters. Many walkers swear by Body Glide, a solid anti-chafing stick sold in running shops and sporting-goods stores. For many, Band-Aid's Friction Block stick is a lifesaver for preventing blisters in spots where your shoe rubs against your foot.

Motion Sickness: To be effective, medication for motion sickness (Dramamine or Marezine) should be taken one hour before you think you'll need it. These medications can also serve as a mild sleep aid. Bonine also treats motion sickness but causes less drowsiness.

Diarrhea: Get used to the fact that you might have diarrhea for a day. (Practice that thought in front of the mirror tonight.) If you get the runs, take it in stride. It's simply not worth taking eight Pepto-Bismol tablets a day or brushing your teeth in Coca-Cola all summer long to avoid a day of the trots. I take my health seriously, and, for me, traveling in India or Mexico is a major health concern. But I find Europe no more threatening to my stomach than the US.

I've routinely taken groups of 24 Americans through Turkey for two weeks. With adequate discretion, we eat everything in sight. At the end of the trip, my loose-stool survey typically shows that five or six travelers coped with a day of the Big D and one person was stuck with an extended weeklong bout.

To help avoid getting diarrhea, eat yogurt, which has enzymes that can ease your system into the country's cuisine.

If you get diarrhea, it will run its course. Revise your diet, don't panic, and take it easy for 24 hours. Make your diet as bland and boring as possible for a day or so (bread, rice, boiled potatoes, clear soup, toast without butter, weak tea). Keep telling yourself that tomorrow you'll feel much better. You will.

If loose stools persist, drink lots of water to replenish lost liquids and minerals. Bananas are effective in replacing potassium, which is lost during a bout with diarrhea.

Don't take antidiarrheal medications if you have blood in your stools or a fever greater than 101°F (38°C)—you need a doctor's exam and antibiotics. A child (especially an infant) who suffers a prolonged case of diarrhea also needs prompt medical attention.

Good news for your health: Europe is getting enthusiastic about not smoking. These days most countries prohibit smoking in enclosed public spaces. Cigarette packages make it really clear: "Smoking kills"; and Berlin's subway—like much of Europe—is now smoke-free.

I visited the Red Cross in Athens after a miserable three-week tour of the toilets of Syria, Jordan, and Israel. My intestinal commotion was finally stilled by a recommended strict diet of boiled rice and plain tea. As a matter of fact, after five days on that dull diet, I was constipated.

Constipation: With all the bread you'll be eating, constipation, the other side of the intestinal pendulum, is (according to my surveys) as prevalent as diarrhea. Get exercise, eat lots of roughage (raw fruits, leafy vegetables, prunes, or bran tablets from home), and everything will come out all right in the end.

Medical Care in Europe

If you're worried about getting sick while traveling, rest assured: Most of Europe offers high-quality medical care that's as competent as what you'll find at home. Plus, the majority of doctors and pharmacists speak at least some English, so communication generally shouldn't be an issue.

Emergencies

If an accident or life-threatening medical problem occurs on the road, get to a hospital. For serious conditions (stroke, heart attack, bad car accident), summon an ambulance. In most countries, you can call 112, the European Union's universal emergency number for ambulance, fire department, or police. Most countries also have a 911 equivalent that works as well. Or you can ask your hotelier, restaurant host, or whoever's

HEALTH AND HYGIENE

around to call an ambulance for you. If you're conscious and don't need immediate life-saving treatment, take a taxi to the hospital.

Be aware that you will likely have to pay out of pocket for any medical treatment, even if your insurance company provides international health care coverage. A visit to the emergency room can be free or cost only a nominal fee, or it can be expensive, depending on where you are and what

*Regardless of the local word for "pharmacy" (*farmacia *in Spanish,* Apotheke *in German,* pharmacie *in French), you can always look for the green cross.*

treatment you need. Make sure you get a copy of your bill so that when you return home, you can file a claim to be reimbursed. If you purchased travel insurance to serve as your primary medical coverage, call the company as soon as possible to report the injury. They can usually work with the hospital directly to get your bills paid (for information on travel insurance, see page 63).

Minor Ailments

If you get sick on your trip, don't wait it out. Find help to get on the road to recovery as soon as possible. Here are your options if you have a non-emergency situation on your hands:

Pharmacies: Throughout Europe, people with a health problem go first to the pharmacy, not to their doctor. European pharmacists can diagnose and prescribe remedies for many simple problems, such as sore throats, fevers, stomach issues, sinus problems, insomnia, blisters, rashes, urinary tract infections, or muscle, joint, and back pain. Most cities have at least a few 24-hour pharmacies from which you can pick up what you need and be on the mend pronto.

When it comes to medication, expect some differences between the way things are done in Europe and at home. Certain drugs that you need a prescription for in the US are available over the counter in Europe. Some drugs go by different names. And some European medication can be stronger than their counterparts in the US, so follow directions and dosages carefully. Also, topical remedies are common in Europe; if you're suffering from body aches and pains, or any swelling, don't be surprised if a pharmacist prescribes a cream to apply to the problem area. If you need to fill a prescription—even one from home—a pharmacy can generally take care of it promptly. If a pharmacist can't help you, he or she will send you to a doctor or a health clinic.

Clinics: A trip to a clinic is actually an interesting travel experience. Every year I end up in a European clinic for one reason or another, and every time I'm impressed by its efficiency and effectiveness.

A clinic is useful if you want to be checked for a non-emergency medical issue, get some tests done, or if your problem is beyond a pharmacist's scope. Clinics in Europe operate just like those in the US: You'll sign in with the receptionist, answer a few questions, then take a seat and wait for a nurse or doctor.

A trip to a clinic generally costs about $75-150. Expect to pay this fee up front, whether you're covered through your health insurance company or a special travel policy. Make sure you get a copy of the bill so you can file a claim when you return home.

House Calls: If you're holed up sick in your hotel room and would rather not go out, the hotel receptionist can generally call a doctor who will come to your room and check you out.

Finding Medical Help

To locate a doctor, clinic, or hospital, ask around at places that are accustomed to dealing with Americans on the road—such as tourist offices and large hotels. Most embassies and consulates maintain lists of physicians and hospitals in major cities (go to www.usembassy.gov, select your location, and look under the U.S. Citizens Services section of that embassy's website for medical services information).

If you're concerned about getting an English-speaking and Western-trained doctor, consider joining IAMAT, the International Association for Medical Assistance to Travelers. You'll get a list of English-speaking doctors in more than 90 member countries who charge affordable, standardized fees for medical visits (membership is free but donation is requested, fee pricing on website, pay provider directly at time of visit, www.iamat.org, tel. 716/754-4883).

Laundry

I met a guy in Italy who wore his T-shirt the right way and then inside out thinking he'd delay the laundry day. A guy in Germany showed me his take-it-into-the-tub-with-you-and-make-waves method of washing his troublesome jeans. You don't need to go to these extremes to have

HEALTH AND HYGIENE

something presentable to wear. Do laundry in your hotel room, find a launderette, or splurge on full-service laundry.

Washing Clothes in Your Room

One of my domestic chores while on the road is washing my laundry in the hotel-room sink. I keep it very simple, using hotel laundry bags to store my dirty stuff, washing my clothes with hotel shampoo, and just improvising places to hang things. But you can pack a self-service laundry kit: a plastic or mesh bag with a drawstring for dirty clothes; concentrated liquid detergent in a small, sturdy, plastic squeeze bottle wrapped in a sealable baggie to contain leakage; and a stretchable "travel clothesline" (a double-stranded cord that's twisted, so clothespins are unnecessary). To make things easier, I bring a quick-dry travel wardrobe that either looks OK wrinkled or doesn't wrinkle. (I test-wash my shirts in the sink at home before I let them come to Europe with me. Some shirts dry fine; others prune up.)

Whistler's laundry

Most European hotels prefer that you not do laundry in your room. Some bathrooms are even equipped with a multilingual "no washing clothes in the room" sign (which, after "eat your peas," may be the most ignored rule on earth). Interpret hoteliers' reticence as "I have lots of good furniture and fine floors in this room, and I don't want your drippy laundry ruining things." But as long as you wash carefully and are respectful of the room, go right ahead.

Sometimes a hotel will remove the sink and tub stoppers in an attempt to discourage washing. Bring a universal drain-stopper from home, try using a wadded-up sock or a pill-bottle lid, or line the sink with your plastic laundry bag and wash in it. Some travelers create their own washing machine with a large, two-gallon sealable baggie: soak in suds for an hour, agitate, drain, rinse.

Wring wet laundry as dry as possible to minimize dripping. Other than a clogged toilet, there's little a hotelier likes seeing less than a pool of water on their hardwood floors. Rolling laundry in a towel and twisting or stomping on it can be helpful (but many accommodations don't provide new towels every day).

Hang clothes in a low-profile, nondestructive way. Suspend them over the bathtub or in a closet. The maid hardly notices my laundry. It's hanging quietly in the bathroom or shuffled among my dry clothes in the closet. Separate the back and front of hanging clothes to speed drying. Some travelers pack an inflatable hanger. Don't hang your clothes out the window—hoteliers find it

Go ahead and ask! There's a good chance you can share the clothesline in the B&B's backyard or on the hotel's roof.

unsightly, and you might find it has blown away when you return from dinner. Laid-back hotels will let your laundry join theirs on the lines out back or on the rooftop.

Smooth out your wet clothes, button shirts, set collars, and "hand iron" to encourage wrinkle-free drying. If your shirt or dress dries wrinkled, hang it in a steamy bathroom or borrow an iron and ironing board from the hotel (nearly all have loaners). A piece of tape is a good ad hoc lint-brush. In very hot climates, I wash my shirt several times a day, wring it, and put it on damp. It's clean and refreshing, and (sadly) in 15 minutes it's dry.

Using a Launderette

For a thorough washing, ask your hotel to direct you to the nearest launderette. In Western Europe, nearly every neighborhood has one; in Eastern Europe, launderettes are much less common. It takes about an hour and $10-15 to wash and dry an average-size load. (Many hostels have coin-op washers and dryers or heated drying rooms.)

Many of Europe's launderettes are completely unstaffed—it's just you, sparse English instructions, and dirty clothes.

Better launderettes have coin-op soap dispensers, change machines, English instructions, and helpful attendants. Others are completely automated—but many of these have pictogram instructions that usually aren't too hard to

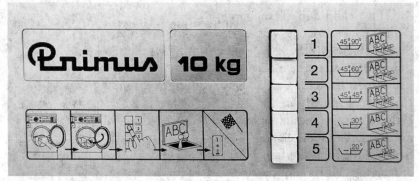

This laundry machine hurdles the language barrier with completely pictographic instructions: Insert your laundry, close the door, select the program, add the soap, and insert coins to start. The five buttons on the right let you select the washing program: The first water temperature (in Celsius) is for the pre-wash cycle, and the second is for the wash cycle. The pictures tell you where to put the soap and softener for each program (notice that the last two skip the pre-wash—no soap needed in compartment A).

parse. Look around for a sign listing the "last wash" time, and stick to it. When it's closing time, an attendant might come by to evict you, or the machines might simply stop operating.

While the exact procedure varies, it usually includes the same steps. Select your machine, put in your clothes, and close the door (which probably needs to be locked with a latch). Add soap, normally in a small reservoir in the top of the washer. If you're planning on visiting a launderette, pack one or two small detergent boxes. If you don't have soap, you can typically buy some at the launderette from an automated dispenser. The soap compartments on most washers have three reservoirs: for pre-wash, the main wash cycle, and softener. (Don't put your main soap into the pre-wash compartment, or it'll be washed away before its time.)

While you might be able to pay at the washer itself, it's more likely that you'll have to insert your money at a central unit. Note the number of your machine, then type that number into the central unit and put in your coins (use exact change if possible—some machines don't give change). Sometimes a central unit dispenses tokens, which you then insert in the machine.

Select your cycle, either at the machine itself or at the central unit. Below I've listed some of the cycles you're likely to see. The first number is the temperature in Celsius for the first cycle (pre-wash), the second is the temperature for the second cycle (main wash), and the third is how long the whole thing lasts.

45° / 90° / 55 m	whites (very hot)
45° / 60° / 50 m	colors (hot)
45° / 45° / 40 m	permanent press (warm)
— / 30° / 30 m	nylon (lukewarm)
— / 20° / 25 m	delicates (cold)

Some washing machines have a built-in spin cycle; however, others leave clothes totally soaked. In this case, put your wet clothes in a special spin-dry machine (usually called a "centrifuge" or something similar) to wring out excess water before moving your clothes to the dryer.

Drying time is generally available in smaller units (5- or 10-minute increments) rather than as a full cycle. Most machines let you choose the drying temperature: low (cool and slow); medium (warmer but still slow); and high (speedy but shrinky). Because both washers and dryers at launderettes can be unpredictable, hand wash anything that you value dearly.

While waiting for your clothes, use the time to picnic, catch up on postcards and your journal, or chat with other customers. Launderettes throughout the world seem to give people the gift of gab. These days, many launderettes have Internet access or Wi-Fi (or ask about an Internet café nearby). If you ask attendants sweetly, they might be willing to transfer your clothes to the dryer, allowing you to slip out for some bonus sightseeing. (In these cases, it's appropriate to thank them by offering a small tip.)

Hiring It Out: Truly full-service places, which fold and sometimes even iron your laundry, are easier—just drop it off and come back in the afternoon—but more expensive. Also pricey, but handiest of all: You can hire your hotel to do your laundry.

Regardless of the cost, every time I slip into a fresh pair of pants, I figure it was worth the hassle and expense.

European Bathrooms

Bathrooms in Europe are nothing to be fearful of. In most cases, they will feel familiar and comfortable. But European bathrooms and plumbing can have their share of quirks. Just keep an open mind, and remember that nothing beats a good bathroom story when you get home.

Your Hotel Bathroom

In Europe, don't expect big bathrooms. Many hotels have tiny facilities that have been retrofitted into the corner of an already modest-size room. Counter space is often limited, and showers can be surprisingly tight, especially if you're a larger person. Be careful bending over to pick up a dropped bar of soap—you might just hit your head on the toilet or sink.

In some bathrooms, you may see a mysterious porcelain thing that looks like an oversized bedpan. That's a bidet. Tourists not in the know use them as anything from a launderette to a vomitorium to a watermelon rind receptacle to a urinal. Locals use them in lieu of a shower to clean the parts of the body that rub together when they walk. Go ahead and give it a try. Just remember the four S's—straddle, squat, soap up, and swish off.

When traveling in Europe, you may need to lower your towel expectations. Like breakfast and people, towels get smaller as you go south. In simple places, bath towels are not replaced every day, so hang them up to dry and reuse. This is also catching on with bigger hotels—even fancy ones—which, in an effort to be eco-friendly, post a sign explaining that they'll replace towels left on the floor, but not those that are hanging to dry. In my experience, pricey hotels rarely stay true to this promise; your towels will probably be replaced no matter where you leave them. On the other end of the spectrum, dorm-style accommodations don't provide towels or soap at all, so you'll have to B.Y.O. Also, most European hotels don't supply washcloths. If this is part of your bath ritual, pack some along in your suitcase.

Shower Strategies

Americans are notorious (and embarrassing) energy gluttons—wasting hot water and leaving lights on as if electricity were cheap. Who besides us sings in the shower? European energy costs are shocking, so many accommodations try to conserve where they can.

Hot Water Hiccups: Most of the cold showers Americans take in Europe are cold only because they don't know how to turn the hot water on. You'll find showers and baths of all kinds. The red knob is hot and the blue one is cold—or vice versa. Unusual showers often have clear instructions posted. Study the particular system, and before you shiver, ask the receptionist for help.

There are some very peculiar tricks. For instance, in Italy

European showers: Each one has its own personality.

and Spain, "C" is for *caldo/caliente*—hot. In Croatia, look for the switch with an icon of a hot-water tank (usually next to the room's light switch). The British "dial-a-shower" features an electronic box under the shower-head—turn the dial to select how hot you want the water and to turn on or shut off the flow of water (this is sometimes done with a separate dial or button). If you can't find the switch to turn on the shower, it may be just outside the bathroom.

No matter where you are in Europe, get used to taking shorter showers. Some places, especially modest accommodations, furnish their bathrooms with little-bitty water heaters that are much smaller than the one in your basement. After five minutes, you may find your hot shower turning very cold.

Handheld Showers: In Europe, handheld showers are common. Sometimes the showerhead is sitting loose in a caddy; other times it's mounted low on the tub. Not only do you have to master the art of lathering up with one hand while holding the showerhead in the other, but you also have to keep it aimed at your body or the wall to avoid spraying water all over the bathroom. To avoid flooding the room, you may find it easier to just sit in the tub and shower that way.

Budget-Hotel Showers: Hostels and budget hotels can offer interesting shower experiences. In some places, the line between shower and bathroom is nonexistent, and there's no shower curtain. The water simply slides into a drain in the middle of the bathroom.

A few hostels and budget hotels actually have coin-operated showers. If you run into one of these, it's a good idea to have an extra token handy to avoid that lathered look. A "navy shower," using the water only to soap up and rinse off, is a wonderfully conservative method, and those who follow you will more likely enjoy some warm *Wasser* (although starting and stopping the water doesn't start and stop the meter).

Shower Cords: The cord that dangles over the tub or shower in many hotels is not a clothesline; only pull it if you've fallen and can't get up. (But if the cord hangs *outside* the tub or shower, it probably controls the light—good luck with this.)

Shared Showers: The cheapest hotels often feature a shared toilet and shower "down the hall." To bathoholics, this sounds terrible. Imagine the congestion in the morning when the entire floor tries to pile into that bathtub! Remember, only Americans "need" a shower every morning. Few Americans stay in these basic hotels; therefore, you've got what amounts to a private bath—down the hall.

Over the years, I've observed that even the simplest places have added lots of private showers. For example, a hotel originally designed with 20 simple rooms sharing two showers may now have been remodeled with private showers in 14 of its rooms. That leaves a more reasonable six rooms rather than 20 to share the two public showers. Those willing to go down the hall for a shower enjoy the same substantial savings with much less inconvenience.

Finding Places to Shower: If you are vagabonding or spending several nights in transit, you can buy a shower in "day hotels" at major train stations and airports, at many freeway rest stops, and in public baths or swimming pools.

Throughout southern Europe, even the cheapest hotel rooms come with a bidet. Europeans use them to stay clean without a daily shower.

Most Mediterranean beaches have free, freshwater showers all the time. I have a theory that after four days without a shower, you don't get any worse, but that's another book.

Toilet Trauma

Every traveler has one or two great toilet stories. Foreign toilets can be traumatic, but they are one of those little things that can make travel so much more interesting than staying at home. If you plan to venture away from the international-style hotels in your Mediterranean travels and become a temporary resident, "going local" may take on a very real meaning.

Squat Toilets: The vast majority of European toilets are similar to our own. But in a few out-of-the-way places, you might find one that consists simply of porcelain footprints and a squat-and-aim hole. If faced with one, remember: Those of us who need a throne to sit on are in the minority. Throughout the world, most humans sit on their haunches and nothing more. Sometimes called "Turkish toilets," these are more commonly found in, well, Turkey.

One of Europe's many unforgettable experiences is the rare squat-and-aim toilet.

Flummoxing Flushers: In Europe, you may or may not encounter a familiar flushing mechanism. In older bathrooms, toilets may come with a pull string instead of a handle (generally with the tank affixed to the wall rather than the toilet itself). In modern bathrooms, you may see two buttons on top of the tank—one performs a regular flush, the other (for lighter jobs) conserves water. In Great Britain, you'll likely come across the "pump toilet," with a flushing handle that doesn't kick in unless you push it just right: too hard or too soft, and it won't go. (Be decisive but not ruthless.)

Toilet Paper: Like a spoon or a fork, this is another Western "essential" that many people on our planet do not use. What they use varies. I won't get too graphic here, but remember that a billion civilized people on this planet never eat with their left hand. While Europeans do use toilet paper, WCs may not always be well stocked. If you're averse to the occasional drip-dry, carry pocket-size tissue packs (easy to buy in Europe) for WCs *sans* TP. Some countries, such as Greece and Turkey, have very frail plumbing, and toilet paper will jam up the WCs. If the bathroom's wastebaskets are full of soiled toilet paper, leave yours there, too.

Paid Toilets: Paying to use a public WC is a European custom that irks many Americans. But isn't it really worth a few coins, considering the cost of water, maintenance, and cleanliness? And you're probably in no state to argue, anyway. Sometimes the toilet is free, but the person in the corner sells sheets of toilet paper. Most common is the tip dish by the entry—the local equivalent of about 50 cents is plenty. Caution: Many attendants leave only bills and too-big coins in the tray to bewilder the full-bladdered tourist. The keepers of Europe's public toilets have earned a reputation for crabbiness. You'd be crabby, too, if you lived under the street in a room full of public toilets. Humor them, understand them, and carry some change so you can leave them a coin or two.

Women in the Men's Room: The women who seem to inhabit Europe's WCs are a popular topic of conversation among Yankee males. Sooner or later you'll be minding your own business at the urinal, and the lady will bring you your change or sweep under your feet. Yes, it is distracting, but you'll just have to get used to it—she has.

Getting comfortable in foreign restrooms takes a little adjusting, but that's travel. When in Rome, do as the Romans do—and before you know it, you'll be Euro-peein'.

Finding a Public Restroom

I once dropped a tour group off in a town for a potty stop, and when I picked them up 20 minutes later, none had found relief. Locating a

HEALTH AND HYGIENE

Going local

decent public toilet can be frustrating. But with a few tips, you can sniff out a biffy in a jiffy.

Coin-op Toilets on the Street: Some large cities, such as Paris, London, and Amsterdam, are dotted with coin-operated, telephone-booth-type WCs on street corners. Insert a coin, the door opens, and you have 15 minutes of toilet use accompanied by Sinatra Muzak. When you leave, the entire chamber disinfects itself.

Some cities have free, low-tech public urinals (called *pissoirs*) that offer just enough privacy for men to find relief... sometimes with a view. Munich had outdoor urinals until the 1972 Olympics and then decided to beautify the city by doing away with them. What about the people's needs? There's a law in Munich: Any place serving beer must admit the public (whether or not they're customers) to use the toilets.

Restaurants: Any place that serves food or drinks has a restroom. No restaurateur would label his WC so those on the street can see, but you can walk into nearly any restaurant or café, politely and confidently, and find a bathroom. Assume it's somewhere in the back, either upstairs or downstairs. It's easiest in large places that have outdoor seating—waiters will think you're a customer just making a quick trip inside. Some call it rude; I call it survival. If you feel like it, ask permission. Just smile, "Toilet?" I'm rarely turned down. American-type fast-food places are very common and usually have a decent and fairly accessible "public" restroom. Timid people buy a drink they don't want in order to use the bathroom, but that's generally unnecessary (although sometimes the secret bathroom door code is printed only on your receipt).

Even at American chains, be prepared

This high-tech public toilet offers a free, private place to do your business.

for bathroom culture shock. At a big Starbucks in Bern, Switzerland, I opened the door to find an extremely blue space. It took me a minute to realize that the blue lights made it impossible for junkies to find their veins.

Public Buildings: When nature beckons and there's no restaurant or bar handy, look in train stations, government buildings, libraries, large bookstores, and upper floors of department stores. Parks often have restrooms, sometimes of the gag-a-maggot variety. Never leave a museum without taking advantage of its restrooms—they're free, clean, and decorated with artistic graffiti. Large, classy, old hotel lobbies are as impressive as many palaces you'll pay to see. You can always find a royal retreat here, and plenty of soft TP.

TRAVEL STYLES

Embracing new experiences is a lot easier to do if you're well prepared. This chapter addresses the special concerns and interests of solo travelers (including issues specific to women), families, seniors, and travelers with disabilities. I also give tips for big-bus tour members and cruise passengers who, despite traveling with a group, also want their independence.

Traveling Solo

I've talked to too many people who put off their travel dreams because they don't want to do it by themselves. If you want to go to Europe but don't have a partner, consider gathering the courage to go it alone. There are plenty of people to meet as you travel, and single travelers often enjoy a montage of fun temporary partners throughout their trip.

Traveling solo has its pros and cons—and for me, the pros far outweigh the cons. When you're on your own, you're independent and in control. You can travel at your own pace, do the things that interest you, eat where

Traveling without a tour, you'll have the locals dancing with you—not for you.

Traveling alone immerses you in Europe.

and when you like, and splurge where you want to splurge. You don't have to wait for your partner to pack up, and you never need to negotiate where to eat or when to call it a day. You go where you want, when you want, and you can get the heck out of that stuffy museum when all the Monets start to blur together. If ad-libbing, it's easier for one to slip between the cracks than two.

Of course, there are downsides to traveling alone: When you're on your own, you don't have a built-in dining companion. You've got no one to send ahead while you wait in line, help you figure out the bus schedule, or commiserate with when things go awry. And traveling by yourself is usually more expensive. With a partner, accommodations cost less because they're shared. Rarely does a double room add up to as much as two singles. If a single room costs $80, a double room will generally be about $100—a savings of $30 per night per person. Other things become cheaper too when you're splitting costs, such as groceries, guidebooks, taxis, storage lockers, and more.

But when you travel with someone else, it's natural to focus on your partner—how you're getting along, whether she meant it when she said she wasn't hungry—and tune out the symphony of sights, sounds, and smells all around you. Traveling on your own allows you to be more present, more open to your surroundings. You'll meet more people—you're seen as more approachable. You're more likely to experience the kindness of strangers.

Solo travel is intensely personal. You can discover more about yourself at the same time you're discovering more about Europe. Traveling on your own is fun, challenging, vivid, and exhilarating. Realizing that you have what it takes to be your own guide is a thrill known only to solo travelers. Your trip is a gift from you to you.

Traveling Alone Without Feeling Lonely

For many people contemplating their first solo trip, their biggest fear is that they'll be lonely. Big cities can be cold and ugly when the only person to talk to is yourself. And being sick and alone in a country where no one knows you is a sad and miserable experience.

Fortunately, combating loneliness in Europe is easy. The continent is full of travelers and natural meeting places, especially in peak season (the built-in camaraderie of other travelers is harder to come by in winter).

Meeting People: You'll run across vaga-buddies every day. If you stay in hostels, you'll have a built-in family (hostels are open to all ages). Or choose small pensions and B&Bs, where the owners have time to talk with you. At most tourist sites, you'll meet more people in an hour than you would at home in a day. If you're feeling shy, cameras are good icebreakers; offer to take someone's picture with his or her camera.

Take a walking tour of a city (ask at the tourist office). You'll learn about the town and meet other travelers, too. If you're staying in a hostel, check its message board—some hostels arrange group tours.

It's easy to meet people on buses and trains. When you meet locals who speak English, find out what they think—about anything. Take your laundry and a deck of cards to a launderette and turn solitaire into gin rummy. You'll end up with a stack of clean clothes and interesting conversations.

Play with kids. Thumb wrestle. Learn how to say "pretty baby" in the native language. If you play peek-a-boo with a baby or fold an origami bird for a kid, you'll make friends with the parents as well as the child.

Try meeting up with other solo travelers through social media. Like-minded individuals can find one another on www.meetup.com, whose worldwide members welcome visitors to wide-ranging events such as photography walks, happy hours, and weekend skiing. Interface with your connections on Facebook to find out if anyone has friends or family in the destinations that you'll be traveling to, then drop them a note about your upcoming visit. Also consider joining a hospitality-exchange network, such as Servas (see page 493), or CouchSurfing, its more low-key alternative (page 225).

Eating Out: I like the old-fashioned, face-to-face social media option of just saying to someone you meet, "Would you like to meet up for dinner?" Some countries have special meals that are more fun to experience with others. You could invite someone to join you for, say, a rijsttafel dinner in the Netherlands, a *smörgåsbord* in Scandinavia, a fondue in Switzerland, a paella feast in Spain, or a spaghetti feed in an Italian trattoria. Wondering whom to ask? People with Rick Steves

Traveling with a Partner

Though I love trekking through Europe by myself, there's nothing like that special lifelong bond that forms between you and the person you've dined with, slept with, and trudged around in the rain with for two weeks straight in a foreign land.

But your choice of travel partner is critical—it can make or break a trip. Traveling with the wrong partner can be like a bad blind date that lasts for weeks. I'd rather do it alone. One summer I went to Europe to dive into as many cultures and adventures as possible. I planned to rest when I got home. My partner wanted to slow life down, get away from it all, relax, and escape the pressures of the business world. Our ideas of acceptable hotels and how much time we wanted to spend eating were quite different. The trip was a near disaster.

Traveling together greatly accelerates a relationship—especially a romantic one. You see each other constantly and make endless decisions. The niceties go out the window. Everything becomes very real; you're in an adventure, a struggle, a hot-air balloon for two. The experiences of years are jammed into weeks. If you haven't traveled with your companion before, consider a trial weekend together before merging dream trips. Any shared trip is a good test of a relationship—often revealing its ultimate course. I'd highly recommend a little premarital travel.

A group of travel buddies defending Caesar's empire atop Hadrian's Wall in Britain

Many people already have their partner—for better or for worse. Couples should take particular care to minimize the stress of traveling together by recognizing each other's need for independence. Too many couples do Europe as a three-legged race, tied together from start to finish. Have an explicit understanding that there's absolutely nothing selfish, dangerous, insulting, or wrong about splitting up occasionally. This is a freedom too few travel partners allow themselves. Doing your own thing for a few hours or days breathes fresh air into your togetherness, making those shared experiences all the more memorable.

Journaling

The best way to document your trip is to pick up a pen and put your experiences to paper. Even in my days as a vagabond backpacker, I was a keen and disciplined journal writer. Journaling the old-fashioned way has no limits, word counts, or caps on creativity.

Great travel journals describe both the inner and outer journey—your physical surroundings and sensory experiences as well as your emotions and thoughts at the time. Transcribing intimate details into your journal will allow you to revisit a place time and time again, whether shared with others or kept to yourself.

Be selective in choosing a journal. I prefer a minimalist booklet with empty pages, lightweight yet stiff enough to both protect the pages and give me something solid to  write on in the absence of a table. Consider a bound book; spiral notebooks tend to fall apart. I write in black ink or mechanical pencil, allowing my simple words to be the focus. Carry your journal with you so you can write throughout the day—while at a bus stop or waiting for a restaurant meal, for instance. If pressed for time while on the go, keep a pocket notebook handy to jot down brief moments or fleeting thoughts. You can expand on these and add them to your actual journal when you have time.

As you write, avoid guidebook-type data and instead focus on the sentimental effects and imagery of your experiences. You don't have to give a chronological account of your journey. In fact, you probably shouldn't. Consider just sitting somewhere interesting and writing about your surroundings or focusing an entry on a specific topic: strange cultural customs or a touching moment, for instance. Throwing in creative essays will sharpen your ability to observe and understand the culture you visited.

Most importantly, don't write just to write. Ten years from now, you won't feel the need to recall the mediocre meal you grabbed at that café or the quality of the hotel's complimentary breakfast. Leave out the boring stuff. You want to include specific details that define the character of a place as well as your personal response. Throw in sketches, mementos, little paper souvenirs like maps and old tickets—anything that takes you back to that moment. Combining these personal touches with candid accounts and reflective musings will create a travel souvenir you'll forever cherish.

guidebooks are like an extended family in Europe. My readers are on the trail of the same travel thrills, and happy to share in the adventure.

If you're going it alone, consider alternatives to formal dining. Try a self-service café, a local-style fast-food restaurant, or a small ethnic eatery. Visit a supermarket deli and get a picnic to eat in the square or a park. Get a slice of pizza from a take-out shop and munch it as you walk along, people watching and window-shopping. Eat in the members' kitchen of a hostel; you'll always have companions. Make it a potluck.

A restaurant feels cheerier at noon than at night, and a maître d' is more likely to seat a solo diner (especially a woman) at a favorable table for lunch than for dinner. If you like company, eat in places so crowded and popular that you have to share a table, or ask other single travelers if they'd like to join you. Assume that many couples would enjoy a third party at their dinner table to stoke the conversation.

Phrase book + big smile = plenty of friends

If you eat alone, be busy. Use the time to learn more of the language. Practice your verbal skills with the waiter or waitress (when I asked a French waiter if he had kids, he proudly showed me a picture of his twin girls). Read a guidebook, a novel, or the *International New York Times.* Do trip planning, draw in your journal, or scrawl a few postcards to the folks back home (for tips on journaling, see the sidebar).

An afternoon at a café is a great way to get some writing done; for the cost of a beverage and a snack, you'll be granted more peace and privacy than at a public fountain or other open space.

At Night: Experience the magic of European cities at night. Go for a walk along well-lit streets. With gelato in hand, enjoy the parade of people, busy shops, and illuminated monuments. You'll invariably feel a sense of companionship when lots of people are around. Take advantage of the wealth of evening entertainment: concerts, movies, puppet shows, and folk dancing. Some cities offer tours after dark. You can see Paris by night on a river cruise.

During the evening, visit any café with wireless and send travel news to your friends and family. You'll find friendly answers in your inbox the next time you have the opportunity to get online.

If you like to stay in at night, get a room with a balcony overlooking a square. You'll have a front-row seat to the best show in town. Call a friend or your family (rates are cheap with an international phone card). Read novels set in the country you're visiting. Learn to treasure solitude. Go early to bed, be early to rise. Shop at a lively morning market for fresh rolls and join the locals for coffee.

Tips for Solo Women Travelers

Thanks to my female staffers and their friends for assembling their top tips for women.

Every year, thousands of women, young and old, travel to Europe on their own. You can, too, by using the same good judgment you use at home. Begin with caution and figure out as you travel what feels right to you. Create conditions that are likely to turn out in your favor, and you'll have a safer, smoother, more enjoyable trip.

Theft and harassment are two big concerns for women. If you've traveled alone in America, you're more than prepared for Europe. In America, theft and harassment

Stay in hostels to swap tales and advice with other adventurous women.

are especially scary because of their connection with assault. In Europe, you'll rarely, if ever, hear of violence. Theft is past tense (as in, "Where did my wallet go?"). As for experiencing harassment, you're far more likely to think, "I'm going to ditch this guy ASAP" than, "This guy is going to hurt me." Here are some tips for safe and pleasant travels:

Use street smarts. Be self-reliant and well prepared, so that you don't need to depend on someone unless you want to—carry cash, a map, a guidebook, and a phrase book. Walk purposefully with your head up; look like you know where you're going. If you get lost in an unfriendly neighborhood, be savvy about whom you ask for help; seek out another woman or a family, or go into a store or restaurant to ask for directions or to study your map.

When you use cash machines, withdraw cash during the day on a busy street, not at night when it's dark with too few people around.

Be proactive about public transportation. Before you leave a city, consider visiting the train or bus station you're going to leave from, so you'll know where it is, how long it takes to reach it, if it feels safe, and what services it has. Reconfirm your departure time. If you're leaving late at night and the bus or train station is sketchy, ask your B&B owner if you can hang out in their lounge or breakfast room—generally untouched in the evening—until you need to head for the station. Cafés, including busy Internet cafés with long hours, are also a safe and productive place to wait.

When taking the train, avoid sleeping in empty compartments. You're safer sharing a compartment with a family. If available, rent a *couchette* for overnight trains. For a small surcharge, you'll stay with like-minded roommates in a compartment you can lock, in a car monitored by an attendant. You'll wake reasonably rested with your belongings intact.

It's possible to ask for a female roommate on overnight trains. (You'll have better luck if the train isn't crowded.) Some countries, such as Spain, are better about accommodating these requests than others. On France's night trains, a one-bed compartment closest to the conductor is set aside for women, but it's the most expensive type of accommodation. In general, ask what your options are, make the request to bunk with other women, and hope for the best—but don't count on it.

Unless you're fluent in the language, accept the fact that you won't always know what's going on. Though it might seem worrisome, there's a reason why the Greek bus driver drops you off in the middle of nowhere. It's a transfer point, and another bus will come along in a few minutes. You'll often discover that the locals are looking out for you.

Learn how to deal with European men. In small towns, men are often more likely to speak English than women. If you never talk to men, you could miss out on a chance to learn about the country. So, by all means, talk to men. Just choose the man and choose the setting.

In northern Europe, you won't draw any more attention from men than you do in America. In southern Europe, particularly in Italy, you'll get more attention than you're used to, but it's usually in the form of the "long look"— nothing you can't handle. But be aware that in the Mediterranean

In Italy, sometimes blondes have more trouble.

Resources for the Woman Traveling Alone

Practical Advice

Gutsy Women: Travel Tips and Wisdom for the Road (Marybeth Bond, 2007). Funny, instructive, and inspiring ideas for solo travelers.

A Journey of One's Own: Uncommon Advice for the Independent Woman Traveler (Thalia Zepatos, 2003). Recommendations on everything from trekking in Nepal to handling sexual harassment.

Safety and Security for Women Who Travel (Sheila Swan and Peter Laufer, 2004). Tips on self-protection.

Traveling Solo: Advice and Ideas for More than 250 Great Vacations (Eleanor Berman, 2008). Advice on specific destinations for women.

Wanderlust and Lipstick: The Essential Guide for Women Traveling Solo (Beth Whitman, 2009). Empowering tales for nervous newbies from experienced women travelers.

Tales from the Road

The Best Women's Travel Writing: True Stories from around the World (Levinia Spalding, ed., published annually). An anthology of funny and inspirational tales.

Expat: Women's True Tales of Life Abroad (Christina Henry de Tessan, ed., 2002). A collection of stories about how the reality of life abroad matches up to the fantasy.

Go Your Own Way: Women Travel the World Solo (Faith Conlon and others, eds., 2007). Cultural revelations mixed with advice for the female traveler.

A Woman's Europe: True Stories (Marybeth Bond, ed., 2004). Europe from a totally female point of view.

Humor

Sand in My Bra and Other Misadventures: Funny Women Write from the Road (Jennifer L. Leo, ed., 2003). Travel shenanigans.

The Unsavvy Traveler: Women's Comic Tales of Catastrophe (Rosemary Caperton, Anne Mathews, and Lucie Ocenas, eds., 2001). A collection of hilarious and cathartic misadventures.

Adventures Abroad

Almost French: Love and a New Life in Paris (Sarah Turnbull, 2003). An amusing look at adopting a famously frosty city.

Eat, Pray, Love: One Woman's Search for Everything Across Italy, India, and Indonesia (Elizabeth Gilbert, 2006). Story of a quintessentially New Age voyage of discovery.

Long Ago in France: The Years in Dijon (M. F. K. Fisher, 1991). Remembrances from the celebrated American food writer of her life in France.

My Life in France (Julia Child, 2006). The inimitably zesty chef's recounting of her early days in Paris.

Tales of a Female Nomad: Living at Large in the World (Rita Golden Gelman, 2001). The true story of the ultimate female traveler, who sells all her possessions and goes on the road.

Without Reservations: The Travels of an Independent Woman and *Educating Alice: Adventures of a Curious Woman* (Alice Steinbach, 2000 & 2004). Travel chronicles from a Pulitzer Prize-winning columnist.

Websites

Hostelbookers (www.hostelbookers.com/article/travel-for-women). A guide to women's travel in Europe and a list of female-friendly European hostels.

JourneyWoman (www.journeywoman.com). A site jam-packed with travel resources just for women.

Nomadic Chick (www.nomadicchick.com). Lessons learned by a young blogger while traveling the world solo.

Wanderlust and Lipstick (www.wanderlustandlipstick.com). A one-stop site for women's travel.

world, when you smile and look a man in the eyes, it's often considered an invitation. Wear dark sunglasses and you can stare all you want.

Dress modestly to minimize attention from men. Take your cue from what the local women wear. For young women, even wearing a shapeless sack and sensible shoes may not ward off unwelcome advances. Try to stay with a group when exploring, and avoid walking alone at night, particularly in unlit areas with few people around. Don't be overly polite if you're bothered by someone; it's important to create boundaries to protect yourself. Use facial expressions, body language, and a loud firm voice to fend off any unwanted attention. If a man comes too close, say "no" firmly and loudly in the local language. That's usually all it takes.

If you feel like you're being followed or hassled, trust your instincts. Don't worry about overreacting or seeming foolish. Start screaming and acting crazy if the situation warrants it. Or head to the nearest hotel and chat up the person behind the desk until your would-be admirer moves on. Ask the hotelier to call you a cab to take you to your own hotel, hostel, or B&B.

Wear a real or fake wedding ring, and carry a picture of a real or fake husband. There's no need to tell men that you're traveling alone, or whether you're actually married or single. Lie unhesitatingly. You're traveling with your husband. He's waiting for you at the hotel. He's a professional wrestler who retired from the sport for psychological reasons.

If you're arranging to meet a guy, choose a public place. Tell him you're staying at a hostel: You have a 10 p.m. curfew and 29 roommates. Better yet, bring a couple of your roommates along to meet him. After the introductions, let everyone know where you're going and when you'll return.

By using common sense, making good decisions, and above all else, having confidence in yourself and your ability to travel on your own, you'll be rewarded with rich experiences—and great stories to tell your friends.

Family Travel

When parents tell me they're going to Europe and ask me where to take their kids, I'm tempted to answer, "to Grandma and Grandpa's on your way to the airport."

It's easy to make the case against taking the kids along. A European vacation with kids in tow is much more about playgrounds and petting zoos than about museums and churches. And traveling with kids is expensive. Out of exhaustion and frustration, you may opt for pricey con-

Leave the Kids at Home?

If you and your partner have 20 days for a family vacation, are on a budget, and are dreaming of an adult time in Europe, consider this plan: Go for 10 days without the kids and really enjoy Europe as adults rather than parents—the savings from leaving them at home will easily cover top-notch child care. Then fly home and spend the other 10 days with your kids—camping, at a water park, or just playing at home. (If your kids have an adult relative somewhere else in the US whom they'd enjoy getting to know better, offer to fly him or her to your house to kid-sit while you're gone.)

veniences like taxis and the first restaurant you find with a kid-friendly menu. Two adults with kids spend twice as much to experience about half the magic of Europe per day than they might without.

But if you can afford it and don't mind accomplishing less as adult sightseers, traveling with your children can be great family fun, creating piles of lifelong memories. Moreover, it's great parenting, as it helps get kids comfortable with the wider world.

Connecting with European families can be a highlight of a family vacation abroad.

With kids, you'll live more like a European and less like a tourist. Your children become your ambassadors, opening doors to new experiences and relationships. Your child will be your ticket to countless conversations. Some of your best travel memories may be of your son floating a wooden boat alongside Parisian garçons in the great pond at Luxembourg Garden, or of your daughter kicking a soccer ball with kids at a park in Madrid. Let them race their new Italian friends around Siena's main square, the Campo, while you sip your Campari.

European families, like their American counterparts, enjoy traveling. You'll find kids' menus, hotel playrooms, and kids-go-crazy zones at freeway rest stops all over Europe. Traveling with an infant or toddler can be challenging, but parents with a babe-in-arms will generally be offered a seat on crowded buses and sometimes allowed to go to the front

TRAVEL STYLES

of the line at museums.

The key to a successful European family vacation is to slow down and to temper expectations. Don't overdo it. Tackle one or two key sights each day, mix in a healthy dose of pure fun, and take extended breaks when needed. If done right, you'll take home happy memories to share for a lifetime.

At What Age Can I Take the Kids?

My children are young adults now, but, after taking them to Europe every year for their first 20 years, it's fun to think back about our European trips during different stages of their  childhood. When they were grade-schoolers, our trips were consumed with basic survival issues, such as eating, sleeping, and occupying their attention. By the time they entered their teens, the big challenge became making our trips educational and fun.

Some parents won't take their kids abroad until they are old enough to truly enjoy the trip. My rule of thumb is that children should be able to stand a day of walking, be ready to eat what's in front of them, and be comfortable sleeping in strange beds. They should be able to carry their own daypacks with some clothes, a journal, and a couple of toys. We found that a child is ready for an international trip at about the same age they're ready for a long day at Disneyland.

Grade-school kids are often the easiest travelers, provided you schedule some kid-friendly activities every day. They're happiest staying in rural places with swimming pools and grassy fields to run around in.

High-schoolers feel that summer break is a vacation they've earned. If this European trip is not *their* trip, you become the enemy. Make it their trip, too, by asking for their help—give each child who's old enough a location to research. Kids can quickly get excited about a vacation if they're involved in the planning stages. Consider your teen's suggestions and make real concessions. A day of shopping or at the beach might be more fun than another ruined abbey.

No matter what age your kids are, it helps to get them enthusiastic about what they'll be seeing in Europe. Before your trip, encourage your kids to learn about the countries, cities, sights, and people they'll be visiting. Even simple Wikipedia articles can provide enough background to pique a child's curiosity. Read books, fiction and non-fiction, set in the place you're going, such as *The Diary of Anne Frank* for Amsterdam or *The Thief Lord* for Venice. Watch movies together, such as *The Sound of Music* for Salzburg, *The Red Balloon* for Paris, or *The Secret of Roan Inish* for Ireland. Your hometown library can be a great resource for age-appropriate books and movies.

Get a jump on foreign phrases. Type out the top 20 or so and put them on the fridge for everyone to learn. Get a copy of the "10 Minutes a Day" book for your country's language—they come with preprinted sticky word labels that your kids will enjoy plastering onto your household items. Capitalize on whatever hobbies or games your children have that may relate to the history of the places you're visiting. Give your kids the chance to try out foreign specialties in advance by eating at ethnic restaurants, or get a cookbook and make meals together at home. Many US cities host celebrations of different cultures—look for festivals held by local communities of Greeks, Italians, Hungarians, or whatever group might be vibrant in your town or relevant to your family.

Travel Documents for Kids

You'll need the proper documents—even babies need passports. For a child of any age, take an official copy of his or her birth certificate, along with a photocopy of his or her passport. These documents are especially important if you have a different last name than your child. For parents of adopted children, it's a good idea to bring their adoption decree as well. Keep these documents separate from your passports, as they'll be a huge help if you end up needing to get a replacement passport for your child.

If you're traveling with a child who isn't yours (say, a niece or grandson), bring along a signed, notarized document from the parent(s) to prove to authorities that you have permission to take the child on a trip. Even a single parent traveling with children has to demonstrate that the other parent has given approval. Specifically, the letter should grant permission for

Family Travel Resources

Books

The Single Parent Travel Handbook (Brenda Elwell, 2002). Good tips for making the most out of traveling solo with your kids.

Cadogan Guides' *Take the Kids* and Fodor's *Around* series. Practical advice on making any destination child-friendly.

Take Your Kids to Europe (Cynthia Harriman, 2007). Lessons from firsthand family-travel experience, especially good for kids ages 6-16.

Travel with Babies and Young Children (Fawzia Rasheed de Francisco, 2008). The lowdown on "painless" travel with youngsters.

Travel with Children: Your Complete Resource (Brigitte Barta with others, 2009). Overall tips, including especially good advice on traveling with infants.

Travels with Baby: The Ultimate Guide for Planning Trips with Babies, Toddlers, and Preschool-Age Children (Shelly Rivoli, 2007). More baby-centered advice, organized by mode of travel, with a section on trips abroad.

What's more fun: a museum or the Eiffel Tower?

Websites

Ciao Bambino (www.ciaobambino.com). Mom-written, destination-focused advice and hotel reviews that focus on family-friendly features.

Travel for Kids (www.travelforkids.com). Fun things to do with kids in locations worldwide.

Travels with Baby (www.travelswithbaby.com). Companion online resources for book of same title (above).

Minitime (www.minitime.com). General resource, with tip sheets and printable packing checklists for babies and children.

the accompanying adult to travel internationally with the child. Include your name, the name of the child, the dates of your trip, destination countries, and the name, address, and phone number of the parent(s) at home.

You may want to bring extra passport photos with you. Since infants and toddlers change so quickly, carry pictures that were taken for the passport, as well as ones taken close to your departure date.

Most parents hold onto their kids' passports, but if you have older children who'll be out on their own, you could get them a money belt or neck pouch for carrying their cash and ID. For younger kids, be ready to drape a lanyard around their necks with emergency contact information, or consider ordering custom dog tags (see www.dogtagsonline.com). Another option is an ID Inside wristband, with a hidden pocket that holds a disposable ID card (www.id-inside.com). You can easily switch out the ID card, updating your hotel name and contact information as you go.

What to Bring

The amount and type of gear you need depends on the age of your child. Since a baby on the road requires a lot of equipment, the key to happiness is a rental car or a long stay in one place. If you're visiting friends or family, they may be able to borrow a car seat, stroller, and travel crib from local friends so you won't have to pack it. If you have older kids, let them know they'll be hauling their own luggage through airports and down cobblestone streets. Pack as light as you can, think hard about whether you'll really need everything (based on your experience taking trips near home)—and trust your judgment.

With little kids, I found having the best gear was more important than packing light. We would rent a car because taking everyone and everything on trains would have been miserable. Once the kids were

older, however, I insisted on being mobile, and we had a family ethic whereby everyone carried their own stuff...so they'd better pack light. (This book's packing tips apply to teens just as much as to adults.)

Infants and Toddlers: It's helpful to have a stroller and a baby carrier. Light umbrella strollers can easily navigate cobblestones—

just make sure you spend a little extra on a solidly built one that can take the bumps, such as Peg Pérego (www.pegperego.com) or Maclaren (www.maclarenbaby.com), and make sure it has a basket underneath for storing overflow items. Carriers are great for keeping your hands free and easier than a stroller on subways and buses.

Prepare to tote more than a tot. A combo purse/diaper bag with shoulder straps is ideal. You can always stow it in your stroller's basket, but be on guard: Purse snatchers target parents (especially while busy, as when changing diapers).

For years, we packed along a travel crib and it worked great—providing a safe and familiar zone for our toddler even in iffy hotel rooms. One travel model—the PeaPod—is a lightweight pop-up tent that fits in a small carry bag (www.kidco.com). BabyBjörn's travel crib is super lightweight and collapses down to the size of a suitcase (www.babybjorn .com). Portable playpens tend to be too heavy and clunky for travel. At a minimum, acclimate your baby to a bring-along sleep-sack blanket, which can be a comforting reminder of home once you are on the road.

Drivers should bring a car seat, buy one in Europe, or arrange one through the car-rental company (usually the most expensive option). Pack a car-seat clip in case you need to secure the car seat to the shoulder-strap seat belt. In addition to being required safety equipment while driving, a car seat can be a stress-saver when traveling by plane, train, or bus. Although it may seem like a bulky carry-on, a car seat is more comfortable for your child to sit in than a seat designed for an adult, and is a familiar place for a nap. Kids are used to car seats and know how to behave in them.

If your child drinks formula, do some research on the manufacturer's website—your usual formula may be available in Europe, but under a different name. Before you fly away, be sure you've packed acetaminophen (easy-dissolving tabs are best), diaper rash cream, a thermometer, and any special medications your baby may need (keeping in mind the air travel rules about liquids).

Older Kids: Today's technology can make the difference between a dream trip and a nightmare. Splurge for a portable DVD player, iPod, netbook, or tablet. Load up with kid-friendly apps, books, movies, and TV shows before you leave. Get a Y-jack so two kids can listen over headphones. There's nothing like a favorite show to help calm your kids before bedtime. A smartphone or a portable gaming device can fill long hours traveling between destinations and soak up time when dinner drags on. Consider giving each of your kids their own digital camera so they can take pictures and make movies from their own perspective.

(Back home, encourage them to get fancy with software to organize and edit photos and video clips.)

Toys: Don't worry about packing too many toys, which take up lots of suitcase space. You can easily buy toys and sports equipment in Europe. For the athletic child, a soccer ball guarantees hours of amusement with newfound friends on foreign turf. When you're in France or Italy, consider purchasing a set of bocce balls (called *boules* or *pétanque* in France); this popular form of outdoor bowling is played on public squares. (The balls are heavy, though, so only get them if you're staying in one place or traveling by car.)

For quiet time in the hotel room, buy a set of Legos once you're in Europe—they're excitingly different from those found in the US. A small indoor Frisbee is also fun.

Flying with Kids

Deciding whether to buy a separate plane ticket for your child under two years of age is a matter of what you can endure in the air: That cute gurgling baby might become the airborne Antichrist as soon as the seat-belt light goes off. If you elect to keep your child on your lap, you'll still pay the tax on the ticket cost for an international flight. The child doesn't get a seat, but many airlines have baby perks for moms and dads who request them in advance—roomier bulkhead seats, bassinets, and baby meals.

After age two, kids are required to have their own seat. Some airlines offer a children's fare, which is typically 85-90 percent of the adult fare. Other airlines simply charge the full fare—a major financial owie. Children's fares may not appear when booking tickets online, so it's worth calling a travel agent to see if they can get you a discount. From age 12 on, kids pay full fare.

As soon as you buy your plane tickets, immediately grab seat assignments so your family has a better chance of being seated together. Inquire about food service on your flight; most international flights still offer a complimentary meal, but be prepared to bring favorite familiar snacks for your crew.

Watching the in-flight movie can help pass a few hours in the air.

Pick flights with few connections; if your child is able to sleep on planes, a red-eye can work well. Decide if you want to sit near the aisle or window. A window seat gives your active child only one escape route, plus the added entertainment of the window. However, a toddler who needs frequent diaper changes and sits quietly may be more comfortable by the aisle.

At the airport, you'll have to clear security with your brood. It's easier for you (and everyone else in line) if you're ready before entering the security line: Take off jackets, untie shoes (children under 12 can leave their shoes on), pull out liquids. All your carry-ons, including children's bags, toys, and blankets, must go through the X-ray machine—explain beforehand that even "teddy" has to ride the conveyor belt. Children who can walk without assistance will be expected to go through the metal detector separately from their parents; babies can be carried through. You may encounter one of the new full-body scanners; you and your children can opt out of this type of screening, but you may be subjected to a thorough pat-down instead.

Some airlines have been phasing out early boarding for families or have resorted to charging for the privilege. If your carrier doesn't offer early boarding, approach the gate agent at a quiet moment and ask if he or she can help. Tire out your tykes before boarding the plane. Some airports have designated play spaces—if you can't find one, feel free to take over an empty gate area. If you fly at night, consider having your child skip that afternoon's nap. While you're waiting to board, get your kids up and moving as much as possible. Finally, when you're on the plane and it's time for sleep, follow normal bedtime routines. Change your child into pajamas, tuck her in with a blanket, and read a story or two.

Be prepared. Have at least one change of clothes and plenty of diapers and wipes for your baby or toddler (Mom and Dad might want to have an extra shirt, just in case). Make sure your electronics are fully charged before boarding. Don't forget to pack earbuds for everything, including handheld games (others on the plane will thank you). For younger kids, have lots of activities and surprises, such as books, stickers, paper, washable markers, dot-to-dot and maze books, Mad Libs, and small stuffed toys.

Jet lag can be kiddie purgatory. If you can tolerate some—OK, maybe a lot of—crankiness on the first day, keep young children awake until a reasonable bedtime. After Junior passes out from exhaustion, hopefully the whole family will sleep through the night and wake up when the locals do. Take it easy at the beginning (maybe even starting with a rural destination), allowing a couple of low-impact days to get over jet lag (for more on dealing with jet lag, see page 400).

Family-Friendly Lodging

Instead of picking up and moving every few days, some families prefer settling down in an apartment or house, using it as their home base, then side-tripping to nearby destinations. Self-catering flats rented by the week, such as *gîtes* in France and villas in Italy, give a family a home on the road. To cut costs, try home-sharing services that let you swap houses with a European family. Not only is it cheaper, but you get to spend time together cooking, watching movies, and just hanging out. It's a cultural experience just to see European TV together. But be aware that European standards on televised sex and nudity are much more relaxed than in the US; you might stumble on some uncensored movies, or even unbridled porn, right next to the Nickelodeon channel.

If you're traveling with older kids, consider hostels. Families can hostel very cheaply (especially in high-priced Scandinavia). Family membership cards are inexpensive, and there's no age limit. Hostels typically have members' kitchens where the family can cook and eat for the price of groceries. Some hostels offer family rooms with enough beds for all of you; these are also likely to offer a range of activities designed for kids.

If your kids love camping, rent a camper van or small RV. Kids and campgrounds—with swings, slides, and plenty of friends—mix wonderfully. Suddenly your family and the Spanish kids over at the next tent are best amigos.

Most hotels, especially those catering to business travelers, have large family rooms. London's big, budget chain hotels allow two kids to sleep for free in their rooms. Bonus: They'll sometimes have a swimming pool. Some European chains, such as KinderHotels, appeal to families by providing playrooms, baby equipment, and professional babysitters.

In some countries, you may need to know the necessary phrases to communicate your needs. If you're a family of four and your children are young, request a triple room plus a small extra child's bed. Traveling with teenagers, you may need two rooms: a double (one big bed) and a twin (a room with two single beds). In much of Europe, a "double" bed is actually two twins put together. These can easily be separated.

Be careful about staying in small hotels or B&Bs with a baby. If your child wakes up in the middle of the night, you're going to wake up everybody else. Some B&Bs won't take children, or impose an age limit (such as no kids under 8); ask before booking.

In very tight European hotel rooms, you might have to stow your kids in the closet...

Choosing lodging close to your daytime activities is smart if your little traveler needs to return for a nap or supplies. Having two adjoining rooms can be better for dealing with sleep issues: One jet-lagged person won't keep everyone else up, and napping will be easier. Request quiet rooms away from the street and bar downstairs. If your child is used to sleeping in his or her own space and you're all in one room, ask for one with a partition, large closet, or other area in which you can separate your child when it's bedtime (baby can even sleep in the bathroom).

If you have young children, child-proof the room immediately on arrival. A roll of masking tape makes quick work of electrical outlets. Place anything breakable up out of reach. (I find the top of a freestanding dresser works great as a kid-free zone.) Proprietors are generally helpful to considerate and undemanding parents.

With a toddler, budget extra to get a bath in your room—a practical need and a fun diversion. Some European showers have a 6-inch-tall "drain extension" and a high lip to create a kid-friendly bathing puddle.

...or, better yet, ask for an extra bed.

For more information on the types of accommodations mentioned above, see the Sleeping chapter.

Feeding Kids on the Road

Start the day with a good breakfast (at hotels, kids sometimes eat free). But even with a big breakfast, don't expect them to power through to a late lunch. A short snack break will help in the long run. Make sure

Find the most scenic perch for your picnic.

to pack along or stop to buy high-quality food as often as possible—a real sandwich, pasta, or yogurt.

Buying bread, cheese, fruit, and drinks in the morning means you can picnic anytime, anywhere. Foreign grocery stores are an adventure for kids, so bring them along and let them help shop. In each country, grocery stores have different kinds of kids' treats, some of which may end up being a real hit—sparking both a country-specific passion and great memories. Another fun (and cheap) option is to get take-out food, such as bratwurst, pizza by the slice, crêpes, or sandwiches, from a street stand. You can eat your meals on a square, at a park, or on the top deck of a tour bus.

Sample gelato, croissants, or chocolate every day (gelato should be twice a day)—whatever is a "specialty" treat of the country you're in. It's a great way to get off your feet and take a break.

At home, you may try to avoid bribes, but the promise of a treat can make a huge difference to everyone's cooperation when you're out and about—and don't have space for a "time out."

An occasional Big Mac or Whopper between all the bratwurst and kraut helps keep the family happy. You'll get your food relatively quickly, and the kids will almost always eat hamburgers, fries, or chicken nuggets. (And, at European fast-food joints, parents can often enjoy their own treat of a beer.)

Eating at European restaurants is a social event, but it can get stressful, since service is much slower than at home. Dinner can easily take two hours, so bring something to occupy the kids

Since many restaurants don't have high chairs, you might have to do a little juggling at mealtime.

while lingering. Skip the white-tablecloth places and hit self-service cafeterias, relaxed cafés, or bars (kids are welcome, though sometimes restricted to the restaurant section or courtyard area). Eat by 7 p.m. to miss the adult crowd. Don't expect high chairs to be available; use your stroller in a pinch.

In restaurants (or anywhere), if your infant is making a disruptive fuss, apologetically say the local word for "teeth" (*dientes* in Spanish, *dents* in French, *denti* in Italian, *Zähne* in German), and annoyed people will become sympathetic.

If you crave a leisurely, peaceful evening out, splurge on a babysitter. Hotels often can get sitters, usually from professional agencies. The service is expensive but worth it. With older kids, we enjoyed an adult break in a nicer, romantic restaurant by giving our teenagers enough money for dinner at a diner and turning them loose for the evening. It was an adventure for them, a welcome break for all involved, and we all shared our stories back at the hotel before bedtime.

Kid-Friendly Sightseeing

Review the day's plan at breakfast with the family. Let your kids make some decisions: choosing lunch spots or deciding which stores to visit. (The cheapest toy selection is usually in large department stores.) Turn your kid into your personal tour guide and navigator. If you use my guidebooks, deputize your child to lead you on my self-guided walks and museum tours.

Since a trip is a splurge for the parents, the kids should enjoy a larger allowance, too. Provide ample money and ask your kids to buy their own treats, *gelati*, postcards, and trinkets within that daily budget. Expect older kids to carry and use the currency. If you don't want your younger child to carry cash, you can be the "banker" and keep a tally of expenses.

Before buying sightseeing passes for your family, consider how many of the covered attractions will be top choices for your kids. It's not worth setting an exhausting whirlwind pace to race to every attraction just to make the pass pay for itself. Instead, make a short list of the places you and your kids really want to see, and calculate whether a pass makes sense; if not, buy individual admissions. And remember that some museums are free for kids under a certain age.

Make getting somewhere as much fun as the destination. Kids love subway maps, train schedules, and plotting routes. The Paris Métro is especially diverting, as many stations have boards that light up the route when you press the button for your destination. Even the automated ticket kiosks are entertaining. Allow time for all of this, rather than just rushing onto a subway train or bus. After a teaching run, let your child lead the family on subway journeys—kids love the challenge. An added perk: Train rides are free for infants and toddlers (and sometimes even for school-age children).

Boat and bus tours can also be a hit. Your kids might not care about the Crown Jewels, but they may go nuts riding the double-decker bus getting there. Boats are also memorable, such as a ride on a Venetian vaporetto or a glide down Amsterdam's canals.

Try a guided walking tour. Some parents are leery of group tours because they're afraid their kids will be the most disruptive members. But your kids will listen to a guide more than they will listen to you.

Hands-on activities, such as this candlemaking demonstration, bring museums to life for kids.

Being in a group of adults can tone down even the wildest child.

Hands-on tours, from cheesemaking to chocolate factories, keep kids engaged. Go to sports or cultural events, but don't insist on staying for the entire event.

European parks provide a wonderland of fun, including puppet shows, pony rides, merry-go-rounds, small zoos, or playgrounds. One of my favorite places to mix kid business with pleasure is Luxembourg Garden in Paris. They have cafés and people-watching for parents, and a play area full of imaginative slides, swings, jungle gyms, and chess games for kids. You'll also find a merry-go-round, pony rides, toy rental sailboats in the main pond, and *guignols* (French marionette shows).

Copenhagen's Tivoli Gardens is like a Hans Christian Andersen fairy tale, with games, marching bands, shows, and rides ranging from vintage cars to a Ferris wheel that resembles a clock. Petzi's World, based on a popular Danish cartoon bear, offers a cuddly array of rides and activities.

Kids need plenty of exercise. Allow time for stops at playgrounds or parks. Small towns often have great public swimming pools, and big cities have recreation centers or water parks (check out Paris' Aquaboulevard). Rent bikes for a quick and easy spin. Local tourist offices can help you dig up these treats.

On days when your troupe will need lots of staying power, don't wear

European amusement parks—such as Denmark's Legoland—are fun for kids of all ages.

them out with too much walking. It's worth taking a taxi to the Louvre to conserve leg power for getting to the *Mona Lisa*. At least every other day, take an extended break. Return to your hotel or apartment after lunch for two hours for napping, reading, or listening to the iPod. What you lose in sightseeing time, you will gain in energy levels.

Consider visiting an amusement park as an end-of-trip reward—the promise of Legoland in Denmark, Blackpool in England, or Disneyland Paris can keep your kids motoring through the more mundane attractions. Europe's open-air folk museums are a bonanza for families; it's worth a detour if your itinerary takes you near one (see page 305).

Big-Sight Survival with Kids

Europe is rich with amazing museums, churches, and art. But unlike you, kids may not appreciate the magnificence of a Michelangelo statue or the significance of an ancient temple frieze. Still, there are ways to liven up big sights. And whenever possible, go early or book ahead for big sights to avoid long lines (see my crowd-beating tips on page 295).

At Notre-Dame Cathedral, replay hunchback Quasimodo's stunt and climb the tower. Kids love being on such a lofty perch, face-to-face with a gargoyle. Using the ArtStart computers in London's National Gallery, kids can enter their interests (cats, naval battles, and so on) and print out a tailor-made tour map for free.

Museum audioguides are great for older children. Our kids liked them because they could pick and choose what they wanted to learn about.

Audioguides keep kids engaged and entertained at museums and on bus tours.

Bigger sights have audioguides tailored to the interests of school-age children. The Louvre, for example, offers themed audio tours on the ancient Egyptians or the life of a musketeer. For younger children, hit the gift shop first so they can buy postcards and have a scavenger hunt to find the pictured artwork. When boredom sets in, try "I spy" games or have them count how many babies or dogs they can spot in all the paintings in the room. Ask at the information desk for activity packets designed for children; you'll find these especially at museums in Great Britain.

Seek out kid-friendly museums. London's Natural History Museum offers a wonderful world of dinosaurs, volcanoes, meteors, and creepy-crawlies. You won't find "do not touch" signs at Florence's Leonardo Museum, where kids can use their energy to power modern re-creations of da Vinci's inventions. If you choose your destination carefully, everyone can enjoy, or at least tolerate, a museum visit.

Precautionary Measures

Even if you have the most well-behaved kids in the world, things happen: Kids wander off, or they get separated from you in a crowd. Whenever you're traveling with children in an unfamiliar place, it's good to have a go-to procedure in place in case something happens. Be sure to give each child a business card from your hotel so they have local contact information (for identification your kids can carry, see page 435).

When using public transportation, make sure everyone knows the final stop and have a backup plan for what to do if you lose each other (for example, plan to meet at your final stop or reconvene at your hotel).

In a crowded situation, having a unique family noise (a whistle or call, such as a "woo-woop" sound) enables you to easily get each other's attention. Consider buying walkie-talkies in Europe to help you relax when the kids roam (don't bring walkie-talkies from home, as ours use a different bandwidth and are illegal in Europe). You can also purchase a cheap pay-as-you-go mobile phone in Europe (explained on page 244); this can also be helpful in case of emergencies.

Europe is not the United States of Litigation. Europeans love children, but their sense of childproofing

The Steves Kids Vote on Britain's Best and Worst

Imagine being a teenager forced to spend a big part of your summer vacation with robo-tourist Rick Steves (alias Dad). Jackie and Andy did that a while ago. What were the highlights? Here are the results of the post-trip interview:

Best City: Blackpool—England's white-knuckle ride capital! The Pepsi Max Big One (one of the world's fastest and highest roller coasters) is still the best. A tip: Avoid the old wooden-framed rides. They're too jerky for parents.

Best Nature Experience: Horseback riding through the Cotswolds with a guide who'll teach you to trot. Wear long pants. One hour is plenty.

Types of Tours: Open-deck bus tours are good for picnic lunches with a moving view. At museums, audioguide tours are nice because you can pick and choose what you want to learn about.

Worst Food: The "black pudding" that so many B&B people want you to try for breakfast...it's a gooey sausage made of curdled blood.

Best New Food: Chocolate-covered digestive biscuits and vinegar on chips (that's British for "French fries").

Most Boring Tour: The Beatles tour in Liverpool: Most kids couldn't

---

public spaces is vastly different from ours. You may find a footbridge across a raging river has child-sized gaps between the railings. Windows in fourth-floor hotel rooms may be easy to open and unscreened. The hot water may scald you in about 30 seconds. Pay attention.

Reflecting and Connecting

Help your kids collect and process their observations. Buy a journal at your first stop, and it becomes a fun souvenir in itself. Kids like cool books—pay for a nice one. The journal is important, and it should feel that way. Encourage the kids to record more than just a trip log: Collect feelings, smells, tastes, reactions to cultural differences, and so on. Grade-school kids enjoy pasting in ticket stubs or drawing pictures of things they've seen (for more on journaling, see page 426).

It can be hard for kids to hang around grown-ups all day, so help

care less about where Paul McCartney went to grade school or a place called Strawberry Fields.

Funniest Activity: The Bizarre Bath walking tour is two hours of jokes and not a bit of history. It's irreverent and dirty—but in a way that parents think is OK for kids.

Best Activities: Leisure (LEZH-ur) Centres in almost every town have good swimming pools.

Best Theater: Shakespeare's Globe in London. First tour the theater to learn about how

and why it was built like the original from 1600. Then buy cheap "groundling" tickets to see the actual play right up front, with your elbows on the stage. The actors involve the audience...especially the groundlings.

Most Interesting Demonstrations: The precision slate-splitting demonstration at the slate mines in North Wales. The medieval knight at the Tower of London who explained his armor and then demonstrated medieval sword fighting tactics—nearly killing his squire.

your kids connect with other children. In hot climates, kids gravitate toward the squares (in cities and villages alike) when the temperature begins to cool in the late afternoon, often staying until late in the evening. Take your children to the European nightspots to observe—if not actually make—the scene (such as the rollerbladers at the Trocadéro in Paris or the crowd at Rome's Trevi Fountain).

Just a few phrases spoken by your kids will open many doors. Make a point of teaching them "thank you," "hello," and "good-bye" in the country's

Journaling trip experiences is fun for kids—and lets them create a personalized souvenir.

language. You'll find nearly everyone speaks English, but small phrases out of the mouths of babes will melt the cool of surly museum guards or harried shop clerks.

Older kids will want to keep in touch with friends at home and European pals they meet on their trip. If you're not traveling with a mobile device, from time to time buy an hour of computer time at an Internet café to placate your teen. Or, for a few euros, kids can purchase an international phone card and chat cheaply with friends back home. If you're traveling with a mobile phone, your kids can use it to text or send photos back to their friends in the US (but be sure you know the charges for international roaming; see page 238).

During the trip, your kids may complain about being parted from their friends or having to visit yet another museum. But don't lose heart—sometimes the pay-off comes years down the road. Your child may surprise you one day by mentioning a painting in Madrid's Prado or recalling a fact about Rome's Colosseum. Besides building memories, your investment in a trip now is a down payment on developing a true citizen of the world.

Savvy Seniors

More people than ever are hocking their rockers and buying plane tickets. Many senior adventurers are proclaiming, "Age matters only if you're a cheese." Travel is their fountain of youth. I'm not a senior—yet—so I put an appeal on the Travel Forums of my website (www.rick steves.com/forums) asking seniors to share their advice. Thanks to the many who responded, here's a summary of top tips from seniors who believe it's never too late to have a happy childhood. (For more suggestions, see page 785.)

Their fountain of youth is Europe!

When to Go: If you're retired and can travel whenever you want, it's smart to aim for shoulder season (April through mid-June, or September and October). This allows you to avoid the most exhausting things about European travel: crowds and the heat of summer.

Travel Insurance: Seniors pay more for travel insurance—but are also more likely to need it. Find out exactly whether and how your medical

---

Resources for Seniors

General Advice

AARP (American Association of Retired People), whose website is full of commonsense travel advice tailored for seniors (www .aarp.org/travel).

The Seasoned Traveler: A Guide for Baby Boomers and Beyond (George Bauer, 2006). Travel basics and special considerations for those over 70.

"Seniors on the Go," Ed Perkins' excellent online column (www .smartertravel.com/senior-travel).

Transitions Abroad's website, offering articles, volunteer programs, and links to more information for those over 60 (www .transitionsabroad.com, click on "Senior Travel").

Unbelievably Good Deals and Great Adventures That You Absolutely Can't Get Unless You're Over 50 (Joan Rattner Heilman, 2008). Making your age pay when traveling.

Retiring or Moving Overseas

The Grown-Up's Guide to Running Away from Home: Making a New Life Abroad (Rosanne Knorr, 2008). How-to guide for expatriate-in-training retirees.

How To Retire Overseas: Everything You Need To Know To Live Well (for Less) Abroad (Kathleen Peddicord, 2010). A primer for deciding how and where to live abroad.

Living Abroad series (Moon Books). A country-by-country series summing up the challenges and rewards of life overseas.

---

insurance works overseas. (Medicare is not valid outside the US except in very limited circumstances; check your supplemental insurance coverage for exclusions.) Pre-existing conditions are a problem, especially if you are over 70, but some plans will waive those exclusions. When considering additional travel insurance, pay close attention to evacuation insurance, which covers the substantial expense of getting you to adequate medical care in case of an emergency—especially if you are too ill to fly commercially. For more on travel-insurance options, see page 59.

Packing: Packing light is especially important for seniors—when you pack light, you're younger. To lighten your load, take fewer clothing items and do laundry more often. Fit it all in a roll-aboard suitcase—don't try to haul a big bag. Figure out ways to smoothly carry your luggage, so you're not wrestling with several bulky items. For example, if you bring a second bag, make it a small one that stacks neatly (or even attaches) on top of your wheeled bag.

Carry an extra pair of eyeglasses if you wear them, and bring along a magnifying glass if it'll help you read detailed maps and small-print schedules. A small notebook is handy for jotting down facts and reminders, such as your hotel-room number or Metro stop. Doing so will lessen your anxiety about forgetting these details, keeping your mind clear and uncluttered.

Medications and Health: It's best to take a full supply of any medications with you, and leave them in their original containers. Finding a pharmacy and filling a prescription in Europe isn't necessarily difficult, but it can be time-consuming. Plus, nonprescription medications (such as vitamins or supplements) may not be available abroad in the same form you're used to. Pharmacists overseas are often unfa-

Seniors can travel as footloose and fancy-free as their teenaged grandkids.

miliar with American brand names, so you may have to use the generic name instead (for example, atorvastatin instead of Lipitor). Before you leave, ask your doctor for a list of the precise generic names of your medications, and the names of equivalent medications. For more on getting medical help in Europe, see page 409.

If you wear hearing aids, be sure to bring spare batteries—it can be difficult to find a specific size in Europe. If your mobility is limited, you'll find more tips and resources later, under "Travelers with Disabilities."

Flying: If you're not flying direct, check your bag—because if you have to transfer to a connecting flight at a huge, busy airport, your carry-on bag will become a lug-around drag. If you're a slow walker, request a wheelchair or an electric cart when you book your seat so you can easily make any connecting flights. Since cramped legroom can be a concern for seniors, book early to reserve aisle seats (or splurge on roomier "economy plus," or first class). Stay hydrated during long flights, and take short walks hourly to minimize the slight chance of getting a blood clot.

Accommodations: If stairs are a problem, request a ground-floor room. Think about the pros and cons of where you sleep: If you stay near the train station at the edge of town, you'll minimize carrying your bag on arrival; on the other hand, staying in the city center gives you a convenient place to take a break between sights (and you can take a taxi on arrival to reduce lugging your bags). No matter where you stay, ask about

your accommodation's accessibility quirks before you book—find out whether it's at the top of a steep hill, has an elevator or stairs to upper floors, and so on.

Getting Around: Subways involve a lot of walking and stairs (and are a pain with luggage). Consider using city buses or taxis instead, and when out and about with your luggage, definitely take a taxi. If you're renting a car, be warned that some countries and some car-rental companies have an upper age limit—to avoid unpleasant surprises, mention your age when you reserve (for details, see the Driving chapter).

Senior Discounts: Just showing your gray hair or passport can snag you a discount at many sights, and even some events such as concerts. (The British call discounts "concessions"; look also for "pensioner's rates.") Always ask about discounts, even if you don't see posted information about one—you may be surprised. But note that at some sights, US citizens aren't eligible for senior discounts (partly because the US is notorious for not reciprocating).

Seniors can get deals on point-to-point rail tickets in Austria, Belgium, Great Britain, Finland, France, Germany, Italy, Spain, and Norway (including the Eurostar Chunnel crossing between Britain and France). Qualifying ages range from 60 to 67 years old. To get rail discounts in some countries—such as Austria, Britain, and Spain, and a second tier of discounts in France—you can purchase a senior card at a local train station (valid for a year, but worthwhile even on a short trip if you take several train rides during your stay). Most railpasses don't offer senior discounts, but passes for Britain and France do give seniors a discount in first class. It's rare, but a few airlines offer discounts to seniors. Always ask.

Sightseeing: Many museums have

Pilgrims of all ages hike from France to Santiago de Compostela in northwest Spain.

elevators, and even if these are freight elevators not open to the public, the staff might bend the rules for older travelers. Take advantage of the benches in museums; sit down frequently to enjoy the art and rest your feet. Go late in the day for fewer crowds and cooler temperatures. Many museums offer loaner wheelchairs. Take bus tours (usually two hours long) for a painless overview of the highlights. Boat tours—of the harbor, river, lake, or fjord—are a pleasure. Hire an English-speaking cabbie to take you on a tour of a city or region (if it's hot, spring for an air-conditioned taxi). Or participate in the life of local seniors, such as joining a tea dance at a senior center. If you're traveling with others but need a rest break, set up a rendezvous point. Some find that one day of active sightseeing needs to be followed by a quiet day to recharge the batteries. For easy sightseeing, grab a table at a sidewalk café for a drink and people-watching.

Educational and Volunteer Opportunities: For a more meaningful cross-cultural experience, consider going on an educational tour such as those run by Road Scholar (formerly Elderhostel), which offers study programs around the world designed for those over 55 (one to four weeks, call or check online for a free catalog, www.roadscholar.org, tel. 800-454-5768). For ideas on volunteer programs, see page 492.

Long-Term Trips: Becoming a temporary part of the community can be particularly rewarding. Settle down and stay a while, doing sidetrips if you choose. You can rent a house or apartment, or go a more affordable route and swap houses for a few weeks with someone in an area you're interested in (for more on apartments and home exchanges, see the Sleeping chapter).

Travelers with Disabilities

Thanks to Susan Sygall and the staff from Mobility International USA for this section.

More and more people with disabilities are heading to Europe, and more of us are looking for the Back Door routes. We, like so many of our non-disabled peers, want to get off the tourist track and experience the real France, Italy, or Portugal. Yes, that includes those of us who use wheelchairs. I've been traveling the "Rick Steves way" since about 1973—and here are some of my best tips.

I use a lightweight manual wheelchair with pop-off tires. I take a backpack that fits on the back of my chair and store my daypack underneath my chair in a net bag. Since I usually travel alone, if I can't carry it

Susan Sygall, in Italy's Cinque Terre

myself, I don't take it. I keep a bungee cord with me for the times I can't get my chair into a car and need to strap it in the trunk or when I need to secure it on a train. I always insist on keeping *my own* wheelchair up to the airline gate, where I then check it at the gate. When I have a connecting flight, I again insist that I use my own chair.

Bathrooms are often a hassle, so I have learned to use creative ways to transfer into narrow spaces. To be blatantly honest, when there are no accessible bathrooms in sight, I have found ways to pee discreetly just about anywhere (outside the Eiffel Tower or on a glacier in a national park). You gotta do what you gotta do, and hopefully one day the access will improve, but in the meantime there is a world out there to be discovered. Bring along an extra pair of pants and a great sense of humor.

I always try to learn some of the language of the country I'm in, because it cuts through the barriers when people stare at you (and they will) and also comes in handy when you need assistance in going up a curb or a flight of steps. Don't accept other people's notions of what is possible—I have climbed Masada in Israel and made it to the top of the Acropolis in Greece.

If a museum lacks elevators for visitors, be sure to ask about freight elevators. Almost all have them somewhere, and that can be your ticket to seeing a world-class treasure.

I always get information about disability groups in the places I am going. See the resources listed on page 458 for a number of helpful organizations. They have the best access information, and many times they'll become your new traveling partners and friends. They can show you the best spots. Remember that you are part of a global family of people with disabilities.

It can be useful to contact tourism offices and local transit providers before you travel. Some even include information on their websites about accessibility for people with disabilities.

Each person with a disability has unique needs and interests. Many of my friends use power wheelchairs, are blind or deaf, or have other disabilities—they all have their own travel tips. People who have difficulty walking long distances might want to think about taking a lightweight wheelchair or borrowing one when needed—many places in Europe have mobility scooter rentals, and bike shops are excellent for tire repairs if you get a flat. Whether you travel alone, with friends, or with an assistant, you're in for a great adventure.

Don't confuse being flexible and having a positive attitude with settling for less than your rights. I expect equal access and constantly let people know about the possibility of providing access through ramps or other modifications. When I believe my rights have been violated, I do whatever is necessary to remedy the situation, so that the next traveler or disabled person in that country won't have the same frustrations.

Keep in mind that accessibility can mean different things in different countries. In some countries, people rely more on human-support systems than on physical or technological solutions. People may tell you their building is accessible because they're willing to lift you and your wheelchair over the steps at the entryway. Be open to trying new ways of doing things, but also ask questions to make sure you are comfortable with the access provided.

Hopefully more books will include accessibility information, which will allow everyone to see Europe "through the Back Door." Let's work toward making that door accessible so we can all be there together.

Tips for Travelers with Disabilities

If you don't travel much, speak to someone with a similar disability who has traveled before. Consult with your travel agent, hotel, airline, and others to understand the services available for your trip, or contact disability organizations overseas at your destination (list available at www .miusa.org).

Tours: If you'd rather not go it alone, several groups run accessible tours to Europe, including:
- **Accessible Journeys:** Wheelchair trips to Britain, France, and Holland (www.disabilitytravel.com, tel. 800-846-4537)
- **Flying Wheels Travel:** Escorted tours to Great Britain and France, plus custom itineraries (www.flyingwheelstravel.com, tel. 877-451-5006)
- **Nautilus Tours and Cruises:** Tours to France, Belgium, and the Netherlands, plus cruises to other destinations (www.nautilustours .com, tel. outside California 800-797-6004, tel. in California 818/591-3159, may close in 2014)
- **Accessible Europe:** Collection of European travel agents and tour operators who specialize in disabled travel (www.accessibleurope .com)

- **Sage Traveling:** Organization helping people with disabilities plan their European vacations and providing accessibility reviews of European destinations (www.sagetraveling.com).

Medical Issues: If needed, see your physician before your trip to identify your health-care needs during the trip. You may want to carry medical-alert information and a letter from your health-care provider describing your medical condition, medications, potential complications, and other pertinent medical information. Carry sufficient prescription medication to last your entire trip. For more on health issues, see page 399.

Medical treatment and hospital care abroad can be expensive. Buying short-term health insurance and emergency assistance policies is a good

idea. Read the policies' definitions of pre-existing conditions to make sure any needs you have are covered (see page 63).

Travelers' Rights: Know your rights as a traveler with a disability. If, under the Americans with Disabilities Act, you feel you have been discriminated against (such as not being allowed on a US tour company's trip to Europe because of your disability), call the US Department of Justice ADA Information Line at 800-514-0301 or 800-541-0383 TTY, or visit www.ada.gov. The US Department of

Many of Europe's newer trains are fully accessible to people who use wheelchairs.

Transportation's Aviation Consumer Protection Division (ACPD) handles complaints regarding the Air Carrier Access Act, and has a toll-free Disability Hotline (tel. 800-778-4838 or 800-455-9880 TTY, http://airconsumer.ost.dot.gov).

Traveling with Service Animals: Allow plenty of time to obtain the necessary documents if you plan to travel with your service animal. It can take weeks or months to obtain the necessary documentation, and guide dogs must meet health standards to avoid quarantines. Refer to the helpful tip sheet available at www.miusa.org/ncde/tipsheets/service dogs. Assistance Dogs Europe (www.assistancedogseurope.org) and the International Association of Assistance Dog Partners (www.iaadp.org) can provide overseas contacts.

Exchange Opportunities: If you are interested in studying, teaching, researching, or volunteering abroad, contact the National Clearinghouse on Disability and Exchange (NCDE) at Mobility International USA for

Resources for Travelers with Disabilities

Mobility International USA (MIUSA): Empowers people with disabilities to take part in international exchange, including work, study, teaching, volunteer, and research opportunities abroad. Their comprehensive website, intended for people with disabilities who want to travel with a purpose (not for leisure/vacation), includes useful tips on air travel, insurance, and general funding, as well as inspiring stories about people with disabilities who have done exchanges in Europe.

MIUSA also publishes the useful book *Survival Strategies for Going Abroad: A Guide for People with Disabilities* (available for free online), offers an online database of disability organizations, periodically sponsors international exchange programs for people with disabilities, and oversees the National Clearinghouse on Disability and Exchange, which publishes *AWAY (A World Awaits You)*, about people with disabilities doing international exchange (www.miusa.org, tel. 541/343-1284, info@miusa.org).

Society for Accessible Travel and Hospitality (SATH): Publishes an online travel magazine and offers travel advice (www.sath.org).

MossRehab ResourceNet: A clearinghouse with links to many accessible travel resources (www.mossresourcenet.org/travel.htm).

Emerging Horizons: Travel info for wheelchair users and slow walkers (www.emerginghorizons.com).

Access Abroad: A good resource for students with disabilities planning to study abroad (www.umabroad.umn.edu/professionals/accessabroad.php).

Flying with Disability: Advice for traveling by air (www.flying-with-disability.org).

Overseas Interpreting Company: For deaf individuals looking for sign-language interpreting in Britain and the European Union (http://overseasinterpreting.com).

Rick Steves' Easy Access Europe: While my guidebook for travelers with mobility challenges is out of print and several years out of date, it still offers lots of helpful information for London, Paris, Bruges, Amsterdam, Haarlem, and the Rhine River. To access the content of this book for free online, go to www.ricksteves.com/easyaccess.

free information and referrals (www.miusa.org/ncde). Whether you're considering traveling abroad to learn a new language, or looking for a way to make your experience more meaningful by volunteering, the NCDE has resources to answer many of your questions.

Visually Impaired: The book *Sites Unseen: Traveling the World Without Sight* (available in Braille and other formats) helps make travel to Europe accessible. Blind author Wendy David talks about her personal experience traveling in the US and Europe, giving tips on riding public transportation, navigating around town, and figuring out currency.

Bus Tour Self-Defense

Many American tourists see Europe on an organized bus tour and don't even consider using a guidebook. Instead, they pay a company to organize their trip and provide a professional guide.

A typical big-bus tour has a professional, multilingual European guide and 40-50 people sharing 50 seats. The tour company is probably very big, booking rooms by the thousands; it often even owns the hotels it uses. Typically, the bus is luxurious and fairly new, with a high, quiet ride, comfy seats, air-conditioning, and a toilet on board. Tour hotels fit American standards—large, not too personal, and offering mass-produced comfort, good plumbing, and double rooms, though often on the outskirts of town.

Some tours deliver exactly what they promise.

Unfortunately, most of the tour groups that unload on Europe's quaintest towns experience things differently from the way independent travelers do. On the biggest tours, groups are treated as an entity: a mob to be fed, shown around, profited from, and moved out. If money is saved, it can be at the cost of real experience. For me, the best travel values are enjoyed not by gazing through the tinted windows of a tour bus, but by experiencing Europe on my own.

Big, cheap bus-tour meals can be another lowlight. Included meals can often be forgettable buffets that hotel restaurants require large groups to take. A common complaint among tourists is that hotel meals don't match the country's cuisine. While this generally isn't true at smaller, family-run hotels and pensions, meals can be a big disappointment in the larger, impersonal tourist hotels.

Generally speaking, the bigger the group, the more you're cut off from Europe's charms. When 50 tourists drop into a "cozy" pub, any coziness is trampled. A good stop for a guide is one with great freeway accessibility and bus parking; where guides and drivers are buttered up with free coffee and cakes (or even free meals); where they speak English and accept credit cards; and where 50 people can go to the bathroom at the same time. *Arrivederci, Roma.*

Many who take an organized bus tour could have managed fine on their own.

All that said, many people find that tours are the best way to scratch their travel itch. Having someone else do the driving, arrange the hotels, and make the decisions takes the stress and work out of travel. Tours can also be the most economical way to see Europe: Large tour companies book thousands of rooms and meals year-round, and with their tremendous economic clout, they can get prices that no individual tourist can match. For instance, on a tour with Cosmos (one of the largest and cheapest tour companies in Europe), travelers get fine rooms with private baths, some restaurant meals, bus transportation, and the services of a European guide—all for less than $150 a day. Considering that many hotel rooms alone cost around $150, that all-inclusive tour price is great. For people looking to travel comfortably and cheaply, tours can be a good option—and if you've got an excellent guide, it can be a great one.

Choosing a Tour

Although I advocate independent travel, I'm not anti-tour. In fact, my company offers tours. I started my career leading big-bus tours for other companies, figured out what didn't work, and then designed my own tours. Three decades later, they're still going strong. (Last year we had our best year ever, taking nearly 12,000 travelers on more than 400 tours with more than three dozen itineraries.)

Our tours sidestep the predictable pitfalls because we pay our guides well and forbid kickbacks (making their focus the tour members' experience, not padding their own paycheck), we keep our groups small (20-28 people), we include plenty of free time and actively teach our tour members how to best use it, and we use friendly, local hotels and restaurants

Comparing Tours

When you're selecting a tour, the cost you're quoted isn't the only factor to consider. Investigate how many people you'll be traveling with as well as what extras you'll be expected to cover. Most tour companies include customer feedback on their websites— look around and see what previous tour members have to say.

When comparing prices, remember that airfare is not included. The chart below illustrates what to expect from a range of tour companies.

	High-End Tours	Rick Steves Tours	Low-End Tours
Price per day	$350-915	$200-300	$120-285
Group Size	20-40	20-28	40-50
Meals	50-75% included	50% included	35-50% included
Sightseeing	All included	All included	Most cost extra
Tips	All except guide's tip included	All included	None included

that other tours are too big to use. We also offer "unguided" tours, which only include transportation and accommodations; these are designed for people who don't want to be tied down to a daily schedule. For all the details, and to get our Tour Catalog and a free Rick Steves Tour Experience DVD (filmed on location during an actual tour), visit www .ricksteves.com or call the Tour Department at 425/608-4217.

There are probably hundreds of tour companies to choose from. The predictable biggies range from high-end expensive (Abercrombie & Kent, Maupintour, and Tauck) to low-end cheap (Cosmos, Globus, Insight, and Trafalgar); every company has a website where you can get more info. Groupon and other sites advertise "flash sale" tours which sound fun and spontaneous, but require you to make a quick decision on a multi-thousand-dollar purchase that's nonrefundable. If you're willing to take the risk (though I wouldn't), scrutinize the fine print and compare rates elsewhere before committing.

No matter which tour company you go with, it's important to do your research. Start by browsing your options online, asking friends, or talking to a travel agent for advice. When considering tours, remember that some of the best sellers are those that promise more sightseeing than is reasonable in a given amount of time. No tour can give you more than 24 hours in a day or 7 days in a week. What a wide-ranging "blitz" tour can do is give you more hours on the bus. Choose carefully among the itineraries available. Do you really want a series of one-night stands? Bus drivers call tours with ridiculous itineraries "pajama tours." You're in the bus from 8:00 a.m. until after dark, so why even get dressed?

Hotel location is important. It can make the difference between a fair trip and a great trip. Beware: Some tour companies save money by parking you in the middle of nowhere. If the tour brochure says you'll be sleeping in the "Florence area," that could be halfway to Bologna (and you'll spend half your sightseeing time on transportation to and from the city center). Centrally located hotels maximize your sightseeing efficiency. Get explicit locations in writing before your trip.

The cheapest bus tours are impossibly cheap. There's literally no profit in their retail price. They can give you bus transportation and hotels for about what the tourist-off-the-street would pay for just the hotels alone. But there's a catch: These tours tend to charge extra for sightseeing, and make money by taking you to attractions and shops from which they receive kickbacks. However, savvy travelers on a tight budget can actually get the last laugh on these tours by thinking of them as a tailored bus pass with hotels tossed in. Skip out of the shopping, don't buy any of the optional tours, equip yourself with a guidebook, and every day you can do your own sightseeing. Just apply the skills of independent travel to the efficient, economical trip shell an organized coach tour provides.

Your Tour Guide

Guides generally prefer to spoon-feed Europe to you—from their menu. Sights may be chosen for their convenience rather than merit. Many tours seem to make a big deal out of a statue in Luzern called the Lion Monument. When the guide declares this mediocre sight is great, obedient tourists "ooh" and "ah" in unison. What makes it "great" for the guide is that the Lion Monument has easy tour-bus parking. However, Leonardo da Vinci's *Last Supper* in Milan may be passed over, because it's expensive to visit and its mandatory reservation system is inconvenient.

To most guides, the best group is one that lets them do the thinking and is happy to be herded around. As long as people on board don't think too much or try to deviate from the plan, things go smoothly and reliably,

The standard European guide does the leading...and you do the following.

Questions to Ask Tour Companies

Nail down the price:

- What does the price include? (How many nights and days? How many meals? Admission to sights? Exactly what kind of transportation?)
- If currency values fluctuate, is the tour price adjusted up or down?
- If the tour doesn't fill up, will the price increase?
- Do singles pay a supplement? Can singles save by sharing rooms?
- Are optional excursions offered? Daily? Average cost?
- Is trip interruption/cancellation insurance included?
- Will the guide and driver expect to be tipped? How much?
- Are there any other costs?

Run a reality check on your dream trip:

- How many travelers will be on the tour?
- Roughly what is the average age and singles-to-couples ratio?
- Are children allowed? What is the minimum age?
- Are hotels located downtown, or are they on the outskirts?
- Does each room have a private bathroom? Air conditioning?
- How many meals are eaten at the hotel? Are menus fixed?
- What is your policy if you have to cancel a tour?
- What are your refund policies before and during the tour?
- How can I see tour evaluations from past customers?

and you really will see (but not necessarily experience) a lot.

Tour companies often put guides in a difficult position. Many companies pay their guides little (or even no) wage. The guides then earn their living from: 1) commissions on the optional daily sightseeing excursions they sell; 2) kickbacks on the souvenirs their group buys from retailers the tour patronizes; and 3) trip-end tips. An experienced and aggressive guide can make $300-500 a day.

Empathize with your guide. Leading a tour is a demanding job with lots of responsibility, paperwork, babysitting, and miserable hours. Very often, guides are tired. They're away from home and family, often for months on end, and are surrounded by foreigners having an extended party that they're probably not in the mood for. Most guides treasure their time alone and keep their distance from the group socially. Each tourist has personal demands, and a big group can amount to one big pain in the bus for the guide.

How to Enjoy a Bus Tour

Be informed. Tour guides call the dreaded tourist with a guidebook an "informed passenger." But a guidebook is your key to travel freedom. Get maps and tourist information from your (or another) hotel desk or a tourist information office. Tour hotels are often located outside the city, which makes tour members more likely to book the tour's optional sightseeing excursions just to get into town. Ask the person behind the desk how to catch public transportation downtown. Taxis are always a possibility, and, with three or four people sharing, they're affordable. Team up with others on your tour to explore on your own.

Remember that it's your trip. Don't let bus tour priorities keep you from what you've traveled all the way to Europe to see. In Amsterdam, some tour companies instruct their guides to spend time in the diamond-polishing place instead of the Van Gogh Museum (no kickbacks on Van Gogh). Skip out if you like. Your guide may warn you that you'll get lost and the bus won't wait. Keep your independence (and your hotel address in your money belt).

Discriminate among optional excursions. While some activities may be included (such as half-day city sightseeing tours), each day one or two special excursions or evening activities, called "options," are offered for $30-50 each. Your guide promotes excursions because he or she profits from them. Don't be pressured. Compare prices. Ask your hotelier, or check a guidebook for the going rate for a gondola ride, Seine River cruise, or whatever. While you are capable of doing plenty on your own, optional excursions can be a decent value—especially when you factor in the value of your time. Some options are cheaper through your tour than from the hotel concierge. Some meals are actually a better value with the group.

Some options, however, aren't worth the time or money. While illuminated night tours of Rome and Paris are marvelous, I'd skip most "nights on the town." On the worst kind of big-bus-tour evening, several bus tours come together for an evening of "local color." Three hundred Australian, Japanese, and American tourists drinking watered-down sangria and watching flamenco dancing on stage to the rhythm of their digital camera bleeps is big-bus tourism at its grotesque worst.

If you shop...shop around. Many people make their European holiday one long shopping spree. This suits your guide and the local tourist industry just fine. Guides are quick to say, "If you haven't bought a Rolex, you haven't really been to Switzerland," or "You can't say you've experienced Florence if you haven't bargained for and bought a leather coat."

Don't necessarily reject your guide's shopping tips; just keep in mind that the prices you see often include a 10-20 percent kickback. Tour guides are clever at dominating your time, making it difficult for shoppers to get out and discover the going rate for big purchases. Don't let them rush you. Never swallow the line, "This is a special price available only to your tour, but you must buy now."

Keep your guide happy. Independent-type tourists tend to threaten guides. Maintain your independence without alienating your guide. Don't insist on individual attention when the guide is hounded by countless others. Wait for a quiet moment to ask for advice or offer feedback.

A well-chosen tour can be a fine value, giving you a great trip and a breakfast table filled with new friends.

If a guide wants to, he can give his entire group a lot of extras—but when he pouts, everyone loses. Your objective, which requires some artistry, is to keep the guide on your side without letting him take advantage of you.

Seek out unjaded locals. The locals most tour groups encounter are hardened businesspeople who put up with tourists because they have to—it's their livelihood. Going through Tuscany in a flock of 50 Americans following the tour guide's umbrella, you'll meet all the wrong Italians. Break away. One summer night in Regensburg, I skipped out. While my tour was still piling off the bus, I enjoyed a beer—while overlooking the Danube and under shooting stars—with the great-great-great-grandson of the astronomer Johannes Kepler.

Cruising in Europe

I once spoke to the CEO of a cruise line, who, in a previous career, sold children's snacks. As bizarre as that connection may seem, he explained to me how adults retain a natural, childlike impulse to explore, coupled with the need for a safe home to return to. While travelers love to get out of their comfort zones, doing so leads many of us to yearn all the more for a refuge or nest. Cruise ships cater to this expertly, by greeting passengers with a welcome table, cold drinks, and friendly smile. On my first cruise, even I remember thinking, as I returned to my ship, "Whew...we're safely back home now."

I'm not pro-cruise or anti-cruise. Taking a cruise can be a fun, affordable, time-efficient, low-hassle, and comforting way to experience Europe—provided you do it smartly. But it's important to choose the right cruise, keep your extra expenses to a minimum, and equip yourself with good information to make the absolute most of your time in port (covered in detail by my *Mediterranean Cruise Ports* and *Northern European Cruise Ports* guidebooks, which equip cruisers with information to travel smartly during their precious shore time). Here are a few insights and suggestions for deciding whether or not to cruise—and then, if you choose to, how to make the best of your experience.

Is Cruising for You?

Short of sleeping on a park bench, I haven't found a more affordable way to see certain parts of Europe than cruising. On a Mediterranean cruise that includes room, board, transportation, tips, and port fees, a couple can pay as little as $100 per night—that's as much as a budget hotel room in many cities. Compared to what it costs to travel on your own—for hotels, railpasses, restaurants, and so on—the base price of mainstream cruises beats independent travel by a mile.

Cruising also works well for travelers who prefer to tiptoe into Europe, rather than dive right in. Cruising can serve as an enticing sampler of bite-sized visits, helping you decide where you'd like to return to and spend more time.

It's also great for retirees (or families traveling with retirees), particularly those with limited mobility. Cruising rescues you from packing up your bags and huffing to the train station every other day. Once on land, accessibility for wheelchairs and walkers can vary dramatically—though some cruise lines offer excursions specifically designed for those who don't walk well. A cruise aficionado who had done the math once told me that, if you know how to find the deals, it's theoretically cheaper to cruise indefinitely than to pay for a retirement home.

Of course, independent, free-spirited travelers may not appreciate the constraints of cruising. For some, seven or eight hours in port is way too short, a tantalizing tease of a place where they'd love to linger for the evening—and the obligation to return to the ship every night is frustrating. If you're self-reliant, energetic, and want to stroll the cobbles of Europe at all hours, cruising probably isn't for you. Even so, even some seasoned globetrotters find that cruising is a good way to travel comfortably on a shoestring budget.

There are different types of cruisers. Some travelers cruise because it's such an efficient way to experience so many ports of call. They appreciate the convenience of traveling while they sleep, waking up in an interesting new destination each morning, and making the most out of every second they're in port. This is the "first off, last on" crowd that attacks each port like a footrace. You can practically hear their imaginary starter's pistol go off when the gangway opens.

Other cruisers come to enjoy the cruise experience itself. They enjoy basking by the pool, taking advantage of onboard activities, dropping some cash at the casino, running up a huge bar tab, and watching ESPN on their stateroom TV.

If you really want to be on vacation, aim for somewhere in the middle. Be sure to experience the ports that really tickle your wanderlust, but give yourself a "day off" every now and again in the less enticing ports to sleep in or hit the beach.

How Cruises Operate

Understanding how the cruise industry makes money can help you take advantage of your cruise experience...and not the other way around. Cruising is a $30-billion-a-year business. Approximately one out of every five Americans has taken a cruise, and each year about 15 million people take one.

In order to compete for passengers and fill megaships, cruise lines offer fares that can be astonishingly low. In adjusted dollars, the price of cruises hasn't risen for several decades. Your cruise fare covers accommodations, all the meals you can eat in the ship's main dining room and buffet, and transportation from port to port. You can have an enjoyable voyage and not spend a penny more on board (though you'd still have some expenses in port). But the cruise industry is adept at enticing you with extras that add up quickly: alcohol, gambling (at onboard casinos), and cruise-company-run excursions. Other temptations include specialty restaurant surcharges, duty-free shopping, fitness classes, spa treatments, and photos.

It's very easy to get carried away—a round of drinks here, a night of blackjack there. First-timers are often astonished when they get their final onboard bill, which can easily exceed the original cost of the trip. But with a little self-control, you can easily limit your extra expenditures, making your supposedly cheap cruise *actually* cheap. You always have the right to say, "No, thanks" to these additional expenses.

Cruise lines are able to remain profitable largely on the backs of their low-paid crews, who mostly hail from the developing world. Crew members work 10 to 14 hours a day (or more), 7 days a week, for up to 10 months at a time—with few or no days off. A base salary of about $1 a day is typical, so most of their income comes from tips (which can add up to what would be considered a very good salary in their homeland). Is this exploitation or empowerment? Socially conscious cruisers wrestle with this question as the trip goes on.

Choosing a Cruise

Selecting a cruise that matches your travel style and philosophy is critical. Each cruise line has its own distinct personality, quirks, strengths, and weaknesses. Cruise lines fall into four basic price categories: mass-market (Royal Caribbean, Norwegian, Carnival, and Costa), premium (Celebrity, Holland America, and Princess), luxury (Azamara Club, Oceania, and Windstar), and ultra-luxury (Crystal, Regent Seven Seas, and Seabourn).

Ask your cruising friends about their favorite cruise lines, examine cruise-line brochures and websites, read reviews online (at www.cruisecritic .com, www.cruisediva.com, www.cruisemates .com, and www.avidcruiser.com), and browse guidebooks (including my *Mediterranean Cruise Ports* guide).

Here are a few factors to keep in mind:

• **Price.** In addition to the base fare, you'll pay taxes and port fees (which can be hundreds of dollars per person), and an "auto-tip" of around $10/day per person will be added to your bill. Also remember to budget for all the aforementioned "extras" you might wind up buying from the cruise line.

• **Destinations.** If you have a wish list of ports, use it as a starting point when shopping for a cruise.

• **Time spent in port.** If exploring European destinations is your priority, look carefully at how much time the ship spends in each port; this can vary by hours from cruise line to cruise line.

• **Ship size.** The biggest ships offer a wide variety of restaurants, activities, entertainment, and other amenities (such as resources for kids)—but foster a herd mentality, and crowded shore experience for passengers. Smaller ships offer fewer crowds, access to out-of-the-way ports, and less hassle when disembarking, but they also have fewer onboard amenities and generally cost much more.

• **Onboard amenities.** Decide which features matter to you most, including food (both quality and variety of restaurants), entertainment, athletic facilities, children's resources, and so on.

Booking a Cruise

While it's possible to book directly with the cruise line, most cruises are booked through travel agencies. There are two different types of cruise-sales agencies: your neighborhood travel agent, where you can get in-person advice, or a giant cruise agency, which sells most of its inventory online or by phone. Several big cruise agencies have user-friendly comparison-shopping websites (such as www.vacationstogo.com, www.cruisecompete.com, and www.crucon.com).

Most cruise lines post their cruise schedules a year or more in advance. The earlier you book, the more likely you'll have your choice of sailing and of cabin type—and potentially an even better price (cruise lines typically offer discounts for booking at least 6-12 months before departure). While last-minute deals (usually within 90 days of departure) are fairly common on Caribbean cruises, they're relatively rare for European ones—and last-minute airfares to Europe can be that much more expensive.

Like cars or plane tickets, cruises are priced very flexibly. In general, for a mass-market cruise, you'll rarely pay the list price. (Higher-end cruises are less likely to be discounted.) It's common to see sales and other incentives, such as reduced fares to free upgrades to onboard credit or other extras.

While most cruise lines are willing to arrange your airfare to and from the cruise, you'll typically save money (and gain flexibility) by booking flights on your own. Allow plenty of time—ideally an overnight—before meeting your cruise; if your flight is delayed and you miss your ship, you're on your own to figure out how you'll meet it at the next port.

Cruising Tips

Eating: Most cruise lines offer a wide range of onboard restaurants: traditional dining rooms (with a semi-formal dress code and assigned seating every night), more casual buffet restaurants, room service whenever you want it, and a variety of specialty restaurants. Avoid this last kind of restaurant if you're on any kind of budget—besides costing you a $10-30 cover charge, certain entrées incur a "supplement" ($10-20). A couple

Excursion Cheat Sheet

This simplified roundup shows which Mediterranean ports are best by excursion and which are doable for on-the-ball travelers who enjoy using a guidebook. For detailed instructions in each destination, see my *Mediterranean Cruise Ports*, dedicated to helping people cruise "through the Back Door." (Baltic cruisers should look for my *Northern European Cruise Ports*.)

Destination (Port)	Excursion?
BARCELONA	No
Shuttle bus from terminal drops you right in town	
PROVENCE (Marseille/Toulon)	Yes
Wide range of worthwhile destinations far from the ugly ports; an excursion can hit several of these with ease	
FRENCH RIVIERA (Nice/Villefranche/Monaco)	No
Entire region is easy to navigate by train or bus	
FLORENCE, PISA, LUCCA (Livorno)	Maybe
These cities are cheap and reasonably easy to reach by public transportation, but excursions offer a no-hassle connection that also includes tours of the major sights in each city	
ROME (Civitavecchia)	Maybe
Easy, direct train trip into town, but an excursion could help you navigate this big city	
AMALFI COAST (Naples/Sorrento)	Yes
Narrow roads of the Amalfi Coast are often snarled by traffic; an excursion gives you peace of mind that the ship won't leave without you	

ordering specialty items and a bottle of wine can quickly run up a $100 dinner bill.

In general, water, coffee, tea, milk, iced tea, and juice are included. Other drinks cost extra: alcohol of any kind, name-brand soft drinks, fresh-squeezed fruit juices, and premium espresso drinks (lattes and cappuccinos). To encourage alcohol sales, many cruise lines limit how much alcohol that guests can bring on board, or prohibit them from bringing any at all.

Destination (Port)	Excursion?
NAPLES AND POMPEII (Naples/Sorrento)	No
Within Naples, everything is easy to reach by foot or bus; the ruins at Pompeii are a quick train ride away	
VENICE	No
Getting downtown is easy by public transportation; even walking there is delightful in this unique city	
SPLIT	No
Port is just a few steps from the easy-to-tour Old Town	
DUBROVNIK	No
Very compact and easy on your own	
ATHENS (Piraeus)	Maybe
Getting downtown is relatively easy, but sights benefit from a good guide, and an excursion offers easy connections	
MOST GREEK ISLANDS	No
Just relax and be on vacation	
EPHESUS (Kuşadası)	Yes
Getting from Kuşadası to Ephesus involves considerable hassle or expense, and a local guide is essential to understand this site	
ISTANBUL	No
The cruise terminals are right in the city, an easy tram ride from all the sights	

Money: Most cruise ships are essentially cashless (except for tips and a few other expenses). Your stateroom key card doubles as a credit card: When buying anything on board, simply provide your cabin number, then sign a receipt for the expense. Because all the extra onboard expenses can add up quickly, it's a good idea to periodically check your current balance (and look for mistaken charges) at the front desk.

These days, cruise lines use a standard "auto-tip" system, in which a set gratuity is automatically billed to each passenger's account and then divided among the crew. Additional tipping is, they'll tell you, "not expected," but it is still most certainly appreciated. In general, the rule of thumb is to give a cash tip at the end of the cruise to those crew members who have provided you with exceptional service.

Communicating: Keeping in touch with home while you're on the ship can be expensive, so it's better to wait until you're in port to make a call or go online.

Most cruise ships offer Wi-Fi and Internet terminals, but access is pricey ($0.50-1/minute) and agonizingly slooooow (remember dial-up?). Calls from your stateroom phone to shore are prohibitively pricey (generally $6-15/minute). If you have a mobile phone—either a US phone with roaming in Europe or a phone using a local European SIM card— you may be able to access land-based networks from within a few miles of shore. But once the ship gets about 10 miles offshore, the onboard mobile phone network switches on, with very high rates (about $2.50-6/minute).

Excursions vs. Independent Sightseeing: Prior to reaching each destination, you'll need to decide whether you want to sightsee on your own or join a shore excursion run by your cruise line. In most ports you can have a satisfying day in port on your own—though the best plan varies depending on the specifics of the destination, and your own level of comfort with navigating Europe independently. For a list of places where excursions make the most sense, see the sidebar on page 470.

A shore excursion efficiently takes you to a carefully selected assortment of sights, with a vetted local guide to explain everything, and is guaranteed to get you back to the ship in time (if an excursion is late, the ship will wait; if you're on your own and you return late, the ship will leave without you). If you don't want to hassle with public transportation, and do want someone to show you the sights, an excursion can be a great option.

But excursions are very expensive, ranging from $40-60/person for a three-hour town walking tour to $100-150/person for an all-day bus tour. Particularly in a place where it's easy to get into the city center on public transportation, you can have a similar experience for far less money. On an excursion, you're doing everything with a large group of people, which takes more time. Excursions tend to include shopping stops, which waste the time of nonshoppers. And at each stop you have to stick with the schedule and get back on the bus, even if you'd prefer to linger somewhere.

Rather than paying a premium to a middleman (your cruise line), you can work directly with local tour guides. Hire a private guide to meet you at the ship and take you on a tour, or, if you're on a tight budget, pay to join a scheduled walking tour around town. For more on local guides, see page 293.

If you decide to go it alone, use a good guidebook and visit the local tourist information office in port. The prospect of missing your ship is daunting, but don't let it scare you into not enjoying shore time on your own terms. As long as you keep a close eye on the time, it's easy to enjoy a very full day in port and be the last tired but happy tourist back onto the ship.

Shopping: At every stop, your cruise line will give you an information sheet highlighting local specialties and where to buy them. But be aware that cruise-recommended shops commonly give kickbacks to cruise lines and guides. This doesn't mean that the shop (or what it sells) isn't good quality; it just means you're probably paying top dollar. Many stores—not just the places working with cruise lines—jack up their rates when ships arrive, knowing they're about to get hit with a tidal wave of rushed and desperate shoppers.

So how can you avoid paying over-the-top, inflated prices? Before spending big money at the obvious tourist shops, be sure to check out local shopping venues, too. Large department stores often have a souvenir section with standard knickknacks and postcards at prices way below those at cruise-recommended shops. Or if you're adept at bargaining, head over to some of Europe's vibrant outdoor flea markets, where you can find local specialties and soft prices. For more shopping tips, see page 319.

Be aware that "local experts" hired by your cruise line are often salesmen in disguise. For instance, that "scholar" who meets you at the dock in Turkey is actually a carpet salesman who will take you to the obligatory ancient sight and then to the carpet shop. Though the demonstrations—whether carpet weaving or glassblowing—are usually interesting, they are just ploys to get you to plunk down your credit card. If you're interested in a particular item, use your newfound knowledge from the demonstration to shop around; you may find something of equal quality for less elsewhere.

PERSPECTIVES

Beyond all the practical considerations of preparing for your trip, there is one more vital task: calibrating your mind for your European experience. When you travel—whether to Europe or around the world—your best souvenir can be a global perspective. This chapter covers a range of ideas, including broadening your perspective through travel, understanding the current European political structure, recognizing the challenges and social issues facing Europe today, and learning how to travel in a socially and environmentally responsible way. Consider this a bit of food-for-thought pre-trip reading.

Broadening Your Perspective Through Travel

In the past few years, I've devoted a lot of time and energy to thinking about travel in a new way: as an invaluable tool for learning how to fit more thoughtfully into our ever-smaller world. I think of this approach as "travel as a political act" (which is also the title of a book I've written; see page 24).

I was raised thinking the world was a pyramid with the US on top and everyone else trying to get there. I believed our role in the world was to help other people get it right...American-style. If they didn't understand that, we'd get them a government that did.

But travel changed my perspective. I met intelligent people—nowhere near as rich, free, or blessed with opportunity as I was—who wouldn't trade passports even if they could. They were thankful to be Nepali,

Estonian, Turkish, Nicaraguan, or whatever. I was perplexed. I witnessed stirring struggles in lands that found other truths to be self-evident and God-given. I learned of Nathan Hales and Patrick Henrys from other nations who only wished they had more than one life to give for their country. I saw national pride that wasn't American. It was a challenging adjustment to my way of thinking—but it opened my mind to a whole new world of experiences I'd otherwise have ignored or derided.

What a difference perspective makes. When I bragged about how many gold medals our American Olympians were winning, my Dutch friend replied, "Yes, you have many medals, but per capita, we Dutch are doing five times as well."

Attitude Adjustment

When American tourists are unhappy, it's usually because of their stubborn desire to find the United States in Europe. Meanwhile, the happiest travelers I meet are truly taking a vacation from America—immersing themselves in different cultures and fully experiencing different people, outlooks, and lifestyles.

Even if you believe American ways are better, your trip will go more smoothly if you don't compare. Things are different in Europe—that's why you go. And European travel is a package deal. Accept the good with the "bad." If you always require the comforts of home, then that's where you'll be happiest. On the other hand, if you're observant and tune into all the little differences, you may find great wisdom in how Europeans do things. Paying for your Italian coffee at one counter and then picking it up at another may seem inefficient, until you realize it's more sanitary: The person handling the food handles no money.

Some Americans' trips suffer because they are treated like "ugly Americans." Those who are treated like ugly Americans are treated that way because they *are* ugly Americans. They aren't bad people, just ethnocentric. These people act as though they "just got off the boat"—putting shoes on train seats, chilling grapes in the bidet, talking loudly in restaurants, taking flash photos during Mass, hanging wet clothes out the hotel window, and consuming energy like it's cheap and ours to waste. But you can't expect the local people to accept you warmly if you don't respect their world and their ways of doing things.

The Ugly American vs. the Thoughtful American

While the ugly American slogs through a sour Europe, mired in a swamp of complaints, the thoughtful American fully experiences wherever he or she is. Ugly Americanism is a disease, but fortunately there is a cure: a change in attitude. The best over-the-counter medicine is a mirror. Here are the symptoms of being an Ugly American...and the treatment.

The Ugly American	The Thoughtful American
...criticizes "strange" customs and cultural differences. She doesn't respect the devout Spanish Catholic's appreciation of his town's patron saint, or doesn't understand the sense of community expressed by the evening promenade in southern Europe.	...seeks out European styles of living and tries new ways of thinking and doing things. You are genuinely interested in the people and cultures you visit. You accept and try to wrap your head around differences.
...demands to find America in Europe. He throws a fit if the air-conditioning breaks down in a hotel. He insists on orange juice and eggs (sunny-side up) for breakfast, long beds, English menus, ice in drinks, punctuality in Italy, and cold beer in England. He measures Europe with an American yardstick.	... is positive and optimistic. You don't dwell on problems or compare things to "back home," and you discipline yourself to focus on the good points of each country. As a guest in another land, you're observant and sensitive. If 60 people are dining with hushed voices in a Belgian restaurant, you know it's not the place to yuk it up.
...uses money as a shield against a genuine experience. She throws money at the locals instead of trying to engage them.	... doesn't flash signs of affluence, especially in poorer countries. You don't joke about the local money or overtip. Your bucks don't talk.
...invades a country while making no effort to communicate with the "natives." He never bothers to learn even the basic survival phrases ("please" and "thank you"), and gets angry when the Europeans he meets "refuse to learn English." Traveling in packs, he talks at and about Europeans in a condescending manner.	...makes an effort to bridge that flimsy language barrier. You find rudimentary communication in any language to be fun. On the train to Budapest, you enter a debate with a Hungarian over the merits of a common European currency—with your 20-word vocabulary. You don't worry about making mistakes—you communicate!

Thank You

Arabic	**shukran**	Greek	**efharisto**
Bulgarian	**blagodarya**	Hebrew	**todah**
Croatian	**hvala**	Hungarian	**köszönöm**
Czech	**děkuji**	Italian	**grazie**
Danish	**tak**	Polish	**dziękuję**
Dutch	**dank u wel**	Portuguese	**obrigado**
English	**thank you**	Russian	**spasiba**
Estonian	**tänan**	Slovak	**d'akujem**
Finnish	**kiitos**	Slovene	**hvala**
French	**merci**	Spanish	**gracias**
German	**danke**	Turkish	**teşekkür ederim**

Europeans judge you as an individual, not by your nationality. I have never been treated like the ugly American. If anything, my Americanness has been an asset in Europe. I've been accepted as an American friend throughout Europe, Russia, the Middle East, and North Africa. I've been hugged by Bulgarian workers on a Balkan mountaintop; discussed the Olympics over dinner in the home of a Greek family; explained to a young, frustrated Irishman that California girls take their pants off one leg at a time, just like the rest of us; and hiked through the Alps with a Swiss schoolteacher, learning German and teaching English.

Go as a guest; act like one, and you'll be treated like one. In travel, as in the rest of life, you often reap what you sow.

Understanding the European Union

A desire for peace and prosperity is powering some sweeping changes in 21st-century Europe. Over the last several generations, the countries of Europe have gone from being bitter rivals to member states in one of the world's biggest economies: the European Union. Bringing together such a diverse collection of separate nations—with different languages and cultures—peacefully, is unprecedented.

Today, the European Union includes most of Western Europe (except Switzerland), the British Isles, and a large chunk of Eastern Europe and Scandinavia. (Croatia joined in 2013, and the Republic of Macedonia, Montenegro, Serbia, Iceland, and Turkey are seeking to become members.) Essentially, the EU is a free-trade zone with its own currency

The European Union: Austria, Belgium, Bulgaria, Croatia, Cyprus, Czech Republic, Denmark, Estonia, Finland, France, Germany, Greece, Hungary, Ireland, Italy, Latvia, Lithuania, Luxembourg, Malta, Netherlands, Poland, Portugal, Romania, Slovakia, Slovenia, Spain, Sweden, and the United Kingdom.

EU Nations

(the euro, used in most member countries). But it's much more than that: The EU is increasingly a political unit that looks, acts, and quacks like a single unified nation-state. While not a "United States of Europe," the EU has an elected Europewide parliament that passes laws on economic policy and some social and foreign policy issues.

Everyone has an opinion on how well the EU works. "Eurocrats" and other optimists see it as a bold and idealistic experiment in unity, mutual

understanding, and shared priorities. "Euroskeptics" view it as a bloated, overly bureaucratic monster that's threatening to wring the diversity and charm out of the Old World; they especially resent that the EU has lashed economically healthy countries to troubled ones. Here's a snapshot of the EU to help you navigate the many interesting conversations you'll have about it with your new European friends.

When I shudder at Switzerland's high taxes, my friend Olle asks, "What's it worth to live in a country with no hunger or homelessness, and where everyone—regardless of the wealth of their parents—has access to good health care and a top-quality education?"

The EU: Past and Present

World War II left 40 million dead and a continent in ruins, and convinced Europeans that they had to work together to maintain peace. Poised between competing superpowers (the US and the USSR), they also needed to cooperate economically to survive in an increasingly

US vs. EU—By the Numbers

	US	EU
Population	316.7 million	504 million
Land area	3.7 million sq. miles	1.7 million sq. miles
Gross domestic product (GDP)	$15.7 trillion	$15.7 trillion
Life expectancy	78.5 years	79.8 years
Infant mortality rate	6 deaths/1,000	4.5 deaths/1,000
Mobile phones	290 million	629 million
Annual military budget	665.5 billion (4.8% of GDP)	248.3 billion (1.6% of GDP)

Statistics from the *CIA's World Factbook*, 2013

globalized economy.

Just after the war ended, visionary "Eurocrats" began the task of convincing reluctant European nations to relinquish elements of their sovereignty and merge into a united body. Starting in 1949, European states gradually came together to form the Common Market (also known as the European Economic Community). In 1992, with the Treaty of Maastricht, the 12 member countries of the Common Market made a leap of faith: They created a "European Union" that would eventually allow capital, goods, services, and labor to move freely across borders.

The by-products would be a common currency, softened trade barriers, EU passports, and the elimination of border checks between member countries.

In 2002, most EU members adopted the euro as a single currency, and for all practical purposes, economic unity was a reality. By 2007, EU membership reached 27 nations, encompassing a vast swath of the continent. With passport checkpoints all but obsolete, the EU is now the world's seventh largest "country" (1.7 million square miles), with the third largest population (more than 500 million people) and the world's

The EU headquarters—a vast and shiny complex of skyscrapers in Brussels—welcomes visitors on guided tours to take a peek at Europe at work.

biggest economy ($15.4 trillion GDP).

The European Union is governed from Brussels and administered through a complicated network of legislative bodies, commissions, and courts that attempt to complement each country's government without encroaching on sovereignty. The EU cannot levy taxes (that's still done through national governments), and it cannot deploy troops without each nation's approval. Unlike America's federation of 50 states, Europe's member states retain the right to opt out of some EU policies. Britain, for example, belongs to the EU but has not adopted the euro as its currency.

It's a delicate balance trying to develop laws and policies for all Europeans while respecting the rights of nations, regions, and individuals. The European response to the Balkan wars in the early 1990s, the Iraq War of the mid-2000s, and the ongoing debt crisis have demonstrated that Europe isn't always prepared to speak with a single voice. An oft-quoted EU slogan is "promoting unity"—that is, economic and political—"while preserving diversity."

Meanwhile, over the last decade, the EU has been pouring money into an ambitious 21st-century infrastructure of roads, high-speed trains, high-tech industries, and communication networks. The goal is to create a competitive, sustainable, environmentally friendly economy that improves the quality of life for all Europeans. To complete these projects, government and private industry have worked hand in hand in a

New roads (such as this one in Ireland) are bringing the infrastructure in Europe up to speed. These EU-funded projects come with a billboard and EU flag reminding drivers where the funding came from.

kind of "democratic socialism" with a global perspective. It's impossible to deny the marked improvements brought about by this investment, as new super-expressways and bullet trains lace the continent ever more efficiently together.

The EU is a bold experiment, and, like any innovation, it's hit a few snags as it's evolved (see next section). Even throughout the debt crisis, the euro has remained relatively strong, and as mentioned earlier, Europe has the world's largest economy (having overtaken the US several years ago). These economic woes are no more a sign of the total failure of European "socialism" than the economic crisis in the US indicated the final collapse of American capitalism.

The EU has evolved in a stuttering way since World War II—two steps forward, one step backward. While some of the media trumpets the steps backward, the EU is here to stay. Far more important than any of its perceived shortcomings is that France and Germany have woven their economies together to the degree that there will never again be a huge war in Europe. Sure, the French and Germans still mix like wine and sauerkraut. Brits still tell insulting jokes about Italians, and vice versa. But Europeans

As Europe unites, historically subjugated peoples are enjoying more autonomy. The Scottish Parliament originated around 1235, was dissolved by England in 1707, and returned in 1999. Its extravagant, and therefore controversial, Edinburgh digs opened in 2004.

don't want to go back to the days of division and strife. Most recognize that a strong and unified Europe is necessary to keep the peace and compete in a global economy. Individual nations still duke it out for world domination...but now the battles are on the soccer field.

European Challenges

Like many places, Europe is grappling with an economic crisis (with resulting strikes and protests) and the ever-present threat of terrorism. Here's a quick rundown on the European reality, and how these issues could affect your trip.

Europe's Economic Crisis

After seeing news reports of violent demonstrations, angry marchers, and frustrated workers rioting, some travelers are wondering if this is still a good time to go to Europe. I'm certainly not an economist. But here's my take on the situation from a travel writer's perspective.

Today Europe is paying the price—in the form of expensive bailouts and painful cutbacks—of what had been taken-for-granted services. Wealthier member countries (mostly in the north) resent being compelled to prop up the euro by rescuing their economically unsound compatriots (the so-called "PIIGS" countries, mostly in the south—Portugal, Italy, Ireland, Greece, and Spain). Meanwhile, troubled countries resent being told what to do by the richer ones, and disgruntled citizens sometimes take to the streets.

When assessing the seriousness of any civil unrest, remember the mantra of commercial news these days: "If it bleeds, it leads." In the era of Walter Cronkite, network news contributed to the fabric of our society by providing solid journalism as a public service without worrying about their bottom line. But today, commercial TV news has to make a profit. In order to sell ads, it has become entertainment masquerading as news. Producers will always grab video footage that makes a demonstration appear as exciting or threatening as possible. Unrest is generally localized—it looks frightening with a zoom lens and much less so with a wide-angle shot.

And also remember that, while we in the US and Europe may consider ourselves in an "economic crisis," the vast majority of people on this planet would love to have our economic problems. By any fair measure, as societies, both the US and Europe are filthy rich. Still, if you're unemployed or if your retirement is suddenly in jeopardy, your times are, indeed, tough.

Europe's economic problems are much like ours here in the US. It seems on both sides of the Atlantic we've conned ourselves into thinking we are wealthier than we really are. Enjoying wild real estate bubbles, we've had houses that were worth half a million suddenly worth a million. Then, when they dropped in value by 50 percent, we felt like we'd lost half a million dollars or euros. Truth be told, we were never millionaires to start with, and what we "lost" we never honestly gained in the first place.

As societies, we've been consuming more goods than we've been producing for a long time. We import more than we export—and things are finally catching up with us. Here in the US, our priorities are warped. Many of our best young minds are going to our finest schools to become experts in finance: rearranging the furniture to skim off the top...aspiring to careers where you produce little while expertly working the system in hopes of becoming unimaginably rich. Recently, surveying the extravagant châteaux outside Paris—such as Vaux-le-Vicomte—I was stuck by how many of them were the homes of financiers. Lately, the US is reminding me of old regime France. It's striking that more than 10 percent of the US economy is tied up in the financial industry.

Europeans and Americans have some of the most generous entitlements in the world combined with aging societies. Because of that, our comfortable status quo is not sustainable. Whenever a society gets wealthy and well educated, it has fewer children. That's simply a force of nature. Western Europe, being one of the wealthiest and best-educated parts of the world, logically has one of the lowest birth rates.

Europe's generous entitlements were conceived in a post-war society with lots of people working, fewer living to retirement, and those living beyond retirement having a short life span. That was sustainable...no problem. Now, with its very low birth rate, the demographic makeup of Europe has flipped upside-down: relatively few people working, lots of people retiring, and those who are retired living a long time. The arithmetic just isn't there to sustain the lavish entitlements.

Politicians in Europe have the unenviable task of explaining to their citizens that they won't get the cushy golden years their parents got. People who worked diligently with the promise of retiring at 62 are now told they'll need to work an extra decade—and even then, they may not have a generous retirement waiting for them. Any politician trying to explain this reality to the electorate is likely to be tossed out, since people naturally seek a politician who tells them what they want to hear rather than the hard truth. And any austerity programs necessary to put a society back on track are also tough enough to get people marching in the streets.

I expect you'll see lots of marches and lots of strikes in Europe in the coming years as they try to recalibrate their economy. Europeans demonstrate: It's in their blood and a healthy part of their democracy. When frustrated and needing to vent grievances, they hit the streets. I've been caught up in huge and boisterous marches all over Europe, and it's not scary; in fact, it's kind of exhilarating. *"La Manifestation!"* as they say in France. All that marching is just too much trouble for many Americans. When dealing with similar frustrations, we find a TV station (on the left or right) that affirms our beliefs and then shake our collective fists vigorously.

When Europe united, the poor countries (such as Ireland, Portugal,

PERSPECTIVES

and Greece) received lots of development aid from the rich ones (mostly Germany and France). I remember when there were no freeways in any of the poor countries. Now they are laced with German-style (and mostly German-funded) superhighways. These countries traded in their lazy currencies for the euro (which is, in a way, the mighty Deutsche mark in disguise, as the European economy is driven and dominated by Germany).

Today, it's no coincidence that the European countries that have received the most development aid are the ones who are the most debt-ridden and at risk of failing. Even with that aid, their productivity has lagged far behind the stronger economies. And, while their workforce doesn't produce as much per capita as German workers, they have a mighty currency tied to Germany. By earning wages and getting aid in euros, these nations enjoyed a false prosperity that they might not have merited—and the bursting real estate bubble made it worse. Before unity, if a nation didn't produce much and slid into crippling debt, the economy could be adjusted simply by devaluing that nation's currency. Today, there's no way to devalue the currency of a particular county on the euro, so this fix is not an option. It's much easier to get into the eurozone than to get out. (One of the biggest questions facing Europe today is: Can and should an economically weak country—namely Greece—leave the eurozone?)

Will Greece and other struggling economies within the EU be safe and stable places to visit as they work out these problems? No one can predict the future for certain. But, as a traveler, I don't worry about it. True, I wouldn't want to be a Greek worker counting on a retirement that may not come. But as a visitor, it's likely that you'll scarcely be aware of these problems. I was just in Greece and enjoyed a warm welcome, great food, and wonderful beaches. Expect a few demonstrations and a few strikes. Expect your loved ones to be worried about you if you are in a country when there's a demonstration. (So be in touch.) But you can also expect rich travel experiences and a society thankful that you decided to spend a slice of your vacation time and money in their country.

Terrorism

While Americans understandably focus on 9/11, Europe has had its own string of modern terrorist tragedies: the Madrid train bombings of March 11, 2004; the London subway bombings of July 7, 2005; and the bombings and shootings by an anti-Islamic Norwegian in Oslo on July 22, 2011. And yet, Europeans seem to have a knack for bouncing back and refusing to give in to the attackers' desire to incite terror. They don't

surrender their emotions and politics to sensational news coverage. Europeans keep the risk and tragedy of terrorism in perspective. As a matter of principle, it seems, they refuse to be terrorized by terrorists.

Of course, terrorism wasn't invented on September 11, 2001. There's never been a superpower that wasn't seen by angry people beyond its borders as an evil empire. All have had insurgents nipping at them. Romans had what they called "barbarians." Habsburgs had "anarchists." Americans have terrorists.

Don't let sensationalism and hysteria get in the way of taking a trip. Numbers don't lie: The odds against being killed by terrorists are astronomical. The facts are that more than 12 million Americans go to Europe every year, and for the last several years, not a single one has been killed by terrorists. I believe that risk is no greater for an American in Milan or Paris than at home in Miami or Pittsburgh. In the mid-2000s, Canada and many European countries issued travel advisories to their citizens for a land they consider more dangerous than their own: the US.

The US State Department issues travel advisories for foreign countries (www.travel .state.gov). Consider these, but don't follow them blindly. Certain warnings (for example, about civil unrest in a country that's falling

Paris' see-through garbage cans give terrorists one less place to hide a bomb.

apart) could be grounds to scrub my mission. But I travel right through most advisories (which can seem politically motivated). A threat against the embassy in Rome doesn't affect my sightseeing at the Pantheon. For other perspectives, check the British (www.fco.gov.uk) and Canadian (www.travel.gc.ca) government travel warnings.

Terrorist threats can suddenly increase security lines or disrupt flight plans; if something unusual is happening in the world, call ahead to confirm flight schedules before heading out. And allow plenty of time to catch your flight. If I get stuck in a long security line, I use the extra time to meditate on the thought, "How has America's place in our world changed... and why?"

Or, if you want to worry about something, worry about this: Each year, more than 30,000 Americans are shot to death in the United States by handguns (8 times the per-capita gun-caused deaths in Europe).

After each attention-grabbing attack, some Americans choose to put their travel

Security on Europe's trains is tighter than ever these days. At this London train station, the police keep a close eye on who boards the Eurostar for Paris.

dreams on hold and stay home. That's OK. I'm still bringing home TV shows that they can watch from the safety of their living room sofas. But those of us who are able would rather enjoy the fun and wonders of Europe firsthand.

Two weeks after 9/11, I was in Padua, the town where Copernicus studied and Galileo taught. The square was filled with college students sharing drinks and discussing America's response to "our new reality." As we talked, I kept dipping little strips of bread into a puddle of olive oil on my plate, tiptoe-style. Watching me do this, my new friend said, "You make the *scarpette*...little shoes."

My Italian wasn't good enough to tell him my thoughts: Travel is a celebration of life and freedom. Terrorists will not take that away from me. My mission in life is to inspire Americans to travel, one by one— "making the little shoes"—to absorb and savor the wonders of Europe.

Learning from Today's History

The economic crisis and terrorism are grabbing headlines, but Europe is also wrangling with other forms of friction. For example, it's next to impossible to keep everyone happy in a multilingual country. Switzerland has four languages, but *Deutsch ist über alles*. In Belgium, tension between the Dutch- and French-speaking halves led to a caretaker government for 541 days—a world record. And Hungarians living in Slovakia had to rely on European Court intervention to get road signs in their native language. Like many French Canadians, Europe's linguistic underdogs will tell you their language receives equal treatment only on cereal boxes, and many are working toward change.

Look beyond the pretty pictures in your tourist brochures for background on how your destination's economic and demographic makeup may be causing problems today or tomorrow. A few months in advance of your trip, begin paying attention to political news so you'll know what's happening (information you'll seldom find in guidebooks).

If you've studied up on local politics, you'll get the most out of opportunities to talk with involved locals about complex current situations. At any pub on the Emerald Isle, you'll get an earful of someone's passionate feelings about "the Troubles." In Istanbul, befriend a Turk over a game of backgammon, and ask how he feels about the rise of Islamic fundamentalism in his proudly secular country. Wherever you go, young, well-dressed people are most likely to speak (and want to practice) English. Universities can be the perfect place to solve the world's problems with a liberal, open-minded foreigner over a cafeteria lunch.

Travel broadens our perspective, enabling us to rise above the 24-hour, advertiser-driven infotainment we call "news" and see things as citizens of our world. By plugging directly into the present and getting the European take on things, a traveler gets beyond traditional sightseeing and learns "today's history."

Social Issues in Europe

Tolerance and celebrating diversity are major tenets of the European Union. But for some Europeans, that's easier said than done. This section offers an admittedly oversimplified overview of immigration, race relations, and gay rights in Europe.

Immigration and Race Relations

Europe is grappling with an influx of immigrants from the developing world. Racial diversity is nothing new in the melting-pot United States (where one-third of the population is non-white), but about 95 percent of people living in Europe are Caucasian. A few places (such as former colonial powers Great Britain and the Netherlands) have seen a steady

Travelers of Color in Europe

People who are not of European descent might be concerned about how they'll be treated abroad. In short, does it matter that you look different from most Europeans? I've collected the following advice from a wide range of people of color who have lived or traveled extensively in Europe.

First off, your Americanness will probably be more notable to the Europeans you meet than the color of your skin. Most Europeans can spot Americans a mile away. And, because American culture is pervasive worldwide, any stereotypes Europeans might have about your race are likely formed by our own popular culture—for example, by actors, musicians, athletes, and characters on popular TV shows. The Obama presidency has also informed the way Europeans think about black Americans, and Americans in general. One African American traveler told me that several Europeans went out of their way to approach her and express their appreciation of Obama.

Travelers of color and mixed-race couples tell me that their most common source of discomfort in Europe is being stared at. While this might seem to indicate disapproval, consider the more likely possibility that it's just a combination of curiosity and impoliteness. Put simply, for many Europeans, you're just not who they're used to seeing. Their response to a person of color likely isn't hostility, but naiveté. (One traveler suggested that this isn't racism, but "rarism"—Europeans reacting not to one's race, but to one's rarity.) When it comes to sensitivity about race, many Europeans are, frankly, pretty clueless. On a recent visit to a Tuscan farm, a gregarious Italian family proudly introduced me to their black kitten, which they'd named "Obama."

influx of transplants from their overseas holdings for many centuries, but most of Europe was largely homogenous well into the 20th century. In the decades since World War II—as Europe has built a new prosperity, and immigrants have arrived seeking a better life—Europe has become much more ethnically diverse.

As immigrants from every corner of the world (mostly Africa, the Middle East, the Caribbean, South Asia, and South America) have come to Europe, many white Europeans have struggled to adapt. Some are frus-

Because the US has grappled more directly with its race issues, many Americans at least pay lip service to a "political correctness" that helps insulate minorities from overtly hateful speech. Europeans tend to be more opinionated and blunt and aren't shy about voicing sweeping generalizations about any topic—including race. Many travelers find this jarring and hurtful, while some consider it weirdly refreshing ("at least it's out in the open").

Travelers of color report being frustrated by racial profiling, particularly at border crossings or airport security. (One traveler speculated that this may have to do with targeting immigrants.) It's possible you'll be more closely scrutinized than other travelers before being allowed to continue on your way.

If you're concerned about how you'll be treated in a specific destination, ask fellow travelers of color what their experiences have been there. An excellent resource for African Americans, including destination-specific reports from several travelers, is http://black travels.blogspot.com. Or check out the "Minority Travelers' Forum" section on my online Travel Forums (www.ricksteves.com/forums).

Will you encounter unfriendliness in your travels? Definitely. Everyone does. But be careful not to over-attribute grumpiness to racism—again, keep in mind the vast difference in cultural context. In the words of one traveler of color: "I think we're more likely to interpret bad behavior from non-Americans as being racist because of our history with white Americans. Often their impatience is just because we're American, and we're clueless about other people's cultures and practices."

No matter your race, the best advice for any traveler is to have a positive attitude. Focus on all the nice Europeans you'll meet, rather than the few unenlightened exceptions. If you feel uncomfortable or mistreated, head somewhere else. And remember that most Europeans are as interested in learning about you as you are in learning about them.

trated by large numbers of immigrants—and now their descendants—who, the critics claim, stick together in tight communities, cling to the culture of their homeland, and are slow to adopt European culture. The immigrants would likely counter that they've found few opportunities to integrate with their European neighbors. Just as in the US, immigrants are sometimes perceived as challenging lifelong residents for jobs, or as taking advantage of the welfare system. Another thorny issue is the friction between European Christianity and the Islamic faith of many immigrants.

Immigration paranoia came to a head in normally peaceful Norway, where, in July 2011, a deranged white-supremacist Christian bombed government offices in Oslo and then went to a pro-immigrant political party's summer camp and gunned down dozens of innocents—mostly teenagers—in cold blood. The gunman's fear that Europe is being "taken over by Islamic fundamentalists" reveals a frightening undercurrent of paranoia and hate that represents a small but growing fringe of the European mindset.

On the other hand, the minority group subject to the most overt racism in Europe isn't made up of new immigrants at all: It's the Roma (or Gypsies). For centuries, white Europeans have regarded this population—which likely shares ancestors with the people of today's India—with suspicion and fear. This feeling is especially pervasive in Eastern Europe, Italy, and Spain, which have large numbers of Roma.

While Europe wrestles with how to accommodate its new populations, travelers of color may encounter a different social reality than the one they're used to back home. For tips on what to expect, see the sidebar on the previous page.

Gay Rights in Europe

In keeping with its generally progressive politics, much of Europe tends to be supportive of gay rights. The European Union specifically includes gay and lesbian citizens in its antidiscrimination laws. The Netherlands—and Amsterdam in particular—has offered equal rights to gays and lesbians for decades. The world's first legal marriage for a gay couple occurred in Amsterdam in 2001.

In general, Northern Europe and larger cities are more progressive when it comes to gay rights. In other places, the record is mixed, with fewer legal rights but pockets of tolerance. Austria has a vibrant gay scene in its cities, and in conservative Catholic Ireland, my readers have reported a generally welcoming environment even in country B&Bs. Paris has a gay mayor and

In progressive Amsterdam, this "Homomonument"—shaped like a giant pink triangle—honors all gays and lesbians who have been persecuted for their sexual orientation.

a gay neighborhood (the Marais), but many rural French communities adhere to an unspoken "don't ask, don't tell" ideology of not flaunting one's sexuality. Italy is a similar story of general acceptance but raised eyebrows in rural areas and in the south. Some of Greece's islands are well-known gay destinations. Eastern European capitals such as Prague and Budapest have liberal attitudes on par with what you'll find in big Western European cities, and the Czech Republic, Hungary, and Slovenia all have legally recognized same-sex unions. But the farther east and south you venture in the former Soviet Bloc, the less progressive things become. Particularly in rural areas of far Eastern Europe, responses range from reasonably accepting to outright hostility. In places such as Romania and Serbia, laws outlawing homosexuality were lifted in recent decades—but acceptance lags behind. For a country-by-country checklist, go to www.wikipedia.org and search for "LGBT rights in Europe."

But the simple fact is that gay and lesbian travelers are more likely than heterosexuals to plan vacations overseas—and the travel industry knows it. Gay travelers are now likely to find themselves on the receiving end of European tourism campaigns. Many guidebooks have sections devoted to gay nightlife, especially city guides like the *Time Out* series. Damron publishes guidebooks for gay and lesbian travelers (www .damron.com). For recommendations online, try websites such as www .outtraveler.com and www.purpleroofs.com. The International Gay & Lesbian Travel Association is a useful tool for locating LGBT travel businesses and destinations (www.iglta.org).

Socially Responsible and Educational Travel

My travels—whether in Egypt, Afghanistan, El Salvador, Turkey, Italy, or the Netherlands—have taught me about my own country as well as the rest of our world. Travel has sharpened both my love of what America stands for and my connection with our world. I've learned to treasure—rather than fear—the world's rich diversity. And I believe that America—with all its power, wisdom, and goodness—can do a better job of making our world a better place. By connecting me with so many people, travel has heightened my concern for people issues: a well-educated electorate, a healthy environment, civil liberties, quality housing, nutrition, health care, and education.

As we learn more about the problems that confront the earth and humankind, more and more people are recognizing the need for the world's industries—including tourism—to function as tools for peace. According to the World Travel and Tourism Council (www.wttc.org), tourism is a $5 trillion-a-year industry (9 percent of world GDP) that employs more than 260 million people. As travelers become more sophisticated and gain a global perspective, the demand for socially, environmentally, and economically responsible means of travel will grow. Peace is more than the absence of war, and if we are to continue enjoying the good things of life—such as travel—the serious issues that confront humankind must be addressed now. Although the most obvious problems relate specifically to travel in the developing world, European travel also offers some exciting socially responsible opportunities.

Understand your power to shape the marketplace by what you decide to buy, whether in the grocery store or in your choice of hotels. In my travels (and in my writing), whenever possible, I patronize and support small, family-run businesses (hotels, restaurants, shops, tour guides). I choose people who invest their creativity and resources in giving me simple, friendly, sustainable, and honest travel experiences—people with ideals. Back Door places don't rely on slick advertising and marketing gimmicks, and they don't target the created needs of people whose values are shaped by capitalism gone wild. Consuming responsibly means buying as if your choice is a vote for the kind of world we could have.

"Voluntourism" and Cultural Exchanges

For some travelers, making the world a better place becomes the driving focus of their trip. Various organizations sponsor "volunteer vacations," work camps, and other service projects in needy countries, including Global Volunteers (www.globalvolunteers.org), Volunteers for Peace (www.vfp.org), and SCI International Voluntary Service (www.sci-ivs .org).

Or consider taking an educational tour; while not explicitly service-oriented, these can do a brilliant job of broadening horizons. I've gone on three trips to Central and South America with the Center for Global Education (at Augsburg College in Minneapolis)—some of the most vivid and perspective-stretching travel experiences I've ever enjoyed (www.augsburg.edu/global; for trip journals of my CFGE experiences in El Salvador and Nicaragua, see www.ricksteves.com/centam). For more resources, see the suggestions in the Overseas Work and Study sidebar, later, or try searching on Google for "volunteer vacation" or "volunteer travel."

Culturally curious travelers can sign up with one of several hospitality exchange organizations. These groups connect travelers with host families with the noble goal of building world peace through international understanding. Guests sightsee less but engage more in everyday life with their hosts—talking, sharing, and learning. You'll arrive as a stranger at new destinations, but leave as a friend.

Although no money changes hands, these exchanges aren't for people simply out to travel cheap—the logistics involved aren't worth it. Most organizations screen members (with varying degrees of stringency) and set ground rules about length of stay. Opening your own home to visitors is encouraged, but not required. Servas is the oldest and largest of these organizations ($85 to join, plus a $25 deposit for a list of hosts, www.usservas.org). London-based Globetrotters Club runs a similar network of hosts and travelers ($30 annual membership, www.globe trotters.co.uk), as do several groups that are free to join, such as Hospitality Exchange (hospex.net) and The Hospitality Club (www.hospitalityclub .org). Other organizations serve specialized audiences (women, Jewish travelers, touring cyclists, gay travelers). Friendship Force International organizes homestay tours for small groups, also with a goal of fostering international goodwill (www.thefriendshipforce.org). Many travelers swear by these exchanges as the only way to really travel, and they treasure their global list of friends.

Student Travel

I feel strongly about the value of students incorporating a little world travel into their university experience. Ninety-six percent of humanity lives outside our borders—and we risk being left in the dust if our next generation of leaders and innovators doesn't know how to effectively engage the world. Sending our students overseas is not a luxury. It's a necessity. Urge the young people in your lives to get a passport and see the world as a classroom.

Good universities all encourage students to take a semester abroad. Interested students can get the details at their campus foreign-study office.

Here's my personal take—from a parent's perspective—on what's to be gained by spending a semester or two overseas. When my son, Andy, was a student at the University of Notre Dame, he enjoyed a fabulous semester abroad in Rome. The fundamental decision for students like Andy—along with whether they should miss fall football season or the fun of spring on campus—is choosing between Europe and the developing world. A semester in Africa or Latin America gives a real-life experience in the rough-and-tumble reality of poverty and powerfully humanizes the often-quoted statistic that "half of humanity is trying to live on $2 a day." Time spent in China or India (whose economies are growing at a much faster pace than their conventional Western European counterparts) introduces a student to emerging economic powerhouses

Overseas Work and Study

If you're adventurous and unattached, the most rewarding European experience can be to get a job or volunteer gig overseas or to enroll at a school abroad. Expatriates enjoy the daily routine and built-in circle of coworkers or classmates (and potential friends). If you're interested in becoming a full-time European, consider these helpful resources. If you're a student, your school can typically help—ask about study-abroad programs at your campus office.

Books

The Alternative Travel Directory: The Complete Guide to Traveling, Studying and Living Overseas (7th ed.)

Directory of Jobs & Careers Abroad (Debora Penrith, 13th ed.)

The Expert Expatriate: Your Guide to Successful Relocation Abroad (Melissa Brayer Hess and Patricia Linderman, 2007)

GenXpat: The Young Professional's Guide to Making a Successful Life Abroad (Margaret Malewski, 2005)

Summer Jobs Worldwide (Susan Griffith, 2012)

Work Abroad: The Complete Guide to Finding a Job Overseas (4th ed.)

Work Your Way Around the World: The Globetrotter's Bible (Susan Griffith, 2012)

Online

BUNAC (www.bunac.org): Facilitates international work and volunteer experiences for students and young people.

Council on International Educational Exchange (www.ciee.org /isp): Offers for-credit programs in 12 European countries.

Expat Exchange (www.expatexchange.com): Postings from expats in virtually every European country.

HelpX (helpx.net): Worldwide listing of farms, homestays, ranches, lodges, B&Bs, and more who invite volunteer helpers to stay short-term in exchange for food and accommodation.

Transitions Abroad (www.transitionsabroad.com): A great resource for anyone considering working or studying abroad.

WorldTeach (www.worldteach.org): Arranges volunteer teaching stints in developing countries.

that will compete with our country throughout that student's work life. But a semester in Europe offers (for many) an opportunity to connect with our roots; follow up on language, art, and history courses already taken; and enjoy that traditional "Grand Tour" of the Old World.

The real education of a semester abroad takes place outside the classroom. It's hard for students to really focus on lectures and homework with so many cultural experiences so close (and parents so far). Each week the buzz is about who's going where on the weekend and how many classes they're skipping to do it. From his base in Rome, Andy would gather a small gang for each three-day weekend: skiing in the Swiss Alps, hiking in the Cinque Terre, biking the Amalfi Coast, or sharing an apartment in Cefalù, Sicily. It came so naturally to him (I wonder why?) that he even formed a tour company for students abroad (www.wsaeurope.com).

Learning the language, making new friends from around the world, flirting with foreigners, getting comfortable with a bustling foreign city, and mastering the late-night scene while going through the motions in classes all add up to a life-changing and unforgettable semester. And it's a bonding experience with fellow students who will be friends for life.

Global Warming and Going "Green"

During a heat wave several years ago in Italy, I switched hotels because it was too hot to sleep without air-conditioning. It was the first time I had done that, and it was a kind of personal defeat—since I've always prided myself on not needing air-conditioning.

As they've sweltered through summer after summer, Europeans (and their visitors) have long embraced the "inconvenient truth" that things are heating up.

There's no doubt in Europe (and among Europeans) that things are warming up. Nearly everywhere in the Alps, summer skiing is just a memory, and—even in the winter—ski resorts are in desperate straits for lack of snow. (These days, new ski lifts in Europe routinely come with plumbing for snowmaking equipment.) Eating outdoors in formerly cool-climate Munich or Amsterdam now feels like a traditional way to dine. Dutch boys now wait years for a frozen canal to skate on. Scandinavia is seeing a spike in summertime visitors from Spain and Italy (seeking a break from the heat).

In general, Europeans are ahead of the curve on environmental issues. In particularly "green" Denmark, you pay for the disposal of a car when you first buy it, and entire towns are competing to see which will be the first to become entirely wind-powered. A few years ago, London introduced a $16 "congestion charge" for drivers entering the city center during peak hours. This cuts down on both pollution and traffic, and the money generated helps fund the city's energy-efficient bus system. Other cities have since followed suit. In a similar effort to reduce reliance on cars, many European cities have become aggressively bike-friendly, with well-groomed bike lanes and even free or very cheap loaner bikes for quick rides within town (for details on biking in Europe, see page 317). Next to Amsterdam's Central Station stands a high-rise garage—not for cars, but for bicycles. While these ideas sound laughably idealistic to some oil-addicted American cynics, Europeans are making them a reality, and environmentally conscious travelers can take advantage of them, too.

A day of reckoning is coming, when honest travelers will agree that flying to Europe pumps more carbon into the atmosphere than our earth can handle to sustain the climate we all find comfortable. Europeans are starting to see "carbon taxes" that force consumers to pay for zeroing out the negative impact their purchases have on the environment. I have friends who, despite cheap airfares, ride the train to minimize the environmental cost of their intra-European travel.

Try to consume responsibly in your travels—do your part to conserve energy. If your hotel overstocks your room with towels, use just one. Carry your own bar of soap and bottle of shampoo rather than rip open all those little soaps and shampoo packets. Bring a lightweight plastic cup instead of using and tossing a plastic glass at every hotel. Turn the light off when you leave your room. Limit showers to five minutes. Return unused travel information (booklets, brochures) to the tourist information office or pass it on to another traveler rather than toss it into a European landfill.

As a business that promotes travel, my company (Europe Through the Back Door) has been exploring the ethics of our work and what we can do to offset our carbon footprint. We're making our office as energy-efficient as possible, and we've made extensive use of 100 percent recycled fabric in the travel bags we manufacture. Given all of the tour members we send abroad, we recently paid for the planting of 80,000 trees in an attempt to be carbon neutral.

There's plenty more that can be done to counterbalance the environmental costs of international travel. Even in small ways, we can make a difference.

PART TWO
BACK DOORS

Europe is your playground...and it's time for recess.

Finding a Back Door of Your Own

The travel skills covered in the first half of this book enable you to open doors most travelers don't even know exist. Now I'd like you to meet my "Back Doors." I'm the matchmaker, and you and the travel bug are about to get intimate. By traveling vicariously with me through these chapters, you'll get a peek at my favorite places. And, just as important, by internalizing this lifetime of magic travel moments, you'll develop a knack for finding your own.

Europe is a bubbling multicultural fondue. A Back Door is a steaming forkful. It could be an all-day walk on an alpine ridge, a sword-fern fantasy in a ruined castle, or a friendly swing with a bell-ringer in a church spire. You could jam your camera with Turkish delights or uncover the village warmth hiding in a cold metropolis. By learning where to jab your fork, you'll put together a travel feast that exceeds your wildest dreams.

Some of my Back Doors are undiscovered towns that have, for various reasons, missed the modern parade. With no promotional budgets to attract travelers, they're ignored as they quietly make their traditional way through just another century. Many of these places won't hit you with their cultural razzle-dazzle. Their charms are too subtle to be enjoyed by the tour-bus crowd. But, learning from the experiences described in this second half of the book, Back Door travelers make their own fun.

Europe's Back Doors

Italy
1. The Cinque Terre
2. Hill Towns
3. Milan, Lakes & Dolomites
4. Naples & Amalfi Coast Area
5. Sicily

Portugal, Spain & Morocco
6. Lisbon
7. Salema
8. Arcos de la Frontera & Spain's White Villages
9. Morocco

France
10. Paris
11. Alsace & Colmar
12. Alps & Mont Blanc

Belgium & the Netherlands
13. Bruges
14. Amsterdam

Germany, Austria & Switzerland
15. Rothenburg & the Romantic Road
16. Hallstatt
17. Gimmelwald

Eastern Europe
18. Prague
19. Kraków
20. Bosnia-Herzegovina

Great Britain
21. London
22. Bath
23. York
24. Blackpool
25. Cotswolds

Ireland
26. Dingle Peninsula
27. Northern Ireland & Belfast

Scandinavia
28. Oslo & the Fjords
29. Ærø

East Mediterranean
30. Peloponnese
31. Istanbul
32. Eastern Turkey

NOTE: The following Back Doors do not appear on this map: Communist Sites in Eastern Europe, Mysterious Britain, Offbeat Europe, A European Sampler, Best Medieval Castle Experiences, and Sites of Nazi Europe.

We'll also explore natural nooks and undeveloped crannies. These are rare opportunities to enjoy Europe's sun, beaches, mountains, and natural wonders without the glitz. While Europeans love nature and are fanatic sun worshippers, they have an impressive knack for enjoying themselves in hellish crowds. Our goal is to experience Europe's quiet alternatives: lonesome stone circles, desolate castles, breezy bike rides, and snippets of the Riviera not snapped up by entrepreneurs.

With a Back Door angle on a big city, you can slip your fingers under its staged culture and actually find a pulse. Even London has a warm underbelly, where you'll rumble with a heart that's been beating for 2,000 years.

And finally, to squeeze the most travel experience out of every mile, minute, and dollar, look beyond Europe. Europe is exciting, but a dip into Turkey or Morocco is well worth the potential diarrhea.

The promotion of a tender place that has so far avoided the tourist industry reminds me of the whaler who screams, "Quick, harpoon it before it's extinct!" These places are this Europhile's cupids. Publicizing them gnaws at what makes them so great. But what kind of a travel writer can keep his favorite discoveries under wraps? Great finds are too hard to come by to just sit on. I keep no secrets.

With ever-more-sophisticated travelers armed with ever-better guidebooks, places I "discovered" 10 or 15 years ago are undeveloped and noncommercial only in a relative sense. And certain places that I really rave about suffer from Back Door congestion now. Every year or so, I revisit my poster-child village discoveries (Gimmelwald, Dingle, Ærø, Salema, and the Cinque Terre), and, while more crowded now, they are still great. At least from my experience, Back Door readers are pleasant people to share Europe with.

People recommended in this book tell me that Back Door readers are good guests who undo the "ugly" image created by the more demanding and ethnocentric American tourists. By traveling sensitively, you're doing a favor for yourself, as well as for the Europeans you'll meet, for the travelers who'll follow you...and for me. Thank you.

These Back Doors combine to give you a chorus line of travel thrills. I've written these chapters to give you the flavor of the places, not for you to navigate by. My various country guidebooks provide you with all the details necessary to splice your chosen Back Doors into a smooth trip. Bon voyage!

ITALY

The Cinque Terre: Italy's Riviera

"A sleepy, romantic, and inexpensive town on the Riviera without a tourist in sight." That's the mirage travelers chase around busy Nice and Cannes. Pssst! Although hardly free of tourists, the most dream-worthy stretch of the Riviera rests in Italy just across the border, between Genoa and Pisa. It's Italy's Cinque Terre.

Leaving the nearest big city, La Spezia, your train takes you into a mountain. Ten minutes later, you burst into the sunlight. Your train nips in and out of the hills, teasing you with a series of Mediterranean views. Each scene is grander than the last: azure blue tinseled in sunbeams, carbonated waves hitting desolate rocks, and the occasional topless sunbather camped out like a lone limpet.

The Cinque Terre (pronounced CHINK-weh TAY-reh), which means "five lands," is a quintet of villages clinging to this most inaccessible bit of Riviera coastline. Each is a variation on the same theme: a well-whittled pastel jumble of homes filling a gully like crusty sea creatures in a tide pool. Like a gangly clump of oysters, the houses grow on each other. Residents are the barnacles—hungry, but patient. And we travelers are like algae, coming in with the tide.

The rugged villages of the Cinque Terre, founded by Dark Age locals hiding out from marauding pirates, were long cut off from the modern world. Only with the coming of the train was access made easy. Today, the villages draw hordes of hikers, and the castles protect only glorious views. To preserve this land, the government has declared the Cinque Terre a national park. Visitors hiking between the towns now pay a small entrance fee (about $7 for a one-day pass), which stokes a fund designed to protect the flora and fauna and keep the trails clean and well maintained.

The government, recognizing how wonderfully preserved these towns are, has long prohibited anyone from constructing any modern buildings. For that reason, today there are no big, comfortable hotels in the area—great news for Back Door travelers because it keeps away the most obnoxious slice of the traveling public: those who need big, comfortable hotels. But rugged travelers, content to rent a room in a private home or simple *pensione,* enjoy a land where the villagers go about their business as if the surrounding vineyards are the very edges of the earth.

I need to warn you that even paradise can experience some setbacks. This region was hit by flash floods in the fall of 2011, with Vernazza and Monterosso getting the worst of it. The townspeople rallied to quickly repair the damage. By the time you visit, the towns and trails likely will be back to normal, much as I describe them below. (But for the latest on Vernazza, check the travel advisory at www.savevernazza.com; for Monterosso, see www.rebuildmonterosso.com.)

Vernazza

Overseen by a ruined castle, with the closest thing to a natural harbor, Vernazza is my Cinque Terre home base. Only the occasional noisy slurping up of the train by the mountain reminds you there's a modern world out there somewhere.

From Vernazza's harbor, wander through the jumble of a tough community living off the sea...or living off travelers who love the sea. The

Vernazza, my home base in the Cinque Terre

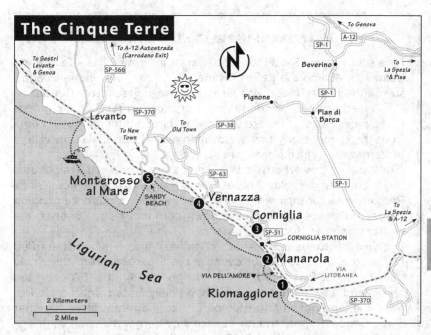

church bells dictate a relaxed tempo. Yellow webs of fishing nets, tables bedecked with umbrellas, kids with plastic shovels, and a flotilla of gritty little boats tethered to buoys provide splashes of color. And accompanying the scene is the soundtrack of a dream...a celebrate-the-moment white noise of children, dogs, and waves.

Vernazza's one street connects the harbor with the train station before melting into the vineyards. Like veins on a grape leaf, paths and stairways reach from Main Street into this watercolor huddle of houses. All of life is summer reruns in this hive of lazy human activity. A rainbow of laundry flaps as if to keep the flies off the fat grandmothers who clog ancient doorways.

Residents spend early evenings doing their *vasche* (laps), strolling between the station and the breakwater. Sit on a bench and study this slow-motion parade.

Sailors who suckle at salty taverns brag that while Portofino sold out, "Vernazza is locally owned." Years ago, fearing the change it would bring, they stopped the construction of a major road into the town and region.

Today, at the top end of town, Vernazza's cruel little road hits a post. No cars enter this village of 600 people. Like the breakwater keeps out the waves at the bottom of the town, the post keeps out the modern storm at the top. But Vernazza's ruined castle no longer says "stay away."

Vernazza: View from a Vineyard

It's a sunny afternoon a thousand years ago in the Cinque Terre, long before it became the Italian Riviera. This string of humble villages, surrounded by terraced vineyards, is a two-day sail from Genoa.

A leathery old farmer, taking a break from tending his grape-vines, picks a cactus fruit to quench his thirst. Suddenly, howls come from the crude, stony tower crowning a bluff that marks his village of Vernazza. Turkish pirates are attacking.

Avoiding powerhouse cities like nearby Genoa and Pisa, pirates delight in the villages. These Cinque Terre towns, famous since Roman times for their white wine, are like snack time for rampaging pirates. Villagers run for cover down corridors buried deep in the clutter of homes that clog Vernazza's ravine.

Nine centuries pass. Another leathery grape-picker is startled by the roar of a smoke-billowing train. Emerging from the newly built tunnel, it flies a red, white, and green flag. It's 1870, and the feudal and fragmented land of Italy is finally united. This first Italian train line, an engineering triumph of fledgling Italy, laces together Turin, Genoa, Rome...and, by chance, tiny Vernazza.

Decades later, in the 1930s, an Italian dictator teams up with a German tyrant. The war they started is going badly. In 1943, the German Führer calls on Vernazza's teenage boys to report for duty. The boys, who are told they'll only work in German farms and facto-ries, know they'll end up as fodder on the front. Rather than dying for Hitler, they become resistance fighters. Running through the night, they climb the ancient terraces into the hills high above the village cemetery.

The 1970s bring on a different battle scene. Hippies exercise their right to lie naked on the Cinque Terre's remote Guvano beach. Outraged, an angry armada of villagers—fully clothed and accompa-nied by a raft of reporters—converges on the rat pack of sunburned urbanite hedonists.

And its breakwater—a broad, inviting sidewalk edged with seaside boul-ders—sticks into the sea like a finger beckoning the distant excursion boats.

The Five-Village Cinque Terre Hike

Follow the fragrant trail through sunny vistas from Riomaggiore to Monterosso al Mare. Since my mind goes on vacation with the rest of me when I'm here, I think of the towns by number for easy orientation. They go—south to north—from one (Riomaggiore) to five (Monterosso).

Next, the age of tourism arrives. In 1978, a college-aged American backpacker, stumbling onto the region, finds the traditions vivid, the wine cheap, and the welcome warm. Inspired by the Cinque Terre and similar places throughout the Continent, he declares the region a "Back Door" and writes what will later become a top-selling guidebook on Europe.

By the 1990s, word of this paradise is out. More and more travelers visit, staying in apartments rather than in hotels. One day, at

the crack of dawn, another invasion comes—this time by land. A platoon of Italian tax inspectors blitzes the sleepy town, rousting out the tourists and cornering locals renting unlicensed rooms. B&B income in Vernazza is suddenly no longer tax-free.

Today, gnarled old men still tend their grapevines. Now Vernazza's castle, named "Belforte" centuries ago for the screams of its watchmen, watches over tourists. And the screams ringing out are of delight from children playing on the beach below.

But the economy has changed. The poor village is now a rich village, living well in its rustic and government-protected shell. Tourism drives the economy as the less-calloused residents feed and house travelers. While the private rooms rented are basic, the cuisine—super-charged by a passion for pasta, pesto, and seafood—is some of Italy's best. The sunny scene is a happy collaboration between locals, travelers, a long past, a lazy present...and no thought of tomorrow.

For a great day, catch the early train to Riomaggiore, hike from towns one through four, and catch the boat from Vernazza to the resort town of Monterosso for some beach time. From there, a five-minute train ride takes you home to Vernazza for the sunset and a seafood dinner.

The first town of the Cinque Terre, Riomaggiore (#1), has seduced famed artists into becoming residents. The biggest non-resort town of the five, Riomaggiore is a disappointment from the station. But the tunnel next to the train tracks takes you to a fascinating tangle of colorful homes leaning on each other as if someone stole their crutches. There's homemade gelato next door to Bar Centrale. And Riomaggiore's beach, an uncrowded cove, is a two-minute walk from town.

From Riomaggiore, follow signs for *Via dell'Amore* ("Walkway of Love"). This photogenic 15-minute promenade leads to Manarola (#2) and is wide enough for baby strollers. While you'll find no beach in Manarola, stairways lead to remote rocks for sunbathing. Uppity little Manarola rules its ravine and drinks its wine while its sun-bleached walls slumber on. Buy a picnic before walking to the beaches of Corniglia.

The Via dell'Amore path connects two Cinque Terre towns—Riomaggiore and Manarola—with grand views.

Corniglia (#3)—the only Cinque Terre town not directly on the water—sits smugly on its hilltop, a proud and victorious king of the mountain. Most visitors—lured to Corniglia by its scrawny, stony beach and the Cinque Terre's best swimming—never tackle the 370 stairs that zigzag up to the actual town. Those who make the Corniglian climb are rewarded by the Cinque Terre's finest wine and most staggering view. Corniglia has cooler temperatures, a windy belvedere, a few restaurants, and more than enough private rooms for rent.

Legend says that the village was originally settled by a Roman farmer who named it for his mother, Cornelia. Since ancient times, when Corniglian wine was so famous that vases found at Pompeii touted its virtues, wine has been this town's lifeblood. Follow the pungent smell of ripe grapes into an alley cellar and get a local to let you dip a straw into her keg.

Ten minutes out of Corniglia on the high trail to Vernazza, you'll see Guvano beach far below. This formerly nude beach made headlines in Italy in the 1970s, as clothed residents in a makeshift armada of dinghies and fishing boats retook their town beach.

The 90-minute hike from Corniglia (#3) to Vernazza (#4) is the wildest and greenest of the coast. The trail is as rugged as the people who've worked the terraced vineyards that blanket the region. Flowers and an ever-changing view entertain you at every step. As you make your sweaty way high above the glistening beaches, you'll ponder paying for your trip with the photos you've shot. The trail descends scenically into Vernazza, from where you can take the train, the boat, or the scenic, up-and-down-a-lot hike to town #5. Trails are rough (some readers report "very dangerous") and narrow, but easy to follow.

Monterosso al Mare (#5), happy to be appreciated, boasts the area's only sandy beach. This is a resort with cars, hotels, paddleboats, and crowds under rentable beach umbrellas. Adventurers in search of no-tan-line coves, refreshing waterfalls, and natural (and dangerous) high dives find them tucked away along the coast between towns #4 and #5.

Regardless of which town you call home, getting around is easy. While these towns are barely accessible by car, the nearly hourly milk-run train connects all five towns for about $2. A ferry provides a more relaxed and scenic town-hopping option.

Traditions ring through the Cinque Terre as persistently as the church bells—which remind residents of the days before tourism. The fishermen out at sea could hear the bells. The men in the vineyards high on the mountain could hear them, too. In one village, the hoteliers tried to stop the bells for the tourists who couldn't sleep. But the people of the village nearly revolted, and the bells ring on.

You'll eat well in the Cinque Terre. This is the home of pesto. Basil— which loves the region's temperate climate—is mixed with cheese (half parmigiano cow cheese and half pecorino sheep cheese), garlic, olive oil, and pine nuts, then poured over pasta. If you become addicted, don't worry: Small jars of pesto are sold in the grocery stores.

And the *vino delle Cinque Terre*, famous throughout Italy, flows cheap and easy throughout the region. If you like sweet, sherrylike wine, try the Sciacchetrà wine—served with a cookie. While 10 kilos of grapes yield 7 liters of wine, 10 kilos of grapes make only 1.5 liters of Sciacchetrà, which is made from near-raisins. If your room is up a lot of steps, be warned:

Sciacchetrà comes with 50 percent more alcohol than regular wine.

In the cool, calm early evening, sit on the Vernazza breakwater nursing a glass of wine. Paint a dream in vineyard greens and Mediterranean blues. Nowhere else does the lure of the Mediterranean, Italy, and village life combine so potently to shipwreck a speedy itinerary.

*For good-value accommodations in **Vernazza**, try Trattoria Gianni (splurge, sea views, near castle, Piazza Marconi 5, tel. 0187-821-003, www.gianni franzi.it) or Albergo Barbara (moderate, sea views, on harbor square, Piazza Marconi 30, tel. 0187-812-398, mobile 338-793-3261, www.albergobarbara .it). For all the travel specifics, see this year's edition of* Rick Steves' Italy.

Hill Towns of Central Italy

Too many people connect Venice, Florence, and Rome with straight lines. Break out of this syndrome, and you'll lick a little of the Italy that the splash of Venice, the finesse of Florence, and the grandeur of Rome were built upon.

The hill towns of central Italy hold their crumbling heads proudly above the noisy flood of the 21st century and offer a peaceful taste of what eludes so many tourists. Sitting on a timeless rampart high above the traffic and trains, hearing only children in the market as the rustling wind ages the weary red-tile patchwork that surrounds me, I find the essence of Italy.

There are a dozen great touristy towns and countless ignored communities casually doing time and drinking wine. See some of each.

The Big-Name Hill Towns

Siena, unlike its rival, Florence, is a city to be seen as a whole rather than as a collection of sights. While memories of Florence consist of dodging Vespas and pickpockets between museums, Siena has an easy-to-enjoy Gothic soul: Courtyards sport flower-decked wells, churches modestly hoard their art, and alleys dead-end into red-tiled rooftop panoramas. Climb to the dizzy top of the 100-yard-tall bell tower and reign over urban harmony at its best. At twilight, first-time poets savor that magic

Siena turns tourists into poets.

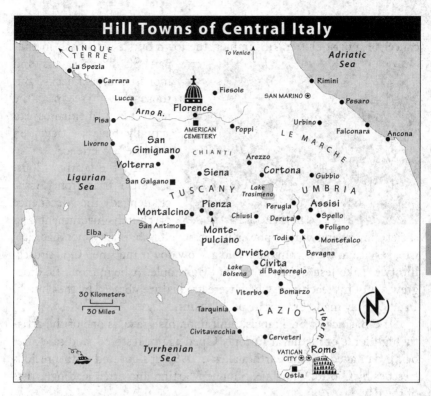

Hill Towns of Central Italy

moment when the sky is a rich blue dome no brighter than the medieval towers that seem to hold it high.

Il Campo, Siena's great central piazza, with its gently tilted floor fanning out from the City Hall tower, is like a people-friendly stage set. It offers the perfect invitation to loiter. Think of it as a trip to the beach without sand or water. Wander among lovers stroking guitars and each others' hair. Il Campo immerses you in a troubadour's world where bellies become pillows. For a picnic dessert on the Campo, try *panforte*, Siena's claim to caloric fame. This rich, chewy concoction of nuts, honey, and candied fruits impresses even fruitcake haters.

The *panforte* of medieval churches is Siena's cathedral. Its striped facade is piled with statues and ornamentation. And the chewy interior, decorated from top to bottom, comes with the heads of 172 popes peering down from the ceiling over the fine inlaid art on the floor. This is as Baroque as Gothic gets.

For those who dream of a city with a traffic-free core, Siena is it. Take time to savor the first European square to go pedestrian (1966), and then, just to be silly, wonder what would happen if they did it in your town.

Assisi, a worthy hometown for St. Francis, is battling a commercial cancer of tourist clutter. In summer, the town bursts with flash-in-the-

pan St. Francis fans and monastic knickknacks. But those able to see past the tacky monk mementos can actually have a "travel on purpose" experience.

In the early 1200s, a simple friar from Assisi challenged the decadence of church government and society in general with a powerful message of simplicity, nonmaterialism, service to the community, and a "slow down and smell God's roses" lifestyle. Like Jesus, Francis taught by example. A huge monastic order grew out of his teachings, which were gradually embraced by the church. In 1939, Italy made Francis its patron saint.

The Basilica of St. Francis, built upon his grave, is one of the artistic highlights of medieval Europe. Open again, restored, and safe after being damaged by the earthquakes of 1997, it's covered with precious frescoes by Giotto, Cimabue, Simone Martini, and other leading artists of the day.

With a quiet hour in the awesome basilica, some reflective reading (there's a bookstore in the courtyard), and a meditative stroll through the

back streets, you can dissolve the tour buses and melt into the magic of Assisi. Grab a picnic and hike to the ruined castle, surrounded by the same Tuscan views and serenaded by the same birdsong Francis enjoyed.

Most visitors are day-trippers. Assisi after dark is closer to a place Francis could call home.

San Gimignano bristles with towers and bustles with tourists. A thrilling silhouette from a distance, Italy's best-preserved medi-

So often photography—and a little wine—bring out the warmth in Italian women.

eval skyline gets better as you approach. With 14 towers still standing (out of an original 60 or so), it's a fun and easy stop. In the 13th century, back in the days of Romeo and Juliet, towns were run by feuding noble families who would periodically battle things out from the protective bases of their respective family towers. Sunset's the right time to conquer San Gimignano's castle. Climb high above the crowds, sit on the castle's summit, and imagine the battles Tuscany's porcupine has endured.

Orvieto, the tourist's token hill town, sits majestically on its throne of volcanic tuff, offering an impressive hill-capping profile to those on the train or *autostrada* to Rome. Its cathedral, with some fascinating Signorelli frescoes, is surrounded by an excellent tourist information office, a fine Etruscan collection at the archaeological museum, and a world-class gelato shop. With three popular gimmicks (ceramics, cathedral, and Classico wine), Orvieto is loaded with tourists by day and quiet by night. Drinking a shot of wine in a ceramic cup as you gaze up at the cathedral lets you experience the essence of Orvieto all at once. Buses run six days a week from Orvieto to Bagnoregio, near the queen of hill towns, Civita di Bagnoregio.

ITALY

Civita di Bagnoregio

Of all the Italian hill towns, Civita di Bagnoregio is my favorite. Less well-known than the famous hill towns mentioned above, it deserves more description.

People who've been here say "Civita" (chee-VEE-tah) with warmth and love. This precious chip of Italy, a traffic-free community with a grow-it-in-the-valley economy, has so far escaped the ravages of modernity. Please approach it with the same respect and sensitivity you would a dying relative, because—in a sense—that's Civita.

Civita teeters atop a pinnacle in a vast canyon ruled by wind and

The perfect hill town, Civita di Bagnoregio

Civita di Bagnoregio

To Lubriano Town

NOTE: MAP NOT TO SCALE;
A WALK ACROSS CIVITA
TAKES APPROX. 5 MINUTES—
BUT DON'T RUSH IT!

Cliffs

Cliffs

OSTERIA
AL FORNO DI AGNESE

ANTICO FORNO TRATTORIA
& CIVITA B&B

LOCANDA
DELLA BUONA
VENTURA

CAMPANILE
(BELL TOWER)

OLIVE PRESS
& BRUSCHETTERIA

MARIA'S
GARDEN

OLD LAUNDRY
& WC

Piazza

CHURCH

ARCH

MAIN   STRADA

ETRUSCAN
COLUMNS

ANTICA
CIVITA
MUSEUM

FOOTBRIDGE

To
Bagnoregio

PALACE

SNACK
BAR

WINE BAR
PEPPONE

WINE CELLAR
& BRUSCHETTE

CAVES &
CHAPEL
CARVED
IN ROCK

Cliffs

Trail to Etruscan
tunnel under Civita

RUINS OF HOUSE
OF ST. BONAVENTURE

erosion. But, while its population has dropped to a handful, the town survives (and even has a website: www.civitadibagnoregio.it).

The saddle that once connected Civita to its bigger and busier sister town, Bagnoregio, eroded away. Today a bridge connects the two towns. A man with a Vespa does the same work his father did with a donkey—ferrying the town's goods up and down the umbilical bridge that connects Civita with a small, distant parking lot and the rest of Italy. Rome, just 60 miles to the south, is a world away.

Entering the town through a cut in the rock made by Etruscans 2,500 years ago, and heading under a 12th-century Romanesque arch, you feel history in the huge, smooth cobblestones. This was once the main Etruscan road leading to the Tiber Valley and Rome. Inside the gate, the charms of Civita are subtle. Those searching for arcade tourism wouldn't know where to look. There are no lists of attractions, orientation tours, or museum hours. It's just Italy. Civita is an artist's dream, a town in the nude. Each lane and footpath holds a surprise. The warm stone walls glow, and each stairway is dessert to a sketch pad or camera.

Sit in the piazza. Smile and nod at each passerby. It's a social jigsaw puzzle, and each person fits. The old woman hanging out in the window monitors gossip. A tiny hunchback lady is everyone's daughter. And cats, the fastest-growing segment of the population, scratch their itches on ancient pillars.

Civita's young people are gone, lured away by the dazzle of more modern places where they can take part in Italy's cosmopolitan parade.

And as old people become frail, they move into apartments in nearby Bagnoregio. Today, Civita's social pie has two slices: the aging, full-time residents; and rich, big-city Italians who are slowly buying up the place for their country escapes. Buoyed by my writing, exposure in German and French travel magazines, and its increasing popularity as a movie backdrop (e.g., for the made-for-TV movie, *Pinocchio*, in 2008), Civita can see up to 200 tourists a day on summer weekends. In summer, visit on a weekday.

Explore the village. The basic grid street plan of the ancient town survives—but its centerpiece, a holy place of worship, rotates with the cultures: first an Etruscan temple, then a Roman temple, and today a church. The pillars that stand like bar stools in the square once decorated the pre-Christian temple.

Step into the church. The heartbeat and pride of the village, this is where festivals and processions start, visitors are escorted, and the town's past is honored. Enjoy paintings by students of famous artists; relics of the hometown-boy Saint Bonaventure; a dried floral decoration spread across the floor; and a cool, quiet moment in a pew.

Just around the corner from the church, on the main street, is Bruschette con Prodotti Locali, Rossana and Antonio's cool and friendly wine cellar. Pull up a stump and let them or their daughters, Arianna and Antonella, serve you *panini* (sandwiches), bruschetta (garlic toast with tomato), wine, and a cake called *ciambella*. The white wine has a taste reminiscent of dirty socks. But it's made right here. After eating, ask to see the cellar with its traditional winemaking gear and provisions for rolling huge kegs up the stairs. Grab the stick and tap on the kegs to measure their fullness.

The ground below Civita is honeycombed with ancient cellars (for keeping wine at the same temperature all year) and cisterns (for collecting rainwater, since there was no well in town). Many of these date from Etruscan times.

Explore further through town, but remember nothing is abandoned. Everything is still privately owned. At Antico Frantoio Bruschetteria, Vittoria shows off the latest in a 2,000-year line of olive presses that have filled her ancient Etruscan cave. Buy a postcard in Italian. Vittoria's sons Sandro and Felice, and her grandsons Maurizio and Fabrizio, run the local equivalent of a lemonade stand, selling bruschetta to visitors. Bread toasted on an open fire, drizzled with the finest oil, rubbed with pungent garlic, and topped with chopped tomatoes—these edible souvenirs stay on your breath for hours and in your memory forever.

At the end of town, the main drag shrivels into a trail that leads past a chapel (once a jail) and down to a tunnel—now barred to entry—that was cut through the hill under the town in Etruscan times. It was widened in the 1930s so farmers could get between their scattered fields more easily.

Civita has only a few restaurants, which cluster near the piazza. At Trattoria Antico Forno ("Antique Oven"), you eat what's cooking. Owner Franco slices and dices happily through the day. Spaghetti, salad, and wine on the Antico Forno patio, cuddled by Civita—I wouldn't trade it for all-you-can-eat at Maxim's.

Spend the evening. After dinner, sit on the church steps with people who've been doing exactly this for 60 years. Children play on the piazza until midnight. As you walk back to your car—that scourge of the modern world that enabled you to get here—stop under a lamp on the donkey path, listen to the canyon... distant voices...*fortissimo* crickets.

Towering above its moat, Civita seems to be fortified against change. But the modern world is a persistent battering ram. Civita will be great for years, but never as great as today.

Virgin Hill Towns

Italy is spiked with similar hill towns. Gubbio, Todi, Volterra, and Arezzo are discovered but rarely visited. Cortona (with a hostel set in a remodeled 13th-century palace), Pienza (a Renaissance-planned town), and Montepulciano (with its dramatic setting) are touristy but also worth the hill-town lover's energy and time.

Any guidebook lists popular hill towns. But if you want to dance at noon with a toothless lady while your pizza cooks, press a good-luck coin into the moldy ceiling of an Etruscan wine cellar, or be introduced to a mediocre altarpiece as proudly as if it were a Michelangelo, then stow your guidebook, buy the best map you can find, and explore.

Many bigger hill towns have a train station nearby (with a shuttle bus beginning its winding climb to the old town center shortly after your train arrives). But to find your own gem, you'll need to leave the train lines. Take the bus, hitch, or rent a car for a few days. If you're using a rail-and-drive pass, all the better—this is car country.

Hill towns, like the Greek Islands, come in two basic varieties: discovered and virgin. The difference, touristically speaking, is that "discovered" towns know what tourism is and have an appetite for the money that comes with it. "Virgin" towns are simply pleased you dropped in.

Sorano, Pitigliano, Poppi, Trevi, and Bagnaia (near Viterbo) have almost no tourism. Bevagna (near Assisi) features Roman ruins and twin dark Romanesque churches on its main square.

Perfect Back Door villages, like hidden pharaohs' tombs, are worth uncovering. Photographers delight in hill towns. Their pictorial collections (such as *Italian Hilltowns*, by Norman F. Carver) are a fine source of information. Study these, circling the most intriguing towns on your map. Talk to travelers who have studied or lived in Italy. Ask locals for their favorites. Scan the horizon for fortified towers. Drive down dead-end roads far from the nearest advertising budget.

Hill towns are a vital slice of the Italian pizza—crumbly crust with a thick, gooey culture. Don't just chase down my favorites or your guidebook's recommendations. Somewhere in the slumber of Umbria and the texture of Tuscany, the ultimate hill town awaits your discovery.

*For good-value accommodations in **Siena**, try the convent-run Alma Domus (budget, request view room, Via Camporegio 37, tel. 0577-44-177, www .hotelalmadomus.it); in **Assisi**, Hotel Ideale (moderate, Piazza Matteotti 1, tel. 075-813-570, www.hotelideale.it); and in **Orvieto**, Hotel Corso (moderate, Corso Cavour 343, tel. 076-334-2020, www.hotelcorso.net). In **Civita**, try Franco Sala's Civita B&B (budget rooms on town square, tel. 076-176-0016, mobile 347-611-5426, www.civitadibagnoregio.it); or, in nearby **Bagnoregio**, Romantica Pucci B&B (moderate, Piazza Cavour 1, tel. 076-179-2121, www.hotelromanticapucci.it). For all the travel specifics, see this year's edition of Rick Steves' Italy.*

North Italy Choices: Milan, Lakes, or Mountains

Italy, Europe's richest cultural brew, intensifies as you plunge deeper. If you like it as far south as Rome, go farther—it gets better. But if Italy's wearing you down, you'll enjoy a milder Italy in the north, complete with the same great cappuccino, gelato, and people-watching.

North Italy's charms come in three packages: urban Milan, romantic lakes, and alpine Dolomites. All are within three hours of Venice, Florence, and each other.

Milan

Milan is today's Italy. The rise of modern Italy can be blamed on cities like Milan. As the saying goes, for every church in Rome, there's a bank in Milan. Italy's second city has a hardworking, fashion-conscious population of more than 1.3 million. From publicists to pasta power lunches, Milan is Italy's industrial, banking, TV, publishing, and convention capital.

Much of Milan is ugly, with a recently bombed-out feeling (a legacy of World War II). Its huge financial buildings are as manicured as its parks are shaggy. As if to make up for its harsh concrete shell, its people and windows are works of art. Milan is an international fashion capital. Even the cheese is gift-wrapped.

Milan's cathedral, the city's centerpiece, is the fourth-largest church in Europe. At 480 feet long and 280 feet wide, forested with 52 sequoia-sized pillars and more than 2,000 statues, the place can seat 10,000 worshippers. Hike up to the rooftop—a fancy crown of spires—for great views of the city, the square, and, on clear days, the Swiss Alps.

Milan's cathedral dominates the main square.

The cathedral square, Piazza Duomo, is a classic European scene. Professionals scurry, label-conscious kids loiter, and young thieves peruse. Facing the square, the Galleria Vittorio Emanuele, Milan's great four-story-high, glass-domed arcade, invites you in to shop or just sip a slow latte. Some of Europe's hottest people-watching turns that pricey cup into a good value. Enjoy the parade. For good luck, locals step on the testicles of the Taurus in the floor's zodiac mosaic. Two girls explained that it's even better if you twirl.

The immense Sforza Castle, Milan's much-bombed and rebuilt brick fortress, is overwhelming at first sight. But its courtyard has a great lawn for picnics and siestas. Its museum features interesting medieval armor, furniture, Lombard art, and a Michelangelo statue with no crowds—his unfinished *Rondanini Pietà*. The Brera Art Gallery, Milan's top collection of paintings, is world class (although you'll see better in Rome and Florence).

La Scala is possibly the world's most prestigious opera house. Opera buffs will love the museum's extensive collection of things that would mean absolutely nothing to the MTV crowd: Verdi's top hat, Rossini's eyeglasses, Toscanini's baton, Fettucini's pesto, and the original scores, busts, portraits, and death masks of great composers and musicians.

Leonardo's ill-fated *Last Supper* is flaking off the refectory wall of the church of Santa Maria delle Grazie. The fresco suffers from Leonardo's experimental use of oil. Decay began within six years of its completion. It's undergone more restoration work than Cher and is now viewable only with a reservation—spots are booked more than a month in advance

Train Connections from Milan

To Basel

To Innsbruck

AUSTRIA

SWITZ.

Chur

Merano

Alpe di Siusi

Lake Maggiore

St. Moritz

Bolzano

Cortina

Dolomites

Calalzo

Lugano

Tirano

Domo.

Lake Como

Trento

Varenna

ITALY

Stresa

Como

Lecco

Gallarate

Bergamo

Lake Garda

Malpensa

Milan

Linate

Desenzano

Verona

Vicenza

Marco Polo

Padua

Venice

Mantova

Cremona

----- Rail
---- Bus

30 Kilometers

30 Miles

Ferrara

Adriatic Sea

To Nice

Genoa

To Cinque Terre

To Florence

Bologna

Ravenna

Med. Sea

ITALY

(best to call them directly, tel. 02-9280-0360 in Italy or from the US 011-39-02-9280-0360; possible to reserve online at www.cenacolovinciano .net, but problematic website often does not show available ticket dates). Most of the original paint is gone, but tourists still enjoy paying $12 to see what's left.

More of Leonardo's spirit survives in Italy's answer to the Smithsonian, the Leonardo da Vinci National Science and Technology Museum. While most tourists visit for the hall of Leonardo's designs illustrated in wooden models, the rest of this vast collection of industrial cleverness is just as fascinating. Plenty of push-button action displays the development of trains, radios, old musical instruments, computers, batteries, and telephones, alongside chunks of the first transatlantic cable.

Italy's Lakes

The Italian Lakes, at the base of Italy's Alps, are a romantic and popular destination for Italians and their European neighbors. The million-euro question is "Which lake?" For a complete dose of Italian-lakes wonder and aristocratic old-days romance, visit Lake Como.

Lined with elegant 19th-century villas, crowned by snow-capped mountains, buzzing with ferries, hydrofoils, and little passenger ships, this is a good place to take a break from the intensity and obligatory turnstile culture of central Italy. Handy, accessible, and offbeat, Lake Como is Italy for beginners. It seems that half the travelers you'll meet on Lago di Como have tossed their itineraries overboard and are actually relaxing. The area's isolation and flat economy have left it pretty much the way the 19th-century romantic poets described it.

On Lake Como, ferries hop from town to town.

While you can circle the lake by car, the road is narrow, congested, and lined by privacy-seeking walls, hedges, and tall fences. This is train-and-boat country. Trains whisk you from intense Milan into the serenity of Lago di Como in an hour. Then, happy-go-lucky ferries sail scenically from port to port.

The town of Bellagio, "the Pearl of the Lake," is a classy combination of tidiness and Old World elegance. If you don't mind that tramp-in-a-palace feeling, it's a fine place to surround yourself with the more adventurous of the soft travelers and shop for umbrellas and ties. The heavy curtains between the arcades create welcome shade and keep the tourists and their poodles from sweating. While Johnnie Walker and jewelry sell best at lake level, the residents shop up the hill.

Menaggio, directly across the lake from Bellagio and just eight miles from Lugano in Switzerland, feels more like a real town than its neighbors. Since the lake is too dirty for swimming, consider its fine public pool.

One hop from Menaggio or Bellagio by ferry, the town of Varenna offers the best of all lake worlds. On the quieter side of the lake, with a romantic promenade, a tiny harbor, narrow lanes, and its own villa, Varenna is the right place to munch a peach and ponder the place where Italy is welded to the Alps. Varenna's volume goes down with the sun. After dark, the *passerella* (lakeside walk) is adorned with lovers pressing silently against each other in the shadows.

The Dolomites

The Dolomites, Italy's dramatic mountainous rooftop, serve alpine thrills with Italian sunshine. The famous valleys and towns of the well-developed region suffer from an après-ski fever, but the bold, snow-dusted mountains and green meadows offer great hikes. The cost for reliably good

Don't forget Italy's Alps, the Dolomites.

weather is a drained-reservoir feeling. Lovers of the Alps may miss the lushness that comes with the unpredictable weather farther north.

A hard-fought history has left this part of Italy bicultural and bilingual, with *der* emphasis on the *Deutsch*. Residents speak German first. Many wish they were still Austrian. In the Middle Ages, the region faced north, part of the Holy Roman Empire. Later it was firmly in the Austrian Habsburg realm. After Austria lost World War I, its South Tirol (Südtirol) became Italy's Alto Adige. Mussolini did what he could to Italianize the region, including giving each town an Italian name. The government has wooed cranky German-speaking locals with economic breaks that make this one of Italy's richest areas (as prices attest). Today, signs and literature in the autonomous province of Südtirol/Alto Adige are in both languages.

In spite of all the glamorous ski resorts and busy construction cranes, local color survives in a blue-aproned, ruddy-faced, long-white-bearded way. There's yogurt and yodeling for breakfast. Culturally as much as geographically, the area feels Austrian. (The western part of Austria is named after Tirol, a village that is now actually in Italy.)

Lifts, good trails, outdoor activity-oriented tourist offices, and a decent bus system make the region especially accessible. But it's expensive. Most towns have no alternative to $120 doubles in hotels, or $80 doubles in private homes. Beds usually come with a hearty breakfast, a rarity in Italy.

The seasons are brutal. The best time to visit—when everything is open and booming, but also at full price and crowded—is from mid-July through September. After a dreary November, the snow hits, and the area bustles with skiers until April. May and early June are dead (though the sedentary sort will enjoy the views and tranquility). The most exciting

Treating the Alps like a beach, in Italy's Dolomites

trails are still under snow, and the mountain lifts are shut down. Most mountain huts and budget accommodations are closed, as the locals are more concerned with preparing for another boom season than catering to the stray off-season tourist.

By car, circle north from Venice and drive the breathtaking Grande Strada delle Dolomiti, or Great Dolomite Road (80 miles: Cortina d'Ampezzo-Pordoi Pass-Sella Pass-Val di Fassa-Bolzano; toll possible). In the spring and early summer, passes labeled "Closed" are often bare, dry, and, as far as local drivers are concerned, wide open. Conveniently for Italian tour operators, no direct public-transportation route covers the Great Dolomite Road.

With limited time and no car, maximize mountain thrills and minimize transportation headaches by taking the train to Bolzano, then catching a public bus into the mountains.

If Bolzano (or "Bozen" to its German-speaking residents) weren't so sunny, you could be in Innsbruck. This arcaded old town of 100,000, with a great open-air market on Piazza Erbe, is worth a Tirolean stroll and a stop at its Dolomite information center. To chill out, see Bolzano's Ice Man, a 5,300-year-old body found frozen with his gear some years ago.

Tourist offices in any Dolomite town are a wealth of information. Before choosing a hike, get their advice. Ideally, pick a hike with an overnight in a mountain hut, and make a telephone reservation. Most huts, called *refugios,* offer reasonable doubles, cheaper dorm *(Lager)* beds, and good, inexpensive meals.

I wouldn't steer you wrong: Hiking through Dolomite meadows is an udderly heifer-vescent experience.

Many are tempted to wimp out on the Dolomites and admire the spires from a distance. They take the cable car into the hills above Bolzano, to the cute but very touristy village of Oberbozen. Don't. Bus into the Dolomites instead.

Europe's largest high-alpine meadow, Alpe di Siusi, spreads high above Bolzano, separating two of the most famous Dolomite ski-resort valleys (Val di Fassa and Val Gardena). Measuring three miles by seven and a half miles, and soaring 6,500 feet high, Alpe di Siusi is dotted by farm huts and wildflowers and surrounded by dramatic (if distant)

Dolomite peaks and cliffs.

The Sasso Lungo Mountains at the head of the meadow provide a storybook Dolomite backdrop, while the bold, spooky Mount Schlern stands gazing into the haze of the Italian peninsula. Not surprisingly, the Schlern, looking like a devilish *Winged Victory*, gave ancient peoples enough willies to spawn legends of supernatural forces. Fear of the Schlern witch, today's tourist-brochure mascot, was the cause of many a broom-riding medieval townswoman's fiery death.

A nature preserve, the alpine meadow is virtually car-free. A gondola whisks visitors up to the park from the valley below. Within the park, buses take hikers to and from key points along the tiny road all the way to the foot of the postcard-dramatic Sasso peaks. Meadow walks are ideal for flower lovers and strollers, while chairlifts provide springboards for more dramatic and demanding hikes.

The Alpe di Siusi is my recommended one-stop look at the Dolomites because of its easy accessibility to those with or without cars, the variety of walks and hikes, the quintessential Dolomite views, and the charm of neighboring Castelrotto as a home base.

Castelrotto/Kastelruth: Your home base in the Dolomites

The town of Castelrotto (population: 2,000; German name: Kastelruth) was built for farmers rather than skiers. It has good bus connections, fine and friendly hotels, and more village character than any town around. Pop into the church to hear the choir practice. And be on the town square at 3:00 p.m. as the bells peal and the moms bring home their preschoolers.

At Europe Through the Back Door, where I work, many consider Italy the greatest country in Europe. If all you have is 10 days, do Venice, Florence, Rome, the hill towns, and the Riviera. If you have more time and seek intensity, head south. But to round out your itinerary with all the best of Italy and none of the chaos, splice in a little of the Dolomites, the lakes, and Milan.

*For good-value (but splurge) accommodations: in **Milan**, try Hotel Grand Duca di York (Via Moneta 1, tel. 02-874-863, www.ducadiyork.com); in **Varenna**, Villa Cipressi (Via IV Novembre 22, tel. 0341-830-113,* *www.villacipressi.it) or Albergo Milano (Via XX Settembre 35, tel. 0341-830-298, www.varenna.net); and in* **Castelrotto/Kastelruth,** *Alla Torre/Gasthof zum Turm (Kofelgasse 8, tel. 0471-706-349, www.zumturm.com). For all the travel specifics, see this year's edition of* Rick Steves' Italy.

Naples, the Amalfi Coast, and Pompeii

Naples Bay rounds out any trip to Italy with an *antipasto misto* of travel thrills. Serene Sorrento, an hour south of Naples' urban intensity, is a great home base and the gateway to the much-drooled-over Amalfi Coast. From the jet-setting island of Capri to the stunning Amalfi Coast towns, from ancient Pompeii to even more ancient Paestum, this is Italy's coast with the most. Naples is Italy intensified, from its best (birthplace of pizza and Sophia Loren) to its worst (home of the Camorra, Naples' "family" of organized crime).

On a quick trip, give the area three days. With Sorrento as your sunny springboard, spend a day exploring the Amalfi Coast, a day split between Pompeii and the town of Sorrento, and a day enjoying the street scene in Naples. Paestum, the crater of Vesuvius, Herculaneum, and the island of Capri are all good reasons to give the area a few more days.

For a blitz day trip from Rome, you could have breakfast on the early Rome-Naples express, do Naples and Pompeii in a day, and be back at your hotel in time for *Letterman.* That's exhausting but more interesting than a third day in Rome. (In the heat of the afternoon, Naples' street life slows and many sights close. Things pick up again in the early evening.)

Sorrento, wedged on a ledge between the mountains and the Mediterranean, is an attractive resort of 20,000 residents and—in the summer—as many tourists. It's as well located for regional sightseeing as it is a pleasant place to stay and stroll. The Sorrentines have gone out of their way to create a completely safe and relaxed place for tourists to spend money. Everyone seems to speak fluent English and work for the Chamber of Commerce. Spritzed by lemon and olive groves, this gateway to the Amalfi Coast has an unspoiled old quarter, a lively main shopping street, a spectacular cliffside setting, and easy public transportation (Circumvesuviana trains run twice hourly to Naples, stopping at Pompeii and Herculaneum en route; and blue or green-and-white SITA buses depart nearly hourly from the Sorrento train station to the Amalfi Coast).

The **Amalfi Coast** offers one of the world's great bus rides: The coastal trip from Sorrento to Salerno will leave your mouth open and

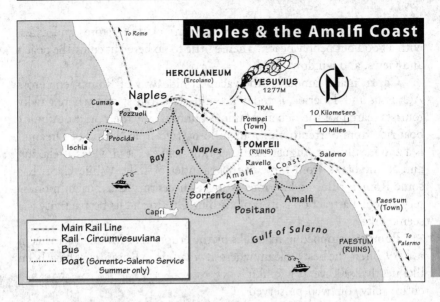

Naples & the Amalfi Coast

your camera smokin'. You'll gain respect for the Italian engineers who built the road—and even more respect for the bus drivers who drive it.

As you hyperventilate, notice how the Mediterranean, a sheer 500-foot drop below, twinkles.

Cantilevered garages, hotels, and villas cling to the vertical terrain. Beautiful sandy coves tease from far below and out of reach. Gasp from the right side of the bus as you head toward Salerno, and the left on the way back to Sorrento. Traffic is so heavy that in the summer cars are allowed to drive only every other day—even-numbered license plates one day, odd the next. (Buses and tourists foolish enough to drive here are exempt from this system.)

The Amalfi Coast towns are pretty but generally touristy, congested, overpriced, and a long hike above tiny beaches. The real Amalfi thrill is the scenic drive.

If you need a destination, consider Positano, an easy day trip from Sorrento. Specializing in scenery and sand, the town of Positano hangs halfway between Sorrento and Amalfi town on the most spectacular stretch of the coast. A three-star sight from a distance, Positano is a pleasant (if expensive) gathering of women's clothing stores and cafés, with a good but pebbly beach. There's little to do here but enjoy the beach and views, and window-shop.

Capri, made famous as the vacation hideaway of Roman emperors Augustus and Tiberius, is today a world-class tourist trap where gawky tourists search for the rich and famous but find only their prices. A quick boat ride from Sorrento, this four-mile-by-two-mile "Island of Dreams" is a zoo in July and August. At other times of year, it provides a relaxing and scenic break from the cultural gauntlet of Italy. While Capri has some Roman ruins and an interesting 14th-century Carthusian monastery, its chief attraction is its famous Blue Grotto and its best activity is a scenic hike.

Pompeii, stopped in its tracks by the eruption of Mount Vesuvius in A.D. 79, offers the best look anywhere at what life in Rome must have been like nearly 2,000 years ago. An entire city of well-preserved ruins is yours to explore. Once a thriving commercial port of 20,000, Pompeii grew from Greek and Etruscan roots to become an important Roman city. Then Pompeii was buried under 30 feet of hot mud and volcanic ash. For archaeologists, this was a shake 'n' bake windfall, teaching them volumes about daily Roman life.

When touring Pompeii, remember this was a booming trading city. Most streets would have been lined with stalls and jammed with customers from sunup to sundown. Chariots vied for street space with shoppers, and many streets were off-limits to chariots during shopping hours (you'll still see street signs with pictures of men carrying vases—this meant pedestrians only). Pompeii's best art is in the Naples Archaeological Museum (see next page).

Herculaneum—smaller, less ruined, and less crowded than its famous sister, Pompeii—offers a closer look at ancient Roman life. Caked and baked by the same eruption in A.D. 79, Herculaneum is a small community of intact buildings with plenty of surviving detail.

Vesuvius, mainland Europe's only active volcano, has been sleeping restlessly since 1944. Complete your Pompeii or Herculaneum experience by scaling the volcano that made them famous. The 4,000-foot summit of Vesuvius is accessible by car, shuttle bus from Pompeii or Herculaneum (about $11 round-trip), or taxi (about $125 round-trip from Naples). From the Vesuvius parking lot, pay about $10 and hike 30 minutes to the top for a sweeping Bay of Naples view, desolate lunar-like surroundings, and hot rocks. On the top, walk the entire crater lip for the most interesting views. The far end overlooks Pompeii. Be still and alone to hear the wind and tumbling rocks in the crater. Any steam? Vesuvius is closed when erupting.

Paestum is one of the best collections of Greek temples anywhere—and certainly the most accessible to Western Europe. Serenely situated, it's surrounded by fields and wildflowers and a modest commercial strip. Founded by the Greeks in the sixth century B.C., it was a key stop on an important trade route. It was conquered first by Romans in the third century B.C. and later by malaria-carrying mosquitoes that kept the site wonderfully desolate for almost a thousand years. Rediscovered in the 18th century, Paestum today offers the only well-preserved Greek ruins north of Sicily.

Naples, a thriving Greek commercial center 2,500 years ago, remains southern Italy's leading city, offering a fascinating collection of museums, churches, eclectic architecture, and crazy traffic. The pulse of Italy throbs in this urban jungle. Like Cairo or Bombay, it's appalling and captivating at the same time, the closest thing to "reality travel" you'll find in Western Europe. But this tangled mess still somehow manages to breathe, laugh, and sing—with a captivating Italian accent.

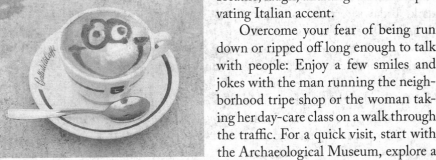

Overcome your fear of being run down or ripped off long enough to talk with people: Enjoy a few smiles and jokes with the man running the neighborhood tripe shop or the woman taking her day-care class on a walk through the traffic. For a quick visit, start with the Archaeological Museum, explore a few streets, and celebrate your survival with pizza.

Naples' Archaeological Museum offers the closest possible peek into the artistic jewelry boxes of Pompeii and Herculaneum. The actual archaeological sites, while impressive, are barren—the best frescoes and mosaics ended up here. The Secret Room (for which you may need to reserve an entry time at the ticket desk) displays R-rated Roman "bedroom" art. A museum highlight is the Farnese Collection—a giant hall of huge, bright, and wonderfully restored statues excavated from Rome's Baths of Caracalla. You can almost hear the *Toro Farnese* snorting.

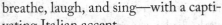

This largest intact statue from antiquity (a third-century copy of a Hellenistic original) was carved out of one piece of marble and restored by Michelangelo.

Marble lovers chisel out time for the Cappella Sansevero, six blocks southeast of the Archaeological Museum. This small chapel is a Baroque explosion mourning the body of Christ, lying on a soft pillow under an incredibly realistic veil—all carved out of marble (by Giuseppe "Howdeedoodat" Sammartino, 1750). Loving statues, each carved from a single piece of marble, adorn the altar. *Despair* (by Francesco Queirolo, 1759) struggles with a marble rope net, while *Modesty* poses coyly under her full-length marble veil (by Antonio Corradini, 1752). For your inner ghoul, descend into the crypt for a creepy look at two 200-year-old studies in varicose veins. Was one decapitated? Was one pregnant?

Take time to explore Naples. This living medieval city is its own best sight. Couples artfully make love on Vespas, while surrounded by more fights and smiles per cobblestone than anywhere else in Italy.

Paint a picture with these thoughts: Naples has the most intact ancient Roman street plan any-where. Imagine life here in the days of Caesar (retain these images as you visit Pompeii), with street-side shop fronts that close up to form private homes after dark. Today is just one more page in a 2,000-year-old story of city activity: all kinds of meetings, beatings, and cheatings; kisses, near misses, and little-boy pisses.

The only thing predictable about this Neapolitan mix is the friendliness of its shopkeepers and the boldness of its mopeds.

Naples: an urban jungle with straight streets and friendly cops

Concerned residents will tug on their lower eyelid, warning you to be wary. Pop into a grocery shop and ask the man to make you his best ham-and-mozzarella sandwich.

For a peek behind the scenes in the shade of wet laundry, venture down a few narrow streets lined by tall apartment buildings. Black-and-white death announcements add to the clutter on the walls. Widows sell cigarettes from plastic buckets. Buy two carrots as a gift for the woman on the fifth floor if she'll lower her bucket down to pick them up. One wave works wonders as six floors of balconies fill up, each with its own

waving family. Walking around, craning my neck upward, I feel like a victorious politician among hordes of supporters. It's a *Laugh-In* wall with each window and balcony vying for a photo: Mothers hold up babies, sisters pose arm in arm, a wild pregnant woman stands on a fruit crate holding her bulging stomach, and an old, wrinkled woman fills her paint-starved window frame with a toothy grin. A contagious energy fills the air. It hurts to say *arrivederci.*

*For good-value accommodations in **Sorrento**, try Hotel Mignon Meublè (moderate, Via Sersale 9, tel. 081-807-3824, www.sorrentohotelmignon.com) or Hotel Minerva (splurge, cliff-hanging views, Via Capo 30, tel. 081-878-1011, www.minervasorrento.com). For all the travel specifics, see this year's edition of* Rick Steves' *Italy.*

Sassy, Spicy Sicily

Jabbing his pole like a one-pronged pitchfork into the slow red river of molten rock, the ashtray salesman pulled out a wad of lava. I scrambled back as he swung it by me and plopped it into a mold. His partner snipped it off with big iron clippers and rammed it into shape. The now shapely mass was dropped into a bucket of water that steamed and hissed. Cooling on a crispy black ledge were a dozen more lava ashtrays, each with the words "Mount Etna, Sicily" molded into it.

As the red lava poured out of its horribly hot trap door, I unzipped the ski parka I'd rented for $1 at the lift. At 11,000 feet, even on a sunny day, it's cold on top of Mount Etna... unless you're three feet from a lava flow.

At the edge of the volcano, I surveyed the island that I had just

Auntie Pasta says, "It's ciao time!"

explored on my scriptwriting mission for a TV show on Sicily. Old lava flows rumbled like buffalo toward teeming Catania. The island's sprawling second city butted up against a crescent beach that stretched all the way to Taormina, the Santorini of Sicily, popular with Italians who dress up to travel. And to my right was the hazy, high, and harsh interior. Two hours later, I had dropped my rental car at the Catania airport and was flying back to Rome, a rough script unfolding on my laptop screen.

Sicily sights are hard to grasp. Its historic and artistic big shots just don't ring a bell. The folkloric traditions, such as marionette theaters promoted by tourist brochures, seem to play out only for tour groups. And the place must lead Europe in litter. But there's

The Greek theater at Sicily's Taormina: With a view like this, no play is a tragedy.

a workaday charm here. If you like Italy for its people, tempo, and joy of living—rather than for its Botticellis, Guccis, and touristic icons—

you'll dig Sicily.

Sicily, standing midway between Africa and Europe, really is a world unto itself. While part of Italy, it's not quite that simple. Even though (with government encouragement) the siesta is fading out of Italian life, it thrives in Sicily. As European safety regulations take hold in the north, with laws requiring helmets on motorbikers, hair continues to fly in the Sicilian wind.

Palermo is the Rome of Sicily, with lavish art, boisterous markets, and holy cannoli. In the market, animals hang like anatomy lessons, sliced perfectly in half. *Fichi di India,* the fist-size cactus fruit that tastes like a cousin of the kiwi, are peeled and yours for less than a buck.

Even in death, Italians know how to look cool.

Palermo offers a great bone experience—skull and shoulders above anything else you'll find in Europe. Its Capuchin crypt is a subterranean gallery filled with 8,000 "bodies without souls" howling silently at their mortality. For centuries, people would thoughtfully choose their niche before they died, and even linger there, getting to know their macabre neighborhood. Then, after death, dressed in their Sunday best, they'd be hung up to dry. The entrepreneurial monk at the door said that for $125 we could take our TV camera inside for an hour. For $2, a tourist can spend all day.

Sicily's slick *autostrada* seems out of place (and way too wide), cutting a nearly deserted swath through the heart of the island. For the tourist, it zips you to some of the best Roman mosaics ever excavated. An emperor's hunting villa at Casale (near the town of Piazza Armerina) shows off 50 lavishly decorated mosaic floors. With the help of a guidebook (Giuseppe di Giovanni's is the best), the duck-driven chariots, bikini-clad triathletes, and amorous love scenes make more sense.

Cefalù was my favorite stop. Steeped in history and bustling with color, it's dramatically set with a fine beach on a craggy coast under a pagan mountain. I dutifully toured Cefalù's museum and cathedral. But the real attraction is on the streets. As the sun grew red and heavy, the old women—still in bathrobes, it seemed—filled their balconies as the

young people (and Vespas) clogged the main drag. Tsk-tsking at the age-old flirting scene, the women gossiped about the girls below.

My friend—ignoring the boy-toy girls—told me of the motorbike he lusted after. It was a classic Vespa from the '70s...with a body that's "round like a woman's." Just then, another guy galloped up on his very round, very blue, classic Vespa. He declared, "It's the only Vespa I've ever owned. I got it when I was 14. That was in 1969. The year man first walked on the moon—that was the year I first rode this Vespa." My friend and a few other guys gathered around almost worshipfully. The old women in the balconies and the mini-skirted flirts no longer existed. Cefalù and its teeming main drag were just Mediterranean wallpaper as that round, blue Vespa dripped in Sicilian testosterone.

Later, at a café overlooking the beach, I sipped my *latte di mandorla* (almond milk) with the locals who seemed to be posted there on duty to make sure that big, red sun went down. Little wooden boats, painted brightly, sat plump on the beach. Above them, the fishermen's clubhouse filled what was a medieval entry through the town wall. I wandered in.

I was greeted warmly by the senior member, "Il Presidente." The men go by nicknames and often don't even know their friends' real names. Since 1944, Il Presidente has spent his nights fishing, gathering anchovies under the beam of his gas-powered *lampara*. When he took the pre-Coleman vintage lamp off its

Travel smart in Sicily: Pay your respects to the Big Cheese.

rusty wall hook, I saw tales of a lifetime at sea in his face. As he showed me the ropes he wove from straw and complained that the new ropes just aren't the same, I lashed him to my budding script.

*For the entire TV script of my Sicily public television program, see www .ricksteves.com/tv. For good-value accommodations in **Palermo,** try Grande Albergo Sole (splurge, Corso Vittorio Emanuele 291, tel. 091-604-1111, www .angalahotels.it) or Hotel Moderno (budget, Via Roma 276, tel. 091-588-683, www.hotelmodernopa.com); in **Cefalù,** Hotel Riva del Sole (moderate, Via Lungomare 25, tel. 092-142-1230, www.rivadelsole.com); in Taormina, Hotel Continental (moderate, Via Dionisio 2a, tel. 094-223-805, www .continentaltaormina.com).*

PORTUGAL, SPAIN & MOROCCO

Lisbon Gold

Barely elegant outdoor cafés, glittering art, and the saltiest sailors' quarter in Europe make Lisbon an Iberian highlight. Portugal's capital is a wonderful mix of now and then. Old wooden trolleys shiver up its hills, bird-stained statues guard grand squares, and people sip coffee in Art Nouveau cafés.

Present-day Lisbon is explained by its past. Her glory days were the 15th and 16th centuries, when explorers such as Vasco da Gama opened new trade routes, making Lisbon the queen of Europe. Later, the riches of Brazil boosted Lisbon even higher. Then, in 1755, an earthquake leveled the city, killing nearly a quarter of its people.

Lisbon was rebuilt on a strict grid plan, symmetrically, with broad boulevards and square squares. The grandeur of pre-earthquake Lisbon survives in only three neighborhoods: Belém, the Alfama, and the Bairro Alto.

While the earthquake flattened a lot of buildings, and its colonial empire is long gone,

A lazy viewpoint overlooking Lisbon's Alfama

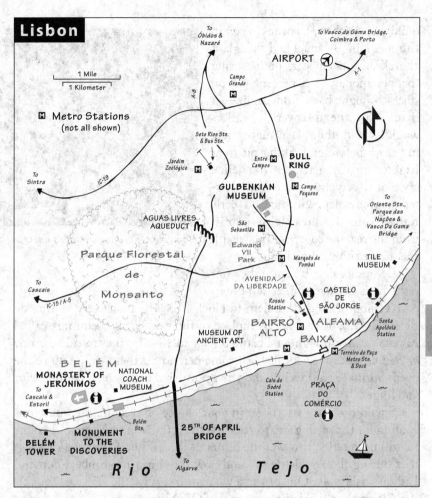

Lisbon's heritage survives. Follow me through a day in Lisbon.

After breakfast, grab a trolley or taxi to Torre de Belém (Belém Tower). The Belém District, four miles from downtown, is a pincushion of important sights from Portugal's Golden Age, when Vasco da Gama and company made her Europe's richest power.

The Belém Tower, built in Manueline style (ornate Portuguese late-Gothic), has guarded Lisbon's harbor since 1555. Today, it symbolizes the voyages that made her powerful. This was the last sight sailors saw as they left—and the first one they'd see when they returned, loaded down with gold, diamonds, and venereal diseases.

Nearby, the giant Monument to the Discoveries honors Portugal's Prince Henry the Navigator and the country's leading explorers. Across the street, the Monastery of Jerónimos is Portugal's most exciting building—with my favorite cloister in Europe. King Manuel had this giant church and its cloisters built—using "pepper money," a 5 percent tax on spices brought back from India—in thanks for the discoveries. Sailors would spend their last night here in prayer before embarking on their frightening voyages. The Manueline style of this giant church and cloister combines late Gothic and early Renaissance features with motifs from the sea, the source of the wealth that made this art possible.

Enjoying the peace of Europe's finest cloister at Lisbon's Monastery of Jerónimos

Before leaving Belém, take your taste buds sightseeing at a famous pastry shop, Pastéis de Belém (a block from the monastery at Rua de Belém 84-92). This is the birthplace of the wonderful cream tart called *pastel de nata* throughout Portugal. But in Lisbon, they're called *pastel de Belém*. Since 1837, locals have come here to get them warm out of the oven. Sprinkle on the cinnamon and powdered sugar, get a *café com leite*, and linger.

Spend the early afternoon in your choice of Lisbon's fine museums waiting for the setting sun to rekindle the action in the Alfama. A colorful sailors' quarter, this was the center of the Visigothic town, a rich district during the Arabic period and now the shiver-me-timbers home of Lisbon's fisherfolk. One of the few areas to survive the 1755 earthquake, the Alfama is a cobbled cornucopia of Old World color.

Wander deep. This urban jungle's roads are squeezed into tangled stairways and confused alleys. Bent houses comfort each other in their romantic shabbiness, and the air drips with laundry and the smell of clams and raw fish. Get lost. Poke aimlessly, sample the ample grapes, avoid rabid-looking dogs, peek through windows. Make a friend, pet a chicken. Taste the *branco seco*—the local dry wine.

Gradually zigzag your way up the castle-crowned hill until you reach a viewpoint, the little green square called Miradouro de Santa Luzia. Rest here and survey the cluttered Alfama rooftops below you. A block away is Largo Rodrigues Freitas, a square with several scruffy, cheap, very characteristic eateries. Treat yourself to the special—a plate of boiled clams.

If you climb a few more blocks to the top of the hill, you'll find the ruins of Castelo de São Jorge. From this fortress, which has dominated the city for more than 1,000 years, enjoy the roaming peacocks and a commanding view of Portugal's capital.

In the late afternoon, for a quintessential Lisbon drink, duck into one of the funky hole-in-the-wall shops throughout town and ask for a *ginjinha* (zheen-zheen-yah). Sold for about a buck a shot, it's a sweet liquor made from the sour cherry-like ginja berry, sugar, and schnapps. The only choices are: with or without berries (*com* or *sem fruta*) and *gelada* if you want it from a chilled bottle out of the fridge—very nice. In Portugal, when someone is impressed by the taste of something, they say, "*Sabe melhor que nem ginjas*" (It tastes even better than ginja).

Spend the evening at a Portuguese bullfight. It's a brutal sport, but the bull lives through it and so will you. The fight starts with an equestrian duel—a fast bull against a graceful horse and rider. Then the fun starts. A colorfully clad eight-man team enters the ring strung out in a line as if to play leapfrog. The leader taunts *O Touro* noisily, and, with testosterone sloshing everywhere, the bull and the man charge each other. The speeding bull plows into the leader head-on. Then—thud, thud, thud—the raging bull skewers the entire charging crew. The horns are wrapped so no one gets gored—just mashed.

In a Portuguese bullfight, the matador is brutalized, too.

The crew wrestles the bull to a standstill, and one man grabs the bull's tail. Victory is complete when the team leaps off the bull and the man still hanging onto the tail "water-skis" behind the enraged animal. This thrilling display of insanity is repeated with six bulls. After each round, the bruised and battered leader limps a victory lap around the ring.

Portugal's top bullring is Lisbon's Campo Pequeno (fights generally on Thu and Sun, mid-June-Sept; other arenas offer fights most Sundays, Easter-Oct). Half the fights are simply Spanish-type *corridas* without the killing. For the real slam-bam Portuguese-style fight, confirm that there will be *grupo de forçados*.

For a modern Lisbon experience, visit Parque das Nações, where Lisbon celebrated the 500th anniversary of Vasco da Gama's voyage to

India by hosting Expo '98 (ride the Metro to the last stop on the red line—Oriente, walk to the water, turn right, and join the people strolling along the riverside). The Vasco da Gama mall has a top-floor beer garden with outside decks that let you drink in the Tejo River view. I ate dinner surrounded by chattering locals, while great platters of fish, meat, fries, salad, and lots of wine and beer paraded frantically in every direction. Despite the food chaos and fab views, somehow the lovers at the next table ignored everything but each other's eyes.

*For good-value accommodations in **Lisbon,** try Hotel Evidencia Lisboa Tejo (splurge, Condes de Monsanto 2, tel. 218-866-182, www.evidenciahoteis .com) or Pensão Residencial Gerês (moderate, Calçada do Garcia 6, tel. 218-810-497, www.pensaogeres.com). For all the travel specifics, see the latest edition of* Rick Steves' Portugal.

Portugal's Sunny Salema

"Let's get the *cataplanas,*" said my friend, urging me to try the fish stew at Ze's Carioca Restaurant in Salema.

Overhearing her, Ze came to our table and said, "I have developed a secret recipe for this specialty. If you don't like it, you don't pay."

"What if we don't like anything else we order?" I asked.

"If you don't pay, I break your fingers," Ze said cheerfully.

We ordered the *cataplanas.* Savoring our meal, we savored one of the last true villages on the Algarve—Salema.

Any place famous as a "last undiscovered tourist frontier" no longer is. But the Algarve of your dreams survives—just barely. To catch it

Salema: Catch the Algarve before it's gone.

before it goes, find a fringe. It took me three tries. West of Lagos, I tried Luz and Burgau, both offering only a corpse of a fishing village, bikini-strangled and Nivea-creamed. Then, just as darkness turned couples into peaceful silhouettes, I found Salema.

Any Algarve town with a beach will have tourism, but few mix tourism and realism as well as little Salema. It's my kind of resort—three beachside streets, many restaurants, a few hotels, time-share condos up the road, a couple of bars, English and German menus, a classic beach with a paved promenade, and endless sun.

Tucked away where a small road hits the beach on Portugal's southwestern tip, Salema is an easy 15-mile bus ride or hitch from the closest train station in Lagos. Don't let the ladies hawking rooms in Lagos waylay you into staying in their city by telling you Salema is full.

With the horn-tooting arrival of the flatbed trucks, the parking lot that separates the jogging shorts from the black shawls becomes a morning market on weekdays. The *1812 Overture* horn of the fish truck wakes you at 8:00 a.m. Then the bakery trailer rolls in, steaming with fresh bread, followed by a fruit-and-vegetables truck, and a five-and-dime truck for clothing and odds and ends. And, most afternoons around 14:00, the red mobile post office stops by (unless the government cuts its funding).

Salema is still a fishing village—but just barely. It has a split personality: The whitewashed old town is for residents, and the more utilitarian other half was built for tourists. Unwritten tradition allocates different chunks of undersea territory to each Salema family. While the fishermen's hut on the beach no longer hosts a fish auction, it provides shade for the old-timers arm-wrestling octopi out of their traps. The pottery jars stacked everywhere are traps, which are tied about a yard apart in long lines and dropped offshore. Octopi, looking for a cozy place to set an ambush, climb inside—making their final mistake.

Salema's tourist-based economy sits on a foundation of sand. Locals hope and pray that their sandy beach returns after being washed away each winter.

In Portugal, restaurateurs are allowed to build a temporary, summer-only beachside restaurant if they provide a lifeguard for swimmers and run a green/yellow/red warning-flag system. The Atlântico Restaurant, which dominates Salema's beach, takes its responsibility seriously—providing lifeguards and flags through the summer...and fresh seafood by candlelight all year long.

Residents and tourists pursue a policy of peaceful coexistence at the beach. Tractors pull in and push out the fishing boats, two-year-olds

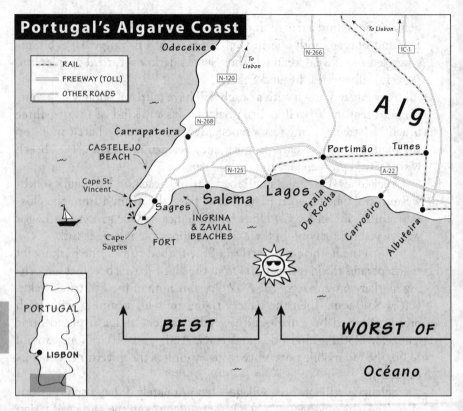

Portugal's Algarve Coast

- ---- RAIL
- ===== FREEWAY (TOLL)
- ===== OTHER ROADS

Odeceixe

To Lisbon

To Lisbon

N-266

IC-1

N-120

A l g

N-268

Carrapateira

CASTELEJO
BEACH

Portimão   Tunes

Cape St.
Vincent

N-125

A-22

Sagres   Salema   Lagos

INGRINA
& ZAVIAL
BEACHES

Praia
Da Rocha

Carvoeiro

Albufeira

Cape
Sagres   FORT

PORTUGAL

LISBON

BEST   WORST OF

Océano

toddle in the waves, topless women read German fashion mags, and old men really do mend the nets. British, German, and Back Door connoisseurs of lethargy laze in the sun, while locals grab the shade.

On the west end of the beach, look for the dinosaur footprints in a big, flat, yellowish raised rock 200 yards past the Atlântico restaurant (beside the rusty pipe sticking out of the cliff). From this beach at low tide, you may be able to climb over the rocks to secluded Figueira Beach, several miles away. While the days of black widows chasing topless Nordic women off the beach are gone, nudity is still risqué today. Over the rocks and beyond the view of prying eyes, Germans grin and bare it.

So often, tourism chases the sun and quaint folksiness. And the quaint folksiness survives only with the help of tourist dollars. Fishermen boost their income by renting spare bedrooms to the ever-growing stream of tan fans from the drizzly North. One year I arrived at 7:00 p.m. with a group of eight people and no reservations. I asked some locals, *"Quartos?"* Eyes perked, heads nodded, and I got nine beds in three homes at $20

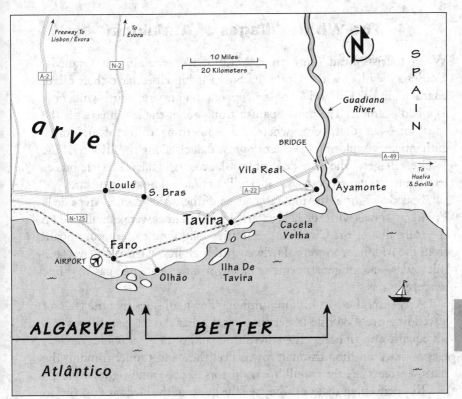

per person. *Quartos* line Salema's main residential street, offering simple rooms with showers, springy beds, and glorious Atlantic views.

If you need to do some touring, drive 15 minutes to the best romantic, secluded beach in the region: Praia do Castelejo, complete with a good restaurant, just north of Cape Sagres.

But Salema's sleepy beauty kidnaps our momentum. Leaving Ze's restaurant with stomachs full and fingers intact, we take a glass of wine from the Atlântico's waterfront bar and sip it with the sunset in a beached paddleboat. Nearby, a dark, withered granny shells almonds with a railroad spike, dogs roam the beach like they own it, and a man catches short fish with a long pole. Beyond him is Cape Sagres—the edge of the world 500 years ago. As far as the gang sipping port and piling olive pits in the beachside bar is concerned, it still is.

For a budget accommodations in **Salema,** *try Casa Duarte (tel. 282-695-206 or 282-695-307). For all the travel specifics, see the latest edition of* Rick Steves' Portugal.

The White Villages of Andalucía

When tourists head south from Madrid, it's generally for Granada, Córdoba, Sevilla, or the Costa del Sol. The big cities have their urban charms, but the Costa del Sol is a concrete nightmare, worthwhile only as a bad example. The most Spanish thing about the south coast is the sunshine—but that's everywhere. For something different and more authentic, try exploring the interior of Andalucía along the "Route of the White Villages." The Ruta de Pueblos Blancos, Andalucía's charm bracelet of cute towns, gives you wonderfully untouched Spanish culture.

Spend a night in the romantic queen of the white towns, Arcos de la Frontera. Towns with "de la Frontera" in their names were established on the front line of the Christians' centuries-long fight to recapture Spain from the Moors, who were slowly pushed back into Africa. Today, these hill towns—no longer strategic or on any frontier—are just passing time peacefully.

Arcos smothers its hilltop, tumbling down all sides like the train of a wedding dress. While larger than most other Andalusian hill towns, it's equally atmospheric. The labyrinthine old center is a photographer's feast. Viewpoint-hop through town. Feel the wind funnel through the narrow streets as drivers pull in car mirrors to fit around tight corners.

Residents brag that only they see the backs of the birds as they fly. To see why, climb to the viewpoint at the main square high in the old town. Belly up to the railing—the town's suicide jumping-off point—and look down. Ponder the fancy cliffside hotel's erosion concerns, orderly orange groves, flower-filled greenhouses, and the fine views toward Morocco.

The thoughtful traveler's challenge is to find meaning in the generally overlooked tiny details of historic towns such as Arcos. On one visit,

In Arcos, locals brag that only they see the backs of the birds as they fly.

Spain's White Villages

I discovered that a short walk from Arcos' church of Santa María to the church of San Pedro (St. Peter) is littered with fun glimpses into the town's past.

The church of Santa María faces the main square. After Arcos was reconquered from the Moors in the 13th century, this church was built—atop a mosque. In the pavement is a 15th-century magic circle: 12 red and 12 white stones—the white ones marked with various constellations. When a child came to the church to be baptized, the parents would stop here first for a good Christian exorcism. The exorcist would stand inside the protective circle and cleanse the baby of any evil spirits. This was also a holy place back in Muslim times. While residents no longer use it, Islamic Sufis still come here in pilgrimage every November.

In 1699, an earthquake cracked the church's foundation. Arches were added to prop it against neighboring buildings. Thanks to these, the church survived the bigger earthquake of 1755 (which destroyed much of Lisbon). All over town, arches support earthquake-damaged structures.

Lately the town rumbles only when the bulls run. Señor González Oca's tiny barbershop (behind the church) is plastered with posters of bulls running Pamplona-style through the streets of Arcos during Holy Week. An American from the nearby Navy base at Rota was killed here by a bull in 1994.

Small towns like Arcos come with lively markets. On my last visit, I was encouraged by the pickle woman to try a *banderilla,* named for the bangled spear that a matador sticks into the bull. As I gingerly slid an onion off the tiny skewer of pickled olives, onions, and carrots, she told me to eat it all at once. Explosive!

An important part of any Spanish market is the meat stall—the *salchichonería*. Since Roman times in Spain, December has been the season to slaughter pigs and cure (salt and dry) every possible bit of meat into various hams and sausages. By late spring, the now-salty meat is cured and able to withstand the heat.

Near the market is a convent. The spiky security grill over the window protects cloistered nuns. Tiny peepholes allow the sisters to look out unseen. I stepped into the lobby to find a one-way mirror and a blind, spinning, lazy Susan-type cupboard. I pushed the buzzer, and a sister spun out some boxes of freshly baked cookies for sale. When I spun back the cookies with a *"No, gracias,"* a Monty Python-esque voice countered, "We have cupcakes as well." I bought a bag of these *magdalenas,* both to support their church work and to give to kids on my walk. Feeling like a religious Peeping Tom, I actually saw—through the not-quite one-way mirror—the sister in her flowing robe and habit momentarily appear and disappear.

Walking on toward St. Peter's, I passed Roman columns plastered into street corners—protection from reckless donkey carts. The walls are scooped out on either side of the windows, a reminder of the days when women stayed inside but wanted the best possible view of any people-action in the streets.

Arcos' second church, St. Peter's, really is the second church. It lost an extended battle with Santa María for papal recognition as the leading church in Arcos. When the pope finally recognized Santa María, pouting parishioners from St. Peter's even changed their prayers. Rather than say, "María, mother of God," they prayed, "St. Peter, mother of God."

The tiny square in front of the church—about the only flat piece of pavement around—serves as the old-town soccer field for neighborhood kids. I joined the game and shared my cupcakes.

Until a few years ago, this church also had a resident bellman who lived in the spire. He was a basket-maker and a colorful character—famous for bringing in a donkey, which grew too big to get back out. Finally, there was no choice but to kill and eat the donkey.

Exploring on, I entered a cool, dark bar filled with very short, old guys. In Spain, any man in his late 80s spent his growth-spurt years trying to survive the brutal Civil War (1936-39). Those who did, generally did so just barely. That generation was a head shorter than the people of the next.

In the bar, the gang—side-lit like a Rembrandt portrait—was fixed on the TV, watching the finale of a long series of bullfights. El Córdobes was fighting. His father, also called El Córdobes, was the Babe Ruth of bullfighting. El Córdobes uses his dad's name even though his dad sued him not to. Today, this generation's El Córdobes is the Ichiro of bullfighting.

Marveling at the bar's fun and cheap list of wines and hard drinks, I ordered a Cuba Libre for $2. The drink came tall and stiff, with a dish of peanuts. Suddenly everyone gasped—all eyes on the TV. El Córdobes had been hooked and did a cartwheel over the angry bull's head. The gang roared as El Córdobes buried his head in his arms and the bull trampled and tried to gore him. The TV repeated the scene many times.

El Córdobes survived and—no surprise—eventually killed the bull. But as he made his victory lap and picked up bouquets from adoring fans, the camera zoomed in on the rip exposing his hip and a 10-inch-long bloody wound. The short men around me would remember and talk about this moment for years.

That evening, I caught the sunset from the viewpoint, then took in dinner at Restaurante El Convento, surrounded by the plants and arches of another old convent—this one long replaced by the best restaurant in town. The walls are decorated with bronzed newspaper pages heralding many culinary awards. As church bells clanged, I poured a *vino tinto con mucho cuerpo* (full-bodied red wine) from the Rioja region, and ordered up the best-quality ham, *jamón ibérico*, from acorn-fed pigs with black feet.

From Arcos, the back road to Ronda is spiked with plenty of undiscovered and interesting hill towns. About half the towns I visited were memorable. Only Arcos (by bus) and Ronda (by train) are easily accessible by public transportation. Other towns are best seen by car. Good information on the area is rare but not necessary. Pick up the tourist brochure on the white towns at a nearby big-city tourist office, get a good map, and fire up your spirit of adventure.

Along with Arcos, here are my favorite white villages:

Zahara, a tiny town with a tingly setting under a Moorish castle, has a spectacular view. During Moorish times, Zahara was contained within the fortified castle walls above today's town. It was considered the gateway to Granada and a strategic stronghold for the Moors by the Spanish Christian forces of the *Reconquista.*

Today, the castle is little more than an evocative ruin with a commanding view (always open, free, and worth the climb). And Zahara is a fine overnight stop for those who want to hear only the sounds of birds,

SPAIN

Zahara reigns in Spain, rising mainly above the plain.

wind, and elderly footsteps on ancient cobbles.

Grazalema, another postcard-pretty hill town (located within huge and rugged Sierra de Grazalema Natural Park), offers a royal balcony for a memorable picnic, a square where you can watch old-timers playing cards, and plenty of quiet, whitewashed streets to explore. Plaza de Andalucía, the main square a block off the view terrace, is the hub for day-trippers. The town has several decent little bars and restaurants, and shops sell the town's famous handmade wool blankets and good-quality leather items. While the area is known as the rainiest place in Spain, the clouds seem to wring themselves out before they reach the town—I've only ever had blue skies.

Estepa, spilling over a hill crowned with a castle and convent, is a freshly washed, happy town that fits my dreams of southern Spain. It's situated halfway between Córdoba and Málaga, but it's light years away from either. Atop Estepa's hill is the convent of Santa Clara, worth three stars in any guidebook but found in none. Enjoy the territorial view from the summit, then step into the quiet, spiritual perfection of the church.

In any of these towns, evening is prime time. The promenade begins as everyone gravitates to the central square. The spotless streets are polished nightly by the feet of families licking ice cream. The whole town strolls—it's like "cruising" without cars. Buy an ice-cream sandwich and join the parade.

*For good-value, moderate accommodations in **Arcos,** try Hotel El Convento (Maldonado 2, tel. 956-702-333, www.hotelelconvento.es) or Hotel los Olivos (Paseo de los Boliches 30, tel. 956-700-811, www.hotel-losolivos.es). For all the travel specifics, see this year's edition of Rick Steves' Spain.*

Morocco: Plunge Deep

Walking through the various souks of the labyrinthine medina, I found sights you could only dream of in America. Dodging blind men and people with clubfeet, I was stoned by smells, sounds, sights, and feelings. People came in all colors, sizes, temperaments, and varieties of deformities. Milky eyes, charismatic beggars, stumps of limbs, sticks of children, tattooed women, walking mummies, grabbing salesmen, teasing craftsmen, seductive scents, half-bald dogs, and little boys on rooftops were reaching out from all directions.

Oooh! Morocco! Slices of Morocco make the *Star Wars* cantina scene look bland. And it's just a quick cruise from Spain. From Tarifa, Gibraltar, or Algeciras, you can catch a boat to Tangier, Morocco. As you step off the boat in Tangier, you realize that the crossing has taken you further culturally than did the trip from the US to Iberia.

Tantalizing Tangier

For decades, the coastal city of Tangier deserved its image as the "Tijuana of Morocco." But that has changed. Tangier was a neglected hellhole for a generation. It was an international city—favored by the West and therefore disdained by the previous king of Morocco, who made it a point to divert national investment *away* from Morocco's fourth city.

The current king, Mohammed VI, who took the throne in 1999, believes Tangier should be a great city once again. To show his support, the first city he visited after his coronation was Tangier. Restorations are now taking place on a grand scale—the beach has been painstakingly cleaned, pedestrian promenades are popping up everywhere, and gardens bloom with lush, new greenery. The difference is breathtaking. The place is still exotic, but likeably exotic.

I'm uplifted by the new Tangier because it is affluent and modern, without having abandoned its roots and embraced Western values. A visit here lets a Westerner marinated in anti-Muslim propaganda see what Islam aspires to be, and can be—and realize it is not a threat.

Tangier's newly pedestrianized Grand Socco—which used to be a perpetual traffic jam—sparkles with the pride of a new affluence.

MOROCCO

But the hotels—and their staffs—are still quirky. Recently when I checked into Hotel Continental, flamboyant Jimmy, who's always around and runs the shop adjacent to the lobby, greeted me. Test him—he knows every telephone area code in the US.

Hotel Continental had me wondering if I'd find the English Patient. Gramophones gathered dust on dressers under dingy lights, and day after day, a serene woman painted a figure-eight in the loose tiles with her mop. My guidebook listed the hotel's phone and email data more accurately than their own printed material—it was a 70-room hotel with not a sheet of paper in its office.

In the morning, roosters and the call to prayer worked together to wake me and the rest of that world. When the sun was high enough to send a rainbow plunging into the harbor amid ferries busily coming and going, I stood on my balcony and surveyed Tangier kicking into gear. Women in colorful flowing robes walked to sweatshops adjacent to the port—happy to earn $8 a day sewing for big-name European clothing lines.

It's a fascinating time for Morocco. The king is modernizing. His queen was a commoner. Moroccans say she's the first queen to be seen in public. They have never seen the king's mother. (They don't even know what she looks like.) Walking the streets, you see a modest new affluence, lots of vision and energy, and no compromise with being Arabic.

Moroccans don't seem to emulate or even care about the US. Al-Jazeera blares on teahouse TVs—with stirring images of American atrocities inflicted on fellow Muslims. But people seem numb to the propaganda. I felt not a hint of animosity to me as an American—something I had been concerned about. Ruled by Spain in the 19th century and France in the 20th, it's a rare place where signs are in three languages...and English doesn't make the cut (they are Arabic, French, and Spanish). In this Muslim city, you'll find a synagogue, Catholic and Anglican churches, and the town's largest mosque— all within close proximity to one another.

The market scene is a wonderland of everything— except pork: mountains of brilliant olives, a full palette of spices, children with knives

Tangier's markets are a barrage on all the senses...including the nose.

happy to perform for my camera. Each animal is slaughtered in accordance with Halal: in the name of Allah, with a sharp knife, its head pointed to Mecca, drained of its blood.

Ferries from Tarifa, Spain, sail to Tangier 15 times daily ($90 round-trip). Even if you're visiting Morocco independently, I recommend hiring a guide to show you around Tangier. You can arrange one through a ferry company in Tarifa (www.frs.es or www.comarit.es) or at the tourist office in Tangier (in the new town at Boulevard Pasteur 29).

Taking a tour to Tangier is easier but less rewarding. A typical day-trip tour includes the round-trip ferry crossing and a guide who meets you at a prearranged point in Tangier. All offer essentially the same five-hour experience: a city bus tour, the famous ride-a-camel stop, a drive through the ritzy palace neighborhood, a walk through the medina, a look at a sales-starved carpet shop, and lunch. Tours generally cost about $90, roughly the same price as a ferry ticket alone—the tour company makes its money off commissions if you shop (book tours directly with the ferry company or through your Tarifa hotel).

Package-tour visitors to Tangier feel like they're being held hostage. Independent travelers melt into the city.

During my stay, I met gracious Moroccans eager to talk and share. About the only time I saw other Western tourists was when I crossed paths with one of the day-tripping tour groups. Those on the tours walked in a tight single-file, clutching their purses and day bags nervously to their bellies like paranoid kangaroos, as they bundled past one last spanking line of street merchants to get safely back onto the ferry to Europe. I was so comfortable, and they were so nervous and embattled. The pathetic scene reminded me of some kind of self-inflicted hostage crisis. Do yourself a favor—visit Tangier on your own.

The Best of Morocco

Rewarding as a visit to Tangier is, you can't fully experience Morocco in a day trip from the Costa del Sol. Plunge deep and your journal will read like a Dalí painting. While Morocco is not easy traveling, it gets rave reviews from those who plug this Islamic detour into their European

MOROCCO

vacation.

Rabat, Morocco's capital, is a good first stop. This comfortable, most-European city in Morocco lacks the high-pressure tourism of the towns on the north coast. Or, for a pleasant break on the beach and a relaxing way to break into Morocco, spend a day at Asilah, between Tangier and Larache.

Taxis are cheap and a real bargain when you consider the comfort, speed, and convenience they provide in these hot, dusty, and confusing cities. Eat and drink carefully in Morocco. Bottled water and bottled soft drinks are safe. The extra-cautious have "well-cooked" written in Arabic on a scrap

0	•	SIFR
1	١	WAAHID
2	٢	ITNEEN
3	٣	TALAATA
4	٤	ARBA'A
5	٥	KHAMSA
6	٦	SITTA
7	٧	SAB'A
8	٨	TAMANYA
9	٩	TIS'A
10	١٠	'ASHRA

of paper and flash it when they order meat. I found the couscous, *tajine*, and omelets uniformly good. The Arabs use different number symbols. Learn them. You can practice on license plates, which list the number twice (using their numbers and "ours"). Morocco was a French colony, so

French is more widely understood than English. A French phrase book is handy. Travel very light in Morocco. You can leave most of your luggage at your last Spanish hotel for free if you plan to spend a night there on your return from Africa.

After Rabat, pass through Casablanca (great movie, dull city) and catch the Marrakech Express south. You'll hang your head out the window of that romantic old train and sing to the passing desert.

Marrakech is the epitome of exotic. Take a horse-drawn carriage from the station to downtown and find a hotel near the Djemaa el Fna, the central square of Marrakech, where the action is. Desert musicians, magicians, storytellers, acrobats, snake charmers, gamblers, and tricksters gather crowds of tribespeople who have come to Marrakech to do their market chores. As a tourist, you'll fit in like a clown at a funeral. Be very careful, don't gamble, and hang onto your wallet. You're in another world, and you're not clever here. Spend an entire day in the colorful medina wandering aimlessly from souk to souk. There's a souk for each trade, such as the dyers' souk, the leather souk, and the carpet souk.

In the medina, you'll be badgered—or "guided"—by small boys all claiming to be "a friend who wants to practice English." They are after money, nothing else. If you don't want their services, make two things

Moroccan road signs: Beware of toboggans.

crystal clear: You have no money for them, and you want no guide. Then completely ignore them. Remember that while you're with a guide, he'll get commissions for anything you buy. Throughout Morocco, you'll be pestered by these obnoxious hustler-guides.

I often hire a young and responsive boy who speaks enough English to serve as my interpreter. It seems that if I'm "taken," the other guides leave me alone. And that in itself is worth the small price of a guide.

The market is a shopper's delight. Bargain hard, shop around, and you'll come home with some great souvenirs. Government emporiums usually have the same items you find in the market, but priced fairly. If you get sick of souks, shop there and you'll get the fair price, haggle-free.

From Marrakech, consider getting to Fès indirectly by taking an exciting seven-day loop to the south. While buses are reliable and efficient throughout Morocco, this tour is best by car, and it's easy to rent a car in Marrakech and drop it off in Fès.

Drive or catch the bus south over the rugged Atlas Mountains to Saharan Morocco. Explore the isolated oasis towns of Ouarzazate, Tinerhir, and Er-Rachidia. If time permits, the trip from Ouarzazate to Zagora is an exotic mud-brick pie. These towns each have a weekly "market day," when the tribespeople gather to do their shopping. This is your chance to stock up on honeydew melons and goats' heads. Stay in Tinerhir and climb to the roof of your hotel for a great view of the busy marketplace.

What century is it?

Venture out of town into the lush fields, where you'll tumble into an almost biblical world. Sit on a rock and dissect the silence. A weary donkey, carrying a bearded old man in a white robe and turban, clip-clops slowly past you. Suddenly, six Botticelli maidens flit like watercolor confetti across your trail and giggle out of sight. Stay tuned. The show goes on.

Bus rides in this part of Morocco are intriguing. I could write pages about experiences I've had on Moroccan buses—good and bad—but I don't want to spoil the surprise. Just ride them with a spirit of adventure, cross your fingers, and keep your bag off the rooftop.

Saharan Adventure

Heading south from Er-Rachidia, a series of mud-brick villages bunny-hop down a lush river valley and into the Sahara. Finally the road melts into the sand, and the next stop is, literally, Timbuktu.

The strangeness of this Alice-in-a-sandy-Wonderland world, untempered, can be overwhelming—even frightening. The finest hotel in Erfoud, the region's major town, will provide a much-needed refuge, keeping out the sand, heat waves, and street kids, and providing safe-to-eat and tasty local food, reliable information, and a good and affordable bed.

But the hotel is only your canteen and springboard. Explore! If you plan to go deep into the desert, hire a guide. Choose one you can understand and tolerate, set a price for his services, and before dawn, head for the dunes.

You'll drive to the last town, Rissani, and then farther south over 15 miles of natural asphalt to the oasis village of Merzouga. There's plenty of tourist traffic at sunrise and in the early evening, so hitching is fairly easy. A couple of places in Merzouga rent spots on their terrace for those who spend the night.

Leave Europe and a warm Islamic welcome awaits.

Before you glows a chain of sand-dune mountains. Climb one. It's not easy. I seemed to slide farther backward with each step. Hike along a cool and crusty ridge. Observe bugs and their tracks. Watch small sand avalanches you started all by yourself. From the great virgin summit, savor the Sahara view orchestrated by a powerful silence. Your life sticks out like a lone star in a black sky. Try tumbling, rolling, and sloshing down your dune. Look back and see the temporary damage one person can inflict on a formerly perfect slope. Then get back in your car before the summer sun turns the sand into a steaming griddle and you into an omelet. Off-season, the midday desert sun is surprisingly mild.

MOROCCO

Merzouga is full of very poor people. The village children hang out at the ruins of an old palace. A ragtag percussion group gave us an impromptu concert. The children gathered around us tighter and tighter, as the musicians picked up the tempo. We shared smiles, warmth, and sadness. A little Moroccan Judy Garland saw out of one eye, the other cloudy as rice pudding. One gleaming six-year-old carried a tiny sleeping brother slung on her back. His crusty little fly-covered face was too tired to flinch. We had a bag of candy to share and tried to get 40 kids into an orderly line to march past one by one. Impossible. The line degenerated into a free-for-all, and our bag became a piñata.

On a student-exchange program, my daughter Jackie became part of her very own Moroccan village family.

Only through the mercy of our guide did we find our way back to Rissani. Camels loitered nonchalantly, looking very lost and not caring. Cool lakes flirted, a distant mirage, and the black hardpan road stretched endlessly in all directions.

Then, with a sigh, we were back in Rissani, where the road starts up again. For us, it was breakfast time, and Rissani offered little more than some very thought-provoking irony. My friends and I could find no "acceptable" place to eat. Awkwardly, we drank germ-free Cokes with pursed lips, balanced bread on upturned bottle caps, and swatted laughing legions of flies. We were by far the wealthiest people in the valley—and the only ones unable to enjoy an abundant variety of good but strange food.

Observing the scene from our humble rusted table, we saw a busy girl rhythmically smashing date seeds; three stoic, robed elders with horseshoe beards; and a prophet wandering through with a message for all that he was telling to nobody.

Our Er-Rachidia hotel was Western-style—as dull and comforting as home. We listened to music and enjoyed the pool, resting and recharging before our next Saharan plunge.

Saharan Nightlife

Desert dwellers and smart tourists know the value of a siesta during the hottest part of the day. But a Saharan evening is the perfect time for a traveler to get out and experience the vibrancy of North African village life. We drove 10 miles north of Erfoud to a fortified mud-brick oasis village. There was no paint, no electricity, not a car in sight—only people, adobe walls, and palm trees. Absolutely nothing other than the nearby two-lane highway hinted of the modern world.

We entered like Lewis and Clark without Sacagawea, knowing instantly we were in for a rich experience. A wedding feast was erupting, and the whole town buzzed with excitement, all decked out in colorful robes and their best smiles. We felt very welcome.

The teeming street emptied through the medieval gate onto the field, where a band was playing squawky, oboe-like instruments and drums. A circle of 20 ornately dressed women made siren noises with tongues flapping like party favors. Rising dust diffused the lantern light, giving everything the grainy feel of an old photo. The darkness focused our attention on a relay of seductively beautiful, snake-thin dancers. A flirtatious atmosphere raged, cloaked safely in the impossibility of anything transpiring beyond coy smiles and teasing twists.

Then the village's leading family summoned us for dinner. Pillows, blankets, a lantern, and a large, round filigreed table turned a stone cave into a warm lounge. The men of this family had traveled to Europe and spoke some English. For more than two hours, the women prepared dinner and the men proudly entertained their New World guests. First was the ritualistic tea ceremony. Like a mad chemist, the tea specialist mixed it just right. With a thirsty gleam in his eye and a large spike in his hand, he hacked off a chunk of sugar from a coffee-can-size lump and watched it melt into Morocco's basic beverage. He sipped it, as if testing a fine wine, added more sugar, and offered me a taste. When no more sugar could be absorbed, we drank it with cookies and dates. Then, with the fanfare of a pack of Juicy Fruit, the men passed around a hashish pipe. Our shocked look was curious to them. Next, a tape deck brought a tiny clutter of music, from Arab and tribal Berber music to James Brown, reggae, and twangy Moroccan pop. The men danced splendidly.

Finally the meal came. Fourteen people sat on the floor, circling two round tables. Nearby, a child silently waved a palm-branch fan, keeping the flies away. A portable washbasin and towel were passed around to start and finish the meal. With our fingers and gravy-soaked slabs of bread, we grabbed spicy meat and vegetables. Everyone dipped eagerly into the delicious central bowl of couscous.

So far, the Moroccan men dominated. Young girls took turns peeking around the corner and dashing off—much like teenyboppers anywhere. Two older women in striking, black-jeweled outfits were squatting attentively in the corner, keeping their distance and a very low profile. Then one pointed to me and motioned in charades, indicating long hair, a backpack, and a smaller partner. I had been in this same village years earlier. I had longer hair and a backpack and was traveling with a short partner. She remembered my 20-minute stay so long ago! People in remote lands enjoy a visiting tourist and find the occasion at least as memorable as we do. So many more doors open to the traveler who knocks.

After a proud tour of their schoolhouse, we were escorted across the field back to our car, which had been guarded by a silent, white-robed man. We drove away, reeling with the feeling that the memories of this evening would be the prize souvenir of our trip.

For good-value accommodations in **Tangier,** *try Hotel Continental (moderate, Dar Baroud 36, tel. 0539-931-024, www.continental-tanger.com) or the swankier Rif & Spa Hotel (splurge, Avenue Muhammad VI 152, tel. 0539-349-300, www.hotelsatlas.com). For more travel specifics, see this year's edition of* Rick Steves' Spain.

MOROCCO

FRANCE

Paris: A Grand Boulevard and a Petite Lane

Paris is the epitome of elegance, a cultural touchstone for art, fashion, food, literature, and good living. Come ready to be charmed by that Parisian *je ne sais quoi*. For me, the true magic of Paris is in its sweeping boulevards and intimate lanes. Start at the Arc de Triomphe, saunter down the grand Avenue des Champs-Elysées, then disappear down Rue Cler.

The Grand Boulevard: Champs-Elysées

My cabbie plunges into the grand traffic circle where a dozen boulevards converge on the Arc de Triomphe. Like referees at gladiator camp, traffic cops are stationed at each entrance to this traffic circus and let in bursts of eager cars. As marble Lady Liberties scramble up Napoleon's arch, heroically thrusting their swords and shrieking at the traffic, all of Paris seems drawn into this whirlpool.

I say to the cabbie, "There must be an accident every few minutes here."

He responds, "In Paris, a good driver gets only scratches, not dents. But bad drivers...If there is an accident here, each driver is considered

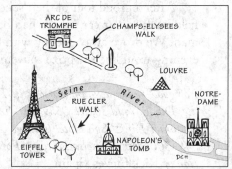

equally at fault. This is the only place in Paris where the accidents are not judged. No matter what the circumstances, insurance companies split the costs fifty-fifty."

It's a game of fender-bender chicken. This circle is the great equalizer. Tippy little Citroëns, their rooftops cranked open like sardine lids, bring lumbering buses to a sudden, cussing halt.

While we're momentarily stalled on the inside lane, I pay and hop out. The cabbie drives away, leaving me under Europe's grandest arch and at the top of its ultimate boulevard. My plan is to stroll the length of the Champs-Elysées (literally, "Elysian Fields"). But first, the flame of France's unknown soldier—flickering silently in the eye of this urban storm—seems to invite me to savor this grandiose monument to French nationalism.

The Arc de Triomphe affords a great Paris view, but only to those who earn it—there are 284 steps to the top. Begun in 1809, the arch was intended to honor Napoleon's soldiers, who, in spite of being vastly outnumbered by the Austrians, scored a remarkable victory at the Battle of Austerlitz. Napoleon died long before the arch was completed, but it was finished in time for his 1840 funeral procession to pass underneath, carrying his remains (19 years dead) home to Paris from exile in St. Helena.

The Arc de Triomphe is dedicated to the glory of all French armies.

Like its Roman ancestors, this arch has served as a parade gateway for triumphal armies (French or foe) and important ceremonies. From 1940 to 1944, a large swastika flew from here as Nazis goose-stepped daily down the Champs-Elysées. In August 1944, Charles de Gaulle led Allied troops under this arch as they celebrated liberation.

Standing under the arch, you're surrounded by names of French victories since the Revolution, the names of great French generals (underlined if they died in battle), and by France's Tomb of the Unknown Soldier. Every day at 6:30 p.m. since just after World War I, the flame is rekindled and new flowers set in place, but any time of day it's a place of patriotic reverence.

Once you've climbed to the top of the arch, look down along the huge axis that shoots like an arrow all the way from the Louvre, up the

FRANCE

Champs-Elysées Walk

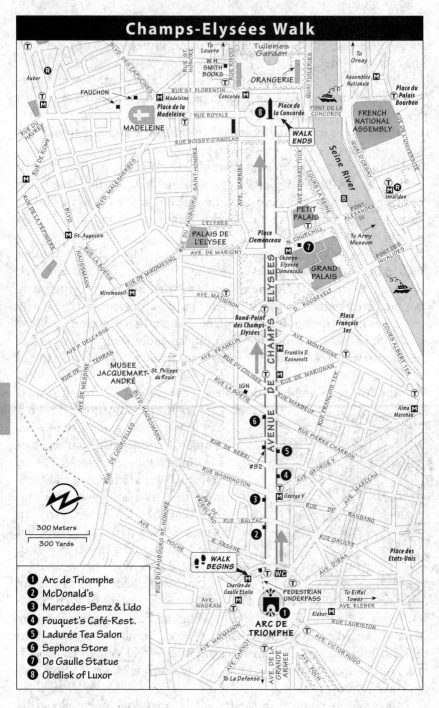

1 Arc de Triomphe
2 McDonald's
3 Mercedes-Benz & Lido
4 Fouquet's Café-Rest.
5 Ladurée Tea Salon
6 Sephora Store
7 De Gaulle Statue
8 Obelisk of Luxor

Champs-Elysées, through the arch, then straight down the Avenue de la Grande-Armée to a forest of distant skyscrapers around an even bigger modern arch in suburban La Défense. Notice the contrast between the skyscrapers in the suburbs and the more uniform heights of buildings closer to the arch. The beauty of Paris—basically a flat basin with a river running through it—is man-made. There's a harmonious relationship between the width of its grand boulevards and the standard height and design of the buildings. This elegant skyline is broken only by venerable historic domes and spires—and the lonely-looking Montparnasse Tower, which stands like the box the Eiffel Tower came in. The appearance of this tower served as a wake-up call in the early 1970s to preserve the historic skyline of downtown Paris.

In the mid-19th century, Baron Georges-Eugène Haussmann set out to make Paris the grandest city in Europe. The 12 boulevards that radiate from the Arc de Triomphe were part of his master plan: the creation of a series of major boulevards, intersecting at diagonals, with monuments (such as the Arc de Triomphe) as centerpieces of those intersections. Haussmann's plan did not anticipate the automobile—obvious when you watch the traffic scene below. But see how smoothly it really functions. Cars entering the circle have the right-of-way (the only roundabout in France with this rule); those in the circle must yield. Parisian drivers navigate the circle like a comet circling the sun—making a parabola. They quickly arc toward the smoothly flowing center. Then, a couple of avenues before their desired exit, they begin working their way back out.

A stroll down the Champs-Elysées will give you Paris at its most Parisian: monumental sidewalks, stylish shops, elegant cafés, and glimmering showrooms. Europe's characteristic love of strolling (a stately paced triathlon of walking, window-shopping, and high-profile sipping) dates from the booming 19th century, when leisure time and cash were abundant for the upper classes.

So, don an aristocratic air. From the Arc de Triomphe, amble gently downhill to the immense and historic square called Place de la Concorde. But before you stroll, you must master the name. Say it: shahn-zay-lee-zay.

Even small-town French kids who haven't traveled beyond a TV screen know that this is their country's ultimate parade ground, where major events all unfold: the Tour de France finale, Bastille Day parades, and New Year's festivities.

In 1667, Louis XIV opened the first section of the street as a short extension of the Tuileries Gardens. This year is considered the birth

Making Scents of It All

Strolling the Champs-Elysées, you'll come to Sephora, the incredible flagship store (at #70-72) of the huge perfume and cosmetics chain. Take your nose sightseeing and glide down Sephora's ramp into a vast hall of cosmetics and perfumes. Grab a disposable white strip from a lovely clerk, spritz it with a sample, and sniff. The store is thoughtfully laid out: The entry hall is lined with new products. In the main showroom, women's perfumes line the right wall and men's line the left—organized alphabetically by company, from Armani to Versace. The mesmerizing music,  chosen just for Sephora, makes you crave cosmetics.

of Paris as a grand city. The Champs-Elysées soon became *the* place to cruise in your carriage. (It still is today—traffic can be jammed up even at midnight.) One hundred years later, the café scene arrived.

The grand café scene survives today, amid pop clothing outlets and music megastores. Two cafés, Fouquet's and Ladurée (two blocks apart on the quiet side of the boulevard), are among the most venerable in Paris. Even elegant cafés like these often have humble roots. (Fouquet's started as a coachmen's bistro.) Today, Parisians keep 12,000 cafés in business.

Fouquet's gained fame as the hangout of French biplane pilots during World War I (Paris was just a few nervous miles from the Western Front). It also served as James Joyce's dining room. Today, it's pretty stuffy—unless you're a film star. The golden plaques at the entrance honor winners of France's Oscar-like film awards, the Césars. While the hushed interior is at once classy and intimidating, the outdoor setting is great for people-watching—and you can pay $10 for the most expensive shot of espresso I found in Paris.

You're more likely to see me hanging out at Ladurée, munching on a *macaron*. This classic 19th-century tea salon/restaurant/*pâtisserie* has an interior right out of the 1860s. Non-patrons can discreetly wander in through the door farthest downhill and peek into the cozy rooms upstairs. The bakery makes cute little cakes and gift-wrapped finger sandwiches.

The traditional *macarons* (which look like tiny hamburgers) come in a pastel palette of flavors from mint to raspberry to rose—these really are worth the journey. Get a frilly little gift box to go, or pay the *rançon* and sit down for a *très elegant* coffee and enjoy the Champs-Elysées show.

From the 1920s through the 1960s, this was a street of top-end hotels, cafés, and residences—pure elegance. Parisians actually dressed up to come here. Then, in 1963, the government pumped up the neighborhood's commercial metabolism by bringing in the RER (commuter train). Suburbanites had easy access, and *pfft*—there went the neighborhood.

The coming of McDonald's—at #140—was a shock to the boulevard. At first it was only allowed to have white arches painted on the window. Today, it legally spills out onto the sidewalk—provided it offers café-quality chairs and flower boxes.

As fast food and pop culture invaded and grand old buildings began to fall, Paris realized what it was losing. In 1985, a law prohibited the demolition of the elegant building fronts that once gave the boulevard a uniform grace. Today, many of the modern businesses hide behind preserved facades. As you stroll, imagine the boulevard pre-'63, with only the finest structures lining both sides all the way to the palace gardens.

The *nouvelle* Champs-Elysées, revitalized in 1994, has new benches and lamps, broader sidewalks, all-underground parking, and a fleet of green-suited workers who drive motorized street cleaners. Plane trees (a kind of sycamore that thrives despite big-city pollution) provide a leafy ambience.

As you stroll, you'll notice the French appetite for good living. The foyer of the famous Lido, Paris' largest cabaret, comes with leggy photos and a perky R-rated promo video. Moviegoing on the Champs-Elysées is popular. Showings *(séances)* with a "v.o." *(version originale)* next to the time indicate the film will be in its original language.

Luxury-car dealerships show off their futuristic "concept cars" alongside their current and classic models. Buying a new Mercedes here is like a fashion makeover—you pick out a leather jacket and purse to match. That new-car smell is a far cry from the 19th century, when this block carried the aroma of horse stables (which evolved into upper-crust limousine garages en route to today's dealerships).

At the Rond-Point des Champs-Elysées, the shopping ends and the park begins. This round, leafy traffic circle is always colorful, lined with flowers or festive seasonal decorations (thousands of pumpkins at Halloween, hundreds of decorated trees at Christmas). Avenue Montaigne, cutting off to the right, is lined by the most exclusive shops in town—places where you need to make an appointment to buy a dress.

Polite Paris

The "mean Parisian" problem is a holdover from Charles de Gaulle days. It's definitely fading, but France's lingering reputation of

rudeness can create a self-fulfilling expectation. If you want to enjoy the French, you can. Make it your goal.

The French, as a culture, are pouting. They used to be the crème de la crème, the definition of high class. Their language was the lingua franca—everyone wanted to speak French. There was a time when the czar of Russia and his family actually spoke better French than Russian. A US passport even has French on it—a holdover from those French glory days.

Enjoy the French.

Modern French culture is reeling—humiliated by two world wars, lashed by Levi's, and crushed by the Big Mac of American culture. And our two cultures aren't natural buddies. The French enjoy subtleties and sophistication. American culture sneers at these fine points. We're proud, brash, and like to think we're rugged individualists. We are a smiley-face culture whose bank tellers are fined if they forget to say, "Have a nice day." The French don't find slap-on-the-back niceness terribly sincere.

Typically, Americans evaluate the French by the Parisians they meet. Big cities anywhere are colder than small towns. And, remember, most of us see Paris at the height of the hot, busy summer, when those Parisians who can't escape on vacation see their hometown flooded with insensitive foreigners who butcher their language and put ketchup on their meat. That's tough to take smiling, and if you're looking for coldness, this is a good place to start.

To make the Parisians suddenly 40 percent friendlier, learn and liberally use these four phrases: *bonjour, s'il vous plaît, merci,* and *pardon.* And to really revel in French friendliness, visit an untouristy part of the countryside and use those four phrases. Oh, and *vive la différence*—celebrate the differences.

A long block past the Rond-Point, at Avenue de Marigny, look to the other side of the Champs-Elysées to find a statue of General Charles de Gaulle. Ramrod straight, he strides out toward the boulevard as he did on the day Paris was liberated in 1944 (6' 4" tall, walking proudly for the length of the Champs-Elysées, as others around him ducked during sporadic gunfire).

From here, it's a straight shot down the last stretch of the boulevard to the sprawling 21-acre square called the Place de la Concorde.

Place de la Concorde, formerly "place de la Révolution"

Its centerpiece is the 3,300-year-old Obelisk of Luxor. It was carted here from Egypt in the 1830s, a gift to the French king. The gold-leaf diagrams on the obelisk tell the story of its laborious journey.

During the French Revolution, this was the Place de la Révolution. A guillotine stood where the obelisk now stands. A bronze plaque memorializes the place where Louis XVI, Marie-Antoinette, and about 1,200 others were made "a foot shorter on top." Invented as a humane alternative to the poorly aimed executioner's axe, the guillotine's efficiency was breathtaking. It took a crew of three: one to manage the blade, one to hold the blood bucket, and one to catch the head and raise it high to the roaring crowd.

Standing in the shadow of that obelisk with your back to the Louvre while you look up the grandest boulevard in Europe, you can't help but think of the sweep of history...and those great *macarons*.

FRANCE

The Petite Lane: Rue Cler

After taking a turn along Paris' showcase of a boulevard, tune into the rhythm of real life—hop in a cab and say, *"Rue Cler, s'il vous plaît."*

The Rue Cler, lined with little food shops, captures the art of Parisian living. Shopping for groceries is an integral part of daily life here for three good reasons: Refrigerators are small (tiny kitchens), produce must be fresh, and it's an important social event. Shopping is a chance to hear about the butcher's vacation plans, see photos of the florist's new grandchild, relax over *un café*, and kiss the cheeks of friends (the French standard is twice for regular acquaintances, three times for friends you

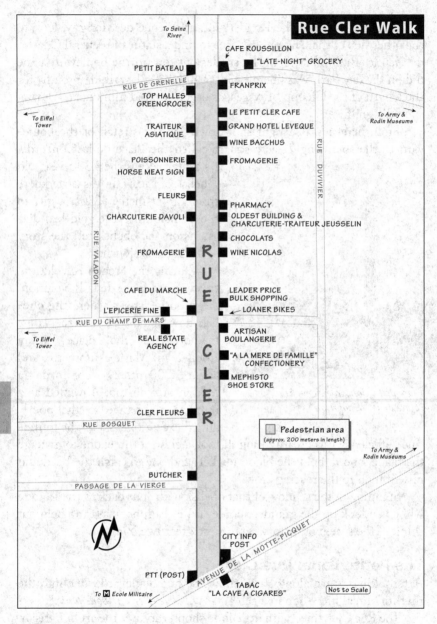

Rue Cler Walk

To Seine River

CAFE ROUSSILLON

"LATE-NIGHT" GROCERY

PETIT BATEAU

RUE DE GRENELLE

FRANPRIX

TOP HALLES GREENGROCER

LE PETIT CLER CAFE

To Eiffel Tower

To Army & Rodin Museums

GRAND HOTEL LEVEQUE

TRAITEUR ASIATIQUE

WINE BACCHUS

POISSONNERIE

FROMAGERIE

HORSE MEAT SIGN

RUE DUVIVIER

FLEURS

PHARMACY

CHARCUTERIE DAVOLI

OLDEST BUILDING & CHARCUTERIE-TRAITEUR JEUSSELIN

CHOCOLATS

FROMAGERIE

WINE NICOLAS

RUE VALADON

RUE CLER

CAFE DU MARCHE

LEADER PRICE BULK SHOPPING

L'EPICERIE FINE

LOANER BIKES

RUE DU CHAMP DE MARS

To Eiffel Tower

REAL ESTATE AGENCY

ARTISAN BOULANGERIE

"A LA MERE DE FAMILLE" CONFECTIONERY

MEPHISTO SHOE STORE

CLER FLEURS

RUE BOSQUET

Pedestrian area
(approx. 200 meters in length)

To Army & Rodin Museums

BUTCHER

PASSAGE DE LA VIERGE

CITY INFO POST

AVENUE DE LA MOTTE-PICQUET

PTT (POST)

To M Ecole Militaire

TABAC
"LA CAVE A CIGARES"

Not to Scale

FRANCE

haven't seen in a while).

Traffic-free Rue Cler offers plenty of space for tiny stores and their patrons to spill into the street. It's an ideal environment for this ritual to survive in and for you to explore. The street is lined with the essential shops—wine, cheese, chocolate, bread—as well as a bank and a post office. And the shops of this community are run by people who've found their niche: boys who grew up on quiche, girls who know a good wine. The people you see in uniform are likely from the Ecole Militaire (military school, Napoleon's alma mater, two blocks away).

There's no better place to assemble the ultimate French picnic. Visit when the market is open and lively, in the morning or early evening (dead on Sunday evening and all day Monday). Remember that these shops are busy serving regular customers. Be polite (say *"Bonjour, Madame/Monsieur"* as you enter and *"Au revoir, Madame/Monsieur"* when you leave), and be careful not to get in the way.

Have the cabbie drop you off at the intersection of Rue Cler and Rue de Grenelle, so you can start your walk where the pedestrian section of Rue Cler does.

Café Roussillon is a neighborhood fixture. Drinks at the bar *(comptoir)* are about half the price of drinks at the tables *(salles)*. Notice the blackboard with a list of wines sold by the little (7 cl.) glass. Also displayed are various *cheque déjeuner* or *ticket restaurant* decals, advertising that this café accepts lunch "checks." In France, an employee lunch subsidy program is an expected perk. Employers issue these voucher checks (worth about $12) for the number of days an employee works in a month. Sack lunches are rare, since a good lunch is sacred.

Each morning, the greengrocer Top Halles receives fresh fruits and vegetables that have been trucked in from farmers' fields to Paris' huge Rungis market—Europe's largest, near Orly Airport—then dispatched to merchants with FedEx-like speed and precision. Good luck finding a shopping bag—locals bring their own two-wheeled carts or reusable bags. Also, notice how the earth-friendly French resist unnecessary packaging.

Parisians—who know they eat best by being tuned into the seasons—shop with their noses. Try it. Smell the cheap foreign strawberries. One sniff of the torpedo-shaped French ones *(gariguettes)* in June, and you know which is better. Find the herbs in the back. Is today's delivery in? Look at the price of those melons. What's the country of origin? It must be posted. If they're out of season, they come from Guadeloupe. Many people buy only local products.

The Franprix across the street is a small Safeway-type store. Opposite

Grand Hôtel Lévêque is an Asian deli *(traiteur asiatique)*. Fast Asian food is popular in Paris. These shops—about as common as bakeries now—are making an impact on Parisian eating habits.

Just past the hotel is a wine shop. Shoppers often save this stop for last, after they have assembled their meal and are ready to pick the appropriate wine. The wine is classified by region. Most "Parisians" (born elsewhere) have an affinity for the wines of their home region. Check out the great prices. Wines of the month—in the center—sell for about $11. You can get a fine bottle for $17. The clerk is a counselor who works with your needs and budget.

Smell the *fromagerie* next door. A long, narrow, canopied cheese table brings the *fromagerie* into the street. Wedges, cylinders, balls, and miniature hockey pucks all powdered white, gray, and burnt marshmallow—it's a festival of mold. The street cart and front window feature both cow and goat cheeses. *Ooh la la* means you're impressed. If you really like

The cheese shop—known as BOF (beurre, oeuf, fromage)—sells butter, eggs, and cheese.

cheese, show greater excitement with more *la*s. *Ooh la la la la.* My local friend once held the stinkiest glob close to her nose, took an orgasmic breath, and exhaled, "Yes, it smells like zee feet of angels." Go ahead...inhale.

Step inside and browse through some of the 200 types of French cheese. A *fromagerie* is lab-coat serious but friendly. Also known as a *crémerie* or a "BOF" (for *beurre, oeuf,* and *fromage)*, this is where people go for butter, eggs, and cheeses. In the back room are *les meules,* the big, 170-pound wheels of cheese (made from 250 gallons of milk). The "hard" cheeses are cut from these. Don't eat the skin of these big ones...they roll them on the floor. But the skin on most smaller cheeses—the Brie, the Camembert—is part of the taste.

At dinner tonight, you can take the cheese course just before or as the dessert. On a good cheese plate you have a hard cheese (perhaps a Comté, similar to a white cheddar), a softer cheese (maybe Brie or Camembert), a bleu cheese, and a goat cheese—ideally from different regions. Because it's strongest, the goat cheese is usually eaten last.

Across the street is the fish shop *(poissonerie)*. Fresh fish is brought into Paris daily from ports on the English Channel, 110 miles away. In fact, fish here is likely fresher than in many towns closer to the sea, because Paris is a commercial hub (from here, it's shipped to outlying towns). Anything wriggling?

Next door, check out the storefront at the Crêperie Ulysée en Gaule. The stones and glass set over the doorway advertise horse meat: *Boucherie Chevaline*. While today this shop serves non-equine souvlaki (the family is Greek) and crêpes, the classy storefront survives from a previous occupant. Created in the 1930s and signed by the artist, it's a work of art fit for a museum.

Wander on past the flower shop and pharmacy (in Europe, the first diagnosis and prescription are made by the pharmacist; if it's out of his league, he'll recommend a doctor). Notice the oldest and shortest building. It's from the early 1800s, when this street was part of a village near Paris and lined with structures like this. Of course, over the years Paris engulfed these surrounding villages, and now the street is a mishmash of architectural styles.

The *charcuterie-traiteur* Davoli sells mouthwatering deli food to go. Because Parisian kitchens are so small, these gourmet delis are handy, even for those who cook. A deli lets hosts concentrate on creating the main course, and then buy beautifully prepared side dishes to complete a fine dinner. Notice the system: Order, take your ticket to the cashier to pay, and return with the receipt to pick up your food.

The Café du Marché, on the corner, is *the* place to sit and enjoy the Rue Cler action. For a reasonable meal, grab a chair and check the chalk menu listing the *plat du jour* (blue plate special). Notice how the recent no-smoking-indoors laws have made outdoor seating and propane heaters a huge hit.

The shiny, sterile Leader Price grocery store (across the street, on the corner) is a Parisian Costco, selling bulk items. Because storage space is so limited in most Parisian apartments, bulk purchases are unlikely to become a big deal here. The latest trend is to stock up on nonperishables by shopping online, pick up produce three times a week, and buy fresh bread daily.

A short side-trip west to 8 Rue du Champ de Mars takes you to L'Epicerie Fine, where gentle Pascal and Nathalie tempt visitors with fine gourmet treats. Their mission in life is to explain to travelers, in fluent English, what the French fuss over food is all about. Let them help you assemble a picnic as they educate you with generous tastes of caramel, balsamic vinegar, and French and Italian olive oil.

Back on the Rue Cler, you'll come upon a *boulangerie*, diagonally across from Café du Marché. Residents debate the merits of *boulangeries*. It's said that a baker cannot be good at both bread and pastry. At cooking school, they major in one or the other. So a baker either bakes bread or makes pastries and has the other done elsewhere. But here, the baker bucks the trend. Rue Cler regulars agree that this man makes both good bread and delicious pastries.

A bit farther along, La Mère de Famille Gourmand Chocolats Confiseries has been in the neighborhood for 30 years. The owner sells modern treats, but has always kept the traditional candies, too. "The old ladies, they want the same sweets that made them so happy 80 years ago," she says. Until a few years ago, chocolate was dipped and decorated right on the premises. As was the tradition in Rue Cler shops, the merchants resided and produced in the back and sold in the front.

Walk on toward the end of Rue Cler. An electronic signpost on the corner directs residents to websites for information—transportation changes, surveys, employment opportunities, community events, and so on. Across the busy street is a *tabac* (tobacco shop). In addition to tobacco, *tabacs* also serve their neighborhoods as a kind of government cash desk. All sell stamps and most sell public-transit tickets and parking cards.

Rue Cler ends where it intersects with Avenue de la Motte-Picquet. The Ecole Militaire Métro stop is just down the street to the right. If you bought a picnic along this walk, head for the nearby benches and gardens: Avenue de la Motte-Picquet leads to two fine parks. Facing Rue Cler, turn right for the Army Museum or left for the Eiffel Tower.

Settle in and enjoy your Parisian feast. *Bon appétit!*

To sleep in Paris' **Rue Cler neighborhood,** *consider the Grand Hôtel Lévêque (moderate, 29 Rue Cler, tel. 01 47 05 49 15, www.hotel-leveque.com) or Hôtel du Champ de Mars (budget, 7 Rue du Champ de Mars, tel. 01 45 51 52 30, www.hotelduchampdemars.com). In the* **Marais neighborhood,** *try the Grand Hôtel Jeanne d'Arc (budget, 3 Rue de Jarente, tel. 01 48 87 62 11, www.hoteljeannedarc.com) or Hôtel Castex (splurge, 5 Rue Castex, tel. 01 42 72 31 52, www.castexhotelparis.com). For all the particulars on Paris, see this year's edition of* Rick Steves' Paris.

Alsace and Colmar: Vintage France

The French province of Alsace stands like a flower-child referee between Germany and France. Bounded by the Rhine River on the east and the well-worn Vosges Mountains on the west, this is a green region of Hansel-and-Gretel villages, ambitious vineyards, and vibrant cities.

Alsace has changed hands several times between Germany and France because of its location, natural wealth, naked vulnerability, and the fact that Germany considered the mountains as the natural border while France saw the Rhine as the dividing line. Centuries as a political pawn between Germany and France have given Alsace a hybrid culture. On doorways of homes, you'll see names like Jacques Schmidt or Dietrich Le Beau. Natives who curse do so bilingually. Half-timbered restaurants serve sauerkraut and escargot.

Wine is the primary industry, topic of conversation, dominant mouthwash, and perfect excuse for countless festivals.

Alsace's wine road, the Route du Vin, is an asphalt ribbon tying 90 miles of vineyards, villages, and feudal fortresses into an understandably popular tourist package. The dry and sunny climate has produced good wine and happy tourists since Roman days.

During the October harvest season, all Alsace erupts into a carnival of colorful folk costumes, traditional good-time music, and Dionysian smiles. I felt as welcome as a grape picker, and my tight sightseeing plans became as hard to follow as a straight line.

If you can pick grapes, you might land a job in October. For a hard day in the vineyards, you'll get room and board, a modest wage, and an intimate Alsatian social experience lubricated liberally, logically, by plenty of wine.

Wine tasting is popular throughout the year. Roadside *dégustation*

signs invite you into wine *caves,* where a producer will serve you all seven Alsatian wines from dry to sweet, with educational commentary (probably in French) if requested. Try Crémant d'Alsace, the Alsatian sparkling wine. *Cave*-hopping is a great way to spend an afternoon on the Route du Vin. With free samples and fine $10 bottles, French wine-tasting can be an affordable sport.

FRANCE

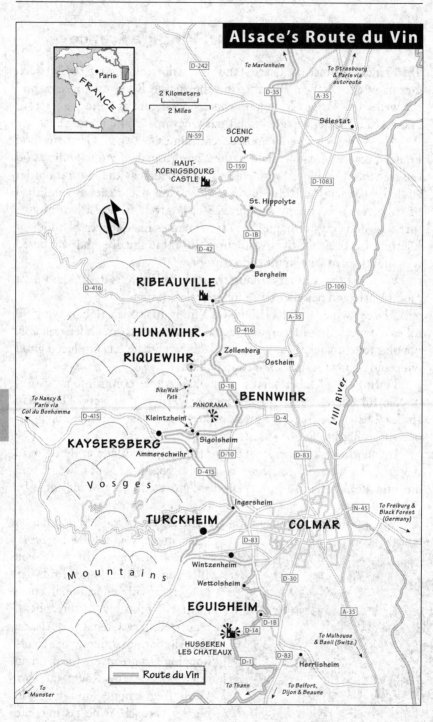

Alsace's Route du Vin

To Marlenheim

To Strasbourg & Paris via autoroute

D-242

D-35

A-35

Sélestat

2 Kilometers

2 Miles

N-59

SCENIC LOOP

D-159

HAUT-KOENIGSBOURG CASTLE

D-1083

St. Hippolyte

D-1B

D-42

Bergheim

D-106

D-416

RIBEAUVILLE

A-35

HUNAWIHR

D-416

RIQUEWIHR

Zellenberg

Ostheim

Bike/Walk Path

D-1B

To Nancy & Paris via Col du Bonhomme

PANORAMA

BENNWIHR

D-415

Kleintzheim

D-4

KAYSERSBERG

Sigolsheim

Ammerschwihr

D-10

D-83

D-415

Vosges

Ingersheim

N-45

To Freiburg & Black Forest (Germany)

TURCKHEIM

COLMAR

D-83

Mountains

Wintzenheim

Wettolsheim

D-30

EGUISHEIM

A-35

D-1B

D-14

HUSSEREN LES CHATEAUX

To Mulhouse & Basil (Switz.)

D-1

D-83

Herrlisheim

Route du Vin

To Munster

To Thann

To Belfort, Dijon & Beaune

The small *caves* are fun, but be sure to tour a larger wine co-op. Beer-drinking Germans completely flattened many Alsatian towns in 1944. The small family-run vineyards of these villages sprang back as large, modern, and efficient cooperatives. Among the best of these is the big and modern Wolfberger Wine Cooperative in Eguisheim (Cave Vinicole d'Eguisheim).

There's more to Alsace than meets the palate. Centuries of successful wine production built prosperous, colorful villages. Countless castles capped hilltops to defend the much-invaded plain, and wine wasn't the only art form loved and patronized by connoisseurs.

Alsatian towns are historic mosaics of gables, fountains, medieval bell towers and gateways, ancient ramparts, churches, and cheery old inns. More than anywhere in France, you'll find plenty of budget beds in private homes ($70-90 doubles, ask at village tourist offices or look for *chambre d'hôte* signs). While Colmar is the best home-base city, petite Eguisheim, with plenty of small hotels, a minimum of tour crowds, and maximum village charm, is the ideal small-town home. Nearby Riquewihr and Kaysersberg are two more crackerjack villages. A scenic path—one of countless in the region—connects these two towns. Take a hike or rent a bike. Drop by a castle or two. Climb the tallest tower and survey Alsace, looking as it has for centuries—a valley of endless vineyards along the Route du Vin.

Colmar

Colmar, my favorite city in Alsace, sees few American tourists but is popular with Germans and the French. This well-pickled old town of 70,000 is a handy springboard for Alsatian explorations.

Historic beauty was usually a poor excuse to be spared the ravages of World War II, but it worked for Colmar. The American and British military were careful not to bomb the half-timbered old burghers' houses, characteristic red- and green-tiled roofs, and cobbled lanes of Alsace's most beautiful city.

Today, Colmar is alive with colorful buildings, impressive art treasures, and German tourists. Schoolgirls park their rickety horse carriages in front of City Hall

German or French? Colmar is both.

FRANCE

and are ready to give visitors a clip-clop tour of the old town. Antique shops welcome browsers, and hoteliers hurry down the sleepy streets to pick up fresh croissants in time for breakfast.

Colmar offers heavyweight sights in a warm, small-town package. By the end of the Middle Ages, the walled town was a thriving trade center filled with rich old houses. The wonderfully restored tanners' quarters is a quiver of tall, narrow, half-timbered buildings. Its confused rooftops struggle erratically to get enough sun to dry their animal skins. Nearby you'll find "La Petite Venise," complete with canals and gondola rides.

Colmar combines its abundance of art with a knack for showing it off. The artistic geniuses Grünewald, Schongauer, and Bartholdi all called Colmar home.

Frédéric-Auguste Bartholdi, who created our Statue of Liberty a century ago, adorned his hometown with many fine, if smaller, statues. Don't miss the little Bartholdi museum, offering a good look at the artist's life and some fun Statue of Liberty trivia.

Four hundred years earlier, Martin Schongauer was the leading local artist. His *Madonna in the Rose Garden* could give a drill sergeant goose bumps. Looking fresh and crisp, it's set magnificently in a Gothic Dominican church. I sat with a dozen people, silently, as if at a symphony, as Schongauer's *Madonna* performed solo on center stage. Lit by 14th-century stained glass, its richness and tenderness cradled me in a Gothic sweetness that no textbook could explain. Even if you become so jaded that you "never want to see another Madonna and Child," give this one a chance.

The Unterlinden Museum, one of my favorite small museums, is housed in a 750-year-old convent next to the tourist office. It has the best collection anywhere of Alsatian folk art and art exhibits ranging from Neolithic and Gallo-Roman archaeological collections to works by Monet, Renoir, Braque, and Picasso. It's a medieval and Renaissance home show. You can lose yourself in a 17th-century Alsatian wine cellar complete with presses, barrels, tools, and aromas.

The highlight of the museum— and for me, the city—is Matthias Grünewald's gripping Isenheim altarpiece. (Working on one panel at a time, conservators have recently completed an extensive restoration

Grünewald's gripping Crucifixion

of this masterpiece.) This is actually a series of paintings on hinges that pivot like shutters. Designed to help people in a hospital suffer through their horrible skin diseases (long before the age of painkillers), it's one of the most powerful paintings ever. Stand petrified in front of it and let the agony and suffering of the Crucifixion drag its fingers down your face. Just as you're about to break down and sob with those in the painting, turn to the happy ending—a psychedelic explosion of Resurrection happiness. It's like jumping from the dentist's chair directly into a Jacuzzi. We know very little about Grünewald except that his work has played tetherball with human emotions for 500 years.

Colmar's tourist information office provides city maps, guides, and a room-finding service. They can also suggest side-trips around Alsace's wine road or into Germany's Black Forest and nearby Freiburg, or a tour of the Maginot Line.

For maximum fun, remember that Colmar goes crazy during its 10-day wine fest in August. You'll enjoy plenty of revelry—feasting, dancing, music, and wine—Alsatian-style.

For good-value accommodations in **Colmar,** *try Hôtel le Rapp (splurge, 1 Rue Weinemer, tel. 03 89 41 62 10, www.rapp-hotel.com) or Maison Marin Jund (budget, 12 Rue de l'Ange, tel. 03 89 41 58 72, www.martinjund.com). For all the travel specifics, see this year's edition of* Rick Steves' France.

From France to Italy over Mont Blanc

Europe's ultimate mountain lift towers high above the tourist-choked French resort town of Chamonix. Ride the Aiguille du Midi *téléphérique* (gondola) to the dizzy 12,600-foot-high tip of a rock needle. As you get

in, remind yourself that this thing has been going back and forth now since 1954; surely it'll make it one more time. Chamonix shrinks as trees fly by, soon replaced by whizzing rocks, ice, and snow, until you reach the top. Up there, even sunshine is cold. The air is thin. People are giddy (those prone to altitude sickness are less giddy). Fun things can happen if you're not too winded to join

Dangle silently for 40 minutes as you glide over the glacier from France to Italy.

FRANCE

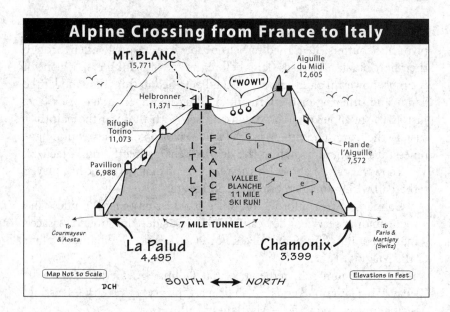

Alpine Crossing from France to Italy

MT. BLANC
15,771

Aiguille
du Midi
12,605

"WOW!"

Helbronner
11,371

Rifugio
Torino
11,073

Plan de
l'Aiguille
7,572

Pavillion
6,988

ITALY FRANCE

VALLEE
BLANCHE
11 MILE
SKI RUN!

G
l
a
c
i
e
r

To
Courmayeur
& Aosta

7 MILE TUNNEL

To
Paris &
Martigny
(Switz)

La Palud
4,495

Chamonix
3,399

Map Not to Scale

Elevations in Feet

DCH

SOUTH ⟷ NORTH

locals in the halfway-to-heaven tango.

The Alps spread out before you. In the distance is the bent little Matterhorn (called "Cervin" in French). You can almost reach out and pat the head of Mont Blanc, at 15,771 feet, the Alps' highest point.

Next, for Europe's most exciting border crossing, get into the tiny red gondola and head south. Dangle silently for 40 minutes as you glide over glaciers and a forest of peaks to Italy. Hang your head out the window; explore every corner of your view. You're sailing a new sea.

Cross into Italy at Helbronner Point (11,371 feet) and descend into the remote Italian Valle d'Aosta. It's a whole different world.

Your starting point for this adventure is Chamonix, a convenient overnight train ride from Paris or Nice. Chamonix is a resort town—packed in August but surprisingly easy and affordable the rest of the year. Like Switzerland's Interlaken, it's a launchpad for mountain worshippers. The town has an efficient tourist information center and plenty of affordable accommodations.

From Chamonix, days of hikes and cable-car rides are within easy reach. The best hikes are opposite the most staggering peaks on the Gran Balcon Sud, a world of pristine lakes, great Mont Blanc range views, and hang gliders lunging off the cliff from the Brévent lift station. Watching these daredevils fill the valley like spaced-out butterflies is a thrilling spectator sport. Probably the best hike—two hours each way—is from the top of the Flégère lift to Lac Blanc. While demanding, the trail is well signed and the views are breathtaking.

For the ultimate ride, take that *téléphérique* to the Aiguille du Midi. This lift is Europe's highest and most spectacular ($60 round-trip from Chamonix, daily 6:00 a.m.-4:30 p.m. in the summer, shorter hours off-season, smart to reserve up to 10 days in advance, www.compagniedu montblanc.com). If the weather is good, forget your budget. Afternoons are most likely clouded and crowded. In August, ride very early to avoid miserable delays. If you plan to dillydally, ride directly to your farthest point and linger on your return.

To both save a little money and enjoy a hike, buy a ticket to the top of the Aiguille du Midi, but ride only halfway back down. This gives you a chance to look down at the Alps and over at the summit of Mont Blanc from your lofty 12,600-foot lookout. Then you descend to the halfway point (Plan de l'Aiguille), where you're free to frolic in the glaciers and hike to Mer de Glace. Then you can catch a train at Montenvers back to Chamonix.

The Alps from atop the Aiguille du Midi, 12,600 feet up

From the top of the Aiguille du Midi, you can continue (weather permitting) over the mountain to Italy. It's a long trip; the last departure is at about 2:00 p.m. The descent from Helbronner Point takes you into the remote Italian Valle d'Aosta, where a dash of France and a splash of Switzerland blend with the already rich Italian flavor and countless castles to give you an easy-to-like first taste of Italy.

The town of Aosta, your best valley home base, is a two-hour bus ride from the base of the lift in La Palud (hourly departures, change in Courmayeur). If a fellow cable-car passenger has a car parked in La Palud, charm a ride to Aosta.

"The Rome of the Alps," as Aosta is called, has many Roman ruins and offers a great introduction to the fine points of Italian life: cappuccino, gelato, and an obligatory evening stroll. An evening here is a fine way to ease into *la dolce vita*.

Chamonix, the Aiguille du Midi, and the Valle d'Aosta—surely a high point in anyone's European vacation.

FRANCE

For good-value accommodations in **Chamonix,** try Hôtel de l'Arve (moderate, 60 Impasse des Anémones, tel. 04 50 53 02 31, www.hotelarve-chamonix .com) or Hôtel Richemond (splurge, 228 Rue du Docteur Paccard, tel. 04 50 53 08 85, www.richemond.fr). For all the travel specifics, see this year's edition of Rick Steves' France.

BELGIUM AND THE NETHERLANDS

Bruges: Pickled in Gothic

With a smile, the shop owner handed me a pharaoh's head and two hedgehogs and said that her husband was busy downstairs finishing off another batch of chocolates. Happily sucking on a hedgehog, I walked out of the small chocolate shop with a $3, 100-gram assortment of Bruges' best pralines—filled-chocolate delights.

Bruggians are connoisseurs of chocolate. You'll be tempted by display windows all over town. Godiva is considered the best big factory brand, but for quality and service, drop by one of the many family-run shops. Pray for cool weather—they close down when it's hot.

With Renoir canals, pointy gilded architecture, vivid time-tunnel art, and stay-awhile cafés, Bruges is a joy. Where else can you bike along a canal, munch mussels and wash them down with the world's best beer, see a Michelangelo, and savor heavenly chocolate, all within 300 yards of a bell tower that jingles every 15 minutes? And do it all without worrying about a language barrier.

The town is Brugge (BROO-ghah) in Flemish, and Bruges (broozh) in French and English. Its name comes from the Viking word for "wharf." Right from the start, Bruges was a trading center. By the 14th century, Bruges had a population of 35,000 (similar to London) and the most important cloth market in northern Europe. But by the 16th century, the harbor had silted up and the economy had collapsed.

Like so many small-town wonders, Bruges is well pickled because

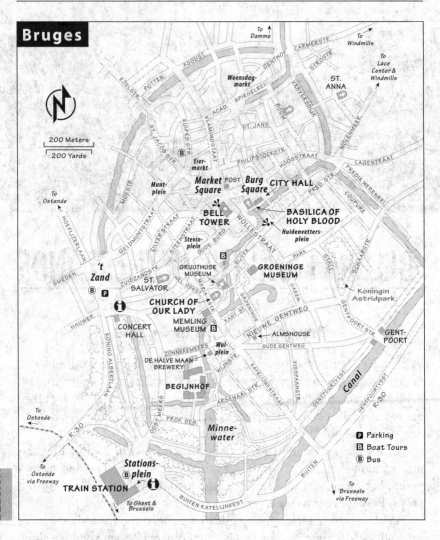

Bruges

(map labels)

To Damme

To Windmills

To Lace Center & Windmills

CARMERSTR.

STROOSTR.

GENTHOF

VEERVERSDIJK

ST. ANNA

MOLENMEER

LAGESTRAAT

PREDIK HERENREI

AUGUST.

EZELSTR.

POTTEN

Woensdag-markt

SPIEGELREI

BLOM.

ST. JANS

ACAD.

VLAMINGSTRAAT

KUIPES STR.

ST. JACOB STR.

PHILIPSTOCKSTR.

HOOGSTRAAT

200 Meters

200 Yards

Eier-markt

To Ostende

MOESTR.

Munt-plein

Market Square   POST   **Burg Square**   **CITY HALL**

FRED. STR.

COUFURE

GELDMUNTSTRAAT

ZILVER STRAAT

STEENSTRAAT

BELL TOWER

WOLLESTRAAT

BASILICA OF HOLY BLOOD

Huidenvetters-plein

Stevin-plein

OUDE BURG

DIJVER

PARK

SCHAARSTR.

HOEFIJZERLAAN

ZUIDZANDSTR.

't Zand

SMEDEN

HEL GEESTR.

GRUUTHUSE MUSEUM

MARIA STR.

GROENINGE MUSEUM

GAREN

GENTPOORT STR.

Koningin Astridpark

ST. SALVATOR

GROENINGE

CHURCH OF OUR LADY

KAST. ST.

NIEUWE GENTWEG

GENT-POORT

HAUWER

CONCERT HALL

MEMLING MUSEUM

Wal-plein

OUDE GENTWEG

—ALMSHOUSE

VISSPAANSTR.

GENTPOORTVEST

ZONNEKEMEERS

DE HALVE MAAN BREWERY

WIJNSTR.

KATELIJNESTRAAT

KONING ALBERTLAAN

BEGIJNHOF

ARSENAAL STR.

Canal

R-30

To Ostende

R-30

OOST MEERS

PROF. SEB.

Minne-water

BUITEN

To Brussels via Freeway

P Parking
B Boat Tours
B Bus

To Ostende via Freeway

Stations-plein

TRAIN STATION

To Ghent & Brussels

BUITEN KATELIJNVEST

To Brussels via Freeway

its economy went sour. But rediscovered by modern-day tourists, Bruges thrives. This uniquely well-preserved Gothic city is no secret, but even with crowds, it's the kind of city where you don't mind being a tourist.

Bruges makes a fine first night on the Continent for travelers arriving from England: It's just 15 minutes by train from Ostende, where boats dock from Dover, and an hour from Brussels, where the Eurostar train arrives from London.

Bruges' Market Square, ringed by great old gabled buildings and crowned by the belfry, is the colorful heart of the city. Under the belfry are two great Belgian french-fry stands, a small metal model of the tower, and a Braille description of the old town.

This bell tower has towered over Market Square since 1300. Climb 366 steps to survey the town. Just before the top, peek into the carillon room. On the quarter hour, the 47 bells are played mechanically with the giant barrel and movable tabs. For concerts, a carillonist plays the manual keyboard with fists and feet rather than fingers. Be there on the quarter hour when things ring. It's *bellissimo* at the top of the hour.

Within a block or three, you'll find a day's worth of sights. The Basilica of the Holy Blood is famous for its relic of the blood of Christ, which, according to tradition, was brought to Bruges in 1150 after the Second Crusade. The City Hall has the oldest and most sumptuous Gothic hall in the Low Countries. The Gruuthuse Museum, a

Bruges: canals, fine beer, a Michelangelo, and even a leaning tower

wealthy brewer's home, is filled with a sprawling smattering of everything from medieval bedpans to a guillotine. The Church of Our Lady, standing as a memorial to the power and wealth of Bruges in its heyday, has a delicate *Madonna and Child* by Michelangelo, said to be the only statue of his to leave Italy in his lifetime. A medieval hospital, now the Memling Museum, contains much-loved paintings by the greatest of the Flemish Primitives, Hans Memling.

Yadda, yadda, yadda...Michelangelo, the blood of Christ, leaning bell towers, and guillotines. You'd expect any medieval powerhouse to show off trinkets from its glory days. But Bruges has fun experiences, too.

The De Halve Maan ("The Half Moon") brewery tour is a handy way to pay your respects to some local favorites: Brugse Zot and Straffe Hendrik, the only beers still made right in Bruges. The happy gang at this working family brewery gives entertaining and informative 45-minute tours in three languages. On the tour, drinkers are reminded that "the components of the beer are vitally necessary and contribute to a well-balanced life pattern. Nerves, muscles, visual sentience, and a healthy skin are stimulated by these in a positive manner. For longevity and lifelong equilibrium, drink Brugse Zot in moderation!"

Belgians are Europe's beer connoisseurs, and this country boasts

BELGIUM

A Stop in Brussels

Bruges isn't the only highlight in Belgium. Consider a short stop in Brussels, one of Europe's underrated cities. If traveling by train, it's easy to do, whether you're transferring in Brussels for Bruges, or just passing through the country. Anyone taking the three-hour train ride between Paris to Amsterdam will stop in Brussels, but few even consider getting out. Each train on this route stops in Brussels, and there's always another train coming in an hour or so. Leave an hour early, arrive an hour late, and give yourself two hours in Brussels. Luckily for the rushed tourist, Brussels Central Station has easy baggage storage and puts you two blocks (just walk downhill) from the helpful tourist office, a colorful pedestrian-only city core, Europe's greatest city square (Grand Place), and its most overrated and tacky

Brussels' Grand Place is the place to kick back with a brew.

sight, the *Manneken-Pis* (a much-photographed statue of a little boy who thinks he's a fountain). Brussels has three stations: Nord, Midi, and Central. Ask if your train stops at Central (middle) Station. If you have to get off at Nord or Midi, don't worry—subway-like connecting trains run every few minutes. You'll have no trouble finding English-speaking help.

The colorful cobblestone Grand Place is the historic and geographic heart of Brussels. As the town's market square for 1,000 years, this was where farmers and merchants sold their wares in open-air stalls. Today the Town Hall dominates the square with its 300-foot-tall tower. Fancy smaller buildings (former guild halls) give the square its grand medieval character, their impressive gabled roofs topped with statues. Any time of day, it's worth swinging by to see what's going on. Concerts, flower markets, endless people-watching—it entertains (as do the streets around it). Shops and cafés sell chocolates, *gaufres* (waffles), beer, mussels, fries, *dentelles* (lace), and flowers. Before heading back for your train, buy a box of chocolates and a bottle of Belgian beer. Pop the top as your train pulls out of the station. Ahhh!

more than 120 varieties of beer and 580 different brands. Duvel ("Devil"), a potent brew, is, even to a Bud Light kind of guy, obviously great beer. Trappist is monk-made beer, and Dentergems is made with coriander and orange peel. Those who don't drink beer enjoy the cherry-flavored Kriek and strawberry-flavored Frambozen. Each beer is served in its own unique glass.

Walk off your beer buzz with a stroll through the Begijnhof (buh-HINE-hof). This quiet courtyard, lined with houses around a church, was for centuries the home of Beguines—women who removed themselves from the world at large to dedicate their lives to God. For reasons of war and testosterone, there were more women than men in the medieval Low Countries. The lay order of Beguines offered single or widowed women a dignified place to live and work. When the order died out, many of its communities were taken over by towns for subsidized housing, but some, like this one, became homes for nuns. You'll find Beguine housing all over Belgium and the Netherlands. Bruges' Begijnhof almost makes you want to don a habit and fold your hands as you walk under its wispy trees and whisper past its frugal little homes.

For more peace, wander back in time to Bruges' four windmills, strung out along a pleasant, grassy canalside park. Joust with a windmill or just have a picnic.

Every once in a while as you travel, you stumble onto a town that somehow missed the 21st-century bus. Ironically, many of these wonderfully preserved towns are so full of Old World charm because, for various reasons, their economies failed. The towns became so poor that no one even bothered to tear them down to build more modern towns. England's Cotswolds lost their export market. Toledo was abandoned as Spain's capital. Stranded-in-the-past Dutch fishing towns were left high and dry as the sea around them was drained and the land reclaimed. And Bruges' harbor silted up.

Today, while some of these towns slumber on, many—like Bruges—enjoy a renewed prosperity by making "tourist dreams come true."

For good-value accommodations in **Bruges,** *try Hotel Heritage (splurge, Niklaas Desparsstraat 11, tel. 050-444-444, www.hotel-heritage.com) or Koen and Annemie Dieltiens' B&B (budget, Waalsestraat 40, tel. 050-334-294, www.bedandbreakfastbruges.be). For all the travel specifics, see the latest edition of* Rick Steves' Amsterdam, Bruges & Brussels.

BELGIUM

Amsterdam's Counter-Culture

Amsterdam is a laboratory of progressive living, bottled inside Europe's most 17th-century city. Like Venice, this city is a patchwork quilt of

canal-bordered islands, anchored upon millions of wooden pilings. But unlike its dwelling-in-the-past cousin, Amsterdam sees itself as a city of the future, built on good living, cozy cafés, great art, street-corner jazz...and a spirit of live-and-let-live.

During its Golden Age in the 1600s, Amsterdam was the world's richest city, an international sea-trading port, and the cradle of capitalism. Wealthy, democratic burghers built a planned city of tree-shaded canals lined with townhouses topped with fancy gables. Immigrants,

Cruise by Amsterdam's stately 17th-century buildings.

Jews, outcasts, and political rebels were drawn here by its tolerant atmosphere, and painters like young Rembrandt captured that atmosphere on canvas.

Approach Amsterdam as an ethnologist observing a fascinating and unique culture. A stroll through any neighborhood is rewarded with things that are commonplace here but rarely found elsewhere. Carillons chime quaintly in neighborhoods selling sex, as young professionals smoke pot with impunity next to old ladies in bonnets selling flowers. Observe the neighborhoods' quirky system of "social control," where an elderly man feels safe in his home knowing he's being watched over by the hookers next door.

Prostitution has been legal since the 1980s (although streetwalking is still forbidden). Most prostitutes opposed legal-

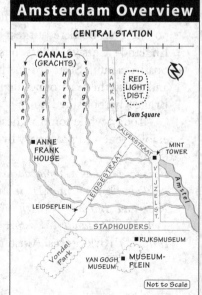

Amsterdam Overview

CENTRAL STATION

CANALS (GRACHTS)

Prinsen
Keizers
Heren
Singel

DAMRAK

RED LIGHT DIST.

Dam Square

■ANNE FRANK HOUSE

KALVERSTRAAT

MINT TOWER

LEIDSESTRAAT

VIJZELST.

LEIDSEPLEIN

Amstel

STADHOUDERS.

■RIJKSMUSEUM

Vondel Park

VAN GOGH MUSEUM

■ MUSEUM-PLEIN

Not to Scale

ization, not wanting the taxes and bureaucratic regulations that came with it.

In an attempt to stem some of the crime associated with the sex trade, Amsterdam has closed about a third of the prostitution windows in recent years. An unintended consequence has been that prices have gone up—both what the women pay and what they charge their customers.

The women are often entrepreneurs, renting space and running their own businesses. Women usually rent their space for eight-hour shifts. A good spot costs $140 for a day shift and $210 for an evening. Popular prostitutes charge $50-70 for a 20-minute visit. They fill out tax returns, and many belong to a loose union called the Red Thread.

The rooms look tiny from the street ("Do they have to do it standing up?"), but most are just display windows, opening onto a room behind or upstairs with a bed, a sink, and little else. Prostitutes are required to keep their premises hygienic, make sure their clients use condoms, and avoid minors.

The law, not pimps, protects prostitutes. If a prostitute is diagnosed with AIDS, she gets a subsidized apartment to encourage her to quit the business. Shocking as this may seem to some, it's a good example of a pragmatic Dutch solution—getting the most dangerous prostitutes off the streets to combat the spread of HIV.

The Dutch people are unique. They may be the world's most handsome people—tall, healthy, and with good posture—and the most open, honest, and refreshingly blunt. They like to laugh. As connoisseurs of world culture, they appreciate Rembrandt paintings, Indonesian food, and the latest French films, but with an un-snooty, blue-jeans attitude.

Un-snooty, but not un-sooty—about a third of the Dutch people smoke tobacco. Holland has a long tradition as a smoking culture, being among the first to import the tobacco plant from the New World. Still, their version of the Surgeon General is finally waking up to the drug's many potential health problems. Warning stickers bigger than America's are required on cigarette packs, and some of them are almost comically blunt, such as: "Smoking will make you impotent...and then you die." (The warnings have prompted gag stickers like "Life can kill you.")

Since 2008, a Dutch law has outlawed smoking tobacco almost everywhere indoors: on trains, and in hotel rooms, restaurants, cafés, and bars. But smoking remains part of an overall diet and regimen that—no denying it—somehow makes the Dutch people among the healthiest in the world. Tanned, trim, firm, 60-something Dutch people sip their

Marijuana in Europe

Compared to the United States, many European countries have a liberal attitude toward marijuana users. They believe that if "harm reduction" is the aim of a nation's drug policy, it makes more sense to treat marijuana as a health problem (and regulate it like alcohol) than as a criminal one. Simply put, many Europeans believe marijuana can be enjoyed responsibly by adults.

Still, drugs are not legal in Europe. The use, sale, and possession of any illegal drug can lead to stiff fines or a jail sentence. While laws against the use of drugs such as cocaine, heroin, LSD, and Ecstasy are strictly enforced, marijuana is more often classified as a "soft drug" and its recreational use tolerated in private or in certain bars.

But even in the most liberal countries, the sale of marijuana is permitted only in certain places. In Amsterdam and other Dutch cities, "coffeeshops"—often sporting red, green, and yellow Rastafarian flags— are allowed to sell small amounts for personal use to

Coffeeshops in Amsterdam offer a wide array of bongs.

beers, take a drag, and ask me why Americans murder themselves with Big Macs.

If you can't avoid tobacco in Amsterdam, why not make it part of your sightseeing? At Rokin 92, the House of Hajenius is a temple of cigars—a "paradise for the connoisseur" showing "175 years of tradition and good taste." To enter this sumptuous Art Deco building with its painted leather ceilings is to step back into 1910. Visitors can sniff fine pipe tobacco from brown-capped canisters. The shop's "personal humidifiers" allow customers to call in an order and have their cigars waiting for them at just the right humidity.

Of course, smokers in Europe's counterculture mecca don't enjoy just tobacco. Throughout Amsterdam, you'll see "coffeeshops"—pubs selling marijuana—with menus that look like the inventory of a drug bust.

Most of downtown Amsterdam's coffeeshops feel grungy and foreboding to American travelers who aren't part of the youth-hostel crowd.

people over 18 (note that the Dutch government is phasing out sales to nonresidents). Recently, Switzerland, Britain, and other countries have also been liberalizing their approach to marijuana.

Remember that you are subject to the laws of the country in which you travel when abroad, so be sensible and err on the side of caution. People who run coffeeshops warn that even a country that is "soft on soft drugs" needs to make a few marijuana arrests each year to maintain its favorable trade status with the United States (which wants European countries to maintain a harder stance on marijuana use).

Be warned that anywhere in Europe, especially in countries adjacent to countries famous for being easy on marijuana, border patrols can be particularly strict. And driving under the influence of any drug is a serious offense that can land you in jail, if not in a car crash.

Because I believe the US's current war on marijuana is as futile and counterproductive as our Prohibition against alcohol was in the 1930s, and because I believe that the responsible recreational use of marijuana among adults is a civil liberty, I am a proud board member of the National Organization for the Reform of Marijuana Laws (NORML). To learn more about my views on this issue, do a Google search for "Rick Steves marijuana." For an overview and country-by-country summary of European drug laws, see the NORML website (www.norml.org).

The neighborhood places (and those in small towns around the country-side) are much more inviting to people without piercings and tattoos.

Paradox is the most *gezellig* (cozy) coffeeshop I found—a mellow, graceful place. The managers, Ludo and Wiljan, and their staff are patient with descriptions and happy to walk you through the options. This is a rare coffeeshop that serves light meals. The juice is fresh, the music is easy, and the neighborhood is charming (two blocks from Anne Frank House at Eerste Bloemdwarsstraat 2, tel. 020/623-5639, www.paradoxcoffeeshop.com).

Ludo explained to me that the Dutch think the concept of a "victim-less crime" is a contradiction in terms. Although hard drugs are illegal, marijuana causes about as much excitement as a bottle of beer. If a tipsy tourist calls an ambulance after smoking too much pot, medics just say, "Drink something sweet and walk it off."

Amsterdam also has several "Smartshops"—bright, clean, fully professional retail outlets that sell a wide array of drugs, many of which are illegal in America. Their "natural" drugs include harmless nutrition boosters (royal jelly), harmful but familiar tobacco, organic versions of popular dance-club drugs (herbal Ecstasy), and joints made from an unpredictable mix of marijuana and other substances, sold under exotic names like "Herbal Love." The best seller: marijuana seeds. Prices are clearly marked, with brief descriptions of the drugs, their ingredients, and effects.

The knowledgeable Smartshop salespeople enjoy talking about these "100-percent-natural products that play with the human senses." Still, my fellow Americans, *caveat emptor!* We've grown used to thinking, "If it's legal, it must be safe. If it's not, I'll sue." While legal in Amsterdam, some of these substances can cause powerful, often unpleasant reactions. If you've never taken drugs recreationally, don't start here. (And these days, you probably don't have the option—drug sales to nonresidents are being phased out throughout the Netherlands.)

The Dutch also like plants you can't smoke, as I learned strolling through one of the oldest botanical gardens in the world. The De Hortus Botanical Garden dates from 1638, when medicinal herbs were grown here. The collection expanded in the 17th and 18th centuries as a wealth of flora was brought from faraway places by the Dutch East India Company. Today, its 6,000 different varieties of plants are spread throughout several greenhouses and a tropical palm house. No mobile phones are allowed because "our collection of plants is a precious community—treat it with respect." The "residents" are described thoughtfully: "A Dutch merchant snuck a coffee plant out of Ethiopia, which ended up in this garden in 1706. This first coffee plant in Europe was the literal grand-daddy of the coffee cultures of Brazil—long the world's biggest coffee producer."

Amsterdam's tolerant culture has attracted some colorful residents. Nick Padalino is one cool cat who—with the help of ultraviolet lights—has found his niche in life. Nick's flowery window display hides an illuminated wonderland: Electric Ladyland, a tiny, unique museum featuring

Electric Ladyland's Nick Padalino glows with pride as he adds more color to Amsterdam's Jordaan district.

black-light art (Tweede Leliedwarsstraat 5-HS, tel. 020/420-3776, www. electric-lady-land.com). Nick lovingly demonstrates fluorescent minerals from all over the world and fluorescence in everyday objects (stamps, candy, and so on). He seems to get a bigger kick out of it than even his customers. Pulling out one of his prize artifacts, Nick says, "This is the historic first fluorescent crayon from San Francisco, from the 1950s. Wow. See the label? It says, 'Use with black light for church groups.' Wow."

Yes, Amsterdam is known for its tolerance of soft drugs—but the Dutch also think progressively about more mundane matters, like transportation. Amsterdam's 765,000 residents own nearly that many bikes. The Dutch average four bikes per family (many people own two: a long-distance racing bike and an in-city bike, often deliberately kept in poor maintenance so it's less enticing to the many bike thieves). The Dutch appreciate the efficiency of a self-propelled machine that travels five times faster than walking, without pollution, noise, parking problems, or high fuel costs. A speedy bicyclist can traverse the historic center in 10 minutes. Pedestrians also enjoy the quiet of a people-friendly town where bikes outnumber cars.

Another way to see the city is by boat: Amsterdam has more canals than Venice. Amsterdam's canals tamed the flow of the Amstel River, creating pockets of dry land to build on. The city's 100 canals are about 10 feet deep, crossed by some 1,200 bridges, fringed with 100,000 Dutch elm and lime trees, and bedecked with 2,000 houseboats. A system of locks near the central train station controls the flow outward to (eventually) the North Sea, and the flow inward of the tides. The locks are opened periodically to flush out polluted water. Some of the boats in the canals look pretty funky by day, but Amsterdam is an unpretentious, anti-status city. When the sun goes down and the lights come on, people cruise the sparkling canals with an onboard hibachi grill and a bottle of wine, and, as my Dutch friends report, "Even scows can become chick magnets."

Amsterdam, a bold experiment in freedom, may box your Puritan ears. Take it all in, then pause to watch the summer sunset—at 10 p.m.— and see the Dutch Golden Age reflected in a quiet canal.

*For good-value accommodations in **Amsterdam**, try The Toren (splurge, Keizersgracht 164, tel. 020/622-6033, www.thetoren.nl) or Hotel Keizershof (moderate, Keizersgracht 618, where Keizers canal crosses Nieuwe Spiegelstraat, tel. 020/622-2855, www.hotelkeizershof.nl). For all the travel specifics, see the latest edition of* Rick Steves' Amsterdam, Bruges & Brussels.

GERMANY, AUSTRIA & SWITZERLAND

Rothenburg and the Romantic Road

Thirty years ago, I fell in love with a Rothenburg in the rough. At that time, the town still fed a few farm animals within its medieval walls. Today its barns are hotels, its livestock are tourists, and Rothenburg is well on its way to becoming a medieval theme park.

But Rothenburg is still Germany's best-preserved walled town. Countless travelers have searched for the elusive "untouristy Rothenburg." There are many contenders (such as Michelstadt, Miltenberg, Bamberg, Bad Windsheim, and Dinkelsbühl), but none holds a candle to the king of medieval German cuteness. Even with crowds, overpriced souvenirs, a Japanese-speaking night watchman, and, yes, even with *Schneeballen*, Rothenburg is still the best. Save time and mileage and be satisfied with the winner.

In the Middle Ages, when Frankfurt and Munich were just wide spots in the road, Rothenburg was Germany's second-largest city, with a whopping population of 6,000. Today, it's the country's most exciting medieval town, enjoying tremendous popularity with tourists.

To avoid the hordes of day-trippers, spend the night. In the deserted moonlit streets, you might hear the sounds of the Thirty Years' War still echoing through turrets and clock towers.

A walking tour helps bring the ramparts alive. The tourist information office on the Market Square offers $10 tours in English led by a local historian—usually an intriguing character (April-Oct and Dec daily at 2:00 p.m., no English tours in Nov or Jan-March; plus the more colorful Night Watchman's tour, Easter-Dec nightly at 8:00 p.m.). A thousand years of history is packed between the cobbles.

For the best view of the town and surrounding countryside, climb the Town Hall tower. For more views, walk the wall that surrounds the old town. This 1.5-mile walk atop the wall is at its most medieval before breakfast or at sunset.

Rothenburg's fascinating Medieval Crime and Punishment Museum, all unusually well explained in English, is full of legal bits and diabolical pieces, instruments of punishment and torture, and even an iron cage—complete with a metal nag gag. Some react with horror, others wish for a gift shop.

St. Jakob's Church contains the one must-see art treasure in Rothenburg: a glorious 500-year-old altarpiece by Riemenschneider, the Michelangelo of German woodcarvers. Pick up the brochure that explains the church's art treasures and climb the stairs behind the organ for Germany's greatest piece of woodcarving.

To hear the birds and smell the cows, take a walk through the Tauber Valley. The trail leads downhill from Rothenburg's idyllic castle gardens to a cute, skinny, 600-year-old castle, the summer home of the town's mayor in the 15th century, Mayor Toppler. While called a castle, the floor plan is more like a four-story tree house. It's intimately furnished and well worth a look. On the top floor, notice the 1945 photo of a bombed-out Rothenburg. From here, walk past the covered bridge and trout-filled Tauber to the sleepy village of Detwang, which is actually older than Rothenburg and has a church with another impressive Riemenschneider altarpiece.

Warning: Rothenburg is one of Germany's best shopping towns. Do it here, mail it home, and be done with it. Lovely prints, carvings, wine glasses, Christmas-tree ornaments, and beer steins are popular.

The Käthe Wohlfahrt Christmas trinkets phenomenon is spreading across the half-timbered reaches of Europe. In Rothenburg, tourists flock to two Käthe Wohlfahrt Christmas stores (just off Market Square). These Santa wonderlands are filled with enough twinkling lights to require a special electric hookup, instant Christmas mood music (best appreciated on a hot day in July), and American and Japanese tourists hungrily filling little woven shopping baskets with \$7-12 goodies to hang on their trees. (OK, I admit it, my Christmas tree sports a few KW ornaments.) Prices have tour-guide kickbacks built into them. I prefer the friendlier Friese shop (on the smaller square just off Market Square), which offers cheaper prices, less glitter, and more variety.

At the English Conversation Club, held every Wednesday night at the Altfränkische Weinstube am Klosterhof hotel/restaurant, locals enjoy a weekly excuse to get together, drink, and practice their fanciest English on each other and on visiting tourists. Anneliese, who runs the Friese shop (see above) and is a regular at the Conversation Club, invites me to join her, so I meander into the pub through candlelit clouds of smoke and squeeze a three-legged stool up to a table already crowded with her family.

Anneliese pours me a glass of wine, then pulls a *Schneeball* (a pow-dered-doughnut-like "snowball") from a bag. Raising a cloud of pow-

dered sugar as she pokes at the name on the now empty bag, she says, "Friedel is the bakery I explained you about. They make the best *Schneeball*. I like it better than your American doughnut. Every day I eat one. But only at this bakery."

Shoving a big doughy ball my way, she says, "You like to eat this?"

I break off a little chunk, saying, "Only a teeny-weeny *bisschen*."

For years, Anneliese has play-fully tried to get me to write good things about *Schneeballen*. I put *Schneeballen* (which originated in a hungrier age as a way to get more mileage out of leftover dough) in that category of penitential foods—like lutefisk—whose only purpose is to help younger people remember the suffering of their parents. Nowadays these historic pastries are pitched to the tourists in caramel, chocolate, and other flavors unknown in feudal times.

As Anneliese finishes the *Schneeball*, we share our favorite slang and tongue twisters. But medieval Rothenburg is waiting. I drain my glass of wine and bid a cheery, *"Tschüss!"*

In the night, I find myself alone with Rothenburg. The winds of his-tory polish half-timbered gables. Following the grooves of centuries of horse carts, I head down to the castle garden. From a distance, the roars

GERMANY

of laughter tumbling like waves out of *Biergarten*s and over the ramparts sound as medieval as they do modern.

Sitting in a mossy niche in the town wall, I finger the medieval stonework. Notching my imaginary crossbow, I aim an arrow into the dark forest that surrounds the city. Even now, it feels good to be within these protective walls.

On the ramparts after dark, I look over a choppy sea of red-tiled roofs to the murky and mysterious moat beyond the wall. The cannons are loaded. Torches illuminate the gory heads of bad guys on pikes that greet visitors at the city gates. With a dash of moonlight and a splash of wine, Rothenburg once again is a crossroads where modern-day travelers meet medieval wayfarers.

Romantic Road

The Romantic Road, which winds scenically from the Rhine to Bavaria through Germany's medieval heartland, is the best way to connect the dots between Frankfurt and Munich. Peppered with pretty towns today because it was such an important and prosperous trade route 600 years ago, this popular road is no secret. But even with the crowds, it's a must.

Along the Romantic Road (and especially just off it), many visitors find the Germany that they have come to see. On the side roads, flower boxes decorate the unseen sides of barns and no unfamiliar car passes unnoticed. Church-steeple masts sail seas of rich, rolling farmland, and fragrant villages invite you to slow down. Stop wherever the cows look friendly or a town fountain beckons. At each village, ignore the signposts and ask an old woman for directions to the next town—just to hear her voice and enjoy the energy in her eyes. Thousands of tourists pass through. Few stop to chat.

After Rothenburg, consider these top stops along the Romantic Road: Dinkelsbühl, Rothenburg's well-preserved medieval sister city, comes with old walls, towers, gateways, and the peaceful green waters of the moat defending its medieval architecture from the 21st century. Würzburg has a fine Baroque prince bishop's Residenz—the Versailles of Franconia—and an oh-wow Baroque chapel. Another lovely carved altarpiece by Riemenschneider (and the unique thimble museum across

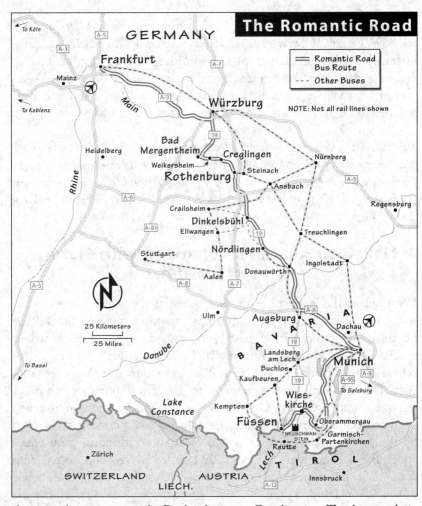

The Romantic Road

GERMANY

To Köln
A-5
A-3
Frankfurt
A-7
Mainz
A-3
To Koblenz
Main
Würzburg
19
Heidelberg
Bad Mergentheim
Weikersheim
Creglingen
Rothenburg
Steinach
Nürnberg
A-3
Rhine
Ansbach
A-6
Regensburg
A-81
Crailsheim
Dinkelsbühl
Ellwangen
19
Treuchlingen
Stuttgart
Nördlingen
Ingolstadt
A-5
Aalen
A-8
A-7
Donauwörth
Ulm
Augsburg
B A V A R I A
Dachau
25 Kilometers
19
25 Miles
Landsberg am Lech
Munich
Danube
Buchloe
A-8
To Basel
Kaufbeuren
19
A-95
To Salzburg
Lake Constance
Kempten
Wies-kirche
Füssen
Oberammergau
Zürich
NEUSCHWAN-STEIN
Reutte
Garmisch-Partenkirchen
SWITZERLAND
AUSTRIA
Lech
T I R O L
LIECH.
A-12
Innsbruck

Romantic Road Bus Route
Other Buses
NOTE: Not all rail lines shown

the street) is just outside Rothenburg at Creglingen. To the south is the flamboyant church called the Wieskirche, near Oberammergau, and "Mad" King Ludwig's Disney-esque Neuschwanstein Castle, near Füssen.

The sections from Füssen to Landsberg and Rothenburg to Weikersheim are most characteristic. (If you're driving with limited time, drive these and then connect Rothenburg and Munich by autobahn.) Caution: The similarly promoted "Castle Road" (between Rothenburg and Mannheim) sounds intriguing but is much less interesting.

A car or bike gives you complete freedom—just follow the brown *Romantische Strasse* signs. This is the best way to connect the castles of the Rhine and the lederhosen charm of Bavaria. Those without wheels have a couple of options. The Deutsche Touring company runs buses daily

GERMANY

between Frankfurt and Munich in each direction (early May-late Oct, tel. 069/719-126-261, www.romanticroadcoach.de). Or you can take public transportation: The larger towns—including Rothenburg, Würzburg, and Füssen—are well connected by train. Some of the more out-of-the-way places (such as Dinkelsbühl, Creglingen, and the Wieskirche) are still reachable, but require a more complicated public-bus connection.

*For good-value accommodations in **Rothenburg**, try Gästehaus Raidel (budget, Wenggasse 3, tel. 09861/3115, www.romanticroad.com/raidel) or Hotel Gerberhaus (splurge, Spitalgasse 25, tel. 09861/94900, www.gerberhaus .rothenburg.de). For all the travel specifics, see this year's edition of* Rick Steves' Germany.

Hallstatt: Austria's Commune-with-Nature Lake District

With one of the longest life spans and one of the shortest work weeks in Europe, Austrians spend their ample free time focusing on the fine points of life: music, a stroll, pastry, and a good cup of coffee. Austrians specialize in good living and *Gemütlichkeit*. A distinctly Austrian concept, and as difficult to translate as it is to pronounce, it means a warm, cozy, friendly, focus-on-the-moment feeling. Even tourists catch on in the Salzkammergut Lake District, where big-city Austrians go to relax.

Far from the urban rat race, though just two hours by train from Salzburg, this is the perfect place to commune with nature, Austrian-style. The Salzkammergut is a lushly forested playground dotted with cottages. Trains, buses, and boats lead the traveler through gentle mountains and shy lakes, winding from relaxed village to relaxed village.

The Salzkammergut's pride and joy is the town of Hallstatt. The minute it popped into view, I knew Hallstatt was my alpine Oz. It's just the right size (900 people), wonderfully remote, and almost traffic-free. A tiny ferry takes you from the nearest train station, across the fjord-like lake, and drops you off on the town's storybook square.

Bullied onto its lakeside ledge

A boat shuttles travelers from the nearest train station to the Back Door town of Hallstatt in Austria.

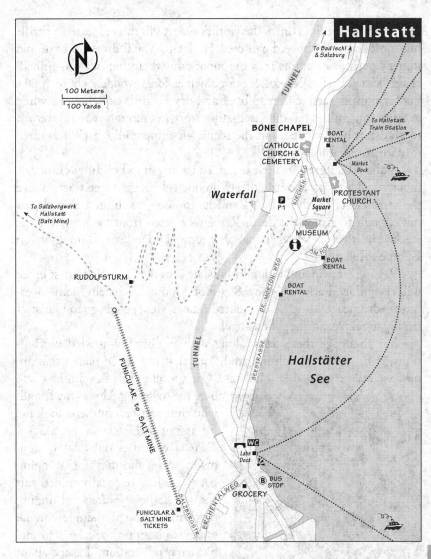

by a selfish mountain, Hallstatt seems tinier than it is. Its pint-size square is surrounded by ivy-covered guest houses and cobbled lanes. It's a toy town. You can tour it on foot in about 10 minutes. Except in August, when tourist crowds trample most of Hallstatt's charm, there's no shortage of pleasant *Privatzimmer* (bed-and-breakfast places).

Nearly three thousand years ago, this area was the salt-mining capital of Europe. An economic and cultural boom put it on the map back in Flintstone times. In fact, an entire 700-year chapter in the story of Europe is called "The Hallstatt Period." A humble museum next to the tourist office shows off Hallstatt's salty past. For a better look, you can tour what the locals claim is the world's oldest salt mine, located a thrilling funicular ride above downtown Hallstatt. You'll dress up in an old miner's outfit, ride trains into the mountain where the salt was mined, cruise subterranean lakes, scream down a long wooden chute (praying for no splinters), and read brief and dry English explanations while entertaining guides tell the fascinating story in German. You can return to Hallstatt by funicular, but the scenic 40-minute hike back into town is (with strong knees) a joy.

Hallstatt outgrew its little ledge, and many of its buildings climb the mountainside, with the street level on one side being three floors above the street level on the other. Land is limited—so limited that there's not enough room for the dead. Remains evicted from the cemetery are stacked neatly in an eerie chapel of decorated bones (see "Boning Up on Europe's Relics").

Passing time in and around Hallstatt is easy. The little tourist office will recommend a hike—the 9,845-foot Mount Dachstein looms overhead—or a peaceful cruise in a rented canoe. Most people go to Hallstatt simply to relax, eat, shop, and stroll.

My challenge these days, along with finding untouristed destinations, is to find vivid cultural traditions that survive in places that are now well discovered...like Hallstatt. On a recent visit, the sun rose late over the towering Alps as my friend, who runs a restaurant here, took me for a spin in his classic boat. It's a *Fuhr*, a centuries-old boat design, made wide and flat for shipping heavy bushels of locally mined salt across shallow waters. Lunging rhythmically on the single oar, he said, "An hour on the lake is for me like a day of vacation." I asked about the oarlock, which looked like a skinny dog-chew doughnut, and he told me, "It's made from the gut of a bull—not of a cow, but a bull."

Returning to the weathered timber boathouse, we passed a teenage boy systematically grabbing trout from the fishermen's pen and killing them one by one with a stern whack to the noggin. Another man

The husband of a woman whose Hallstatt B&B I've recommended for years takes me and my TV crew out in his handmade, traditional Fuhr boat.

carried them to the tiny fishery to be gutted by a guy who, 40 years ago, did the stern whacking. A cat waited outside the door, confident his breakfast would be a good one. And restaurateurs and homemakers alike—their dining rooms decorated with trophies of big ones that didn't get away—lined up to buy fresh trout to feed the hungry tourists, or a good fish to cook for a special friend.

Traditions are embattled everywhere by a bullying modern world. Yet they manage to survive. Despite tourism—and sometimes thanks to tourism—traditional Europe hangs in there. To cloak yourself in the *Gemütlichkeit,* flowers, and cobblestones of Austria's Salzkammergut Lake District, visit Hallstatt.

*For good-value (but splurge) accommodations in **Hallstatt,** try Gasthof Simony (Marktplatz 105, tel. 06134/8231, www.gasthof-simony.at) or Gasthof Zauner (Marktplatz 51, tel. 06134/8246, www.zauner.hallstatt.net). For all the travel specifics, see the current edition of* Rick Steves' Vienna, Salzburg & Tirol.

Gimmelwald: The Swiss Alps in Your Lap

When told you're visiting Gimmelwald, Swiss people assume you mean the famous resort in the next valley, Grindelwald. When assured that Gimmelwald is your target, they lean forward, widen their eyes, and—with their singsongy Swiss German accent—they ask, "Und how do you know about Gimmelvald?"

"Downtown" Gimmelwald

The traffic-free village of Gimmelwald hangs nonchalantly on the edge of a cliff high above Lauterbrunnen Valley, 30 minutes south of Interlaken by car or train. This sleepy village has more cow troughs than mailboxes. The songs of birds and brooks and the crunchy march of happy hikers constantly remind you why so many travelers say, "If heaven isn't what it's cracked up to be, send me back to Gimmelwald."

Gimmelwald, an ignored station on the spectacular Schilthorn cable car, should be built to the hilt. But, led by a visionary schoolmaster,

SWITZERLAND

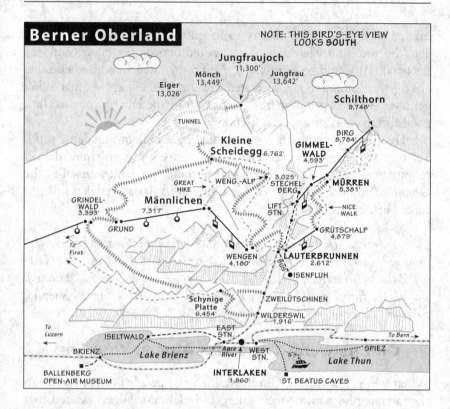

Berner Oberland

NOTE: THIS BIRD'S-EYE VIEW LOOKS **SOUTH**

Jungfraujoch 11,300'

Eiger 13,026'

Mönch 13,449'

Jungfrau 13,642'

Schilthorn 9,748'

TUNNEL

BIRG 8,784'

Kleine Scheidegg 6,762'

GIMMEL-WALD 4,593'

GREAT HIKE

WENG.-ALP

3,025' STECHEL-BERG

MÜRREN 5,381'

GRINDEL-WALD 3,393'

Männlichen 7,317'

LIFT STN.

NICE WALK

GRUND

GRÜTSCHALP 4,879'

To First

WENGEN 4,180'

LAUTERBRUNNEN 2,612'

ISENFLUH

Schynige Platte 6,454'

ZWEILÜTSCHINEN

WILDERSWIL 1,916'

To Luzern

ISELTWALD

EAST STN.

To Bern

BRIENZ

Lake Brienz

Aare River

WEST STN.

SPIEZ

Lake Thun

BALLENBERG OPEN-AIR MUSEUM

INTERLAKEN 1,860'

ST. BEATUS CAVES

the farming community managed to reclassify its land as an "avalanche zone"—too dangerous for serious building projects. So while developers gnash their teeth, sturdy peasants continue to milk cows and make hay, thus surviving in a modern world only by the grace of a government that subsidizes such poor traditional industries.

Gimmelwald is a community in the rough. Take a walk—you can tour it in 15 minutes. Its two streets, a 700-year-old zig and zag, are decorated by drying laundry, hand-me-down tricycles, and hollowed stumps bursting proudly with geraniums. Little-boy cars are parked next to the tiny tank-tread cement mixers and mini-tractors necessary for taming this alpine environment. White-bearded elves smoke hand-carved pipes, and blond-braided children play "barn" instead of "house." Stones called *schindeln* sit like heavy checkers on old rooftops, awaiting nature's next move. While these stones protect the slate from the violent winter winds, in summer it's often so quiet that you can hear the cows ripping tufts of grass.

Notice the traditional log-cabin architecture. The numbers on the buildings are not addresses, but fire insurance numbers. The cute little hut near the cable-car station is for storing and aging cheese, not hostelers. Small as Gimmelwald is, it still has daily mail service. The postman comes down from neighboring Mürren each day (by golf cart in summer, sled in winter) to deliver mail and pick up letters at the communal mailbox.

There's nothing but air between Gimmelwald and the rock face of the Jungfrau nearly four miles away. Small avalanches across the valley look and sound like distant waterfalls. Kick a soccer ball wrong and it ends up a mile below on the Lauterbrunnen Valley floor.

Most Gimmelwalders have one of two last names: von Allmen or Feuz. To keep prescriptions and medical records straight, the doctor in nearby Lauterbrunnen goes by birth date first, then the patient's name.

The people of Gimmelwald systematically harvest the steep hillside. Entire families cut and gather every inch of hay as thoroughly as children of America's Great Depression once polished their dinner plates. After harvesting what the scythe can reach, they pull hay from nooks and crannies by hand.

Half a day is spent on steep rocks harvesting what a machine can cut in two minutes on a flat field. It's tradition. It's like breathing. And there's one right way to do it.

To inhale the Alps and really hold it in, sleep high in Gimmelwald. Poor but pleasantly stuck in the past, the village has a creaky hotel, happy hostel, decent pension, and a couple of B&Bs.

Walter Mittler's Hotel Mittaghorn sits at the top end of Gimmelwald. The black-stained chalet has eight balconies and a few tables shaded by umbrellas on its tiny terrace. Everything comes with huge views. Sitting as if anchored by pitons into the steep, grassy hillside, the hotel is disturbed only by the cheery chatter of hikers and the two-stroke clatter of passing tractors.

Evening fun in Gimmelwald is found in the hostel (with lots of young Alp-aholic hikers eager to share information on the surrounding mountains) and, depending on Walter's mood, at Hotel Mittaghorn. If you're staying at Walter's, enjoy his simple supper and coffee schnapps, then sit on the porch

In a Back Door–style hotel, you get more by spending less. Here, the shower's down the hall, and the Alps are in your lap.

and watch the sun caress the mountaintops to sleep as the moon rises over the Jungfrau.

Starting early in the morning, the bright modern cable car swooshes by with 30 tourists gawking out the windows. In Gimmelwald, the modern world began in 1965 when it got the cable car. Before that, mothers ready to give birth had to hike an hour downhill to the valley floor for a ride into Interlaken. Many mothers didn't make it all the way to the hospital. Outside of Interlaken, a curve in the road is named for a Gimmelwald baby...born right there.

Today, the Schilthornbahn is the all-powerful lift that connects the valley floor with the mountain communities of Gimmelwald and Mürren on its way to the 10,000-foot Schilthorn summit. This artificial vein pumps life's essentials—mail, bread, skiers, hikers, schoolkids, coffins, hang gliders, and tourists—to and from each community.

From Gimmelwald, ride the cable car up to the peak of the Schilthorn, capped by a revolving restaurant called Piz Gloria ($95 round-trip, discounts early and late). Lifts go twice hourly, involve two transfers, and take 30 minutes. Watch the altitude meter go up, up, up.

For the most memorable breakfast around, ride the early cable car to the summit, where you'll find the restaurant and a thrilling 360-degree view. Sip your coffee slowly to enjoy one complete circle. Drop into the theater to see clips from the James Bond movie *On Her Majesty's Secret Service*, in which the restaurant is blown up. Then go outside for the real thrills. Frolic on the ridge. Watch hang gliders methodically set up and jump into airborne ecstasy.

While you can hike down from the summit, the first station below the summit, Birg, is the best jumping-off point for high-country hikes.

Two minutes from the Birg station, I'm completely alone—surrounded by a harsh and unforgiving alpine world. Anything alive is here only by the grace of nature. A black ballet of rocks is accompanied by cowbells and a distant river. Wisps of clouds are exclamation points. The Alps put you close to God. A day like today has Lutherans raising their hands and holy rollers doing cartwheels.

I make it to my target, a peak that stands dramatically high above Gimmelwald. After a steep descent, I step out of the forest at the top end of the village I call home. Walking over a pastel carpet of gold clover, bellflowers, milk kraut, and daisies, I'm surrounded by butterflies and cheered on by a vibrant chorus of grasshoppers, bees, and crickets.

The finish line is a bench that sits at the high end of Gimmelwald—one of my "savor Europe" depots. A great dimension of travel is finding the right spot and just sitting still. Crickets rattle congratulatory casta-

Thrill-seeking hang gliders are a common sight on alpine peaks. Here, an absent-minded hang glider prepares for his last takeoff.

nets, a river blurts out of a glacier, and Mürren crowns a bluff above me, keeping all the fancy tourists where they belong. An alpine farm that has intrigued me for years still sits high above the tree line, forever alone amid distant flecks of brown and white cows and goats.

Christian, the accordion player, who went up to the fields early this morning, chugs by on his mini-truck towing a wobbly wagonload of hay. His kids bounce like cartoon characters on top.

Enjoying this alone is fine. But sharing this bench with a new friend, with the sun of a daylong hike stored in your smiling faces, is even better.

If you're interested in the alpine cream of Switzerland, it's best seen from nearby peaks and ridges (the Jungfrau, Kleine Scheidegg, or the Schilthorn). If you're looking for Heidi and an orchestra of cowbells in a Switzerland that you thought existed only in storybooks—take off your boots in Gimmelwald.

From Interlaken into the Jungfrau Region

When the 19th-century Romantics redefined mountains as something more than cold and troublesome obstacles, Interlaken became the original alpine resort. Ever since then, tourists have flocked to the Alps "because they're there." Interlaken's glory days are long gone, its elegant old hotels eclipsed by more jet-setting alpine resorts. Today, Interlaken's shops are filled with chocolate bars, Swiss Army knives, and sunburned backpackers.

I had always considered Interlaken overrated, but I've come to understand that it's only a springboard for alpine adventures. Stop in

SWITZERLAND

Interlaken for shopping, banking, email, and telephone chores, and to pick up information on the region. Then head south into the Berner Oberland.

You have several options (see the map at the beginning of this chapter). Vagabonds who just dropped in on the overnight train can do a loop trip, going down Grindelwald Valley, over the Kleine Scheidegg ridge, and then into Lauterbrunnen. From there you can head on out by returning to Interlaken, or settle into Gimmelwald for the alpine cuddle after the climax. Those with more time (or less energy) go directly to the village of Gimmelwald (skipping Grindelwald) and explore the region from that home base.

Loop-trippers should get an early start and catch the private train from the Interlaken East station to Grindelwald (discounted with a Eurail Pass or Eurail Select Pass; covered by the Swiss Pass railpass). Don't sleep in touristy Grindelwald, but take advantage of its well-informed tourist information office and buy a first-class mountain picnic at its co-op grocery. Then ascend by train into a wonderland of white peaks to Kleine Scheidegg, or even higher by gondola to Männlichen (show your pass at ticket windows for varying discounts for train and gondola). It's an easy one-hour walk from Männlichen down to Kleine Scheidegg.

Now you have successfully run the gauntlet of tourist traps and reached the ultimate. Before you towers Switzerland's mightiest mountain panorama. The Jungfrau, the Mönch, and the Eiger boldly proclaim that they are the greatest. You won't argue.

Like a saddle on the ridge, Kleine Scheidegg gives people something to hang onto. It has a lodge (with $58 dorm bunks) and an outdoor restaurant. People gather here to marvel at tiny rock climbers dangling from ropes halfway up the icy Eiger. You can splurge for the expensive ride from here to the towering Jungfraujoch ($125 round-trip from Kleine Scheidegg, discounts early and late)—expect crowds on sunny summer days, especially after a stretch of bad weather. The ride's impressive, but I couldn't have asked for more than the *Mona Lisa* of mountain views that I enjoyed from Kleine Scheidegg.

From Kleine Scheidegg, start your hike down into the less-touristy

Lauterbrunnen Valley. The hike is easy. My gear consisted only of shorts (watch the mountain sun), tennis shoes, a tourist brochure map, and a bib to catch the drool.

It's lunchtime as you hike into your own peaceful mountain world. Find a grassy perch, and your picnic will have an alpine ambience that no restaurant can match. Continuing downhill, you may well be all alone and singing to the rhythm of your happy footsteps. The gravelly walk gets steep in places, and you can abbreviate your hike by catching the train at one of two stations you'll pass along the way. As the scenery changes, new mountains replace the ones you've already seen. After two hours, you enter the car-free town of Wengen. Avoid the steep, dull hike from Wengen to Lauterbrunnen by taking the train down to the valley floor, where you can continue by bus and cable car up the other side of the valley to the village of Gimmelwald.

This is the scenic but very roundabout way to Gimmelwald. For a much more direct route, take the train from the Interlaken East station to Lauterbrunnen, transfer to the bus for the Schilthornbahn cable-car station near Stechelberg, then ride the cable car up to Gimmelwald.

For more adventures in the Alps, turn to "Alpine Escapes".

*For good-value accommodations in **Gimmelwald**, try Hotel Mittaghorn (budget, open April–Oct, email answered May–Sept only, tel. 033-855-1658, www.ricksteves.com/mittaghorn), or Maria and Olle Eggimann's B&B (moderate, tel. 033-855-3575, oeggimann@bluewin.ch). For all the travel specifics, see the latest edition of Rick Steves' Switzerland.*

EASTERN EUROPE

Czech Out Prague

Prague has always been historic. Now it's fun, too. No place in Europe has become so popular so quickly. And for good reason: The capital of the Czech Republic—the only Central European capital to escape the bombs of the last century's wars—is a people-friendly and entertaining showcase for Czech culture.

Prague is slinky with sumptuous Art Nouveau facades, offers tons of cheap Mozart and Vivaldi, and brews some of the best beer in Europe. It's an explosion of pent-up entrepreneurial energy jumping for joy after 40 years of communist rule. Its low prices will make your visit enjoyable and, with a few skills, nearly stress-free. From Munich, Berlin, or Vienna, it's roughly a five-hour train ride (day or overnight) to Prague...your train won't even stop at the border.

Prague, the golden city of a hundred spires

Praha, as residents call their town, is big, with 1.2 million people. For the quick visit, think of the town as small and focus on its relatively compact historic core.

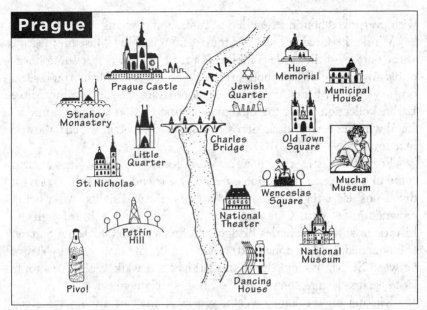

Prague

Strahov Monastery
Prague Castle
VLTAVA
Jewish Quarter
Hus Memorial
Municipal House
Little Quarter
Charles Bridge
Old Town Square
St. Nicholas
Mucha Museum
Petřín Hill
National Theater
Wenceslas Square
Pivo!
Dancing House
National Museum

Prague is charming, safe, and ready to show you a good time.

Your Prague visit deserves at least two full days. With this much time, spend a morning seeing the castle and a morning in the Jewish Quarter—the only two chunks of sightseeing that demand any brainpower. Spend your afternoons strolling Charles Bridge and loitering around Old Town. Split your evenings between beer halls and classical concerts.

Prague Castle—which Czechs consider the biggest in Europe—has served as home to Czech rulers for more than a thousand years. The highlight is St. Vitus Cathedral, where locals go to remember Saint Wenceslas, patron saint of the Czechs. This "good king" of Christmas-carol fame was not a king at all, but a wise, benevolent Duke of Bohemia. After being assassinated in 935, Wenceslas became a symbol of Czech nationalism. His tomb sits in an extremely fancy chapel.

Apart from the underwhelming Royal Palace, there's little else of importance to see in Prague Castle. Its lower end is the gimmicky Golden Lane—once lined with goldsmith shops, now filled

A good guide gives meaning to a great city like Prague.

EASTERN EUROPE

with overpriced boutiques, galleries, cafés, and gawking tourists.

While the Golden Lane is a tourist trap, the Toy Museum (nearby, at the bottom of the castle complex) is a treat. Its two entertaining floors of old toys and dolls are thoughtfully described in English. You'll see a century of teddy bears, 19th-century model train sets, and an incredible Barbie collection. Find the buxom 1959 first edition and you'll understand why these capitalistic sirens of material discontent weren't allowed here until 1989.

From the castle, the "King's Walk" leads into town. This ancient route of coronation processions, pedestrian-friendly and full of playful diversions, laces together most of Prague's essential sights. After being crowned in St. Vitus Cathedral, the new king would walk through the historic town, cross Charles Bridge, and finish at the Old Town Square. If he hurried, he'd be done in 20 minutes. Like the main drag in Venice between St. Mark's and the Rialto Bridge, this walk mesmerizes tourists. Use it as a spine, but venture off it—especially to eat.

Kicking off the King's Walk, you leave the castle following steep and cobbled Nerudova street towards the river. It's lined with old buildings still sporting the characteristic doorway signs (such as the lion, three violinists, and house of the golden suns) that served as street addresses. The surviving signs are carefully restored and protected by law. They represent the family name, the occupation, or the various passions of the people who once inhabited the houses. (If you were to replace your house number with a symbol, what would it be?) In 1770, in order to collect taxes more effectively, a court decree mandated the introduction of street numbers instead of these quaint house names. This neighborhood's many old noble palaces are now generally used as foreign embassies and offices of the Czech Parliament.

Prague's much-loved Charles Bridge will be undergoing a lengthy renovation over the next few years, but should remain open to pedestrians.

The much-loved Charles Bridge is my vote for Europe's most pleasant quarter-mile stroll. Commissioned by the Holy Roman Emperor Charles IV in the 1350s, its chorus line of time-blackened Baroque statues mix it up with street vendors and musicians. Be on the bridge when the sun is low for the best light, people-watching, and photo opportunities. (Although a multi-year restoration on the bridge means it may be partly covered with scaffolding during your visit, you can still walk the bridge's entire length.)

After crossing the bridge, follow the shop-lined street to the Old Town Square. The focal point for most visits, this has been a market square since the 11th century. Today, many of the old-time market stalls have been replaced by cafés, touristy horse buggies, and souvenir hawkers.

The square's centerpiece, the Hus memorial—unveiled in 1915, 500 years after Jan Hus was burned—symbolizes the long struggle for Czech freedom. The statue of the Czech reformer stands tall, as he did against both Rome and the Habsburgs. Behind Hus, a mother with her children represents the ultimate rebirth of the Czech nation.

A few blocks past the Old Town Square stretches the centerpiece of urban, modern Prague: Wenceslas Square. The most dramatic moments in modern Czech history were played out on this stage. The Czechoslovak state was proclaimed here in 1918. In 1969, Jan Palach set himself on fire here to protest the puppet Soviet government. And the massive demonstrations here 20 years after his death led to the overthrow of the communist government. Czechs still remember the night in 1989 when they gathered, hundreds of

Prague's Wenceslas Square: When there's a revolution, this is where the action is.

thousands strong, filling the square. Jangling their key chains at the presidential palace, they chanted, "It's time to go now." Their message was heard, and the next morning they woke up a free nation.

The great sights of Prague chronicle the struggle of the Czech people against the outside world. They also recall the struggles of the Jewish people within Czech society. I find Prague's Josefov the most interesting Jewish Quarter in Europe.

Two thousand years ago the Romans dispersed the Jews. But "time was their sanctuary which no army could destroy," as their culture survived in enclaves throughout the Western world. The main intersection

Eastern Europe: From Surviving to Thriving

The former "Warsaw Pact" is changing fast. Having decisively left the communists in their dust, the people here are racing West...and getting there in a hurry. Several Eastern European countries have joined the European Union, shifting the geographical center of Europe from Brussels to Prague. In fact, most people here now insist on being called *Central* Europeans. Borders have melted away, each year a new country adopts the euro currency, and even the grumpy old *babushki* ladies who sell flowers on the street are retiring.

From a traveler's perspective, today's Eastern Europe offers many of the conveniences of Western Europe (many English-speaking locals, ATMs, and Internet cafés), but retains a sense of pioneer excitement (unusual languages, foods, and currencies). And it's less expensive than most of the West.

This section covers three top sightseeing stops in this region: the tourist mecca of Prague, the delightful "next Prague" of Kraków, and the off-the-beaten-path Bosnian city of Mostar. But these destinations are just the beginning...use them as springboards for exploring a vast, beautiful, and diverse region.

Simmering in a Budapest thermal bath, surrounded by hedonistic Hungarians, is a quintessential Eastern European experience.

In **Hungary,** explore Eastern Europe's de facto "capital city," Budapest. Peel back the layers of history in this grand metropolis, home to ancient Romans, nomadic Magyars, conquering Ottomans,

of Prague's Jewish Quarter was the meeting point of two medieval trade routes. Jewish traders settled here in the 13th century and built a synagogue.

When the pope declared that Jews and Christians should not live together, this Jewish Quarter was walled in and became a ghetto. In the 16th and 17th centuries, Prague's ghetto—with 11,000 inhabitants—was one of the biggest in Europe.

Europe's Jews relied mainly on profits from lending money (forbid-

reconquering Habsburgs, and modern-day Hungarian freedom fighters. Browse the truly great Great Market Hall, sampling some spicy paprika. Take in an inexpensive performance at the opulent Opera House, which gives Vienna's—just up the Danube—a run for its money. Relax by soaking with potbellied, Speedo-clad chess players under gorgeous Baroque domes at a thermal bath.

In **Croatia,** set sail on the shimmering Adriatic, to a remote island whose name you can't pronounce but whose wonders you'll never forget. Lie on a beach in the hot summer sun, listening to the lapping waves as a Venetian-style bell tower overhead clangs out the hour. Stroll on boardwalks through the Plitvice Lakes' waterfall wonderland. Ponder the fading scars of a recent war, and admire how skillfully the residents have revitalized their once-troubled region. Dine on a seafood feast and sip a glass of wine as you watch the sunset dip into the watery horizon.

In **Slovenia,** corkscrew your way up impossibly twisty mountain roads to panoramic vistas of cut-glass peaks. Sip a coffee at a sun-bathed outdoor café, and help the Slovenian college students at the next table polish their near-perfect English. Glide across an idyllic mountain lake to a church-topped island in the shadow of the Julian Alps. (For details, see "Alpine Escapes".)

On a recent visit to Eastern Europe, some of my favorite experiences came off the beaten path. At a humble vineyard buried deep in the Hungarian countryside, the proud vintner told me how this land had been in his family for generations, before being seized by the communists. The communist winemaking industry—interested in squeezing out quantity rather than quality—ruined his vines, but he's spent the last decade painstakingly restoring them to their former greatness. He poured me a generous taste, then threw his head back and taught me the tongue-twisting Hungarian "Cheers": *Egészségedre!* Sipping his full-bodied blend of red wines, I had to think he was off to a great start.

den to Christians) and community solidarity to survive. While their money protected them, it was often also a curse. Throughout Europe, when times got tough and Christian debts to the Jewish community mounted, entire Jewish communities were evicted or killed.

In the 1780s, Emperor Josef II, motivated more by economic concerns than philanthropy, eased much of the discrimination against Jews. In 1852, the walls were torn down, and the neighborhood—named Josefov in honor of the emperor who provided this small measure of

Pondering Jewish history

tolerance—was incorporated as a district of Prague.

In 1897, ramshackle Josefov was razed and replaced with a new modern town. This is what you'll see today: an attractive neighborhood of mostly Art Nouveau buildings, with a few surviving historic Jewish buildings. By the 1930s, Prague's Jewish community was hugely successful. Yet of the 35,000 Jews living in the area in 1939, just 8,000 survived the Holocaust to see liberation in 1945. Strangely, the museums of the Jewish Quarter are, in part, the work of Hitler. He preserved parts of Josefov to be his "museum of the exterminated race." Seven sites (six synagogues and a cemetery) scattered over a three-block area make the tourists' Jewish Quarter. Each has a fascinating exhibit, and one ticket includes admission to all but one.

The Pinkas Synagogue, a site of Jewish worship for 400 years, is a poignant memorial to the victims of the Nazis. Its walls are covered with the handwritten names of 77,297 Czech Jews who were sent from here to gas chambers at Auschwitz and other camps. (You'll hear the somber reading of the names as you ponder this sad sight.) When the communists moved in, they closed the synagogue and erased virtually everything. With freedom in 1989, the Pinkas Synagogue was reopened and all the names rewritten.

The Old Jewish Cemetery is the quarter's most photographed site. As you wander among 12,000 evocative tombstones, remember that from 1439 until 1787, this was the only burial ground allowed for the Jews of Prague. Tombs were piled atop each other because of limited space, the sheer number of graves, and the Jewish belief that the body should not be moved once buried. With its many layers, the cemetery became a small plateau. And as things settled over time, the tombstones got crooked and mystically

picturesque.

The "Old-New" Synagogue—"new" 700 years ago—has always been the most important synagogue and central building in Josefov. Standing like a bomb-hardened bunker, it feels as though it's survived plenty of hard times. Stairs take you down to the street level of the 13th century and into the Gothic interior. Built in 1270, it's the oldest synagogue in Central Europe.

Down the street from Josefov is the surreal sight of a giant metronome slowly ticking away. Locals know this marks the spot of a 100-foot-tall sculpture of Stalin—destroyed in 1962, a few years after Khrushchev revealed the communist tyrant's crimes in a "secret" speech.

It's hard to imagine the gray and bleak Prague of the communist era. Before 1989, the city was a wistful jumble of possibility. Cobbled lanes were shadowed by sooty, crusty buildings. Thick, dark timbers bridging narrow streets kept decrepit buildings from crumbling. Consumer goods were plain and uniform, stacked like Legos on thin shelves in shops where customers waited in line for a beat-up cabbage, tin of ham, or bottle of ersatz Coke. The Charles Bridge was as sooty as its statues, with no commerce except a few shady characters trying to change money. Hotels had two-tiered pricing: one for people of the Warsaw Pact nations and another (five or six times as expensive) for capitalists. This made the run-down Soviet-style hotels as expensive for most tourists as a fine Western one. At the train sta-

Before the fall of communism, Czech freedom lovers found inspiration at Prague's graffiti-covered wall dedicated to John Lennon—an icon of Western freedom in the 1980s. Authorities whitewashed it countless times, but the spirited graffiti kept coming back. Even today, after being independent since 1989, Czechs treasure their freedom and their Lennon wall.

tion, frightened but desperate characters would meet arriving foreigners to rent them a room in their flat. They were scrambling to get enough hard Western cash to buy batteries or Levis at one of the hard-currency stores.

With capitalism came entrepreneurial con artists. There's no particular risk of violent crime, but green, rich tourists do get taken by con artists. Be on guard when changing money (even at banks) for bad arithmetic and inexplicable pauses while tellers count back your change. Understand the exact price before ordering at restaurants. Paying with cash is safer than using a credit card.

Taxis here are notorious rip-offs. Prague is walkable and also has fine public transportation, but if you prefer taxis, use only registered ones (marked with a company logo and phone number). My rule of thumb: Know the approximate local rate. If overcharged, pay what you think is fair, and walk away.

A newly affluent Prague has spiffed up its fine architecture. Prague is the best Art Nouveau town in Europe, with fun-loving facades gracing streets all over town. Art Nouveau, born in Paris, is "nouveau" because it wasn't inspired by Rome. It's neo-nothing...a fresh answer to all the revival styles of the later 19th century and an organic response to the Eiffel Tower art of the Industrial Age. The streets of Josefov, the Mucha window in the St. Vitus Cathedral, and Hotel Evropa on Wenceslas Square are just a few Art Nouveau highlights.

If you like Art Nouveau, you'll love the Mucha Museum—one of Europe's most enjoyable little galleries. I find the art of Alfons Mucha (MOO-kah, 1860-1939) insistently likeable. This popular artist's posters, filled with Czech symbols and expressing his people's ideals and aspirations, were patriotic banners arousing the national spirit. With the help of an abundant supply of slinky models, Mucha was a founding father of the Art Nouveau movement.

In the evening, Prague booms with live (and inexpensive) theater, opera, and classical, jazz, and pop music. You'll choose from half a dozen classical "tourist" concerts daily in Prague's ornate Old Town halls and churches. The music is crowd-pleasing: Vivaldi, best of Mozart, pop arias, and works by local boys Anton Dvořák and Bedřich Smetana. Leafleteers are everywhere, handing out their announcements of the evening's events.

Even if Mozart himself were performing, many visitors

As Eastern Europe races into the future, cities such as Prague are cleaning up their industries, giving elegant facades a face-lift, and replacing asphalt with charming cobbles and pedestrian zones.

would rather spend the evening at a Prague beer hall. *Pivo* (beer) is a frothy hit with tourists. After all, the Czechs invented Pilsner-style lager in nearby Plzeň, and the result, Pilsner Urquell, is on tap in many pubs. Budvar, another local beer, is popular with Anheuser-Busch's attorneys. Czechs are the world's most enthusiastic beer drinkers—adults drink an average of 80 gallons a year. In many Czech restaurants, a beer hits your table like a glass of water does in the United States. Be careful. *Pivo* for lunch has me sightseeing for the rest of the day on Czech knees. *Na zdraví* means "to your health" in Czech. After a few *pivos*, fun-loving Czechs stumble on their own words, raising their mugs and bellowing "*Nádraží*" (which means "train station").

For good-value accommodations in **Prague,** *try Hotel Julián (moderate, Elišky Peškové 11, Praha 5, tel. 257-311-150, reception tel. 257-311-145, www.julian.cz) or the Athos Travel room-booking service (tel. 241-440-571, www.a-prague.com). For all the travel specifics, see the latest edition of* Rick Steves' Prague & the Czech Republic.

Charming Kraków

The top stop in Poland is Kraków. Of all the Eastern European cities laying claim to the boast "the next Prague," Kraków is for real. And enjoying a drink on its marvelous Main Market Square, you'll know why. The biggest square in medieval Europe remains one of Europe's most gasp-worthy public spaces.

Knowing this is one of Europe's least expensive countries, I choose the fanciest café on Kraków's fanciest piece of real estate and order without even considering the price. Sinking deep into my chair and sipping deep into my drink, I ponder the bustle of Poland, two decades after it won its freedom.

Vast as it is, the square has a folksy intimacy. It bustles with street musicians, fragrant flower stalls,

Poland's top tourist attraction promises to be "the next Prague." Tourism has brought Kraków prosperity—great restaurants, comfy hotels, and plenty of welcoming sights.

Kraków's Old Town

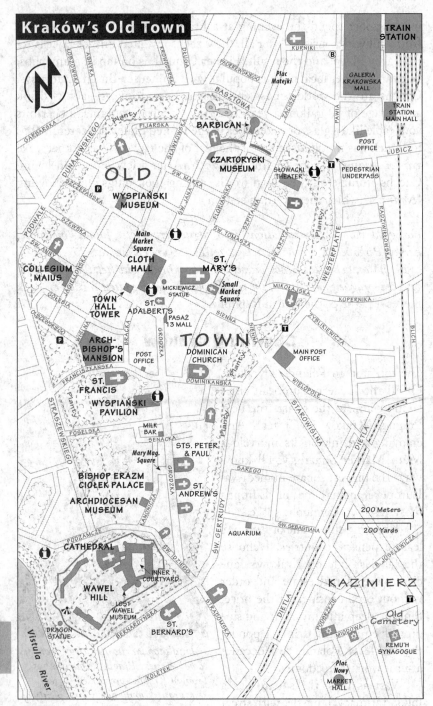

cotton-candy vendors, loitering teenagers, businesspeople commuting by bike, gawking tourists, and the lusty coos of pigeons. This square is where Kraków lives...and where visitors like me find themselves hanging out. To my left, activists protest Poland's EU membership. To my right, teens practice break-dancing moves.

The folk band—swaggering in their colorful peasant costumes—give me a private little concert. Feeling flush, I tip them royally. (Perhaps too royally. Be warned: A big tip gets you "The Star-Spangled Banner.")

Kraków is the Boston of Poland: a captivating old-fashioned city buzzing with history, intriguing sights, colorful eateries, and college students. Even though the country's political capital moved from here to Warsaw 400 years ago, Kraków remains Poland's cultural and intellectual center.

Flat and easy to navigate, Kraków is made for walking. A greenbelt called the Planty rings the Old Town, where the 13th-century protective walls and moat once stood (a great place for a stroll or bike ride).

Street musicians play "The Star-Spangled Banner" for big spenders.

With its diverse sights, Kraków can keep a speedy tourist busy for three days. Most sights are inside the Planty park, except for the historic Wawel Castle grounds and the Jewish quarter in Kazimierz. You'll want to side-trip to the notorious Auschwitz Concentration Camp. And most visitors also visit Wieliczka Salt Mine—my vote for the deepest art gallery in Europe.

Kraków grew wealthy from trade in the 12th century. Traders passing through were required to stop here for a few days and sell their wares cheap. Local merchants then sold those goods with big price hikes...and Kraków thrived. It became Poland's capital.

Tatars invaded in 1241, destroying the city. Krakovians took this opportunity to rebuild their streets in a near-perfect grid around the spectacular Main Market Square. King Kazimierz the Great sparked Kraków's golden age in the 14th century. He established the university that still defines the city (and counts Copernicus and Pope John Paul II among its alumni).

But Kraków's power waned and the capital moved to Warsaw. Two

EASTERN EUROPE

EU Enlargement and the "New Europe"

The Czech Republic, Slovakia, Poland, Hungary, Slovenia, and five other countries joined the European Union in 2004, with Bulgaria and Romania joining in 2007. Today, Croatia, the Republic of Macedonia, Turkey, and Iceland are also candidates for membership. (For more on the EU, see page 477.) Though EU membership—and investment—should ultimately benefit everybody, old members and new members have both had their doubts.

For example, new EU member Poland survived the communist era without collectivizing its small family farms. But now that they've joined the EU, collectivization is mandatory. Traditional Czech cuisine is also in jeopardy. EU hygiene standards dictate that cooked food can't be served more than two hours old. My Czech friend complained, "This makes many of our best dishes illegal." Czech specialties, often simmered, taste better the next day.

A wise Czech grandmother put it best. In her lifetime, she had lived in a country ruled from Vienna (Habsburgs), Berlin (Nazis), and Moscow (communists). She said, "Now that we're finally ruled from Prague, why would we want to turn our power over to Brussels?"

For their part, longstanding EU members have been skeptical about taking on more countries. Wealthy nations have already spent vast fortunes to improve the floundering economies of poorer member countries (such as Portugal, Greece, and Ireland). Most of the new members expect a similar financial-aid windfall, especially during these uncertain economic times. Westerners also fret about an influx of cheap labor from the East. Finally, Western Europeans worry about their political power being diluted. In the "New Europe," Poland or the Czech Republic might emerge with a leading role.

As the New Europe takes shape, players on both sides will continue to define their new roles and seek compromise. So far, the general consensus in the East is that joining the European Union was the right move. In a few years, the Hungarians, Poles, Czechs, and their neighbors will all be working harder than ever and enjoying more coins jangling in their pockets...and they expect those coins will be euros.

centuries later, Poland was partitioned by neighboring powers. Warsaw ended up as a satellite of oppressive Moscow, and Kraków became a poor provincial backwater of Vienna. But despite Kraków's reduced prominence, Austria's comparatively liberal climate helped turn the city into a haven for intellectuals and progressives (including a young Russian revolutionary named Vladimir Ilyich Lenin).

Kraków emerged from World War II virtually unscathed. But when the communists took over, they decided to give intellectual (and potentially dissident) Kraków an injection of good Soviet values—in the form of heavy industry. They built Nowa Huta, an enormous steelworks on the city's outskirts, dooming the city to decades of smog. Thankfully, Kraków is now much cleaner than it was 15 years ago.

Entering through the main gate of the Old Town wall, past an outdoor gallery for struggling art students, walk down Floriańska street to one McDonald's worth a visit. When renovating this building, workers discovered a Gothic cellar. They excavated it and added seating. Today, you can super-size your ambience by dining on a Big Mac and fries under a medieval McVault.

Even better, keep your eyes open for a *bar mleczny* ("milk bar"). In the communist era, the government subsidized the food at these cafeterias to provide working-class Poles with an affordable meal out. The tradition continues, and today Poland still subsidizes your milk-bar meal. Prices are astoundingly low—soup for less than a dollar. And, while communist-era fare was gross, today's milk-bar cuisine is tastier. Just head to the counter, point to what you want, and get a quick and hearty meal for half the cost of McDonald's.

Got milk? Poland does. In milk bars, a throwback to the communist era, you can fill your tank cheaply.

St. Mary's Church—overlooking the main square—marks the center of Kraków. From its taller tower (actually the city's watchtower), a bugler plays half a tune at the top of each hour. During the 1241 Tatar invasion, the story goes, a watchman in the tower saw the enemy approaching and sounded the alarm. Before he could finish the tune, an arrow pierced his throat—which is why even today, the music stops *subito* partway through. Today's buglers are firemen—serving as fire lookouts first...and musicians second.

Wawel (VAH-vehl) Hill towers over old Kraków. This hill, with its castle, cathedral, and complex of sights, is a symbol of Polish royalty and independence. It's sacred ground to every Pole, and the country's leading tourist attraction. Crowds and a ridiculously complex admissions system for the hill's many historic sights can be exasperating. Thankfully, for most non-Polish visitors, a stroll through the cathedral and around the castle grounds covers the site adequately and requires no tickets. Wawel's many museums are mildly interesting but skippable.

Wawel Cathedral is Poland's national church—its Westminster Abbey. The national mausoleum, it holds the tombs of Poland's most important rulers and historical figures. The interior is slathered in Baroque memorials and tombs. Everyone visits the tomb of Kazimierz the Great. But even Kazimierz is outdone by a black crucifix marking the relics of St. Jadwiga, the beloved 14th-century "king of Poland" (the sexist bigwigs of the day refused to call her "queen") who helped Christianize Lithuania and was sainted by John Paul II in 1997. All the candles flickering here indicate she's popular with Poles today.

The Wawel Castle museums may be forgettable. But the complex has one "sight" which—while invisible—attracts travelers from around the world: chakra. Hindus

A glass of wine and a salad with a serenade on Kraków's floodlit main square caps one of the best days Europe has to offer.

believe the chakra is part of a powerful energy field that connects all living things. There are seven points on the surface of the earth where this chakra energy is most concentrated. These points include Jerusalem, Mecca, Rome...and Kraków's Wawel Hill. Look for peaceful people with their eyes closed. One thing's for sure: They're not thinking of Kazimierz the Great. The Wawel administration seems creeped out by all this. They've done what they can to discourage this ritual, but believers still gravitate from far and wide to hug the wall in the castle courtyard. (Just for fun, ask a Wawel tour guide about chakra and watch him squirm—they're forbidden to talk about it.)

A 20-minute walk beyond Wawel takes you to the historic center of Jewish Kraków, Kazimierz. After King Kazimierz the Great encouraged

Jews to come to Poland in the 14th century, a large Jewish community settled in and around Kraków. According to legend, Kazimierz (the king) established Kazimierz (the village) for his favorite girlfriend—a Jewish woman named Ester—just outside the Kraków city walls. Kazimierz was an autonomous community, with its own Town Hall, market square, and city walls. By 1800, the walls came down, Kazimierz became part of Kraków, and the Jewish community flourished. By the start of World War II, 65,000 Jews lived in Kraków (mostly in Kazimierz), making up more than a quarter of the city's population. Only a few thousand Kraków Jews survived the war.

Today's Kraków has only about two hundred Jewish residents. Kazimierz still has an empty feeling, but the neighborhood has enjoyed a renaissance of Jewish culture lately following the popularity of Steven Spielberg's *Schindler's List* (which takes place, and was partly filmed, in Kazimierz). The spirit of the Jewish tradition survives in the neighborhood's evocative synagogues, soulful cemeteries, and the lilting klezmer folk concerts put on by restaurants.

Kazimierz has two Jewish cemeteries, both more undiscovered and powerful than the famous one in Prague. Locals shop at Plac Nowy's market stalls, a gritty factory-workers-on-lunch-break contrast to Kraków's touristy main square. Fans of Spielberg's Holocaust movie—and the compassionate Kraków businessman who did his creative best to save the lives of his Jewish workers—can see Schindler's actual factory, in the Podgórze district across the river from Kazimierz. The factory was converted into a museum to celebrate non-Jews who, like Schindler, risked their lives to save Holocaust victims.

Most of Kazimierz's Jews were killed at Auschwitz, a Nazi concentration camp in the Polish town of Oświęcim (a 70-minute drive west of Kraków). This is one of Europe's most moving sights and certainly the most important of all the Holocaust memorials. (For more on Auschwitz, see "Sobering Sites of Nazi Europe".)

Also near Kraków is the remarkable Wieliczka Salt Mine,

A bright and fun generation of new young guides (with or without cars) all across Eastern Europe are proud to share their cities and cultures, making your visit especially meaningful.

which has been producing salt since at least the 11th century. Under Kazimierz the Great, one-third of Poland's income came from these precious deposits. Wieliczka miners spent much of their lives underground, rarely emerging into daylight. To pass the time, 19th-century miners began carving figures, chandeliers, and eventually even an entire chapel out of the salt.

The tour shows how the miners lived and worked (using horses that lived their lives underground, never seeing the light of day). It takes you through some impressive underground caverns, past subterranean lakes, and introduces you to some of the mine's many salt sculptures (including an army of salt elves and a life-size statue of this region's favorite son, Pope John Paul II). Your jaw will drop as you enter the enormous Chapel of the Blessed Kinga. Don't miss the extremely salty relief of the Last Supper.

Your walk finishes over 400 feet below the surface, where a traditional miners' lift hoists you back up to a sunlit world that seems particularly bright.

*For good-value accommodations in **Kraków**, splurge at one of the Donimirski Boutique Hotels (three swanky locations in or near the Old Town, www.donimirski.com), or sleep cheaper at Globtroter Guest House (budget, Pl. Szczepanski 7, tel. 12-422-4123, www.globtroter-krakow.com). For all the travel specifics, see the latest edition of Rick Steves' Eastern Europe.*

Off the Beaten Path in Bosnia-Herzegovina

Looking for a change of pace from Croatia's Dalmatian Coast, I drove from Dubrovnik into the city of Mostar, in Bosnia-Herzegovina. Almost everyone doing this trip takes the scenic coastal route. But, with a spirit of adventure, I took the back road instead: inland first, then looping north through the Serb part of Herzegovina.

Bosnia-Herzegovina's three main ethnic groups—Serbs, Croats, and Bosniaks—are descended from the same ancestors and speak closely related languages. The key distinction is that they practice different religions: Orthodox Christianity, Roman Catholicism, and Islam, respectively. For the most part, there's no way that a casual visitor can determine the religion or loyalties of the people just by looking at them. Studying the complex demographics of the former Yugoslavia, you gain a respect for the communist-era dictator Tito—the one man who could hold this place together peacefully. (To learn more about the conflicts in the former Yugoslavia, see www.ricksteves.com/yugo.)

Bosnia-Herzegovina is one nation, historically divided into two regions: Bosnia and Herzegovina. But the 1995 Dayton Peace Accords gerrymandered the country along other lines, giving a degree of autonomy to the area where Orthodox Serbs predominate. This "Republika Srpska" rings the core of Bosnia on three sides. When asked for driving tips, Croats—who, because of ongoing tensions with the Serbs, avoid this territory—insist that the road I want to take doesn't even exist. From the main Croatian coastal road just south of Dubrovnik, directional signs

send you to the tiny Croatian border town—but ignore the large Serb city of Trebinje just beyond.

And yet, Trebinje more than exists...it is bustling and prosperous. As I enter the town, police with Ping-Pong paddle stop signs pull me over—you must drive with your headlights on at all hours. The "dumb tourist" routine gets me off the hook. I enjoy a vibrant market scene,

The Bosnian-Serb city of Trebinje enjoys a bright and busy Saturday market.

and get cash at an ATM to buy some produce. (Even here—in perhaps the most remote place I've been in Europe—ATMs are plentiful.)

Bosnia-Herzegovina's money is called the "convertible mark." I don't know if they are thrilled that their money is now convertible, but I remember a time when it wasn't. I stow a few Bosnian coins as souvenirs. They have the charm of Indian pennies and buffalo nickels. Some bills have Cyrillic lettering and Serb historical figures, while others use "our" alphabet and show Muslims or Croats. Like everything else in Bosnia-Herzegovina, the currency is a careful balancing act.

Later, after a two-hour drive on deserted roads through a rugged landscape, I arrive at the humble crossroads village of Nevesinje. Towns in this region all have a "café row," and Nevesinje is no exception. It's lunchtime, but as I walk through the town, I don't see a soul with any food on their plate—just drinks. Apparently locals eat (economically) at home, then enjoy an affordable coffee or drink at a café.

A cluttered little grocery—the woman behind the counter happy to make a sandwich—is my solution for a quick meal. The salami looks like Spam. I take my sandwich to an adjacent café and pay the equivalent of a US quarter for a cup of strong Turkish (or "Bosnian") coffee, with highly caffeinated mud in the bottom. Then I munch, drink, and watch the street scene.

Big men drive by in little beaters. High-school kids crowd around the window of the photography shop, which has just posted their class graduation photos. The girls on this cruising drag prove you don't need money to have style. Through a shop window, I see a newly engaged couple picking out a simple ring. One moment I see Nevesinje as very different from my hometown...but the next, it seems just the same.

Looking at the curiously overgrown ruined building across the street, I notice bricked-up, pointed Islamic arches, and realize it was once a mosque. In its backyard—a no-man's-land of bombed-out concrete and glass—a single half-knocked-over turban-

This charred mosque is a poignant reminder of more difficult times in Nevesinje...and of what has been lost.

topped tombstone still manages to stand. The prayer niche inside, where no one prays anymore, faces an empty restaurant.

After an hour's drive over a twisty mountain road, I cross into the Muslim-Croat part of Bosnia-Herzegovina, and arrive at the city of Mostar.

Mostar: Mending Broken Bridges

Mostar provided me with one of the richest travel experiences I've had in years. With jarring reminders of a recent war, but an inspiring resilience and a vibrant humanity, the city left me both exhilarated and exhausted.

Before the war, Mostar was famous for its 400-year-old, Turkish-style stone bridge. The Old Bridge's elegant, single-pointed arch—commissioned by the Otto-

Mostar's symbol is its Old Bridge...with stoic grace and echoes of Turkey.

man Sultan Süleyman the Magnificent—was a symbol of Mostar's Muslim society, and of the town's status as the place where East met West in Europe.

Then, during the 1990s, Mostar became a poster child for the excesses of the Bosnian war. First, the Croats and Bosniaks forced out the Serbs. Then they turned their guns on each other—staring each other down across a front line that ran through the middle of the city. Across the world, people wept when the pummeled Old Bridge—bombarded by Croat paramilitary artillery shells from the hilltop above—finally collapsed into the river.

Now, the bridge has been painstakingly rebuilt, and Mostar is thriving. As they have for generations, young men swan-dive from the bridge 75 feet down into the Neretva (which remains icy cold even in summer).

As if reaffirming their zest for life, young Mostarians plunge off their beloved Old Bridge into the chilly river below.

Done both for the sake of tradition and to impress girls, this custom was carried on even during the time the destroyed bridge was temporarily replaced by a wooden one. On hot summer days, you'll see divers making a ruckus and collecting donations at the top of the bridge. They tease and tease, standing up on the railing and pretending they're about to jump...then get down and ask for more money. Once they collect about $50, one of them will take the plunge.

The city's Bosniak core—where most visitors spend their time—offers an illuminating and unique glimpse of a culture that's both devoutly Muslim and fully European. Surrounding the Old Bridge is a cobbled Old Town, which has been fully restored since the war. Here you can poke into several mosques, tour old-fashioned Turkish-style houses, shop your way through a bazaar of souvenir stands, and hear the call to prayer warbling across the rooftops.

Climbing up the hill from the Old Bridge is the lively, colorful Coppersmiths' Street—a shopping zone with the flavor of a Turkish bazaar: blue-and-white "evil eyes" (believed in the Turkish culture to keep bad spirits at bay), old Yugoslav army kitsch, and hammered-copper decorations (continuing the long tradition that gave the street its name).

I stop in at the Turkish-style Biščević House. Dating from 1635,

EASTERN EUROPE

it's typical of old houses in Mostar, which mix Oriental style with Mediterranean features. It's surrounded by a high wall—protection from the sun's rays, from thieves...and from prying eyes. A fountain gently gurgles in the courtyard, enjoyed by the house's free-range pet turtles. Removing my shoes to enter the house, I climb a wooden staircase to the cool, shady, and airy living room. Privacy latticework allows the women to peek down discreetly to see what is happening in the courtyard. At the back of the house is the gathering room. This space—designed in a circle so people can face each other, cross-legged, for a good conversation—has a dramatic view overlooking the Neretva. Heading back down to reclaim my shoes, I find a turtle clambering over them.

A few steps outside the touristy Old Town, burned-out husks of buildings and bullet holes everywhere are a constant reminder that the city is still recovering—physically and psychologically. In the back of my mind, I'm prodded by the chilling thought that, just a few years ago, these people—who make me a sandwich, direct me to a computer terminal in the cybercafé, stop for me when I cross the street, show off their paintings, and direct the church choir—were killing each other.

And yet, as in any conflict, most people here were innocent bystanders who felt trapped by an unwanted, unnecessary war. In fact, I didn't meet anyone in Mostar who called the war anything but a tragic mistake. And many are eager to share their lessons from living through those unthinkably difficult times.

I meet Alen, a thirty-something Muslim who immigrated to Florida during the war, and is now back home in Mostar. Alen strolls with me through his hometown, offering an eyewitness account of its darkest hour. He points to a tree growing out the window of a bombed-out building. Seeming to speak as much about Mostar's people as its vegetation, he says, "It's a strange thing in nature: Figs can grow with almost no soil."

There are blackened ruins everywhere. When I ask why—after more than 15 years—the ruins still stand, Alen explains, "Confusion about who owns what. Surviving companies have no money. The bank of Yugoslavia, which held the mortgages, is now gone. No one will invest until it's clear who owns the buildings."

We visit a small cemetery congested with more than a hundred white-marble Muslim tombstones. Alen points out the dates. Everyone died in 1993, 1994, or 1995. This was a park before 1993. When the war heated up, snipers were a constant concern—they'd pick off anyone they saw walking down the street. Bodies were left for weeks along the main boulevard, which had become the front line. Mostar's cemeteries were too exposed, but this park was relatively safe from snipers. People bur-

New cemeteries in downtown Mostar are crammed with graves from a grotesque three-year period.

ied their loved ones here...under cover of darkness.

Alen says, "In those years, night was the time when we lived. We didn't walk...we ran. And we dressed in black. There was no electricity. If the Croat fighters didn't kill us with their bullets, they killed us with their rabble-rousing pop music. It was blasting from the Croat side of town."

The symbolism of the religious conflict is powerful. Ten minarets pierce Mostar's skyline like proud exclamation points. There, twice as tall as the tallest minaret, stands the Croats' new Catholic church spire. Standing on the reconstructed Old Bridge, I look at the hilltop high above the town, with its single, bold, and strongly floodlit cross. Alen says, "We Muslims believe that cross marks the spot from where they shelled this bridge...like a celebration."

Alen takes me to Masala Square (literally, "Place for Prayer"), which is designed for big gatherings. Muslim groups meet here before departing to Mecca on the Hajj. But tonight, there's not a hint of prayer. It's prom night. The kids are out, and Bosnian hormones are sloshing everywhere. Being young and sexy is a great equalizer. With a beer, loud music, desirability, twinkling stars—and no war—your country's GDP doesn't really matter.

The next day, I decide to grab a lunch for my trip from Mostar back to Croatia. I stop at a tiny grocery store, where a woman I befriended the day before—a gorgeous person, sad to be living in a frustrating economy, and stiff from a piece of shrapnel in her back that doctors decided was safer left in—makes me a hearty ham sandwich. As she slices, I gather the rest of what will be a

Despite the hardships of war—such as a chunk of shrapnel in the back—the resilient people of Mostar are putting their city and their lives back together.

fine picnic meal on wheels.

As I sort through conflicting emotions on my way out of town, I drive over patched bomb craters in the pavement. In similarly war-torn Sarajevo, they've filled these scars with red concrete as memorials: "Sarajevo roses." Here they are black like the rest of the street—but knowing what they are, they show up red in my mind.

*For good-value accommodations in **Mostar**, consider the simple, central Villa Fortuna (budget, Rade Bitange 34, tel. 036/580-625, www.villafortuna .ba) or the Muslibegović House, a preserved traditional Turkish house (splurge, Osman Đikića 41, tel. 036/551-379, www.muslibegovichouse.com). For all the travel specifics, see the latest edition of* Rick Steves' Croatia & Slovenia.

Communist Sites in Eastern Europe

Until 1989, Eastern Europe was a foreboding place—a dark and gloomy corner of the "Evil Empire." Three decades ago, my Polish friends were taking in their windshield wipers at night. (If stolen, they were impossible to replace.) Bomb craters appeared in front of Bulgarian train stations...and no one talked about it. People ran their kitchen faucets so neighbors in their flimsy apartment flats couldn't hear them listening to Radio Free Europe. Teenagers were allowed one rock concert a year—which happened to be scheduled the same time as Easter Mass. And train conductors checked my ticket before slipping secretively with me into the bathroom to change money at black-market rates.

Happily, over the past 20 years, the people here have dropped the "Eastern" and are embracing the "European"...and they're not looking back. The obligatory grays and preachy reds of communism live on only in history books, museums, and cheesy theme restaurants. Freedom is a generation old, and—for better or for worse—McDonald's, MTV, and mobile phones are every bit as entrenched here as anywhere else in Europe. But the curious traveler can still uncover some time-travel communist sites—some kitschy and fun, others somber and moving.

Berlin, Germany
Berlin, once the western outpost of the Soviet Bloc, is filled with poignant memories of its communist days. And now that the city has been free and united for nearly two decades, there's a playful nostalgia—or "*Ost*-algia" (*Ost* is German for "east")—for what some consider happier times...back when "everybody had a job."

Today, theme eateries serve dreary food from the 1960s with a Cold

War "ambience." Enjoying a creamy vanilla ice-cream sundae in eastern Berlin's Café Sibylle, I pondered the odd stone carving that hung overhead: an ear and half a moustache. The sundae, which comes with a shot of liquor, was the standard treat back then. And the ear and moustache are all that's left of what was the largest statue of Josef Stalin in Germany.

The café stands on what was the showpiece boulevard of communist Berlin. Its original buildings were completely leveled by the Soviet Army in 1945. When Stalin decided this main drag should be a showcase street, he had it rebuilt and named it Stalinallee. Today this street, lined with "workers' palaces"—apartment flats done in the bold "Stalin Gothic" style so common in Moscow in the 1950s—has been restored and renamed for Karl Marx. Socialist Realist reliefs on the buildings and lampposts celebrate triumphs of the working class.

One symbol of the old days still shines: Look at the old pedestrian lights, and you'll realize that at least some communists had a sense of humor. The perky red and green men—*Ampelmännchen*—were nearly replaced by far less jaunty Western signs. But after an uproar from "Ost-algic" residents, the East German signals have survived.

The jaunty former East German traffic lights survive at the request of "Ost-algic" East Berliners.

Little remains of the grandest souvenir of Cold War Berlin, the infamous Berlin Wall. The 100-mile "Anti-Fascist Protective Rampart," as it was called by the East German government, was erected almost overnight in 1961 to stop the outward flow of people (three million leaked out between 1949 and 1961). Guides are quick with all the stats: The 13-foot-high Wall had a 16-foot tank ditch, a no-man's-land (or "death strip") that was 30-160 feet wide, and 300 sentry towers. During the Wall's 28 years, border guards fired 1,693 times and made 3,221 arrests, and there were 5,043 documented successful escapes (including 565 by East German guards).

The carnival atmosphere of those first years after the Wall fell is gone, but hawkers still sell "authentic" pieces of the Wall, flags of the DDR (East Germany), and military paraphernalia to gawking tourists. When it fell, the Wall was literally carried away by the euphoria.

What managed to survive has been nearly devoured by persistent "Wall-peckers." A low-key row of cobbles traces the Wall's former path around the city. A short stretch of the Wall survives at Zimmerstrasse. And a section at Bernauer Strasse (near the Nordbahnhof S-Bahn station) is part of the fascinating Berlin Wall Documentation Center.

The biggest surviving stretch of the Wall is the colorful East Side Gallery. Nicknamed "the world's longest outdoor art gallery," it stretches for nearly a mile and is covered with murals painted by artists from around the world. This segment of the Wall makes a poignant walk.

Checkpoint Charlie, the famous border checkpoint between the American and Soviet sectors, is long gone. But its memory is preserved by the Museum of the Wall at Checkpoint Charlie. During the Cold War, the House at

Berlin's East Side Gallery: once a link in the imposing Wall...and now an art gallery

Checkpoint Charlie stood defiantly—spitting distance from the border guards—showing off all the ingenious escapes over, under, and through the Wall. Today, while the drama is over and hunks of the Wall stand like victory scalps at its door, this museum still tells a gripping history—including those heady days when people-power tore down the Wall.

Budapest, Hungary

If communism was a religion during the Cold War, Budapest was Eastern Europe's sin city. Since Hungary's milder "goulash communism" allowed tourists from within the Soviet Bloc a taste of the decadent West, Budapest was famous for rock concerts, a sport shop selling Adidas, and the first McDonald's behind the Iron Curtain.

That McDonald's still stands, a few steps off the main pedestrian street, Váci utca. Munching a burger here, ponder that back then, there was nothing fast or cheap about Western "fast food." A Happy Meal was a splurge. People traveled here from other communist countries to wait in a line that stretched around the block for a burger and a Coke. Ronald McDonald stood on the street corner like a heretic prophet cheering on the downtrodden proletariat, while across the street, wannabe capitalists drooled over window displays featuring fancy tennis shoes that cost

The House of Terror is a sobering reminder of Hungary's "dual occupation"—first Nazis, then communists.

two months' wages.

But just a generation earlier, Hungary was still as oppressive as its neighbors. And today, Budapest's House of Terror—long the headquarters of communist Hungary's secret police—documents a terrible story. When the communists moved into Budapest, their secret police took over the former Nazi headquarters. It was here that Hungarians suspected of being enemies of the state were given sham trials, tortured, and executed.

The museum's atrium features a Soviet tank and a vast wall covered with portraits of victims of this building. Exhibits cover gulag life, Socialist Realist art, and propaganda. Leaving the museum, you pass a chilling finale. The "wall of victimizers" is lined with photos of members and supporters of both the Nazi and communist secret police—many of whom are still living, and who were never brought to justice.

When regimes fall, so do their monuments. Just like statues of Saddam Hussein bit the dust in Baghdad, across Eastern Europe statues of Stalin, Lenin, and their local counterparts came crashing to the ground.

In Budapest, a clever entrepreneur gathered these stony reminders of communist tyranny into a "Memento Park" where tourists flock to get a taste of the communist era. A visit here is a lesson in Socialist Realism, the art of communist Europe. Under the communists, creativity was discouraged. Art was acceptable only if it furthered the goals of the state. Aside from a few important figureheads,

This monument—in Budapest's Memento Park—represents a strong communist soldier racing into the future. But cynical Hungarians of the time had a different interpretation: a thermal-bath attendant running after a customer who forgot his towel.

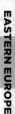

EASTERN EUROPE

individuals didn't matter. Everyone was a cog in the machine—a strong and stoic automaton—an unquestioning servant of the nation.

Wandering through Budapest's Memento Park, you're entertained by a jumbled collection of once fearsome and now almost comical statues, seeming to preach their ideology to each other, as locals and tourists take funny photos mocking them. The gift shop hawks a fun parade of communist kitsch. On my last visit I picked up a CD featuring 20 patriotic songs—*The Greatest Hits of Communism*—and a Stalin vodka flask.

More Communist Sites

Many other places that suffered through communism have similar points of interest.

Prague, Czech Republic: On a thriving shopping street near the bottom of Prague's Wenceslas Square, wedged ironically between an American fast-food joint and a casino, stands the Museum of Communism. It re-creates slices of communist life—from a bland store counter to a typical classroom (where a poem on the chalkboard extols the virtues of the tractor).

A few blocks away at the top of Wenceslas Square is a blocky building that housed Czechoslovakia's rubber-stamp Parliament back when they voted with Moscow. Between 1994 and 2008, this building was home to Radio Free Europe. After communism fell, RFE lost some of its funding and could no longer afford its Munich headquarters. In gratitude for its broadcasts—which

The communist era left Eastern Europe with some decent public transportation, but ugly train stations were erected—like this one, in Prague. The low ceilings still make the individual feel like staying in line.

had kept the people of Eastern Europe in touch with real news—the Czech government offered the building to RFE for one Czech koruna a year. Today, RFE has relocated, and this building is run by the National Museum. Visitors are welcome to stroll its halls ($4.50 to enter), but you can pop in and enjoy the Prager café for free—sitting in the same big leather chairs that communist big shots did a generation ago.

At Olomouc's astronomical clock, the white bands honor saints...while the dark bands trumpet communist bigwigs.

Olomouc, Czech Republic: This appealing university town in Moravia (the eastern half of the Czech Republic) has a distinctive communist astronomical clock. Like Prague's famous clock, the one in Olomouc was intentionally destroyed by the Nazis in World War II. Today's version was rebuilt in 1953 by the communists—with their tacky flair for propaganda. This one-of-a-kind clock made in the Socialist Realist style is adorned with earnest chemists and heroic mothers rather than saints and Virgin Marys. High noon is marked by a proletarian parade, when, for six minutes, a mechanical conga line of milkmaids, clerks, blacksmiths, medics, and teachers are celebrated as the champions of everyday society. As with any proper astronomical clock, there's a wheel with 365 saints, so you'll always know whose special day it is. But this clock comes with a Moscow-inspired bonus—red bands on the wheel splice in the birthdays of communist leaders, including Lenin and Stalin.

Gdańsk, Poland: Just a 20-minute walk from Gdańsk's colorful Hanseatic quarter are the dreary shipyards that Lech Wałęsa called the "cradle of freedom." Here the "Roads to Freedom" museum tells the story of the Solidarity movement of 1980, which started Eastern Europe's march to liberty. The engaging exhibit—housed in the very shipyards where the first labor strikes began—includes a replica of a sparsely stocked communist-era grocery store, the original list of 21 demands posted by the protestors, images of the newly minted Polish pope who inspired them, and plenty

This monument—towering over the Gdańsk shipyard, where it inspired the birth of Solidarity—commemorates striking workers who were killed when the communist regime opened fire on them in 1970.

of bushy-mustachioed photos of the strike's leader, Lech Wałęsa. Wałęsa achieved rock-star status during the Gdańsk shipyard strikes, when—according to legend—the portly electrician hopped over a wall to become the leader of the protestors. He went on to become Poland's first post-communist president.

Warsaw, Poland: The Polish capital was devastated by World War II, then rebuilt largely by the Soviet regime. Towering over the seas of communist apartment blocks is the tallest building in Poland, the 760-foot Palace of Culture and Science. This massive skyscraper, dating from the early 1950s, was a "gift" from Stalin that the people of Warsaw couldn't refuse. Residents call it "Stalin's Penis" (using cruder terminology than that). Because it was to be "Soviet in substance, Polish in style," Soviet architects toured Poland to absorb local culture before starting the project. Since it's designed to show off the strong, grand-scale Soviet aes-

The harrowing, communist-style Palace of Culture and Science was a "gift" from Stalin to the people of Warsaw. (Talk about a white elephant.)

thetic and architectural skill, everything about the building is just plain big.

Tallinn, Estonia: In 2003, a wealthy Estonian-American opened a Museum of Estonia's Occupations. In the basement, between the toilets, stands an army of Soviet-era statues of communist leaders.

Any Town in Eastern Europe: Keep your eyes open for old communist-era loudspeakers. Locals remember growing up with these mouthpieces of government boasting of successes ("This year, despite many efforts of sabotage on the part of certain individuals in service of imperialist goals, we have surpassed the planned output of steel by 195 percent"); calling people to action ("There will be no school tomorrow as all will join the farmers in the fields for an abundant harvest"); or quelling disturbances ("Some citizens may have heard about alien forces in our society taking advantage of this week's anniversary to spread unrest. This is to reassure you that the situation is firmly under control and nothing is happening. Nevertheless, for their own safety, we suggest all citizens stay home").

These days, as I walk through the streets of Eastern Europe, it occurs to me that Stalin—whose estate gets no royalties for all the postcards and vodka flasks featuring his mug—must be spinning in his communist grave.

For all the specifics, see the latest editions of Rick Steves' Budapest *or* Rick Steves' Eastern Europe.

GREAT BRITAIN

London: A Warm Look at a Cold City

I've spent more time in London than in any other European city. It lacks the grandeur of Rome, the warmth of Munich, and the elegance of Paris, but its history, traditions, people, markets, museums, and entertainment keep drawing me back.

London has changed dramatically in recent years, and many visitors are surprised to find how "un-English" it is. Whites are now a minority in major parts of this city that once symbolized white imperialism. Arabs have nearly bought out the area north of Hyde Park. Chinese takeouts outnumber fish-and-chips shops. Eastern Europeans pull pints in British pubs. Many hotels are run by people with foreign accents (who hire English chambermaids), while outlying suburbs are home to huge communities of Indians and Pakistanis. London is learning—sometimes fitfully—to live as a microcosm of its formerly vast empire.

London is a world in itself, a barrage on all the senses, an urban jungle sprawling over 600 square miles and teeming with eight

The London Eye towers over Big Ben.

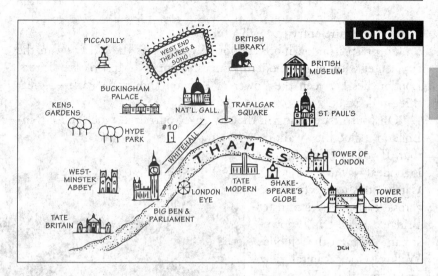

million people. As a first stop for many travelers, this huge city can be overwhelming. On my first visit I felt like Oliver Twist asking for more soup. Here are a few ideas to soften and warm this hard and cold city.

Have fun seeing the predictable biggies. Blow through the city on the open deck of a double-decker tour bus. Ogle the crown jewels in the Tower of London and see the Houses of Parliament in action. Cruise the Thames River, and take a spin on the London Eye. Hobnob with the tombstones in Westminster Abbey, and visit with Leonardo da Vinci, Botticelli, and Rembrandt in the National Gallery. Enjoy Shakespeare in a replica of the Globe Theatre, then marvel at a glitzy, fun musical at a modern-day theater. Whisper across the dome of St. Paul's Cathedral and rummage through our civilization's attic at the British Museum. Enjoy some of Europe's best people-watching at Covent Garden and snap to at Buckingham Palace's Changing of the Guard. Sip your tea with pinky raised and clotted cream dribbling down your scone.

Have you tried London lately?

Any guidebook recommends these worthwhile must-sees. But go beyond the big museums, churches, and castles. Take walks (self-guided and with a local guide), hit the offbeat museums, and seek out experiences that don't require entry through a turnstile.

To grasp London more comfortably, see it as the old town in the city center without the modern, congested sprawl. Most of the visitors' London lies between the Tower of London and Hyde Park—a great three-mile walk.

On your first evening in the city, give yourself a "pinch-me-I'm-in-London" floodlit walking tour. If you just flew in, this is an ideal way to fight jet lag. Catch a bus to the first stop across (east of) Westminster Bridge. Side-trip downstream along the Jubilee Walkway for a capital view. Then, for that "Wow, I'm really in London!" feeling, cross back over the bridge to view the floodlit Houses of Parliament and Big Ben up close.

To thrill your loved ones (or stoke their envy), call home from a pay phone near Big Ben at about three minutes before the hour. As Big Ben chimes, stick the receiver outside the booth and prove you're in London: ding dong ding dong...dong ding ding dong. It's an audio postcard.

Then cross Whitehall, noticing the Winston Churchill statue in the park. (He's electrified to avoid the pigeon problem that stains so many other great statues.) Walk up Whitehall toward Trafalgar Square. Stop at the barricaded and guarded little Downing Street to see #10, home of the British prime minister. Chat with the bored bobby. From Trafalgar, walk to hopping Leicester Square and continue to youth-on-the-rampage Piccadilly, through safely sleazy Soho (north of Shaftesbury Avenue) up to Oxford Street. From Piccadilly or Oxford Circus you can taxi, bus, or subway home.

To nibble on London one historic snack at a time, take any of the focused two-hour walking tours of the city. For about $12, local historians take small groups through the London story, one entertaining page at a time. Choose from London's Plague, Dickens' London, Legal London, the Beatles in London, Jack the Ripper's London (which is the most popular, even though guides admit it's a lousy walk), Harry Potter's London, and many more. Some walks focus on the various "villages" of London, such as trendy Chelsea and leafy Hampstead.

The South Bank of the River Thames, rapidly becoming gentrified, is a thriving arts and cultural center. From Westminster Bridge to the

Tower Bridge, the slick Jubilee Walkway is a trendy jogging, yuppie pub-crawling walk—lined with fun and offbeat sights. The London Eye observation wheel offers the city's highest public viewpoint (450 feet). Featuring modern art, the great Tate Modern on the South Bank is connected with the sedate St. Paul's Cathedral on the North Bank by the pedestrian Millennium Bridge. Skip the South Bank's outrageously amateurish, heavily promoted, and overpriced "London Dungeon," but consider Shakespeare's Globe Theatre and the Imperial War Museum.

For megatons of things military, the impressive Imperial War Museum covers the wars of the last century. You'll see heavy weaponry, love notes from the front, Vargas Girl pinups, Monty's Africa-campaign tank, and Schwarzkopf's Desert Storm uniform. Trace the development of the machine gun, watch footage of the first tank battles, and hold your breath through the gruesome "WWI trench experience." You can even buy WWII-era toys. The section on the Holocaust is one of the best on the subject anywhere. The museum doesn't glorify war, but chronicles the sweeping effects of humanity's most destructive century.

My favorite way to learn history is to stroll with a guide, as if beach-combing. You pick up obscure shards of a neighborhood's distant past, unlocking unexpected stories. On a bright, brisk January morning, I joined a guide, David Tucker, who runs a tour company called London Walks (www.walks.com).

From London Bridge, David pointed downriver past the Tower of London and said, "During the Second World War, Nazi bombers used the Thames as a guide on their nightly raids. When moonlit, they called it a 'silver ribbon of tin foil.' It led from the English Channel right to our mighty dockyards. Even with all the city lights carefully blacked out, those bombers easily found their targets. Neighborhoods on both banks of the river went up in flames. After the war, the business district on the North Bank was rebuilt, but the South Bank...it was long neglected."

Turning his back to St. Paul's Cathedral, he pointed to a vast complex of new buildings, displaying the restored, trendy South Bank, and continued, "Only now has the bombed-out South Bank been properly rebuilt. There's a real buzz in London about our South Bank."

We walked down to the beach. The Thames is a tidal river, and at low tide it's littered with history. Even today, many of the beaches are red with clay tiles from 500-year-old roofs. Picking up a chunky piece of tile worn oval by the centuries, with its telltale peg hole still clearly visible, the guide explained that these tiles were heavy, requiring large timbers for support. In the 16th century, when shipbuilding for the Royal Navy made these timbers more costly and rare, lighter slate tiles became the preferred roofing material. Over time, the heavy, red-clay tiles migrated from the rooftops to the riverbank...to the pockets of beachcombers like us.

Like kids on a scavenger hunt, we studied the pebbles. David picked up a chalky white tube to show me. It was the fragile stem of an 18th-century clay pipe. Back then, when tobacco was sold with disposable one-use pipes, used pipes were routinely tossed into the river. David tossed it down. Thinking, "King George may have sucked on this," I picked it up.

Climbing back to street level, we prowled through some fascinating relics of the South Bank neighborhood that survived both German bombs and urban renewal. Scaling steep stairs, we visited the Operating Theatre Museum, a crude surgical theater where amputations were performed in the early 1800s as medical students watched and learned. Down the street, the last surviving turret of the original London Bridge is the decorative centerpiece of an old hospital yard. We wandered through the still-bustling Borough Market to see farmers doing business with city shopkeepers.

Walking through this area put us through a time warp. David led us into a quiet courtyard, where we looked up at three sets of balconies climbing the front of an inn. He explained, "Courtyards like this provided struggling theater troupes—like young William Shakespeare's—with a captive audience."

Remember those roving troupes when you visit the Globe Theatre, a rebuilt version of the stage that eventually became their home. To see Shakespeare in a replica of the half-timbered, thatched theater for which he wrote his plays, attend a play at the Globe. This open-air, round theater does the plays as Shakespeare intended, with no amplification ($8 to stand, $25-55 to sit, late April-early Oct, usually nightly, www.shakespeares-globe.org). The $8 "groundling" tickets—while open to rain—are the most fun. Playing the part of  a crude peasant theatergoer, you can walk around, munch a picnic dinner, lean your elbows on the stage, and even interact with the actors. I've never enjoyed Shakespeare as much as here, performed as the Bard intended it...in the "wooden O." The theater is open to tour when there are no plays; the Shakespeare exhibit is worthwhile (and open even during afternoon plays).

Here's a cheap Globe Theatre tip: Plays are long. Many groundlings, who are allowed to come and go as they please, leave before the end. Peasants with culture hang out an hour before the finish and beg or buy a ticket off someone leaving early.

Shakespeare is just the first act here in the world's best theater city. Choose from top musicals, comedies, thrillers, sex farces, and more. Over the years I've enjoyed *Harvey*, starring Jimmy Stewart; *The King and I*, with Yul Brynner; *My Fair Lady; A Chorus Line; Cats; Starlight Express; Les Misérables;* and *Chicago*. Performances are generally nightly except Sunday (though Shakespeare's Globe has shows on Sunday), usually with one matinee a week. Matinees are cheaper and rarely sell out. Ticket prices are comparable to New York, ranging from about $25 to $100. Most theaters are marked on London tourist maps and cluster in the Piccadilly-Trafalgar area.

Unless you want this year's smash hit, getting a ticket is generally easy. You'll be enticed by ads all over the Tube; the *Official London Theatre Guide* and the *Entertainment Guide* (free at box offices, hotels, and tourist offices) list everything in town. While very popular shows sell out early, nearly-as-popular shows may offer discounted tickets to fill seats, even at short notice. If you're interested in a particular show, call or check the theater's website carefully to see if they're offering any deals (see "cheap theater tricks," later). Otherwise, drop by the famous "tkts" booth at Leicester (pronounced "Lester") Square, which sells discounted tickets for top-price seats to shows on the same day or up to a week in advance (Mon-Sat 10:00 a.m.-7:00 p.m., Sun 11:00 p.m.-4:00 p.m., lines often form early, must book in person but lists of shows and discounts are at www.tkts.co.uk).

Prebooking theater tickets from home is smart if there's a show you must see, it's very popular, and your time in London is quite limited (for example, on weekends, plays are more likely to sell out). First do your homework to figure out what you want (browse your options at www .officiallondontheatre.co.uk). Once you've decided on a show, the easiest option is to book through the theater's website; most will link you to a preferred ticket vendor, usually www.ticketmaster.co.uk or www .seetickets.com. Another option is to call the theater box office. Whether you book online or over the phone, you pay with your credit card. A service charge of about $5 per ticket is typical if you book direct with the theater.

Avoid buying tickets through third-party, middleman agencies, which mark up their prices dramatically. These agencies are worthwhile only if a show you've just got to see is sold out at the box office.

Cheap theater tricks: Most theaters offer cheap returned tickets, standing room, matinees, senior or student standby deals, and sometimes discounted same-day seats. These "concessions" are indicated with a "conc" or "s" in the listings. Picking up a late return can get you a great seat at a cheap-seat price. Even if a show is "sold out," there's usually a way to get a seat. Call the theater box office and ask how.

I buy the second-cheapest tickets directly from the theater box office. Many theaters are so small that there's hardly a bad seat. After the lights go down, "scooting up" is less than a capital offense.

If your theatergoing puts you in a literary frame of mind, visit the British Library. While the library contains 180 miles of bookshelves filling London's deepest basement, two beautiful rooms filled with state-of-the-art glass display cases show you the printed treasures of our civilization. You'll see ancient maps; early gospels on papyrus; illuminated manuscripts from the early Middle Ages; the Gutenberg Bible; the Magna Carta; pages from Leonardo's notebooks; original writing by the titans of English literature, from Chaucer and Shakespeare to Dickens and Wordsworth; and music manuscripts from Beethoven to the Beatles.

On Sunday, enjoy an hour of craziness at Speaker's Corner in Hyde Park. By noon, there are usually several soapbox speakers, screamers, singers, communists, or comics performing to the crowd of onlookers. "The grassroots of democracy" is actually a holdover from when the gallows stood here and the criminal was allowed to say just about anything he wanted to before he swung. I dare you to raise your voice and  gather a crowd—it's easy to do. If you catch the London double-decker bus tour from Speaker's Corner Sunday at 10 a.m., you'll return at noon for the prime-time action.

Kew Gardens are lively and open daily. Cruise the Thames or ride the Tube to London's favorite gardens for plants galore and a breezy respite from the city. The Royal Botanic Gardens of Kew are, for most visitors, a delightful opportunity to wander among 33,000 different types of plants. Garden lovers could spend days exploring Kew's 300 acres. For a quick visit, spend a fragrant hour wandering through three buildings: the Palm House, a humid Victorian world of iron, glass, and tropical plants built in 1844; a Waterlily House that Monet would swim for; and the Princess of Wales Conservatory, a modern greenhouse with many different climate zones growing countless cacti and bug-munching carnivorous plants. Then climb up to the Rhizotron and Xstrata Treetop Walkway, a 200-yard-long scenic steel catwalk that puts you high in the canopy 60 feet above the ground.

Antiques buffs, people-watchers, and folks who brake for garage sales love to haggle at London's street markets. There's good early-morning market activity somewhere every day of the week. There are markets for fish, fruit, used cars, antiques, clothing, and on and on. Portobello Road (shops open Mon-Sat; market Sat only 5:30 a.m.-5:00 p.m.) and Camden Lock (daily 10:00 a.m.-6:00 p.m.) are just two of the many colorful markets that offer great browsing. But don't expect great prices. These days, the only people getting a steal at London's markets are the pickpockets.

No visit to London is complete without enjoying a pint in a woody

pub. Pubs are an integral part of English culture. You'll find all kinds, each with its own personality. Taste the different beers. If you don't know what to order, ask the bartender for a half pint of his or her favorite. Real ale, pumped by hand from the basement (look for the longest handles on the bar), is every connoisseur's choice. For a basic American-type beer, ask for a lager. Teetotalers can get lemon-lime soda pop by asking for a "lemonade." Children are welcome in most pubs but won't be served alcohol until they turn 18. Order some pub grub and talk to the people. Enjoy a public house. By getting beyond the bobbies and beefeaters—by meeting the people—you see London take on a personality you can't capture on a postcard.

*For good-value accommodations in London's **Victoria Station neighborhood**, try Luna Simone Hotel (moderate, 47 Belgrave Road, tel. 020/7834-5897, www.lunasimonehotel.com). In **South Kensington**, stay at the Aster House (hotelesque splurge, 3 Sumner Place, tel. 020/7581-5888, www.asterhouse .com). Near **Kensington Palace**, consider the London Vicarage Hotel (moderate, 10 Vicarage Gate, tel. 020/7229-4030, www.londonvicaragehotel.com). For all the travel specifics, see this year's edition of* Rick Steves' London, Rick Steves' England, *or* Rick Steves' Great Britain.

Elegant and Frivolous Bath

Two hundred years ago, this city of 85,000 was the Hollywood of Britain. Today, the former trendsetter of Georgian England invites you to take the 90-minute train ride from London and sample its aristocratic charms. If ever a city enjoyed looking in the mirror, Bath's the one. It has more "government-listed" or protected buildings per capita than any town in England. The entire city, built of the creamy warm-tone limestone called "Bath stone," beams in its cover-girl complexion.

An architectural chorus line, Bath is a triumph of the Neoclassical style of the Georgian era, with buildings as competitively elegant as the society they once housed. If you look carefully, you'll see false windows built in the name of balance (but not used, in the name of tax avoidance) and classical columns that supported only Georgian egos. Two centuries ago, rich women wore feathered hats atop three-foot hairdos, and the very rich stretched their doors

Bath: Georgian on my mind

and ground floors to accommodate this high fashion. But today, many of the owners of these beautiful buildings can't afford to maintain them, so the soot of the last century remains on the extra-tall walls.

Bath's town square, a quick walk from the bus and train station, is a bouquet of tourist landmarks, including the Abbey, the Roman and medieval baths, the royal "Pump Room," and a Georgian flute player complete with powdered wig.

A good day in Bath starts with a tour of the historic baths. Even

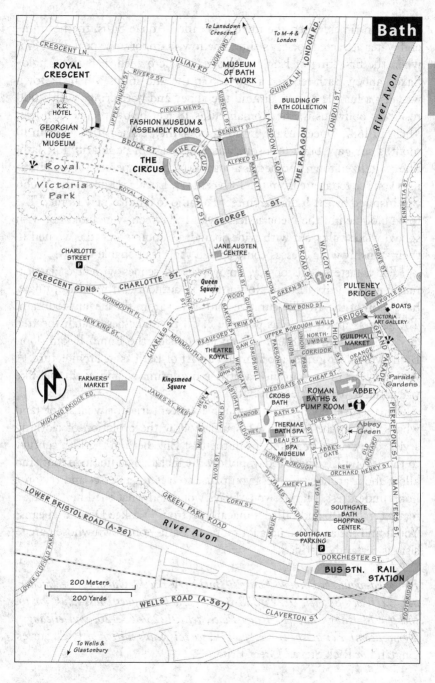

in Roman times, when the town was called Aquae Sulis, the hot mineral water attracted society's elite. The town's importance peaked in 973, when the first king of England, Edgar, was crowned in Bath's Anglo-Saxon abbey. Bath reached a low ebb in the mid-1600s, when the town was just a huddle of huts around the abbey and hot springs with 3,000 residents oblivious to the Roman ruins 18 feet below their dirt floors. Then, in 1687, Queen Mary, fighting infertility, bathed here. Within 10 months she gave birth to a son...and a new age of popularity for Bath. The revitalized town boomed as a spa resort. Ninety percent of the buildings you see today are from the 18th century. Local architect John Wood was inspired by the Italian architect Palladio to build a "new Rome." The town bloomed in the Neoclassical style, and streets were lined not with scrawny sidewalks but with wide "parades," upon which the women in their stylishly wide dresses could spread their fashionable tails.

For a taste of aristocracy, enjoy tea and scones with live classical music in the nearby Pump Room. For an authentic, if repulsive, finale, have a sip of the awfully curative Bath water from the elegant fountain. To make as much sense as possible of all this fanciness, catch the free city walking tour that leaves from just outside the Pump Room door. Bath's volunteer guides are as much a part of Bath as its architecture. A walking tour gives your visit a little more intimacy, and you'll feel like you actually have a friend in Bath.

In the afternoon, stroll through four centuries of what's hot (and what's not) in the Fashion Museum. Follow the evolution of clothing styles, one decade at a time, from the first Elizabeth in the 16th century to the second Elizabeth today. Follow the included audioguide tour, and allow about an hour—unless you pause to lace up a corset and try on a hoop underdress. Haven't you always wondered what the line, "Stuck a feather in his cap and called it macaroni," from "Yankee Doodle" means? You'll find the answer (and a lot more) in Bath—one town whose narcissism is certainly justified.

*For good-value accommodations in **Bath**, try Brocks Guest House (moderate, 32 Brock St., tel. 01225/338-374, www.brocksguesthouse.co.uk) or the cheaper 14 Raby Place (14 Raby Place, tel. 01225/465-120, murieljeanguy @gmail.com). For all the travel specifics, see this year's edition of* Rick Steves' England *or* Rick Steves' Great Britain.

York: Vikings, Bygone Days, and England's Top Church

Historians run around York like kids in a candy shop. But the city is so fascinating that even nonhistorians find themselves exploring the past

York's massive Minster

with the same delight they'd give a fun-house hall of mirrors.

York is 200 miles north of London (just two hours by train). For a practical introduction to the city, start your visit by taking one of the free, entertaining, and informative guided walking tours (leaving morning, afternoon, and summer evenings from Exhibition Square). To keep the day open for museums and shopping and enjoy a quieter tour (with a splash of ghostly gore), take the evening walk. The excellent guides are likeably chatty and opinionated. By the end of the walk, you'll know the latest York city gossip, several ghost stories, and what architectural "monstrosity" the "insensitive" city planners are about to inflict on the public.

With this introductory tour under your belt, you're getting the hang of York and its history. Just as a Boy Scout counts the rings in a tree, you can count the ages of York by the different bricks in the city wall: Roman on the bottom, then Danish, Norman, and the "new" addition—from the 14th century.

The pride of the half-timbered town center is the medieval butchers' street called the Shambles, with its rusty old hooks hiding under the eaves. Six hundred years ago, bloody hunks of meat hung here, dripping into the gutter that still marks the middle of the lane. This slaughterhouse of commercial activity gave our language a new word. What was once a "shambles" is now ye olde tourist shopping mall.

York's four major sights—the York Castle Museum, the Jorvik Viking Centre, the best-in-Europe National Railway Museum, and the huge and historic York Minster cathedral—can keep a speedy sightseer busy for two days.

Charles Dickens would feel right at home in York's Castle Museum. English memorabilia from the 18th, 19th and 20th centuries are cleverly displayed in a huge collection of craft shops, old stores, living rooms, and other intimate glimpses of bygone days.

As towns were being modernized in the 1930s, the museum's founder, Dr. Kirk, collected entire shops and reassembled them here. In Kirkgate, the museum's most popular section, you can wander through a Lincolnshire butcher's shop, Bath bakery, coppersmith's shop, toy shop, and barbershop.

The shops are actually stocked with the merchandise of the day. Eavesdrop on English grannies as they reminisce their way through the museum's displays. The general store is loaded with groceries and candy, and the sports shop has everything you'd need for a game of 19th-century archery, cricket, skittles, or tennis. Anyone for "whiff-whaff" (Ping-Pong)? In the confectionery, Dr. Kirk beams you into a mouth-watering world of "spice pigs," "togo bullets," "hum bugs," and "conversation lozenges."

Fiddling around old York

In the period rooms, three centuries of Yorkshire living rooms and clothing fashions paint a cozy picture of life centered around the hearth. Ah, a peat fire warming a huge brass kettle while the aroma of freshly baked bread soaks into the heavy, open-beamed ceilings. After walking through the evolution of romantic valentines and unromantic billy clubs, you can trace the development of early home lighting—from simple waxy sticks to the age of electricity. An early electric heater has a small plaque explaining, "How to light an electric fire: Switch it on!"

Dr. Kirk's "memorable collection of bygones" is the closest thing in Europe to a time-tunnel experience, except perhaps for the Jorvik Viking Centre just down the street.

A thousand years ago, York was a thriving Viking settlement called Jorvik (YOR-vik). While only traces are left of most Viking settlements, Jorvik is an archaeologist's bonanza, the best-preserved Viking city ever excavated.

If you sailed the "Pirates of the Caribbean" north several latitudes and back in time 1,000 years, you'd have Jorvik. More a ride than a museum, this exhibit drapes the abundant harvest of this dig in Disney cleverness. You'll ride a little people-mover for 12 minutes through the re-created Viking street of Coppergate. It's the year 975, and you're in

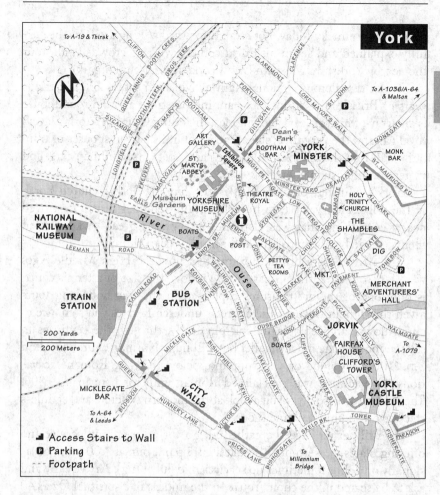

the village of Jorvik. Slowly glide through the reconstructed village. Everything—sights, sounds, even smells—has been carefully re-created. You experience a Viking village. Next, your time-traveling train rolls you through the actual excavation site, past the actual remains that inspired the reconstructed village. Stubs of buildings, piles of charred wood, broken pottery—a time-crushed echo of a once-thriving town. Everything is true to the original dig—even the face of one of the mannequins was computer-modeled from a skull dug up here.

Your ride ends at a gallery filled with artifacts from every aspect of Viking life: clothing, cooking, weapons, clever locks, jewelry, even children's games. The gift shop—the traditional finale of any English museum—capitalizes nicely on your newly developed fascination with Vikings in England (www.jorvik-viking-centre.co.uk).

Innovative 20 years ago, Jorvik and its cousins all over England seem tired and gimmicky today. For straightforward Viking artifacts, beautifully explained and set in historical context with no crowds at all, tour the nearby Yorkshire Museum (www.yorkshiremuseum.org.uk).

York's thunderous National Railway Museum shows 200 illustrious years of British railroad history. Fanning out from a grand roundhouse is an array of historic cars and engines, including Queen Victoria's lavish royal car and the very first "stagecoaches on rails." Even spouses of train buffs will find the exhibits on dining cars, post cars, Pullman cars, and vintage train posters interesting.

York's Minster, or cathedral, is the largest Gothic church north of the Alps. Henry VIII, in his self-serving religious fervor, destroyed nearly everything that was Catholic—except the great York Minster. Henry needed a northern capital for his Anglican church.

The Minster is a brilliant example of how the High Middle Ages were far from dark. The Great East Window, the size of a tennis court, is only one of the art treasures explained in the free hour-long tours given throughout the day. The church's undercroft gives you a chance to climb down, archaeologically and physically, through the centuries to see the roots of the much smaller but still huge Norman church (built in A.D. 1100) that stood on this spot and, below that, the Roman excavations. Constantine was proclaimed Roman emperor here in A.D. 306. The undercroft also gives you a look at the modern concrete and stainless steel save-the-church foundations.

To fully experience the cathedral, go for an evensong service (no offering plates, no sermon; Tue-Sat at 5:15 p.m., Sun at 4:00 p.m., occasionally on Mon, sometimes no services mid-July-Aug). Arrive early and ask to be seated in the choir. You're in the middle of a spiritual Oz as 40 boys sing psalms—a red-and-white-robed pillow of praise, raised up by the powerful pipe organ. You feel as if you have elephant-size ears, as the beautifully carved choir stalls—functioning as giant sound scoops—magnify the thunderous, trumpeting pipes. If you're lucky, the organist will run a spiritual musical victory lap as the congregation breaks up. Thank God for York. Amen.

For good-value accommodations in **York,** *try Abbeyfields Guest House (moderate, 19 Bootham Terrace, tel. 01904/636-471, www.abbeyfields.co.uk) or Airden House (moderate, 1 St. Mary's, tel. 01904/638-915, www.airden house.co.uk). For all the travel specifics, see this year's edition of* Rick Steves' England *or* Rick Steves' Great Britain.

Blackpool: Britain's Coney Island

For over a century, until the last generation, Blackpool—located on the coast north of Liverpool—was where the factory workers and miners

of Yorkshire and Lancashire spent their holidays. Working blokes took their families to this queen of North England resorts both for good fun for the kids and a bit of high-quality entertainment.

Cheap airfares to Spain have stolen most of its business, but Blackpool parties on. Tacky, tatty, and rundown, today's Blackpool is struggling to remain England's glittering city of fun.

British people flock to Blackpool to soak up the seaside resort's atmosphere.

It's ignored by American guidebooks, and many would say for good reason. But if you want to spend a day finding bits of old-time seaside elegance while dodging drunken hen-and-stag parties, this six-mile beach promenade affords a fascinating glimpse of an England few travelers experience.

When I told Brits I was Blackpool-bound, their expressions soured and they asked, "Oh, God, why?" My response: Because it's an ears-pierced-while-you-wait, tipsy-toupee place, offering a stale-beer look at lowbrow England at play.

Blackpool is dominated by the Blackpool Tower—a giant amusement center that seems to grunt, "Have fun." You pay about $27 to get in, and after that the fun is free. Work your way up through layer after layer of noisy entertainment: circus, bug zone, space world, dinosaur center, aquarium, and the silly house of horrors. The finale at the tip of this 518-foot-tall symbol of Blackpool is a smashing view, especially at sunset.

The tower's gilded ballroom, festooned with Old World elegance, is part of what makes Blackpool residents believe their town is worthy of a UNESCO world-heritage listing. A relay of organists keep pensioners waltzing, fox-trotting, and doing the tango below a banner proclaiming Shakespeare's invitation to dance, "Bid me discourse, I will enchant thine ear." Dancers, many of whom have been coming here regularly for fifty years, are happy to share an impromptu two-step lesson.

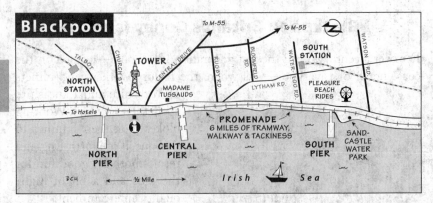

Hop a vintage trolley car to survey Blackpool's beach promenade. The cars, which rattle constantly up and down the waterfront, are more fun than driving. Each of the three amusement piers has its own personality. Are you feeling sedate (north pier), young and frisky (central pier), or like a cowboy dragging a wagon full of children (south pier)?

Stroll the Promenade. A million greedy doors try every trick to get you inside. Huge arcade halls advertise free toilets and broadcast bingo numbers into the streets. The randy wind machine under a wax Marilyn Monroe blows at a steady gale, and the smell of fries, tobacco, and sugared popcorn billows everywhere. Milk comes in raspberry or banana in this land where people under incredibly bad wigs look normal. I was told that I mustn't leave without having my fortune told by a Gypsy spiritualist, but, at $10 per palm, I'll read them myself.

Don't miss an evening at a play or an old-time variety show. Blackpool claims to be England's second-best theater town (after London) and always has a few razzle-dazzle music, dancing girl, racy humor, magic, and tumbling shows. I enjoy the "old-time music hall" shows. The shows are corny—neither hip nor polished—but it's fascinating to be surrounded by hundreds of partying British seniors, swooning again and waving their hankies to the predictable beat. Busloads of happy widows come from all corners of North England to giggle at racy jokes. A perennial favorite is *Funny Girls*, a burlesque-in-drag show that delights footballers and grannies alike.

Blackpool's "Illuminations" light up the night every year from early September through early November. Blackpool (the first city in England to switch on electric streetlights, in 1879) stretches its season by illuminating its six miles of waterfront with countless blinking and twinkling lights. The American inside me kept saying, "I've seen bigger and I've seen better," but I filled his mouth with cotton candy and just had some simple fun like everyone else on my specially decorated tram.

For a fun forest of amusements, Blackpool Pleasure Beach is tops. These 42 acres of rides (more than 125, including "the best selection of white-knuckle rides in Europe"), ice-skating shows, cabarets, and amusements attract seven million people a year, making Pleasure Beach one of England's most popular attractions. Its roller coasters include the Pepsi Max Big One, among the world's highest (235 feet), fastest (85 mph), and least likely to have me on board.

For me, Blackpool's top sight is its people. You'll experience England here like nowhere else. Grab someone's hand and a big baton of "rock" (rock candy), and stroll. Appreciate the noisy 20-somethings pulling down their pants to show off the new tattoos on their backsides. Ponder the horrible thought of actually retiring here and spending your last years dog-paddling through this urban cesspool of fun, wearing plaid pants and a bad toupee.

British people imagining sunshine at the beach in Blackpool

Blackpool is a scary thing to recommend. I probably overrate it. Many people (ignoring the "50 million flies can't all be wrong" logic) think I do. If you're not into kitsch and greasy spoons (especially if you're a nature lover and the weather happens to be good), skip Blackpool and spend more time in nearby North Wales or England's Lake District. But if you're traveling with kids—or still are one yourself—visit Blackpool, Britain's fun puddle: where so many Brits go, even if few will admit it.

*For good-value accommodations in **Blackpool**, try Beechcliffe Private Hotel (moderate, 16 Shaftesbury Ave., tel. 01253/353-075, www.beechcliffe.co.uk). For all the travel specifics, see this year's edition of* Rick Steves' England *or* Rick Steves' Great Britain.

Cotswold Villages: Inventors of Quaint

The Cotswold region, a 25-by-90-mile chunk of Gloucestershire, is a sightseeing treat: crisscrossed with hedgerows, raisined with storybook villages, and sprinkled with sheep.

As with many fairy-tale regions of Europe, the present-day beauty of the Cotswolds was the result of an economic disaster. Wool was a huge industry in medieval England, and the Cotswold sheep grew it best. Wool money built lovely towns and palatial houses as the region prospered. Local "wool" churches are called "cathedrals" for their scale and wealth. Stained-glass slogans say things like "I thank my God and ever shall, it is the sheep hath paid for all."

It's hard to go wrong in the Cotswolds.

With the rise of cotton and the Industrial Revolution, the wool industry collapsed, mothballing the Cotswold towns into a depressed time warp. Today visitors enjoy a harmonious blend of man and nature: the most pristine of English countrysides decorated with time-passed villages, gracefully dilapidated homes of an impoverished nobility, tell-me-a-story stone fences, and "kissing gates" you wouldn't want to experience alone. Appreciated by throngs of 21st-century romantics, the Cotswolds are enjoying new prosperity.

Towns are small, and everyone seems to know everyone. The area is provincial, yet ever so polite, and chatty residents commonly rescue themselves from a gossipy tangent by saying, "It's all very...ummm...yyya."

The north Cotswolds are best. Two of the region's coziest towns, Chipping Campden and Stow-on-the-Wold, are eight and four miles, respectively, from Moreton-in-Marsh, which has the best public transportation connections. Any of these three towns makes a fine home base for your exploration of the thatch-happiest of Cotswold villages and walks.

Chipping Campden is just touristy enough to be convenient. This market town, once the home of the richest Cotswold wool merchants, has some incredibly beautiful thatched roofs. Both the great British historian G. M. Trevelyan and I call Chipping Campden's High Street the finest in England.

Walk the full length of High Street (like most market towns, wide enough for plenty of sheep business on market days). On one end, you'll find impressively thatched homes. Walking north on High Street, you'll pass the 17th-century Market Hall, the wavy roof of the first great wool mansion, a fine and free memorial garden, and, finally, the town's famous 15th-century Perpendicular Gothic "wool" church.

Stow-on-the-Wold has become a crowded tourist town, but most

Imprisoned by the charm of the Cotswolds

visitors are day-trippers, so nights, even in summer, are peaceful. Stow has no real sights other than the town itself, some good pubs, antique stores, and cute shops draped seductively around a big town square. The tourist office sells a handy walking-tour brochure called *Town Trail*. A visit to Stow is not complete until you've locked your partner in the stocks on the green.

Moreton-in-Marsh, an easy home base for those without a car, is like Stow or Chipping Campden without the touristic sugar. Rather than gift and antique shops, you'll find streets lined with real shops: ironmongers selling cottage nameplates and carpet shops strewn with the remarkable patterns that decorate B&B floors. A shin-kickin' traditional market of 100-plus stalls fills High Street each Tuesday as it has for the last 400 years. The Cotswolds have an economy outside of tourism, and you'll feel it in Moreton.

Stanway, Stanton, and Snowshill, between Stow and Chipping Campden, are my nominations for the cutest Cotswold villages. Like marshmallows in hot chocolate, they nestle side by side—awaiting your arrival.

Stanway, while not much of a village, is notable for its manor house. The Earl of Wemyss, whose family tree charts relatives back to 1202, opens his melancholy home and grounds to visitors just two days a week in the summer ($11, June-Aug house open and 300-foot-tall fountain flows Tue and Thu only 2:00-5:00 p.m., tel. 01386/584-469, www.stanwayfountain.co.uk).

The 14th-century Tithe Barn predates the manor and was originally where monks, in the days before money, would accept one-tenth of whatever the peasants produced. While the Tithe Barn is no longer used to greet motley peasants with their feudal "rents," the lord still gets rent from his vast landholdings and hosts community fêtes in his barn.

The Earl of Wemyss opens his quirky and fascinating manor house to the public and personally greets his guests.

Stepping into the obviously very lived-in palace, you're free to wander pretty much as you like, but keep in mind that a family does live here. The place feels like a time warp. Ask the ticket-taker (inside) to demonstrate the spinning rent-collection table. In the great hall, marvel at the one-piece oak shuffleboard table and the 1780 Chippendale exercise chair (half an hour of bouncing on this was considered good for the liver).

The manor dogs have their own cutely painted "family tree," but the earl admits that his last dog, C. J., was "all character and no breeding." The place has a story to tell. And so do the docents stationed in each room—modern-day peasants who, even without family trees, probably have relatives going back just as far in this village. Really. Talk to these people. Probe. Learn what you can about this side of England.

Stanway and neighboring Stanton are separated by a row of oak trees and grazing land, with parallel waves echoing the furrows plowed by medieval farmers. Let someone else drive so you can hang out the window under a canopy of oaks as you pass stone walls and sheep.

In **Stanton,** flowers trumpet, door knockers shine, and slate shingles clap: a rooting section cheering visitors up the town's main street. The church, which probably dates back to the ninth century, betrays a pagan past. Stanton is at the intersection of two lines (called ley lines) connecting prehistoric sites. Churches such as Stanton's, built on a pagan holy ground, are dedicated to St. Michael. You'll see his well-worn figure above the door as you enter. Inside, above the capitals in the nave,

find the pagan symbols for the moon and the sun. But it's Son worship that's long established, and the list of rectors goes back to 1269. Finger the back pew grooves, worn away by sheepdog leashes. (A man's sheepdog accompanied him everywhere.)

Snowshill, another nearly edible little bundle of cuteness, has a photogenic triangular square with a characteristic pub at its base. Snowshill Manor is a dark and mysterious old palace filled with the lifetime collection of the long-gone Charles Paget Wade. It's one big, musty celebration of craftsmanship, from finely carved spinning wheels to frightening samurai armor to tiny elaborate figurines carved by long-forgotten prisoners from the bones of meat served at dinner. Taking seriously his family motto, "Let Nothing Perish," he dedicated his life and fortune to preserving things finely crafted. The house (whose management made me promise not to promote it as an eccentric collector's pile of curiosities) really shows off Mr. Wade's ability to recognize and acquire fine examples of craftsmanship. It's all very...ummm...yyya.

The Cotswolds are walkers' country. The English love to walk the peaceful footpaths that shepherds walked back when "polyester" meant two girls. They vigorously defend their age-old right to free passage. Once a year, the Ramblers, Britain's largest walking club, orga-

If you'd rather be riding, rent a horse.

nizes a "Mass Trespass," when each of England's 50,000 miles of public footpaths is walked. By assuring each path is used at least once a year, they stop landlords from putting up fences. Most of the land is privately owned and fenced in, but you're welcome (and legally entitled) to pass through, using the various sheep-stopping steps, gates, and turnstiles provided at each stone wall.

After a well-planned visit, you'll remember everything about the

Cotswolds—the walks, churches, pubs, B&Bs, thatched roofs, gates, tourist offices, and even the sheep—as quaint.

For good-value accommodations in **Chipping Campden**, *try Sandalwood House B&B (moderate, Back Ends, tel. 01386/840-091, sandalwoodhouse @hotmail.com); in* **Stow-on-the-Wold**, *Cross Keys Cottage (moderate, Park Street, tel. 01451/831-128, rogxmag@hotmail.com); and in* **Moreton-in-Marsh**, *Treetops B&B (London Road, tel. 01608/651-036, www.treetops cotswolds.co.uk). For all the travel specifics, see this year's edition of* Rick Steves' England *or* Rick Steves' Great Britain.

Mysterious Britain

Stonehenge, Holy Grail, Avalon, Loch Ness...there's a mysterious side of Britain steeped in lies, legends, and at least a little truth. Haunted ghost walks and Nessie the Monster stories are profitable tourist gimmicks.

But the cultural soil that gives us Beowulf, Shakespeare, and "God Save the Queen" is fertilized with a murky story that goes back to 3000 B.C., predating Egypt's first pyramids.

As today's sightseers zip from castle to pub, they pass countless stone circles, forgotten tombs, man-made hills, and figures carved into hillsides whose stories will never be fully understood.

Certain traveling druids skip the beefeater tours and zero right in on this side of Britain. With a little background, even the skeptic can appreciate Britain's historic aura.

Britain is crisscrossed by lines connecting prehistoric Stonehenge-type sights. Apparently prehistoric tribes intentionally built sites along this huge network of ley lines, which some think may have functioned together as a cosmic relay or circuit.

Glastonbury, two hours west of London and located on England's most powerful ley line, gurgles with a thought-provoking mix of history and mystery. As you climb the Glastonbury Tor, notice the remains of the labyrinth that made the hill a challenge to climb 5,000 years ago.

In A.D. 37, Joseph of Arimathea—Jesus' wealthy uncle—supposedly brought vessels containing the blood and sweat of Jesus to Glastonbury, and with them, Christianity to England. (Joseph's visit is plausible—long before Christ, residents traded lead to merchants from the Levant.) While this story is "proven" by fourth-century writings and accepted by the Church, the King-Arthur-and-the-Holy-Grail legends it inspired are not.

Those medieval tales came when England needed a morale-boosting folk hero to inspire its people during a war with France. They pointed to the ancient Celtic sanctuary at Glastonbury as proof of the greatness of the fifth-century warlord, Arthur. In 1911, his supposed remains (along with those of Queen Guinevere) were dug up from the abbey garden, and Glastonbury became woven into the Arthurian legends. Reburied in the abbey choir, their gravesite is a shrine today. Many think the Grail trail ends at the bottom of the Chalice Well, a natural spring at the base of Glastonbury Tor.

In the 16th century, Henry VIII, on his church-destroying rampage, wrecked the powerful Glastonbury Abbey. For emphasis, he hung and quartered the abbot, sending the parts of his body on four national tours...at the same time. While that was it for the abbot, two centuries later Glastonbury rebounded. In an 18th-century tourism campaign, thousands signed affidavits stating that water from the Chalice Well healed them, and once again Glastonbury was on the tourist map.

Today, Glastonbury and its tor are a center for searchers, too creepy for the mainstream church, but just right for those looking for a place to recharge their crystals. Since the society that built the labyrinth worshipped a mother goddess, the hill, or tor, is seen by many today as a Mother Goddess symbol.

After climbing the tor (great view, easy parking, always open), visit the Chalice Well at its base. Then tour the evocative ruins of the abbey, with its informative visitors center and a model of the church before Henry got to it. Don't leave without a browse through the town. The Rainbow's End café (two minutes from the abbey at 17 High Street) is a fine place for salads and New Age people-watching. Read the notice board for the latest on midwives and male bonding.

From Glastonbury, as you drive across southern England, you'll see giant figures carved on hillsides. The white chalk cliffs of Dover stretch across the south of England, and almost anywhere you dig you hit chalk. While most of the giant figures are creations of 18th- and 19th-century humanists reacting against the coldness of the Industrial Age, three Celtic figures (the Long Man of Wilmington, the White Horse of Uffington, and the Cerne Abbas Giant) have, as far as history is concerned, always been there.

The **Cerne Abbas Giant** is armed with a big club and an erection. For centuries, people fighting infertility would sleep on Cerne Abbas. And, as my English friend explained, "Maidens can still be seen leaping over his willy."

Cerne Abbas Giant: "Maidens can still be seen leaping over his willy."

Stonehenge, England's most famous stone circle, is an hour's drive from Glastonbury. Built in phases between 3000 and 1000 B.C. with huge stones brought all the way from Wales or Ireland, it still functions as a remarkably accurate celestial calendar. A study of more than 300 similar circles in Britain found that each was designed to calculate the movement of the sun, moon, and stars, and to predict eclipses in order to help early societies know when to plant, harvest, and party. Even in modern times, as the summer solstice sun sets in just the right slot at Stonehenge, pagans boogie. Modern-day tourists and druids are kept at a distance by a fence, but if you're driving, Stonehenge is just off the highway and worth a stop ($12). You must make an advance reservation (an extra $25) to enter the stone circle, but even a free look from the road is impressive.

Why didn't the builders of Stonehenge use what seem like perfectly adequate stones nearby? There's no doubt that the particular "blue stones" used in parts of Stonehenge were found only in (and therefore brought from) Wales or Ireland. Think about the ley lines. Ponder the fact that many experts accept none of the explanations of how these giant stones

Stonehenge is surrounded by a rope. This is as close as most visitors get.

were transported. Then imagine congregations gathering here 5,000 years ago, raising thought levels, creating a powerful life force transmitted along the ley lines. Maybe a particular kind of stone was essential for maximum energy transmission. Maybe the stones were levitated here. Maybe psychics really do create powerful vibes. Maybe not. It's as unbelievable as electricity used to be.

The nearby stone circle at **Avebury,** 16 times the size of Stonehenge,

is one-sixteenth as touristy. You're free to wander among 100 stones, ditches, mounds, and curious patterns from the past, as well as the village of Avebury, which grew up in the middle of this 1,400-foot-wide Neolithic circle.

Spend some time at Avebury. Take the mile-long walk around the circle. Visit the fine little archaeology museum and pleasant Circle Restaurant next to the National Trust store. The Red Lion Pub (also within the circle) has good, inexpensive pub grub. As you leave, notice the pyramid-shaped, 130-foot-high Silbury Hill. This man-made mound of chalk, more than 4,000 years old, is a reminder that you've only scratched the surface of Britain's fascinating prehistoric and religious landscape.

A fine way to mix Neolithic wonders and nature is to explore one of England's many turnstile-free moors. You can get lost in these stark and sparsely populated time-passed commons, which have changed over the centuries about as much as the longhaired sheep that seem to gnaw on moss in their sleep. Directions are difficult to keep. It's cold and gloomy, as nature rises like a slow tide against human constructions. A crumpled castle loses itself in lush overgrowth. A church grows shorter as tall weeds eat at the stone crosses and tilted tombstones.

Dartmoor is the wildest moor—a wonderland of green and powerfully quiet rolling hills in the southwest, near the tourist centers of Devon and Cornwall. Crossed by only two or three main roads, most of the area is either unused or shared by its 34,000 villagers as a common grazing land—a tradition since feudal days. Dartmoor is best toured by car, but it can be explored by bike, rental horse, thumb, or foot. Bus service is meager. Several national park centers provide maps and information. Settle into a small-town B&B or hostel. This is one of England's most remote corners—and it feels that way.

Dartmoor, with more Bronze Age stone circles and huts than any other chunk of England, is perfect for those who dream of enjoying their own private Stonehenge sans barbed wire, police officers, parking lots, tourists, and port-a-loos. Ordnance Survey maps show the moor peppered with bits of England's mysterious past. Down Tor and Gidleigh are especially thought-provoking.

Word of the wonders lurking just a bit deeper into the moors tempted me away from my B&B in Gidleigh. Venturing in, I sank into the powerful, mystical moorland. Climbing over a hill, surrounded by hateful but sleeping towers of ragged granite, I was swallowed up. Hills followed hills followed hills—green growing gray in the murk.

Where was that 4,000-year-old circle of stone? I wandered in a world of greenery, eerie wind, white rocks, and birds singing but unseen. Then the stones appeared, frozen in a forever game of statue-maker. For endless centuries they had waited patiently, still and silent, for me to come.

I sat on a fallen stone as my imagination ran wild, pondering the people who roamed England so long before written history documented their story. Grabbing the moment, I took out my journal. The moor, the distant town, the chill, this circle of stones. I dipped my pen into the cry of the birds to write.

*For good-value accommodations in **Dartmoor**, try Easton Court (moderate, just east of Chagford, tel. 01647/433-469, www.easton.co.uk). For all the travel specifics, see this year's edition of* Rick Steves' England.

IRELAND

The Dingle Peninsula: A Gaelic Bike Ride

Be forewarned: Ireland is seductive. In many areas, traditions are strong and stress is a foreign word. I fell in love with the friendliest land this side of Sicily. It all happened in the *Gaeltacht*—an area of traditional culture where the government protects the old Irish ways. Shaded green on many maps, this cultural region is fragmented into geographical areas that fringe the west coast of the Emerald Isle. *Gaeltacht* means a place where Irish (or Gaelic) is spoken. But Irish culture is more than just the ancient language. You'll find it tilling the rocky fields, singing in the pubs, and lingering in the pride of the small-town preschool that brags "all Irish." Signposts are in Irish only, with many in the old Irish lettering. If your map is in English...good luck. Modern Irish yuppies report that the old Irish language is cool and on the rise.

The Dingle Peninsula—green, rugged, and untouched—is my favorite *Gaeltacht*. (In 2005 the government dictated that Dingle use its Gaelic handle, An Daingean, which you may see on some signs. But most tourist information, and nearly everyone there—locals and tourists alike—still refers to it as Dingle.) While the big tour buses clog the neighboring Ring of Kerry before heading east to kiss the Blarney Stone, in Dingle it still feels like the fish and the farm actually matter. Twenty fishing boats sail from Dingle. And a nostalgic whiff of peat continues to fill its nighttime streets, offering visitors an escape into pure Ireland. For more than 30 years, my Irish dreams have been set here, on this sparse but lush peninsula where residents are fond of saying, "The next parish is Boston."

Of the peninsula's 10,000 residents, 1,500 live in Dingle town (An Daingean). Its few streets, lined with ramshackle but gaily painted shops and pubs, run up from a rain-stung harbor. During the day, teenagers—already working on ruddy beer-glow cheeks—roll kegs up the streets and into the pubs in preparation for another tin-whistle night.

Fishing once dominated Dingle, and the town's only visitors were students of old Irish ways. Then, in 1970, the movie *Ryan's Daughter* introduced the world to Dingle. The trickle of its fans grew to a flood, as word spread of its musical, historical, gastronomical, and scenic charms—not to mention Fungie the friendly dolphin, who hangs out in the harbor.

The Dingle Peninsula Circle—By Bike or Car

The Dingle Peninsula is 10 miles wide and 41 miles long, from Tralee to Slea Head (Ceann Sleibhe in Gaelic). The top of its mountainous spine is Mount Brandon—at 3,130 feet, the fourth-tallest peak in Ireland.

While only tiny villages lie west of Dingle town, the peninsula is home to half a million sheep. The weather on this distant tip of Ireland is often misty, foggy, and rainy. Good and bad weather blow by in a steady meteorological parade. With stops, the 30-mile circuit (go with the traffic, clockwise) takes five hours by bike or three hours by car.

Enjoy the Emerald Isle on two wheels.

Leaving Dingle town, it becomes clear that the peninsula is an open-air museum. It's littered with monuments reminding visitors that the town has been the choice of Bronze Age settlers, Dark Age monks, English landlords, and Hollywood directors. In the front yard of the Milestone B&B what could be an ancient border marker has stood there since the time of the Celts—one of more than 2,000 stony pieces in the puzzle of prehistoric life here.

Across the bay, the manor house of Lord Ventry is surrounded by palms, magnolias, fuchsias, and fancy flora introduced to Dingle by the Englishman who once owned the peninsula. His legacy—thanks only to the mild, Gulf Stream-protected weather—is the fuchsias that line the

Dingle: Before Tourism and After

I love envisioning towns the way they were before tourism and the modern world brought prosperity. Dingle town, on the once-bleak southwest tip of Ireland, is now more upscale. Ireland, long one of Europe's poorest corners, became one of its richest during the "Celtic Tiger" economic boom from the mid-1990s to the mid-2000s (until the economic downturn hit it hard). These days, towns are painted a rainbow of pastels (which tourists think are traditional), and residents no longer make soil from sand and seaweed in order to grow their potatoes.

peninsula roads. And just down the road, locals point to the little blue house that once kept Tom Cruise and Nicole Kidman cozy during the filming of *Far and Away*.

Near a two-room schoolhouse, a street sign warns *Taisteal go Mall*—slow down. Near the playground, students hide out in circular remains of a late Stone Age ring fort. In 500 B.C., it was a petty Celtic chieftain's headquarters—a stone-and-earth stockade filled with little stone houses. So many of these ring forts survived the centuries because of superstitious beliefs that they were "fairy forts."

In the little town of Ventry (Ceann Tra'), talk with the chatty Irish you'll meet along the roadside. I once met an elfish, black-clad old man here. When I asked if he was born here, he breathed deeply and said, "No, 'twas about six miles down the road." When I told him where I was from, a faraway smile filled his eyes as he looked out to sea and sighed, "Aye, the shores of Americay."

The wet sod of Dingle is soaked with medieval history. In the darkest depths of the Dark Ages, when literate life almost died in Europe, peace-loving, bookwormish monks fled the chaos of the Continent and

Dingle Peninsula Loop Trip

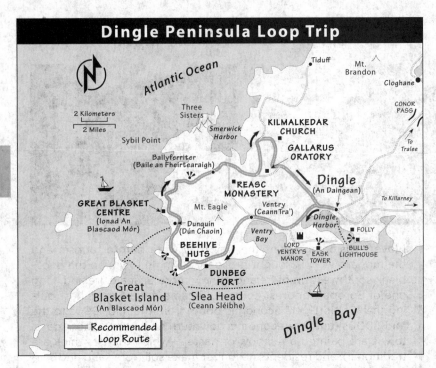

its barbarian raids. They sailed to this drizzly fringe of the known world and lived their monastic lives in lonely stone igloos or "beehive huts," which you'll see dotting the landscape.

Several groups of these mysterious huts, called *clochans*, line the road. Built without mortar by seventh-century monks, these huts take you back. Climb into one. You're all alone, surrounded by dank mist and the realization that it was these monks who kept literacy alive in Europe. To give you an idea of their importance, Charlemagne, who ruled much of Europe in the year 800, imported Irish monks to be his scribes.

It was from this peninsula that St. Brendan, the semi-mythical priest-explorer, is said to have set sail in the sixth century in search of a legendary western

The Irish seem to have all the time in the world to share craic *(conversation) with you.*

paradise. Some think he beat Columbus to North America...by almost a thousand years!

Rounding Slea Head, the point in Europe closest to America, the rugged coastline offers smashing views of deadly black-rock cliffs and the distant Blasket Islands (Na Blascaodai). The crashing surf races in like white horses, while long-haired sheep—bored with the weather, distant boats, and the lush countryside—couldn't care less.

Just off the road you'll see the scant remains of the scant home that was burned by the movie-star equivalent of Lord Ventry as he evicted his potato-eating tenants in the movie *Far and Away*.

Ireland's top attraction—the friendliest people in Europe

Even without Hollywood, this is a bleak and godforsaken place. Sand and seaweed heaped on the clay eventually became soil. The land created was marginal, just barely growing potatoes. Ragged patches of this reclaimed land climb the hillsides. Rocks were moved and piled into fences.

Stacks of history can be read into the stones. From the air, Ireland looks like alligator skin—a maze of stone fences. With unrivaled colonial finesse, the British required Irish families to divide their land among all heirs. This doomed even the largest estates to fragmentation, shrinking lots to sizes just large enough to starve a family. Ultimately, of course, the land ended up in the possession of British absentee landlords. The tiny rock-fenced lots that carve up the treeless landscape remind the farmers of the structural poverty that shaped their history. And weary farmers have never bothered with gates. Even today they take a hunk of wall down, let their sheep pass, and stack the rocks again.

Study the highest fields, untouched since the planting of 1845, when the potatoes never matured and rotted in the ground. You can still see the vertical ridges of the potato beds—a reminder of that year's Great Potato Famine, which eventually, through starvation or emigration, cut Ireland's population by one-quarter.

Take your time at the Gallarus Oratory (c. A.D. 700)—the sightseeing highlight of your peninsula tour. One of Ireland's best-preserved early Christian churches, its shape is reminiscent of an upturned boat. Its watertight dry-stone walls have sheltered travelers and pilgrims for 1,300 years.

From the oratory, continue up the rugged one-lane road to the crest of the hill, then coast back into Dingle—hungry, thirsty, and ready for...

The enduring Gallarus Oratory

Dingle Pubs

Dingle is a pub-crawl waiting to happen. Even if you're not into pubs, give Dingle's a whirl. The town is renowned among traditional musicians as a place to get work ("€40 cash a day plus drink"). There's music most nights and with nary a cover charge. The scene is a decent mix of locals, Americans, and Germans. While two pubs—the Small Bridge Bar (An Droichead Beag) and O'Flaherty's—are the most famous for their atmosphere and devotion to traditional Irish music, make a point to wander the town and follow your ear.

When you say "a beer, please" in an Irish pub, you'll get a pint of "the tall blonde in the black dress"—Guinness. If you want a small beer, ask for a half pint. Never rush your bartender when he's pouring a Guinness. It takes time—almost sacred time. If you don't normally like Guinness, try it in Ireland; it doesn't travel well and is better in its homeland. Murphy's is a very good Guinness-like stout, but a bit smoother and milder.

The Irish government passed a law in 2004 making all pubs and restaurants in the Republic smoke-free; Northern Ireland followed in 2007. (Hotels, however, can still have designated smoking rooms.) Smokers now take their pints outside, turning alleys into covered smoking patios. An incredulous Irishman responded

On a Dingle evening, follow your ear to a music-filled pub.

to the law by saying, "What will they do next? Ban drinking in pubs? We'll never get to heaven if we don't die."

In an Irish pub, you're a guest on your first night; after that, you're a regular. Women traveling alone need not worry—you'll become part of the pub family in no time.

It's a tradition to buy your table a round, and then for each person to reciprocate. If an Irishman buys you a drink, thank him by saying, "*Go raibh maith agat*" (guh-rev-mah-a-gut). Offer him a toast in Irish— "*Slainte!*" (slahn-chuh). A good excuse for a conversation is to ask to be taught a few words of Irish. You've got a room full of native speakers who will remind you that every year, 10 languages go extinct. They'd love to teach you a few words of their favorite language.

Craic (pronounced "crack") is the art of conversation—the sport that accompanies drinking in a pub. People are there to talk. Join in. Ireland—small as it is—has many dialects. People from Cork (the big city of Ireland's south coast) are famous for talking very fast (and in a squeaky voice)...so fast that some even seem to talk in letters alone. Those from Kerry are famous for being a bit out of it. One joke goes that when the stupidest man in county Cork moved to county Kerry, it raised the average IQ in both areas.

Traditional Irish Music

Traditional music is alive and popular in pubs throughout Ireland. "Sessions" (musical evenings) may be planned and advertised or impromptu. Traditionally, musicians just congregate and play. There's generally a fiddle, flute or tin whistle, guitar, *bodhrán* (goat-skin drum), and maybe an accordion. Things usually get going around 9:30 and the "last call" (last chance to order a drink before closing) is around "half eleven" (11:30 p.m.), sometimes later on weekends.

The *bodhrán* is played with two hands: one wielding a small two-headed club and the other stretching the skin to change the tone and pitch. The wind and string instruments embellish melody lines with lots of improvised ornamentation. Occasionally the fast-paced music will stop, and one person will sing a lament in a slightly nasal style called *shan nos* (Gaelic for "old style"). This is the one time when the entire pub will stop to listen, as sad lyrics fill the room. Stories—ranging from struggles against English rule to tragic love songs—are always heartfelt. Spend a lament studying the faces in the crowd.

The music comes in sets of three songs. Whoever happens to be leading determines the next song, only as the song the group is playing is about to be finished. If he wants to pass on the decision, it's done with eye contact and a nod.

A session can be magic, or it can be lifeless. If the chemistry is right, it's one of the great Irish experiences. The music churns intensely while the group casually enjoys exploring each others' musical styles. The drummer dodges the fiddler's playful bow. Sipping their pints, they skillfully maintain a faint but steady buzz. The floor on the musicians' platform is stomped paint-free, and barmaids scurry artfully through

Irish pubs—a blur of banjo pickin', flute tootin', great beer, and new friends

the commotion, gathering towers of empty, cream-crusted glasses. With knees up and heads down, the music goes round and round. Make yourself right at home, "playing the boot" (tapping your foot) under the table in time with the music.

Great Blasket Island (An Blascoad Mór)

Great Blasket (An Blascoad Mór in Gaelic), a rugged, uninhabited island off the tip of Dingle Peninsula, seems particularly close to the

Ghost town on Great Blasket Island

soul of Ireland. Its population, once as many as 160 people, dwindled until the last handful of residents was moved by the government to the mainland in 1953. These people were one of the most traditional Irish communities of the 20th century—symbols of an antique culture. They had a special closeness to their island, combined with a knack for vivid storytelling. From this poor, simple, but proud fishing and farming community came three writers of international repute whose works—basically tales of life on the island—are translated into many languages. In shops all over the peninsula, you'll find *Peig* (by Peig Sayers), *Twenty Years A-Growing* (Maurice O'Sullivan), and *The Islandman* (Tomás O'Crohan).

Today, Great Blasket is a grassy three-mile poem, overrun with memories. With fat rabbits, ruffled sheep, abandoned stone homes, and a handful of seals, it's ideal for windblown but thoughtful walks.

A ferry runs hourly, depending on weather and demand, from Dunquin, at the tip of the Dingle Peninsula, to Great Blasket (10:30 a.m.-4:30 p.m., but not in winter). Scenic, two-hour Blasket Island circuit cruises leave from Dunquin Harbor. Boats also depart from Dingle town several times a day in summer.

Before visiting the islands, stop at the state-of-the-art Great Blasket Centre (Ionad An Blascaod Mór, on Dingle Peninsula facing the islands, tel. 066/915-6444). This center creatively gives visitors the best possible look at the heritage, language, literature, life, and times of Blasket islanders. See the fine video, hear the sounds, read the poems, browse through old photos, and then gaze out the big windows at those rugged islands and imagine. Even if you never got past limericks, the poetry of these people—so pure and close to each other and nature—is an inspiration.

For good-value accommodations in **Dingle**, *try Bambury's Guesthouse (splurge, Mail Road, tel. 066/915-1244, www.bamburysguesthouse.com) or the simpler Sráid Eoin House (moderate, John Street, tel. 066/915-1409, www.sraideoinbnb.com). For all the travel specifics, see this year's edition of* Rick Steves' Ireland.

Northern Ireland and Belfast

Ireland is a split island still struggling with questions left over from its stint as a British colony. While the island won its independence back in the 1920s, the predominantly Protestant northern section opted to stick with its Pope-ophobic partners in London. While somewhere between a headache and a tragedy for locals, this adds up to some fascinating travel opportunities for you and me. And recent history has given everyone some good, solid reasons to be hopeful.

With so many people working so hard to bring Ireland together, a browse through Belfast will give you more faith in people than despair over headlines. The peace process jolted forward in 2010, when British Prime Minister David Cameron issued a surprisingly forthright apology for the British Army's actions during the infamous 1972 Bloody Sunday incident, in which unarmed civilians were shot.

Make your visit to Ireland complete by including Northern Ireland. This is a British-controlled six-county section of a nine-county area called Ulster. It offers the tourist a very different but still very Irish world. The British-ruled counties of Northern Ireland, long a secret enjoyed and toured mainly by the country's own inhabitants, are finally being recognized by international travelers.

Today tourists in Northern Ireland are no longer considered courageous (or reckless). When locals spot you with a map and a lost look on your face, they're likely to ask, "Wot yer lookin fer?" in their distinctive Northern accent. They're not suspicious of

With this Union Jack bulldog street mural, a Belfast Protestant neighborhood makes its Unionist feelings pit-bull clear.

you, but trying to help you find your way. You're safer in Belfast than in any other UK city—and far safer than in most major US cities. You have to look for trouble to find it here. Just don't seek out spit-and-sawdust pubs in working-class neighborhoods to talk politics.

Include Belfast in your Irish travel plans. Here's an itinerary that will introduce you to this capital city and Ireland's best open-air folk museum. At the same time, you'll meet some of the friendliest people in Europe and learn firsthand about their struggle.

Belfast

Seventeenth-century Belfast was only a village. With the influx, or "plantation," of Scottish and English settlers, Belfast boomed, spurred by the success of the linen, rope-making, and shipbuilding industries. The Industrial Revolution took root with a vengeance. While the rest of Ireland remained rural, Belfast earned its nickname, "Old Smoke," when many of the brick buildings you'll see today were built. The year 1888 marked the birth of modern Belfast. After Queen Victoria granted city status to this town of 300,000, citizens built its centerpiece, City Hall.

Belfast is the birthplace of the *Titanic*—and many other ships that didn't sink. In 2012—to mark the 100th anniversary of the Titanic disaster—a modern new attraction opened in Belfast's shipyard, telling the ill-fated ship's fascinating and tragic story. Nearby, two huge, mustard-colored cranes (the biggest in the world, nicknamed Samson and Goliath) rise like skyscrapers above the harbor. They stand idle now, but serve as a reminder of this town's former shipbuilding might.

Despite the economic downturn, it feels like a new morning in Belfast. It's hard to believe that the bright and bustling pedestrian center

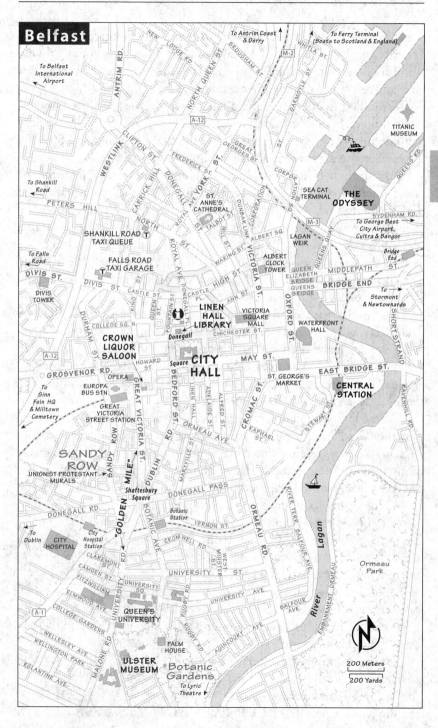

Belfast

To Antrim Coast & Derry

To Ferry Terminal (Boats to Scotland & England)

To Belfast International Airport

TITANIC MUSEUM

NEW LODGE RD.

ANTRIM RD.

NORTH QUEEN ST.

BROUGHAM ST.

WHITLA ST.

GARMOYLE ST.

QUEENS RD.

CLIFTON ST.

FREDERICK ST.

GREAT GEORGES ST.

To Shankill Road

WESTLINK

CARRICK HILL

DONEGALL ST.

ROYAL AVE.

YORK ST.

CORPORATION ST.

SEA CAT TERMINAL

THE ODYSSEY

PETERS HILL

ST. ANNE'S CATHEDRAL

SYDENHAM RD.

To George Best City Airport, Cultra & Bangor

SHANKILL ROAD TAXI QUEUE

NORTH ST.

TALBOT ST.

HILL ST.

DUNBAR LINK

ALBERT SQ.

LAGAN WEIR

To Falls Road

FALLS ROAD TAXI GARAGE

WARING ST.

VICTORIA ST.

ALBERT CLOCK TOWER

QUEEN ELIZABETH BRIDGE

MIDDLEPATH ST.

Bridge End

DIVIS ST.

DIVIS ST.

CASTLE ST.

KING ST.

QUEEN ST.

HIGH ST.

ANN ST.

QUEENS BRIDGE

QUEENS QUAY

BRIDGE END

DIVIS TOWER

DURHAM ST.

FOUNTAIN ST.

DONEGALL PL.

LINEN HALL LIBRARY

VICTORIA SQUARE MALL

OXFORD ST.

WATERFRONT HALL

To Stormont & Newtownards

COLLEGE SQ. N.

CHICHESTER ST.

SHORT STRAND

CROWN LIQUOR SALOON

Donegall Square

CITY HALL

MAY ST.

EAST BRIDGE ST.

RAVENHILL RD.

GROSVENOR RD.

HOWARD ST.

OPERA

ST. GEORGE'S MARKET

CENTRAL STATION

To Sinn Fein HQ & Milltown Cemetery

EUROPA BUS STN.

GREAT VICTORIA STREET STATION

GREAT VICTORIA ST.

BEDFORD ST.

ORMEAU AVE.

LINEN HALL ST.

ADELAIDE ST.

ALFRED ST.

CROMAC ST.

RAPHAEL ST.

STEWART ST.

SANDY ROW

Unionist Protestant Murals

SANDY ROW

"GOLDEN MILE"

DUBLIN RD.

Shaftesbury Square

DONEGALL PASS

MARYVILLE ST.

ORMEAU RD.

RIVER Lagan

DONEGALL RD.

Botanic Station

VERNON ST.

To Dublin

CITY HOSPITAL

City Hospital Station

CROMWELL RD.

UNIVERSITY ST.

WESTMINSTER ST.

Ormeau Park

CLAREMONT ST.

CAMDEN ST.

FITZWILLIAM ST.

UNIVERSITY RD.

UNIVERSITY SQ.

RUGBY RD.

UNIVERSITY AVE.

AGINCOURT AVE.

BALFOUR AVE.

RIVER Lagan

EMBANKMENT ORMEAU

ELMWOOD AVE.

COLLEGE GARDENS

A-1

QUEEN'S UNIVERSITY

MALONE RD.

WELLESLEY AVE.

WELLINGTON PARK

ULSTER MUSEUM

PALM HOUSE

Botanic Gardens

To Lyric Theatre

EGLANTINE AVE.

200 Meters

200 Yards

N

was once a subdued, traffic-free security zone. Now there's no hint of security checks, once a tiresome daily routine. These days both Catholics and Protestants are rooting for the Belfast Giants ice-hockey team, one of many reasons to live together peacefully.

Still, it's a fragile peace and a tenuous hope. Mean-spirited murals, hateful bonfires built a month before they're actually burned, and pubs with security gates are reminders that the island is split...and 800,000 Protestant Unionists prefer it that way.

A visit to Belfast is easy from Dublin. Consider this plan for the most interesting Dublin-Belfast day trip: With the handy two-hour Dublin-Belfast train ($64 "day-return" tickets, pricier on weekends), you can leave Dublin early and catch the Belfast City Hall tour at 11 a.m. After browsing through the pedestrian zone, ride a shared black taxi (see below) through the Falls Road neighborhood. At 3:00 p.m., head out to the Ulster Folk and Transport Museum in Cultra. Picnic on the evening train back to Dublin.

The well-organized day-tripper will get a taste of both Belfast's Industrial Age glory and its recent Troubles. It will be a happy day when the sectarian neighborhoods of Belfast have nothing to be sectarian about. For a look at a couple of the original home bases of the Troubles, explore the working-class neighborhoods of Falls Road (Catholic) and Shankill Road or Sandy Row (Protestant).

At the intersection of Castle and King Streets, you'll find the Castle Junction Car Park. This nine-story parking garage's basement (entrance on King Street) is filled with old black cabs—and the only Irish-language signs in downtown Belfast. These shared black cabs efficiently shuttle residents from outlying neighborhoods up and down the Falls Road and to the city center. All cabs go up the Falls Road to Milltown Cemetery, passing lots of murals and the head-quarters of Sinn Fein (the Irish Republican Army's political wing). Sit in front and talk to the cabbie. Easy-to-flag-down cabs run every minute or so in each direction on Falls Road. Forty trained cabbies also do one-hour tours (www.taxitrax.com).

At the Milltown Cemetery, walk past all the Gaelic crosses down to the far right-hand corner (closest to the highway), where the IRA Roll of Honor is set apart from the thousands

Murals reinforce political walls.

of other graves by little green railings. They are treated like fallen soldiers. Notice the memorial to Bobby Sands and nine other hunger strikers. They starved themselves to death in the nearby Maze prison in 1981, protesting for political prisoner status as opposed to terrorist criminal treatment. The prison closed in 2000.

The Sinn Fein office and bookstore are near the bottom of Falls Road. The bookstore is worth a look. Page through books featuring color photos of the political murals that decorate the buildings. Money raised here supports the families of deceased IRA members.

A sad corrugated structure called the Peace Wall runs a block or so north of the Falls Road (along Cupar Way), separating the Catholics from the Protestants in the Shankill Road area. This is just one of 17 such walls in Belfast.

While you can ride a shared black cab through the Protestant Shankill Road area (leave from North Street near the intersection with Millfield Road), the easiest way to get a dose of the Unionist side is to walk Sandy Row—a working-class-Protestant street behind the Hotel Europa (said to be Europe's most-bombed hotel). From Hotel Europa, walk a block down Glengall Street, then turn left for a 10-minute walk along a working-class Protestant street. A stop in the Unionist memorabilia shop, a pub, or one of the many cheap eateries here may give you an opportunity to talk to a local. You'll see a few murals filled with Unionist symbolism. The mural depicting William of Orange's victory over the Catholic King James II (Battle of the Boyne, 1690) stirs Unionist hearts.

Most of Ireland has grown disillusioned with the violence wrought by the IRA and the Protestants' Ulster Volunteer Force (UVF). They are now seen by many as having evolved into rival groups of gangsters who actually work together, Mafia-style, to run free and wild in their established territories.

Maybe the solution can be found in the mellowness of Ulster retirement homes, where old "Papishes" with their rosaries and old "Prods" with their prayer books sit side by side talking to the same heavenly father. But that kind of peace is elusive. An Ulster Protestant on holiday in England once told me with a weary sigh, "Tomorrow I go

Children march in a Protestant Orange parade: Political differences are taught at an early age.

IRELAND

back to my tribe."

For a trip into a cozier age, take the eight-mile train ride to the 180-acre Ulster Folk and Transport Museum at Cultra. The Folk Museum is an open-air collection of 34 reconstructed buildings from all over the nine counties of Ulster, designed to showcase the region's traditional lifestyles. After wandering through the old town site (church, print shop, schoolhouse, humble Belfast row home, and so on), you'll head into the country to nip into cottages, farmhouses, and mills. Many houses are warmed by peat fires and friendly attendants. The museum can be dull or vibrant, depending upon your ability to chat with the people staffing each building.

The adjacent Transport Museum (downhill, over the road from the folk museum) traces the evolution of transportation from its beginning 7,500 years ago, when someone first decided to load up an ox, and continues to the present, with an interesting exhibit on the sinking of the Belfast-made *Titanic*, expanded for the 100th anniversary of its sinking. In the next two buildings, you roll through the history of bikes, cars, and trains. The car section goes from the first car in Ireland (an 1898 Benz), through the "Cortina Culture" of the 1960s, to the adventures of John DeLorean (with a 1981 model of his sleek sports car).

Speeding on the train back to Dublin, gazing at the peaceful and lush Irish countryside while pondering DeLorean, the *Titanic*, and the Troubles, your illusion of a fairy-tale Europe has been muddled. Belfast is a bracing dose of reality.

*For good-value accommodations in **Belfast**, try Malone Guest House (moderate, 79 Malone Road, tel. 028/9066-9565, www.maloneguesthousebelfast .com) or Jurys Inn (moderate, Fisherwick Place, tel. 028/9053-3500, www .jurysinns.com). For all the travel specifics, see this year's edition of Rick Steves' Ireland.*

SCANDINAVIA

Norway in a Nutshell: Oslo and the Fjords

Oslo is the smallest of the Nordic capitals, but this brisk little city is a scenic *smörgåsbord* of history, sights, art, and Nordic fun. As an added bonus, you'll be inspired by a city that simply has its act together. Add on a "Norway in a Nutshell" excursion over the mountains and to the fjords, and this is potentially one of Europe's best three-day packages of sightseeing thrills.

I am always struck by how peaceful Oslo feels. A congestion fee keeps most cars out of the town center, while underground tunnels take nearly all the rest under the city. The old train station facing the fjord boat landing is now the Nobel Peace Center, which explains the unique vision of Alfred Nobel: the inventor of dynamite who dedicated his fortune to the celebration of peacemakers. The brick City Hall—where the prize is awarded—towers high above the harbor action. On every visit, matching memories from my childhood trips here, I see a

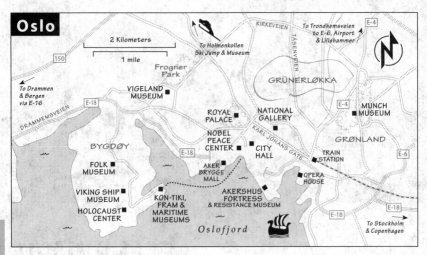

Oslo

2 Kilometers
1 mile
150
To Drammen & Bergen via E-16
E-18
DRAMMEMSVEIEN
BYGDØY
FOLK MUSEUM
VIKING SHIP MUSEUM
HOLOCAUST CENTER
KON-TIKI, FRAM & MARITIME MUSEUMS
Oslofjord
To Holmenkollen Ski Jump & Museum
Frogner Park
VIGELAND MUSEUM
ROYAL PALACE
NOBEL PEACE CENTER
AKER BRYGGE MALL
CITY HALL
AKERSHUS FORTRESS & RESISTANCE MUSEUM
KIRKEVEIEN
TÅSENVEIEN
GRÜNERLØKKA
NATIONAL GALLERY
KARL JOHANS GATE
To Trondhemsveien to E-6, Airport & Lillehammer
E-4
MUNCH MUSEUM
GRØNLAND
TRAIN STATION
OPERA HOUSE
E-6
E-18
To Stockholm & Copenhagen
E-4
E-4

weather-beaten sailor standing at the stern of his boat, hoping to sell the last of the shrimp he caught before sunrise.

On May 17, Norway's national holiday, Oslo bursts with flags, bands, parades, and pride. Blond toddlers are dressed up in colorful ribbons, traditional pewter buckles, and wool. But Oslo—surrounded by forests, near mountains, and on a fjord—has plenty to offer the visitor year-round.

Oslo's most popular sights tell an exciting story of Viking spirit. From the City Hall, hop the ferry for the 10-minute ride to Bygdøy. This cluster of sights reflects the Norwegian mastery of the sea. Some of Scandinavia's best-preserved Viking ships are on display here. Rape, pillage, and plunder were the rage 1,000 years ago in Norway. There was a time when much of a frightened Western Europe closed every prayer with, "And deliver us from the Vikings, amen." Gazing up at the prow of one of those sleek, time-stained vessels, you can almost hear the shrieks and smell the armpits of those redheads on the rampage.

Nearby, Thor Heyerdahl's balsa raft, *Kon-Tiki,* and the polar ship *Fram* illustrate Viking energy channeled in more productive directions. The *Fram,* serving both Nansen and Amundsen, ventured farther north and south than any other ship.

Just a harpoon toss away is Oslo's huge open-air Norwegian Folk Museum. The Scandinavians were leaders in the development of these cultural parks, which are now popular throughout Europe. More than 150 historic log cabins and buildings from every corner of the country are gathered together on 35 acres. Inside each house, a person in traditional garb is happy to answer questions about life in that part of Norway. Don't miss the 1,000-year-old wooden-stave church.

The place is lively only June through mid-August, when buildings are open and staffed. (Otherwise the indoor museum is fine, but the park is just a walk past lots of locked-up log cabins.) On summer Sundays, you'll enjoy a music-and-dance show at 2:00 p.m. (mid-May-mid-Sept only). If you don't take a tour, glean information from the $2 guidebook and the informative attendants ($20, daily mid-May-mid-Sept 10:00 a.m.-6:00 p.m.; shorter hours off-season; www.norskfolkemuseum.no).

You can also visit Oslo's 700-year-old Akershus Fortress. Its fascinating Nazi-resistance museum shows how one country's spirit cannot be crushed, regardless of how thoroughly it's occupied by a foreign power. The castle itself is interesting only with a guided tour (www.mil .no/felles/ak).

Oslo's avant-garde City Hall, finished in 1950, was a communal effort of Norway's greatest artists and designers. Tour the interior. More than 2,000 square yards of bold, colorful murals are a journey through the collective mind of modern Norway. City halls, rather than churches, are the dominant buildings in this your-government-loves-you northern corner of Europe. The main hall of the City Hall actually feels like a temple to good government—the altar-like mural celebrates "work, play, and civic administration." Each December, the Nobel Peace Prize is awarded in this room.

Norway has given the world two outstanding modern artists: Edvard Munch (pronounced "monk") and Gustav Vigeland. Oslo's Munch Museum is a joy. It's small, displaying an impressive collection of one man's work, rather than numbing you with art by countless artists from countless periods. You leave the Munch Museum feeling like you've learned something about one artist, his culture, and his particular artistic "ism"—expressionism. Happily, Munch's famous *Scream*, stolen from

Norwegian art in Oslo's Frogner Park

this museum in 2004, was recovered two years later. You can see another version of *Scream* at Oslo's centrally located National Gallery.

Thirty years of Gustav Vigeland's creativity—in the form of 192 bronze and granite sculptures—are featured at Oslo's Frogner Park. The centerpiece is the 46-foot-tall totem pole of tangled bodies known as the *Monolith of*

Life. This, along with the neighboring Vigeland Museum, is a must on any list of Oslo sights.

When the sun's out, all of Oslo's parks are packed. Norwegians are avid sun-worshippers, and a common ailment here is *"solsting"* (a fun twist on sunburn). American visitors will notice a lot of nudity: topless women and naked kids. Scandinavia has a casual approach to nudity. (I'm not talking just mixed saunas. Many Americans are amazed at what's on prime-time TV here.) Parents let their kids run naked in city parks and fountains. It's really no big deal. My friend tells me, "If you ever end up in a Norwegian hospital and need an X-ray, I hope you're not modest. Women strip to the waist and are casually sent from the doctor's office down the hall past the waiting public to the X-ray room. No one notices...no one cares." Norwegians are quick to point out the irony that while America goes into a tizzy over a goofy "wardrobe malfunction," or a president who had a hard time keeping his zipper up, it's the US that statistically has the biggest problem with sex-related crimes.

While traditional Oslo sightseeing is contained in the monumental and classically Norwegian city center, a short walk takes you to the city's two trendy multiethnic zones: Grünerløkka and Grønland.

Grünerløkka—with its funky shops, old hippies, and bohemian cafes—is the Greenwich Village of Oslo. In the 19th century, it was a planned working-class neighborhood. As the factories faded, the low rents attracted artistic types. They injected a creative and edgy ambience to the district, which in turn attracted young professionals looking to spice up their lives. Eventually the prices will rise too high, and the creative types who gave the area its color in the first place will be forced out. Today, Grünerløkka is still enjoying the alternative crowd...but its bohemian days are numbered.

Bordering Grünerløkka is Oslo's rough-and-tumble immigrant zone—a stretch of a street called Grønland. It's a hit with locals and tourists because this is where Turks, Indians, Pakistanis, and the rest of Oslo's growing immigrant community congregate. Over a quarter of the city's residents are not ethnic Norwegians. These new Norwegians provide a much-needed and generally appreciated labor force.

Oslo's entrepreneurial immigrants also have opened wonderful ethnic restaurants—literally adding spice to the otherwise pretty drab local cuisine. Colorful greengrocers' carts spill onto sidewalks, and the various kebabs and spicy *börek*—about $4 to go—make the cheapest meals in town. Dueling tandoori restaurants actually offer meals for under $15—unheard of in Oslo, which has been called Europe's most expensive city. I'll buy that. Norwegians cope with the high cost of dining out with the *engangsgrill* ("one-time grill"). These foil grills—which cost about $4 at a supermarket—are all the rage. On balmy evenings, the city is perfumed with the smoky fragrance of one-time grills as the parks fill up with Norwegians eating out on the cheap.

Without relatives, life in Oslo on a budget is possible only if you have a good guidebook and take advantage of money-saving options. Budget tricks like picnicking and sleeping in private homes offer the most exciting savings in this most expensive city.

One Day for the Fjords?

If you go to Oslo and don't get out to the fjords, you should have your passport revoked. Norway's greatest claim to scenic fame is its deep and

lush fjords. Sognefjord, Norway's longest (120 miles) and deepest (more than a mile), is tops. Anything but Sognefjord is, at best, foreplay. This is it: the ultimate natural thrill Norway has to offer.

For the best one-day look at fjords, do "Norway in a Nutshell." This series of well-organized train, ferry, and bus connections lays this most beautiful fjord country before you on a scenic platter. Ambitious and energetic travelers can see the whole shebang in a day; with more time or less energy,

Norway's Sognefjord

consider an overnight in Bergen (or along the fjord).

Every morning, northern Europe's most spectacular train ride leaves Oslo at about 8:00 a.m. for Bergen. Cameras smoke as this train roars over Norway's mountainous spine. The barren, windswept heaths, glaciers, deep forests, countless lakes, and a few rugged ski resorts create a harsh beauty. The railroad is an amazing engineering feat. Completed in 1909, it's 300 miles long and peaks at 4,266 feet—which, at this Alaskan latitude, is far above the tree line. You'll go under 18 miles of snow sheds, over 300 bridges, and through 200 tunnels in just less than seven hours (about $260 one-way, second-class railpass-holders pay $10 to reserve, reservations required; in peak season—July through August—book several weeks in advance).

At Myrdal, a 12-mile spur line ($50 one-way, or $35 with a railpass) drops you 2,800 breathtaking feet in 55 minutes to the village of Flåm on Sognefjord. This is a party train. The engineer even stops the train for

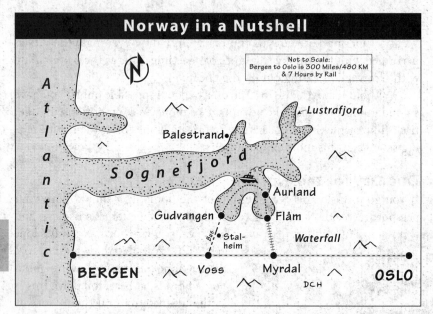

photographs at a particularly picturesque waterfall.

While most "Norway in a Nutshell" tourists zip immediately from the train onto the scenic fjord boat in Flåm, those with time enjoy an overnight stop on the fjord.

Flåm is a handy tourist depot with several simple hotels. Aurland, a few miles north of Flåm, is more of a town. It's famous for producing some of Norway's sweetest *geitost*—goat cheese. Aurland has as many goats as people (1,900). Nearly every train arriving in Flåm connects with a bus or boat to Aurland, also on Sognefjord. While nearby Bergen is famous for its rain—more than six feet a year—Sognefjord is a relative sun belt, with only two feet of rain a year.

The train from Myrdal to Flåm is quite scenic, but the ride doesn't do the view justice. For the best single-day activity from Flåm, take the train to Berekvam (halfway back up to Myrdal), then hike or bike (rentable from the Flåm tourist office) the gravelly construction road back down to Flåm. Bring a picnic and extra camera batteries.

From Flåm, "Nutshellers" catch the most scenic of fjord cruises. Sightseeing boats leave throughout the day ($53 one-way, discounts with a student card). For 90 minutes, camera-clicking tourists scurry on the drool-stained deck like nervous roosters, scratching fitfully for a photo to catch the magic. Waterfalls turn the black-rock cliffs into a bridal fair. You can nearly reach out and touch the sheer, towering walls. The ride is one of those fine times, like being high on the tip of an Alp, when a warm camaraderie spontaneously combusts among the strangers who came together for the experience. The boat takes you up one narrow arm (Aurlandsfjord) and down the next (Nærøyfjord) to the nothing-to-stop-for town of Gudvangen, where waiting buses ($16) shuttle you back to the main train line at Voss. From Voss, return to Oslo or carry on into Bergen for a short evening visit.

Bergen, Norway's second city and historic capital, is an entertaining place. You can finish the day there by browsing the touristy but fun wharf area, or zipping up the funicular to the top of 1,000-foot-tall "Mount" Fløyen for city and fjord views, before spending the night in Bergen—or, for maximum efficiency, catching the overnight train back to Oslo. Back in Oslo's station, as you yawn and stretch and rummage around for a cup of morning coffee, it'll hit you: You were gone for 24 hours, experienced the fjord wonder of Europe, and saw Bergen to boot.

For good-value accommodations in **Oslo,** *try Thon City Hotel Stefan (splurge, Rosenkrantz Gate 1, tel. 23 31 55 00, www.thonhotels.no/stefan) or Oslo Budget Hotel (budget, Prinsens Gate 6, tel. 22 41 36 10, www.budgethotel .no). Sleep cozy near the palace at Ellingsen's Pensjonat (moderate, Holtegata 25, tel. 22 60 03 59, www.ellingsenspensjonat.no). For all the travel specifics, see the latest edition of* Rick Steves' Scandinavia.

Ærø: Denmark's Ship-in-a-Bottle Island

Few visitors to Scandinavia even notice Ærø, a sleepy, 6-by-22-mile island on the southern edge of Denmark. Ærø has a salty charm. Its tombstones are carved with such sentiments as: "Here lies Christian Hansen at anchor with his wife. He'll not weigh until he stands before God." It's a peaceful and homey island, where baskets of strawberries

sit in front of farmhouses—for sale on the honor system.

Ærø's capital, Ærøskøbing, makes a fine home base. Temple Fielding called it "one of five places in the world that you must see." Many Danes agree, washing up on the cobbled main drag in waves with the landing of each ferry. The town's preservation is mandated by law.

Main Street, Ærøskøbing

Ærøskøbing is a town-in-a-bottle kind of place. Wander down lanes right out of the 1680s, when the town was the wealthy home port to more than 100 windjammers. The post office dates to 1749, and cast-iron gaslights still shine each evening. Windjammers gone, the harbor now caters to German and Danish holiday yachts. On midnight low tides, you can almost hear the crabs playing cards.

A warm and traditional welcome awaits you at an old-fashioned Danish country inn.

The Hammerich House, full of old junk, is a 1900s garage sale of a museum open daily in summer. The Bottle Peter Museum is a fascinating house with a fleet of more than 750 different bottled ships. Old Peter Jacobsen died in 1960 (and is probably buried in a glass bottle), leaving a lifetime of his tedious little creations for visitors to squint and marvel at.

Touring Ærø by car is like sampling chocolates with a snow shovel. It's much better to enjoy a breezy 15-mile tour of Ærø's subtle charms by bike. Borrow a bike from your hotel or rent one from Pilebækkens Cykler at the top of town, and bring a map. Note that this can be a strenuous ride if you're unused to cycling.

Ready? Leave Ærøskøbing west on the road to Vrå, going past many of the U-shaped farms that are typical of this island. The three sides block the wind and are used for storing cows, hay, and people. *Gaard* (farm) shows up in many surnames. Bike along the coast in the protection of the dike, which turned the once-salty swampland to your left into farmable land. Pedal past a sleek modern windmill and Borgnæs, a pleasant cluster of mostly modern summer cottages. (At this point, bikers with one-speeds can shortcut directly to Vindeballe.)

After passing a secluded beach, climb uphill over the island's summit

Ærø's "night watchman" offers spirited tours of his quaint little burg.

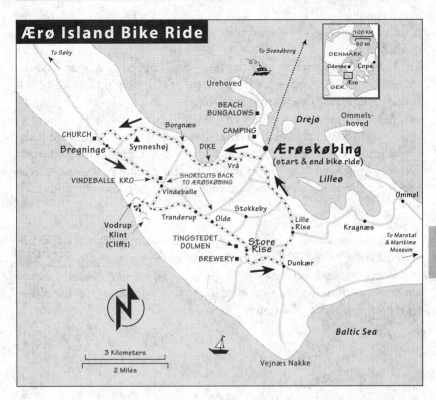

Ærø Island Bike Ride

To Søby

To Svendborg

Urehoved

DENMARK

Odense • Cope.

Ærø

GER.

100 KM

50 MI

BEACH
BUNGALOWS

Borgnæs

CHURCH

Bregninge

Synneshøj

CAMPING

DIKE

Vrå

Drejø

Ommels-
hoved

Ærøskøbing

(start & end bike ride)

VINDEBALLE KRO

SHORTCUTS BACK
TO ÆRØSKØBING

Vindeballe

Lilleø

Ommel

Tranderup

Vodrup
Klint
(Cliffs)

Olde

TINGSTEDET
DOLMEN

Stokkeby

Lille
Rise

Kragnæs

Store
Rise

To Marstal
& Maritime
Museum

BREWERY

Dunkær

3 Kilometers

2 Miles

Baltic Sea

Vejnæs Nakke

to Bregninge. Unless you're tired of thatched and half-timbered cottages, turn right and roll through Denmark's "second-longest village" to the church. Peek inside. Then roll back through Bregninge, head a mile down the main road to Vindeballe, and take the Vodrup turnoff to the right.

A road leads downhill to dead-end at an ancient site on a rugged bluff called Vodrup Klint. If I were a pagan, I'd stop here to worship. Savor the sea, the wind, and the chilling view.

Backtrack and pedal to Tranderup, past a lovely farm and a potato stand. At the old town of Olde, you'll hit the main road. Turn right toward Store Rise—marked by its church spire in the distance. Just behind the church is a 6,000-year-old Neolithic burial place, the Langdysse (Long Dolmen) Tingstedet. Hunker down. Ærø once had more than 200 of these. Only 13 survive.

Inside the Store Rise church, notice the little ships hanging in the nave, the fine 12th-century altarpiece, and Martin Luther in the stern making sure everything's theologically shipshape.

Continue down the main road passing the church. Consider a stop at the microbrewery, built on the site of an 1884 dairy. Wing by the hopeful forest of modern windmills whirring on your right and continue to Dunkær.

For the homestretch, take the small road, signed *Lille Rise,* past the topless windmill. Except for "Lille Rise," it's all downhill as you coast home past great sea views to Ærøskøbing.

After a power tour of big-city Scandinavia, Ærø offers a perfect time-passed island on which to wind down, enjoy the seagulls, and pedal a bike into the essence of Denmark. After a break in this cobbled world you may understand the sailors who, after the invention of steam-driven boat propellers, decided that building ships in bottles was more their style.

For good-value accommodations in Ærø, try Pension Vestergade (moderate, Vestergade 44, tel. 62 52 22 98, www.vestergade44.com) or Det Lille Hotel (moderate, Smedegade 33, tel. 62 52 23 00, www.det-lille-hotel.dk). For all the travel specifics—including a more thorough description of the bike ride— see the latest edition of Rick Steves' Scandinavia.

A EUROPEAN SAMPLER

Offbeat Europe

No one planning a trip to Europe needs to be reminded to see Big Ben and the Leaning Tower. But did you know that you can spelunk the sewers of Paris, quaff homebrewed beer with German monks, or ski in Scotland in summer? It's these unexpected experiences that are often the most memorable part of a trip. Here are a few that I've especially enjoyed writing home about.

Salzburg's Super-Soaker Prince: Salzburg's 17th-century Hellbrunn Castle entertains with a garden full of trick fountains and tour guides sadistically soaking tourists. At the touch of a button, paths (and pedestrians) get doused and benches turn into fountains. It's silly fun, especially with kids on a sunny day ($13, closed Nov-mid-March, www.hellbrunn.at).

Belgium's Little Squirt: For more dribbling diversions, stop by Brussels' *Manneken-Pis*,

a statue of a young boy urinating, and the irreverent mascot of this great Belgian city. You'll find this little squirt three blocks off the main square, La Grand Place. He'll probably be aiming through some clever outfit—by tradition, costumes for the lad are sent to Brussels from around the world. Go figure. Cases displaying scores of these colorful getups are on display in Brussels' City Museum.

Frankfurt's Red Light Towers: Near Frankfurt's central station, people killing time between trains can visit one of about 20 "Eros Towers"—each a five-story brothel filled with hookers. Frankfurt's prostitutes,

Belgium's little squirt

who are legal and taxed, note that business varies with the theme of the trade show at the nearby convention center. While Frankfurt's annual auto show is boom time, hookers complain that the world's largest annual book fair is a complete bust. (No, I'm not a customer.) Beware—drug addicts and pushy barkers make this neighborhood feel unsafe after dark.

Europe's Skinniest Park: Paris' skinny, two-mile-long Promenade Plantée Park is a narrow garden walk on a viaduct once used for train

A sliver of a park slices through downtown Paris.

tracks. The elevated park, which cuts through lots of modern condos, gives a fun peek into the workaday lives of Parisians today. Staircases lead to the street level, where artsy, offbeat shops (whose rent is subsidized by the city government) fill the viaduct's arches. The park runs from Place de la Bastille, along Avenue Daumesnil to Saint-Mandé.

Skiing in Edinburgh: If you'd rather be skiing, the Midlothian Ski Centre, just outside Edinburgh, has an artificial brush-skiing hill with a chairlift, two slopes, a jump slope, and rentable ski gear (www.midlothian.gov.uk). While you're actually skiing over what seems like a million toothbrushes, it feels like snow skiing on a slushy day. It's open nearly year-round (call to confirm before showing up, probably closed when it snows). Beware: Doctors are used to treating an ailment called "Hillend Thumb"—digits dislocated when people fall and get tangled in the brush.

The Tide Went Out and Never Came Back: Holland is twice as big today as it was 300 years ago. Why? Because the Dutch have been "reclaiming" land from the sea using dikes and windmill-powered pumps. During the process, many tiny islands—home to traditional fishing villages—were stranded high and dry in the middle of Dutch farmland. The fishing village of Schokland, once on an island in the Zuider Zee, is one such village. The village has a now-useless lighthouse, and you can walk right up to a buoy that once bobbed in the harbor. A bent and rusty propeller from a WWII Allied bomber is displayed just outside the museum...a reminder that when farmers first tilled their new soil, they uncovered more than just muck and mollusks.

Roman Pyramid: You don't need to go to Egypt to see an ancient

Pyramid power in Rome

pyramid. Standing 90 feet tall, Rome's pyramid was built in 12 B.C. as a tomb for the Roman Gaius Cestius, after the Cleopatra and Mark Antony scandal brought exotic Egyptian styles into vogue. Later the pyramid was incorporated into Rome's city wall.

Rome's Fake Dome: Rome's St. Ignazio church (near the Pantheon) is a riot of Baroque illusions. As you walk into the church, admire the dome. Keeping your eyes on the dome, walk under and past it. It's false. When the church was built, a nearby mon-

astery didn't want its light blocked by a huge dome, so the flat roof was instead skillfully painted to look like a dome.

The Original Ice Man: The South Tirol Museum of Archaeology in Bolzano, Italy, is an excellent museum. It features "Ötzi the Ice Man," a 5,300-year-old body found frozen with his gear in a glacier by some German hikers in 1991. With the help of informative displays and a great audioguide, you'll learn about life in this prehistoric period way before ATMs. You'll see a

Boning Up on Europe's Relics

Centuries ago, relics were an important focus of worship. These holy relics, often bones, were the "ruby slippers" of the medieval age.

They gave you power—got your prayers answered and helped you win wars—and ultimately helped you get back to your eternal Kansas.

The bones of monks were venerated, and sometimes even artistically arranged in crypts and chapels. In **Rome's** Capuchin Crypt, hundreds of skeletons decorate the walls to the delight—or disgust—of the always wide-eyed visitor. The crypt offers unusual ideas in home decorating, as well as a chance to pick up a few of Rome's most interesting postcards. A similar Capuchin Crypt is a highlight of many visits to **Palermo** in Sicily. In **Évora,** Portugal, osteophiles make a pilgrimage to the macabre "House of Bones" chapel at the Church of St. Francis, lined with the bones of thousands of monks.

Cappuccin monks have a thought-provoking habit of hanging their dead brothers out to dry for all to see...for ever and ever, amen.

Overcrowding in cemeteries has prompted unusual solutions. Austria's tiny town of **Hallstatt** is crammed between a mountain and a lake. Space is so limited that bones get only 12 peaceful buried years in the church cemetery before making way for the newly dead. The result is a fascinating chapel of bones in the cemetery. Each skull is lovingly named, dated, and decorated, with the men getting ivy, and the women, roses. Hallstatt stopped this practice in

convincing reconstruction of Ötzi, and yes, you will actually get to see the man himself—lying peacefully inside a specially built freezer ($13, www.iceman.it).

Choco-Sightseeing: Along with its rich culture, Europe is loved for its delicious chocolate. All day long, rivers of molten chocolate work their way through factories into small foil packages. While chocolate factories generally give tours only to clients or groups, many have museums, showrooms, video presentations, and free tasting rooms where visitors

Head to Hallstatt's Bone Chapel.

the 1960s, about the same time the Catholic Church began permitting cremation.

Kutná Hora's ossuary, an hour by train from Prague, is decorated with the bones of 40,000 people, many of them plague victims. The monks who stacked these bones 400 years ago wanted viewers to remember that the earthly church is a community of both the living and the dead. Later bone-stackers were more into design than theology—creating, for instance, a chandelier made with every bone in the human body.

Some cities, such as Paris and Rome, have catacombs. Many cities opened up a little extra space by de-boning graveyards, which used to surround medieval churches. During the French Revolution, **Paris** experienced a great church cemetery landgrab. Skeletons of countless Parisians were dug up and carefully stacked along miles of tunnels beneath the city.

Seekers of the macabre can bone up on Europe's more obscure ossuaries, but any tourist will stumble onto bones and relics. Whether in a church, chapel, or underground tunnel in Europe, you might be surprised by who's looking at you, kid.

Kutná Hora's ossuary, decorated Early Ghoulish

A EUROPEAN SAMPLER

are welcome. Chocoholics love the Imhoff Chocolate Museum in Köln. Their self-proclaimed "Mmmuseum" takes you on a well-described-in-English tour from the origin of the cocoa bean to the finished product. You can see displays on the culture of chocolate and watch treats trundle down the conveyor belt in the functioning chocolate factory, the museum's highlight. The top floor's exhibit of chocolate advertising is fun. Sample sweets from the chocolate fountain, or take some home from the fragrant choc-full gift shop ($11, www.schokoladenmuseum.de).

Skinny-Dipping in Downtown Munich: Munich's Central Park, the Englischer Garten, offers a variety of offbeat things to explore. Up to 300,000 residents commune with nature here on a hot summer day...many of them buck naked. Nudism, denoted by the code letters "F.K.K." (Freikörperkultur, free body culture), is perfectly legal and widely practiced here. It's quite a spectacle to most Americans (they're the ones riding their bikes into the river and trees).

Well-Fed Geese: At various farms in France's Dordogne region, you can watch *la gavage:* farmers force-feeding geese to fatten up their livers for the local specialty, foie gras. In a kind of peaceful, mesmerizing trance, the farmer rhythmically grabs a goose by the neck, pulls him under his leg and stretches him up, slides a tube down to the belly, and fills it with corn. He pulls the trigger to squirt the corn, slowly slides the tube up the neck and out, holds the beak shut for a few seconds, lets that goose go, and grabs the next. As their livers swell, the geese take on a special shape—like they're waddling around with a full diaper under their feathers (a mouthwatering symbol for foie gras fanatics). While some people consider this treatment inhumane, the farmers have their own perspective: The free-range geese are calm, in no pain, and have an expandable liver and no gag reflex. They ask: Are these geese really any worse off than the many hormone-fed farm animals slaughtered after living in cages?

Munich's English Garden offers more than nude sunbathing. Surfers "hang ten" in the rapids of the city's little river.

Foie gras in the making

Monk Brewers: Imagine a fine Bavarian Baroque church at a monastery that serves hearty food and perhaps the country's best beer, in a carnival setting full of partying Germans. That's the Andechs monastery, crouching happily between two lakes at the foot of the Alps, just south of Munich. Come ready to eat tender chunks of pork, huge soft pretzels, spiraled white radishes, and savory sauerkraut, and to drink Andecher monk-made beer—so good that it would almost make celibacy tolerable. Everything is served in medieval portions; two people can split a meal. Andechs has a fine picnic center offering first-class views and second-class prices (tel. 08152/3760, www.andechs.de). From Munich without a car, take the S-8 train to Herrsching and catch a sporadic shuttle bus or taxi, or hike three miles. Don't leave before strolling up to see the church.

A Swiss Urban River Promenade: In Bern, join the merchants, students, and carp in a lunchtime float down the Aare River. The Bernese, proud of their health and their clean river, have a wet tradition. On hot summer days, they hike upstream and float back down to the excellent (and free) riverside baths and pools *(Aarebad)* just below the Parliament building. While the locals make it look easy, this can be dangerous—the current is swift. If you miss the last pole, you're history. If the river is a bit much, you're welcome to enjoy just the pools, and watch this fast-flowing fun from the sidelines.

If you miss the last pole, you're history.

Paris' Historic Sewers: In Paris, the Sewer Tour takes you along a few hundred yards of an underground water tunnel, lined with interesting displays, well-described in English, that explain the evolution of the world's longest sewer system. Flush hard: If you lined up Paris' sewers end to end, they would reach beyond Istanbul ($6, closed Thu-Fri, located where Pont de l'Alma greets the Left Bank).

The Peat Spa of Třeboň: The small Czech town of Třeboň is famous for its spa, where people come from near and far to soak in peat. Immersed in a *One Flew Over the Cuckoo's Nest* ambience, patrons are ushered to a changing cubicle, strip naked, then climb into a big steel tub. The peat muck only flows

at the top of the hour, when the attendant pulls a plug and you quickly disappear under a rising sea of dark-brown peat broth...like a gurgling sawdust soup. When finished, you shower and lie facedown (in what feels like a nurse's office with a pile of dirty sheets stacked in the corner) for a vigorous massage. You walk out with your shirt stuck to your skin by a mucky massage cream...wondering what soaking in that peat soup was supposed to accomplish (tel. 384-754-457, www.berta.cz, sestra @berta.cz).

Swiss Military Readiness: Travelers marvel at how Swiss engineers have conquered their Alps with the world's most-expensive-per-mile road system. But no one designs a Swiss bridge or tunnel without designing its destruction. Each comes with built-in explosives so that, in the event of an invasion, the entire country can be blasted into a mountain fortress. When driving, notice ranks of tank barriers lined up like giant Tic-Tacs along strategic roadsides. As you approach each summit, look for the explosive patches ominously checkering the roads.

In Switzerland, fake barns hide guns and underground shelters.

But the Swiss are realizing that the cost of maintaining their strategic defense initiative is no longer justified. In fact, many of the country's 15,000 secret underground military installations are being decommissioned, and some are being opened to the public as museums.

The Fortress Fürigen Museum of War History offers a rare glimpse into Swiss military preparedness. This little country dug some 20,000 bunkers into the sides of the Alps—and the Festung Fürigen, built during World War II, is one of the few open to the public. Tour the kitchen, hospital, dorms, and machine-gun nests ($6, April-Oct open to public weekends only, tel. 041-618-7340, www.nidwaldner-museum .ch). It's in Stansstad on Lake Luzern, a 15-minute train ride from Luzern.

Ride the Luge: The *Sommerrodelbahn* ("summer toboggan run") is one of the most exhilarating alpine experiences. Speed demons spend entire summer days riding chairlifts up in order to "luge" down the concrete bobsled courses on oversize skateboards. You sit with a brake stick between your legs. Push to go fast. Pull to stop. Luge courses are normally open daily in the summer from roughly 9:00 a.m. to 5:00 p.m., and each ride costs $5-10. The course banks on the corners, and even a first-timer can go very, very fast. Most are careful on their first run and really rip on their second. To avoid a slow-healing souvenir, keep both hands on your stick. You'll rumble, windblown and smile-creased, across the finish line with one thought on your mind—"Do it again!"

You've got several luge options. In the French mountain resort of Chamonix, at the base of Mount Blanc, two concrete courses run side by side (the slow one marked by a tortoise and the fast one marked by a hare). In Austria, south of Salzburg on the road to Hallstatt, you'll pass two metal courses: one near Wolfgangsee (scenic with grand lake views) and one at Fuschlsee (half as long and cheaper).

In Germany and Austria, near "Mad" King Ludwig's Neuschwanstein Castle, you'll find two courses. One is in Austria, just beyond Biberwier (under Zugspitze, Germany's tallest mountain); the Biberwier Sommerrodelbahn is the longest in Austria at 4,000 feet. And just a mile from Neuschwanstein is Germany's Tegelberg course—because it's metal rather than concrete, it's often open when the other course has closed at the least sprinkle of rain.

Head for the hills, or go underground. Anywhere in Europe, the offbeat sights are a fun way to get some distance from the crowds and lighten up a heavy-duty museum itinerary.

The Flavors of Europe

In my quest to experience Europe as the locals do—intimately and on all fronts—I make a point to eat well. In a given year, I'm lectured by a Belgian woman who tells me that the guts are the absolute best part of a crab. I crunch into the cartilage of a prized plate of pigs' ears on a

back street in Madrid. And I pay a ransom for barnacles, gathered at great risk by teams of divers off the coast of Galicia in northwest Spain. (How do you eat barnacles? With a simple twist, rip, and bite.) Eating well wherever I go, I find my budget survives and my trip is always the better for it. While each country vies for my favor, France and Italy contribute most to my noticeably expanding waistline.

To fully enjoy the art of eating in France, my daughter Jackie and I decide to take an all-day class with a renowned Parisian cook. We prowl through the market with her, gather the needed ingredients, cook it all up in her kitchen, and (of course) devour the delicious fruits of our labor...all spiced with lots of tips, philosophy, and attitude.

When it comes to cuisine, there's no false modesty among French chefs. Our chef cooks with strong principles: "In France, we love fat because fat is where the flavor is...never cook with a wine you wouldn't drink...in America, you just don't have a great leek culture...it's always a good thing to let your meat rest, you know...water is the friend of the enemy...pat your pears."

Wandering with her from shop to shop and through a bustling market, we learn plenty: Baking and pastry are separate arts; a chef can't do both well. (Go to a *boulangerie* for bread, and a *patisserie* for pastry.) Fish shops need to indicate how the fish was caught: *pêché en* means fished rather than farmed; *élevé en* is "raised" on a fish farm. Poultry sold with the head attached is a sign of freshness.

My favorite discovery: a bottle of Fleur de Sel, the top crust of hand-harvested sea salt (generally from Brittany). This grappa of salt—which you sprinkle by the pinch—is $10 very well spent.

After Jackie flies home, I continue my dogged quest for great-yet-affordable taste treats on the road—this time by working on the restaurant listings in my Paris guidebook.

Restaurateurs dazzle me with their cooking: gizzard salads, made of fresh greens with rich kidneys and gizzards; crêpes, where something magic happens to Emmentaler cheese when it's cooked in all that butter; escargot, with a hot plate to keep the sauce steamy for dipping the crunchy bread into the garlic.

I experience high-class eating with Dominique—as fragile and elegant as her petite restaurant—who forces me to empathize with those force-fed geese by force-feeding *me* the foie gras. And I enjoy quality food at budget prices in a Greek restaurant with plastic tables. I ask, "Do you have yogurt with honey?" They say, "Sure, we're Greek," and bring me a bowl that takes me straight to Santorini.

In Paris, you can't escape the desserts: the ritual cracking of the caramelized crust of a crème brûlée...the tangy peach sorbet drenched in liqueur that you lap up like a thirsty puppy...and plates of pastel mini-macaroons (pistachio, rose, mint, or raspberry) served with tea at the palatial Laudrée café on the Champs-Elysées.

I'm not a food sophisticate, but I love people—especially cooks—who love their work. Monsieur Isaac, the self-proclaimed "ace of falafels" in the Jewish Quarter, brags, "I've got the biggest pita on the street...and I fill it up!"

When I head south to Italy, it seems the entire country is singing, *"Mangia, mangia."* In the rugged Riviera villages of the Cinque Terre, people are famously passionate about their food. In Vernazza, Giovanni makes

pasta. "I like the pasta too much," he says, holding a belly far bigger than mine.

Alessandro has clearly found his niche. Rolling his cart into Vernazza for the weekly market as he has every Tuesday for 23 years, he sells porcini mushrooms, dried cod, and sturdy parmesan cheese to Vernazzan shoppers who've proudly never set foot in a big city mall.

Valerio, a waiter in my favorite Riviera restaurant, is evangelical about the beauties of anchovies. Knowing I want to teach Americans the wonders of Italian anchovies, he brings me a plate with the little fish prepared four ways and says, "It's not harsh and cured in salt like yours in America. I know, people in America say, 'Pizza—but hold the anchovies.' Our anchovies were swimming yesterday—they are fresh. Taste this."

Farther south and far from the sea, the Tuscan landscape is dotted with *agriturismos*. These traditional family farms rent out spare rooms to make ends meet—and to show off Italy's knack for fine country living. Signora Gori, who runs a noble old farm, takes me on a walk through her estate. As a horrendous chorus of squeals comes from a rustic slaughterhouse on the horizon, she says, "This is our little Beirut." But the view is lush, pristine, and tranquil.

Taking me into a room dominated by a stainless steel table piled with red sides of pork, she declares, "And here we make the prosciutto." Burly men in aprons squeeze the blood out of hunks of meat the size

of dancing partners. Then they cake the ham in salt to begin a curing process that takes months. While the salt helps cure the meat, a coating of pepper seals it. In spooky but great-smelling rooms, racks of hanging hams age. A man, dressed and acting like a veterinarian, tests each ham by sticking it with a horse-bone needle and giving it a sniff.

Passing a sty dominated by a giant pig nicknamed Pastenetto ("the little pastry"), Signora Gori escorts me into the next barn, where fluffy white lambs jump to wobbly attention in their hay. Backlit, it's a dreamy, almost biblical scene. Picking up a baby lamb, she explains, "We use unpasteurized milk in making the pecorino cheese. This is allowed but only with strict health safeguards. I must really know our sheep."

This close-to-the-land-and-animals food production is part of Italy's Slow Food movement (www.slowfood.it). Advocates believe there's more to life than increasing its speed. They produce and serve food in the time-honored way. It may be more labor-intensive and expensive, but it's tastier and—just as important—connects consumers more directly with their food. They know who made it and how.

On the far side of the farm, the son empties his last bucket of purple grapes into the dump truck, and it—in turn—unloads into a grinder that munches through the bunches. The machine spits stems one way and juice (with mangled grapes) the other. Following that promising little river into the cellar, we're surrounded by tall vats of aging grape juice. My guide jokes that while making wine is labor-intensive, right now the grapes are doing all the work. And as they ferment, we head home to dinner.

Around a long, rustic table polished by many decades of feasting, the entire Gori family—three generations surrounded by heirlooms from many more—gathers and welcomes their American guest. It's a classic Tuscan table: simplicity, a sense of harmony, no hurry, and a glass of fine red wine.

A key word for your Tuscan travels is *corposo*—full-bodied. Lifting the elegant glass to my lips, I sip, while enjoying the pride in the eyes of a family so comfortably and happily rooted in their heritage and cultural soil. Entirely satisfied, I say, *"Corposo."* They say, *"Si, bravo."*

As I dip my bread in extra-virgin olive oil and savor a slice of their prosciutto, my friends explain that great wine goes best with simple food. With each bite and every sip, I better understand the art of Tuscan living—and why I'll always hunger to return to Europe.

Alpine Escapes

Even those who know a Rocky Mountain high find something special about the Alps. In the Alps, nature and civilization mix it up comfortably, as if man and mountain shared the same crib.

Imagine walking to the long, legato tones of an alpenhorn. Then, just when you need it most, there's a mechanical lift to whisk you silently and effortlessly—if not cheaply—to the top of that staggering ridge or peak, where your partner can snap a photo of you looking ruggedly triumphant. You'll pass happy yodelers, sturdy grannies, and dirndl'd moms with apple-cheeked kids.

You can hike...or frolic...from France to Slovenia and never come out of the Alps.

While the most famous corners are now solidly in the domain of tour groups, much of the best alpine charm is folded away in no-name valleys, often just over the ridge from the Holiday Inns and the slap-dancing stage shows.

Here are a few places that will make your alpine adventures more than a scenic hike.

Log-Cabin Villages: Both Switzerland and Austria have isolated log-cabin villages, smothered with alpine goodness, set in a flower-speckled world of serene slopes, lazy cows, and musical breezes. While both Taveyanne and Fallerschein are barely accessible by car, they're worth circling on the map if you suspect you may have been Kit Carson in a previous life.

The village of Taveyanne is in the French-speaking part of Switzerland, two miles off the road from Col de la Croix to Villars (or take the footpath from Villars). It's just a jumble of log cabins and snoozing cows stranded all alone at 5,000 feet. The only business in town is the Refuge de Taveyanne, where the Siebenthal family serves hearty meals—great fondue and a delicious *croute au fromage avec oeuf*—in a rustic setting. Who needs electricity? There's a huge charred fireplace with a cannibal-size cauldron, a prehistoric cash register, low-beamed ceilings,

Alpine Escapes

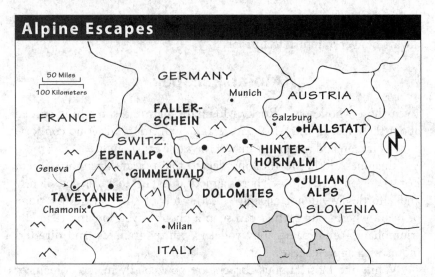

50 Miles
100 Kilometers

GERMANY

Munich

AUSTRIA

FRANCE

FALLER-
SCHEIN

Salzburg

•HALLSTATT

SWITZ.
EBENALP•

HINTER-
HORNALM

Geneva

•GIMMELWALD

TAVEYANNE

DOLOMITES

JULIAN
ALPS

Chamonix•

SLOVENIA

• Milan

ITALY

N

and well-hung ornamental cowbells. For a memorable experience—and the only rentable beds in the village—rent one of five mattresses in their primitive loft (accessed by an outdoor ladder, bathroom outside, $17/person, open June-mid-Oct, closed Tue except July-Aug, tel. 024-498-1947, www.taveyanne.ch).

The similarly remote village of Fallerschein is in western Austria, south of Reutte. Thunderstorms roll down its valley as if it were God's bowling alley. But the blissfully simple pint-size church on the high ground seems to promise that this huddle of houses will remain standing. The people sitting on benches are Austrian vacationers or clandestine lovers who've rented cabins. (Fallerschein is notorious as a hideaway for those having affairs.) The town is 4,000 feet high at the end of a one-mile road near Namlos, on the Berwang road south of Reutte, in Austria's Tirol.

Hinterhornalm over Gnadenwald: The same mountains that put Innsbruck on the vacation map surround Hall. For a lazy look at life in the high Alps around these towns, drive up to 5,000-foot Hinterhornalm and walk to a remote working farm.

Begin your ascent in Gnadenwald, a chalet-filled village sandwiched between Hall and its Alps. Pay $7 at the toll hut, then wind your way upward, marveling at the crazy amount of energy put into this road, to the rustic Hinterhornalm Berg restaurant. This place serves hearty food with a cliff-hanger of a view (generally open daily mid-May-Oct 10:00-18:00, often closed due to weather, mobile 0664/211-2745). Hinterhornalm is a hang-gliding springboard. On sunny days, it's a butterfly nest of thrill-seekers ready to fly.

From there, it's a level 20-minute walk to Walderalm, a cluster of three dairy farms with 70 cows that share their meadow with the clouds.

A firsthand look at fairy-tale alpine culture is just a hike away at Walderalm, near Gnadenwald.

The cows—cameras dangling from their thick necks—ramble along ridgetop lanes surrounded by cut-glass peaks. The ladies of the farms serve soup, sandwiches, and drinks (very fresh milk in the afternoon) on rough plank tables. Below you spreads the Inn River Valley and, in the distance, tourist-filled Innsbruck.

Ebenalp in Appenzell: Switzerland's Appenzell is a region whose forte is cow culture rather than staggering peaks. Its only famous peak, Säntis, is a modest 8,200 feet high. For a fun angle on alpine culture, go five miles south of Appenzell town to Wasserauen and ride the lift to the top of nearby Ebenalp ($30 round-trip). From its summit, enjoy a sweeping view of a major chunk of Switzerland. Then hike down about 15 minutes to a prehistoric cave home (its tiny museum is always open). Wander in and through; as you emerge into the light, you'll pass a hermit's home (a tiny museum, always open) and the Wildkirchli, a 400-year-old cave church that housed hermit monks from 1658 to 1853. Farther along the path and clinging precariously to the cliffside is Berggasthaus Aescher. This rugged guest house, originally built to accommodate those who came here to pray with a hermit monk, now bunks hikers communing with nature.

Rather than sleep in the unmemorable town of Appenzell, stay in the Berggasthaus Aescher ($50/dorm bed, includes breakfast and comforter, no sheets required or provided, no towels available, Family Knechtle-Wyss, 12

A Swiss cliff-hanger of a hideaway: Berggasthaus Aescher on Ebenalp

minutes by steep trail below top of lift, closed Sun nights and Nov-April, tel. 071-799-1142, www.aescher-ai.ch). This old house has only rainwater and no shower. The goats live inside a neighboring hut. The Berggasthaus is sometimes quiet and sometimes festive (locals party until the wee hours on weekends). While Saturdays can be packed with more hikers than mattresses, you'll usually get a small woody dorm to yourself.

The hut is actually built onto the cliffside; the back wall is rock. Study this alpine architecture—and geology—from the toilet. Sip your coffee on the deck, behind a curtain of water dripping from the gnarled overhang a hundred yards above. Leave a note in the guest book, which goes back to 1940.

From this perch, cows look like dandruff littering meadows on the far side of the valley. In the distance, below Säntis, an hour's walk away, is the alpine lake Seealpsee and Wasserauen. Only the hang gliders, like neon jellyfish, tag your world as 21st-century.

Slovenia's Julian Alps: Tiny, undiscovered Slovenia (part of Yugoslavia until 1992) offers fine alpine scenery with a Slavic twist. The northwestern corner of Slovenia is crowned by the Julian Alps, which are laced with hiking paths, blanketed with deep forests, and speckled with ski resorts and vacation chalets. Beyond every ridge is a peaceful alpine village nestled around a quaint Baroque steeple.

Visiting Lake Bled's picturesque island is a must. Hire a traditional *pletna* boat to row you out to the island, which is capped by a super-cute church. Ninety-eight steps lead from the dock up to the Church of the Assumption on top. Grooms prove themselves "fit for marriage" by carrying their brides all the way up.

The single best day in the Julian Alps is spent driving up and over the breathtaking Vršič (vur-SHEECH) Pass and back down via the Soča (SOH-chah) River Valley. There are 50 hairpin turns—24 on the way up, 26 on the way back down—each one numbered and labeled with the altitude in meters. Curling on twisty roads between the peaks, visitors enjoy stunning high-mountain scenery, thought-provoking World War I sights, and charming hamlets.

A humble little Orthodox chapel up the steps at switchback #8 honors the at least 10,000 Russian POWs who built this road during World War I. In 1916, an avalanche thundered down the mountains, killing hundreds of workers. The chapel was built where the final casualty was found.

The road crests at just over 5,000 feet, where a mountain hut offers stunning alpine views (hike up to the hut for a snack or drink on the grand view terrace). Twisting back down the other side of the mountains, the road deposits drivers in the valley of the Soča River. The Soča—with water somehow both crystal clear and spectacularly turquoise—is a mecca for kayakers and other whitewater adventurers, who call it "Adrenaline Valley."

Beautiful as it is, the Soča Valley saw some of the fiercest fighting of World War I. Known as the Soča Front—or the Isonzo Front in Italian—the million casualties here gave it the nickname "Valley of the Cemeteries." The fighting here between the Italian and Austro-Hungarian armies was waged not in the valleys, but at the tops of the mountains.

The valley's World War I sights are concentrated in the humble village of Kobarid. This town was immortalized by Ernest Hemingway, who drove a Red Cross ambulance nearby (and later wrote about Kobarid in *A Farewell to Arms*).

Kobarid's excellent museum offers a haunting look at the tragedy of the Soča Front. The tasteful exhibits, with a pacifist tone, focus not on the guns and heroes, but on the big picture of the front and on the stories of the common people who fought and died here.

For a powerful finale to your museum visit, head up to the hilltop just above town. Built in Fascist style under Mussolini (in 1938), this octagonal pyramid holds the remains of 7,014 Italian soldiers. Names are listed alphabetically, along with mass graves for more than 1,700 unknown soldiers *(militi ignoti)*.

Only Slovenia combines alpine thrills, World War I history, and Slavic culture...all within yodeling distance of Austria and Italy.

Italy's Dolomites: Italy's own stretch of Alps is just over the border from Slovenia's. For details, turn to "North Italy Choices: Milan, Lakes, or Mountains".

And More Alps: For even more high-mountain thrills, read about these three destinations—"From France to Italy over Mont Blanc"; "Hallstatt: Austria's Commune-with-Nature Lake District"; and "Gimmelwald: The Swiss Alps in Your Lap."

A EUROPEAN SAMPLER

Best Medieval Castle Experiences

Castles excite Americans. Medieval fortresses are rotting away on hilltops from Ireland to Israel, from Sweden to Spain, lining the Loire and guarding harbors throughout the Mediterranean. From the west coast of Portugal to the crusader city of Rhodes, you'll find castle thrills lurking in every direction.

Europe's Best Castles

Life in the Middle Ages was actually a lot like the people: nasty, brutish, and short. In cities, there was some measure of safety and security, but the countryside was the domain of outlaw bands of "merry men," who invaded farms and villages to fill their pockets and satisfy their thirst for violence. In those days, the difference between robbers and armies was only a matter of "how big."

Most countryside castles began not as palaces for princes, but as armored bunkers for landowners, protecting their harvest, hired hands, and any foolhardy traveler who might pass through (some castles also "protected" key roads and rivers, extorting tolls from all who passed).

A real castle had all the romance of a fallout shelter. Sure, it had a lofty tower or two, but only to spot trespassers and to give attackers second thoughts. When the bad guys came knocking, a negotiated ransom was the typical outcome—not a swashbuckling battle.

In the 17th and 18th centuries, large-scale European wars made these castles handy tactical tools. But for the most part, they became obsolete against ever-growing armies and cannons (and between wars, better law enforcement made the countryside safer). Most castles fell into ruin, used as quarries to build more practical things.

Suddenly, in the late 19th century, everything changed. Under the Prussian leadership of Bismarck, the Germanic cluster of mini-states quickly came together as a single powerful nation. There was a great surge in German nationalism, and a popular obsession with "roots," both real and Romantic. Wagner's fairy-tale operas and King Ludwig II's re-created castles epitomized the new German "pop history," which was rewritten to express the ideal spirit of German-ness instead of its grim reality. Modern tourism took root during this same time. So there was not only a patriotic spirit, but also an economic incentive behind the "reinterpreting" of castles in a Romantic style. A few short decades later, Walt Disney made the fairy-tale castle his trademark, and ("authentic" or not) the rest is history.

What travelers see today is a muddle of Middle Age bunker mentality and 150-year-old Romantic renovation...which also happens to be real. While confusing, this weird mix makes for great sightseeing.

Visiting Europe can overwhelm you with too many castles to tour in too little time. To help you prioritize, here are my favorites: 10 medieval castles—some forgotten, some discovered—where the winds of the past really howl.

Carcassonne, France

Before me lies Carcassonne, the perfect medieval city. Like a fish that everyone thought was extinct, Europe's greatest Romanesque fortress-city somehow survives.

Medieval Carcassonne is a 13th-century world of towers, turrets, and cobblestones. It's a walled city and Camelot's castle rolled into one, frosted with too many day-tripping tourists. At 10:00 a.m., the salespeople stand at the doors of their main-street shops, their gauntlet of tacky temptations poised and ready for their daily ration of customers. But an empty Carcassonne rattles in the early morning or late-afternoon breeze. Enjoy the town early or late, or off-season. Spend the night.

Best stormed early or late

I was supposed to be gone yesterday, but it's sundown and here I sit—imprisoned by choice—curled in a cranny on top of the wall. The moat is one foot over and 100 feet down. Happy little weeds and moss upholster my throne. The wind blows away many of the sounds of today, and my imagination "medievals" me.

Twelve hundred years ago, Charlemagne stood below with his troops, besieging this fortress-town for several years. As the legend goes, just as food was running out, a cunning townswoman had a great idea. She fed the town's last bits of grain to the last pig and tossed him over the wall. Splat. Charlemagne's restless forces, amazed that the town still had enough food to throw fat party pigs over the wall, decided they'd never succeed in starving the people out. They ended the siege, and the city was saved. Today, the walls that stopped Charlemagne open wide for visitors (www.carcassonne-tourisme.com).

Warwick Castle, England

From Land's End to John O'Groats, I searched for the best castle in Britain. I found it. With a lush, green, grassy moat and fairy-tale fortifications, Warwick Castle will entertain you from dungeon to lookout (www.warwick-castle.com). Standing inside the castle gate, you can see the mound where the original Norman castle of 1068 stood. Under this mound (or motte), the wooden stockade (bailey) defined the courtyard as the castle walls do today. The castle is a 14th- and 15th-century fortified shell holding an 18th- and 19th-century royal residence surrounded by dandy gardens, landscaped by Lancelot "Capability" Brown in the 1750s.

Warwick Castle—for kings and queens of any age

There's something for every taste—an educational armory, a terrible torture chamber, a knight in shining armor on a horse that rotates with a merry band of musical jesters, a Madame Tussauds re-creation of a royal weekend party with an 1898 game of statue-maker, a queenly garden, and a peacock-patrolled, picnic-perfect park. The great hall and staterooms are the sumptuous highlights. The "King Maker" exhibit (it's 1471 and the townsfolk are getting ready for battle...) is highly promoted but not quite as good as a Disney ride. Be warned: The tower is a one-way, no-backing-out, 250-step climb offering a view not worth a heart attack. Even with its crowds of modern-day barbarians and its robber-baron entry fee ($36), Warwick's worthwhile.

Eltz Castle, Germany

Burg Eltz is my favorite castle in all of Europe. Lurking in a mysterious forest, it's furnished throughout as it was 500 years ago. Thanks to smart diplomacy and clever marriages, Burg Eltz was never destroyed. It's been in the Eltz family for 850 years.

The first *burg* (castle) on the Elz creek was built in the 12th century

Eltz Castle, near Cochem, on Germany's Mosel River

to protect a trade route. By about 1490, the castle looked like it does today: the homes of three big landlord families gathered around a tiny courtyard within one formidable fortification. Today, the excellent 45-minute tour winds you through two of those homes (the third is the caretaker's residence). The elderly countess of Eltz traces her family back 33 generations; you'll see a photo of her family. She enjoys flowers, and has had the castle's public rooms adorned with grand floral arrangements every week for the last 40 years.

It was a comfortable castle for its day: 80 rooms made cozy by 40 fireplaces and wall-hanging tapestries. Many of its 20 toilets were automatically flushed by a rain drain. The delightful chapel is on a lower floor. Even though "no one should live above God," this chapel's placement was acceptable because its altar fills a bay window, which floods the delicate Gothic space with light. The three families met—working out common problems as if sharing a condo—in the large "conference room." A carved jester and a rose look down on the big table, reminding those who gathered that they were free to discuss anything ("fool's freedom"—jesters could say anything to the king), but nothing discussed could leave the room (the "rose of silence").

Burg Eltz is between Koblenz and Cochem, about an hour's drive from the Rhine River. The only way to see the inside of the castle is with a 45-minute tour (in English, included with $11 admission ticket, www.burg-eltz.de).

Rheinfels Castle, Germany's Rhineland

Sitting like a dead pit bull above St. Goar, this mightiest of Rhine castles rumbles with ghosts from its hard-fought past (www.st-goar.de). Burg Rheinfels (built in 1245) withstood a siege of 28,000 French troops in 1692. But in 1797, the French Revolutionary army destroyed it.

Rheinfels was huge. Once the biggest castle on the Rhine, it spent the 19th century as a quarry. So today, while still mighty, it's only a small fraction of its original size. This hollow but interesting shell offers your single best hands-on ruined-castle experience on the river.

The massive Rheinfels was the only Rhineland castle to withstand Louis XIV's assault during the 17th century. For centuries, the place was self-sufficient and ready for a siege. Circling the central courtyard, you'd find a bakery, pharmacy, herb garden, animals, brewery, well, and livestock. During peacetime, 300-600 people lived here; during a siege, there could be as many as 4,000.

Any proper castle was prepared to survive a six-month siege. With 4,000 people, that's a lot of provisions. The count owned the surrounding farmland. Farmers—in return for the lord's protection—got to keep 20 percent of their production. Later, in more liberal feudal times, the nobility let them keep 40 percent. (Today, the German government leaves workers with 60 percent after taxes ... and provides a few more services.)

Hike around the castle perimeter. Notice the smartly placed crossbow-arrow slit. Thoop...you're dead. While you're lying there, notice the fine stonework on the chutes high above. Uh-oh ... boiling pitch ... now you're toast.

In about 1600, to protect their castle, the Rheinfellas cleverly booby-trapped the land just outside their walls by building tunnels topped by thin slate roofs and packed with explosives. By detonating the explosives when under attack, they could kill hundreds of approaching invaders. In

Even in ruins, Rheinfels is mighty.

1626, a handful of underground Protestant Germans blew 300 Catholic Spaniards to (they assumed) hell.

You're welcome to wander through a set of never-blown-up tunnels. But be warned: It's pitch-dark, muddy, and claustrophobic, and with confusing dead-ends. Assuming you make no wrong turns, it's a 200-yard-long adventure, never letting you walk taller than a deep crouch. It cannot be done without a light (bring a flashlight or buy candles, available at the castle entrance).

A door blasted through the castle wall takes you to the small, barren prison. You walk through a door prisoners only dreamed of 400 years ago. (They came and went through the little square hole in the ceiling.) The holes in the walls supported timbers that thoughtfully gave as many as 15 miserable residents something to sit on to keep them out of the filthy slop that gathered on the floor. Twice a day, they were given bread and water. Some prisoners actually survived for more than two years in this dark hole. While the town could torture and execute, the castle had permission only to imprison criminals in these dungeons. According to town records, the two men who spent the most time down here—2.5 years each—died within three weeks of regaining their freedom. Perhaps after a diet of bread and water, feasting on meat and wine was just too much.

Germany's Rhine River is filled with castle-crowned hills. These can be enjoyed conveniently by train, car, or boat. The best 50-mile stretch is between Koblenz and Mainz. The best one-hour cruise is from St. Goar to Bacharach (www.k-d.com).

Château de Chillon, Switzerland

Set romantically at the edge of Lake Geneva near Montreux, this wonderfully preserved 13th-century castle is worth a side-trip from anywhere in southwest Switzerland. Château de Chillon (shee-yon) has never been damaged or destroyed—it's always been inhabited and maintained. Its oldest fortifications date to the 11th century, and the castle was expanded by the Savoy family in the 13th century, when this became a prime location—at a crossroads of a major trade route between England, France, and Rome. It was the Savoys' fortress and residence, with four big halls (a major status symbol) and impractically large lake-view windows (their powerful navy could defend against possible attack by sea).

Shimmering Château de Chillon

When the Bernese invaded in 1536, the castle was conquered in just two days, and the new governor made Château de Chillon his residence (and a Counter-Reformation prison). Inspired by the Revolution in Paris, the French-speaking people on Lake Geneva finally kicked out their German-speaking Bernese oppressors in 1798. The castle became—and remains—the property of the Canton of Vaud. It has been used as an armory, a warehouse, a prison, a hospital, and a tourist attraction. Rousseau's writings first drew attention to the castle, inspiring visits by Romantics such as Lord Byron and Victor Hugo, plus other notables including Dickens,

Goethe, and Hemingway.

Follow the English brochure, which takes you on a self-guided tour through fascinatingly furnished rooms (www.chillon.ch). The dank dungeon, mean weapons, and 800-year-old toilets will excite even the dullest travel partner.

Reifenstein Castle, Italy

For an incredibly medieval kick in the pants, get off the autobahn one hour south of Innsbruck at the Italian town of Vipiteno (called "Sterzing" by

residents who prefer German). With her time-pocked sister just opposite, Reifenstein Castle bottled up this strategic valley leading to the easiest way to cross the Alps.

Reifenstein offers castle connoisseurs the best-preserved medieval-castle interior I've ever seen. Take a tour (in German and Italian, tel. 339-264-3752). You'll discover the mossy past as you learn how the cistern col-

Rugged Reifenstein Castle

lected water, how drunken lords managed to get their keys into the keyholes, and how prisoners were left to rot in the dungeon (you'll look down the typical only-way-out hole in the ceiling). In the only surviving original knights' sleeping quarters (rough-hewn plank boxes lined with hay), you'll see how knights spent their nights. Lancelot would cry a lot.

Moorish Ruins of Sintra, Portugal

The desolate ruins of a 1,000-year-old Moorish castle overlook the sea and the town of Sintra, just west of Lisbon. Ignored by most of the tourists who flock to the glitzy Pena Palace (capping a neighboring hill-

Run with the winds of the past in Europe's countless ruined castles. Here in Portugal, with a little imagination, you're under attack over a thousand years ago.

top), the ruins of Sintra offer a reminder of the centuries-long struggle between Muslim Moorish forces and Christian European forces for the control of Iberia. From 711 until 1492, major parts of Iberia (Spain and Portugal) were occupied by the Moors. Contrary to the significance that Americans place on the year 1492, Europeans remember the date as the year the Moors were finally booted back into Africa. For most, these ruins are simply a medieval funtasia of scramble-up-and-down-the-ramparts delights and atmospheric picnic perches with vast Atlantic views in an enchanted forest (www.parquesdesintra.pt). With a little imagination, it's A.D. 800, and you're under attack.

Castle Day: Neuschwanstein, Hohenschwangau, and the Ehrenberg Ruins

Three of my favorite castles—two famous, one unknown—can be seen in one busy day. "Castle Day" takes you to Germany's Disney-like Neuschwanstein Castle, the more stately Hohenschwangau Castle at its foot, and the much older Ehrenberg Ruins across the Austrian border in Reutte.

Make the Austrian town of Reutte your home base. (It's just over the German border, three Alp-happy hours by train west of Innsbruck.)

From Reutte, catch the early bus across the border to touristy Füssen, the German town nearest Neuschwanstein. (Planning ahead, note the times buses return to Reutte.) From Füssen, you can walk, pedal a rented bike, or ride a bus a couple of miles to Neuschwanstein.

Neuschwanstein is the greatest of King Ludwig II's fairy-tale castles. His extravagance and Romanticism earned this Bavarian king the title "Mad" King Ludwig...and an early death. His castle is one of Europe's most popular attractions.

You can reserve by calling 08362/930-830 (or by visiting www.ticket-center-hohenschwangau.de). If you don't book ahead, arrive by 8:00 a.m. to buy a ticket—you'll likely be touring soon after. Your ticket lists appointed times for you to visit Ludwig's boyhood home,

Some of Europe's most popular attractions, such as "Mad" Ludwig's castles, sell tickets with entry times. If you don't reserve ahead or arrive early, you'll risk not getting in at all.

Hohenschwangau Castle, and then the neighboring Neuschwanstein on the hill. If you arrive late, you'll spend a couple of hours in the ticket line and may find all tours booked.

Hohenschwangau Castle, where Ludwig grew up, offers a good look at his life. Like its more famous neighbor, it takes about an hour to tour. Afterward, head up the hill to Ludwig's castle in the air.

Neuschwanstein Castle, which is about as old as the Eiffel Tower, is a textbook example of 19th-century Romanticism. After the Middle Ages ended, people disparagingly named that era "Gothic," or barbarian. Then, all of a sudden, in the 1800s it was hip to be square, and neo-Gothic became the rage. Throughout Europe, old castles were restored and new ones built—wallpapered with chivalry. King Ludwig II put his medieval fantasy on the hilltop not for defensive reasons, but simply because he liked the view.

The lavish interior, covered with damsels in distress, dragons, and knights in gleaming armor, is enchanting. (A little knowledge of Wagner's operas

"Mad" King Ludwig's Neuschwanstein Castle

goes a long way in bringing these stories to life.) Ludwig had great taste—for a mad king. Read up on this political misfit—a poetic hippie king in the realpolitik age of Bismarck. After Bavarians complained about the money Ludwig spent on castles, the 40-year-old king was found dead in a lake under suspicious circumstances, ending work on his medieval fantasy-come-true. After the tour, climb farther up the hill to Mary's Bridge for the best view of this crazy yet elegant castle.

This is a busy day. By lunchtime, catch the bus back to Reutte and get ready for a completely different castle experience.

Pack a picnic and your camera, and with the help of some directions, walk 30 minutes out of town to the Ehrenberg Castle Ensemble, the brooding ruins of four castles that once made up the largest fort in Tirol. If Neuschwanstein was the medieval castle dream, Ehrenburg is the medieval castle reality. Grab a sword fern, shake your hair free, and unfetter that imagination.

The impressive "castle ensemble" was built to defend against the Bavarians and to bottle up the strategic Via Claudia trade route, which cut through the Alps as it connected Italy and Germany. Today, it's a "castle museum," showing off 500 years of military architecture in one swoop. The European Union is helping fund the project because it promotes the heritage of a multinational region—Tirol—rather than a country.

The fortified Klause "toll fort" on the valley floor—which levied duties along the Via Claudia in Roman times—is flanked by Ehrenberg and a sister castle (Fort Claudia) on the opposite side. After locals rained cannon balls on Ehrenberg from the bluff above it, a much bigger castle—Schlosskopf—

The brooding Ehrenberg Ruins

was built higher up. Over the centuries it became completely overgrown and concealed. Today, the trees have been shaved away and the castle excavated.

You can see Ehrenberg's castles reconstructed on Reutte's restaurant walls. Ask at your hotel where you can find a folk evening full of slap-dancing and yodel foolery. A hot, hearty dinner and an evening of Tirolean entertainment is a fitting way to raise the drawbridge on your memorable "Castle Day."

*For good-value accommodations in **Carcassonne**, try the Hôtel le Montmorency (splurge, 2 rue Camille Saint-Saëns, tel. 04 68 11 96 70, www .hotels-carcassonne.net); in **St. Goar**, Hotel am Markt (moderate, Markt 1, tel. 06741/1689, www.hotel-am-markt-sankt-goar.de); near **Reutte**, Moserhof Hotel (moderate, Planseestrasse 44, in nearby Breitenwang, tel. 05672/62020,* *www.hotel-moserhof.at); and in* **Füssen,** *Altstadthotel zum Hechten (moderate, Ritterstrasse 6, tel. 08362/91600, www.hotel-hechten.com). For all the travel specifics, see this year's editions of the pertinent Rick Steves' country guides.*

Sobering Sites of Nazi Europe

Fondue, nutcrackers, Monet, Big Ben...gas chambers. A trip to once-upon-a-time Europe can be a fairy tale. It can also help tell the story of Europe's 20th-century fascist nightmare. While few travelers go to Europe to dwell on the horrors of Nazism, most people value visiting the memorials of fascism's reign of terror and honoring the wish of its survivors—"Never forget." These sites are committed to making the point that intolerance and fascism are still alive and strong. Their message: Fascism can emerge from its loony fringe if we get complacent and think the horrors of Hitler could never happen again.

Memorial at the Dachau concentration camp

Why are these sites worth a bit of your vacation? Because you can learn from them. Genocide is as recent as conflicts in Yugoslavia, Rwanda, and Sudan. Even today, Machiavellian politicians can hijack great nations, artfully manipulating fear, patriotism, and mass media to accomplish their aggressive agendas.

Concentration Camps

The most sobering of all Nazi sites are concentration and extermination camps. Of the many concentration-camp memorials in Europe, the most moving is Auschwitz-Birkenau (near Kraków, Poland). Three others are also evocative and convenient to visit: Dachau (just outside Munich), Mauthausen (between Vienna and Salzburg), and Terezín (near Prague).

No sight in all of Europe is as powerful as **Auschwitz-Birkenau** (www.auschwitz.org). This Nazi concentration camp in the Polish town of Oświęcim (a 70-minute drive west of Kraków) was the site of the systematic murder of more than a million innocent people.

Nazi Sites

Oslo

Copenhagen

SACHSEN-
HAUSEN

Haarlem • Amsterdam   Berlin •   Warsaw •

• Mechelen   BUCHEN-
      • Irrel   WALD   **AUSCHWITZ-**
          TEREZIN •   **BIRKENAU**
Nürnberg •   Prague •   • Kraków

Paris •   **DACHAU** •
      Munich •   • Vienna
      Berchtes-   **MAUTHAUSEN**
          gaden

ORADOUR-
SUR-
GLANE

Rome •

Auschwitz was the biggest, most notorious concentration camp in the Nazi system...strategically located in the heart of Jewish Europe. Since the Middle Ages, Poland was known for its tolerance of Jews. By the beginning of World War II, Poland had Europe's largest concentration of Jews: 3.5 million. During the Holocaust, the Nazis murdered 4.5 million Jews in Poland (many brought in from other countries). Today, only a few thousand Jews live in all of Poland.

A visit to Auschwitz is obligatory for Polish students. You'll often see Israeli high school groups walking through the grounds waving their Star of David flags. Many people, including Germans, leave flowers and messages. One of the messages reads: "Nations who forget their own history are sentenced to live it again."

There are two camps: Auschwitz I and Auschwitz II (better known as Birkenau). Most visitors begin at Auschwitz I. After seeing a grippingly graphic video, you cross under the notorious gate with the cruel message *Arbeit Macht Frei* ("Work sets you free") and into the rows of barracks—each containing an exhibit.

People being transported here, thinking they were going to a new homeland, were encouraged to bring luggage. After they were killed, everything of value was plundered by the Nazis. In these barracks, room after room is literally full to the ceiling of prisoners' personal effects: eyeglasses; fine Jewish prayer

"Work sets you free."

A EUROPEAN SAMPLER

shawls; crutches and prosthetic limbs; shoes; suitcases; and even human hair.

The "Death Block," from which nobody ever left alive, is particularly evocative. The Starvation Cell held prisoners selected to starve to death when a fellow prisoner escaped. The Dark Cell, crammed with 30 people at a time, had only a small window for ventilation. If it became covered with snow, the prisoners suffocated.

Seven hundred people at a time could be gassed in the Auschwitz crematorium. This wasn't efficient enough for the Nazis, so they built a far bigger death camp two miles away. From Auschwitz, a shuttle bus takes visitors to part two of their visit: Birkenau.

At first sight, it's clear: Birkenau is all about the efficient mass production of death. It held 100,000 prisoners and could cremate 16,000 a day. From the top of the guard tower, survey the staggering scope of Birkenau: a few wooden barracks housing exhibits, and a vast field of chimneys—all that remains of the other barracks—stretching nearly as far as the eye can see.

Train tracks lead through the middle of the camp to the dividing platform, where a Nazi doctor would evaluate each prisoner. If he pointed right, the prisoner was sentenced to death, and trudged—unknowingly—to the gas chamber. If he pointed left, the person would be registered and generally worked to death. It was here that families from all over Europe were torn apart forever.

Beyond the dividing platform, the tracks arrive at the finale of this wrenching visit: the ruins of the gas chambers and crematoria. As they

Birkenau: remembering the Holocaust's mass production of death

entered the undressing rooms, people were given numbered lockers, conned into thinking they were coming back. (The Nazis didn't want a panic.) Then they piled into the "shower room," where they were murdered with poison gas. Their bodies were then burned in one of four giant crematoria. Finally, their ashes were dumped into a ghostly lake.

The Auschwitz crematoria were destroyed by the Nazis as the Soviet army approached, leaving today's haunting ruins. The Soviets arrived on

January 27, 1945, and the nightmare of Auschwitz was over. The Polish parliament quickly voted to turn these grounds into a museum, so that the world would understand, and never forget, the horror of what happened here.

Dachau, near Munich, is a much tamer concentration-camp experience (closed Mon except holidays, www.kz-gedenkstaette-dachau.de). While some visitors complain that Dachau is too "prettied-up," it gives a powerful look at how these camps worked. Built in 1933, this first Nazi concentration camp offers a compelling voice from our recent, grisly past, warning and pleading "Never Again"—the memorial's theme. On arrival, pick up the mini-guide and check when the next documentary film in English will be shown. The museum, the movie, the chilling camp-inspired art, the reconstructed barracks, the gas chambers, the cremation ovens, and the memorial shrines will chisel into you the hidden meaning of fascism.

Mauthausen town sits cute and prim on the romantic Danube at the start of the very scenic trip downstream to Vienna. But nearby, atop a now-still quarry, linger the memories of a horrible slave-labor camp. Mauthausen is a solemn place of meditation and continuous mourning. Fresh flowers adorn yellowed photos of lost loved ones. The home country of each victim has erected a gripping monument. You'll find yourself in an artistic gallery of grief, resting on a foundation of Never Forget. Retrace the steep and treacherous steps of the camp's inmates— the "stairway of death" *(Todesstiege)*—to and from the quarry where they worked themselves to death. Mauthausen offers an English booklet, a free audioguide, an English movie, and a painful but necessary museum (www.mauthausen-memorial.at).

Just outside of Prague is **Terezín** concentration camp (Theresienstadt in German, www.pamatnik-terezin.cz). This particularly insidious place was dolled up as a model camp for Red Cross inspection purposes. Inmates put out their own newspaper, and the children put on cute plays. But after the camp passed its inspection, life returned to slave labor and death. Ponder the touching collection of Jewish children's art, also on display in the Pinkas Synagogue in Prague's Jewish Quarter.

You can also visit **Sachsenhausen** near Berlin (www.gedenkstaette -sachsenhausen.de), **Buchenwald** near Weimar (www.buchenwald.de), and many others.

Germany and Austria

Since destruction and death are fascist fortes, only relatively insignificant bits and pieces of Hitler's Germany survive. But as time passes, today's

Germans are increasingly aware of the need to remember the horrors that began in their country.

Hitler got his start—and had his strongest support—in the beer halls of **Munich.** The Munich City Museum (Münchner Stadtmuseum) traces the origin and development of Nazism. To uncover Nazi sites in Munich, take the Hitler and the Third Reich walking tour by Radius Tours (www.radiustours.com). Ironically, we have the Nazis to thank for the accuracy of Munich's postwar reconstruction. When Allied bombings were imminent, Nazi photographers documented Munich's great architecture—allowing it to be rebuilt exactly as it was after the war.

Berlin, now that its Wall is history, is giving its Nazi chapter a little more attention. Most original Nazi sites are hidden. To help you find them, take the Infamous Third Reich Sites walking tour by Original Berlin Walks (www.berlinwalks.de). But don't even bother looking for "Hitler's Bunker"—it's long gone.

Berlin has several Nazi-related museums and memorials. The Topography of Terror exhibit illustrates SS tactics (in the ruins of the former SS/Gestapo headquarters, near what was Checkpoint Charlie). The adjacent four small "mountains" are made from the rubble of the bombed-out city. The chilling Book Burning Monument commemorates the 20,000 books that were burned on Berlin's Bebelplatz at the order of the Nazis. Glance into the glass floor in the middle of the square (on Unter den Linden) to see a huge underground room with empty shelves. The gripping Käthe Kollwitz Museum is filled with art inspired by the horrors of Berlin's Nazi experience. Berlin's New Synagogue was burned on Kristallnacht in 1938, but has since been restored. The excellent Jewish Museum Berlin, which focuses on Jewish culture, was designed by the American architect Daniel

As Hitler consolidated his power in the 1930s, he arrested 96 members of the German Parliament who opposed him. He sent them to concentration camps, where most perished. This monument, outside the renovated Reichstag where they once worked, is their memorial.

Libeskind. The zigzag shape of the zinc-walled building is pierced by voids, symbolic of the irreplaceable cultural loss caused by the Holocaust (www.jmberlin.de). In nearby **Wannsee** (near Potsdam), you can tour the house where Hitler's cronies came up with the "Final Solution" of the

Holocaust (www.ghwk.de).

There was resistance to Hitler even in Berlin. In front of the glass-domed Reichstag is a row of slate slabs imbedded in the ground memorializing the 96 politicians who were murdered and persecuted because their politics didn't agree with Chancellor Hitler's. Near the Kulturforum museums is a former military headquarters (Bendlerblock) where conspirators plotted an ill-fated attempt to assassinate Hitler—and where they were also shot for the crime. It's now the site of the German Resistance Memorial (Gedenkstätte Deutscher Widerstand, free audioguide available, www.gdw-berlin.de). Just outside the city is the Plötzensee Prison, where Nazi enemies were imprisoned and executed (www.gedenkstaette-ploetzensee.de).

Berlin's Memorial to the Murdered Jews of Europe consists of 2,711 gravestone-like pillars. Completed in 2005, it is the first formal German government-sponsored Holocaust memorial. It's controversial for the focus—just Jews. The government promises to build memorials to the other groups targeted by Hitler. The pillars are made of hollow concrete, each chemically coated for easy removal of graffiti. The number of pillars, symbolic of nothing, is simply how many fit on the provided land. Is it a labyrinth...symbolic cemetery... intentionally disorienting? The meaning is entirely up to the visitor. Beneath the field of concrete pillars is the state-of-the-art information center. This studies the Nazi system of extermination, humanizes the victims, traces stories of individual families and collects vivid personal accounts, and lists 200 different places of genocide. The memorial's location—where the Berlin Wall once stood—is coincidental. It's just a place where lots of people can easily experience it. The bunker of Nazi propagandist Joseph Goebbels was discovered during the work and left buried (under the northeast corner of the memorial). Hitler's bunker is just 200 yards away, under a nondescript parking lot. Such Nazi sites are intentionally left hidden to discourage neo-Nazi elements from turning them into shrines (www.stiftung-denkmal.de).

Berlin's Memorial to the Murdered Jews of Europe is a moving monument to one of history's greatest tragedies.

In **Nürnberg**, the ghosts of Hitler's showy propaganda rallies still rustle in the Rally Grounds (now Dutzendteich Park), down the Great Road, and through the Congress Hall. The north wing of the hall houses the Nazi Documentation Center, with a "Fascination and Terror" exhibit that examines the causes and consequences of the Nazi phenomenon (www.museen.nuernberg.de). Across town is the Nürnberg Trials Courtroom—where high-ranking Nazi officers answered to an international tribunal after the war ended.

The town of **Berchtesgaden,** near the Austrian border, is any German's choice for a great mountain hideaway—including Hitler's.

The remains of Hitler's Obersalzberg headquarters, with its extensive tunnel system and Nazi Documentation Center, will interest WWII buffs (www.obersalzberg.de).

Just north of Trier in the town of **Irrel** is the Westwall Museum, with tourable bunkers that made up part of the Nazis' supposedly impenetrable western fortification (closed in winter, www.westwall-museum.de).

Hitler's Eagle's Nest, high above Berchtesgaden, is a fascinating bit of Bavaria and an easy side-trip from Salzburg.

On **Vienna**'s Judenplatz, you'll find the Austrian Holocaust Memorial—a library turned inside out to remind visitors that each victim had a story. Nearby is the Judenplatz Museum, displaying the ruins of a forgotten 14th-century synagogue unearthed during the memorial's construction (www.jmw.at).

The Netherlands and Scandinavia

In **Amsterdam**, Anne Frank's House gives the cold, mind-boggling statistics of Nazi cruelty some much-needed intimacy by telling the heartbreaking story of a young girl who became one of those statistics. Even bah-humbug types who are dragged in because it's raining and their spouses read the diary find themselves caught up in Anne's story (www.annefrank.org).

The small town of **Haarlem**, 20 minutes by train from Amsterdam, has its own Anne Frank-type story. Touring a cozy apartment above a clock shop just off the busy market square, you'll see Corrie Ten Boom's

"Hiding Place." The sight was popularized by an inspirational book and movie about this woman and her family's experience hiding Jews from Nazis. Tipped off by an informant, Nazis raided their house but didn't find the Jews, who were hiding behind a wall in Corrie's bedroom. Because the Nazis found a suspiciously large number of ration coupons, they sent the Ten Boom family to a concentration camp. Only Corrie survived (www.corrietenboom.com).

Amsterdam's Dutch Theater, which was used as an assembly hall for local Jews destined for Nazi concentration camps, is a powerful memorial. On the wall, 6,700 family names represent the 104,000 Dutch Jews deported and killed by the Nazis. The nearby Jewish History Museum—four historic synagogues joined together by steel and glass to make one modern complex—tells the story and struggles of Judaism through the ages (www.jhm.nl).

While Hitler controlled Europe, each country had a courageous, if small, resistance movement. All over Europe you'll find streets and squares named after the martyrs of the resistance. Any history buff or champion of the underdog will be inspired by the patriotism documented in Europe's Nazi-resistance museums—the most extensive is Amsterdam's Dutch Resistance Museum. You'll see propaganda movie clips, study a forged ID card under a magnifying glass, and read of ingenious, daring efforts to hide Jews from the Germans (www.verzets museum.org).

In **Mechelen**, Belgium, the new Kazerne Dossin Memorial, Museum, and Documentation Centre on the Holocaust and Human Rights is fascinating (www.kazernedossin.be), as are resistance museums in **Copenhagen** (www.frihedsmuseet.dk) and **Oslo** (www.mil.no/felles /nhm). Oslo's Norwegian Holocaust Center is actually located in the former home of Nazi collaborator Vidkun Quisling (www.hlsenteret.no).

Poland

Poland was hit harder by World War II than any other country—more than six million Poles died, half of them Jews. But the Poles—Jewish or not—did not go quietly. Monuments around the capital city remember their valiant, though eventually unsuccessful, uprisings.

In 1940 and 1941, a million and a half Jews were moved into a ghetto in **Warsaw**. By 1943, only a tenth of the ghetto's Jews survived—the rest had died from disease or been shipped to concentration camps. The survivors staged the Ghetto Uprising against their Nazi oppressors, but almost all of them were eventually killed in the fighting, captured and executed, or sent to concentration camps. Today the former ghetto—leveled during the war—has been rebuilt as a dull residential zone, but a few monuments scattered around the area honor the uprising's heroes. The Museum of the History of Polish Jews is built on a site that was part of the Warsaw ghetto (www.jewishmuseum.org.pl).

A year after the Ghetto Uprising, as the Soviet army approached, a Polish resistance army staged the 1944 Warsaw Uprising against the Nazis, which resulted in the deaths of nearly a quarter of a million Warsaw civilians. Both of these events are depicted in the Oscar-winning film *The Pianist*. Today, you can still visit the neighborhoods and landmarks where these brave uprisings began. A high-tech museum about the 1944 Uprising tells the story eloquently (www.1944.pl).

The real Oskar Schindler—hero of the film *Schindler's List*—lived and worked in the Polish city of **Kraków**. Fans of the film can visit Schindler's factory (near the Kraków-Zabłocie train station), which has been converted into a museum (www.mhk.pl). The Jarden Bookshop, located in Kraków's Jewish Quarter, offers *Schindler's List* tours (www.jarden.pl).

The Czech Republic

After completing his "final solution," Hitler had hoped to build a grand museum of the "decadent" Jewish culture in **Prague**. Today, the museums and synagogues of Prague's Jewish Quarter (Josefov), containing artifacts the Nazis assembled from that city's once-thriving Jewish community, stand together as a persistently unforgettable memorial (see "Czech Out Prague").

France

Paris commemorates the 200,000 French victims of Hitler's camps with the Memorial de la Déportation. Walking through this evocative park, on the tip of the Ile de la Cité just behind Notre-Dame, is like entering a work of art. Walk down the claustrophobic stairs into a world of concrete, iron bars, water, and sky. Inside the structure, the eternal flame, triangular niches containing soil from various concentration camps, and powerful quotes will etch the message into your mind. Then gaze at the 200,000 lighted crystals—one for each person who perished.

Rivaling Auschwitz as the most moving sight of all is the martyred village of **Oradour-sur-Glane,** in central France (www.oradour.org). This town, 15 miles northwest of Limoges, was machine-gunned and burned in 1944 by Nazi SS troops. Seeking revenge for the killing of

one of their officers, they left 642 men, women, and children dead in a blackened crust of a town under a silent blanket of ashes. The poignant ruins of Oradour-sur-Glane—scorched sewing machines, pots, pans, bikes, and cars—have been preserved as an eternal reminder of the reality of war. When you visit, you'll see the simple sign that greets every pilgrim who enters: *Souviens-toi*...Remember.

EAST MEDITERRANEAN

Greece's Peloponnesian Highlights

The Peloponnesian Peninsula stretches southwest from Athens. Studded with antiquities, this land of ancient Olympia, Corinth, and Sparta offers plenty of fun in the eternal Greek sun, with pleasant fishing villages, sandy beaches, bathtub-warm water, and none of the tourist crowds that plague the much-scrambled-after Greek Isles.

Greece has been much in the news because of its economic crisis. But, for travelers, the essential Greek experience—sea, sun, ancient ruins, and wonderful food—remains unchanged, impervious to the battering of global tides.

Nafplio and Its Historic Side-Trips

The charming Peloponnesian port town of Nafplio is small, cozy, and strollable. Though it has plenty of tourism, Nafplio is both elegant and proud. It's a must-see on any Greek visit because of its historical importance (the first capital of an independent Greece), its accessibility from Athens (an easy 2.5-hour drive or bus ride), and its handy location as a home base for touring the ancient sites at Mycenae and Epidavros (both described later). Nafplio has great pensions, appealing restaurants, a thriving evening scene, inviting beaches nearby, and a good balance of local life and tourist convenience.

Nafplio's harbor is guarded by three castles: one on a small island, another just above the old town, and a third capping a tall cliff above the

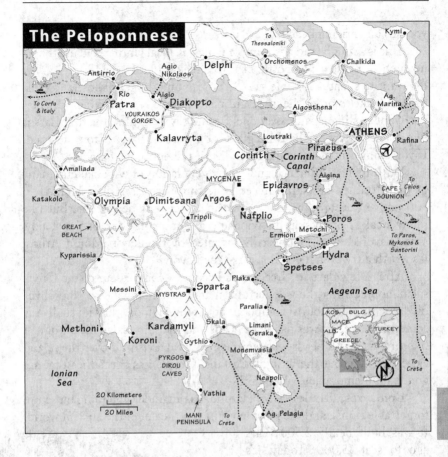

The Peloponnese

To Corfu & Italy
To Thessaloniki
Kymi
Antirrio
Agio Nikolaos
Delphi
Orchomenos
Chalkida
Rio
Aigio
Patra
Diakopto
Aigosthena
Ag. Marina
VOURAIKOS GORGE
Kalavryta
Loutraki
ATHENS
Amaliada
Corinth
Corinth Canal
Piraeus
Rafina
MYCENAE
Epidavros
Aigina
To Chios
Katakolo
Olympia
Dimitsana
Argos
CAPE SOUNION
GREAT BEACH
Tripoli
Nafplio
Poros
Metochi
Ermioni
To Paros, Mykonos & Santorini
Kyparissia
Hydra
Spetses
Messini
Plaka
Sparta
Aegean Sea
MYSTRAS
Paralia
Methoni
Kardamyli
Skala
Limani Geraka
KOS
BULG.
MACE.
Koroni
Gythio
Monemvasia
ALB.
TURKEY
GREECE
Ionian Sea
PYRGOS DIROU CAVES
Neapoli
To Crete
20 Kilometers
20 Miles
Vathia
MANI PENINSULA
To Crete
Ag. Pelagia

EAST MEDITERRANEAN

city. All three are wonderfully floodlit at night. Just looking from the town up to its highest castle makes you need a tall iced tea.

But this old Venetian outpost, built in the days when Venice was the economic ruler of Europe, is the best-preserved castle of its kind in Greece and well worth the climb. (A fun Nafplio pastime is asking various residents exactly how many steps there are. Most estimates fall between 850 and 1,000, but you'll never hear the same answer twice.) From the highest ramparts, you can see several islands and look deep into the mountainous interior of the Peloponnese. Below

Nafplio's castle towers over the town.

you lies an enticing beach.

This is a rough land with simple wines. A local vintner told me there's no such thing as a $50 bottle of fine Greek wine. I asked him, "What if I want to spend $30?" He said, "You can buy three $10 bottles." With dinner, I like to order the infamous resin-flavored *retsina* wine. It makes you want to sling a patch over one eye and say, "Arghh." The first glass is like drinking wood. The third glass is dangerous: It starts to taste good. If you drink any more, you'll smell like it the entire next day.

With its new affluence and a new generation of winemakers (many of them trained abroad), Greece is getting better at wine. More than 300 native varietals are now grown in Greece's wine regions. But like many locals, I often skip the wine and go for a cold beer, or the cloudy, anise-flavored ouzo. Supposedly invented by monks on Mount Athos, it's worth a try even if you don't like the flavor.

After a few days in Greece, you become a connoisseur of the Greek salad, appreciating the wonderful tomatoes, rich feta cheese, and olive-oil drenching. If a tourist complains about Greek food, they'll usually say something like, "It was fish with heads and the same salads every day." I like tiny fish with heads—squeeze lemon luxuriously all over them, and eat everything but the wispy little tails. Greece has specialties that are good and memorable—often both.

Epidavros, 18 miles east of Nafplio, has an underwhelming museum, forgettable ruins...and the most magnificent theater of the ancient world. It was built nearly 2,500 years ago to seat 15,000. Today, it's kept busy reviving the greatest plays of antiquity. You can catch performances of ancient Greek comedies and tragedies on weekends from June through August. Try to see Epidavros either early or late in the day. The theater's marvelous acoustics are best enjoyed in near-solitude. Sitting in the most distant seat as your

Epidavros' state-of-the-art acoustics

partner stands on the stage, you can practically hear the *retsina* rumbling in her stomach.

Thirty minutes north of Nafplio are the ruins of **Mycenae,** with a fine museum. This was the capital of the Mycenaeans, who won the Trojan War and dominated Greece 1,000 years before the Acropolis and other Golden Age Greek sights. As you tour this fascinating fortified

First Stop: Athens

Wherever you go all over the world (Mexico City, Dublin, Turkey, Egypt...you name it), it's smart to bone up on history and art in the capital city's big museum before tackling the ruins that dot the countryside. Athens is no exception. The Greek capital is big and crowded...but its "big four" sights are must-sees: the stunning Acropolis (with its showpiece Parthenon); the newly opened Acropolis Museum; the Ancient Agora; and the remarkable National Archaeological Museum.

Far and away the world's best collection of ancient Greek art, the National Archaeological Museum takes you chronologically from 7000 B.C. to A.D. 500, through beautifully displayed and well-described exhibits (and in air-conditioned comfort). Take this museum as seriously as you can, as if cramming for a big test. Trace the evolution of Greek art, study a guidebook, take a guided tour, and examine the ancient lifestyles painted on the vases.

In Athens' National Archaeological Museum, you'll see textbook examples of lifelike, graceful Golden Age Greek art—such as Poseidon of Artemision *(who's missing his trident).*

Finally, after gaining a rudimentary knowledge of Greek art here, head for the hills—prepared to resurrect all that B.C. rubble.

citadel, imagine that the Mycenaeans were as mysterious to Socrates and Plato as those guys are to us. The classical Greeks marveled at the huge stones and workmanship of the Mycenaean ruins. They figured that only a race of giants (Cyclopes) could build with such colossal rocks...and called it "cyclopean" architecture.

Visitors today can gape at the Lion's Gate, peer into a deep ancient cistern, and explore the giant *tholos* tomb. The tomb, built in 1500 B.C., stands like a huge stone igloo, with a smooth subterranean dome almost 50 feet wide and more than 40 feet tall. The most important Mycenaean artifacts, like the golden "Mask of Agamemnon," are in the National Archaeological Museum in Athens.

EAST MEDITERRANEAN

Olympia

Visiting ancient Olympia is a Peloponnesian pilgrimage for modern tourists. Olympia's once-majestic temple columns—toppled like a tower of checkers by an earthquake—are as evocative (with the help of the excellent museum) as anything from ancient times.

Olympia was a mecca of ancient Greek religion—its greatest sanctuary and one of its most important places of worship. Ancient Greeks came here only every four years, during the religious festival that featured the Olympic Games. The original Olympic Games were more than an athletic festival. They served a political purpose: to develop a Panhellenic ("cross-Greek") identity. Every four years, wars between bickering Greeks were halted for a sacred one-month truce, and leading citizens from all corners would assemble here.

On your mark, get set...go!

Athletes, who were usually aristocratic youth, would stay here to train for months. There were no losers...except those who quit and cheated. Drinking animal blood—the Red Bull of the day—was forbidden. Official urine drinkers tested for this ancient equivalent of steroids.

Today, modern visitors just can't resist lining up on that original starting block from the first Olympic Games in 776 B.C.

The Mani Peninsula and Southern Peloponnesian Coast

The Mani Peninsula—the southern tip of mainland Greece (in fact, of the entire Continent, east of Spain)—feels like the end of the road. It's stark and sparse. If Greece had an OK Corral, this is where it would be. The awe-inspiring, fortified ghost- and hill-town of Vathia is vendetta-ville—it seems everyone lived in a fort and sat in corners looking outward for danger.

Today, Mani's population is a tiny fraction of what it once was. Many of its former residents either fled the country for the promise of faraway lands like America, or were killed in the violent bickering that seems to be a tradition.

Only goats thrive here. While mountains edged with abandoned terraces hint that farming was once more extensive, olives have been the only Mani export for the last two centuries.

In the days of old, people hid out tucked in the folds of the mountains, far from the coast and marauding pirate ships. Empty, ghostly hill towns clamber barnacle-like up distant ridges and are fortified for threats from both without and within. Cisterns that once sustained hardy communities by catching pure rainwater are now mucky green puddles that would turn a goat's stomach. The farther south you go, the bleaker conditions become. And yet, many Mani towns feature sumptuous, old, fresco-slathered churches...pockets of brightness that survive in this otherwise parched land.

The deserted hill town of Vathia is typical of the desolate Mani Peninsula.

The tragic history and rugged landscape provide an evocative backdrop—making hedonism on the Mani coast all the more hedonistic. **Kardamyli,** a humble beach town, has a "Bali in a dust storm" charm. This handy base for exploring the Mani Peninsula works like a stun gun on your momentum. On my last trip, I could have stayed here for days, just eating well and hanging out. It's the kind of place where travelers plan their day around the sunset.

Stepping out of my room and onto the shady veranda, I bonked my head on a lemon. Then, strolling to the taverna on the beach, I enjoyed memories of a long-ago Mani dinner: Settling my chair into the sand under a bare and dangling lamp at sunset, preparing to eat an octopus, I had enjoyed a faint but refreshing spritzing. Looking around for the source of the mist, I saw a tough young Greek in a swimsuit the size of a rat's hammock tenderizing a poor octopus to death by whipping it like a wet rag, over and over, on a big flat rock. The octopus would be featured that night on someone's dinner plate—but not mine.

Twenty years later, I settled in at Lela's Taverna under a leafy canopy. Lightbulbs still swung in the breeze—but, no longer naked, they were dressed in gourd lampshades. Lela, bent and cloaked in black, scurried as a fleeting rainstorm drove a few people inside. In a land where "everybody's grandma is the best cook," ancient Lela is appreciated for how she gives her *tzatziki* a fun kick, and for the special way she marinates her olives.

I sat under an eave enjoying the view. I've always loved gazing into the misty Mediterranean, knowing the next land is Africa. Inky waves

Monemvasia is one of the most striking sights of Greece.

churned as a red sun set. The light morphed, as it does each evening, from solar to incandescent.

More treats line the coast east of the Mani Peninsula. **Monemvasia,** a Gibraltar-like rock with a Crusader-style stone town at its base, has ruins all across its Masada-like summit. It's connected by a causeway to the mainland. Reaching the summit of Monemvasia is a key experience on any Peloponnesian visit.

Although it's famous and "on the way," skip **Mystras.** Yes, it was once the cultural capital of the Byzantine Empire, but today there's just not much to see. Mystras spills down a mountain over the town and the scant ancient ruins of **Sparta.** Sparta—where mothers famously told their sons to "come home with your shield... or on it"—is a classic example of how little a militaristic society leaves as a legacy for the future.

Cockcrow on Hydra

Probably the best small town in this part of Greece is just offshore from the Peloponnesian Peninsula. Hydra—less than two hours south of Athens by hydrofoil—offers the ideal "Greek island" experience, without a long journey across the Aegean.

Hydra has one real town, no real roads, no cars, and not even any bikes. Zippy water taxis whisk you from the quaint little harbor to isolated beaches and tavernas. Sure-footed beasts of burden laden with everything from sandbags and bathtubs to bottled water climb stepped lanes. Behind each mule-train toils a human pooper-scooper; I imagine picking up after your beast is required. On Hydra, a traffic jam is three donkeys and a fisherman.

Mules take the place of cars on Hydra.

To Greece or Not to Greece?

Some travelers think they can squeeze Greece into a few days at the end of a trip through Europe. But if that's all the time you've got, I question the sanity of investing a lot of effort, money, and stress just to spend a couple of days in huge, polluted Athens and take a quick trip to an island—especially when you consider that 500 years before Christ, southern Italy was called "Magna Graecia" (Greater Greece). You can find excellent Greek ruins at Paestum, just south of Naples.

But with more time, Greece merits a visit. In the summer, Greece is the most touristed, least explored country in Europe. It seems that nearly all of its visitors are in a few places, while the rest of the country casually goes about its traditional business.

You'll get to Greece fastest by flying. Popular budget air carriers such as easyJet (www.easyjet.com) offer cheap flights from various European cities. For more on these and other low-cost flight options, see "Flying Within Europe" in Flying. If you're beginning or ending your multi-country trip in Greece, it's especially smart to consider flying into one city and out of another.

Italy used to be the tourist's launch pad for Greece. But by car or train, it takes two days of solid travel to get from Rome to Athens, and two days to get back. By boat, it's a long overnight trip (Eurail covers Ancona or Bari, Italy, to Patra, Greece, on Superfast Line, www.superfast.com; and gets you a 30-50 percent discount from Brindisi, Italy, to Patra, Greece, on Hellenic Mediterranean Lines, www.ferries.gr/hml; also see www.youra.com/intlferries).

The island once had plenty of spring water. But today Hydra's very hard water is shipped in from the mainland. No wonder showering (lathering and rinsing) is such an odd, frustrating experience.

The island is a land of tiny cats, tired burros, and roosters with big egos. While it's generally quiet, dawn teaches visitors the exact meaning of "cockcrow." The end of night is marked with much more than a distant cock-a-doodle-doo: It's a dissonant chorus of cat fights, burro honks, and what sounds like roll call at an asylum for crazed roosters. After the animal population gets that out of its system, the island slumbers a little longer.

Tourists wash ashore with the many private and public boats that come and go, but few venture beyond the harborfront. I decided to head uphill, and my small detour became a delightful little odyssey. While I had no intention of anything more than a lazy stroll, one inviting lane after another drew me up, up, up to the top of the town. Here, shabby homes enjoyed grand views, tired burros ambled along untethered, and island life trudged on, oblivious to tourism.

Over the crest, I followed a paved riverbed (primed for the flash floods that fill village cisterns each winter) down to the remote harbor hamlet of Kaminia—where 20 tough little fishing boats jostled within a breakwater. Children jumped fearlessly from rock to rock to the end of the jetty, ignoring an old man rhythmically casting his line.

A rickety woven-straw chair and a tipsy little table were positioned just right, overlooking the harbor. The heavy reddening sun commanded, "Sit." I did, sipping ouzo and observing a sea busy with taxi boats, the "flying dolphin" hydro-foils that connect this oasis with Athens, freighters—like castles of rust—lumbering slowly along the horizon, and a cruise ship anchored like it hadn't moved in weeks.

Ouzo, my anise-flavored drink of choice on this trip, and the plastic baggie of pistachios purchased back in town were a perfect complement to the set-

A sunset laced with ouzo...classic Greece

ting sun. Blue and white fishing boats jived with the chop. I'd swear the cats—small, numerous as the human residents of this island, and oh so feminine—were watching the setting sun with me. An old man flipped his worry beads, backlit by the golden glitter on the harbor. Three men walked by, each reminding me of Spiro Agnew.

As darkness settled at Kodylenia's Taverna, my waiter—who returned here to his family's homeland after spending 20 years in New Jersey, where he "never took a nap"—brought a candle for my table. The soft Greek lounge music tumbling out of the kitchen mixed everything like an audio swizzle stick. I glanced over my shoulder to the coastal lane home...thankfully, it was lamplit.

Walking home, under a ridge lined with derelict windmills, I tried to envision Hydra before electricity, when spring water flowed and the community was powered by both wind and burros. At the edge of town I passed the Sunset Bar, filled with noisy cruise-ship tourists, and was thankful I'd taken the uphill lane when I left my hotel that morning. Locals, proud of the extravagant yachts moored for the night, like to tell of movie stars who make regular visits. But the island is so quiet that, by midnight, all the high rollers seem to be back on board watching movies. Sitting on a ferry cleat the size of a stool, I scanned the harbor—big flat-screen TVs flickered from every other yacht.

Back in Hydra town, I observed the pleasant evening routine of strolling and socializing. Dice clattered on dozens of backgammon boards, entrepreneurial dogs and soccer-goal-oriented children busied themselves, and a tethered goat chewed on something inedible in its low-profile corner. From the other end of town came the happy music of a christening party. Dancing women filled the building, while their children mimicked them in the street. Farther down, two elderly, black-clad women sat like tired dogs on the curb.

Succumbing to the lure of the pastry shop, I sat down for our day-end ritual: honey-soaked baklava. I told the cook I was American. "Oh," he said, shaking his head with sadness and pity, "you work too hard."

I answered, "Right. But not today."

For good-value accommodations in **Hydra,** *try Hotel Leto (splurge, Hydra Town, tel. 22980-53385, www.letohydra.gr) or the smaller Alkionides Pension (budget, Hydra Town, tel. 22980-54055, www.alkionidespension .com). For all the travel specifics, see the most recent edition of* Rick Steves' Greece: Athens & the Peloponnese.

Turkey's Hot

Turkey is a proud new country. It was born in 1923, when Kemal Atatürk, the father of modern Turkey, rescued it from the buffet line of European colonialism. He divided mosque and state, expanded women's civil rights, replaced Arabic script with Europe's alphabet, and gave the battle-torn, corrupt, and demoralized remnants of the Ottoman Empire the foundation of a modern nation. Because of Atatürk, today's 74 million Turks have a flag—and reason to wave it. For a generation, many young Turkish women actually worried that they'd never be able to really love a man because of their love for the father of their country.

At the same time, Turkey is a musty

EAST MEDITERRANEAN

Where Greece Meets Turkey

Athens and the Peloponnese are a fine place to begin your Greek vacation. But to mix in some cultural variety, go to Turkey. It's closer than you might think: Historic rivals Greece and Turkey practically flow into each other in the eastern Aegean. The Greek isles of Sámos, Rhodes, and Kos are each connected daily by boat to Turkey. This short boat ride gives you more of a cultural change than the flight from the US to Athens.

Leaving Greece via Sámos offers a look at one of my favorite Greek islands and drops you in Kuşadasi, a pleasant place to enter Turkey and a 20-minute drive from Ephesus (both described in this chapter).

Sámos—green, mountainous, diverse, and friendly—has tourist crowds, but not as bad as other Greek islands. Bus transportation on the island is fine. And it's cheap to crisscross Sámos on your own moped. Pounding over potholes, dodging trucks, stopping to gaze across the sea at the hills of Turkey, and being spanked happily by the prickly wind and Greek sun, you will find that a moped ride around Sámos is exhilarating.

The tourist map shows plenty of obscure sights on Sámos. Gambling that the Spiliani monastery was worth the detour, I traded potholes for gravel and wound my way up the hill. The road ended at a tiny church overlooking the sunburned island. Behind the church was the mouth of a cave, with whitewashed columns carved like teeth into the rock. I wandered into the drippy, dank darkness, cool and quiet as another world. Sitting still, I could almost hear the drip-by-drip growth of the stalagmites and the purr of my brain. The only motion was the slight flicker of slender candles. I was ready to venture out of Christendom and into Islam.

archaeological attic, with civilization stacked upon dusty civilization. The more archaeologists dig, the more they learn that Turkey, not Mesopotamia, is the cradle of Western civilization.

I find Turkey even tastier, friendlier, cheaper, and richer in culture and history than Greece. But the average Turkish person looks like a character the average American mother would tell her child to run from. It's important that we see past our visual hang-ups and recognize Turks as the sincere and friendly people they are.

Those who haven't been to Turkey wonder why anyone would choose to go there. Those who have been there dream of returning. Tourists are learning that the image of the "terrible Turk" is false, created to a great degree by the country's unfriendly neighbors. Turks are quick to

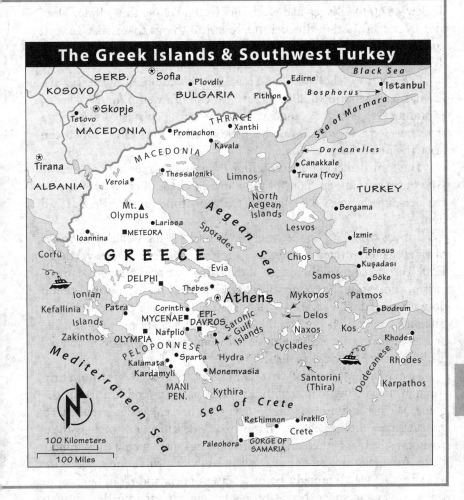

The Greek Islands & Southwest Turkey

remind visitors that, surrounded by Syria, Iraq, Iran, Georgia, Bulgaria, and Greece, they're not exactly living in Mr. Rogers' neighborhood.

Many visitors are put off by Turkey's "rifles on every corner" image. Turkey is not a police state. Its NATO commitment is to maintain nearly a million-man army. Except far to the east, where this million-man army is dealing with Kurdish separatists, these soldiers have little to do but "patrol" and "guard"—basically, loiter in uniform.

Today's Turkey is on the move. It's looking West and getting there. Eager to join the European Union, Turkey has pushed to modernize— its widespread Internet access, mobile phones, and slick bus system rival the status of many EU members. I once had a forgotten plane ticket express-mailed across the country in 24 hours, for $5. Only half of

Turkey's 42,000 villages had electricity in 1980. Now they all do. Does all this modernization threaten the beautiful things that make Turkish culture so Turkish? An old village woman assured me, "We can survive TV and tourism because we have deep and strong cultural roots."

English is widely spoken, and tourism is booming. Even the Turkish lira has been reborn. In 2005, a new Turkish lira went into circulation, trimming off six zeroes; and in 2009, the currency started sporting a fresh new look. Now $1 is worth a little over 1.50 liras...and tourists can leave their calculators at home.

Travel in Turkey is relatively cheap. Vagabonds order high on menus. And buses, which offer none of the romantic chaos of earlier years, take travelers anywhere in the country nearly any time for as little as $5 an hour.

Turkey knows it's on the fence between the rising wealth and power of an ever-more-united Europe and a forever-fragile-and-messy Middle East. Turks recognize the threat of the rising tide of Islamic fundamentalism, and, while the country is 99 percent Muslim, most want little to do with the Iranian-style rule that steadily blows the dust of religious discontent over their border. But fundamentalists are making inroads, and as these men walk by with veiled women in tow, modern-minded Turks grumble—a bit nervously.

Two months after the first Gulf War, I enjoyed my ninth trip through Turkey, this time with 22 travel partners and a Turkish co-guide. We had a life-changing 15 days together, enjoyed a level-headed look at Islam, took a peek at a hardworking developing country with its act impressively together, and learned how our mass media can wrongly shape America's assessment of faraway lands. No survey was necessary to know that we all brought home a better understanding of our world. But a survey did show that 14 people bought carpets (mostly less than $1,000, one for $3,000), eight people had diarrhea (seven for less than two days, one for six days), and nine of us learned to play backgammon well enough to challenge a Turk in a smoky teahouse. For the price of a Big Mac, we bought tea for 20 new friends, played backgammon until the smoke didn't bother us, and rocked to the pulse of Turkey. Oh, those tiny handmade dice...cockeyed dots in a land where time is not money.

Turkey reshuffles your cards. A beautiful girl is called a pistachio. A person with a beautiful heart but an ugly face is called a Maltese plum—the ugliest fruit you'll ever enjoy. Much of Turkey is scrambling into the modern Western world, but the Turkish way of life is painted onto this land with indelible cultural ink. If you're able to put your guidebook aside and follow your wanderlust, you'll still find sleepy goats playing Bambi on rocks that overlook a nomad's black tent. High above on the hillside, the lone but happy song of the goatherd's flute plays golden oldies. His wife bakes bread and minds the children, knowing her man is near.

Turkey is like abstract art, a riveting movie without a plot, a melody of people, culture, and landscape that you just can't seem to stop whistling.

Güzelyurt—Cappadocia Without Tourists

Cappadocia is rightly famous as the most bizarre and fascinating bit of central Turkey that accepts credit cards. The most exciting discovery I made on my last trip was a town on the edge of Cappadocia called Güzelyurt.

Güzelyurt means "beautiful land." The town is a harmonious blend of cultures, history, architecture, and religions. Walk down streets that residents from 3,000 years ago might recognize, past homes carved into the rocks, enjoying friendly greetings of *"merhaba."* Scowling sheep-dogs, caged behind 10-foot-high rookeries, give the scene just enough tension.

Walk to a viewpoint at the far side of town, toward the snowy slopes of the Fuji-like volcano (Mt. Hasan) that rules the horizon. Before you is a lush and living gorge. The cliff rising from the gorge is stacked with building styles: Upon the 1,600-year-old church sit troglodyte caves, Selcuk arches, and Ottoman facades. And on the horizon gleams the tin dome of the 20th-century mosque, with its twin minarets giving you a constant visual call to prayer. The honey that holds this architectural baklava together is people.

Put your camera away, shut your mouth, and sit silently amidst the sounds of 1000 B.C. Children play, birds chirp, roosters crow, shepherds chase goats, and mothers cackle. (Ignore that distant motorbike.)

Below you, sleeping in the greens and browns of this land of simple living, is the church of St. Gregorius. Built in 385, it's thought by Gregorian fans to be the birthplace of church music, specifically the Gregorian chant. Its single minaret indicates that it's preserved as a mosque today in a valley where people call God "Allah."

Who needs three-star sights and tourist information offices? In Güzelyurt, we dropped by the City Hall. The mayor scampered across town to arrange a lunch for us in his home. He welcomed us Christians, explaining, "We believe in the four books"—his way of saying, "It doesn't matter what you call him, as long as you call him." He showed us the names of his Greek Christian friends, kept as safe and sacred as good friends could be in his most precious and holy possession, the family Quran bag.

The lady of the house made tea. Overlapping carpets gave the place a cozy bug-in-a-rug feeling. As the lady cranked up the music, we all began to dance like charmed snakes until our fingers could snap no more. A small girl showed me a handful of almonds and said, "Buy dem." *Badem* is Turkish for almond, and this was her gift to me. Enjoying her munchies, I reciprocated with a handful of Pop Rocks. As the tiny candies exploded in her mouth, her surprised eyes became even more beautiful.

The town's name is spelled proudly across its volcanic backdrop. The black bust of Atatürk seems to loom just as high over the small market square. The streets are alive with the relaxed click of victorious *tavla* (backgammon) pieces. The men of the town, who seem to be enjoying one eternal cigarette break, proudly make a point not to stare at the stare-worthy American visitors searching for postcards in a town with no tourism.

Güzelyurt, in central Turkey, is a short bus ride from Aksaray. It's near the Ihlara Valley, famous for its five-mile hike through a lush valley of poplar groves, eagles, vultures, and early Christian churches.

Belisirma, near Güzelyurt, is even more remote. With a population of "100 homes," Belisirma zigzags down to its river, which rushes through a poplar forest past the tiny Belisirma Walley Wellkome Camping (one bungalow). A group of bangled women in lush purple wash their laundry in the river under the watchful eyes of men who seem to have only a ceremonial function. Children on donkeys offer to show off the troglodyte church carved into the hill just past the long, narrow farm plots. A lady, her face framed in the dangling jewelry of her shawl, her net worth hanging in gold around her neck, points to my postcard, a picture of a little girl holding a baby sheep. The girl is her niece. They call the card "Two Lambs."

14 Days in Turkey

Turkey offers the most enjoyable culture shock within striking distance of Europe. But it's a rich brew, and, for most, two weeks is enough for a good first look. Here's my recommendation for the best two-week visit to Turkey. (This plan is tried and tested, as it's the route our guided

tours follow.)

Flying to Istanbul is about as tough as flying to Paris. When planning your trip, remember that flying "open jaw" into Istanbul and home from Athens can make for a diverse and efficient itinerary.

Spend your first two days in Istanbul. Take a taxi from the airport to the old Roman racetrack called the Hippodrome, near the Blue Mosque in the Sultanahmet district, where you'll find several decent hotels and hostels.

For an easygoing first evening, walk over to the Blue Mosque and enjoy the park. Spend the next day doing the historic biggies: Topkapı Palace, Blue Mosque, and the Hagia Sophia (Aya Sofya) church. The latter was completed in 537, when Istanbul was called Constantinople and was the leading city in Christendom. It was the largest dome in Europe until Brunelleschi built Florence's

Impressive from the outside, Istanbul's Blue Mosque is named for the deeply hued tiles inside.

Islam in a Pistachio Shell

Five times a day, God enjoys a global wave as the call to prayer sweeps from the Philippines to Morocco to the US at the speed of the sun. The muezzin chants, "There is only one God, and Muhammad is his prophet."

Islam is the fastest-growing religion on earth. Unbiased listings place Muhammad above Jesus on rankings of all-time most influential people. For us to understand Islam by studying Osama bin Laden and al-Qaeda would be like a Turk understanding Christianity by studying Timothy McVeigh and the Ku Klux Klan.

Traveling in an Islamic country is an opportunity to better understand this religion. Just as it helps to know about spires, feudalism, and the saints to comprehend your European sightseeing, a few basics on Islam help make your sightseeing in Muslim countries more meaningful.

Muslims in modern-day Turkey—a mix of East and West

The Islamic equivalent of the Christian bell tower is the minaret, which the muezzin climbs to chant the call to prayer. In a kind of architectural Darwinism, the minarets have shrunk as calls to prayer have been electronically amplified; their height is no longer so necessary—or worth the expense. Many small, modern mosques have one tin mini-minaret about as awesome as my little toe.

Worshippers pray toward Mecca, which, from Turkey, is roughly in the same direction as Jerusalem, but not quite. In Istanbul, Hagia Sophia was built 1,400 years ago as a church, its altar niche facing Jerusalem. Since it became an out-of-sync-with-Mecca mosque, the Muslim focus-of-prayers niche is to the side of what was the altar.

A mosque is a shoes-off place. Non-Muslims are welcome to drop in. The small stairway that seems to go nowhere is symbolic of the growth of Islam (Muhammad had to stand higher and higher to talk to his growing following). Today every mosque has one of these as a kind of pulpit. No priest ever stands on the top stair, which is symbolically reserved for Muhammad.

The "five pillars" of Islam are the core tenets of the faith, basic to an understanding of a religious force that is bound to fill our headlines for years to come. Followers of Islam should:

1. Say and believe, "There is no other God but Allah, and Muhammad is his Prophet."

2. Pray five times a day. Modern Muslims explain that it's important to wash, exercise, stretch, and think of God. The ritual of Muslim prayer works this into every day—five times.

3. Give to the poor (one-fortieth of your wealth, if you are not in debt).

4. Fast during daylight hours through the month of Ramadan. Fasting is a great social equalizer and helps everyone to feel the hunger of the poor.

5. Make a pilgrimage to Mecca. Muslims who can afford it, and who are physically able, are required to go on a pilgrimage (hajj) to the sacred sites in Mecca and Medina at least once in their lifetime. This is interpreted by some Muslims as a command to travel. Muhammad said, "Don't tell me how educated you are, tell me how much you've traveled."

Prayer services in a mosque are segregated; women worship in back, men in front. For the same reason I might find it hard to concentrate on inner peace in a yoga class full of women, Muslim men decided prayer would go better without the enjoyable but problematic distraction of bent-over women between them and Mecca. How Muslims can have more than one wife is a bigamistery to many. While polygamy is illegal (and has never been practiced by most folks) in Turkey, Islam does allow a man to have as many wives as he can love and care for equally (up to four). This originated as Muhammad's pragmatic answer to the problem of too many unattached women caused by the deaths of so many men in the frequent wars of his day. Religious wars have been as common in Islam as they have been in Christendom.

These basics are a simplistic but honest attempt by a non-Muslim to help travelers from the Christian West understand a very rich but often misunderstood culture that is worthy of our respect. These days, religious extremists can polarize entire populations. And those who profit from the related strife—either from weapons sales, or by turning serious news into light entertainment just to sell more advertisements—are clever at riding the bloody coattails of any religious conflict. Therefore, we need all the understanding we can muster.

EAST MEDITERRANEAN

great dome in the Renaissance, almost a thousand years later.

Bone up on Anatolian folk life in the Turkish and Islamic Arts Museum (next to the Hippodrome), then taxi to the bustling New District (Beyoğlu) for dinner in the Nevizade Sokak restaurant arcade, where Istanbul's beautiful people and tourists alike enjoy the funky elegance. If you like baklava, stroll the district's main drag, İstiklal street, in search of a pastry shop. From the heartbeat of modern Istanbul, Taksim Square, catch a cab home. A less touristy dinner option is the Ortaköy district, in the shadow of the Bosphorus bridge.

The next morning, browse the bustling Grand Bazaar and Spice Market. After lunch, take an intercontinental cruise up the Bosphorus. If you disembark in "Asian" Istanbul (the part of the city that lies east of the Bosphorus), you can taxi quickly to the station to catch your overnight train to Ankara.

This gets you to the country's capital by 8:00 a.m. As you munch feta cheese, olives, tomatoes, and cucumbers for breakfast in the dining car, it dawns on you that you're far from home.

Ankara has two blockbuster sights. The Museum of Anatolian Civilizations is a prerequisite for meaningful explorations of the ancient ruins that litter the Turkish countryside. The Atatürk Mausoleum shines a light on the recent and dramatic birth of modern Turkey and gives you an appreciation of the country's love of its version of George Washington. For a happening scene, a great view, and a look at modern Turkey, ride to the top of the Ankara tower.

From Ankara, it's a four-hour bus ride to exotic and evocative Cappadocia, an eroded wonderland of cave dwellings that go back to the early Christian days, when the faithful fled persecution by hiding in Cappadocian caves. Cappadocia gives you a time-tunnel experience, with its horse carts, strangely eroded mini-Matterhorns (called "fairy chimneys"), traditional crafts, and labyrinthine underground cities. Don't miss the Back Door town of Güzelyurt (described earlier).

From mysterious Cappadocia, cross the Anatolian Plateau to Konya, the most conservative and orthodox Muslim city in Turkey, home of the Mevlevi order and the Whirling Dervishes. The dance of the dervish connects a giving god with our world. One hand is gracefully raised, and the other is a loving spout as the dervish whirls faster and faster in a trance the modern American attention span would be hard-pressed to understand.

Then follow the steps of St. Paul over the Taurus Mountains to the Mediterranean resort of Antalya. You can hire a *gulet* (a Turkish yacht) to sail the Mediterranean coast to your choice of several beachside attrac-

Exotic terrain, ornery transport...Cappadocia

tions. After a free day on the beach, travel inland to explore the ruins of Aphrodisias and its excellent museum.

Nearby is Pamukkale, a touristy village and Turkey's premier mineral spa. Soak among broken ancient columns in a mineral spring atop the white cliff, terraced with acres and acres of steamy mineral pools. Watch frisky sparrows hop through a kaleidoscope of white birdbaths.

For the final leg of your two-week swing through Turkey, head west to the coastal resort of Kuşadası. Nearby is my favorite ancient site, the ruins of Ephesus. For a relaxing finale, take a Turkish *hamam* (bath with massage) in Kuşadası before flying back to Istanbul from nearby İzmir or catching the daily boat to the entertaining island of Sámos in Greece (see the "Where Greece Meets Turkey" sidebar on page 732). Boats and planes take travelers from Sámos to other Greek islands and on to Athens.

Some Hints to Make Turkey Easier

Good information is rare here, especially in the East. Bring a good guidebook from home. Take advantage of my book, *Rick Steves' Istanbul*, or Lonely Planet's guidebook to Turkey. Maps are easy to get in Turkey and useful to have.

Eat carefully. Find a cafeteria-style restaurant and point. Choose your food personally by tasting and pointing to what you like. Joke around with the cooks. They'll love you for it. The bottled water, soft drinks, *chai* (tea), and coffee are cheap and generally safe. Watermelons are a great source of safe liquid. If you order a glass of tea, your waiter will be happy to "process" your melon, giving it to you peeled and in little chunks on a big plate.

Learn to play backgammon before you visit Turkey. Backgammon, the national pastime, is played by all the men in this part of the world. Join in (women, too). It's a great way to instantly become a contributing member of the teahouse scene.

Really get away from it all. Catch a *dolmuş* (a shared van or taxi) into the middle of nowhere. Get off at a small village. If the bus driver thinks you must be mistaken or lost to be getting off there, you've found the right place. Explore the town, befriend the children, trade national dance lessons. Act like an old friend returning after a 10-year absence, and you'll be treated like one.

You'll be stared at all day long. Preserve your sanity with a sense of humor. Joke with the Turks. Talk to them, even if there's no hope of communication. One afternoon, in the town of Ercis, I was waiting for a bus and writing in my journal. A dozen people gathered around me, staring with intense curiosity. I felt that they needed entertainment. I sang the Hoagy Carmichael classic, "Huggin' and Chalkin'." When the bus came, I danced my way on board, waving good-bye to the cheering fans. From then on, my singing entertained most of eastern Turkey.

Make invitations happen and accept them boldly. While exploring villages with no tourism, I loiter near the property of a large family. Very often the patriarch, proud to have a foreign visitor, will invite me to join him cross-legged on his large, bright carpet in the shade. The women of the household bring tea, then peer at us from around a distant corner. Shake hands, jabber away in English, play show and tell, pass around photos from home, take photos of the family, and get their addresses so you can mail them copies. They'll always remember your visit. And so will you.

Greek and Turkish travel agencies are more helpful than they look.

*For good-value accommodations in **Istanbul**, see page 746. In **Güzelyurt**, try Hotel Karballa (budget, Çarşı içi, tel. 382/451-2103, www.karballahotel .com) or Kadir's Antique Gelveri Houses (budget, Yukarı Mahalle Aksaray 37, tel. 382/451-2089, www.cappadociakadirshouses.com). In **Kuşadasi**, consider Grand Onder Otel (moderate, Atatürk Bulvari Girsi Yat Limani Karsisi, tel. 256/618-1690, www.onderotel.com). In **Sámos** (Greece), try Sámos City Hotel* *(moderate, 11 The. Sofouli, tel. 22730-283-778, www.samoshotel.gr). For more about Turkey, see the latest edition of* Rick Steves' Istanbul.

Istanbul Déjà Vu

When I was in my twenties, I finished eight European trips in a row in Turkey. I didn't plan it that way—it was the natural finale, the sub-

conscious cherry on top of every year's travel adventures. Recently, realizing I hadn't set foot in Istanbul for nearly a decade, I made a point to return to the city where East meets West. The comforting simi-larities and jarring differences between today's Istanbul, and the Istanbul I remember, filled the trip both with nostalgia and with vivid examples of how change is sweeping the planet.

The moment I stepped off my plane, I remembered how much I enjoy this country. Marveling at the efficiency of Istanbul's Atatürk Airport, I popped onto the street and into a yellow *taksi*. Seeing the welcoming grin of the unshaven driver who greeted me with a *"Merhaba,"* I just blurted out, *"Çok güzel."* I forgot I remembered the phrase. It just came to me—like a baby shouts for joy. I was back in Turkey, and it was "very beautiful" indeed. My first hours in Turkey were filled with similar déjà vu moments like no travel homecoming I could remember.

As the *taksi* turned off the highway and into the tangled lanes of the tourist zone—just below the Blue Mosque—all the tourist-friendly busi-nesses still lined up, providing a backdrop for their chorus line of barkers shouting, "Yes, Mister!"

I looked at the dirty kids in the streets and remembered a rougher time, when kids like these would earn small change by hanging out the passenger door of ramshackle vans. They'd yell "Topkapı, Topkapı, Topkapı" (or whichever neighborhood was the destination) in a scram-ble to pick up passengers in the shared minibuses called *dolmuş*. (The *dolmuş*—a wild cross between a taxi, a bus, and a kidnapping vehicle—is literally and appropriately translated as "stuffed.")

While Turkey's new affluence has nearly killed the *dolmuş*, the echoes of the boys hollering from the vans bounced happily in my memory: "Aksaray, Aksaray, Aksaray...Sultanahmet, Sultanahmet, Sultanahmet."

I remembered my favorite call was for the train station's neighborhood: "Sirkeci, Sirkeci, Sirkeci" (SEER-kay-jee).

Istanbul, now with a population of almost 15 million, is thriving. The city is poignantly littered both with remnants of grand (if eventually corrupt) empires, and with living, breathing reminders of the harsh reality of life in the developing world. Sipping my tea, I watched old men shuffle by, carrying nothing but walking as if still bent under the towering loads they had carried all of their human-beast-of-burden lives.

And yet, this ancient city is striding into the future. During my visit, everyone was buzzing about the upcoming completion of the new tunnel

under the Bosphorus, which will give a million commuters in the Asian suburbs of Istanbul an easy train link to their places of work in Europe. This tunnel is emblematic of modern Turkey's commitment to connecting East and West, just as Istanbul bridges Asia and Europe. I also see it as a concrete example of how parts of the developing world are emerging as economic dynamos.

Stepping out of my shoes, I entered the vast and turquoise (and therefore not-quite-rightly-named) Blue Mosque. Hoping for another déjà vu, I didn't get it. Something was missing. Yes...gone was the smell of countless sweaty socks, knees, palms, and foreheads soaked into the ancient carpet upon which worshippers did their quite physical prayer workouts. Sure enough, the Blue Mosque had a fresh new carpet—with a subtle design that keeps worshippers organized in the same way that lined paper tames printed letters.

The prayer service let out, and a sea of Turks surged for the door. Being caught up in a crush of locals—where the only way to get any personal space is to look up—is a connecting-with-humanity ritual for me. I seek out these opportunities. It's the closest I'll ever come to experiencing the exhilaration of bodysurfing above a mosh pit. Going outside with the worshipping flow, I scanned the dark sky. That scene—one I had forgotten was so breathtaking—played for me again: hard-pumping seagulls powering through the humid air in a black sky, surging into the light as they crossed in front of floodlit minarets.

Walking down to the Golden Horn inlet and Istanbul's churning waterfront, I crossed the new Galata Bridge, which made me miss the dismantled and shipped-out old Galata Bridge—so crusty with life's struggles. Feeling a wistful nostalgia, I thought of how all societies morph with the push and pull of the times.

But then I realized that, while the old bridge is gone, the new one has been engulfed with the same vibrant street life—boys casting their lines, old men sucking on water pipes, and sesame-seed bread rings filling cloudy glass-windowed carts. It reminded me how stubborn cultural inertia can be.

Istanbul's new Galata Bridge retains the lively spirit of the old one, with a lower level for eateries, pedestrians, and fishermen.

On the sloppy adjacent harborfront, the venerable "fish and bread boats" were still rocking in the constant chop of the busy harbor. In a humbler day, they were 20-foot-long open dinghies— rough boats with battered car tires for fenders—with open fires for grilling fish, literally fresh off the boat. For a few coins, the fishermen would bury a big white fillet in a hunk of fluffy white bread, wrap it in newsprint, and I was on my way...dining out on fish.

In recent years, the fish and bread boats had been shut down—they had no license. After a popular uproar, they came back. They're a bit more hygienic, no longer using newspaper for wrapping, but still rocking in the waves and slamming out fresh fish.

Wandering under stiletto minarets, I listened as a hardworking loudspeaker—lashed to the minaret as if to a religious crow's nest— belted out a call to prayer. Noticing the twinkling lights strung up in honor of the holy month of Ramadan, I thought, "Charming—they've draped Christmas lights between the minarets." (A Turk might come to my house and say, "Charming—he's draped Ramadan lights on his Christmas tree.") I marveled at the multigenerational conviviality at the Hippodrome—that long, oblong plaza still shaped like a chariot race-course, as it was 18 centuries ago. Precocious children high-fived me and tried out their only English phrase: "What is your name?" Just to enjoy their quizzical look, I'd say, "Seven o'clock." As I struggle to understand their society, I guess my mischievous streak wanted them to deal with a little confusion as well.

In Turkey, I have more personal rituals than in other countries. I cap my days with a bowl of *sütlaç*. That's rice pudding with a sprinkle of cinnamon—still served in a square and shiny stainless steel bowl with a matching spoon, not much bigger than a gelato sampler.

And I don't let a day go by in Turkey without enjoying a teahouse game of backgammon with a stranger. Boards have become less characteristic; they're now cheap and mass-produced, almost disposable. Today's dice—plastic and perfect—make me miss the

It's enlightening to visit a place where you are the cultural spectacle.

tiny handmade "bones" of the 20th century, with their disobedient dots. But some things never change. To test a fun cultural quirk, I tossed my dice and paused. As I remembered, a bystander moved for me. When it comes to backgammon, there's one right way...and everybody knows it. And in Turkey, perhaps as a result of its ruthless history, when starting a new game, the winner of the last game goes first.

With each backgammon game, I think of one of my most precious possessions back home: an old-time, hand-hewn, inlaid backgammon board, with rusty little hinges held in place by hasty tacks, and soft, white wood worn deeper than the harder, dark wood. Twenty years after taking that backgammon board home, I open it and still smell the tobacco, tea, and soul of a traditional Turkish community. There's almost nothing in my world that is worn or has been enjoyed long enough to absorb the smells of my life and community. It's a reminder to me of the cost of modernity. And when the feel and smell of my old backgammon board takes me back to Turkey, I'm reminded how, in the face of all that modernity, the endangered though resilient charm of traditional cultures is something to value.

Today in Turkey, the people—like those dots on the modern dice—line up better. The weave of a mosque carpet provides direction. There's a seat for everyone, as the *dolmuş* are no longer so stuffed. Fez sales to tourists are way down, but scarves worn by local women (a symbol of traditional Muslim identity) is way up. Each of my déjà vu moments shows a society confronting powerful forces of change while also wanting to stay the same.

*For good-value accommodations in **Istanbul**, consider Aya Sofya Pensions SC (moderate, along Soğukçeşme Sokak, tel. 0212/513-3660, www.ayasofya pensions.com) or Uyan Hotel SC (moderate, Utangaç Sokak 25, tel. 0212/516-4892 or 0212/518-9255, www.uyanhotel.com). For all the travel specifics, see the most recent edition of* Rick Steves' Istanbul.

Eastern Turkey

Istanbul and the western Turkish coast—while still fascinating, cheap, and eager to please—are moving toward European-style mainstream tourism.

For the most cultural thrills, head east. Tour inland Anatolia with abandon, using Ankara as a springboard. From here, buses transport you to the region, culture, and era of your choice.

Find a town that has yet to master the business of tourism, like Kastamonu (5 hours northeast of Ankara). The business hotel where I stayed was cheap ($20 doubles) and comfortable, but not slick. I handed a postcard to the boy at the desk, hoping he could mail it for me. He looked it over a couple of times on both sides, complimented me, and politely handed it back. As I left, he raised his right hand like a cigar-store Indian and said, "Hello." While changing money, I was spotted by the bank manager, who invited me into his office for tea. Since I was his first American customer, he wanted to celebrate.

Outside, a gaggle of men wearing grays, blacks, and browns were shuffling quietly down the street. A casket floated over them as each man jostled to the front to pay his respects by "giving it a shoulder."

Turkey is a land of ceremonies. Rather than relying on a list of festivals, travel with sharp eyes, flexibility, and some knowledge of the folk culture. Life

here is punctuated with colorful, meaningful events. As the dust from the funeral procession clears, you may see a proud eight-year-old boy dressed like a prince or a sultan. The boy is celebrating his circumcision, a rite of passage that some claim is an echo of the days of matriarchal Amazon rule, when entry into the priesthood required c-c-c-castration. This is a great day for the boy and his family. Turks call it the "happiest wedding"—because there are no in-laws.

Having an interpreter helps you explore and mingle with meaning, but it's not required. Many older Turks speak German. The friendliness of Turkey is legendary among those who have traveled beyond the cruise ports. While relatively few small-town Turks speak English, their eagerness to help makes the language barrier look much less formidable.

Enjoy jabbering with the people you meet. If Turkish sounds tough to you, remember, it's the same in reverse. Certain sounds, like our "th," are tricky. My friend Ruth was entertained by the tortured attempts Turks made at pronouncing her name: "Woooott." Any English-speaking Turk can remember

In Turkey, you don't need museums—they're living in the streets.

spending long hours looking into the mirror, slowly enunciating: "This and these are hard to say. I think about them every day. My mouth and my teeth, I think you see, help me say them easily."

Throughout Turkey, travelers cringe at the sight of ugly, unfinished construction that scars nearly every town with rusty tangles of steel rebar waiting to reinforce future concrete walls. But in Turkey, unfinished buildings are family savings accounts. Inflation here can be ruinous. Anyone in need of a hedge against inflation keeps a building under construction. Whenever there's a little extra cash, rather than watch it evaporate in the bank, Ahmed will invest in the next stage of construction. It's the goal of any Turkish parent to provide each child with a house or apartment with which to start adult life. A popular saying is, "Rebar holds the family together."

If you're looking for a rain forest in Turkey, go to the northeast, along the Black Sea coast, where it rains 320 days a year. This is the world's top hazelnut-producing region and home of the Laz people. A highlight of one tour (which I led through Eastern Turkey with 22 American travelers and a Turkish co-guide) was spending an evening and a night with a Laz family. Actually the families of three brothers, they all lived in one large three-layered house provided to them by their elderly parents.

The people in our group were the first Americans that the 16 people who lived there had ever seen. We were treated to a feast. In Turkey, it's next to impossible to turn down this kind of hospitality. As we praised the stuffed peppers, members of our group discreetly passed Pepto-Bismol tablets around under the table. (The pouring tea didn't quite mask the sound of ripping cellophane.)

After dinner, we paid our respects to the grandma. Looking like a veiled angel in white, she and her family knew she would soon succumb to her cancer. But for now, she was overjoyed to see such a happy evening filling her family's home.

When we wondered about having an extended family under one roof, one of the sons said, "If a day goes by when we don't see each other, we are very sad." To assure harmony in the family, the three brothers married three sisters from another family. They also assured us that entertaining our group of 22 was no problem. If we weren't there, they'd have had as many of their neighbors in.

No Turkish gathering is complete without dancing, and anyone who can snap fingers and swing a Hula-Hoop can be comfortable on the living-room dance floor of new Turkish friends. Two aunts, deaf and mute from meningitis, brought the house down with their shoulders fluttering like butterflies. We danced and talked with four generations until after midnight.

Stepping into the late-night breeze, I noticed that what had seemed to be a forested hillside was now a spangled banner of lights shining through windows, each representing a "Third World" home filled with as many "family values" as the one we were a part of that night. So much for my stereotypical image of fanatical Muslim hordes. Before we left the next morning, our friends tossed a gunnysack of hazelnuts into our bus.

For decades, this eastern end of Turkey's Black Sea coast was a dead end, butting up against the closed border of Soviet Georgia. But today the former USSR is ringed by sprawling "Russian markets" rather than foreboding guard posts.

From Finland to Turkey, we found boxy Lada automobiles overloaded with the lowest class of garage-sale junk, careening toward the nearest border on a desperate mission to scrape together a little hard cash. In the Turkish coastal town of Trabzon, 300 yards of motley tarps and blankets displayed grandpa's tools, pink and yellow "champagnski," Caspian caviar (the blue lid is best), battered samovars, fur hats, and nightmarish Rube Goldbergian electrical gadgetry. A Georgian babushka lady with a linebacker's build, caked-on makeup, and bleached-blonde hair offered us a wide selection of Soviet pins, garish plastic flowers, and practically worthless ruble coins.

To satisfy my group's strange appetite for godforsaken border crossings, we drove out to the Georgian border. No one knew if we could cross or not. As far as the Turkish official was concerned, "No problem." We were escorted through the mud, past pushcarts bound for flea markets and huge trucks mired in red tape. In this strange economic no-man's-land, the relative prosperity of Muslim Turkey was clear. Just a prayer call away from Georgia, a sharp little Turkish mosque with an exclamation-point minaret seemed to holler, "You sorry losers, let us help you onto our boat." Young Georgian soldiers with hardly a button on their uniforms checked identity cards, as those who qualified squeezed past the barbed wire and through the barely open gate. A soldier told us we couldn't pass. In search of a second opinion, we fetched an officer who said, "Visa no, problem"—a negative that, for a second, I misinterpreted as a positive.

Driving inland from the Black Sea under 10,000-foot peaks, our bus crawled up onto the burnt, barren, 5,000-foot-high Anatolian plateau to Erzurum, the main city of Eastern Turkey (24 hours by bus from Istanbul). Life is hard here. Blood feuds, a holdover from feudal justice under the Ottomans, are a leading cause of imprisonment. Winters are below-zero killers. Villages spread out onto the plateau like brown weeds, each with the same economy: ducks, dung, and hay.

But Allah has given this land some pleasant surprises. The parched plain hides lush valleys where rooftops sport colorful patches of sun-dried apricots, where shepherd children still play the eagle-bone flute, and where teenage boys prefer girls who dress modestly. And you can crack the sweet, thin-skinned hazelnuts with your teeth.

Entering a village, we passed under a banner announcing, "No love is better than the love for your land and your nation." Another ducks, dung, and hay town, it took us warmly into its callused hands. Each house wore a tall hat of hay—food for the cattle and insulation for the winter. Mountains of cow pies were neatly stacked and promised warmth and cooking fuel for the six months of snowed-in winter that was on its way. A man with a donkey cart wheeled us through town. Veiled mothers strained to look through our camera's viewfinder to see their children's mugging faces. The town's annually elected policeman bragged that he keeps the place safe from terrorists. Children scampered around women beating raw wool with sticks—a rainbow of browns that would one day be woven into a carpet to soften a stone sofa, warm up a mud-brick wall, or serve as a daughter's dowry.

Driving east from Erzurum, we set our sights on 17,000-foot Mount Ararat, which is in the part of Turkey inhabited by Kurds. Villages growing between ancient rivers of lava expertly milk the land for a subsistence living. After a quick reread of the flood story in Genesis, I realized this powerful, sun-drenched, windswept land had changed little since Noah docked.

On a ridge high above our bus, I could make out the figure of a lone man silhouetted against a bright blue sky waving at us. A few years ago, he could have been a guerrilla. Once a deadly internal conflict, Turkey's fight with its persistent Kurdish insurgency has pretty much died down in the last decade. But the turmoil in Iraq—and the prospect that those Kurds could form an autonomous nation—has reignited this prickly issue. One thing is for sure: Turkey does not want to share a border with an independent Kurdistan.

When I got up early the next morning to see the sunrise over Mount Ararat, I could make out a long convoy of Turkish army vehicles. It reminded me that these days it takes more than 40 days of rain to fix things. Our world is a complicated place in which the nightly news is just a shadow play of reality. To give it depth, you need to travel.

For the entire script of my Eastern Turkey public television program, check out www.ricksteves.com/tvr.

PART THREE
APPENDIX

SAMPLE ROUTES

After years of designing bus tours, brainstorming with my guides, and helping travelers plan their itineraries, I've come up with some fun and efficient three-week plans. These itineraries are fast but realistic if you plan well and travel smart. They're roughly the routes our guided bus tours follow, and are also the routes covered in my various country guidebooks.

Great Britain in 22 Days

While this three-week itinerary is designed to be done by car, it can be done by train and bus or, better yet, with a BritRail & Drive Pass (best car days: Cotswolds, North Wales, Lake District, Scottish Highlands, Hadrian's Wall). For three weeks without a car, I'd probably cut back on the recommended sights with the most frustrating public transportation (South and North Wales, Ironbridge Gorge, and the Scottish Highlands). Lacing together the cities by train is very slick. With more time, everything is workable without a car.

Day 1: Arrive in London, catch bus to Bath. Get over your jet lag in Bath (3 nights).

Day 2: Enjoy Bath.

Day 3: Pick up your rental car and day-trip to the stone circle at Avebury and the towns of Wells and Glastonbury.

Day 4: Visit South Wales, including St. Fagans Museum and Tintern Abbey. Head for the Cotswolds and sleep in Chipping Campden (2 nights).

Day 5: Explore the Cotswolds and Blenheim Palace.

Day 6: Visit Stratford, Warwick Castle, and Coventry. Sleep in Ironbridge Gorge (1 night).

Day 7: Explore Ironbridge Gorge, then head to North Wales. Explore the towns and terrain around Snowdonia National Park and sleep in Conwy (2 nights).

Day 8: Enjoy more highlights of North Wales.

Day 9: Stop by Liverpool to enjoy Beatles sights, then head to Britain's tacky but fun "Coney Island," Blackpool (1 night).

Day 10: Explore the southern Lake District, home-basing in the Keswick area (2 nights).

Day 11: Tour the northern Lake District.

Day 12: Drive up through the Scottish Lowlands to the west coast of Scotland, overnighting in Oban (1 night).

Day 13: Explore the scenic Scottish Highlands, looking for the Loch Ness monster. End your day in Edinburgh (3 nights).

Day 14: Another Highlands adventure, or begin touring Edinburgh.

Day 15: More time in Edinburgh.

Day 16: Visit Hadrian's Wall and the Beamish Museum, arriving in Durham in time for an evensong at the cathedral (1 night).

Day 17: Explore the North York Moors, winding up in York. Turn in your car and check into your hotel (2 nights).

Day 18: Enjoy York.

Day 19: Take an early train to London and begin exploring the city (3 nights).

Day 20: Enjoy London.

Day 21: More time in London.

Day 22: Fly home.

Ireland in 23 Days

This three-week itinerary is designed to be done by car, although most of it can be done by train and bus. For three weeks without a car, spend your first three nights in Dublin using buses and taxis. Cut back on the recommended sights with the most frustrating public transportation (Ring of Kerry, Valley of the Boyne, Connemara, and Counties Mayo, Wexford, and Donegal). You can book day tours by bus for some of these areas through local tourist offices. For at least two people traveling together, taxis—while expensive—can work in a pinch if the bus schedule doesn't fit your plans (i.e., Cork to Kinsale, Dublin to Trim). If you have time for only one idyllic peninsula on your trip, I'd suggest the Dingle Peninsula over the Ring of Kerry.

Day 1: Fly into Dublin, pick up your rental car, and visit the ancient Glendalough monastic settlement in the Wicklow Mountains. Sleep in Kilkenny (2 nights).

Day 2: Explore Kilkenny, with a side-trip to the Rock of Cashel.

Day 3: Move on to Waterford. Sleep in Waterford (2 nights).

Day 4: Visit County Wexford sights (Hook Head Lighthouse, Kennedy Homestead, *Dunbrody* Famine Ship, Irish National Heritage Park).

Day 5: Drive to Cobh, explore the town, then continue on to Kinsale (2 nights).

Day 6: Enjoy Kinsale.

Day 7: Visit Muckross House and Farms, then move on to Kenmare (1 night).

Day 8: Tour the Ring of Kerry, ending in Dingle (3 nights).

Day 9: Drive or bike the Dingle Peninsula loop.

Day 10: Make a day trip out to the Blasket Islands or relax in Dingle (this is a good laundry/rest day).

Day 11: Head north to Galway, stopping along the way at the dramatic Cliffs of Moher. Explore the Burren region and enjoy the Dunguaire Castle medieval banquet in Kinvarra before settling down in Galway (2 nights).

Day 12: Spend the day in Galway.

Day 13: Take a boat out to the Aran Islands, where you'll sleep (1 night).

Day 14: Tour the wild Connemara area and County Mayo, winding up in Westport (1 night).

Day 15: Drive to Northern Ireland, ending in Derry (2 nights).

Day 16: Side-trip to Donegal.

Day 17: Enjoy Derry, then drive to Portrush (2 nights).

Day 18: Explore the Antrim Coast.

Day 19: Head into Belfast and explore Northern Ireland's capital (1 night).

Day 20: Drive to the Valley of the Boyne sights, then on to Dublin. Drop off your car and check into your hotel or B&B (3 nights).

Day 21: Enjoy Dublin.

Day 22: More time in Dublin.

Day 23: Fly home.

France in 22 Days

This itinerary is designed to be done by car, but works by train with liberal use of buses, minivan tours, and taxis. A France Flexipass with nine train days works well. A France Rail & Drive Pass is another good option—a car is especially efficient in Normandy, the Dordogne, and Provence. If you have only two weeks, do your Paris sightseeing at the start of your trip, skip Honfleur, and fly home from Nice. *Bonne route!*

Day 1: Fly into Paris, pick up your car, visit Giverny and Honfleur, and overnight in Honfleur (1 night). Save Paris sightseeing for the end of your trip.

Day 2: Spend today at D-Day sights: Arromanches, American Cemetery, and Pointe du Hoc (and Caen Memorial Museum, if time allows). Dinner and overnight in Bayeux (1 night).

Day 3: Visit the Bayeux tapestry and church, then go to Mont St. Michel. Sleep on Mont St. Michel (1 night).

Day 4: Spend your morning on Mont St. Michel, then head for *châteaux* country in the Loire Valley. Tour Chambord, then stay in Amboise (2 nights).

Day 5: Do a day-trip, touring Chenonceaux and Cheverny or Chaumont. Save time at the end of the day for Amboise and its sights.

Day 6: Head south to the Dordogne region, stopping at Oradour-sur-Glane en route. End in your choice of Dordogne villages, where you'll sleep (2 nights).

Day 7: Browse the town and market of Sarlat and tour the Font-de-Gaume cave.

Day 8: Head to the Languedoc region, have lunch in Puycelci or Albi, and spend the evening in Carcassonne (1 night).

Day 9: Enjoy a morning in Carcassonne, then on to Provence with a stop at the Pont du Gard aqueduct. Stay in Arles (2 nights).

Day 10: All day for Arles and Les Baux.

Day 11: Visit Avignon or a Provençal hill town such as Roussillon, then depart for the Riviera, staying in Nice or Villefranche-sur-Mer (2 nights).

Day 12: Sightsee in Nice and Monaco.

Day 13: Make the long drive north to the Alps, and sleep in Chamonix (2 nights).

Day 14: With clear weather, do the mountain lifts up to Aiguille du Midi and beyond.

Day 15: Devote another half-day to the Alps (in Chamonix or Annecy). Then head for Burgundy, ending in Beaune for a wine-tasting. Sleep in Beaune (1 night).

Day 16: Spend the morning in Beaune, then move on to Colmar (2 nights).

Day 17: Enjoy Colmar and the Route du Vin villages.

Day 18: Return to Paris, visiting Verdun and Reims en route. Collapse in your Paris hotel (4 nights).

Day 19: Sightsee Paris.

Day 20: More time in Paris.

Day 21: Finish up your sightseeing in Paris, and consider side-tripping to Versailles.

Day 22: Fly home.

Scandinavia in 22 Days

This itinerary, designed to be done by car, can also be done by public transportation (train, bus, and boat). Doing this itinerary by train is

most efficient with a little reworking: I'd go overnight whenever possible on any train ride six or more hours long. Streamline by doing North Zealand, Odense, and Ærø as a three-day side-trip from Copenhagen. Take the overnight train from Copenhagen to Stockholm (via Malmö), skipping Växjö and Kalmar. The Bergen/Setesdal/Århus/Copenhagen leg is possible on public transit, but Setesdal (between Bergen and Kristiansand) is not worth the trouble if you don't have a car. Consider flying out of Bergen.

Day 1: Arrive in Copenhagen (3 nights).

Day 2: Sightsee Copenhagen.

Day 3: More time in Copenhagen.

Day 4: Head through North Zealand and into Sweden. Spend the night in Växjö (1 night).

Day 5: Explore Växjö, then continue through Glass Country to Kalmar, where you'll sleep (1 night).

Day 6: Continue on to Stockholm (2 nights).

Day 7: Sightsee Stockholm.

Day 8: All day in Stockholm, then take the night boat to Helsinki.

Day 9: Enjoy the day in Helsinki before returning to Stockholm on the night boat.

Day 10: Head to the town of Uppsala, then on to Oslo (3 nights).

Day 11: Sightsee Oslo.

Day 12: More time for Oslo.

Day 13: Go north to Lillehammer, in the Gudbrandsdal Valley. Sleep in the Jotunheimen area (1 night).

Day 14: Explore the Jotunheimen Mountains and head for the fjords. Sleep in the Lustrafjord area or Aurland (1 night).

Day 15: Gawk at the Sognefjord, taking the "Norway in a Nutshell" route to Bergen (2 nights).

Day 16: Spend the day in Bergen.

Day 17: Take the long drive south through the Setesdal Valley to Kristiansand (1 night).

Day 18: Catch the boat to Denmark, where you'll explore Jutland, stopping in Århus and Legoland. Sleep in Århus or near Legoland in Billund (1 night).

Day 19: Continue south to the salty island of Ærø, where you'll sleep in the village of Ærøskøbing (2 nights).

Day 20: Enjoy Ærø.

Day 21: Head back north to Copenhagen, via Odense (Hans Christian Andersen House) and Roskilde (Viking ships).

Day 22: Fly home.

Spain and Portugal in 22 Days

While this itinerary is designed to be done by car, it works by train and bus. For three weeks without a car, I'd simplify it by flying "open jaw" into Barcelona and out of Lisbon. From Barcelona, fly or take the speedy AVE train to Madrid (see Toledo, Segovia, and El Escorial as side-trips); take the early, direct train from Madrid to Granada (leaving at about 9:05 a.m.); bus along Costa del Sol to Tarifa (day-trip to Morocco); bus to Arcos de la Frontera, Sevilla, and Algarve; and take the train to Lisbon, your final destination. This skips Salamanca, Coimbra, and Nazaré. If you're taking

the train from Lisbon back to Madrid, you can sightsee your way in three days (via Coimbra and Salamanca), or simply catch the night train straight to Madrid.

Day 1: Arrive in Barcelona (2 nights).

Day 2: Enjoy Barcelona's sights.

Day 3: Sightsee Barcelona, then take afternoon AVE train (or flight) to Madrid (2 nights).

Day 4: Sightsee Madrid.

Day 5: Pick up your rental car and drive to El Escorial palace on your way to Segovia (1 night).

Day 6: Sightsee Segovia before driving to Salamanca (1 night).

Day 7: See the sights in Salamanca, then cross the Portuguese border and head for Coimbra (2 nights).

Day 8: All day for Coimbra.

Day 9: Visit Batalha and/or Fátima en route to Nazaré for the afternoon and night (1 night).

Day 10: Sightsee Nazaré, then visit Belém on the way into Lisbon (2 nights).

Day 11: All day for Lisbon.

Day 12: Morning in Lisbon, then head to Portugal's south coast, the Algarve. Sleep in Salema (2 nights).

Day 13: Enjoy a beach day, and consider a side-trip to Cape Sagres.

Day 14: Head east across the Spanish border to Sevilla (2 nights).

Day 15: All day for Sevilla. Consider a flamenco show tonight.

Day 16: Follow Andalucía's Route of White Villages to the hill town Arcos de la Frontera (1 night).

Day 17: See Arcos, then head south to Jerez (sherry bodegas and horse shows), and on to Tarifa (2 nights).

Day 18: Use Tarifa as a home base for a day trip into Morocco.

Day 19: Visit Gibraltar and drive to Granada (2 nights).

Day 20: All day to enjoy Granada and visit the Alhambra.

Day 21: Leave early and drive through La Mancha to Toledo (1-2 nights).

Granada's Alhambra is a Moorish masterpiece.

Day 22: Spend the day in Toledo. Sleep again in Toledo or move on to Madrid for another overnight or a late flight home.

Germany, Austria, and Switzerland in 23 Days

Although this itinerary is designed to be done by car, you can do it by train with minor modifications. If traveling by train, sleep in Füssen rather than Reutte, sleep on the train from Vienna to Zürich on your way to the Swiss Alps (skipping Hall and Appenzell), skip French-speaking Switzerland, skip the Black Forest, and add two days in Berlin, connecting it with night trains.

Day 1: Arrive in Frankfurt, pick up your car, and drive to Rothenburg (2 nights).

Day 2: Sightsee the medieval walled town of Rothenburg.

Day 3: Drive along the Romantic Road route to Reutte, Austria (2 nights).

Day 4: Using Reutte as a home base, spend the day at castles near Füssen and other sights in Bavaria.

Day 5: Drive to Munich and begin exploring the city (2 nights).

Overlooking the Rhine

Day 6: All day in Munich.

Day 7: Drive over the Austrian border to Salzburg and see the town (1 night).

Day 8: Tour the *Sound of Music* country, the Salzkammergut Lake District. Spend the night in tiny Hallstatt (1 night).

Day 9: Visit Mauthausen Concentration Camp and follow the Danube into Vienna (3 nights).

Day 10: All day to enjoy Vienna.

Day 11: Another day for Vienna.

Day 12: Make the long drive into Switzerland, ending in the Swiss village of Appenzell. Sleep in Appenzell or in the mountain hut at Ebenalp (1 night).

Day 13: Drive west to the Berner Oberland, and stay in the high-altitude village of Gimmelwald (2 nights).

Day 14: Enjoy a free day in the Alps, with great hikes and spectacular views.

Day 15: Spend some time in Bern, then drive west to Murten (2 nights).

Day 16: Using Murten as a home base, day-trip south through the French Swiss countryside to Lake Geneva.

Day 17: Drive to the Black Forest, spending the night in the village of Staufen (1 night).

Day 18: Tour the Black Forest on your way north to Baden-Baden (2 nights).

Day 19: Relax and soak in the baths at Baden-Baden.

Day 20: Drive to the Rhine, take a river cruise, and visit some castles. Sleep in the riverside town of Bacharach (1-2 nights).

Day 21: Explore the Mosel Valley, including one of Europe's best castles: Burg Eltz. Return to spend the night in Bacharach, or sleep in the cute Mosel village of Beilstein.

Day 22: More time on the Rhine, or visit Köln and/or Frankfurt. To extend your trip, take a night train to Berlin.

Day 23: Fly home (or enjoy some time in Berlin).

Best of Italy in 22 Days

This trip works well either by car or by rail with a few modifications. For the longer segments served by faster trains, you can buy reserved tickets through a US travel agent or upon arrival in Italy. Pay as you go for short, unreserved runs, such as Milan to Varenna or the hops between villages in the Cinque Terre. In the Dolomites, consider basing yourself in Bolzano. From Venice, go directly to the Cinque Terre, then do Florence and Siena. A car is efficient in the hill towns of Tuscany and Umbria, but a headache elsewhere. Sorrento is a good home base for Naples and the

Amalfi Coast. Skip Paestum unless you love Greek ruins. To save Venice for last, start in Milan and see everything but Venice on the way south, then sleep through everything you've already seen by catching the night train from Naples or Rome to Venice. This saves you a day and gives you an early arrival in Venice.

Day 1: Arrive in Milan (1 night).

Day 2: Pick up your rental car and drive to Lake Como. Sleep in Varenna (2 nights).

Day 3: Enjoy romantic Lake Como.

Day 4: Drive to the Dolomites with a three-hour stop in Verona. Sleep in the alpine town of Castelrotto (2 nights).

Day 5: Explore the Dolomites (hikes, lifts, mountain bikes, horseback riding).

Day 6: Drive to Venice (2 nights).

Day 7: All day for Venice.

Day 8: Go to the Cinque Terre, on the Italian Riviera, and set up in the village of Vernazza (2 nights).

Day 9: All day to enjoy the Cinque Terre (great beaches and hikes).

Day 10: Head to Italy's art capital, Florence (2 nights).

Day 11: Spend the day sightseeing in Florence.

Day 12: Drive to Siena via Pisa (2 nights).

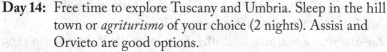

Day 13: Sightsee Siena.

Day 14: Free time to explore Tuscany and Umbria. Sleep in the hill town or *agriturismo* of your choice (2 nights). Assisi and Orvieto are good options.

Day 15: More free time in Tuscany and Umbria.

Day 16: Drive early to the Amalfi Coast. Sleep in Sorrento (3 nights).

Day 17: Spend the day sightseeing in Sorrento, with a side-trip to Pompeii.

Day 18: Using Sorrento as a home base, day-trip to Paestum via the Amalfi Coast.

Day 19: Drive to Rome, drop off your rental car, and explore Italy's capital (3 nights).

Day 20: Enjoy Rome.

Day 21: More time for Rome.

Day 22: Finish up your sightseeing in Rome, and fly home.

The Best of Western Europe in 23 Days

This far-reaching itinerary makes most sense by train; a Eurail Global Pass for 21 consecutive days is a good fit. Taking two night trains avoids two long travel days. The day trips from Munich to Salzburg and from Florence to Siena keep the hotel situation streamlined and take advantage of excellent public transportation services. With your railpass, the Rhine cruise is covered, and you get a discount on the Romantic Road bus that runs Frankfurt-Rothenburg-Füssen-Munich (though the train is preferable, entirely covered, and faster). While the route can be done by car (with certain adjustments), this plan is heavy on big cities, where cars are worthless and expensive to park.

Day 1: Arrive at Amsterdam's Schiphol airport, and stay in the nearby town of Haarlem (2 nights).

Day 2: Using Haarlem as a home base, day-trip to Amsterdam.

Day 3: Cross the German border to the Rhine River Valley. Explore the quaint riverside town of Bacharach (2 nights).

Day 4: Cruise the best stretch of the Rhine (between Bacharach and St. Goar), then tour St. Goar's Rheinfels Castle. Return to Bacharach by train.

Day 5: Take the train to Rothenburg and sightsee (1 night).

Day 6: After a morning in Rothenburg, take the Romantic Road bus to Munich (1 night).

Day 7: Spend the day in Munich, or consider day trips: a bus tour to "Mad" King Ludwig's fairy-tale castles or a train from Munich to Salzburg (1.5 hours each way). Take a night train to Venice.

Day 8: All day to enjoy Venice (1 night).

Day 9: Head from Venice to Florence (3 nights).

Day 10: Spend the day in Florence's museums.

Day 11: Using Florence as a home base, side-trip to Siena.

Day 12: Head for Rome (3 nights).

Day 13: Sightsee Rome.

Day 14: More time in Rome.

Day 15: Take the train to the Cinque Terre and set up in the village of Vernazza (2 nights).

Day 16: Today's a "vacation from your vacation" in the Cinque Terre. Hit the beach or hike the Riviera trails.

Day 17: Train into the Swiss Alps, and sleep in the mountain town of Gimmelwald (3 nights).

Day 18: Alps Appreciation Day: Spend the day enjoying the hiking and high-mountain scenery.

Day 19: More time in the Alps. If the weather's bad, side-trip to Bern or Luzern.

Day 20: Take a morning train from Interlaken to Paris (3 nights), then spend the afternoon sightseeing.

Day 21: All day for Paris.

Day 22: More time in Paris, maybe with a day trip to Versailles.

Day 23: Fly home.

The Best of Eastern Europe in 22 Days

This ambitious, once-over-lightly, far-reaching itinerary works best by public transportation. Most of the time, you'll take the train. There are a few exceptions: Bled and Ljubljana are better connected by bus. To get from Bled to Plitvice, take the bus to Ljubljana, the train to Zagreb, and then the bus to Plitvice. To get from Plitvice to the coast, take the bus to Split. The Dalmatian Coast destinations are connected to each other by boat or bus (no trains). No single railpass covers all of the trains, but point-to-point tickets are cheap to buy as you go.

The massive Hungarian Parliament watches over Budapest from the bank of the Danube.

By car, this itinerary is exhausting, with lots of long road days. It makes more sense to connect long-distance destinations by night train (e.g., Prague to Kraków) and then strategically rent cars for a day or two in areas that offer inviting day-trip destinations difficult to reach by public transit (e.g., the Czech or Slovenian countryside).

Day 1: Arrive in Prague and begin sightseeing (2 nights).

Day 2: All day in Prague.

Day 3: All day for more Prague. Take a night train to Kraków.

Day 4: Arrive in Kraków and check into your hotel (2 nights). Spend the day sightseeing in Kraków.

Day 5: Using Kraków as a home base, day-trip to Auschwitz.

Day 6: Finish up in Kraków, maybe including a side-trip to Wieliczka Salt Mine. Then take the overnight train (via Füzesabony in summer) to the charming Hungarian town of

Eger (1-2 nights); if the Eger night train is not available, take the night train to Budapest instead, and continue to Eger in the morning.

Day 7: Spend the day enjoying Eger.

Day 8: Take the train to Budapest, check into your hotel, and begin sightseeing (3 nights).

Day 9: All day in Budapest.

Day 10: More time in Budapest.

Day 11: Catch the direct nine-hour train to Ljubljana, Slovenia, where you'll sleep (no night-train option, 2 nights).

Day 12: Spend the day touring Ljubljana.

Day 13: Go to Lake Bled and explore the lake and surrounding mountains. Sleep in the town of Bled (2 nights).

Day 14: Rent a car for a day trip around the Julian Alps.

Day 15: Cross into Croatia to Zagreb for a few hours of sightseeing, then take an early-evening bus to Plitvice Lakes National Park. Sleep in a Plitvice hotel (1 night).

Day 16: Spend the morning hiking the waterfall wonderlands of Plitvice, then take an afternoon bus to the Dalmatian Coast. Sleep in Split (2 nights).

Day 17: Sightsee Split.

Day 18: Island-hop by boat to the island town of Korčula, or bus to Mostar for a taste of Bosnia. Sleep in Korčula or Mostar (2 nights).

Day 19: Spend the day relaxing in Korčula or Mostar.

Day 20: Take the boat or bus to Dubrovnik, and check into your hotel (2 nights).

Day 21: All day for exploring Dubrovnik.

Day 22: Fly home.

Greece (Athens and the Peloponnese) in 15 Days

This itinerary works best by car. To stretch this plan to three weeks, visit the mysterious monastery-topped stone formations at Meteora, or spend more time on your choice of Greek isles, such as Mykonos or Santorini.

Day 1: Arrive in Athens and begin sightseeing (3 nights).

Day 2: Sightsee in Athens.

Day 3: More time in Athens.

Day 4: Take the boat to Hydra (2 nights).

Day 5: Sightsee in Hydra.

Day 6: Take boat back to Athens, pick up your rental car, and drive to Delphi (1 night).

Day 7: Sightsee in Delphi, then drive to Olympia (1 night).

Day 8: Sightsee in Olympia, then drive to Kardamyli (2 nights).

Day 9: Relax in Kardamyli.

Day 10: Take the Mani Peninsula loop drive, then continue on to Monemvasia (2 nights).

Day 11: Sightsee in Monemvasia.

Day 12: Explore Mycenae en route to Nafplio (2 nights).

Day 13: Sightsee in Nafplio and take a side-trip to Epidavros.

Day 14: Return to Athens (1 night), where you'll drop off the rental car.

Day 15: Fly home, or continue to Mykonos and/or Santorini by plane or boat.

Europe's Best Whirlwind Two-Month Trip

Let's assume you have two months, plenty of energy, and a desire to see as much of Europe as is reasonable. Fly into London and travel around with a two-month railpass (Global Pass). You'll spend two months on the Continent and use any remaining time in Great Britain, before or after you start your railpass (because Eurail passes don't cover Great Britain). Budgeting about $1,750 for a two-month first-class Eurail pass, $120 a day for room and board, and about $20 a day for sightseeing and entertainment, the entire trip will cost about $10,150 per person. (This does not include airfare—generally $1,000-1,500.) It can be done. Rookies on a budget do it all the time—often for less.

If I were planning my first European trip and wanted to see as much as I comfortably could in two months (and I had the experience I now have to help me plan), this is the trip I'd take. I have to admit, I itch just thinking about this itinerary.

Several of these destinations are included in this book's "Back Doors" section. In these cases, I've noted which chapter you can turn to for more details and accommodations suggestions. For one fat book covering many of the stops mentioned below, consider my *Rick Steves' Best of Europe* guidebook.

London and Side-Trips—5 days

London is Europe's great entertainer; it's wonderfully historic. Culturally milder than the Continent, it's the best starting point for a European adventure. The English speak English, but their accents will give you the sensation of understanding a foreign language.

From London's airports, you'll find easy train or subway access to the hotels. To get your bearings, catch a "hop-on, hop-off" orientation bus tour (departs every 20 minutes) from the park in front of Victoria Station. Give the London Eye a spin and tour the spiffed-up British Museum. Every day will be busy and each night filled with a play and a pub. For more on London, see page 634.

Spend your remaining time in the English countryside: Bath (see page 642), the Cotswolds (see page 651), York (see page 645), and the university city of Cambridge. But the Continent beckons. Paris is less than three hours away by Eurostar train (at least 15 trains/day). Cheaper seats can sell fast. To save money, order your tickets up to six months ahead (www.ricksteves.com/eurostar). If you'll be ending your trip in London, plan for your return: Reserve the accommodations of your choice and get tickets to a hot play.

Europe's Best Two-Month Trip

Paris—3 days

Ascend the Eiffel Tower to survey a Paris studded with architectural gems and historical one-of-a-kinds. You'll recognize the Louvre, Notre-Dame, the Arc de Triomphe, Sacré-Cœur, and much more (to avoid the ticket lines, book an entry time in advance at www .toureiffel.fr).

Take a walk covering Paris' biggies. From the Latin Quarter, head to Notre-Dame, the Deportation Monument to Nazi victims, and Sainte-Chapelle. Cross the Seine over the famous Pont Neuf. Walk by the Louvre, through the Tuileries Gardens, and up the Avenue des Champs-Elysées to the Arc de

Paris' Eye-ful Tower

Triomphe.

Be sure to experience the Louvre, Orsay Museum (Impressionism), Rodin Museum (*The Thinker* and *The Kiss*), Napoleon's Tomb, a jazz club, and Latin Quarter nightlife. Spend an evening in Montmartre soaking in the spiritual waters of the Sacré-Cœur and browsing among the tacky shops and artists of the Place du Tertre. Pick up the *Pariscope* entertainment guide. Most museums are closed on Monday or Tuesday.

Learn the Paris Métro (subway)—it's fast, easy, and cheap. Ask your hotelier to recommend a small family-owned restaurant for dinner. For more on Paris, see page 556.

Side-trip to Europe's greatest palace, Louis XIV's Versailles (take the RER-C train to the end of the line: Versailles R.G.). Another great side-trip is the city of Chartres, with its wonderful Gothic cathedral (cathedral tours by historian Malcolm Miller, usually Mon-Sat at noon and 2:45 p.m., no tours last half of August and January-February).

Start your Eurail pass when you leave Paris. Take the overnight train to Madrid (14 hours), or take a detour...

Loire Valley—2 days

On the way to Spain, explore the dreamy châteaux of the Loire Valley. Make Amboise your headquarters. Stay at the luxurious Le Manoir les Minimes (www.manoirlesminimes.com) or the half-timbered Hôtel le Blason (www.leblason.fr), or enjoy bed and breakfast at Au Charme Rabelaisien with the charming Madame Viard (www.au-charme -rabelaisien.com). Consider an all-day bus tour of the *châteaux*. For the simplest approach to *château* sightseeing, skip the Loire and see Vaux-le-Vicomte, the epitome of a French *château*, just a 45-minute side-trip from Paris.

Madrid—2 days

On arrival, reserve your train out. Reservations are required on long trains in Spain and on all trains when using a railpass.

Take a taxi or the subway to Puerto del Sol to find a central hotel. Try Hotel Europa (www.hoteleuropa.net) or Hostal Acapulco (www .hostalacapulco.com).

Bullfights, shopping, and museums will fill your sunny days. Madrid's three essential sights are the Prado Museum (Goya, El Greco, Velázquez, Bosch), Reina Sofía (Picasso's *Guernica*), and the Royal Palace (one of Europe's most lavish interiors). Bullfights are on Sundays and holidays throughout the summer (check at hotel, buy tickets at arena). Tourists and pickpockets alike enjoy El Rastro, a huge flea market that sprawls every Sunday.

From Madrid, side-trip to Toledo (30 minutes by AVE train, or about an hour by bus or shared taxi).

Toledo—1 day

Save a day for this perfectly pre-served historic capital, home of El Greco and his masterpieces. Back in Madrid, take the night train to Lisbon (about 9 hours). Night trains make sense for long distances in Iberia, and there is no daytime train to Lisbon. But remember, domestic shuttle flights can cost less than $50.

Toledo: Spain's historic capital and El Greco's hometown

Lisbon—2 days

Lisbon, Portugal's friendly capital, can keep a visitor busy for days. Its highlight is the Alfama. This salty old sailors' quarter is a photogra-pher's delight. You'll feel rich here in Europe's bargain basement (see page 534).

Side-trip to Sintra for its eclectic Pena Palace and mysterious ruined Moorish castle. Circle south for a stop on Portugal's south coast, the Algarve (train from Lisbon to Lagos, about 3.5-4.5 hours).

Algarve—2 days

Settle down in Salema, the best beach village on the south coast of Portugal (see page 538). Cross into Andalucía for flamenco, hill towns, and Sevilla.

Sevilla and Andalucía—3 days

After strolling the *paseo* of Sevilla, the city of flamenco, sleep at Hotel Amadeus (lovingly decorated with a music motif, www.hotelamadeus sevilla.com) or the homey Pensión Córdoba (www.pensioncordoba.com). Then head for the hills and explore Andalucía's White Villages. Arcos de la Frontera is a good home base (see page 542). From Sevilla, ride the speedy AVE train back to Madrid. From there, fly or catch the quick AVE day train (or slower night train) to Barcelona.

Barcelona—2 days

Tour the Picasso Museum, relax, shop, and explore the Gothic Quarter. Stay at the simple Hostería Grau (www.hostalgrau.com) or the palatial but affordable Hotel Granvía (www.hotelgranvia.com). Catch a train to Arles, France (about 5.5-7.5 hours with 1 or 2 transfers).

Provence or French Riviera—2 days

Your best home base for Provence is Arles (Hôtel Régence, www .hotel-regence.com). Tour the Papal Palace in Avignon and ramble among Roman ruins in Nîmes (nearby Pont du Gard bridge) and Arles (amphitheater).

Most of the Riviera is crowded, expensive, and stressful, but if you're set on a Riviera beach, Nice is where the jet set lies on rocks. Tour Nice's great Chagall Museum and stay at B&B Nice Home Sweet Home (www .nicehomesweethome.com). Then dive into intense Italy.

Cinque Terre—2 days

The Cinque Terre is the best of Italy's Riviera. You will find pure Italy in these five sleepy, traffic-free little villages between Genoa and Pisa. Although it's become fairly well known, and parts may still be recovering from 2011's flash floods, the Cinque Terre remains the ultimate Italian coastal paradise (see page 503).

As you finish a day-long Riviera hike, your home village, Vernazza, comes into view.

Florence—1 day

Florence is steeped in history and art. Europe's Renaissance art capital is packed in the summer but worth the headaches. Reserve ahead for the Uffizi Gallery at www.polomuseale.firenzemusei.it (the museum's sometimes troublesome site) or at middleman sites such as www.uffizi.com or www.tickitaly.com (pricey but reliable). You can also avoid Uffizi lines by purchasing a Firenze Card (grants admission to several museums) when you arrive in the city, or ask your hotelier to reserve a spot for you when you book your room. Stay at Casa Rabatti (cheap, homey, casarabatti @inwind.it), Hotel Accademia (elegant, marbled, more expensive, www .hotelaccademiafirenze.com), or Soggiorno Battistero (mid-range, www .soggiornobattistero.it).

Extras You May Want to Add

More England—Bath, York, Cambridge, and the Cotswolds

Ireland—Dublin, Dingle Peninsula

Scotland—Edinburgh, St. Andrews, the Highlands, Isle of Skye

French Alps—Chamonix, Aiguille du Midi

Belgium—Bruges, Brussels

Poland—Kraków, Warsaw, Gdańsk

Hungary—Budapest, Eger, Pécs, Sopron

Slovenia—Lake Bled, Julian Alps, Ljubljana

Croatia—Dubrovnik and the Dalmatian Coast, Plitvice Lakes National Park, Rovinj and Istria

Spain's South Coast and Morocco

Southern Italy—Naples and the Amalfi Coast

Greece—Athens, the Peloponnese, the islands

Russia—St. Petersburg, Moscow (visa required in advance)

More extras—Visiting, resting, and a little necessary slack for laundry and postcards; travel days to avoid sleeping on the train

Hill Towns of Tuscany and Umbria—2 days

This is where dreams of Italy are fulfilled. Visit Siena and Civita di Bagnoregio (see page 510 and page 513).

Rome—3 days

Devote your first day to classical Rome: Tour the Colosseum, Forum, Capitoline Hill (and its museum), and Pantheon. Linger away the evening at Piazza Navona. Chocolate *tartufo* ice cream is mandatory.

For your second day, visit Vatican City. Tour the Vatican Museum and Sistine Chapel (to skip the line, buy a ticket and reserve an entry time online at http://mv.vatican.va). When you're done, head into St. Peter's Basilica and climb to the top of the dome for a grand view. Take advantage of the Vatican's post office, which is better than Italy's. Picnickers will find a great open-air produce market three blocks before the Vatican Museum entrance.

Spend your third morning at Ostia Antica, ancient Rome's seaport (like Pompeii, but just a subway ride away from Rome). In downtown Rome, visit Piazza Barberini for its Bernini fountain and Capuchin Crypt (thousands of bones in the first church up Via Veneto). In the early evening, join Romans doing the "Dolce Vita stroll" from Piazza del Popolo to the Spanish Steps. Have dinner on Campo de' Fiori. Explore Trastevere, where yesterday's Rome lives out a nostalgic retirement.

Stay near the Vatican Museum at Hotel Alimandi Tunisi (www .alimanditunisi.com) or near the train station at Hotel Oceania (www .hoteloceania.it). Take a train to Venice (about 5-8 hours, or an overnight train).

Venice—2 days

Cruise the colorful canals of Venice. Grab a front seat on boat #2 for an introductory tour down the Grand Canal. Stay near the Rialto Bridge at Pensione Guerrato (www.pensioneguerrato.it) or near St. Mark's Square at Hotel Campiello (www.hcampiello.it). The Accademia Gallery showcases the best Venetian art. Tour the Doge's Palace and St. Mark's, and catch the view from the Campanile bell tower. Then wander, leave the

In Venice, it's fun to get lost.

tourists, and get as lost as possible. Don't worry—you're on an island, and you can't get off. Catch the night train to Vienna (about 11 hours).

Vienna—2 days

Savor the elegance of Habsburg Vienna, Paris' eastern rival. This grand capital of the mighty Austrian Empire is rich in art history and Old World charm. Stay at tidy Pension Hargita (www.hargita.at) or the classier Pension Suzanne (www.pension-suzanne.at). Side-trip east for a look at Prague (4.5 hours by train).

Prague—2 days

Prague, a magnificently preserved city, is a happening place and the easiest first excursion into Eastern Europe (see page 604).

Salzburg—1 day

Mozart's gone, but you'll find his chocolate balls everywhere. Baroque Salzburg, with its music festival and *Sound of Music* delights, is touristy in a way most love. Sleep cheap at Institute St. Sebastian (www.st-sebastian -salzburg.at) or pricier at Gasthaus zur Goldenen Ente (www.ente.at).

Tirol and Bavaria—2 days

Tour "Mad" King Ludwig's fairy-tale castle at Neuschwanstein (reserve in advance to avoid waiting in line, www.ticket-center -hohenschwangau.de) and Bavaria's heavenly Wieskirche. Visit the Tirolean town of Reutte and its hill-crowning ruined castles. Running along the overgrown ramparts of the Ehrenberg ruins, your imagination works itself loose, and suddenly you're notching up your crossbow and ducking flaming arrows (see page 709).

Switzerland—3 days

Pray for sun. For the best of the Swiss Alps, establish a home base in Switzerland's rugged Berner Oberland, south of Interlaken.

Surrounded by Austria's Ehrenberg ruins

The traffic-free and quiet village of Gimmelwald above the Lauterbrunnen Valley is everything an Alp lover could possibly want (see page 597).

Switzerland's best big city is Bern and best small town is Murten. The country is crisscrossed with unforgettably scenic train rides. Be careful: Mixing sunshine and a full dose of alpine beauty can be intoxicating.

King of the Alps, high above Gimmelwald

Munich—2 days

Munich, the capital of Bavaria, has a great palace, museums, and the world's best street singers. But they probably won't be good enough to keep you out of the beer halls. You'll find huge mugs of beer, bigger pretzels, and even bigger beer maids. The Hofbräuhaus is the most famous (near Marienplatz in the old town center). Good places to stay include Hotel Münchner Kindl (www.hotel-muenchner-kindl.de) and Hotel Monaco (www.hotel-monaco.de). Take the train to Rothenburg (2.5-3 hours).

Munich's thriving Marienplatz

Rothenburg and the Romantic Road—1 day

The always-popular queen of quaint German towns, Rothenburg, lies in the heart of medieval Germany (see page 589). Then head for the Rhine.

Rhine/Mosel River Valleys and Köln—2 days

Take a Rhine cruise (covered by the German Pass or any Eurail Pass that includes Germany) from Bingen to Koblenz to enjoy a parade of old castles. The best hour of the cruise is from Bacharach to St. Goar. In St. Goar, hike up to the Rheinfels castle (see page 705). Stay in Bacharach at Hotel Kranenturm (www.kranenturm.com) or up at the Jugendherberge Stahleck hostel (www.diejugendherbergen.de) with panoramic Rhine views.

Cruise along the sleepy Mosel Valley and tour Cochem's castle, Trier's Roman ruins, and the impressive medieval castle Burg Eltz (see page 704). Then go to Germany's capital, ever-vibrant Berlin (a 4.5-hour train ride from Köln).

Berlin—2 days

Berlin, capital of a united Germany, with its great art and stunning Reichstag dome, is worth two busy days. For accommodations, try homey Pension Peters (www.pension-peters-berlin.de) or the classy Hotel Astoria (www.hotelastoria.de). Then take the train from Berlin to Copenhagen (about 6.5 hours by day; or take the longer night train-plus-ferry via Malmö, Sweden).

Climb Berlin's Reichstag dome.

Copenhagen—1 day

Finish your continental experience with a blitz tour of the capitals of Scandinavia: Copenhagen, Stockholm, and Oslo. To save money and time, avoid expensive hotels by sleeping on trains and ferries. From Malmö, Sweden (near Copenhagen), you can take an overnight train to Stockholm or Oslo, and from Copenhagen you can reach Oslo on an overnight cruise.

Leave your bags at the Copenhagen train station. Tour the city during the day and spend the evening at Tivoli, just across the street from

SAMPLE ROUTES

the train station. Catch a night train to Stockholm (via Malmö, no night train on Saturdays, about 8 hours; otherwise hourly on the x2000 high-speed train, 5.5 hours). If you'd like to stay overnight in Copenhagen, try a comfortable B&B (Peter Eberth and the staff at Bed & Breakfast Denmark can help you find a good place, www.bbdk.dk).

Stockholm—2 days

With its ruddy mix of islands, canals, and wooded parks, Stockholm is a charmer, studded with fine sights: the 17th-century *Vasa* warship, Europe's best open-air folk museum at Skansen, and a gas-lamped old town. Sleep in the elegant Norrmalm neighborhood at the Stureparkens Gästvåning (www.stureparkens.nu) or on the centrally located island of Gamla Stan at the Rica Hotel Gamla Stan (www.rica.se). Catch the late-afternoon train to Oslo (6-8 hours; night train only in summer).

Oslo—1 day

After a busy day wandering through Viking ships, the *Kon-Tiki,* and the Nazi Resistance Museum, and climbing the ski jump for a commanding view of the city and its fjord, you'll be famished. It's red-nosed Rudolph with lingonberries for dinner (see page 675).

Scenic Train, Fjord Country, and Bergen—2 days

For the best look at the mountainous fjord country of west Norway, do "Norway in a Nutshell," a combination of spectacular train, boat, and bus rides (see page 675). Catch the morning train from Oslo over the spine of Norway to Bergen. You can do the Nutshell in a day, but you'll have more fjord fjun if you stay overnight near Flåm in Aurland at the funky Vangsgården Guest House (www.vangsgaarden.no). Enjoy a day in salty Bergen. Stay downtown at Guest House Skiven (www.skiven.no), or catch the night train back to Oslo (about 7 hours, no night train on Saturday).

SAMPLE ROUTES

Oslo—1 day

Take a second day in Oslo. There's plenty to do. Hop an overnight cruise back to Copenhagen (16 hours).

Copenhagen—1 day

Another day in Copenhagen. *Smörgåsbords*, Viking *lur* horns, and healthy, smiling blonds are the memories you'll pack on the night train south to Amsterdam (about 16 hours).

Amsterdam—2 days

Amsterdam is a study in contrast: Prostitutes shimmy in the Red Light District while marijuana smoke wafts from coffeeshops, all against a backdrop of 17th-century buildings and elegant canals (see page 582). If you prefer a small-town home base, consider day-tripping into Amsterdam from nearby Haarlem (Hotel Amadeus Haarlem, www.amadeus-hotel.com; or Hotel Malts, www.maltshotel.nl). You'll discover great side-trips in all directions.

After touring crazy Amsterdam and biking through the tulips, you can get to England via a cheap flight (1 hour), the train (5-6 hours via Brussels and the Chunnel), or boat (about 11 hours). Or, easier still, consider avoiding the return to London by flying out of Amsterdam.

Final Thoughts

This 61-day Whirlwind Tour is just a sampler. There's plenty more to see, but I can't imagine a better first two months in Europe. The itinerary includes opportunities for several nights on trains or ferries. This could save you hundreds of dollars in hotel costs, and also frees up your days for doing more interesting things than sitting on a train or boat.

On this itinerary, with a Eurail pass good for two calendar months (e.g., May 15 through midnight July 14), validate when you leave Paris and expire (the Eurail pass, not you) on arrival in Amsterdam. You'll have spent 53 days, leaving eight days of railpass time to slow down or add options.

Bon voyage!

Rick's readers—his Road Scholars—have a wealth of travel information to share. I've collected just the tip of the iceberg. To read many more hot-out-of-the-rucksack tips on more than 100 different travel topics (and to contribute your own) visit our Travel Forums at www.ricksteves.com/forums. Thanks to all those who take the time to share their travel intelligence. This sampling of travelers' tips was drawn from the packing, shoes, flying, senior savvy, scams, communicating, and chocoholic sections of the Travel Forums.

Packing: Creative Extras

■ I use a **cloth pencil bag** with a plastic window to corral my passport, itinerary, emergency contact papers, and other important information. I use one of the holes along the edge to clip it inside my bag for extra security.

■ **Sarong**: A large piece of lightweight material, it can be used as a quick-drying towel, blanket, pillow, etc.

■ **Inflatable hangers**: Clothes dry faster.

■ The two most useful medicines: **Tylenol** is a general analgesic and helps reduce fatigue. **Benadryl** is a great sedative and sleep aid.

■ Small **suction cups with hooks**: To hang a toiletry bag from the mirror in small bathrooms and to dangle money belt from the youth-hostel shower wall.

■ **Half a tennis ball** works as a stopper in any sink!

■ **Earplugs** for the night the hostel gets rowdy!

■ Small **plastic baggie**: To save theater stubs, train tickets, subway tickets, and all kinds of other tiny souvenirs.

■ **Starched pants:** Pre-trip, have your blue jeans and khakis laundered and heavily starched at your local dry cleaner. They'll look great for as many days as you can stand wearing them.

■ **Dental floss** or **fishing line**: Strong, versatile, waterproof, nearly weightless. Tied backpack together when it broke, doubled as a shoelace, etc.

■ **Sleep machine/alarm clock**: In noisy hotel rooms, the sleep machine (which emits various soothing sounds) is a true godsend.

■ **Local CDs**: We rented a car, and in each country we visited we bought CDs of traditional music. We'd be driving down German side roads, passing maypoles, and listening to tubas.

■ Comfy **slippers**: If your feet aren't happy, YOU aren't happy. Pamper them!

■ A portable **motion-detector alarm** ($30 from Radio Shack): Place near the hotel door or window. If someone moves the door or window, the motion sensor emits a high-pitched sound similar to a fire alarm.

■ If you have a fancy camera, a little **black electrician's tape** across the brand name discourages thieves. What appears to be a generic camera is almost worthless to those who regularly "hunt" Canon, Leica, Nikon, and so on.

■ I **"cinch-tied"** the opening of my backpack to make it less accessible for would-be thieves (punched holes in the band at the top of the bag and ran an extendable cable lock through the holes, pulled it tight, and locked it).

■ A **small headlamp** instead of a flashlight. Better for reading in bed, and frees your hands.

■ **Post-It notes** to flag guidebooks.

■ Women, pack some yeast infection cream or **Monistat** one-day suppositories—difficult to find in some countries.

■ Body Shop's Peppermint Cooling **Foot Spray** and Peppermint Cooling **Foot Lotion** in small, travel-size bottles: Soothe tired, aching feet.

■ Tiny **musical instrument**: If you can play a harmonica, the spoons, the bones, or another tiny instrument, bring it. Playing music can break the ice, start friendships, and even earn you a free meal!

■ **Pillowcase**: To put your backpack/travel bag in while you sleep on it on an overnight train. It's another obstacle thieves must overcome. Also, set up the Coke-can warning system on your compartment door (a few pennies in an empty can).

■ Put extra camera lenses in a **thick ankle sock**. You can toss them in your daypack without worrying about damage and they take up less room than bulky lens cases.

■ Pack a **picture of your hometown** and a **small map** to locate it.

■ Tie something distinctive, like a **ribbon**, to your luggage handle for quick spotting at airport carousels.

■ **Mailing tubes**: To collect prints and posters; also handy for small items and breakables.

■ Combo **journal/scrapbook**: Buy a fancy (lightweight) journal and take colored pens and a glue stick. As you write each day, add creative touches by sketching in color, pasting in museum tickets, or even cutting/pasting local brochures, etc.

Shoes: Walking Softly

■ My **Ecco Gore-Tex hiking shoes** scrambled thru Scottish Highlands and County Kerry, muddy bogs, wet grass, and muck, not to mention cobbled medieval rambles. Excellent grip. It's not a heavy shoe, and the waterproofing is a good idea.

GRAFFITI WALL

■ Last year I took a pair of **Merrell men's walking shoes** to Italy. The best part is they are an oxford-type lace-up shoe, but with a cross-training-type sole. We used them for light jogging before breakfast, all-day sightseeing, and for dining out in dressy restaurants.

■ I've had great luck with any shoes made by **Montrail**. The soles are specifically designed to handle the added weight of, say, a backpack. You can find them at most outdoor stores.

■ I've loved my **Dr. Martens** since my punk-rock years in the early '80s and have yet to find a more comfortable walking shoe. However, these shoes have about a two-week breaking-in period, during which they're pretty darn uncomfortable.

■ I picked up a pair of **Campers** before going to Rome, and I was very pleased. They are light, comfortable, and stylish. In fact, many an Italian foot was shod exactly like mine.

■ I took one pair of **Rockport Pro Walkers** to Europe for two weeks, and they were wonderful. Comfortable and stylish, they went with everything. With only one pair of shoes, I was careful to shake a little foot powder into them every night to keep them from smelling too bad.

■ **Hush Puppies** work for me. A cloudburst in Siena soaked me and my shoes. They dried out and looked as good as new. Mine are roomy enough for thick socks, which helps for long walks. The smooth black leather looks great with a little touching up. I wear orthotics and they fit fine in the shoes. I carry a lightweight pair of flip-flops for showering and wearing around my hotels or B&Bs.

■ I purchased a pair of **Mephisto Diva boots** (workboot styling) for $67 at the Chaussures Magfred shoe store on the Rue Cler in Paris (back here in the States at the time, they cost $295!). My feet really like these boots! I got great shoes, and a great souvenir from France.

■ I have tried several different brands, but always come back to **Dansko**. I have traveled to Europe on several occasions and have worn the sandals and/or the clogs without any problems. You can purchase discounted Dansko footwear with slight imperfections at www.danskooutlet.com.

■ **Okabashi** shoes are $15, vegan, recyclable, dishwasher safe, and recommended by the American Chiropractic Association. I walked 30 miles in them in one day while on vacation. I was tired, but my feet were not.

■ I traveled Europe for six weeks with an 18-pound backpack and one pair of shoes: **Teva Hydro Rodiums**. They were great for everything—walking, hiking, whatever. They're light, breathable, and dry very quickly. No socks necessary, either, unless it's cold.

■ Before a month-long trip to France, my doctor recommended FitFlops sandals for their terrific arch support. They saved the day. I bought the Pietra version for their upbeat styling. Ah, my feet were in heaven!

■ I've worn **Birkenstock Arizonas** for years. They have one type with a padded sole that is really comfortable for standing and walking. They have microfiber straps, and the Birk clerk said the shoes were originally designed for diabetics. Translation: No blisters. Bonus: They slip off easily to allow a few minutes of barefooted bliss.

■ I wanted shoes that would be comfortable for walking all day, have a certain amount of "Euro" style, and cost less than $150. I settled on a pair of Keen Austins. Perfetto! I wore them right out of the box, all day, every day, for two weeks. I have wider feet, so the wider toe box was very comfortable.

■ As a doctor who treats foot and ankle problems, here are a few tips: Buy quality, break them in first, get used to walking before you go (maybe you'll discover that foot problem before you leave and have it treated here), take along some **Advil** or other pain reliever, and consider the use of **prescription orthotics**. They will make your foot do what you hope the "right" shoe will do—but often doesn't.

■ I find that a good pair of **hiking shoes** (low-cut, lightweight boots) can be more supportive than most shoes. A hiking shoe with a nylon or steel shank (a supportive sole stiffener) and some ankle support can take most of the load off your feet when you're walking on cobblestones or hard pavement.

■ As a physical therapist, I would recommend taking two pairs of shoes with good socks. If you are on your feet a lot, simply **changing shoes** every eight hours prevents foot discomfort.

■ Even though they're rubber-soled, I always pack a pair of **Tingley Moccasin Stretch Storm Rubbers** in case it rains. They look like shoes and really keep a rainy day from becoming soggy.

■ If your feet still hurt after a long day, regardless of your shoes, try this: Put about four inches of **cold water** in the tub, sit on the side, and put your bare feet in the water. The cold water will numb your aching feet and help reduce swelling. You could also stick your bare feet in any other cold water, like a stream.

■ If you're prone to blisters, try this: Use your **underarm antiperspirant** on your feet. I'll use it on my heel, arch, toes, and on the top of my foot. Blisters come from heat, heat comes from friction, and the body's response is sweat. Antiperspirant saves your socks and your feet. Remember to use antiperspirant, not deodorant. If you use deodorant, you'll just have nice-smelling blisters.

■ After two trips to Europe that were uncomfortable for my feet, I've finally found a solution. I switched to more technical socks. Good socks are as important as good walking shoes. Use a pair of **light running socks** that are blended (not 100 percent cotton) and designed to wick away moisture.

■ **SmartWool** makes a great sock. They keep your feet relatively dry and odor-free.

GRAFFITI WALL

■ Extra pair of **insoles**: For when shoes get wet. Overnight, I pulled the insoles out of the pair I wore and let the shoes and insoles air out. A second pair of insoles is much lighter than a second pair of shoes.

Flying Smart

■ Can't get enough **frequent-flier miles** to take your whole family to Europe? Use your US award to get your family to a busy airport such as Newark/New York, Washington, DC, or Miami, where there are cheap departures. Using half the frequent-flier miles we'd need to get to Europe, we got free flights to Newark, where our $300 round-trip tickets to London were less than half of what we'd pay from Colorado.

■ While looking for airfare, my only destination requirement was that we hadn't been there before. I started monitoring airfares to about 15 cities. Barcelona won out! My point: If you are trying to travel on a budget, don't worry about where you are going as long as it's an adventure. Plus the savings in this case, over $700, paid for a week's worth of accommodations.

■ With earplugs known as **Earplanes**, I overcame my problems with ear air-pressure equalization during flights.

■ For the flight over, take **earplugs**, **ski socks**, and a large **water bottle** (fill it at a drinking fountain after you go through airport security). Once the plane takes off, remove your shoes and put on the warm socks. Rather than constantly bugging flight attendants for water, you'll have your own.

■ On long flights with small kids, bring a **tiny flashlight**. The light will quiet a crying toddler.

Senior Savvy

■ Know as much as possible about your hotel/hostel/room etc. before you leave. Being able to plan how to get to your **accommodations** is a necessity. For example, staying in castles may be romantic, but don't forget that they're built on high points (like mountains or hills). Make sure that you know how you're going to get to the top. You don't want to carry your heavy backpack and a roll-along up a dirt trail with lots of steps. Research your accommodations or suffer.

■ Remember that **hostels** frequently have bunk beds. You may get a top bunk. If you have problems getting up to it, politely ask if someone will change with you. Most of the time one of the young people will oblige. Buy them a drink in the bar or a bottle of water to show your appreciation.

■ We visit Paris often, buy a transit pass, use the **bus system** exclusively, and eliminate all of those Métro stairs. A large system map is posted at most bus stops, and a pocket map is available at Métro ticket booths (a magnifying glass is helpful with the small print). We make a point of never being in a hurry (we're on vacation), so waiting at a bus stop is no problem. Another advantage of the Paris bus is being able to see the street life and neighborhoods (not seen on the Métro).

■ On our last trip to **Germany**, I noticed that discounts are available on most of the **boat trips** on the Rhine and the Bodensee—on certain days. If you are staying in a departure city such as Rudesheim or Friedrichshafen for several days, schedule your excursion for a discounted day. You can probably check online ahead of time. These trips are a wonderful way to relax.

■ At 69, I am now an "older traveler." Compared with being a "younger traveler" as I was in 1969, things have improved for me. In general, Europeans respect older people. Although nobody gives me their seat on the Métro (yet), I have noticed that younger people gladly engage with me in conversation and seem interested in me as a person. I recommend that senior travelers stay in **hostels** occasionally. The ones I've been in welcome people of all ages. You have an opportunity to meet all types of people.

■ **London** is a very good deal for the over-60 crowd. Ask for the **senior rate** at museums, theaters, and so on. In quite a few places, we got reduced rates and, in several, admission was free. You will have to show proof of age.

■ On our last trip to Europe, we smiled and politely asked if the establishment offered a **senior discount**, even when it was not posted that one was available. In nearly every instance we got one. Sometimes it saved us as much as half price. Don't be afraid to ask, but remember to smile.

■ We just returned from a wonderful trip to Germany with my 79-year-old mother-in-law. It soon became apparent that she was having trouble realizing the fact that we "weren't in Kansas anymore." My tip to seniors: Please keep an **open mind**. Your hotel accommodations may not provide washcloths, Kleenex, or more than one wastebasket. If you don't expect things to be like they are in the States, you'll have a much better time and so will your companions.

■ My wife and I, both seniors, took a tour of Spain, Morocco, and Portugal. After the long transatlantic flight and a day of riding in the bus, my wife's ankles swelled up appreciably. The tour guide had my wife keep her legs high the next two nights (by putting a bolster pillow under the foot end of the mattress) and drink **lots of water** both days. The swelling was gone by the second day. Moral: Drink lots of water on the way over and during each day!

■ For peace of mind, compile a **checklist** of all the things you need to do to get your house ready before leaving on vacation. Then, check off the items and take the list with you. This way there is no worrying, "Did I turn off the stove?"

■ People who wear hearing aids should bring **spare batteries** along and not plan to purchase them in Europe. I thought I had taken enough batteries, but my hearing aids quit near the end of our trip. I went to pharmacies but no one had what I needed, nor did they know where I might purchase that particular size. Luckily, I finally discovered the last set in the bottom of my toiletries bag.

■ Carry a **small notebook** to write down things to remember: train reservations to be made, events you want to record in your journal, and so on.

■ Those of us 60 and over traveling by train in **Great Britain** can take advantage of their Senior Railcard—buy online or from a station ticket office for £28 (valid for one year, www.senior-railcard.co.uk). The 33 percent savings on most rail fares quickly justifies the cost.

■ At 65+ with bad backs, we hired a **taxi** in Sorrento to take us sightseeing, a $300 splurge that was worth every cent.

■ My partner and I stayed in a **"youth" hostel** for the first time and thought we'd be the oldest people there. Not so! This was the wonderful La Primula hostel near **Menaggio, Italy**. At our table was a 60-ish couple from Sydney and a 79-year-old British woman who was backpacking alone through Europe! All three were a delight, but especially the backpacker, who said she stays in hostels for the evening company.

■ Most major museums have **loaner wheelchairs** available, and you'll find this information on their websites. (If they don't mention it, call or email to ask.) Also, be sure to request, in advance, assistance at the airport. This is a free service that airlines are happy to provide.

■ We have found that many museums in Europe do have **elevators** even though they have no sign telling about them. Just ask! You will be taken to a small, carefully hidden elevator, and most often escorted to your floor.

■ Seniors in **Belgium** (over 65 and departing after 9:00 a.m.) get a huge discount on train fares.

■ Seniors, before traveling outside the US, make sure your **travel insurance** covers air-ambulance evacuation. I traveled with my 92-year-old father and he became very ill. We had to evacuate him by air ambulance and it cost me $10,000. Thankfully he's fine now. But we could have saved so much anguish if we had been prepared.

■ When planning train travel, look for routing with transfers that won't require stairs. Check station maps online beforehand to scope out the location of escalators and elevators.

■ I traveled for a month in Italy with my 65-year-old mother. We stayed in hotels located as centrally as possible to the sights we wanted to see, and broke most of our days into two parts (with at least an hour of **feet-up time** after lunch). We were happy to **splurge on cabs** from the train station to the hotel (easier than hauling your own luggage up and down stairs in the subway or bus). We had a great trip by not trying to fit too much into each day and enjoying **people-watching** from cafés when our feet were tired.

■ I went on a trip with a piece of small luggage that converts into a backpack.

I'm in good shape, walk every day, and watch what I eat, but I'm 64 and the backpack eventually made my shoulders ache. The pain lasted for months. I will use **wheeled luggage** from now on.

Tourist Scams

■ At a reliable-looking **Budapest** restaurant, the handheld credit-card machine apparently read one amount but actually charged our bank a different, higher amount. Our $40 meal got posted as $800, which the bank paid. And because we entered our PIN, the bank refused to refund the money. So try not to use your debit card and PIN at restaurants—use cash if possible.

■ In **Rome** we needed to catch a cab to the Vatican. The taxi driver covered the meter with his hat as he pulled up; when we asked for the meter, he insisted it was a fixed price. We simply asked to get out and found another cab that took us there without incident. The only fixed price is to/from the airports. Our Rick Steves tour guide had warned us about this exact scam ahead of time.

■ My friend and I were walking down the steps of the Cascada fountain in **Barcelona's** Citadel Park when we were approached by several girls with clipboards, asking us to sign their petitions. We politely refused, but they were persistent and three of them surrounded me, blocked my path, and physically shook me by the shoulders. It wasn't until I got to the bottom of the steps that I realized my skirt pocket zipper was open and my wallet was missing. When I retraced my steps, I saw my wallet lying on the ground and the girls looking at me with a "Who, us?" expression. They got away with €10-15 and my T10 Metro card.

■ My husband and I traveled to **London** with my parents and were sold discounted tickets to the National Gallery. We each paid the discount rate of £10 to the man who approached us. He gave us official tickets and a brochure. When we handed the tickets over at the museum, the people at the front desk laughed and told us the museum is free!

■ When we first arrived in **Rome**, we got a taxi from the Termini station (without getting a quote ahead of time). When we arrived, the price was €28 (crazy amount!) I was surprised, but I handed him two €20 bills. He took them and then showed me two fives as if that's all I handed him. I had just arrived and was very confused, so I paid the difference and realized what happened right after he drove off. After that, I asked every taxi driver for a cost before I got in and carried smaller bills.

■ While in **Barcelona**, we stopped our car (a new Renault with French plates) to look at something, and a man on a scooter rode up and asked for directions. While we were talking to him, his partner apparently slit our rear tire. Several blocks later I pulled over to change the flat tire, and the same two men arrived—disguised with motorbike helmets—to give directions to a "tire shop."

I had the trunk lid open to access the spare tire, thus limiting my view into the interior of the car. While the first man was trying to convince me to go with him to the shop, the other man was in the car going through our stuff, including my wife's purse. A local woman on a balcony started screaming at the two thieves; I closed the trunk lid, started shouting and waving the tire wrench, and the two of them dropped the purse and ran off. When I returned the car, I mentioned to the agent that we had been to Barcelona, and he said, "Did you have your tires slit?"

■ High tourist areas like around Sacré-Cœur in **Paris** and the Spanish Steps in **Rome** have rip-off artists that try to make "friendship" bracelets right on your arm. I didn't have problems with these people because I totally ignored them. However, some of my friends didn't listen to my advice and ended up having to buy the bracelets.

■ Pickpockets in Europe's larger cities sometimes dress like businessmen. I observed a pickpocket rush onto a subway train car in **Rome** just as the doors were closing. He was dressed very nicely with his sport coat draped over one arm, and was holding a newspaper in the other. As my husband and I were close to the doors, I observed this man's fingers working the zipper on the woman's handbag just next to me! I looked up and he gave me a "LOOK" that was meant to frighten me. The moral of the story: You need to watch your surroundings, not just for people that "look" like they might steal from you, but at everyone!

■ A scam that seems prevalent in **Paris** is for a person to "find" a ring on the ground and then ask if it is yours. He then remarks that it is gold and offers to sell it to you. The rings are placed on the ground ahead of time. If you buy it, you'll soon find out that the gold ring that you paid 50 euros for was actually worth 50 cents. Beware of people asking if you dropped your wallet, ring, or anything else that they "found and picked up."

■ When I was in **Vienna**, my friend and I wanted to buy tickets to that evening's opera. We were walking around Stephensdom and were approached by a rather official-looking lady in a long velvet cape who was selling opera tickets. There were at least eight more of these people walking around in the square; all were selling tickets. She spoke perfect English and said she worked for the opera house and that they sold tickets in the square to help shorten the lines at the box office. She had a clipboard complete with a seating chart of the opera house. We bought what we thought were very good seats at a reasonable price, and were given a receipt. Later that night, we were sadly turned away—the opera had in fact been sold out for a month. We were told by the box office employees that the people in capes often sell fake tickets to tourists. They warned us that the only safe place to purchase tickets was from the box office.

■ Our change for dinner at a **Bolzano** restaurant should have been around €6. We received what certainly looked like three €2 coins. I was in the process of collecting a set of euro coins from each country we traveled to, so I examined the coins to see which country they came from. These coins looked really strange. They turned out to be 500-lira coins, which of course aren't worth anything but look amazingly like a €2 coin. We called the waitress right back and showed them to her. She just shrugged her shoulders, took them back and gave us euros instead. So watch your money.

■ We experienced the "**lost leather jacket salesman**" scam in **Rome**. Luckily, I had read Rick's Graffiti Wall and knew about it. My husband played along with the guy, showing him how to get to the train station and giving him a map. He gave us two "leather" jackets as a thank you. Then he asked for money for gas. I pulled out a €5 note and told him that was all we had. After several minutes of me trying to give back the jackets and him insisting that we must have more money, he gave up and drove away. I now have two vinyl jackets and a great story to tell.

■ The only "scam" we encountered was the **Value-Added Tax refund system**. In order to request a VAT refund, you have to get your paperwork stamped at the departure airport after you have gone through immigration. In **Rome**, we were told the VAT refund office was in another terminal, even though we were in the international departure terminal, so it would be better to get the stamp in Munich, where we connected. In **Munich**, only one person knew where the office was, and she said it was closed. So there was no way to get this stamp before we left, and there's no refund without the stamp. When I asked the Lufthansa rep about this, she said it happens all the time.

■ In **Budapest**, you will see attractive women walking up and down Váci street. They are not prostitutes. They approach young men, pull out a map, and pretend they're Eastern European tourists looking for directions, then ask you to have a drink with them at a nightclub. Just say no—otherwise they'll take you to a bar where the only access is via elevator and the Cokes are $20 apiece. Of course, they'll order Cognac. While we were not victims, I did meet a Brit who paid £100 for three drinks.

■ My husband gave me a strange look as we stood in a very crowded car on the **Paris** Métro. A boy was picking his back pocket. We were wearing money belts and were not worried because we wanted to see the boy's expression when he finally discovered the phrase book that he thought was a wallet. It was priceless—he was so disappointed. He even let it slip back down into the pocket. Guess it's all part of the European experience, as Rick says.

■ I have found that a few minutes of pre-planning will save you the stress of using a potentially **crooked taxi** from airports and train stations to your destination: Ask your hotel when you book your room! They will tell you a range of what it should cost. Write it down and show it to the cabbie before you get in. Only agree to the ride once the price is set, and don't get out and/or pay until you are clearly where you need to be.‑

■ In Naples, a common scam is for a couple of guys to try and sell you a killer **digital camera** for an irresistible price. But when the moment arrives to take the camera into possession, the second guy (with a big coat) switches the camera bag for one hidden behind his back—which has a big rock in it. After I found my rock, I chased them down the street, but they had a car and driver waiting to leave me in the dust...$300 lighter.

■ Watch out for the **shell game**, like Rick says! I was waiting for a friend and I saw people gathered around nearby. I went over and watched for a while. It looked so easy. I was finding the ball every time, so I decided to play once. I thought for sure I knew where it was, but it wasn't there, of course. The people in the crowd kept urging me to get my money back by playing again. I shouldn't have listened to them. I lost again, of course! Never even get close to those games.

■ In **Eastern Europe**, watch out for vendors giving change in the wrong currency. I was in a rush and the vendor in the Prague train station gave me Hungarian bills as change, instead of Czech currency. Since I was unfamiliar with the currency, I didn't recognize it until much later.

■ While at an ATM in **Paris**, a guy at the neighboring ATM asked me a question, saying he didn't understand what his screen was telling him. Meanwhile, his friend was getting ready to take the currency my ATM was dispensing. Moral: Use only "single" ATMs in an uncrowded area, and pay strict attention.

■ In **Rome**, avoid the young men who carry around roses. They work on flattery and hand roses to women while dishing out a load of compliments. One such man literally shoved a dozen such roses in my hands despite my disapproval, then he turned to my husband and demanded money for them (and he would not allow me to put them back into his hands after I had repeatedly said I did not want any). I got wise and started literally shoving these men out of my way whenever I saw them approaching.

■ At a well-known, very touristy, upscale coffee shop in **Vienna**, we had a check for about €14. The waiter took our €20 bill and disappeared. After we tracked him down and insisted on getting change, he threw €2 on our table and walked away. I will visit less touristy places from now on.

■ While visiting gravesites at the Père-Lachaise Cemetery in **Paris**, my girlfriend and I were "befriended" by a very knowledgeable gentleman at Chopin's grave. He told us he worked there and said, "I'll show you a shortcut to Jim Morrison's grave." Well, an hour later, and quite frankly after an excellent tour of not only the well-known graves but also little-known facts, he led us outside of the cemetery to "Jim Morrison's favorite café." At this point, we knew it wasn't free, and we offered him €5. He was obviously upset and asked for more "for his family." I said I was sorry and I wished he had been up front about the cost. We could tell he was going to start a scene so we said "sorry" again and hightailed it out of there. After sharing my story I've learned of other "friendly tour" scams that have actually ended quite violently.

■ On my last trip, two men claimed they were police and flashed IDs (and quickly put them away), then asked for my identification with the casual after-thought, "Passport is okay." I said, "Hold up your ID so I can read it carefully." The men looked shocked, then became abusive. I said, "I am now going to scream for a real policeman. Would you like to wait and talk to him?" They ran away. This type of scam always takes place away from crowds and out of sight of uniformed policemen. Never be afraid to scream loudly for assistance. I did that once on a bus; I screamed *"Aiuto! Ladro!"* ("Help! Thief!"), and the Italians almost killed the poor thief, shoving her off the bus.

■ My husband and I arrived at **Paris**' Gare du Nord train station and proceeded to read the map to find out how to get to our hotel via the Métro. One guy came up and advised us to buy tickets from the ticket machine. When we were at the machine trying to read the French, another guy came out and "helped" us buy tickets. Later, what was supposed to be a three-day ticket turned out to be a one-way, single-use ticket. We paid him €48, the price shown on the ticket machine, but he must have canceled the transaction and bought us the single-trip ticket instead.

■ In **Paris**, at a boutique across the street from the Louvre, the shop owner presented me with a receipt for €25 for my two T-shirts, but gave me a receipt for €250 to sign for the credit-card purchase. When I called him on it, he claimed it was a mistake. I have no doubt that it was intentional, so watch what you sign.

■ When we visited France, we as Americans started wondering why we were getting quarters in our pockets from change. We finally figured it out when we realized that the €1 coin is the same size as the American quarter. I finally caught on after we bought tickets at a Métro station and realized that the cashier had made this exchange.

■ Be warned when buying from **street artists**. A lot of the "original" artwork (mostly the watercolors) is actually just printed by computer on watercolor paper.

■ Beware of letting your round-trip tickets out of sight on the overnight train from Kraków to Prague (or any other **Eastern European routes**, for that matter). The "conductor" took my round-trip ticket as I got into the *couchette* and assured me that I'd get it back in the morning. Come morning, he said he gave it to me, then later said he put it in my *couchette*. Then he went through the motions of looking in his pockets, but I was screwed. My round-trip ticket was gone and he'd likely sell it for the 25 bucks it was worth. If possible, get a round-trip ticket that is physically two separate pieces of paper, and then only

GRAFFITI WALL

give the conductor the one necessary for that leg of the trip.

■ On a Sunday in **Barcelona**, I was going from the Picasso Museum to the Palau de la Música Catalana. In order to get there as quickly as possible I headed through one of the side streets—a big mistake! I vaguely noticed three young men standing off to the side. Everything happened very fast. One came in front of me, snatched my travel purse—which I carry across one shoulder and round my neck—with enough force to break the tough strap. He took off down an alley. The incident made me more conscious of keeping to the more frequented streets.

■ When traveling, use **ATMs** only when the bank is open. An ATM machine ate our card, and when we went back to the bank in the morning, we found out that it was missing. There were charges already made before we could cancel the card. Train stations and airports often have the best ATMs, with lots of people around to help.

■ We were targeted on the Via Nationale in **Rome**. As we walked to our hotel, a passerby pointed to my wife's back. We were shocked to see her entire back covered with some kind of whitish brown substance. The man, dressed in a business suit, held his nose, pointed to the sky (birds), and quickly offered a tissue to help us clean up. As we took his tissue and set our backpack on the ground to get more tissue out, another guy swooped in, grabbed the backpack, and started to quickly move away. Fortunately I saw him do it, took three quick steps right at him and yelled. He set the backpack down and took off.

■ On the way to the airport on the **Paris** RER, we encountered people working in groups asking for signatures on a petition to help the disabled. They were very aggressive and shoved the petition on my lap and over my bag. They unzipped the bag and tried to pick it, but I protested very loudly.

Connecting with Locals

■ Sincere **admiration** opens doors. Admiring someone's dog/cat/flowers/ motorcycle/garden/whatever is a great way to start a conversation.

■ Meet friendly locals in the **Czech Republic** by attending a hockey game. I am a 26-year-old woman who turned loneliness into lots of fun this way. I'm planning my second solo trip, and the hockey arena will be my first stop!

■ When you're on a train, **make conversation**. Many Europeans want to practice English as much as you may want to practice their native language.

■ One night in **Paris**, we noticed a hundred or so people on the Pont Neuf, so we checked it out. Locals our age were just hanging out drinking beer, wine, Coke—even smoking pot. Everyone was simply relaxing. My wife and I found a nice spot to sit, bought a few beers, and hung out until well past 1 a.m. No police and no trouble, just a lot of fun.

■ Make **eye contact**. After a week in Rome, I hadn't really met a soul. So I thought about it—and I realized that I hadn't actually looked at anyone! Being a big-city dweller, I was in the habit of avoiding eye contact with people on the streets. That evening, I made plenty of eye contact, and within an hour I was having the time of my life with new friends at a nearby trattoria!

■ **Irish nightlife** centers around the pubs. To meet locals, arrive a bit early to snag a big table with several extra chairs. As the night gets busier, people always ask to share the table. Every time I've tried this, I've met a fun montage of great people.

■ A couple of tips: **Eat by yourself** in busy restaurants. You may be seated at a table of locals with an empty chair, or they may come and sit by you. And fake ignorance. Even if you know the answer, just ask that cute German girl a question. It could lead to a long conversation.

■ When I'm taking public transportation, I like to engage with people by asking **simple questions** (like making sure I'm on the right train, or where to get off), which signals to locals that I'm a traveler looking to connect.

■ The easiest way to meet locals is to **be where they are**. They're not watching the 10:10 a.m. bell-ringing festival or prowling through souvenir shops. They're living their normal lives: the guy at the car wash, people at the town pool. Visitors are always welcome for a buck or two. Just wander the shopping area of any little town and strike up conversations.

■ Don't be so stuck on your schedule that you miss out on **once-in-a-lifetime opportunities**. We had just parked our car in a small German town, and a kindly gentleman walking by made a comment about the tight squeeze and how lucky we were to find a place. In chatting with him, we learned that he had served with Rommel in North Africa. Our schedule was suffering, so we said our good-byes. Later it dawned on me that I had missed the chance to discuss real history with a participant. I was too concerned with my plans to take the time to buy the guy a beer, so I missed out on an experience I can never recapture.

■ **Pictures of grandchildren** are great icebreakers!

■ If you belong to a **service club** like Kiwanis or Rotary, check the Internet for club meetings.

■ Just as you want to meet local folks when abroad, look kindly on **foreign travelers** in the United States. They just might be looking for the same kind of experience.

■ Everywhere I've traveled a **polite, genuine smile** is the best icebreaker.

■ Attending **church services** can be a great way to meet people. Neighborhood churches (rather than famous cathedrals and huge "downtown" churches) are the best, since visitors are less common there, and people go out of their way to make you feel welcome. Many have a welcoming coffee-and-cookies time after Mass.

GRAFFITI WALL

■ Try **second-class seating** on trains. You'll find lively locals instead of stuffy businessmen and American tourists.

■ Track down your **European roots**! The highlight of my recent European adventure was visiting my Italian relatives—a truly priceless experience. Before I left for Europe, I sent my relatives a brief letter. I introduced myself, let them know when I would be in Italy, and told them I would be interested in meeting them. They quickly responded, offering me a ride from the train station and a place to stay. They met me at the station and brought me to their small village. I was the only tourist in town, and all 500 inhabitants of the village (many of them my relatives) seemed as excited to meet me as I was honored to meet them.

■ While in **Germany**, be sure to visit one of the many thermal baths that are found in just about any large town. These places are only frequented by Germans. If you have the courage, pay a bit extra and visit the saunas. Clothing inside a sauna is not optional—it's forbidden! And in most places, men and women sauna together. How's that for an icebreaker?

■ I just returned from St. Petersburg, Russia. I handed out pencils (with pictures of American dollar bills) and candy to the children. I was the talk of the town. I found the people to be very appreciative of me, the dorky American tourist, thanks to **candy** and **funny-looking pencils**.

■ Don't know anyone in your destination? You might just make contact over the Internet. Last fall I visited Croatia. Before going I posted to an Internet **travel bulletin board**. A Croatian journalist responded to several of my posts. He gave me lots of good ideas, and when I asked about getting to some of the more remote places in Istria, he responded that he would love to show me his country. I was a little wary about meeting him—but I knew the minute I met him that everything was okay. My new online pal drove me around Istria and showed me things few tourists see.

■ I collect **little pins** from places I've been and display them on my favorite travel hat. When I'm on the road, the hat gets piles of attention. People comment, want to look at it, and ask which pin was from my home city. I bring a few pins from my home, which I give as gifts to new friends.

■ Try to **speak their language**. After a seemingly futile attempt to communicate in French, many of the locals would laugh and switch to English and we were fine. The French appreciated our efforts (and we learned as we went).

■ We made **personal business cards** on our computer and passed these out to people we met as we traveled. Today we still receive email from folks we met.

■ Rick's 3-in-1 German, Italian, and French **phrase book** was my best friend during a recent adventure throughout Europe. I quickly learned that one of the most important phrases was, "Which is your favorite dish/cheese/wine/etc.?" By asking this in restaurants and open-air markets, it shows an interest in the menu and respect for the waiter or vendor and his opinion. The usual result: a great dish, and friendly conversation to boot.

■ Join a club, seek out weekend soccer teams, go to town meetings, visit public swimming pools, shop in small markets, attend school concerts and sporting events, go to nightclubs, attend personal appearances and book-signings in bookstores, track down travel slide shows, go to church, use public transportation, use barbers/hairdressers, buy from small vintners—there are many **low-key ways** to meet locals. Be courteous, inquisitive, and willing to participate when appropriate. Show people you are interested in them and their lives, not just the tourist traps, and your trip suddenly becomes more meaningful.

■ One of the best ways to meet people is to **bring children** with you! We took our two kids for two months around Europe. We did something we would never do in the States: We bribed them. We told them if someone told us how well-behaved or polite they were, they would get $3. We didn't realize how great our kids could be! They discovered right away that saying "please" and "thank you" in the local language, smiling, and saying "good day," earned them a smile and a pat on the head. The money actually became a secondary reward, and they worked harder at learning how to say foreign words and making connections with people than we did.

■ Before a trip overseas, go to your chamber of commerce/hospitality association/tourist board, and they will usually give you **small flags** or **lapel pins** of your state to give away to friends you make in your travels.

■ I break barriers by **complimenting** people and stating (in the native language) when I like something. In a restaurant in Croatia, I saw the cook and said, *"Dobro"*—Croatian for "good." Soon the entire staff was smiling at me, and when I left an hour later I felt more like a friend than just another tourist.

■ The best thing I did to strike up conversation with locals was to sew my **state flag's patch** to my pack. So many people of all nationalities asked me what it was.

■ Along with "please" and "thank you," it is really useful to learn to say, in the **local language**, "You have a beautiful country. We are having a wonderful time." Say it over and over. You will be happy and so will everyone else.

■ I notice that whenever I **attempt a few words** of the native language, the people I'm speaking to are always more open and willing to share great "insider" information with me.

■ **Food** is truly universal, so if possible, I ask questions about what I'm eating, how it's made, if it's a personal favorite, and so on. People appreciate my genuine interest in their food and cultures and seem delighted to explain the "special ingredient" that makes their dish so good. A great souvenir is bringing the recipe of a favorite place home.

■ In **Germany**, I shared a bench along the river with an older German lady. We

GRAFFITI WALL

sat in silence for a few minutes until three very good-looking men jogged past. I looked at her, looked at the guys, raised my eyebrows, and said, "Yummm." She laughed, and the ice was broken. We had a fun chat and agreed to meet again the next day. When I showed up, she had brought a German dessert to share with me.

■ Wherever you go, do something local—like a **flea market**. This is a great way to mingle with residents (and see what they shop for).

■ Before a recent trip to Paris, I accidentally stuck a **picture of my dog** in the book I was reading. When we got to our hotel, the picture fell out, and I instantly learned I had a great conversation-starter. For the rest of the trip, I was showing off my dog like a proud parent. Love of animals is an international language!

■ Here's one good way to meet people in England: Ask to **photograph their dogs**! All last summer in England I was on a self-appointed mission to photograph as many Jack Russell terriers as I could. Dog owners love to show off their dogs, demonstrate their best tricks, and tell stories.

■ With four of us traveling together, we knew we were at a disadvantage when it came to "mingling with the locals." To make sure that we did get to have stories to relate over dinner, we **separated several times** during the day.

■ Remember, the locals you meet are **individuals**, not tourist attractions who cease to exist when you put away your camera.

Chocoholics Unite

■ **Cadbury** chocolate bars are awesome. The Dairy Milk, Crunchie, and Wispa bars are fantastic. Also, when in **London**, try the hot chocolate—tastes just like a liquid Dairy Milk bar.

■ The very best chocolates in **Bruges** have to be at the **Jan de Clerck** chocolate shop. Rich dark chocolate filled with delicious concoctions that make you want more. Truffles...WOW. All made right on the premises by Mr. de Clerck himself.

■ The best chocolate is in **Germany**. Milka and Ritter Sport are great! The Kinder Überaschung (Kid's Surprise) eggs are very popular. Also, during Christmas they come out with Advent calendars that have chocolate hidden behind the flip-open door for each day. Eating those made the wait bearable. In **London**, visit Charbonnel et Walker, 28 Old Bond Street, near Kensington, for the best chocolates anywhere.

■ My favorite European chocolate: **Ritter Sport**. It's German, but it's sold all over Europe. Ritter Sport is a square bar that comes in a million varieties. My favorite is praline (dark blue wrapper).

■ One word: Sprungli, Zürich, Bahnhofstrasse...OK, that was three words, but when in **Zürich**, go to the Sprungli shop on Bahnhofstrasse and enjoy...

mmmm...makes my mouth water just thinking about it.

■ We did the equivalent of a pub crawl in **Bruges** and sampled truffles at all the small chocolate shops. By noon we were on a major sugar buzz.

■ Once I met a man on a plane who told me he was the chocolate taster for Hershey's and his job was to travel the world tasting chocolate. His favorite? **Belgian**.

■ Did you know they put the equivalent of 1.5 cups of milk into every huge **Cadbury Dairy Milk bar**? At last, a palatable solution to the specter of osteoporosis!

■ A good friend from **Brussels** explained that "**Mary's**" had the best chocolate. He noted that there are two stores of every type, which are appointed by the King. One is a large, commercial place (Godiva in this case) and one is a small place, where the King actually buys his goods. Mary's is that place.

■ If you are a chocoholic, then you must tour the **Cadbury factory** (train to Birmingham, then train to Bournville, then a 10-minute walk, www.cadbury world.co.uk). Upon entering, you're greeted with the most heavenly smell, a lively tour, and an entire chocolate bar! As you munch, you walk through the history of chocolate.

■ Try the hot chocolate in **Paris** to truly experience it the way it was meant to be. The best place is Angelina near the Louvre, across from the Tuileries on Rue de Rivoli. Order the Africain, a pot of liquid pleasure. We loved Angelina so much that we named our cat after it.

■ After two trips to **Paris**, walking everywhere and tasting along the way, we've found our favorite chocolatier. It's **Puyricard** (on Avenue Rapp in the seventh arrondissement).

■ The chocolate factory alone is reason enough to visit **Köln, Germany**. They offer tours with a history of chocolate-making and a great look at all the machines in action.

GRAFFITI WALL

RESOURCES

Whether you're preparing for your trip, or simply looking to do a little armchair travel, consider joining me on my public television series and my public radio show. The map on the next page shows many of the places you can travel along with me over the airwaves.

Rick Steves' Europe on Public Television

Our television series, *Rick Steves' Europe,* airs in high definition on nearly 300 public television stations across the United States. We've also produced several specials, including *Rick Steves' Andalucía, Rick Steves' European Christmas* (celebrating family holiday traditions in seven different European cultures), *Rick Steves' Iran* (made in the hope of humanizing that proud if perplexing nation), and *Rick Steves' Symphonic Journey* (a visual and musical tour of European composers and countries, ranging from Edvard Grieg in Norway to Giuseppe Verdi in Italy).

Producer Simon Griffith, cameraman Karel Bauer, writer/host Rick Steves, and David—working together to bring the best of Europe home to you on public television.

All 100 TV shows are available on DVD, so you can see any show whenever the travel bug bites (you can get up to eight

These are just some of the places covered on my TV show, Rick Steves' Europe.

regional shows per DVD or the entire series with specials in one 50-hour boxed set). You can also watch shows on demand at www.hulu.com and shorter segments on YouTube or via video podcasts at iTunes. For all the scripts, shooting news, streaming video bloopers, and to order DVDs, visit www.ricksteves.com/tv.

Travel with Rick Steves on Public Radio

My weekly hour-long radio show, *Travel with Rick Steves*, is broadcast by about 200 public radio stations around the country. It's also available as a free on-demand podcast, with archives going back more than seven years.

Travel with Rick Steves is a great way for you to hear a wide variety of experts and authors explain what tickles their travel fancy, and pick up some travel tips along the way. My guests lead us into all corners of the world and include some of today's top travel writers, guidebook authors, accomplished naturalists and adventure travelers, experts on art and photography, foodies and flight crews.

The show also provides a venue for my enthusiastic and well-traveled community of listeners—my "Road Scholars"—to ask questions and share their own travel stories and tips. Even if you're not planning a trip to a particular destination, *Travel with Rick Steves* brings you the flavor of places near and far, and stimulates your imagination—taking you on a vicarious journey for an hour each week.

Hundreds of hours of interviews are organized by destination and available for free at my website. Pack them along on your mobile device to bring added understanding and joy to your travels (as they do mine). For a list of radio stations airing Travel with Rick Steves, upcoming topics, and details on how to join in the conversation yourself, see www .ricksteves.com/radio.

Rick Steves' Audio Europe

My free smartphone app, *Rick Steves Audio Europe,* makes it easy to download destination-specific travel interviews from my public radio shows. You'll also find my free audio tours covering many of Europe's top sights. The app is available for your iPhone, iPad, iPod, or Android device, and can found at www.ricksteves.com/audio europe, iTunes, and Google Play.

Travel Literature

Consider some trip-related recreational reading. A book on the court of Louis XIV brings Versailles to life. Books such as James A. Michener's *Iberia* (for Spain and Portugal) or *Poland,* Irving Stone's *The Greek Treasure* for Greece and Turkey, William Wordsworth's poems for England's Lake District, and Leon Uris' *Trinity* for Ireland are real trip bonuses. After reading Stone's *The Agony and the Ecstasy,* you'll visit dear friends in Florence—who lived there 500 years ago.

Personal accounts are fun and vivid, such as *Notes from a Small Island* by Bill Bryson (on Britain), Peter Mayle's Provence books (on himself), and the Travelers' Tales series (on Ireland, France, Paris, Provence, Italy, Tuscany, Spain, Prague, Greece, and Turkey; www.travelerstales. com). Bibliotravel.com provides user-generated lists of suggested reading sorted by destination.

To get in an adventurous mood, start with Mark Twain's classic, witty travelogue, *The Innocents Abroad* (and follow it up with *A Tramp Abroad*, which takes you to Germany, Switzerland, and bits of France and Italy).

To glimpse life in Italy, consider Frances Mayes' *Under the Tuscan Sun*, Tim Parks' *Italian Neighbors*, Jan Kubik's *Piazzas and Pizzas*, or John Berendt's *The City of Falling Angels*. Christina Björk's *Vendela in Venice* is aimed at kids but is also enjoyable for adults.

For the flavor of France, try M. F. K. Fisher's *Two Towns in Provence*, Polly Platt's diplomatic *French or Foe?* and *Savoir-Flair!*, Thad Carhart's *The Piano Shop on the Left Bank*, Sarah Turnbull's *Almost French*, Ernest Hemingway's *A Moveable Feast*, Adam Gopnik's *Paris to the Moon*, or Carol Drinkwater's *The Olive Farm*. To sample Spain, consider *Driving Over Lemons* by Chris Stewart or *It's Not About the Tapas* by Polly Evans. For understanding the Basque region (divided between Spain and France), Mark Kurlansky's *The Basque History of the World* is essential.

Tony Hawks' *Round Ireland with a Fridge* affords a goofy look at the Irish, *The Emperor's New Kilt* by Jan-Andrew Henderson deconstructs the myths surrounding the tartan-clad Scots, and Susan Allen Toth's *My Love Affair with England* explores the country's charms and eccentricities.

For Germany, consider the travel memoir *The Bells in Their Silence: Travels through Germany*, by Michael Gorra. Marcus Zusak's award-winning novel, *The Book Thief*, follows a young German girl during and after World War II.

To get a sense of Greece, consider Patricia Storace's *Dinner with Persephone*, Tom Stone's *The Summer of My Greek Taverna*, Henry Miller's *The Colossus of Maroussi*, or Gerald Malcolm Durrell's *My Family and Other Animals*. Travelers to Turkey might enjoy Alev Lytle Croutier's novel, *Seven Houses*, or Yashar Kemal's classic tale, *Memed, My Hawk*.

If you're a mystery fan, try the detective series by Anne Perry (Victorian London) or Lindsey Davis (ancient Rome); Alan Furst's WWII spy novels; or Steven Saylor's Roma Sub Rosa historical mysteries. The stylish detective Aimée Leduc prowls through Paris in Cara Black's mysteries; Colin Dexter's Inspector Morse is on the case in Oxford; and Donna Leon's world-weary Guido Brunetti investigates in Venice.

History buffs recommend Ross King's *Brunelleschi's Dome* (on how the stunning dome of Florence's cathedral was built) and his *Michelangelo and the Pope's Ceiling* (the story behind the Sistine Chapel); Jan Morris' and H. V. Morton's books on Italy; Salley Vickers' *Miss Garnet's Angel* (Venice); Colleen McCullough's Masters of Rome series; Edward

Rutherfurd's *London, Sarum, The Forest,* and *Dublin;* Nigel Tranter's trilogies (Scotland); Ken Follett's *The Pillars of the Earth* (cathedral epic set in England); and Hilary Mantel's powerful reimagining of Tudor England in *Wolf Hall.*

The Diary of Anne Frank tells the story of a young Jewish girl hiding out from the Nazis in Amsterdam. Corrie ten Boom's autobiography, *The Hiding Place,* offers another angle with the story of a Christian family caught hiding Jews in Haarlem (near Amsterdam). For a harrowing account of survival in a Nazi concentration camp, consider the much-lauded *Night* by Elie Wiesel.

For literature lovers, there's Victor Hugo's *The Hunchback of Notre-Dame,* set in medieval Paris; Voltaire's 18th-century French satire *Candide;* Czech existentialist Franz Kafka's disturbing *The Metamorphosis;* James Joyce's Irish odyssey, *Ulysses;* and the British classics by Jane Austen, Charles Dickens, the Brontë sisters, D. H. Lawrence, William Shakespeare, C. S. Lewis, and so on.

For more complete country-by-country lists of recommended reading (and viewing), see www.ricksteves.com/travelreading. You'll also find additional suggestions from fellow travelers in the "Recommended Novels for Your Travels" section at our Travel Forums (www.ricksteves .com/forums).

Europe in Film and TV

Austria
The Third Man (1949). Carol Reed film starring Orson Welles, shot in a bombed-out and Soviet-occupied Vienna with noir foreboding.
The Sound of Music (1965). Beloved Julie Andrews musical, partially set in pre-WWII Switzerland and Austria.
Amadeus (1984). Giggling Mozart climbs the court ladder in Vienna.
Before Sunrise (1995). Ethan Hawke sightsees, talks, romances, and talks some more with Julie Delpy in Vienna.

Croatia
Underground (1995). Award-winning satire follows two friends—and the history of Yugoslavia—through World War II, the Cold War, and the Yugoslav wars.

Czech Republic
The Unbearable Lightness of Being (1988). Adaptation of Milan Kundera's novel, chronicling a love affair during the Prague Spring.

Kolya (1996). A Czech man's life takes an unexpected turn as the Communist bloc starts to fall apart.

France

Grand Illusion (1937). French WWI prisoners of war hatch a plan to escape a German POW camp. Directed by Jean Renoir, the movie was later banned by the Nazis for its anti-fascism message.

Jules and Jim (1962). François Truffaut, a filmmaker of the French New Wave school, shows Parisian streets and the love they inspire.

Jean de Florette (1986) and *Manon of the Spring* (1986). Marvelous tale of greed and intolerance follows a hunchback as he fights for the property he inherited.

Saving Private Ryan (1998). Steven Spielberg's intense and brilliant story of the D-Day landings and their aftermath.

Amélie (2001). Charming young waitress searches for love in Paris.

Before Sunset (2004). Romantic drama of a young American man and young French woman who spend an afternoon together in Paris.

Marie Antoinette (2006). Kirsten Dunst stars as the infamous French queen (with a Californian accent) at Versailles.

La Vie en Rose (2007). The glamorous yet turbulent life of the fabled singer Edith Piaf (many scenes shot in Paris).

Midnight in Paris (2011). Woody Allen's sharp comedy shifts between today's Paris and the 1920s mecca of Picasso, Hemingway, and Fitzgerald.

Germany

The Marriage of Maria Braun (1979). Gritty meditation on post-WWII Germany, seen through the romantic woes of a young woman.

Mephisto (1981). Allegorical tale about one man's artistic approach to the Nazis' rise to power.

Wings of Desire (1987). Set in Berlin, Wim Wenders' best film shows an angel who falls in love and falls to earth.

Immortal Beloved (1994). After Beethoven's death, an assistant puzzles over the identity of the composer's secret lover.

Run Lola Run (1998). Art-house phenomenon set in Berlin, combining action, love, and mobsters with a time-twisting plot.

Good Bye, Lenin! (2003). Funny, poignant look at a son's struggle to re-create communist Eastern Europe for his mother.

Downfall (2004). The Führer's final days in his Berlin bunker.

Sophie Scholl: The Final Days (2005). Beautiful, devastating account of a student who defied Hitler.

The Lives of Others (2006). A member of the East Germany's secret police becomes too close to the lives he surveils.

Great Britain

Mary Poppins (1964) and *My Fair Lady* (1964). Two beloved musical films, ideal if you're traveling with children.

A Man for All Seasons (1966). Sir Thomas More faces down Henry VIII.

The Elephant Man (1980). Stark portrayal of the cruelty of Victorian London.

My Beautiful Laundrette (1986). Compelling story of two gay men (with Daniel Day-Lewis) in urban London.

Hope and Glory (1987). Semi-autobiographical story of a boy growing up during WWII's London blitz.

Sammy and Rosie Get Laid (1987). Another portrayal of London—and the racial tensions found in its multiethnic center.

Braveheart (1995). Mel Gibson helps the Scots overthrow English rule in the 13th century.

Persuasion (1995). The classic Jane Austen tale of status, partially filmed in Bath.

Pride and Prejudice (1995). Among the many versions of Jane Austen's classic, this BBC miniseries starring Colin Firth is the winner.

Rob Roy (1995). Liam Neeson struggles against feudal landlords in 18th-century Scotland.

Sense and Sensibility (1995, with Emma Thompson, Hugh Grant, and Kate Winslet) and *Emma* (1996, with Gwyneth Paltrow). Other Austen adaptations set in 19th-century England.

Shakespeare in Love (1999). Clever, romantic taste of Tudor-era London set in the original Globe Theatre.

The Queen (2006). Helen Mirren expertly channels Elizabeth II in the days after Princess Diana's death.

The Tudors (2007-2010). Showtime's racy, entertaining, loosely accurate chronicle of the marriages of Henry VIII.

Sweeney Todd (2007) and *Sherlock Holmes* (2009). Two highly stylized films capturing the gritty Victorian milieu.

The King's Speech (2010). Colin Firth as the stuttering King George VI on the cusp of World War II.

Greece

Never on Sunday (1960). Melina Mercouri plays a beautiful woman with a shady background in this depiction of postwar Greece.

Zorba the Greek (1964). Shows how Greek culture can free even the most uptight Englishman.

Z (1969). Thriller about the assassination of a crusading politician—and the rise of the Greek junta—in the 1960s.

The Trojan Women (1971). Euripides' classic tragedy of Troy's female aristocracy in chains, featuring Katharine Hepburn, Vanessa Redgrave, and Irene Pappas.

Clash of the Titans (1981). The myth of the Greek hero Perseus retold by an all-star cast including Laurence Olivier, Claire Bloom, and Maggie Smith.

Alexander (2004). Colin Farrell stars as the Macedonian military genius who conquered the known world.

Troy (2004). Brad Pitt portrays the petulant warrior Achilles from Homer's *The Iliad*.

Mamma Mia! (2008). Meryl Streep headlined this frothy ABBA-themed musical, filmed on the mainland and on the islands of Skiathos and Skopelos.

Hungary

Sunshine (1999). Starring Ralph Fiennes, somewhat melodramatically traces three generations of an aristocratic Jewish family in Budapest.

Ireland

Man of Aran (1934). Classic documentary about the life on the Aran Islands in the early 20th century.

Odd Man Out (1947). Film noir about the early IRA, with a great scene filmed in Belfast's Crown Bar.

Ryan's Daughter (1970). David Lean's epic WWI love story, filmed near Dingle.

The Field (1990). An Irish farmer fights to keep his land.

The Commitments (1991) and *The Secret of Roan Inish* (1995). Two comedic films adapted from books by Roddy Doyle and Rosalie K. Fry; set in Dublin and charming Donegal County, respectively.

In the Name of the Father (1993). Starring Daniel Day-Lewis, a biopic of accused bomber Gerry Conlon.

Michael Collins (1996). Liam Neeson as the Irish Free State revolutionary.

Angela's Ashes (1999). The Frank McCourt memoir of a poverty-stricken childhood in Limerick.

The Wind That Shakes the Barley (2006). The struggle for independence from Britain told through the story of two brothers.

Italy

Rome, Open City (1945). Roberto Rossellini's war drama, set in the Eternal City during the Nazi Occupation during World War II.

Bicycle Thieves (1949). A poor man looks for his stolen bicycle in busy Rome in this inspirational classic of Italian Neorealism.

Roman Holiday (1953). Audrey Hepburn and Gregory Peck sightsee the city on his scooter.

Ben-Hur (1959) and *Spartacus* (1960). Two campy big-budget Hollywood flicks bring ancient Rome to life.

La Dolce Vita (1960). Director Federico Fellini tells a series of stories that capture the Roman character.

A Room with a View (1985). Florence's appeal to turn-of-the-century English travelers, as seen through the eyes a young woman and her love abroad.

Cinema Paradiso (1990). Drama about the friendship between a film projectionist and a little boy in post-WWII Sicily.

Enchanted April (1991). Filmed in Portofino, an all-star British cast fall in love, discuss relationships, eat well, and take naps in the sun.

Il Postino (1995). Poet Pablo Neruda befriends his Italian postman, who uses a newfound love for Italian poetry to woo a local beauty.

Life Is Beautiful (1997). Set in a Tuscan town, this Oscar winner follows the experiences of an imaginative Jewish-Italian man.

Bread and Tulips (2000). A harassed Italian housewife discovers beauty, love, and her true self in Venice.

Gladiator (2000). Russell Crowe is a Roman general turned gladiator in this crowd-pleasing Oscar-winner.

Best of Youth (2003). Warm-hearted story of two brothers takes place in several Italian locations and spans the last several decades of Italian history.

Netherlands and Belgium

The Diary of Anne Frank (1959). A fine version of Anne's story.

Soldier of Orange (1977). Epic tale about the Nazi occupation and Dutch Resistance during WWII (and a good book).

Girl with a Pearl Earring (2003). The artist Vermeer falls in love with his servant in Delft.

Black Book (2006). Filmed in Holland, a sexy blonde bombshell fights for the Dutch Resistance.

In Bruges (2008). A dark and violent comedy filmed just where you'd think.

Poland

The Decalogue (1989). Television drama that explores the meanings of the Ten Commandments with a fictional narrative set mostly in modern Warsaw.

Schindler's List (1993). Oscar winner about a German factory owner's inspirational efforts to save his Polish-Jewish employees from deportation to concentration camps.

The Pianist (2002). Oscar-winning movie about the plight of a Jewish musician hiding in Warsaw during the Holocaust.

Portugal

According to Pereira (1996). Marcello Mastroianni is the namesake in this adaptation of the Antonio Tabucchi novel, detailing one editor's reaction to Spanish Fascism.

Capitães de Abril (2000). The 1974 coup that overthrew the right-wing Portuguese dictatorship, told from the perspective of two young army captains.

Amália (2008). The story of Portugal's beloved fado singer Amália Rodrigues, who rose from poverty to international fame.

Scandinavia

The Seventh Seal (1957, a knight questions the meaning of life), *Smiles of a Summer Night* (1955, turn-of-the-century frolic), and *Fanny & Alexander* (1983, children overcome their father's death). Worthwhile films by Oscar-winning Swedish director Ingmar Bergman.

Song of Norway (1970). Musical based on the life of Norwegian composer Edvard Grieg.

My Life as a Dog (1985). Bittersweet tale of a young boy in 1950s Sweden.

Babette's Feast (1987). The original foodie movie, set in rural 19th-century Denmark.

Pelle the Conqueror (1988). Examines Swedish immigration to Denmark in the 19th century.

Kristin Lavransdatter (1995). A condensed version of the epic novel about the life of a Norwegian woman in the 14th century.

Smilla's Sense of Snow (1997). Dramatic adaptation of Peter Høeg's best seller, partly set in Copenhagen.

The Singing Revolution (2006). Enjoyable documentary about Estonia's musical fight for freedom (www.singingrevolution.com).

The Girl with the Dragon Tattoo (2011). Hollywood's version of Stieg Larsson's first Millennium novel, with lots of action in Stockholm.

Slovenia

The Death of Yugoslavia (1995). Six-hour BBC documentary series featuring interviews with all the key players (it's difficult to find on DVD, but try searching for "Death of Yugoslavia" on YouTube).

No Man's Land (2002). Slovenian-produced war drama about the Bosnia-Herzegovina conflict.

Spain

For Whom the Bell Tolls (1943). Based on Hemingway's novel about an American volunteer fighting in the Spanish Civil War.

The Sun Also Rises (1957). Hemingway (and Hollywood) look at Spain in the 1920s and 1930s (with an enactment of the famous running of the bulls).

Woman on the Verge of a Nervous Breakdown (1988), *All About My Mother* (1999) and *Volver* (2006). Director Pedro Almodóvar's piquant films about relationships in the post-Franco era.

L'auberge Espagnole (2002). The loves and lives of European students sharing an apartment in Barcelona.

Vicky Cristina Barcelona (2008). Woody Allen directs Javier Bardem as a macho Spanish artist romancing two American women, when suddenly his stormy ex-wife (Penélope Cruz) re-enters his life.

Switzerland

The Eiger Sanction (1975). Clint Eastwood directed and starred in this spy thriller, partially shot in Kleine Scheidegg.

North Face (2008). Excruciatingly realistic reimagining of the disastrous 1936 attempt by an Austrian/German team to scale the Eiger's "wall of death."

Turkey

Gallipoli (1981). Tells the story of the famous Turkish WWI battle from the perspective of two Australian soldiers (including a very young Mel Gibson).

Hamam (also titled *Steam: The Turkish Bath*, 1997). An Italian inherits a traditional public bath, or *hamam*, in Istanbul.

Distant (2004). Award-winning story of a photographer and his unemployed cousin trying to connect in snow-covered Istanbul.

European National Tourist Offices

Austria: www.austria.info
Belgium: www.visitbelgium.com
Croatia: http://us.croatia.hr, tel. 212/279-8672
Czech Republic: www.czechtourism.com
Denmark: See Scandinavia.
Estonia: www.visitestonia.com
Finland: See Scandinavia.
France: www.franceguide.com
Germany: www.germany.travel
Great Britain: www.visitbritain.com
Greece: www.visitgreece.gr
Hungary: www.gotohungary.com, tel. 212/695-1221
Ireland: www.discoverireland.com, tel. 800-742-6762
Italy: www.italia.it, tel. 212/245-5618
Luxembourg: www.visitluxembourg.com
Morocco: www.visitmorocco.com
Netherlands: www.holland.com
Norway: See Scandinavia.
Poland: www.poland.travel
Portugal: www.visitportugal.com
Scandinavia: www.goscandinavia.com
Slovenia: www.slovenia.info
Spain: www.spain.info
Sweden: See Scandinavia.
Switzerland: www.myswitzerland.com, tel. 877-794-8037
Turkey: www.goturkey.com, tel. 212/687-2194

City Name Variations

English Name	European Name
Athens (Gre.)	Athina in Greek, Athenes in German
Bolzano (Italy)	Bozen in German
Bratislava (Slovakia)	Pressburg in German, Pozsony in Hungarian
Basel (Switz.)	Bâle in French
Bruges (Bel.)	Brugge in Flemish
Brussels (Bel.)	Bruxelles in French
Cologne (Ger.)	Köln (or Koeln)
Copenhagen (Den.)	København

Cracow (Pol.)	Kraków
Dubrovnik (Cro.)	Ragusa in Italian and German
Florence (Italy)	Firenze
Gdańsk (Pol.)	Danzig in German
Geneva (Switz.)	Genève in French, Genf in German
Genoa (Italy)	Genova (not Geneva)
Gothenburg (Sweden)	Göteborg
The Hague (Neth.)	Den Haag, 'S Gravenhage
Helsinki (Fin.)	Helsingfors in Swedish
Lisbon (Port.)	Lisboa
London (Brit.)	Londres in French
Munich (Ger.)	München (or Muenchen) in German, Monaco di Baviera in Italian
Naples (Italy)	Napoli in Italian, Neapel in German
Nice (Fr.)	Nizza in Italian
Nuremberg (Ger.)	Nürnberg (or Nuernberg)
Padua (Italy)	Padova
Pamplona (Spain)	Iruña in Euskara (Basque)
Paris (Fr.)	Parigi in Italian
Prague (Czech.)	Praha
Rome (Italy)	Roma
San Sebastián (Spain)	Donostia in Euskara (Basque)
Venice (Italy)	Venezia in Italian, Venedig in German
Vienna (Aus.)	Wien in German, Bécs in Hungarian, Dunaj in Slovene, Vídeň in Czech, Viedeň in Slovak
Warsaw (Pol.)	Warszawa in Polish, Warschau in German

Metric Conversion

1 inch	=	25 millimeters	1 ounce	=	28 grams
1 foot	=	0.3 meter	1 pound	=	0.45 kilogram
1 yard	=	0.9 meter	Temp. (°F)	=	9/5 °C + 32
1 mile	=	1.6 kilometers	1 kilogram	=	2.2 pounds
1 sq. yd.	=	0.8 square meter	1 kilometer	=	0.62 mile
1 acre	=	0.4 hectare	1 centimeter	=	0.4 inch
1 quart	=	0.95 liter	1 meter	=	39.4 inches

RESOURCES

Clothes Sizing Conversion

Most items are sized differently in the US, the UK, and continental Europe. Use these conversion tables as general guidelines. I've also included shortcuts for figuring out sizes. When a range is given (e.g., shoe size 36-37), it means that the European size straddles the American one (half-sizes are rare on the Continent)—look for a 36 that runs large, or a 37 that runs small.

Women's Sizes

Pants, Dresses & Suits

US	2	4	6	8	10	12	14	16	18	20
Europe	32	34	36	38	40	42	44	46	48	50
UK	6	8	10	12	14	16	18	20	22	24

Shortcut: From US to Europe—add 30; from US to UK—add 4.

Blouses & Sweaters

US	32(S)	34(S)	36(M)	38(M)	40(L)	42(L)
Europe	40	42	44	46	48	50
UK	34	36	38	40	42	44

Shortcut: From US to Europe—add 8; from US to UK—add 2.

Shoes

US	5½	6	6½	7	7½	8	8½	9	9½	10
Europe	35-36	36	37	37-38	38	38-39	39	40	41	42
UK	3	3½	4	4½	5	5½	6	6½	7	7½

Shortcut: From US to Europe—add about 31; from US to UK—subtract 2½.

Men's Sizes

Suits & Jackets

US/UK	34	36	38	40	42	44	46	48	50	52
Europe	44	46	48	50	52	54	56	58	60	62

Shortcut: From US to Europe—add 10; US and UK use the same sizing.

Shirts

US/UK	14(S)	14½(S)	15(M)	15½(M)	16(L)	16½(L)	17(XL)
Europe	36	37	38	39	40	41	42

Shortcut: From US to Europe—multiply by 2 and add about 8; US and UK use the same sizing.

Shoes

US	7½	8	8½	9	9½	10	10½	11	11½	12
Europe	39	39-40	40	41	42	43	44	45	45-46	46
UK	7	7½	8	8½	9	9½	10	10½	11	11½

Shortcut: From US to Europe—add about 32-34; from US to UK—subtract about ½.

Children's Sizes

Clothing

US/UK	2	4	6	8	10	14/13	16/15
Europe	1	2	5	7	9	10	12

Shortcut: From US to Europe—subtract 1-2 for smaller children and subtract 4 for juniors; US and UK use the same sizing.

Girls' Shoes

US	9½	10	11	12	13	1	2	3	4
Europe	26	26-27	27-28	28-29	30	31	32-33	33-34	35
UK	8	8½	9½	10½	11½	12½	13½	1½	2½

Shortcut: From US to Europe—for sizes up to 13 add 16-17, and for sizes 1 and up add about 30; from US to UK—subtract about 1½, except sizes 1 and 2, to which you'll add 11½.

Boys' Shoes

US	11½	12	12½	13	1	2	3	4	5
Europe	29	29-30	30-31	31	33	34	35	36	37-38
UK	11	11½	12	12½	13½	1½	2½	3½	4½

Shortcut: From US to Europe—for sizes up to 13 add 17½-18, and for sizes 1 and up add about 32; from US to UK—subtract about ½, except size 1, to which you'll add about 12½.

European Weather

The following climate chart can be helpful in planning your itinerary, although I have never found European weather to be particularly predictable. The first line shows the average daily high temperature; second line, average daily low; third line, average days without rain.

	J	F	M	A	M	J	J	A	S	O	N	D
AUSTRIA • Vienna												
	34°	38°	47°	58°	67°	73°	76°	75°	68°	56°	45°	37°
	25°	28°	30°	42°	50°	56°	60°	59°	53°	44°	37°	30°
	16	17	18	17	18	16	18	18	20	18	16	16
BELGIUM • Brussels												
	40°	44°	51°	58°	65°	72°	73°	72°	69°	60°	48°	42°
	30°	32°	36°	41°	46°	52°	54°	54°	51°	45°	38°	32°
	10	11	14	12	15	15	14	13	17	14	10	12
CROATIA • Dubrovnik												
	53°	55°	58°	63°	70°	78°	83°	82°	77°	69°	62°	56°
	42°	43°	57°	52°	58°	65°	69°	69°	64°	57°	51°	46°
	18	15	20	20	21	24	27	28	23	20	14	16
CZECH REPUBLIC • Prague												
	31°	34°	44°	54°	64°	70°	73°	72°	65°	53°	42°	34°
	23°	24°	30°	38°	46°	52°	55°	55°	49°	41°	33°	27°
	18	17	21	19	18	18	18	19	20	18	18	18
DENMARK • Copenhagen												
	37°	37°	42°	51°	60°	66°	70°	69°	64°	55°	46°	41°
	29°	28°	31°	37°	45°	51°	56°	56°	51°	44°	38°	33°
	14	15	19	18	20	18	17	16	14	14	11	12
FINLAND • Helsinki												
	26°	25°	32°	44°	56°	66°	71°	68°	59°	47°	37°	31°
	17°	15°	20°	30°	40°	49°	55°	53°	46°	37°	30°	23°
	11	10	17	17	19	17	17	16	16	13	11	11
FRANCE • Paris												
	43°	45°	54°	60°	68°	73°	76°	75°	70°	60°	50°	44°
	34°	34°	39°	43°	49°	55°	58°	58°	53°	46°	40°	36°
	14	14	19	17	19	18	19	18	17	18	15	15
FRANCE • Nice												
	50°	53°	59°	64°	71°	79°	84°	83°	77°	68°	58°	52°
	35°	36°	41°	46°	52°	58°	63°	63°	58°	51°	43°	37°
	23	22	24	23	23	26	29	26	24	23	21	21

How Europe Compares to North America

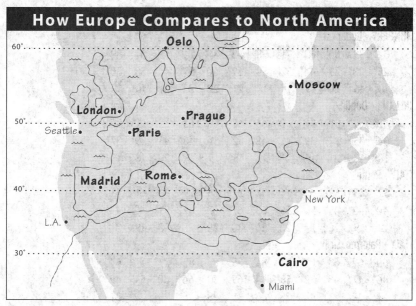

Wondering what clothes to pack? Europe and North America share the same latitudes and a similar climate. This map shows Europe superimposed over North America (shaded) with latitude lines. Use the map as a general weather guide. For example, London and Canada's Vancouver are located at a similar latitude and are both near the sea, so you can assume their climates are nearly the same. But you can't go by latitude alone. Rome and New York City should have similar weather, but Rome is hotter because it's surrounded by the warm Mediterranean. Inland areas have colder winters, so Prague can get as chilly as Minneapolis. Elevation affects climate as well. For more info, see the climate chart here and www.weatherbase.com. Bon voyage!

J	F	M	A	M	J	J	A	S	O	N	D

GERMANY • Munich

35°	38°	48°	56°	64°	70°	74°	73°	67°	56°	44°	36°
23°	23°	30°	38°	45°	51°	55°	54°	48°	40°	33°	26°
15	12	18	15	16	13	15	15	17	18	15	16

GREAT BRITAIN • London

43°	44°	50°	56°	62°	69°	71°	71°	65°	58°	50°	45°
36°	36°	38°	42°	47°	53°	56°	56°	52°	46°	42°	38°
16	15	20	18	19	19	19	20	17	18	15	16

GREECE • Athens

55°	57°	60°	68°	77°	86°	92°	92°	84°	75°	66°	58°
44°	44°	46°	52°	61°	68°	73°	73°	67°	60°	53°	47°
15	17	20	21	23	26	29	28	26	23	18	16

	J	F	M	A	M	J	J	A	S	O	N	D

HUNGARY • Budapest

34°	39°	50°	62°	71°	78°	82°	81°	74°	61°	47°	39°
25°	28°	35°	44°	52°	58°	62°	60°	53°	44°	38°	30°
18	16	20	19	18	17	21	22	23	21	16	18

IRELAND • Dublin

46°	47°	51°	55°	60°	65°	67°	67°	63°	57°	51°	47°
34°	35°	37°	39°	43°	48°	52°	51°	48°	43°	39°	37°
18	18	21	19	21	19	18	19	18	20	18	17

ITALY • Rome

52°	55°	59°	66°	74°	82°	87°	86°	79°	71°	61°	55°
40°	42°	45°	50°	56°	63°	67°	67°	62°	55°	49°	44°
13	19	23	24	26	26	30	29	25	23	19	21

ITALY • Palermo, Sicily

60°	62°	63°	68°	74°	81°	85°	86°	83°	77°	71°	64°
46°	47°	48°	52°	58°	64°	69°	70°	66°	60°	54°	49°
19	20	23	24	28	28	31	29	26	23	22	21

MOROCCO • Marrakech

65°	68°	74°	79°	84°	92°	101°	100°	92°	83°	73°	66°
40°	43°	48°	52°	57°	62°	67°	68°	63°	57°	49°	42°
24	23	25	24	29	29	30	30	27	27	27	24

NETHERLANDS • Amsterdam

40°	42°	49°	56°	64°	70°	72°	71°	67°	57°	48°	42°
31°	31°	34°	40°	46°	51°	55°	55°	50°	44°	38°	33°
9	9	15	14	17	16	14	13	11	11	9	10

NORWAY • Oslo

28°	30°	39°	50°	61°	68°	72°	70°	60°	48°	38°	32°
19°	19°	25°	34°	43°	50°	55°	53°	46°	38°	31°	25°
16	16	22	19	21	17	16	17	16	17	14	14

POLAND • Kraków

32°	34°	45°	55°	67°	72°	76°	73°	66°	56°	44°	37°
22°	22°	30°	38°	48°	54°	58°	56°	49°	42°	33°	28°
15	13	19	15	19	15	15	16	18	17	15	15

PORTUGAL • Lisbon

57°	59°	63°	67°	71°	77°	81°	82°	79°	72°	63°	58°
46°	47°	50°	53°	55°	60°	63°	63°	62°	58°	52°	47°
16	16	17	20	21	25	29	29	24	22	17	16

PORTUGAL • Faro (Algarve)

60°	61°	64°	67°	71°	77°	83°	83°	78°	72°	66°	61°
48°	49°	52°	55°	58°	64°	67°	68°	65°	60°	55°	50°
22	21	21	24	27	29	31	31	29	25	22	22

J	F	M	A	M	J	J	A	S	O	N	D

SLOVENIA • Ljubljana

36°	41°	50°	60°	68°	75°	80°	78°	71°	59°	47°	39°
25°	25°	32°	40°	48°	54°	57°	57°	51°	43°	36°	30°
18	17	20	17	15	14	19	19	20	17	15	16

SPAIN • Madrid

47°	52°	59°	65°	70°	80°	87°	85°	77°	65°	55°	48°
35°	36°	41°	45°	50°	58°	63°	63°	57°	49°	42°	36°
23	21	21	21	21	25	29	28	24	23	21	21

SPAIN • Almería (Costa del Sol)

60°	61°	64°	68°	72°	78°	83°	84°	81°	73°	67°	62°
46°	47°	51°	55°	59°	65°	70°	71°	68°	60°	54°	49°
25	24	26	25	28	29	31	30	27	26	26	26

SWEDEN • Stockholm

30°	30°	37°	47°	58°	67°	71°	68°	60°	49°	40°	35°
26°	25°	29°	37°	45°	53°	57°	56°	50°	43°	37°	32°
15	14	21	19	20	17	18	17	16	16	14	14

SWITZERLAND • Geneva

38°	42°	51°	59°	66°	73°	77°	76°	69°	58°	47°	40°
29°	30°	36°	42°	49°	55°	58°	58°	53°	44°	37°	31°
20	19	22	21	20	19	22	20	20	21	19	21

TURKEY • Istanbul

46°	47°	51°	60°	69°	77°	82°	82°	76°	68°	59°	51°
37°	36°	38°	45°	53°	60°	65°	66°	61°	55°	48°	41°
13	14	17	21	23	24	27	27	23	20	16	13

INDEX

A

Aare River: 691
AARP: 64, 451
Abrasions, first aid for: 408
Accommodations: *See* Sleeping; *and specific destinations*
Active travel: 312–319
Addresses, locating: 358–359
Ærø: 681–684; map, 683; sleeping, 684
Affordability: 5, 8, 15–21. *See also* Budgeting; Money-saving tips
African-American travelers: 488–489
Agriturismos: 210, 695–696
Aiguille du Midi: 573, 575
Airbnb: 214, 224–225
Airfares (airlines): 87–105; budget, 99–104; budgeting for, 16; flight-booking tips, 92–95; frequent-flier miles, 96–99; mobile apps, 259; money-saving tips, 89–90; and seasons, 37; websites, 30
Airports: car rental fees, 146; with children, 440; packing tips, 71–72; for senior travelers, 452; sleeping in, 231; VAT tax refunds, 184
Air travel: 87–105; carry-on considerations, 68, 70–71, 96–97; checking in and taking off, 95–96; with children, 439–441; to Europe, 87–99; within Europe, 40, 67, 99–105; fear of flying, 91; Graffiti Wall, 785; insurance, 61, 66; and itinerary planning, 39; jet lag, 400–402, 403–404; mobile apps, 259; online research, 30, 87–89, 102–103; for senior travelers, 452; vs. train travel, 104–105; travel agents for, 90, 92; websites, 30
Akershus Fortress (Oslo): 677
Aksaray: 736
Algarve Coast: 538–541; itineraries, 773; map, 540–541
Alpe di Siusi: 522–523
Alpine huts: 316
Alpine lifts: 315
Alps: 697–701; Italian Dolomites, 520–524, 701; luges, 692–693; map, 698; Mont Blanc, 573–576; Slovenia, 700–701; Swiss, 597–603, 697–698, 699–700
Alsace: 569–573; map, 570
Amalfi Coast: 524–526; map, 525
Ambien: 96, 402

Amsterdam: 582–588; itineraries, 47, 780; literature, 803; map, 582; Nazi sights, 718–719; sleeping, 588
Andalucía: 542–546; itineraries, 773; map, 543
Andechs Monastery: 690–691
Andorra: 52
Ankara: 740, 747
Antalya: 740–741
Aosta: 575
Apartment rentals: 213–217
Appenzell: 699–700
Arc de Triomphe (Paris): 557, 559
Arcos de la Frontera: 542–545; sleeping, 546
Arezzo: 516
Arles: 47
Asilah: 550
Assisi: 512; sleeping, 517
Athens: 32, 725, 769
ATMs: 167–172
Attitude adjustment: 475, 477
Audio Europe, Rick Steves: 7, 259, 263, 303, 801
Auschwitz-Birkenau Concentration Camp: 712–715
Austria: 698; Ehrenberg Ruins, 711, 777; Hallstatt, 594–597; information, 810; itineraries, 50, 762–764, 776–777; map, 762; movies, 803; Nazi sights, 715–718; sight reservations, 299; sleeping, 210; weather, 814
Avebury: 659

B

Back Doors: defined, 500, 502; map, 501
Back Door travel philosophy: 13–14
Backpacks: 71–72
Baggage: carry-on restrictions, 68, 70–71, 96–97; checking at train stations, 128–129; insurance, 66; packing tips, 72–74; train safety, 133–134
Bagnoregio: *See* Civita di Bagnoregio
Bakeries: 376–377
Bank card scams: 180–181
Banking: *See* Money
Barcelona: itineraries, 774; scams, 788–789, 793
Bargaining: 323–324

Bars: 373. *See also specific destinations*
Bath: 642–644; map, 643; sleeping, 644
Bathrooms: 415–421; for disabled travelers, 455
Bavaria: itineraries, 777
Bed-and-breakfasts (B&Bs): 208–213
Beer: 385, 386–387, 390, 393, 579, 581
Belfast: 670–674; map, 671; sleeping, 674
Belgium: 577–581; cuisine, 384–385; information, 810; itineraries, 775; language, 344; movies, 807; offbeat sights, 685–686; weather, 814
Belisirma: 736
Bellagio: 520
Berchtesgaden: 718
Bergen: 679–681; itineraries, 779
Berlin: Communist sites, 626–628; itineraries, 778; Nazi sights, 716–717
Berlin Wall: 627–628
Bern: 691
Berner Oberland: 597–603; map, 598
Bevagna: 516
Biking: 316–319. *See also specific destinations*
Blackpool: 649–651; map, 650; sleeping, 651
Black Sea: 748–749
Blasket Island: 668–669
Bled, Lake: 700
Blisters, first aid for: 408
Blogs (blogging): 273–274
Blue Guides: 29
Boat cruises: 465–473; websites, 30
Bolzano: 522, 789–790
Bone Crypt (Rome): 688
Books, recommended: 801–803
Border crossings: 56, 152–153; VAT tax refunds, 184
Bosnia-Herzegovina: 620–626
Breakfast: 374
Britain: *See* Great Britain
Bruges: 577–581; map, 578; sleeping, 581
Brussels: 580; *Manneken-Pis*, 580, 685–686
Buchenwald: 715
Budapest: 628–630; scams, 788, 790
Budgeting: 15–21; general tips, 17–21; relative prices, 19. *See also* Money-saving tips
Burg Eltz: 704–705
Buses: 129, 138–141, 283–285; schedules, 139–140; stations and tickets, 140; tours, 292–293, 459–465; websites, 30

C
Cabs: *See* Taxis
Cadogan Guides: 29
Cafés: 373, 375. *See also specific destinations*
Cafeterias: 364, 375–376
Cameras: *See* Digital cameras; Photography
Camper rentals: 158, 232
Camping (campgrounds): 228–233, 441
Cappadocia: 735–736
Capri: 526
Carbon neutrality and travel: 496–497
Car buying: 157–158
Carcassonne: 703–704; sleeping, 711
Car leasing: 157–158
Car rentals: 67, 144–158; age limits, 152; booking, 147; choosing a car, 149–150; companies, 147–149; expenses, 145–147; insurance, 66, 153–156; picking up and dropping off, 150, 156–157; theft-proofing, 330–331
Carry-on bags: 69–72, 73, 96–97
Car-sharing programs: 148–149
Car travel (driving): 144–166; documents, 58, 150–152; driving tips, 159–162; gasoline, 163; GPS devices, 83, 164–165; maps, 163–165; navigating, 163–166; parking, 162; rail-and-drive passes, 116, 119; road signs, 160; vs. train travel, 145, 151; websites, 30
Casablanca: 551
Cash machines: *See* ATMs
Castelrotto: 523; sleeping, 524
Castles and palaces, best: 702–712; maps, 702, 709
Cefalù: 531–532; sleeping, 533
Cell phones: *See* Mobile phones
Cerne Abbas Giant: 658
Chamonix: 573–576, 693; sleeping, 576
Champs-Elysées (Paris): 556–563; map, 558
Charles Bridge (Prague): 606–607, 611
Château de Chillon: 707–708
Checkpoint Charlie (Berlin): 628
Children: 432–450; air travel, 439–441; appropriate age for travel, 434–435; eating, 442–444; leaving at home, 433; packing tips, 437–439; precautionary measures, 447–448; reflecting and connecting, 448–450; resources, 436; sightseeing tips, 444–447; sleeping, 441–442; travel documents, 435, 437

Chip-and-PIN cards: 178–179
Chipping Campden: 652–653; sleeping, 656
Chocolate: 384, 397–398, 688–689, 797–798
Churches: sightseeing strategies, 303–304
Cinque Terre: 503–510; hiking, 313, 506–510; itineraries, 774; map, 505
City name variations: 810–811
Civita di Bagnoregio: 513–516; map, 514; sleeping, 517
Classes: 4
Climate: 814–817
Climate change: 495
Clochans: 664–665
Clothing: packing tips, 74–78; shopping, 322–323; size conversion, 322–323, 812–813
Colds, first aid for: 407
Collision damage waiver (CDW) insurance: 66, 153–156
Colmar: 571–573; sleeping, 573
Combo-tickets: 298–299
Communication: *See* Language
Communist sites: 626–633
Como, Lake: 519–520
Concentration camps: 712–715
Consolidators: 90, 92, 148
Constipation: 409
Convent accommodations: 223
Conversation Clubs: 310–311
Cooking schools: 311
Copenhagen: 719; itineraries, 47, 778–779, 780
Corniglia: 508–509
Cotswolds, the: 651–656; map, 652
CouchSurfing: 225–226, 311
Creative worriers: 8–9
Credit cards: 67, 175–178; car rentals, 154–155; lost or stolen, 180–181, 336–337, 338; scams, 180–181
Creglingen: 593
Croatia: 609; cuisine, 387–388; information, 810; itineraries, 51; language, 345; movies, 803; sleeping, 212–213; weather, 814
Crowds, avoiding: 295–299
Cruises: 465–473; websites, 30
Cuisine: 384–398. *See also* Eating
Cultural exchanges: 492–493
Currency and exchange: 172–174; mobile apps, 260
Customs regulations: 186

Cybercafés: *See* Internet access
Czech Republic: Communist sites, 630–631; cuisine, 387; information, 810; itineraries, 776; language, 345; movies, 803–804; Nazi sights, 720; Prague, 604–613; Trebon, 691–692; weather, 814

D
Dachau Concentration Camp: 715
Dartmoor: 659–660; sleeping, 660
Da Vinci, Leonardo: 297, 518–519
Debit cards: *See* Credit cards
Denmark: Ærø, 681–684; folk museums, 306; information, 810; sleeping, 212; weather, 814
Dental checkups: 400
Department stores: 320, 322, 383
Deutsche Bahn: 121–123
Diarrhea: 408–409
Digital cameras: 263–272; accessories, 264–266; managing images on the road, 267–268; packing tips, 83; sharing your trip, 272–276; tricks for a good shot, 268–272
Dingle Peninsula: 661–669; map, 664; sleeping, 669
Dinkelsbühl: 592
Disabled travelers: 454–459
Doctors: 409–411
Dolomites: 520–524, 701
Dordogne: 690
Drinking water: 368–369, 403
Drinks: 368–370, 380–381
Driver's licenses: 67, 150–152
Driving: *See* Car travel
Drugstores: 410–411, 452
Dublin: 672, 674
Dynamic currency conversion (DCC): 176–177

E
Eastern Europe: 604–633; Communist sites, 626–633; cuisine, 387–388; itineraries, 51, 52, 767–768
Eastern Turkey: 747–751; map, 747
East Mediterranean: 722–751
Eating: 361–398; breakfast, 374; budgeting for, 16–17, 18, 361–362; with children, 442–444; country cuisines, 384–398; on cruises, 469–470; flavors of Europe, 693–697; mobile apps, 259–260; money-saving

tips, 375–384; ordering your meal, 366–368; restaurants, 362–373; for solo travelers, 424, 427; tipping, 181, 372–373; for vegetarians, 364–365. *See also* Markets; *and specific destinations*
Ebenalp: 699–700
Ebooks: 262
Economic crisis: 482–484
Edinburgh: 686–687
Educational opportunities: 454
Educational travel: 491–495
Eguisheim: 571
Ehrenberg Ruins: 711, 777
Eiger: 602
Elder travelers: *See* Senior travelers
Electricity: adapters and converters, 84–85
Electronic guidebooks: 262
Electronics: for children, 438–439; mobile apps, 258–262; packing tips, 81, 83–85. *See also* Digital cameras
Eltz Castle: 704–705
Email: *See* Internet access
Emergencies: 409–410
England: *See* Great Britain
Englischer Garten (Munich): 690
Entertainment: budgeting for, 17; guides for, 290–291
Ephesus: 732, 741
Epidavros: 724
Er-Rachidia: 552
Erzurum: 750–751
Estepa: 546
Estonia: Communist sites, 632; information, 810; language, 345
Eurailpasses: *See* Railpasses
Euro currency: 169
European gestures: 355–356
European homes, staying in: 223–226
European Union (EU): 477–481, 616
Eurostar: 114
Evacuation insurance: 64
Évora: 688
Exchange opportunities: 457, 459
Exercise: 404, 445
Extroverts: 10–12
Eyewitness Travel: 27

F
Facebook: 272–273
Fallerschein: 698
Family travel: *See* Children
Ferries: 141–143; websites, 30

Fès: 551–552
Fever, first aid for: 407
Finland: folk museums, 306; information, 810; language, 345; weather, 814
First aid: 407–409
First-aid kit: 81
Fjords of Norway: *See* Norway fjords
Flåm: 680
Flea markets: *See* Markets
Flight insurance: 66
Flims, recommended: 803–809
Florence: itineraries, 47, 774
Flying: *See* Air travel
Foie gras: 690, 694
Food: *See* Eating; Picnics
Foreign study: 454, 493–495
Fortress Fürigen Museum of War History: 692
France: 556–576; Carcassonne, 703–704; cuisine, 388–389, 694; information, 810; itineraries, 50, 52, 53, 757–759, 771–772, 774; language, 344, 349, 350; literature, 801–803; map, 758; movies, 804; Nazi sights, 720–721; offbeat sights, 686, 690; sight reservations, 299; sleeping, 210; weather, 814
Frankfurt: 686
Frank's (Anne) House (Amsterdam): 718
Frequent-flier miles: 96–99
Friends, crashing with: 226–227
Frommer's Guides: 27
Füssen: 593; sleeping, 712

G
Gallarus Oratory: 665–666
Gasoline: 163
Gay travelers: 490–491
Gdansk: 631–632
Germany: 589–594; castles, 704–707, 709–712, 777; Communist sites, 626–628; cuisine, 389–390; folk museums, 306; information, 810; itineraries, 49, 50, 52, 762–764, 777–778; language, 344, 349, 350; literature, 802; map, 762; movies, 804–805; Nazi sights, 712–718; offbeat sights, 686, 689, 690–691; sight reservations, 299; sleeping, 210; weather, 815
Gidleigh: 660
Gimmelwald: 597–603; sleeping, 603
Glacier Express: 52–53
Glastonbury: 656–657
Global Greeter: 310

Global warming: 495–497
Globe Theatre (London): 638–639
Glossary of terms: happy talk, 350; tap water, 369; thank you, 477; vegetarian phrases, 365
Gnadenwald: 698–699
GPS devices: 83, 164–165
Graffiti Wall: 6–7, 781–798
Grande Strada delle Dolomiti: 522
Grazalema: 546
Great Blasket Island: 668–669
Great Britain: 634–660; with children, 448–449; cuisine, 385–387; folk museums, 307; information, 810; itineraries, 49–51, 754–756, 770, 775; language, 344, 352–353; literature, 801–803; map, 755; movies, 805; mysterious sites, 656–660; sight reservations, 299; sleeping, 209–210; Warwick Castle, 704; weather, 815
Great Dolomite Road: 522
Greece: 722–731; cuisine, 390–391; economic crisis, 482, 483–484; information, 810; itineraries, 769; literature, 802; maps, 733, 769; movies, 805–806; sleeping, 212; weather, 815
"Green" travel: 495, 502
Grindelwald: 602
Group travel: 4–5, 20–21
Gubbio: 516
Guidebooks: 21–29, 289; electronic, 262; hiking, 314; Rick Steves, 23–26, 68; for women travelers, 430–431
Guided tours: See Tours
Guvano Beach: 506, 508
Güzelyurt: 735–736; sleeping, 742

H
Haarlem: 718–719
Haggling: 323–324
Hallstatt: 594–597, 688–689; map, 595; sleeping, 597
Headaches: 407
Health concerns: 399–411; basic first aid, 407–409; disabled travelers, 457; senior travelers, 452; while traveling, 402–405; women travelers, 405–406; before you go, 399–400
Health insurance: 63–64, 399–400, 410
Helbronner Point: 574, 575
Hellbrunn Castle (Salzburg): 685
Herculaneum: 526
Hiking: 313–314, 316; alpine huts, 316.

See also specific destinations
Hill towns of Italy: 510–517; map, 511
Hinterhornalm: 698–699
Hohenschwangau Castle: 709–710, 777
Holland: See Netherlands
Home-base strategy: 46–47
Hostels: 217–223, 441; general tips, 218–223; glossary of terms, 218; memberships, 58, 67, 217–218; official vs. independent, 217–218
Hotel runners: 196–197
Hotels: 198–207; budget, 199–201; chain, 201–202; finding, 202–203; general tips, 203–207; reservations, 191–198; room types and costs, 198–199. See also Sleeping
House swapping: 227–228
Hungary: 608–609; Communist sites, 626–633; folk museums, 307; information, 810; itineraries, 52; language, 345; movies, 806; weather, 816
Hydra: 728–731; sleeping, 731

I
IAMAT: 401, 411
Ice Man: 687–688
Imhoff Chocolate Museum (Köln): 689
Immigration (immigrants): 487–490
Immunizations: 399
Information sources: 21–33, 799–810; for children, 436; for disabled travelers, 458; film and TV, 803–809; guidebooks, 21–29; Internet, 4, 29–33; Rick Steves, 6–7, 23–26, 799–801; for seniors, 451; travel literature, 801–803; for women travelers, 430–431; work and study, 494; and your travel dreams, 3–5
Insurance: 59–66; car, 66, 153–156; medical, 63–64, 399–400, 410
Interlaken: 601–603
International Driving Permits (IDP): 67, 150–152
International Student Identity Card (ISIC): 58, 60, 67
Internet access: 253–256; at train stations, 129
Internet calling: 247–249
Internet resources (websites): 4, 29–33; accommodations, 30, 192, 203, 214–215, 224–226; air travel, 30, 87–89, 102–103; for children, 436; for

disabled travelers, 458; health, 401; tourist information, 810; train tickets, 112–113; translating foreign Websites, 254; for women travelers, 431; work and study, 494
Internet security: 256–257
Interruption insurance: 61–63
Ireland: 661–674; cuisine, 385–387; folk museums, 307; information, 810; itineraries, 49, 50, 756–757, 775; literature, 801, 802; map, 756; movies, 806; sleeping, 210; weather, 816
Irish music: 667–668
Irrel: 718
Islam: 738–739
Istanbul: 737, 740, 743–747; sleeping, 742, 747
Italy: 503–533; cuisine, 391–392, 695–697; information, 810; itineraries, 47, 51, 764–765, 774–776; language, 344, 349, 350; literature, 801–803; map, 765; movies, 807; offbeat sights, 687; Reifenstein Castle, 708; sight reservations, 299; sleeping, 210, 223; weather, 816
Itinerary planning: 33–53; best and worst sights, 49–53; general considerations, 39–41; high-speed town-hopping, 47–48; home-base strategy, 46–47; seasonal considerations, 34–39; in Seven Steps, 41–46; for sights, 295; whirlwind two-month tour, 770–780

J
Jet lag: 400–402, 403–404, 440–441
Jewish Quarter (Kraków): 618–619
Jewish Quarter (Prague): 605, 607–611
Jorvik (York): 646–648
Journaling: 426, 448
Julian Alps: 700–701
Jungfrau Region: 601–603

K
Kaminia: 730
Kardamyli: 727
Kastamonu: 747
Kastelruth: See Castelrotto
Kew Gardens: 640–641
Kids: See Children
KISS ("Keep it simple, stupid!"): 9
Kleine Scheidegg: 602–603
Kobarid: 701
Köln: 778, 798

Konya: 740
Kraków: 613–620; map, 614; Nazi sights, 720; sleeping, 620
Kusadasi: 741; sleeping, 742
Kutná Hora: 689

L
Landsberg: 593
Language: 340–356, 486–487; creative communication, 346, 348, 351; European gestures, 355–356; family tree, 344–345; international words, 347; tongue-twisters, 349; translation mobile apps, 260; using simple English, 343, 346; Yankee-English phrase book, 352–353. See also Glossary of terms
Last Supper (da Vinci): 297, 518–519
Laundry: 411–415
Lauterbrunnen Valley: 599, 602–603
Let's Go guidebooks: 27, 229
Lines, avoiding: 295–299
Lisbon: 534–538; itineraries, 773; map, 535; sleeping, 538
Literature: 801–803
Lodging: See Sleeping; and specific destinations
Loire Valley: itineraries, 772
London: 634–642; car buying, 158; itineraries, 47, 49, 770; map, 635; scams, 788; sleeping, 223, 642
Loneliness: 10–12, 424, 427–428
Lonely Planet guidebooks: 26–27
Lost or stolen items: 335–339
Ludwig II castles: 709–711, 777
Luges: 692–693
Luggage: See Baggage
Luxembourg: information, 810

M
Madrid: itineraries, 47, 772–773
Mail: 359
Manarola: 508
Mani Peninsula: 726–728
Manneken-Pis: 580, 685–686
Männlichen: 602
Maps: 289–290; driving, 163–165; legend, 5; mobile apps, 260–261; transit, 277–278; websites, 30. See also Map Index
Marijuana: 584–585
Markets: 320, 382–383; bargaining, 323–324. See also specific destinations

Marrakech: 551–552
Matterhorn: 574
Mauthausen: 715
McDonald's: 378, 628
Mechelen: 719
Medical care: 409–411
Medical checkups: 67, 399–400
Medical insurance: 63–64, 399–400, 410
Medications: 67, 80, 339, 400, 452
Medieval castles, best: 702–712; maps, 702, 709
Meeting locals: 10–12, 310–311, 424; becoming a temporary European, 307–312; Graffiti Wall, 793–797; scams, 333–335
Meet-the-Locals Programs: 310
Memento Park (Budapest): 629–630
Menaggio: 520, 787
Merzouga: 553
Metric system: 357–358, 811
Metro: *See* Subways
Michelin Green Guides: 27
Midlothian Ski Centre (Edinburgh): 686–687
Milan: 517–519; sleeping, 523
Minivan excursions: 294
Minority travelers: 488–489
Mobile phones: 67, 83, 238–247; apps, 258–262
Monemvasia: 728
Money: 167–186; on cruise ships, 471–472; scams, 180–181, 332. *See also* Budgeting
Money belts: 78, 120, 327–328
Money-saving tips: airfares, 16, 89–90; eating, 375–384; railpasses, 117–119; sleeping, 189–191, 199–202; train tickets, 115. *See also* Budgeting
Mont Blanc: 573–576
Monterosso al Mare: 506–507, 509
Montreux: 707
Moorish Ruins of Sintra: 708–709
Moreton-in-Marsh: 652–653; sleeping, 656
Morocco: 547–555; information, 810; itineraries, 51; map, 550; weather, 816
Mosel River Valley: 778
Mosques: sightseeing strategies, 303–304
Mostar: 622–626; sleeping, 626
Motion sickness: 408
Mount Brandon: 662
Mount Vesuvius: 526–527
Movies, recommended: 803–809

Moving overseas: 451
Munich: 690, 716; itineraries, 47, 777; scams, 790; sleeping, 223
Mürren: 599, 600
Museums: with children, 446–447; for disabled travelers, 455; senior travelers, 453–454
Museum sightseeing strategies: 301–303
Mycenae: 724–725
Myrdal: 679–680
Mystras: 728

N
Nafplio: 722–724
Naples: 527–529; map, 525
Naples Bay: 524–527; map, 525
Nazi sites: 712–721
Netherlands: 582–588; cuisine, 392–393; folk museums, 306; information, 810; itineraries, 780; language, 344; literature, 803; movies, 807; Nazi sights, 718–719; offbeat sights, 687; sight reservations, 299; weather, 816
Neuschwanstein Castle: 709–710, 777
Nevesinje: 621–622
"New Europe": 616
Northern Ireland: 669–674
Norway: 675–681; folk museums, 306; information, 810; itineraries, 51; weather, 816
Norway fjords: 51, 679–681; itineraries, 779; map, 680
Norwegian Folk Museum: 306, 676–677
Numbers and stumblers: 357–359
Nürnberg: 718

O
Oberammergau: 593
Oberbozen: 522
Offbeat sights: 685–693
Off-season travel strategies: 37–39
Old Bridge (Mostar): 622–623
Olomouc: 631
Olympia: 726
Online photo-and video-sharing: 274–275
Online resources: *See* Internet resources
Open-air folk museums: 305–307
Oradour-sur-Glane: 720–721
Organized tours: *See* Tours
Orvieto: 513; sleeping, 517
Oslo: 675–679; itineraries, 51, 779; map, 676; Nazi sights, 719; sleeping, 681

Ötzi the Ice Man: 687–688
Ouarzazate: 552

P

Packing: 69–86; baggage restrictions, 68, 70–71; checklist of essentials, 82; with children, 437–439; clothing, 74–78; documents, money, and travel info, 78–79; electronics, 81, 83–85; Graffiti Wall, 781–782; optional bring-alongs, 85–86; senior travelers, 451–452; toiletries and personal items, 79–81; what to pack, 72–74
Paestum: 527
Palermo: 531, 688; sleeping, 533
Pamukkale: 741
Paris: 556–568, 694; Champs-Elysées, 556–563; itineraries, 47, 771–772; maps, 558, 564; Nazi sights, 720; offbeat sights, 686, 689, 691; Rue Cler, 563–568; scams, 789, 790, 791–792; sleeping, 568
Passports: 54–57, 66; for children, 435, 437; lost or stolen, 337–338; photocopy of, 58–59, 66, 326
Peak-season travel strategies: 34–36
Peloponnesian Peninsula: 722–728, 769; map, 723
Perspectives: 474–497
Pharmacies: 410–411, 452
Phone cards: 250–251
Phones: 234–252; calling chart, 236–237; communicating over, 354–355; dialing, 234–235, 238. See also Mobile phones
Photo books: 275
Photography: 263–272; accessories and gadgets, 264–266; flashes at sights, 301; managing images on the road, 267–268; sharing your trip, 272–276; tricks for a good shot, 268–272. See also Digital cameras
Physicians: 409–411
Pickpockets: 279, 326–330
Picnics (picnicking): 378–382; general tips, 380–382; shopping at markets, 382–383. See also Markets
Pienza: 516
Piz Gloria: 600
Poland: Communist sites, 631–632; cuisine, 387; information, 810; itineraries, 52; Kraków, 613–620; language, 345; movies, 808; Nazi sights, 719–720; weather, 816

Police reports: 336–337
Pompeii: 526
Portobello Road Market (London): 641
Portugal: 534–541; cuisine, 393; information, 810; itineraries, 51, 761–762; language, 344, 349; map, 761; Moorish Ruins of Sintra, 708–709; movies, 808; sleeping, 212; weather, 816
Positano: 525–526
Post offices: 359
Prague: 604–613; Communist sites, 630–631; itineraries, 776; Nazi sights, 720; sleeping, 613
Prague Castle: 605–606
Praia do Castelejo: 541
Pregnant travelers: 406
Prescriptions: 67, 80, 339, 400, 452
Priorities: 49–53
Promenade Plantée Park (Paris): 686
Prostitution: 582–583
Provence: itineraries, 774; literature, 801
Pubs: 363, 385–386, 641, 666–667

R

Rabat: 550–551
Race relations: 487–490
Radio, Rick Steves': 7, 800–801
Railpasses: 58, 67, 115–121; comparing plans, 117–119; glossary of terms, 116; vs. tickets, 108–110; using, 119–120
Rail travel: See Train travel
Recreational activities: 312–319
Reifenstein Castle: 708
Rental cars: See Car rentals
Rental properties: 213–217
Researching: See Information sources
Reservations: hotels, 191–198; sights, 297–298, 299; train seats, 122–124, 131
Responsible travel: 491–495
Restaurants: 362–373; bills, 370–372; with children, 443–444; drinks, 368–370; etiquette, 363–366; finding, 362–363; ordering your meal, 366–368; tipping, 181, 372–373. See also Eating; and specific destinations
Restrooms: 415–421; for disabled travelers, 455
Retiring overseas: 451
Reutte: 709; sleeping, 711–712
Rheinfels Castle: 705–707
Rhine River Valley: 778

Rhodes: 732
Rick Steves Audio Europe: *See* Audio Europe, Rick Steves
Rick Steves' Back Door travel philosophy: 13–14
Ricksteves.com: 6–7
Rick Steves guidebooks: 23–26, 68
Rick Steves' television show: 7, 799–800
Riomaggiore: 506–508
Rissani: 553–554
Riviera: itineraries, 774. *See also* Cinque Terre
Road Scholar: 454
Romantic Road: 592–594; itineraries, 778; map, 593
Rome: itineraries, 775–776; offbeat sights, 687; scams, 788–791, 793
Room-finding services: 197, 224–226
Rothenburg: 589–592; itineraries, 778; sleeping, 594
Rough Guides: 27
Route du Vin: 569–573; map, 570
Route of the White Villages: 542–546; map, 543
Rue Cler (Paris): 563–568; map, 564
Russia: itineraries, 775; visas, 57–58
RV (recreational vehicles) camping: 232

S
Sachsenhausen: 715
Safe sex: 404
Safety: *See* Scams; Terrorism; Theft
Saharan Morocco: 552–555
St. Goar: 705, 707, 778; sleeping, 711
Salema: 538–541; sleeping, 541
Salzburg: 685; itineraries, 776
Salzkammergut: 210, 594
Sámos: 732; sleeping, 742–743
Sandwich shops: 376–377
San Gimignano: 512–513
Sasso Lungo Mountains: 523
Scams: 331–335; bank card, 180–181; Graffiti Wall, 788–793; taxis, 286–287
Scandinavia: 675–684; cuisine, 394; folk museums, 306; information, 810; itineraries, 51, 759–760, 778–780; language, 344; map, 760; movies, 808; Nazi sights, 718–719; sleeping, 212
Schilthorn: 597–598, 600
Schindler's List (movie): 619, 720, 808
Schlern: 523
Schokland: 687
Scotland: cuisine, 387; itineraries, 49, 775

Scrapbooks: 275
Seasons: 34–39
Senior discounts: 453
Senior travelers: 450–454; Graffiti Wall, 785–788
Sephora (Paris): 560
Service animals, traveling with: 457
Sevilla: itineraries, 773
Sewers of Paris: 691
Sexually transmitted diseases (STDs): 404
Sharing your trip: 272–276
Shipping packages: 359–360
Shoes: 77, 406, 782–785
Shopping: 319–324; budgeting for, 17; cruise ship, 473; customs regulations, 186; VAT refunds, 182–186, 321–322; where to shop, 320–321
Shoulder-season travel strategies: 36–37
Showers: 416–418
Sicily: 529–533; map, 530; sleeping, 533
Siena: 510–511; sleeping, 517
Sightseeing: budgeting for, 17; with children, 444–447; general strategies for, 295–307; passes and combo-tickets, 298–299, 444; senior travelers, 453–454. *See also specific destinations*
SIM cards: 240–241, 244–247
Sintra Moorish Ruins: 708–709
Slea Head: 665
Sleeping: 187–233; budgeting for, 16–17, 18; with children, 441–442; finding right room, 187–191; money-saving tips, 189–191; phones, 249; reservations, 191–198; reservations form, 194; senior travelers, 452–453; on trains, 136–138; types of accommodations, 198–233; websites, 30, 192, 203. *See also specific destinations*
Slideshows: 276
Slovakia: language, 345
Slovenia: 609, 700–701; cuisine, 387–388; information, 810; itineraries, 775; language, 345; movies, 809; sleeping, 212–213; weather, 817
Smartphones: 83, 241, 242–243; mobile apps, 258–262
Snowshill: 655
Soca River Valley: 700–701
Social issues: 487–491
Socially responsible travel: 491–495
Social media: 272–275
Social networking mobile apps: 261

Social networking websites: 31
Sognefjord: 51, 679–681; map, 680
Solo travelers: 4–5, 422–424, 427–432; women, 428–432
Sommerrodelbahn: 692–693
Sorrento: 524; itineraries, 47; sleeping, 529
Souvenirs: 321–322
Spain: Andalucía, 542–546; cuisine, 394–395; information, 810; itineraries, 51, 761–762, 772–774, 775; language, 344, 349, 350; map, 761; movies, 809; sight reservations, 299; sleeping, 212; weather, 817
Sparta: 728
Stanton: 654–655
Stanway: 653–654
State Department, U.S.: 58, 401
Stockholm: itineraries, 779
Stonehenge: 658–659
Stow-on-the-Wold: 652–653; sleeping, 656
Street food: 377
Strikes: 133
Student cards: 58, 60, 67
Student travelers: 493–495
Study abroad: 454, 493–495
Subways: 279–283; senior travelers, 453
Supermarkets: 383–384
Sweden: folk museums, 306; information, 810; itineraries, 778; weather, 817
Swelling, first aid for: 407
Swiss Alps: 597–603, 697–698, 699–700; hiking, 313–314, 316
Switzerland: Château de Chillon, 707–708; cuisine, 395–398; folk museums, 307; Gimmelwald, 597–603; information, 810; itineraries, 51–52, 762–764, 777; map, 762; movies, 809; offbeat sights, 691, 692; sleeping, 210; weather, 817

T
Tallinn: 632
Tangier: 547–549; sleeping, 555
Tapas: 396–397
Taveyanne: 697–698
Taxes: VAT refunds, 182–186, 321–322
Taxis: 285–288; between cities, 287–288; hotel tips, 197; scams, 286–287
Telephones: See Mobile phones; Phones
Television show, Rick Steves': 7, 799–800

Temperatures: 358; average monthly, 814–817
Temporary European: 307–312
Terezín Concentration Camp: 715
Terrorism: 484–486
Theft (thieves): 279, 325–339; insurance, 65, 146; tips for avoiding, 326–330. See also Scams
Thoughtful Americans: 476
Timbuktu: 552
Time Out guidebooks: 29
Time zone: 357
Tinerhir: 552
Tipping: 181–182; taxis, 285–286
Tirol: itineraries, 777
Todi: 516
Toilets: 415–421; for disabled travelers, 455
Toledo: itineraries, 773
Tour guides: 293–294, 462–463; tipping, 181
Tourist information: offices, 290, 810; websites, 29, 32
Tourist scams: See Scams
Tours: 291–294; by bike, 319; by boat, 465–473; by bus, 292–293, 459–465; with children, 445; for disabled travelers, 456–457; guided vs. on your own, 4–5; by minivan, 294; walking and guided, 291–292; whirlwind two-month, 770–780
Train stations: 124–132; buying tickets, 125–126; schedules, 126–128; sleeping in, 230–231
Train travel: 106–138; vs. air travel, 104–105; benefits of, 106–108; boarding trains, 130–132; vs. car travel, 145, 151; costs and time, 111; first vs. second class, 112–113; Glacier Express, 52–53; glossary of terms, 116, 127; point-to-point tickets, 110–115; schedules, 121–122, 126–128; seat reservations, 122–124, 131; sleeping on trains, 136–138, 231; for solo women travelers, 428–429; tickets, 108–115, 125–126; on the train, 132–136; websites, 30. See also Railpasses
Transportation: 277–288; budgeting for, 16; with children, 447; mobile apps, 259; public transit tips, 277–279; senior travelers, 453. See also Air travel; Biking; Buses; Car travel; Taxis; Train travel

Travel agents: 90, 92
Travel booking mobile apps: 258–259
Travel booking websites: 30
Travel documents: 54–59; for children, 435, 437; lost or stolen, 336–338; packing, 79; photocopies of, 58–59, 66, 326
Traveler's checks: 172
Travel guides: *See* Guidebooks
Travel industry: 22
Travel insurance: 59–66, 450–451
Travel laundry: 411–415
Travel literature: 801–803
Travel magazines and books: 3–4
Travel partners: 4–5, 20–21, 425
Travel photography: *See* Photography
Trebinje: 621
Trebon: 691–692
Trip-cancellation insurance: 61–63
Trip costs: 17
Turkey: 731–751; cuisine, 398; information, 810; literature, 801, 802; maps, 733, 737, 747; movies, 809; visas, 57; weather, 817
Tuscany: cuisine, 695–697; itineraries, 775
TV, recommended: 803–809

U

Ugly Americans: 476
Umbria: itineraries, 775
Urinary tract infections: 405–406

V

Valle d'Aosta: 574–575
Value-added tax (VAT): 182–186, 321–322
Varenna: 520; sleeping, 523–524
Vathia: 726
Vatican City (Rome): 359, 775–776
VAT refunds: 182–186, 321–322
Vegetarians: 364–365
Venice: itineraries, 47, 764, 776
Ventry: 663
Vernazza: 504–506
Vesuvius: 526–527
Video-sharing: 274–275
Vienna: 718; itineraries, 776; scams, 789, 791
Visas: 57–58
Visitor information: *See* Tourist information

Voice over Internet Protocol (VoIP): 247–248
Volterra: 516
Volunteer opportunities: 454
"Voluntourism": 492–493
Voss: 681
Vrsic Pass: 700–701

W

Walderalm: 699
Walking: 312; tours, 291–292
Walking shoes: 77, 406, 782–785
Wannsee: 716–717
Warsaw: Communist sites, 632; Nazi sights, 719–720
Warwick Castle: 704
Wasserauen: 699–700
Water, drinking: 368–369, 403
Weather: 814–817; mobile apps, 260; seasons, 34–39; websites, 31
Web resources: *See* Internet resources
Wengen: 603
Western Europe: itineraries, 765–767
Western Union: 174–175
Wheelchairs: 454–455
White villages of Andalucía: 542–546; map, 543
Wieliczka Salt Mine: 619–620
Wi-Fi: 129, 242–243, 253–256
Wildkirchli: 699
Wiring money: 174–175
Women travelers: 428–432; dealing with men, 429, 432; health issues, 405–406; packing tips, 78; resources, 430–431
Work abroad: 494
World War II: literature, 803; Nazi sites, 712–721
Würzburg: 592–593

Y

Yankee-English phrase book: 352–353
Yeast infections: 405–406
York: 645–648; map, 647; sleeping, 648
York Minster: 648
Youth hostels: *See* Hostels

Z

Zahara: 545–546

MAP INDEX

Europe: vi-vii

Part One: Travel Skills
Budgeting & Planning
Sample Itinerary: 41

Flying
Multiple-City Flights: 93

Trains & More
Point-to-Point Rail Tickets: Cost &
   Time: 111
Crossing the English Channel: 114
Eurail Countries: 117

Money
Euroland: 168

City Transportation
A Sample Subway Trip: 281

Perspectives
EU Nations: 478

Part Two: Back Doors
Europe's Back Doors: 501

Italy
The Cinque Terre: 505
Hill Towns of Central Italy: 511
Civita di Bagnoregio: 514
Train Connections from Milan: 519
Naples & the Amalfi Coast: 525
Sicily: 530

Portugal, Spain & Morocco
Lisbon: 535
Portugal's Algarve Coast: 540
Spain's White Villages: 543
Morocco: 550

France
Paris Overview: 556
Champs-Elysées Walk: 558
Rue Cler Walk: 564

Alsace's Route du Vin: 570
Alpine Crossing from France to Italy: 574

Belgium and the Netherlands
Bruges: 578
Amsterdam Overview: 582

Germany, Austria & Switzerland
The Romantic Road: 593
Hallstatt: 595
Berner Oberland: 598

Eastern Europe
Prague: 605
Kraków's Old Town: 614

Great Britain
London: 635
Bath: 643
York: 647
Blackpool: 650
The Cotswolds: 652
Mysterious Britain: 656

Ireland
Dingle Peninsula Loop Trip: 664
Belfast: 671

Scandinavia
Oslo: 676
Norway in a Nutshell: 680
Ærø Island Bike Ride: 683

A European Sampler
Offbeat Europe: 685
Alpine Escapes: 698
Europe's Best Castles: 702
Castle Day: 709
Nazi Sites: 713

East Mediterranean
The Peloponnese: 723
The Greek Islands &
   Southwest Turkey: 733
14 Days in Turkey: 737
Eastern Turkey: 747

Appendix
Great Britain in 22 Days: 755
Ireland in 23 Days: 756
France in 22 Days: 758
Scandinavia in 22 Days: 760
Spain and Portugal in 22 Days: 761
Germany, Austria, and
 Switzerland in 23 Days: 762
Best of Italy in 22 Days: 765
The Best of Western Europe in 23 Days:
 766

The Best of Eastern Europe
 in 22 Days: 768
Greece (Athens and the Peloponnese)
 in 15 Days: 769
Europe's Best Two-Month Trip: 771
Rick Steves' Europe on
 Public Television: 800
How Europe Compares to North
 America: 815

Audio Europe™

RICK STEVES AUDIO EUROPE

Rick's Free Travel App

Get your FREE **Rick Steves Audio Europe**™ app to enjoy…

- Dozens of self-guided tours of Europe's top museums, sights and historic walks
- Hundreds of tracks filled with cultural insights and sightseeing tips from Rick's radio interviews
- All organized into handy geographic playlists
- For iPhone, iPad, iPod Touch, Android

With Rick whispering in your ear, Europe gets even better.

Find out more at ricksteves.com

Join a Rick Steves tour

Enjoy Europe's warmest welcome... with the flexibility and friendship of a small group getting to know Rick's favorite places and people. It all starts with our free tour catalog and DVD.

Great guides, small groups, no grumps.

See more than three dozen itineraries throughout Europe

ricksteves.com

Free information and great gear to

▶ Explore Europe

Browse thousands of articles, video clips, photos and radio interviews, plus find a wealth of money-saving tips for planning your dream trip. You'll find up-to-date information on Europe's best destinations, packing smart, getting around, finding rooms, staying healthy, avoiding scams and more.

▶ Travel News

Subscribe to our free Travel News e-newsletter, and get monthly updates from Rick on what's happening in Europe!

▶ Travel Forums

Learn, ask, share—our online community of savvy travelers is a great resource for first-time travelers to Europe, as well as seasoned pros.

Rick Steves' Europe Through the Back Door, Inc.

turn your travel dreams into affordable reality

▶ Rick's Free Audio Europe™ App

The Rick Steves Audio Europe™ app brings history and art to life. Enjoy Rick's audio tours of Europe's top museums, sights and neighborhood walks—plus hundreds of tracks including travel tips and cultural insights from Rick's radio show—all organized into geographic playlists. Learn more at ricksteves.com.

▶ Great Gear from Rick's Travel Store

Pack light and right—on a budget—with Rick's custom-designed carry-on bags, wheeled bags, day packs, travel accessories, guidebooks, journals, maps and Blu-ray/DVDs of his TV shows.

130 Fourth Avenue North, PO Box 2009 • Edmonds, WA 98020 USA
Phone: (425) 771-8303 • Fax: (425) 771-0833 • ricksteves.com

Rick Steves
www.ricksteves.com

EUROPE GUIDES
Best of Europe
Eastern Europe
Europe Through the Back Door
Mediterranean Cruise Ports
Northern European Cruise Ports

COUNTRY GUIDES
Croatia & Slovenia
England
France
Germany
Great Britain
Ireland
Italy
Portugal
Scandinavia
Spain
Switzerland

CITY & REGIONAL GUIDES
Amsterdam, Bruges & Brussels
Barcelona
Budapest
Florence & Tuscany
Greece: Athens & the Peloponnese
Istanbul
London
Paris
Prague & the Czech Republic
Provence & the French Riviera

Rome
Venice
Vienna, Salzburg & Tirol

SNAPSHOT GUIDES
Berlin
Bruges & Brussels
Copenhagen & the Best of Denmark
Dublin
Dubrovnik
Hill Towns of Central Italy
Italy's Cinque Terre
Krakow, Warsaw & Gdansk
Lisbon
Madrid & Toledo
Milan & the
Munich, Bavaria & Salzburg
Naples & the Amalfi Coast
Northern Ireland
Norway
Scotland
Sevilla, Granada & Southern Spain
Stockholm

POCKET GUIDES
Athens
Barcelona
Florence
London
Paris
Rome
Venice

NOW AVAILABLE:
eBOOKS, DVD & BLU-RAY

TRAVEL CULTURE
Europe 101
European Christmas
Postcards from Europe
Travel as a Political Act

eBOOKS
*Nearly all Rick Steves guides
are available as eBooks. Check
with your favorite bookseller.*

RICK STEVES' EUROPE DVDs
10 New Shows 2011–2012
Austria & the Alps
Eastern Europe
England & Wales
European Christmas
European Travel Skills & Specials
France
Germany, BeNeLux & More
Greece & Turkey
Iran
Ireland & Scotland
Italy's Cities
Italy's Countryside
Scandinavia
Spain
Travel Extras

BLU-RAY
Celtic Charms
Eastern Europe Favorites
European Christmas
Italy Through the Back Door
Mediterranean Mosaic
Surprising Cities of Europe

PHRASE BOOKS & DICTIONARIES
French
French, Italian & German
German
Italian
Portuguese
Spanish

JOURNALS
Rick Steves' Pocket Travel Journal
Rick Steves' Travel Journal

PLANNING MAPS
Britain, Ireland & London
Europe
France & Paris
Germany, Austria & Switzerland
Ireland
Italy
Spain & Portugal

Contributor

Cameron Hewitt

Cameron Hewitt has researched, written for, and edited the last 10 editions of *Europe Through the Back Door*. He has researched various guidebooks and led tours for Rick Steves' travel company since 2000. While he's visited almost every European country, his favorite area is Central and Eastern Europe, where he co-authors Rick Steves' guidebooks on Eastern Europe, Croatia & Slovenia, and Budapest. When he's not traveling, Cameron lives in Seattle with his wife, Shawna.

Chapter Images

This list identifies the panoramic images at the beginning of each chapter and credits their photographers.

	Photographer
Getting Started	
Paris	Rick Steves
Budgeting and Planning	
Florence, Italy	Rick Steves
Paper Chase	
Important Travel Documents	Rhonda Pelikan
Pack Light	
Packing Light in Germany	Dominic Bonuccelli
Flying	
Flying to the Netherlands	Cameron Hewitt
Trains and More	
Railway in Switzerland	Rick Steves
Driving	
Driving in Great Britain	Rick Steves
Money	
Money Montage	David C. Hoerlein
Sleeping	
Casa Rabatti, Florence	Rick Steves
Phones and Technology	
Surfing the Internet	Dominic Bonuccelli
City Transportation	
The Tube, London	Rick Steves
Sightseeing and Activities	
Ballooning in Cappadocia, Turkey	Dominic Bonuccelli
Theft and Scams	
Begging in Rome	Rick Steves

Language and Communication
Olive Oil Tasting in Lucca, Italy — Dominic Bonuccelli
Eating
Fondue in Switzerland — Dominic Bonuccelli
Health and Hygiene
French Pharmacy — Dominic Bonuccelli
Travel Styles
Kalmar Castle, Sweden — Dominic Bonuccelli
Perspectives
Turkey — Rick Steves
Italy
Vernazza, Cinque Terre — Dominic Bonuccelli
Portugal, Spain & Morocco
Lisbon — Rick Steves
France
Champs-Elysées, Paris — Rick Steves
Belgium and the Netherlands
Bruges — Rick Steves
Germany, Austria & Switzerland
Rothenburg, Germany — Rick Steves
Eastern Europe
Prague, Czech Republic — Rick Steves
Great Britain
Parliament, London — Rick Steves
Ireland
Blasket Islands — Pat O'Connor
Scandinavia
Frogner Park, Oslo — Sonja Groset
A European Sampler
Tegelberg Luge, Bavaria — Dominic Bonuccelli
East Mediterranean
Nafplio, Greece — Carol Ries
Appendix
Canoeing on the Dordogne — Rick Steves

How Was Your Trip?

If you enjoyed a successful trip with the help of this book and would like to share your discoveries, please fill out the survey at www.ricksteves.com /feedback. Thanks in advance for your feedback—it helps a lot. We're all in the same traveler's school of hard knocks...and it's OK to compare notes. Your feedback helps us improve this book for future travelers!

For our latest travel tips, tap into our information-packed website: www.ricksteves.com. For any updates to this book, check www.ricksteves .com/update.

Europe Through the Back Door is more than Rick Steves. All 80 of us are pooling our travel experience and working hard to help you enjoy the trip of a lifetime!

Acknowledgments

Danke to Cameron Hewitt for his travel savvy, editing, and commitment to excellence. *Dank u wel* to Risa Laib for managing my guidebook series so lovingly. And *grazie* to the following for sharing their knowledge in their fields of travel expertise: Dave Hoerlein (artful maps, public-transit tips); Wide World Books & Maps (guidebooks, www.wideworldtravelstore.com); Tim Tattan (radio); Brooke Burdick (audio tours); Joan Robinson and Ann Neel (women's packing tips); Kent Corrick (travel insurance); Todd and Carla Hoover (cruisers extraordinaire); Elizabeth Holmes (travel agents, overseas flights, www.elizabethholmes.com); Laura Terrenzio and Gretchen Strauch at ETBD (train travel); Alfred Celentano at Europe by Car and our colleagues at Auto Europe (car rental and leasing); Steve Breedlove at Bank of America Merrill Lynch (money); Cory Mead (technology); Alan Spira, M.D., and Craig Karpilow, M.D. (health for travelers); Lisa Friend (family travel and health advice); Amy Lysen (CouchSurfing); France Freeman (home exchange); Kevin Williams (alternative accommodations); Tara Swenson (health advice); Arlan Blodgett and Stewart Hopkins (photography); Deanna Russell (tours); Susan Sygall (travelers with disabilities); Jennifer Hauseman (gay travelers); Audrey Edwards and Leiane Cooke (travelers of color); Rich Sorensen (website); Andy Steves (foreign study abroad); and Aaron Harting (green travel).

Merci for support from my entire well-traveled staff at ETBD, including Gene Openshaw, Steve Smith, Rich Sorensen, and in particular, Anne Kirchner for keeping things in order while I'm both in and out. *Spasiba* also to Pat Larson, Sandie Nisbet, and John Givens at Small World Productions for introducing so many travelers to this book through our original public television series, *Travels in Europe with Rick Steves*. *Muchas gracias* to Simon Griffith for directing and producing our current *Rick Steves' Europe* television series with such passion and artistry.

Finally, *tusen takk* to my parents for dragging me to Europe when I didn't want to go.